HP-UX 11i
Tuning and Performance

Hewlett-Packard® Professional Books

HP-UX

Cooper/Moore	HP-UX 11i Internals
Fernandez	Configuring CDE
Madell	Disk and File Management Tasks on HP-UX
Olker	Optimizing NFS Performance
Poniatowski	HP-UX 11i Virtual Partitions
Poniatowski	HP-UX 11i System Administration Handbook and Toolkit, Second Edition
Poniatowski	The HP-UX 11.x System Administration Handbook and Toolkit
Poniatowski	HP-UX 11.x System Administration "How To" Book
Poniatowski	HP-UX 10.x System Administration "How To" Book
Poniatowski	HP-UX System Administration Handbook and Toolkit
Poniatowski	Learning the HP-UX Operating System
Rehman	HP-UX CSA: Official Study Guide and Desk Reference
Sauers/Ruemmler/Weygant	HP-UX 11i Tuning and Performance
Weygant	Clusters for High Availability, Second Edition
Wong	HP-UX 11i Security

UNIX, LINUX, WINDOWS, AND MPE I/X

Mosberger/Eranian	IA-64 Linux Kernel
Poniatowski	UNIX User's Handbook, Second Edition
Stone/Symons	UNIX Fault Management

COMPUTER ARCHITECTURE

Evans/Trimper	Itanium Architecture for Programmers
Kane	PA-RISC 2.0 Architecture
Markstein	IA-64 and Elementary Functions

NETWORKING/COMMUNICATIONS

Blommers	Architecting Enterprise Solutions with UNIX Networking
Blommers	OpenView Network Node Manager
Blommers	Practical Planning for Network Growth
Brans	Mobilize Your Enterprise
Cook	Building Enterprise Information Architecture
Lucke	Designing and Implementing Computer Workgroups
Lund	Integrating UNIX and PC Network Operating Systems

SECURITY

Bruce	Security in Distributed Computing
Mao	Modern Cryptography: Theory and Practice
Pearson et al.	Trusted Computing Platforms
Pipkin	Halting the Hacker, Second Edition
Pipkin	Information Security

WEB/INTERNET CONCEPTS AND PROGRAMMING

Amor	E-business (R)evolution, Second Edition
Apte/Mehta	UDDI
Chatterjee/Webber	Developing Enterprise Web Services: An Architect's Guide
Kumar	J2EE Security for Servlets, EJBs, and Web Services
Mowbrey/Werry	Online Communities
Tapadiya	.NET Programming

HP-UX 11i
Tuning and Performance

Robert F. Sauers

Chris P. Ruemmler

Peter S. Weygant

http://www.hp.com/go/retailbooks

PRENTICE
HALL
PTR
Prentice Hall PTR
Upper Saddle River, New Jersey 07458
www.phptr.com

Library of Congress Cataloging-in-Publication Data

A CIP catalog record for this book can be obtained from the Library of Congress.

Editorial/production supervision: *Mary Sudul*
Cover design director: *Jerry Votta*
Cover design: *DesignSource*
Manufacturing manager: *Maura Zaldivar*
Acquisitions editor: *Jill Harry*
Editorial assistant: *Brenda Mulligan*
Marketing manager: *Dan DePasquale*
Publisher, HP Books: *Mark Stouse*
Manager and Associate Publisher, HP Books: *Victoria Brandow*

 © 2004 Hewlett-Packard Corp.
Published by Prentice Hall PTR
Pearson Education, Inc.
Upper Saddle River, New Jersey 07458

Prentice Hall books are widely used by corporations and government agencies for training, marketing, and resale.

The publisher offers discounts on this book when ordered in bulk quantities. For more information, contact Corporate Sales Department, Phone: 800-382-3419; FAX: 201- 236-7141;
E-mail: corpsales@prenhall.com
Or write: Prentice Hall PTR, Corporate Sales Dept., One Lake Street, Upper Saddle River, NJ 07458.

Other company and product names mentioned herein are the trademarks or registered trademarks of their respective owners.

Printed in the United States of America
1st Printing

ISBN 0-13-143349-0

Pearson Education LTD.
Pearson Education Australia PTY, Limited
Pearson Education Singapore, Pte. Ltd.
Pearson Education North Asia Ltd.
Pearson Education Canada, Ltd.
Pearson Educación de Mexico, S.A. de C.V.
Pearson Education — Japan
Pearson Education Malaysia, Pte. Ltd.

To my wife Kay and my son Matthew—
I couldn't have done this without your
support and encouragement.
—*Robert F. Sauers*

To Sue and Alex—
Thanks for always being there for me.
—*Chris P. Ruemmler*

For Richard McClure—
Thanks for your patience and understanding.
—*Peter S. Weygant*

CONTENTS

PREFACE

Maximizing the performance of Unix systems is a challenge that requires a specialized understanding of operating system behavior, knowledge of the design and tuning capabilities of the applications that run on the system, and an intimate acquaintance with system and application performance measuring tools that assist in tuning. Operating system behavior changes as improvements are made for scalability and significant new features are added. New hardware designs offer the potential for improved performance when the operating system and application takes advantage of the new designs. The behavior of applications can change not only with new versions of the application itself, but also with new versions of the underlying operating system.

Although application design and tuning is crucial to getting the best possible performance, the number of applications and application vendors are so numerous that it is impractical to discuss specific application tuning in detail. Therefore, this book focuses on Hewlett-Packard's HP-UX Operating System and the HP 9000 and Integrity Systems on which it runs. This edition adds significant content on networking, Java, new hardware designs, especially Itanium Processor Family (IPF) designs, and HP-UX 11i-specific performance issues. The authors are most familiar with HP-UX, and therefore, the specific operating system architecture and tuning suggestions presented in this book apply directly to HP-UX. The authors also have experience working with a variety of applications and provide guidance on tuning based on their knowledge of how applications and the system interact.

We start by presenting a general discussion of performance management in Chapters 1 and 2 and by developing a performance management methodology in Chapter 3. It is important to realize that performance management is more than crisis-oriented problem solving. Next, in Chapter 4, we look at how the operating system kernel is instrumented to provide data that are used to analyze what is happening on the system. Chapter 5 provides suggestions and guidelines for choosing among the many system performance tools that are available and a discussion of the advantages and disadvantages of each tool.

Hardware system design is covered in detail in Chapter 6, from component modules through the system itself. Chapters 7 through 10 concentrate on providing an understanding of the major operating system resources (CPU, Memory, Disk and Network) that are utilized by applications and can become bottlenecks to good performance. The authors feel that it is not possible to properly tune a system without understanding how the operating system works. Therefore, operating system design from a performance perspective is discussed in each of these chapters followed by the applicable performance metrics and suggestions for tuning to improve resource utilization.

Tuning the operating system alone can provide only a piece of the solution to performance optimization of a system. Application optimization is discussed in the chapters on Compiler Performance Tuning, Java Run-time Performance Tuning, Designing Applications for Performance and Application Profiling. The appendices include an alphabetical reference of the various performance tools, a lexicon of the naming of the versions of HP-UX, and lists of the tuneable parameters that can be dynamically or automatically tuned while the system and its applications are running.

We sincerely hope that you find this book to be useful and valuable in keeping your HP-UX systems running optimally.

ABOUT THE AUTHORS

ROBERT F. (Bob) SAUERS is Chief Architect for Mission Critical and Disaster Tolerant Solutions in HP's High Availability R&D Lab. As an engineer, consultant and software architect for over 25 years with Hewlett-Packard Company, he has worked directly with customers on the architecture, design, implementation and troubleshooting of highly available and high performing computing environments as well as the porting of software applications. He established and ran the HP-UX porting and benchmarking center where many of this book's techniques were developed, and created the HP-UX tuning class this book is based on. Bob has traveled worldwide to solve complex performance and availability problems for customers. His focus is now on the architecture of High Availability and Disaster Tolerant solutions, and works with customers to help them choose the best solution based upon business needs. Bob started his career working at the Naval Ship Research and Development Center where he worked in the area of structure-borne vibration and acoustics. He received Bachelor of Engineering Science in Mechanics and Master of Science in Computer Science degrees from Johns Hopkins University.

CHRIS P. RUEMMLER is an HP Software Engineer in HP's kernel R&D lab where he is responsible for HP-UX performance. He was graduated from the University of California at Berkeley in 1993 with a Masters degree in Computer Science. For the last ten years at HP, he has been involved in various areas of HP-UX performance, specializing in commercial application performance, compilers, and I/O-related issues, and has solved many complex customer performance problems, thus providing real-world experience for his knowledge of performance.

PETER S. WEYGANT (pweygant@psw-consulting.com) is an information engineering specialist with PSW Consulting, Inc. Formerly a Learning Products Engineer at Hewlett Packard, he has been a technical writer and consultant in the computer industry for over twenty years. He has developed training and documentation on relational database technology, high availability solutions, and the HP-UX operating system. He is the author of *Clusters for High Availability: A Primer of HP Solutions* in the Hewlett-Packard Professional Books series.

ACKNOWLEDGMENTS

This book is the result of the combined efforts of Bob Sauers and Chris Ruemmler who created the technical content, and Peter Weygant who provided assistance with writing, editing, formatting and graphics. A number of other individuals also deserve credit for their assistance. The following individuals provided invaluable assistance by reading and commenting on the manuscript, offering suggestions for technical changes and additions, and helping to detect and correct many defects:

    Joseph Coha

    Eric Hamilton

    Richard Hank

    Rick Jones

    Tara Krishnaswamy

    Cliff Mather

    Leonard McCrigler

    Harshad Parekh

    Mark Riley

    Reza Taheri

    Michael Yoder

We are thankful for all of the time spent after normal work hours and the thoroughness with which all of these people did the reviews. The authors are solely responsible for any errors or deficiencies that remain.

Many others have our thanks as well. Martin Whittaker, our HP Executive Sponsor, provided significant moral support and assisted us in lining up reviewers, technical resources, resolving last-minute issues, and made excellent suggestions for content. Jill Harry, our Executive Editor from Prentice Hall PTR, provided encouragement and just the right amount of "cracking the whip" when necessary to keep us on schedule. Mary Sudul provided essential technical assistance and coordination during the detailed, painstaking, and tedious copy editing, proofreading, and formatting processes.

Finally, thanks to the hundreds of HP students who participated in performance tuning classes given by Bob over the years, to those HP engineers with whom both Bob and Chris worked on customer benchmarking and performance problem issues. Their questions and insights along with the real-world customer-oriented point-of-view helped to shape this book from the beginning with the first edition into the second edition.

## CHAPTER 1

Introduction to Performance Management

Application developers and system administrators face similar challenges in managing the performance of a computer system. Performance management starts with application design and development and migrates to administration and tuning of the deployed production system or systems. It is necessary to keep performance in mind at all stages in the development and deployment of a system and application. There is a definite overlap in the responsibilities of the developer and administrator. Sometimes determining where one ends and the other begins is more difficult when a single person or small group develops, administers and uses the application. This chapter will look at:

- Application Developer's Perspective
- System Administrator's Perspective
- Total System Resource Perspective
- Rules of Performance Tuning

1.1 Application Developer's Perspective

The tasks of the application developer include:

- Defining the application
- Determining the specifications
- Designing application components
- Developing the application codes
- Testing, tuning, and debugging
- Deploying the system and application
- Maintaining the system and application

•Estimating and monitoring the growth of the application over time

1.1.1   Defining the Application

The first step is to determine what the application is going to be. Initially, management may need to define the priorities of the development group. Surveys of user organizations may also be carried out.

1.1.2   Determining Application Specifications

Defining what the application will accomplish is necessary before any code is written. The users and developers should agree, in advance, on the particular features and/or functionality that the application will provide. Often, performance specifications are agreed upon at this time, and these are typically expressed in terms of user response time or system throughput measures. These measures will be discussed in detail later. Of course, there are always trade offs being made between performance, features and cost. For instance, it may only be possible to meet a performance specification with a larger system or by allocating more engineering resources for design.

1.1.3   Designing Application Components

High-level design should be performed before any code is actually written. Performance should begin to play a part at this point in the development process. Choices must be made as to what operating system services are to be used. Trade-offs such as ease of coding versus algorithm efficiency appear to be easily made at this stage, but they can often negatively affect performance once the application is deployed.

Not considering performance at this phase of the life cycle condemns the application to a lifetime of rework, patches, and redesign. The designer should also be considering ways to design instrumentation for transaction rate and other application-specific measurements that cannot be made by general-purpose tools.

1.1.4   Developing the Application Codes

After high-level design is complete, the developer creates the actual codes in one or more computer languages. Codes are based on the application specifications, including performance specifications, developed in conjunction with users.

1.1.5   Testing, Tuning, and Debugging

All too often, performance does not become an issue until the application has been written and is in the testing phase. Then it quickly becomes apparent that the application performs poorly or will not meet the response or throughput requirements of the user.

1.1.6   Deploying the System and/or Application

If not discovered sooner, performance deficiencies normally become quite apparent once the system and/or application is deployed out to the user community. Complaints that the performance is poor may be frequent and loud once the system is fully operational.

1.1.7   System and Application Maintenance

Once the system is operational, the developers work on making changes in the application, which may include adding new features, fixing bugs, and tuning for performance. It is often too late to have a big impact on performance by making slight modifications to the application. Developers may have to consider large-scale application redesign in order to meet performance specifications. The overlap of the duties of the developer and the system administrator begins here.

1.2   System Administrator's Perspective

The tasks of the system administrator include:

• Making the system available to others
• Monitoring the usage of the system
• Maintaining a certain level of performance
• Planning for future processing needs

1.2.1   Making the System Available to the Users

This may include such responsibilities as loading the system and application software, configuring devices, setting up the file system, and adding user and group names.

1.2.2   Monitoring the Usage of the System

Measuring the utilization of various system resources is done for several reasons. Monitoring CPU and disk utilization can provide the basis for chargeback accounting. Identifying and documenting the various applications being used allows management to understand the trends in resource usage within the system. And of course, monitoring is the quickest way to detect problems.

1.2.3   Maintaining a Certain Level of System Performance

System administrators often see performance tuning as a response to user complaints. After monitoring and analyzing system performance, administrators must take appropriate action to ensure that performance returns to acceptable levels. System or application tuning may be necessary to improve responsiveness.

1.2.4   Planning for Future Processing Needs

This involves predicting the size of systems needed either for new applications or for growth of existing applications.

Almost any change to a system or application will have some impact on performance. Proposed changes must be weighed against the potential resulting change in performance. Performance management is the process of measuring, evaluating, and modifying the level of performance that a system and application provide to their users, and assessing the effect of proposed changes. It is important to understand that performance management is a proactive function and not a reactive one. It is not very pleasant to be told by either the users or management that the computer system is not living up to expectations, and that you, the system administrator or developer, need to do something about it.

1.3 Total System Resource Perspective

To understand performance management, it is necessary to understand the various system resources that interact to affect the overall performance of the system. Traditionally, system administrators viewed performance as the interaction of three system resources: *central processing unit*, *memory*, and *I/O*. Figure 1-1 shows this view. The Central Processing Unit, or CPU, is

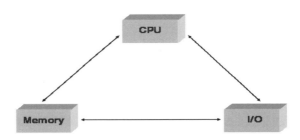

Figure 1-1   Interaction of System Resources

the hardware that executes the program codes, which exist as one or more *processes*. Each process may run as one or more *threads*, depending on the operating system (OS) version or variant. The part of the OS that controls the CPU resource is the process management subsystem, which handles the scheduling of the processes that want to use the CPU.

Memory is the part of the computer that stores the instructions and data. Physical memory is typically semiconductor Random Access Memory (RAM). Virtual memory includes physical memory and also the *backing store* (which is the overflow area used when memory is fully utilized) that is typically on disk. The Memory Management Subsystem controls this resource. Processes may be swapped and/or paged in and out as demands for memory change.

The I/O resource includes all of the peripheral devices such as hard disk drives, tape drives, and networking connections attached to the computer system. These I/O resources may be of various capacities and interface types. From a performance standpoint, the I/O resources involve the movement of data to and from the computer rather than the utilization of the space on a device. The File System and disk I/O Management subsystems control the disk resource. The Networking Stack and drivers control the networking resources. Disk and networking are the two most important areas of the I/O resource that can cause performance issues.

When one of these resources is completely consumed and is the source of a performance problem, we often conclude that there is a bottleneck. For example, if memory is completely utilized and response is slow, then there is a memory bottleneck. However, reality is always more complicated. We will see later that it is not sufficient to use 100% utilization as the sole criterion for defining a resource bottleneck.

Figure 1-1 shows the primary resources: CPU, memory, and I/O, or disk. The double-sided arrows between them are meant to emphasize that the resources are interrelated and that relieving a given bottleneck will often move the bottleneck to a different part of the system. Several years ago, one of the authors was involved in a performance problem on a database server system. Analysis showed that the CPU was saturated and was limiting the throughput of the database. After the system was upgraded with a faster CPU, the performance was limited by the disk subsystem. It was then necessary to better distribute the tables of the database across multiple disk drives. It is often the case that one system resource that is bottlenecked can mask another resource problem.

1.4 Rules of Performance Tuning

Here is the first of several "Rules of Performance Tuning."

RULE 1: When answering a question about computer system performance, the initial answer is always: "It depends."

(These rules will often be referred to by just the number, or the short form. So, here we would say: "**Rule #1**" or "It depends.") The following shows the application of the rule in a typical consulting situation.

From Bob's Consulting Log—On arriving at a customer site for a performance consultation, one of the first questions we were asked was, "What will happen if I add twenty users to my system?" The answer was, of course, "It depends!" Implicit in this question, though unspoken, was the fact that performance was actually *satisfactory* at the time. But the customer did not know whether any resources were at or near the saturation point.

Of course, when you say, "It depends," you have to qualify the dependencies—what does good performance for added users depend on? Does each extra user require additional memory, or does the application support additional users without requiring more memory? Will more data storage be needed for the new users? This book aims to show you how to understand what the dependencies are, to ask the right questions, to investigate, to weigh the dependencies, and then to take appropriate action.

The weighing of dependencies brings us to the second "Rule of Performance Tuning."

RULE 2: Performance tuning always involves a trade-off.

When an administrator tries to improve the performance of a computer system, it may be necessary to modify operating system parameters, or change the application itself. These modifications are commonly referred to as performance tuning, that is, tuning the system kernel, or tuning the application. Tuning the kernel involves changing the values of certain *tunable parameters* followed by possibly relinking the kernel and rebooting the system. Application tuning involves adjusting the design of the application, employing the various compiler optimization techniques, and choosing the appropriate trade-offs among the various kernel services that will be discussed more fully in Chapter 13, "Designing Applications For Performance". Application tuning also may involve adjusting any tunable parameters of the application itself, if any are available.

When analyzing the performance of a system, it is extremely important to consider how the application makes use of system resources, and how the application is designed to work. Some performance problems that manifest themselves as OS or system issues are really caused by the design of the application. Tuning the system may have only a small impact on the overall performance if the application design is the major cause of the lack of good performance. Fixing application performance problems is difficult if not impossible since:

•Source codes to externally purchased applications are seldom available

•In-house development teams seldom have the resources to redesign the application to fix real-time performance issues for those applications where source code is available

•The initial focus of application development is seldom performance

•Independent Software Vendors (ISVs) do not usually respond quickly to performance problems

•Major performance issues are usually only resolved during development of a major revision of the application

•Major performance issues usually require radical redesigns of the application

Remember that changing the application, when possible, will almost always have the greatest chance of significantly improving performance.

System tuning requires an understanding of how the operating system works, and a knowledge of the dependencies that affect performance. Choosing a particular modification always involves trading one benefit for another. For example, tuning to improve memory utilization may degrade file system performance. Understanding the needs of the application and this interaction between memory and file system permits the selection of the appropriate trade-off. Cost or risk may also be involved in the trade-off. Choosing RAID (Redundant Arrays of Inexpensive Disks, see "RAID Modes" on page 258 for more information) disk configurations for data integrity may be less expensive than alternative mirroring solutions that often improve performance. It may be more cost-effective to purchase a CPU upgrade rather than spend days or weeks analyzing how the application could be changed to improve performance.

In the case of a bottleneck, it is necessary to strike a balance between the demand for a resource and the availability of that resource. In order to relieve a given bottleneck, we must either increase the availability of a resource or decrease demand for it. Figure 1-2 shows this balance. A more complex view analyzes the demand for and availability of resources over time.

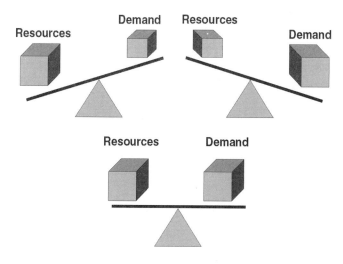

Figure 1-2   Balancing Resources and Demands

Shifting some of the demand for a resource from a high demand time period to one of lower demand is a way of balancing resource and demand without reducing the total demand. One way to view this graphically is shown in Figure 1-3. When possible, shifting batch jobs, reporting, or other functions to hours of the day when the online transaction load is lower may significantly improve the performance during the heavy transaction period. This may have an effect of smoothing out the demands on the system resources, resulting in better overall utilization of the system.

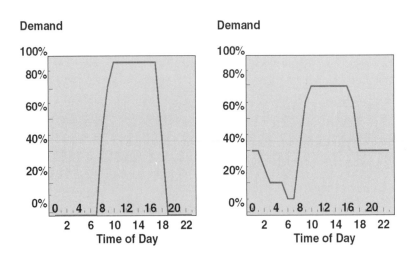

Figure 1-3   Balancing Demand Over Time

Another trade-off that should be considered is tuning for the most common situations versus tuning for the occasional performance problem. For example, consider a database application that usually is used in an online transaction manner. Sometimes, however, other functions such as backups or batch reporting are performed. Online performance usually benefits by having a large database buffer area. The other functions may benefit more by having a large system buffer cache. One must decide which of these is more common and more important, and then tune for that situation. The only other way would be to change the configuration of the system when some of these offline or batch operations are occuring.

The traditional view of system resources is, however, incomplete. HP-UX systems are often used in a distributed environment where many computer systems are joined in a cooperative network. Other important resources, such as the network and graphics, are not included in the traditional view.

A fuller view of system resources is shown in Figure 1-4. Again, the double-sided arrows denote that all the resources are intertwined, and that relieving one bottleneck will likely result in a new one.

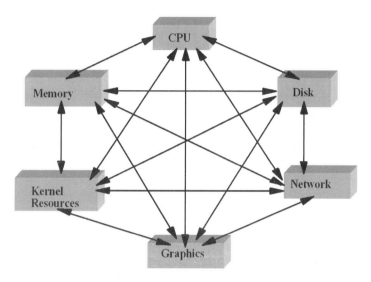

Figure 1-4   Complete View of System Resources

The general I/O resource, which includes direct-connected terminal I/O and magnetic tape, is *not* included in Figure 1-4. Network-connected terminals, such as those connected via a terminal server, are included in the network resource. However, network-connected terminals use the same *termio* subsystem as direct-connected terminals. The *termio* subsystem can consume a large amount of the CPU resource to process the characters as they are transmitted from the terminals.

The network resource includes system-to-system connections, network-connected terminals, and other smarter clients such as PCs. Network transports such as Ethernet, SNA, and X.25 are included here. Applications that consume this resource include virtual terminal, file transfer, remote file access, electronic mail, X/Windows or Motif applications, and networked inter-process communication (IPC) methods such as sockets and remote procedure calls (RPCs).

Client/Server applications are very complex. One must consider the traditional resource consumption on the server and client systems, plus the network resource consumption and latency involved in communication between the client and server programs.

Kernel resources are system tables that provide the mechanism for file access, intrasystem inter-process communication (IPC), and process creation.

The graphics resource typically involves specialized hardware and software that provides graphics capabilities. This resource will not be discussed in detail in this book. The tuning possibilities for the graphics resource are limited to upgrading to a faster CPU, upgrading to faster graphics hardware, or tuning the specialized graphics software, for which the typical user does not have the source code (X-11, PHIGS, etc.).

It is useful to look at each of these resources separately for the purpose of analysis. The various performance monitoring tools, which will be discussed in Chapter 5 "Survey of Unix Performance Tools" on page 51, provide data from a particular set of metrics, and may not provide data for all the system resources shown above.   It will be demonstrated that no single tool provides all the data needed to monitor overall system performance.

An important aspect of resource analysis is that it is invasive, as shown in another rule.

RULE 3: Performance cannot be measured without impacting the system that is being measured.

Rule #3 is a loose interpretation of the Heisenberg principle. Physicist Werner Heisenberg discovered that he could not measure both the speed and the position of an atomic particle, since the act of making the measurement perturbed the system that was being measured. This is also true of computer systems. The following is an example from Bob's consulting experience.

From Bob's Consulting Log—I was called in to evaluate a database server system used for On-line Transaction Processing (OLTP). There were several hundred users on the system, and memory was configured at 128 MB. There had been complaints of poor performance. I did preliminary measurements with *vmstat* and *glance*. Then I started using *gpm*, the graphical version of *glance*, for more detailed measurements. The system started thrashing and exhibiting a very different behavior: application processes were being starved of CPU. The system was already at the verge of a severe virtual memory problem, and I pushed it over the edge by running *gpm*, which consumes much more virtual memory than the other tools (over 5 MB).

Making measurements consumes resources. The level of resource consumption caused by performance data collection and presentation depends upon:

- The type, frequency, and number of measurements
- Data presentation method (text and/or graphics)
- Whether the data is being stored to disk
- The source of the data (to be discussed later)
- General activity on the system (the busier the system is, the more data is generated)

Different tools consume varying amounts of memory, CPU, and disk bandwidth (if the data is being recorded in a file). It is important to realize that it is not possible to collect performance data without consuming resources and even changing the *system* that is being measured. There may not be sufficient system resources available to run the tool. The added overhead due to using the tools may push the system over the edge. In that case, what is being measured is no longer the same system. For instance, if memory consumption is already very high and the tool requires a large amount of memory just to run, memory thrashing may occur (if it is not already occurring) and change the characteristics of what is being measured. The "Catch-22" with this situation is that the poorer the system's performance, the more measurements must be made to provide information about what the system is doing. One must decide what level of impact is acceptable in order to acquire the necessary information.

Finally, there is no single tool for all your needs.

> ## RULE 4: No single performance tool will provide all the data needed to solve performance problems.

The perfect performance tool that solves all performance problems in all situations simply does not exist. It is necessary to develop familiarity with multiple tools so that all needs can be met. In fact, it is sometimes useful to cross-check measurements between the various tools to ensure that the tool itself is reporting information correctly. In other words, if the data doesn't make sense, question the tool!

## CHAPTER 2

Performance Management Tasks

Performance Management is a job function and a process that may be performed by the System Administrator, or by a person whose job is to monitor system performance. Performance Management is a process that starts when the computer purchaser considers what system to buy, and it continues throughout the life of that system. Unfortunately, the role of performance management is sometimes left until a performance crisis occurs, as in the following example.

From Bob's Consulting Log—We were called in to a situation where performance was so bad that users and management were complaining loudly. However, the problem had existed for several months, and no one had bothered to collect any performance data, so it was impossible to tell if the situation had suddenly become worse, or if it had degraded gradually. Worse still, there was no log of changes to the system to help in figuring out whether some system adjustment had degraded performance.

Performance management tasks include:

• Workload Estimation

• Benchmarking

• Performance Characterization

• Performance Forecasting or Prediction

• Application Optimization

• Capacity Planning

• Performance Problem Diagnosis and Resolution

Each of these tasks fits into the performance management system life cycle that is shown in Figure 2-1.

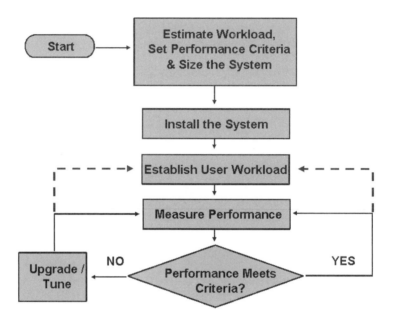

Figure 2-1   Performance Management Life Cycle

2.1 Workload Estimation

Workload estimation begins when a new application is being designed, or when an existing application is to be ported to a new system platform. Examples of data required for workload estimation are:

- Number of users
- Types of transactions
- Mix of transactions
- Transaction rate
- Amount of data
- Throughput (amount of work to be accomplished in a given time interval)
- Response time (acceptable average amount of time per transaction)

When a similar workload does not exist, workload estimation involves guessing the values for the data listed above. Otherwise, the data should be estimated based on real values from a working application and system.

2.2 Benchmarking

Performance criteria are typically set along with the workload estimation. Both are needed to appropriately size the system. *Benchmarking* is sometimes conducted to prove that the system sizing accurately meets the workload and performance criteria. Benchmarking is a very complex and time-consuming activity that tests the system and application in a controlled environment. Deciding whether to use an industry-standard benchmark or to define and create a custom user-benchmark is very difficult. There are trade-offs associated with each.

For instance, industry-standard benchmarks can be very useful in comparing systems from different vendors and in determining relative performance differences among several systems from the same vendor. However, the industry-standard benchmark is not usually an accurate reflection of the actual application environment unless the workload of the benchmark fairly closely matches the actual application workload. A well-defined and characteristic subset of the actual application environment used as a benchmark will provide the most complete prediction of performance. This process is usually quite expensive to define, create or port, and execute. The trade-off, then, is one of time and money versus accuracy.

There are commercially-available tools that can simulate users, transactions, and batch jobs to help execute the benchmark. Nevertheless, benchmarking requires a significant investment in hardware, software tools, and time for design and implementation.

2.3 Performance Characterization

After the system and application are installed, and users begin putting a real workload on the system, *performance characterization* is done, first with baseline measurements and later with historical measurements. The performance professional keeps monitoring system performance and checks it against the performance criteria that were set before the system was installed.

Some organizations use Service Level Agreements to guarantee a certain level of performance to the user organizations. In order to monitor compliance with Service Level Agreements, it is necessary to continually monitor performance against the performance criteria. It may become necessary to upgrade the hardware, to tune the operating system, or to optimize the application to comply with the terms of the Service Level Agreement. This is a two-way agreement in which the user organization defines and fixes the workload, and the performance organization guarantees the level of performance. Performance monitoring becomes an ongoing task that continues throughout the life of the system.

2.4 Performance Forecasting or Prediction

Performance managers may want to predict when resources may be saturated on the system. This prediction is based on historical performance of the current application and the current growth rate of the business. This task is often called *performance prediction* or *forecasting*. By accurately predicting resource consumption, necessary hardware or software upgrades may be ordered in advance and installed before users complain that performance is degrading unacceptably as the workload naturally increases.

2.5 Application Optimization

Application optimization is an important activity before and during application development and when performance problems arise. Knowledge of the operating system is necessary so that decisions can be made about selecting various system services. Compiler optimization features can be used to improve application performance in certain circumstances. Profiling tools can be used to determine where an application is spending its time. Databases, for instance, may include tools that provide information that can be used to tune the application to improve performance. Refer to Chapter 11, "Compiler Performance Tuning", Chapter 12, "Java Run-time Performance Tuning", Chapter 13, "Designing Applications for Performance", and Chapter 14, "Application Profiling" for a discussion of application optimization.

It is very important to start with analysis of the application itself, because that is where the greatest performance improvement can actually occur. It is often necessary to have source code to the application to correct many application performance problems. However, analyzing how the application *uses* system resources can yield ideas on how to improve the application's performance. Especially where applications spend most of their time in user mode, it is necessary to focus on the application rather than the system. Another example is with database applications. Adding an index to a database table can suddenly and significantly improve application performance.

From Bob's Consulting Log—I was called into a situation halfway around the world in Kuala Lumpur, Malaysia. An important customer was using a database application that usually provided excellent response times. However, at certain times during the day, the system seemed to freeze and users had to wait for five minutes before getting a response. After I analyzed the system for several hours, the problem occurred. I asked my host to take me to the people whom I had noted were consuming a lot of system resources. I found that one user was running a batch reporting job. After asking to look at the job, I determined that the job locked the entire database when it ran. It then became a very simple task of changing the locking mode from database to table or row. Suddenly performance for all of the users improved to the normal level.

2.6 Capacity Planning

Capacity planning techniques may also be a part of the performance professional's job. Capacity planning involves answering "What if ?" questions such as:

- What size system will be needed if fifty more users are added?
- How will response time degrade if a new application is added to the system?
- Will performance improve if the CPU is upgraded to a faster model?

• Do I add an application server or upgrade an existing one?

Capacity planning is a complex activity that requires an intimate knowledge of the application and accurate measurements of system resource utilization related back to the business transactions.

Capacity planning software packages that are commercially available use either modeling or simulation techniques to project answers to the "What if ?" question. Use of capacity planning software requires measurement and analysis of data from tools such as *PerfView/Analyzer* or *sar*, both of which are discussed in Chapter 5, "Survey of Unix Performance Tools". Measurements are made at certain key times, such as peak periods during the day, as well as during peak business cycle periods such as end-of-month, end-of-quarter, and end-of-year.

Further discussion of capacity planning is beyond the scope of this book.

2.7 Performance Problem Resolution

Each of the preceding activities is proactive in that an attempt is made to predict and prevent performance problems. Even if the system is currently performing satisfactorily, performance management is required so that changes in performance can be readily and speedily detected. Unfortunately, no matter how much planning is accomplished, *performance problem resolution* is still needed when problems arise. Performance problems manifest themselves when users complain of poor response time or when the user department complains that the workload cannot be processed in the appropriate time. Problems often arise at very inopportune times and therefore create emotional, reactive, and time-constrained environments. For these reasons, performance problem resolution requires crisis management skills and techniques. It is too late to employ performance management techniques when a performance crisis occurs. The type, quantity, and frequency of data collected in the course of performance problem resolution is also quite different from the data collected during performance management activities. Therefore, performance problem resolution is often a large part of the performance professional's role.

All of the activities that are part of performance management require performance tools to provide objective data that shows what the system and application are doing, and how well (or poorly) it is performing. A variety of performance tools will be discussed in great detail in Chapter 5, "Survey of Unix Performance Tools".

## CHAPTER 3

A Performance Management Methodology

Although performance management and crisis management (including performance problem resolution) require different techniques and data collection, the same basic methodology can be used for both. Performance management uses the following steps:

- Assessment
- Measurement
- Interpretation and Analysis
- Identification of Bottlenecks
- Tuning or Upgrading the System

The flow chart in Figure 3-1 summarizes the performance methodology that will be discussed in detail, step by step.

3.1 Assessment

Assessment often involves asking lots of questions, as the following example shows.

From Bob's Consulting Log—I spent the entire morning asking people a lot of questions about the application, the system configuration, and how users perceived the performance problem. At lunch, the person who hired me said he was surprised that I had not yet logged onto the system. I told him my approach is to ask questions first and collect system data second. Later that day, I did obtain some data from the system, but the most important clue to the nature of the problem came from interviewing the users.

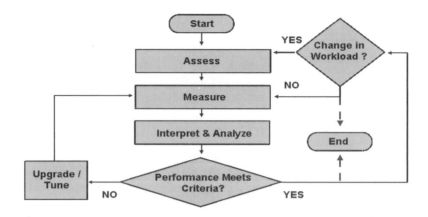

Figure 3-1   Performance Management Methodology

These questions are necessary to help you understand your limits as a performance professional, as well as those things that you can change. The following items must be learned during the assessment phase:

- System configuration
- Application design
- Performance expectations
- Known peak periods
- Changes in the system configuration or the application
- Duration of the problem, if applicable
- The options
- The politics

3.1.1   System Configuration

System configuration includes both hardware and software configuration. The number of disk drives, how data are distributed on the disks, whether the disks are used with mounted file systems or used in raw mode, the file system parameters, and how the application makes use of them—all of these factors are examined during a system configuration assessment. Memory size, the amount of lockable memory, and the amount of swap space are scrutinized in assessing the virtual memory system configuration. You will need to know the processor type and the number in the system. Finally, the kernel (operating system) configuration must be understood, and the values of tunable kernel parameters should be identified. Knowing all these items in advance will make carrying out the various performance management functions much easier.

3.1.2 Application Design

Understanding the design of the *application* is equally important. It may not be possible for you as a performance specialist to thoroughly understand the design and workings of the application. Optimally, there should be someone with whom the application design can be discussed.

Such things as inter-process communication (IPC) methods, basic algorithms, how the application accesses the various disks, and whether the application is compute- or I/O-intensive are examples of the knowledge you will need. For instance, with relational databases, it is important to understand whether or not the Relational Database Management System (RDBMS) software supports placing a table and the index that points to it on different disk drives. Some RDBMS products support this and some do not; when this capability is present, it is an important tuning technique for improving database performance. Modern design techniques such as creating multi-threaded applications and the deployment of applications on multi-processor systems require new skills to analyze how the application works and its use of system resources.

You should expect consumer complaints and comments to be in terms of the application. However, measurements will be based upon the available metrics, which are mostly kernel-oriented. If you can't translate system measurements into application-specific terms, it will be difficult to explain in a meaningful way what the measurements indicate in terms of necessary changes in the system.

3.1.3 Performance Expectations

You will need to learn the *performance expectations* of the system's users. It is very important to know, in advance, the measurable criteria for satisfactory performance. This is the only way to know when performance tuning is successful and when it is time to monitor performance rather than actively attempt to improve it. Objective rather than subjective measures must be elicited. Being told that response time must be less than two seconds and is currently five seconds or more is much more useful than being told that performance is "lousy."

Understanding performance expectations is a complicated task. The perception of actual system performance and the definition of satisfactory performance will change depending upon one's perspective and role. Understanding expectations includes the need for eliciting success criteria. In another words, you need to know whether the users or owners of the application and system will agree with you that you have finished tuning the system and application.

3.1.3.1 Response Time

Users of the system typically talk about poor response time. They are mostly concerned with how long it takes to get a response from the system or application once the enter key is pressed. For instance, a user who is entering invoices into an accounts payable system expects to have data verification and data insertion completed within several seconds, at most. Engineers who use a computer-aided design application expect to see the image of the part being analyzed rotated in real-time. Otherwise, they get frustrated with what they consider to be poor performance. Response time is the most commonly used measure of system performance and is typically quoted as one of the following:

- An average of a fractional second (sometimes called sub second) or seconds
- A certain confidence level
- A maximum response time

Typical confidence levels are 90%–98%. For example, one would say that the desirable average response time is two seconds, 95% of the time, with a maximum transaction response time of five seconds.

What is a good value for response time? While the automatic answer "It depends" is certainly true, it is useful to have a range of values for response time to use as a guideline. Users of a text editor or word processing package don't want to have to wait to see the characters echoed on the screen as they are typed. In this case, sub-second response time of approximately 250 milliseconds would be considered optimal. In a transaction processing environment one must understand the environment before developing good response time values. Some of the factors are as follows:

- Transaction complexity
- Number of users
- Think time between transactions
- Transaction types and ratios

Transaction Complexity   This deals with the amount of work which the system must perform in order to complete the transaction. If the transaction is defined as requiring three record lookups followed by an update, that transaction is much more complex than one that is a simple read. The complexity associated with typical Computer-Aided Design (CAD) applications is very high. Many CPU cycles and perhaps disk I/Os are necessary for simple interactive tasks, such as rotating a model of an object on the display.

Number of Users   The number of users influences the sizing of any system that is required to support a given workload and response time.

Think Time   As the think time between transactions increases, more work can be supported by the system in the idle periods between transactions. *Heads down* environments provide almost no think time between transactions. This is a typical data input environment. Conversely, customer service environments often provide very long think times, since most of time the customer service representative is speaking with the caller by telephone and casually accessing various databases as the telephone conversation proceeds.

Transaction Types and Ratios It is necessary to look at the types of transactions and the ratios of the number of each transaction type to the total. Read-intensive applications can provide rapid response times to queries. Insert- and particularly update-intensive applications require more CPU cycles and often disk I/Os to complete the transaction. Table 3-1 gives guidelines for acceptable response times.

Table 3-1 Typical Application Response Times (based on the author's experience)

Transaction Type	Acceptable Response Time in Seconds
Interactive CAD applications	< 1
Text editing or word processing	1/4
Read-intensive, low complexity	< 1
Read-intensive, medium to high complexity	1–2
Update-intensive, low to medium complexity	5
Update-intensive, high complexity	5–15
Long think-time environments	2–3
Batch run	N/A

Users perceive performance as poor when update response time exceeds 5 seconds and when there is no preparation to be done by the user to get ready for the next transaction. Read performance must be no more than 1–2 seconds to keep users satisfied.

After installing the computer system and the application, some system administrators or performance managers have been known to create dummy workloads on the systems before letting any users access the applications or the system. The initial users perceive a certain response time following their inputs. As more users are added, the dummy workload is reduced, thus providing a constant response time to the users. This trick attempts to address another issue with the perception of actual performance. Users prefer consistent responsiveness rather than variable responsiveness. If someone decides to run some resource-intensive batch jobs while interactive users are on the system, interactive performance will typically degrade. End-of-month processing will usually consume a very large amount of system resources, making it necessary to either keep the interactive users off the system while it is being run, or to run it in off-hours.

Users can tolerate and accept consistently poor response time rather than response that is good one minute and poor the next. The acceptable variance in response time changes as the average response time itself changes. Users will tolerate an average response time of 1.5 seconds with a variance of ± 1 second much less than they will tolerate an average response time of 3 seconds with a variance of ± .25 second. One problem associated with attempting to prevent variability in performance is that when throughput is favored in tuning the system, the chance of experiencing variability in response time is greatly increased.

Predictability is another way of looking at consistency of performance. Predictability makes the job of the performance professional easier when forecasting future resource consumption. It also allows the appropriate setting of expectations for performance, as the following analogy shows.

The public transportation department announces that buses on a particular bus route are scheduled to arrive at each stop an average of every ten minutes. In a given thirty-minute period, three buses arrive all at once and the next one arrives forty minutes later. This schedule meets the stated criteria. However, it will make the people waiting for the fourth bus very unhappy. It would be much better for the waiting passengers if the buses were to arrive consistently ten minutes apart. It would also be perceived well if the buses were to arrive predictably at certain clock times.

3.1.3.2   Throughput

Information system *management personnel* are typically interested in throughput, rather than response time. If the demands of the organization require that a certain amount of work must be processed in an average day, then management is concerned whether the system can process that workload, rather than caring whether response time is one second or two seconds. Throughput is often quoted as work per unit time. Examples of throughput measures are:

• Three thousand invoices processed per hour

• Five CAD modeling runs per day

• All end-of-month processing must complete within three days

• Overnight processing must complete in the nine off-peak hours

It is not possible to develop guidelines for good throughput values. Throughput is driven by business needs, and the system must be sized to support those requirements. Capacity planning is done to ensure that as business requirements grow, the system will be able to handle the workload. It should be easy to predict in advance whether a system will be able to provide a specified throughput. The workload is considered a batch workload and the average time to complete a unit of work can be measured with a simple benchmark.

In reality, the situation is never that simple. Users are typically very vocal, and poor response time often reaches the ears of management. The point of this discussion is that the definition of performance may change from person to person; attitudes about response time and throughput must be examined to determine what users consider to be acceptable performance. Although the overall methodology is the same, tuning for response time and for throughput are different. Another way of putting this is that there is one strategy for approaching performance, but there are many different tactics.

3.1.4 Known Peak Periods

It is useful to identify *known peak periods* in advance, so that unusual spikes in the data can be readily explained. For instance, it is often mentioned that resource utilization in an office environment peaks at 11:00 a.m. and between 2:00–3:00 p.m. during the normal work day. Processing requirements typically grow at the end of the month or the end of a quarter. Expecting peaks at these times can save time when analyzing the data. Additionally, if the peaks are absent, it may be a clue that something unusual is preventing full system utilization.

3.1.5 Sudden Changes

Anyone who has worked in technical support has experienced callers complaining that the system "suddenly" is no longer working correctly or that performance has suddenly degraded. The following is a familiar dialogue:

From Bob's Consulting Log—

Consultant: Has anything changed in the application or the system?
Client: No, nothing has changed.
Consultant: Are you sure that nothing has changed?
Client: I'm quite sure nothing has changed.

(Three days later, after a lot of investigation ...)

Consultant: Did you notice that your database administrator (DBA) dropped some indexes?
Client: Oh! I didn't think **those** changes would make a difference.

The task of investigating changes that may have been made to the system is quite an art. However, the importance of this part of the assessment should not be minimized.

3.1.6 Duration of the Problem

When doing performance problem diagnosis, identifying the *duration of the problem* involves several issues:

- How long does the performance problem last?
- When does the performance problem occur?
- How long has the performance problem existed?
- When did it begin?

It is important to understand *the length of time that the problem lasts* to detect whether it occurs only sometimes, because of a spike in resource utilization, or constantly. In each of these situations, tuning requires a different approach.

Knowing *when the performance problem occurs* means that data collection can be planned and minimized, as an alternative to collecting performance data for days or weeks to capture data when the problem manifests itself.

Finally, *the length of time that the performance problem has existed* influences the probability of determining if anything in the system or application has been changed. If the problem has existed for a long time (weeks or months), it is very unlikely that any changes will be discovered. One can also question the seriousness of the situation if the users have been living with the problem for months.

3.1.7   Understanding the Options

Understanding the options lets you determine what recommendations should be offered. If there is no capital budget for purchasing computer hardware, you can look for other ways to resolve the performance problem. Perhaps tuning the operating system or application is a viable alternative to upgrading the CPU to a faster model. In contrast, if time constraints dictate that the problem must be resolved quickly and deterministically, then upgrading the CPU to a faster model would probably be more expeditious than spending an unpredictable amount of time attempting to improve or redesign the application.

3.1.8   Understanding the Politics

It may be necessary to *understand the politics of the organization* before revealing the cause of the problem or before recommending the changes to be implemented. Knowledge of the politics may help narrow the scope of the question you are trying to answer. It may be that the user organization wants to gain more control of the system, and it is trying to gather evidence to support this cause. The Information Technology (IT) department (also called Information Systems in some organizations) may be trying to allocate computing resources fairly, and it may not be possible to make changes that improve the situation for only one group. Finally, you may have been called in simply to provide objective data to justify the purchase of a larger, faster system.

3.2 Measurement

The next phase of the performance management methodology involves measuring actual system or application performance. For this phase, performance tools are used to perform the data collection and presentation.

Measurement is based upon the answers to several interrelated questions that must be answered before any data is collected.

- Which performance tools are available?
- What is the purpose of the measurement?
- Is the measurement baseline- or crisis-oriented?
- How long should the data be collected, and at what intervals?

- What data metrics are to be collected?
- How well are the metrics documented?
- How accurate are the data presented by the tool?
- Are certain system resources already saturated?
- How do these measurements relate to the organization's business needs?

3.2.1 Tool Availability

Some performance tools come standard with the HP-UX Operating System. Others are available as separately purchasable products. The availability of the various tools on the system being measured will constrain the answers to the other questions. Tool familiarity also affects the answer to this question. Comfort and experience with using a tool often limit the use of other tools even if other tools are more useful in a given situation. However, the best tool for a given purpose should be used to make the measurements, even if that tool must be purchased.

3.2.2 Purpose of the Measurement: Baseline versus Crisis

The purpose of the data collection must be determined in advance in order to select the correct set of tools for gathering the data. It is important to measure performance on the system when performance is acceptable. This type of measurement is called a *baseline measurement*. Think of a baseline as a signature or profile which can be used for purposes of comparison at those times when performance is not acceptable or is degrading. Baseline measurements require fewer metrics and a longer sampling interval, because a particular problem is not being investigated. Instead, the goals are to characterize system performance only, and to watch for trends.

An analogy to baseline measurements is a routine physical exam. The physician takes certain vital signs like blood pressure, pulse rate, temperature, and blood tests, including cholesterol counts. A visual inspection by the physician is correlated with the internal measurements and an historical record is kept to monitor trends over time. Any unusual symptoms are investigated immediately so that the physician can treat the problem before it becomes chronic.

Baseline measurements should be reviewed to develop conclusions about system performance without the immediate goal of altering performance by tuning the system or application. Baseline measurements should be archived for historical purposes. They can then be used to:

- Review performance trends over time
- Compare against current performance when investigating or diagnosing current performance problems
- Provide data for performance forecasting
- Develop and monitor service level agreements
- Provide data for capacity planning

Data collected and archived over time does not typically need to be as voluminous and detailed as for performance problem resolution.

Performance crises usually result from failing to manage performance. *Crisis measurements* (those typically made during performance problem diagnosis) require much more detail so that performance problems can be adequately investigated. The additional detail involves additional metrics as well as more frequent measurement, resulting in a much larger volume of data. The purpose of crisis measurements is to characterize *current* system performance in detail so that appropriate tuning can be done. Managing a performance crisis is much more difficult when there are no baselines against which a comparison can be made.

Baseline measurements should be made, archived, and reviewed periodically so that future performance crises can be prevented, and dangerous performance trends acted upon before they become serious. As the data ages, less and less detail is required. As changes in the system occur, for example, adding users or making changes in the application, new baseline measurements should be taken. Another tactic is to compare baselines from similarly configured systems, to help understand the variances before problems occur.

Baseline measurements can help provide the necessary translation between the language of performance tools and the needs of users. If the data can be presented and reviewed prior to a crisis, then communication during the crisis should be easier.

Baseline measurements should include information that is not related to existing sources. For instance, reviewing the "Other Application" category in MeasureWare can indicate if new work is being added, or whether the trend is to move work away from existing applications.

3.2.3   Duration and Interval of the Measurement

Some tools are good for displaying performance metrics in real-time. Other tools are better for collecting performance metrics in the background over a long period for casual analysis later. If performance problem diagnosis is the goal of the data collection and the problem manifests itself consistently or after a short time, then real-time performance tools would be the best choice. The amount of data produced by real-time performance tools is quite large. Therefore, this type of data should not be gathered for long periods of time since there is a large storage requirement, and it is difficult to review large volumes of data. Performance problems that cannot be readily reproduced, or those that occur unpredictably or only occasionally, will warrant longer-term data collection. Tools that provide summarization and detail capabilities are the best choice.

If performance characterization or forecasting is the goal, longer-term trending tools would be the tools of choice. Chapter 5, "Survey of Unix Performance Tools" on page 51 will discuss in detail the individual tools and when they are best used. The duration of the measurement should greatly influence selection of the tool or tools that will be used to collect the data.

The measurement interval must also be determined. Sampling intervals for baseline measurements should be measured in minutes or hours rather than seconds to reduce the volume of data that will be collected. Sampling intervals for crisis measurements or for performance problem resolution need to be shorter and are measured in seconds. If performance problems are of short duration, i.e., tend to spike, sampling intervals must also be short: typically one to five seconds. The shorter the sampling interval, the higher the overhead of making the measurement. This is of particular concern if one or more of the system resources are already saturated.

3.2.4   Particular Metric Needs

Performance tools come from various sources, and people get used to using certain ones, depending on their background. These then become their favorite tools, whether or not they are best for the job. Some tools were written for specific purposes; for example, *vmstat* was written specifically to display virtual memory and CPU metrics, but not disk statistics. The tool chosen should be useful in diagnosing the performance issue at hand.

3.2.5   Metric Documentation

There are several hundred performance metrics available from the kernel. These metrics were developed over time, and some are better documented than others. Some of the metrics may have a one-line description that is incomprehensible. Only by reviewing kernel source code can one hope to determine the meaning of some of the more esoteric metrics. Of course, the availability of kernel source code is limited, as is the desire to review it.

For example, the manual page for the tool *vmstat* defines the field *at* as the number of address translation faults. Those of us who are familiar with hardware components of modern computers might readily conclude that this field counts the number of Translation Lookaside Buffer (TLB) faults. This would be a very desirable metric, since it would give one indication of how well the CPU address translation cache is performing. Unfortunately, only by reviewing the kernel source code can one determine that the *at* field in the *vmstat* report is really referring to the number of page faults, a virtual memory system metric.

Good documentation is needed to determine what metrics are important to the purpose of the measurement and to learn how to interpret them.

3.2.6   Metric Accuracy

In order to understand completely why some performance metrics are inaccurate, one must understand how the kernel is designed. For instance, although most CPU hardware clocks measure time in microseconds, the granularity of the HP-UX system clock is 10 milliseconds. Most Unix-based operating systems record CPU consumption on a per-process basis by noting which process was running when the clock ticked. That process is charged for consuming CPU time during the *entire* clock tick, whether or not it used all of the tick. So, the saying "garbage in, garbage out" applies to performance tools in a loose sense. If the source of the data is inaccurate, the data will be inaccurate.

The standard Unix performance tools use the kernel's standard sources of data. This method of determining global and per-process CPU utilization was fine in the early days of Unix when systems were much slower. Newer methods have been developed by Hewlett-Packard to more accurately characterize system performance. Tools developed by HP get their data from the new sources in the kernel, which provides for greater metric accuracy. The IEEE POSIX

(P1004) committee, the Open Group, and the Performance Working Group (PWG) are all reviewing HP's implementation for adoption into a standard that could be implemented in other versions of Unix.

3.2.7   Saturation of Certain System Resources

When one or more system resources are saturated, it may be necessary to concentrate on particular metrics in order to determine the source of the saturation. However, merely invoking a performance tool causes additional overhead. The tool chosen should be one that does not exacerbate the saturation of the resource of concern. Tool overhead will be discussed more fully in Chapter 4, "Kernel Instrumentation and Performance Metrics" on page 39 and Chapter 5, "Survey of Unix Performance Tools" on page 51.

3.2.8   Relationship Between the Metric and the Application

Metrics by their nature usually count how many times some piece of code or hardware is used. The relationship of a given metric to a particular application and to the needs of its users must be established by analysis and interpretation of the data, plus a complete understanding of the application.

3.2.9   Qualitative versus Quantitative Measurements

One last point about measurements. The preceding discussion involved quantitative measures of how the system is performing. Other, equally important measures of system performance are qualitative in nature. There is a management style called "Management by Wandering Around," or MBWA, in which the manager visits a wide variety of managed personnel and asks questions that help to monitor the pulse of the organization. In the performance arena, MBWA becomes "Measuring by Wandering Around." Talk to the users. Ask them how they perceive system and application performance. Find out *why* they might feel that performance is bad. Watch how they interact with the system. It's possible that the users may be interacting with the system in a way that the application designers never imagined, and that is causing the application to behave poorly.

Another type of qualitative measurement can be made by interacting with the system directly and noting its responsiveness or the lack of it. Logging on the system, initiating a simple command like *ls(1)* for a directory listing, and noting the response might result in a qualitative measure of interactive performance.

3.2.10   Summary

In summary, the reasons for making measurements are:

• Measurements are key to understanding what is happening in the system.
• Measurements are the *only* way to know what to tune.

In addition, it is necessary to measure periodically in order to proactively monitor system and application performance so that problems can be prevented or resolved quickly.

3.3 Interpretation and Analysis

After making the measurements, it is necessary to review the voluminous amount of data that were collected. Some of the performance tools present the data as tables of numbers. Other tools offer summarization of the data in graphical form. Regardless of the presentation method, interpretation of the data is complex. One must first understand what the metrics mean. Then, it is necessary to know how to interpret the numbers; in other words, what number indicates a performance problem. This is no easy task! **Rule #1** comes into play here. A good value or a bad value for a given performance metric *depends* upon many factors.

From Bob's Consulting Log—I was involved in a sizing exercise where we had to determine what system was needed to support the application running 125 users with a response time of < 5 seconds. We started out with a basic system and looked at the load average metric, which was 250. We also saw that the response time was well above 5 seconds (some took 5 minutes!), and we were only simulating 75 users.

After upgrading the CPU to a faster one, we re-ran the test, and the load average dropped to 125. We were now able to simulate all 125 users, but response time was still unsatisfactory. Finally, we upgraded to the most powerful processor currently available. Now, the load average was 75. Most people would cringe at that number, saying response time should be terrible. However, all transactions completed in under 5 seconds for all 125 users. The moral is: Don't be scared by large numbers. What really matters is that you meet the performance requirements of the application.

The value for a given metric that can be considered good or bad will be discussed in-depth in the tuning section for each major system resource.

Some of the general factors that affect setting rules of thumb for performance metrics are:

- Type of system: multi-user or workstation
- Type of application: interactive or batch, compute- or I/O-intensive
- Application architecture: single system or client/server, multi-tiered, parallel system
- Speed of the CPU
- Type of disk drives
- Type of networking

3.3.1 Multi-User versus Workstation

A multi-user system experiences many more context switches than a workstation normally does. Context switches consume some of the CPU resource. Additionally, the high number of users typically causes a lot of I/O, which puts demands on the CPU and disk resources. Workstations that are used for graphics-intensive applications typically have high user CPU utilization numbers (which are normal) but lower context switch rates, since there is only one user. Applications on a multi-user system usually cause random patterns of disk I/O. Workstation applications often cause sequential patterns of disk I/O. So, these factors affect the optimal values for the CPU and disk metrics.

3.3.2   Interactive versus Batch, Compute-Intensive versus I/O-Intensive

Workstations can support highly interactive applications, for example, X/Windows or Motif applications that require a lot of interaction. These can be business applications, such as customer service applications that provide several windows into different databases. Alternatively, technical applications such as CAD programs support interactive input to draw the part on the screen. Compute-bound applications on a workstation sometimes act like batch applications on a multi-user systems. Batch applications consume a large amount of CPU, as do compute-intensive applications. Interactive applications cause many more context switches and more system CPU utilization than do batch or compute-intensive applications. Batch applications use less memory than highly interactive applications. Compute-intensive applications can touch more pages of memory than individual I/O-intensive applications. The optimal values for the CPU and memory metrics are affected by these factors.

3.3.3   Application Architecture

An application may be architected in several ways. It can be monolithic, that is, one large program that runs entirely on a single system. Parallel applications are designed to make better use of the components of the single computer system (especially a Symmetric Multi-Processing (SMP) system) to improve throughput or response. In contrast, an application can be distributed as in a multi-tiered client/server environment. In this case, parallel processing does not necessarily provide the same benefits. For these reasons, understanding the architecture is necessary before deciding what measurements to make and how to interpret the data.

3.3.4   Performance of the CPU

The higher performing the CPU, the greater the CPU resource that is available. Applications can get more work done during the time-slice they are allocated, and may be able to satisfy their current need for the CPU resource completely, rather than having to wait for another turn. This factor affects the *run queue* metric.

3.3.5   Type of Disks

Newer technology disk drives are faster, have higher capacity, and can support more I/Os per second than can older disks. The number of disk channels also affects the number of disk I/Os that are optimal. Caches on disks can dramatically improve the overall response times of disk I/Os.

3.3.6   Type of Networks

Networks continue to get faster and faster as well. High speed networks can move a lot of data between servers with high bandwidth and low latency. The network bandwidth has actually increased much more significantly over the years than the bandwidth of disks. Improvements in link throughput and connectivity technologies such as Dense Wave Division Multiplexing (DWDM) fiber links allow for high speed and low latency between systems separated by miles.

3.4   Identifying Bottlenecks

With all these factors in mind, the goal of data interpretation and analysis is to determine if there is a particular bottleneck. Once a particular bottleneck is identified, tuning to improve performance can be initiated. Characteristics of bottlenecks are:

- A particular resource is saturated.
- The queue for the resource grows over time.
- Other resources may be starved as a result.
- Response time is not satisfactory.

3.4.1   Resource Saturation

Resource saturation is often thought of as 100% utilization. The entire resource is consumed. Additional requests for the resource are required to wait. However, this is not sufficient as proof of a bottleneck. Two examples reinforce this point.

Disk utilization is determined by periodically monitoring whether there are any requests in the queue for each disk drive. The total number of requests in the queue is not factored into the disk utilization metric. Although 100% disk utilization is an indicator of a busy disk, it does not mean that the disk cannot support more I/Os.

The idle loop in the kernel is used to compute CPU utilization. On a workstation executing a compute-intensive application, CPU utilization is probably 100% for a long period of time. However, if no other processes are waiting for the CPU, and response time is satisfactory, there is no bottleneck.

There are utilization metrics for the CPU, memory, network, and disk resources.

3.4.2   Growing Resource Queue

Resource queue growth over time is a strong indicator of a bottleneck, in conjunction with the utilization metric. The queue for a resource tends to grow when demand increases and when there is not enough resource available to keep up with the requests. It is easier to develop rules of thumb for queue metrics than for utilization metrics.

3.4.3   Resource Starvation

Resource starvation can occur when one resource is saturated and another resource depends upon it. For instance, in a memory-bound environment, CPU cycles are needed to handle page faults. This leaves less of the CPU resource for application use.

3.4.4   Unsatisfactory Response Time

Unsatisfactory response time is sometimes the final arbiter of whether or not a bottleneck exists. The CPU example given above demonstrates this point. If no other processes are waiting for the CPU, and the application produces the results in a satisfactory time period, then there is no bottleneck. However, if the CPU is saturated and response or throughput expectations are not being met, then a CPU bottleneck exists.

3.4.5   Bottleneck Summary

Multiple metrics should always be reviewed to validate that a bottleneck exists. For example, the CPU utilization metric is a measure of saturation. The run queue metric is a measure of queue growth. Both metrics are needed to establish that a CPU bottleneck is present. Multiple tools should be used to validate that there is not a problem with a particular tool yielding misleading data. Consider the following analogy.

A three-lane highway is built to accommodate a certain maximum traffic flow, for example, twenty vehicles per minute distributed across the three lanes. This would be considered 100% utilization. Additional traffic entering the highway would be forced to wait at the entrance ramp, producing a queue. Suppose that a tractor/trailer overturns and blocks two lanes of the highway. Now, the same amount of traffic must funnel through the one remaining open lane. With the same number of cars on the road, the highway is now more than saturated. The queue builds at the entrance ramps. Resource starvation occurs, since two lanes are closed. The time it takes to travel a given distance on the highway now becomes unacceptably long.

Once a bottleneck is identified, it can possibly be alleviated. However, alleviating one bottleneck may result in the emergence of a new one to investigate.

3.5 Tuning or Upgrading

Once the bottleneck is identified, there are two choices. Either the amount of the resource can be increased, or the demand for the resource can be reduced. Tuning techniques will be discussed along with the particular bottlenecks. However, there are some general tips that can be applied to tuning bottlenecks:

- Determine whether the data indicate a particular bottleneck.
- Devise a simple test for measuring results.
- Do not tune randomly.

- Use heuristics and logic in choosing what to tune.
- Look for simple causes.
- Develop an action plan.
- Change only one thing at a time.
- Prioritize the goals.
- Know when to stop tuning.

3.5.1   Determine Whether There Is a Particular Bottleneck

This is the first tip to apply. Using the multiple characteristics of a bottleneck, determine if the data indicate a particular bottleneck. There is no use in tuning disk I/O on a system that is CPU-bound.

3.5.2   Devise a Simple Test for Measuring Results

When something in the operating system or application is tuned, it is advisable to quantitatively measure whether performance has improved or degraded. The test should be simple, short, and repeatable, so that it can be performed as each tuning step is taken.

3.5.3   Do Not Tune Randomly

There was once a system administrator who always tuned the size of the buffer cache, no matter what the bottleneck. Tuning the wrong thing can make the situation worse rather than better. Use knowledge of how the kernel works to help decide the cause of the bottleneck. Always try to visualize what the data *should* look like and compare it to the actual data before assuming that a cause has been found.

3.5.4   Use Heuristics and Logic

Use heuristics to select the most likely cause of the bottleneck. Experience can point to a particular bottleneck rather quickly. Watching the access lights on the disk drives can quickly indicate which disk drives may be saturated even before you look at the metrics. Use the qualitative measures as well as the quantitative metrics. Logically work through the possible causes and potential tuning solutions. Experience in tuning systems will tell which tuning alternatives offer the largest probability of success.

3.5.5   Look for Simple Causes

By looking for simple causes, easier and less expensive solutions can be tried. This is the K. I. S. S. principle: Keep it Simple, Stupid! Simple causes tend to occur more frequently, and simple solutions should be tried first. For example, tuning a system parameter is easier and less costly than modifying the design of an application. Either tactic might result in performance improvements, but one is clearly a better solution than the other.

3.5.6   Develop an Action Plan

Write up an ordered, prioritized list of measurements and tuning actions. The list can sometimes be turned over to other people for execution. Include contingencies in case some of the steps do not result in improvement. Analyze the results after performing each step of the plan.

3.5.7   Change Only One Thing at a Time!

Otherwise, the cause of the bottleneck cannot be found. If you attempt to tune multiple things at once, the benefits from one type of tuning can be counteracted by the degradation caused by a different type of tuning.

3.5.8   Prioritize Goals

Often, you may have multiple goals when developing a tuning solution. Prioritizing the goals can solve the problem caused by different goals requiring different solutions. It is usually possible to tune for response time or for throughput, but not both. In a transaction-processing environment, one should tune for the most frequent type of transaction, or the most important.

3.5.9   Understand the Limits of the Application's Architecture

Some applications cannot fully utilize a system. An example is a single-threaded process flow designed with no parallelism. Adding a CPU to such an application may not increase performance.

Instrumenting an application (adding code to measure specific events or code paths) to provide performance metrics can also create this problem if the instrumentation is not created with parallelism in mind. For example, incrementing a single global counter may be a choke point, as in the following code design:

```
while not done {
    do transaction work
    lock
    increment global counter
    unlock
}
```

3.5.10   Know When to Stop

Finally, knowing when to stop tuning is very important. Setting the performance expectations in advance is the easiest way to establish completion. Getting the user to agree to success criteria in advance is important for deciding not only when to stop tuning, but when you can declare success. Baselines can be used to help establish that performance has returned to a normal level. The "eternal hope syndrome" will not occur if the performance expectations are met through tuning.

From Bob's Consulting Log—I spent several days at a customer site improving performance by a factor of 50%. Once the customer saw the extent of the improvement, she insisted I do additional work to improve things even more. Soon it became clear that we had already maxed out the performance improvement and then wasted several more days trying to eke out just a little bit extra.

It is not useful to spend a lot of time on gaining 1% improvement in performance. Optimizing a part of the application that is executed only once and consumes less than 5% of the total execution time is just not worth it.

Kernel Instrumentation and Performance Metrics

The ability to make measurements is crucial to any performance management activity. Without measurements, there is no objective data that shows where a system bottleneck is. Also, there is no way to objectively evaluate the effects of tuning the system or the application. The only alternative is to tune randomly, but even with random tuning, the outcome cannot be evaluated without measurements.

This chapter discusses several topics related to how performance data is gathered and which items of data are interesting:

- Approaches to Measuring

- Kernel Instrumentation

- Performance Metrics Categories

4.1 Approaches to Measuring

Making measurements involves gathering data and processing it so that it is usable. There are several common approaches to acquiring data to measure activity in a computer system. They fall into three groups:

- External hardware monitors

- Internal hardware monitors

- Internal software monitors

4.1.1   External Hardware Monitors

External hardware monitors usually involve probes, such as printed circuit boards which plug into the computer backplane or attach directly to the integrated circuits on the CPU board itself. These hardware monitors are triggered by events such as instruction execution or hardware interrupts. The accumulation of data typically occurs so rapidly that some external storage mechanism is required to save the data in real-time so that it can be analyzed later.

Advantages (+) and disadvantages (-) of hardware monitors are as follows:

+ Extremely accurate

+ Non-invasive to operating system

+ No overhead

- Expensive to build

- Difficult to set up and use

- Require specialized hardware

- Hardware must be redesigned with each change of CPU

- Large volume of data

- Difficult to tie individual data items to individual processes

- Difficult to measure resources other than the CPU

- Difficult to relate to the user's application

Although hardware monitoring provides very accurate results, these disadvantages preclude its use outside of laboratory environments.

4.1.2   Internal Hardware Monitors

Newer generation (PA-RISC 2.0 and newer and all IPF-based) high-end systems include internal hardware monitors for critical internal system components such as the caches and the TLB (Chapter 6, "Hardware Performance Issues" on page 107). These components are so frequently accessed that measuring their utilization is extremely important. Because of the frequent access, it would be prohibitive in terms of overhead to provide these measurements with software monitors. The increase in cost to place these monitors in the CPU chip is insignificant to the overall cost of the system for high-end systems.

The HP-UX operating system does not have hooks to access these counters. The counters are accessed only via low-level instructions. Only the performance tool *Caliper* has the ability to access these counters. Metrics include:

•TLB hit/miss statistics

•cache hit/miss statistics

4.1.3   Internal Software Monitors

Internal software monitors are created by placing instrumentation points within the source code of the operating system kernel or the application code to acquire the performance data. Advantages (+) and disadvantages (-) of software instrumentation are as follows:

+ Relatively easy to implement
+ Easy to monitor many different resources, including networks
+ Easy to link individual processes with the data
+ Can easily be turned on or off
+ Can run safely in production environments
+ Runs on various models of CPU without change
+ Gives very accurate measures of transaction response time based on the application's definition of a transaction
+ Conducive to general purpose software analysis tools

- Is invasive to the operating system
- Contends for the same resources that it is measuring, which affects accuracy

Data from internal software monitors is so general purpose and easy to analyze that this kind of instrumentation is quite common on Unix systems. HP-UX incorporates three types of software instrumentation: sampling, counters, and event traces.

4.1.3.1   Periodic Sampling

Sampling is normally performed by the kernel. The kernel schedules itself periodically to take a sample, which is like taking a picture of what is happening. Each sample will contain particular information that is measurable and desired by some performance tool.

The software clock on HP-UX systems ticks at a rate of 10 milliseconds. Since counting is synchronous with respect to the system clock, accuracy of the counting is limited to the clock rate. Today's computer hardware operates at much higher frequencies than in the past: from 800 MHZ to several gigahertz (GHZ) or more. Since early Reduced Instruction Set Computers (RISC) such as PA-RISC typically complete one hardware instruction every hardware clock cycle, a computer operating at 800 MHZ would complete as many as 8 million instructions in one 10 millisecond software clock cycle. In this case, multiple short-lived processes could be created, perform their work, and terminate. The counting mechanism would not accurately account for these short-lived processes. Later PA-RISC and all Extremely Parallel Instruction Computers (EPIC) such as IPF execute multiple instructions per clock cycle and this accentuates the problem even more.

However, sampling can be a very accurate way of measuring CPU consumption of long-running CPU-bound applications. Any error caused by other short-lived processes running becomes very insignificant.

There are several ways of addressing this situation. An obvious solution would be to have the software clock tick more often. Although easy to implement, it is not a common solution. This is because the kernel does a lot of work when the software clock ticks, and a faster clock rate would cause higher overhead but would not provide the process-accounting accuracy desired. A more difficult solution would involve inventing a new method of capturing performance information in Unix.

Sampling is performed by Unix systems whenever the system clock ticks. When the clock ticks, the kernel takes note of which process, if any, is running, and allocates CPU time for the entire tick to that process. It also keeps track of what state the kernel is in so as to allocate global CPU utilization to the appropriate state. The kernel takes care of other housekeeping at the same time; for example, it checks to see if a higher priority process is ready to run. Sampling is commonly used for global and per-process CPU utilization and disk utilization metrics.

Process profiling, used for application optimization, also employs a sampling technique which is incorporated into the kernel. At the clock tick, the kernel determines which procedure or system call the process is currently executing, so that the profiler can determine how much time is being spent on which part of the process. Some newer operating system versions skew the profile clock from the main system clock to prevent beating between the two clocks, similar to when two audio tones very close in frequency cause an audible beating phenomenon. Profiling will be discussed in more detail in Chapter 14, "Application Profiling" on page 437.

4.1.3.2   Event-Driven Sampling

Rather than acquiring data based on a time interval, event sampling occurs whenever the event happens. For instance, if a page-out or a context switch occurs, it is counted immediately. Since event-driven sampling is related to the event rate, it has an inconsistent overhead. It is highly accurate, however, and especially useful for process profiling: whenever a procedure is called, a counter is incremented.

4.1.3.3   Counters

Counters are commonly found in various Unix systems to measure kernel activity. They were inserted into the kernel code at certain "interesting" points by the originators of the System V and Berkeley Unix variants, and were designed for use with specific performance-analysis tools. This same instrumentation can be found today on almost every version of Unix. Because of this, one advantage of these counters is that they are considered "standard" on multiple versions of Unix.

Counters can be thought of as answering two questions: "How Many?" and "How Much?" They record the number of times a particular event occurs or how much of a particular resource is used. Answering the question "What?" is up to the tool when it is accessing a particular counter. Examples are the number of page-outs (a virtual memory function) that occur and the amount of CPU that a process has used. The kernel merely increments a counter during the execution of a particular section of code. Counters are almost always turned on, counting the occurrence of various events and providing very little detail. The overhead of collecting this information is unknown and cannot be measured with software tools, but it is estimated to be very low, and an acceptable cost of monitoring system performance. Additional resources are consumed to access and report the data.

Because HP-UX is a combination of Berkeley and System V Unix, it contains counters to support both the Berkeley and System V performance tools which will be discussed in Chapter 5, "Survey of Unix Performance Tools" on page 51. For example, in HP-UX 10.0, the majority of the standard counters can be found in the file */usr/include/sys/vmmeter.h*. (Note that accessing these counters on an SMP system may yield incorrect results.) A number of structures and individual counters defined in this include file produce measurements of the CPU and of memory resources. These counters are used by all the standard Unix performance tools. However, most of these tools have been changed to access these counters by calling *pstat(2)* instead of referencing them directly.

4.1.3.4   Accessing Counters Through /dev/kmem

Counters in a Unix system are traditionally and typically accessed through the pseudo-driver */dev/kmem*. This pseudo-driver provides access to kernel run-time memory by a user process with appropriate permissions. Accessing performance metrics via */dev/kmem* is not recommended on any HP-UX system, since the kernel has a much more accurate way of providing utilization metrics. See the sections on *pstat(2)* and kernel event traces for learning better means of gathering performance metric data.

As an example of how counters can be accessed directly, it is possible to create a program that reads the data in the structure *vmtotal* which is defined in *vmmeter.h*. Acquiring data from the instrumentation defined in *vmmeter.h* alone is a time consuming, multi-step process:

1. Determine the metric names by perusing the numerous system include files.

2. Call *nlist()* for each metric name to find the address in the kernel.

3. Open the */dev/kmem* special device file.

4. For each of the metrics:

      - Position the driver to the address.

      - Read the variable or structure.

5. Report the results.

The code shown below gives an example of the old way of accessing performance metrics. It may be the only way to access counters on some non-HP operating systems. The technique is not recommended for use with HP-UX 10.0 and later, and it is no longer supported.

```
#include <nlist.h>
#include <fcntl.h>
#include <unistd.h>
main()

struct nlist nl[2];
struct vmtotal vmt;
int ierr;
int fd;
int value;
int address;

nl[0].n_name = "vmtotal";
nl[1].n_name = "";

if ((ierr = nlist("/vmunix",nl)) == -1) {
    printf("error from nlist call\n");
    exit(1);
    }
if (fd = open ("/dev/kmem",O_RDONLY)) == -1) {
    perror(open:  ");
    exit(2);
    }
if ((ierr = lseek(fd,nl[0].n_value,SEEK_SET)) == -1) {
    perror("lseek:  ");
    exit(3);
    }
if (ierr = read(fd,vmt,sizeof(vmt)) == -1) {
    perror("read:  ");
    exit(4);
    }
close(fd);
printf("Structure vmtotal:  ... ... ..
```

4.1.3.5   Accessing Counters Through *pstat(2)*

Due to the overhead required to read the data periodically for all of the desired metrics, some vendors have developed a system call like the *pstat(2)* call in HP-UX. *Pstat(2)* transfers a block of data to the user process all at once, at much lower overhead. However, *pstat(2)* is not intended for use by the casual application programmer because kernel source code is required to fully understand all of the counters. It is the job of the various performance reporting tools to document the counters they report. Making calls to *pstat(2)* is the only supported way to access performance metrics with a user-written or non-HP application. In fact, most of the standard Unix performance tools have been modified to use *pstat(2)* instead of */dev/kmem*. The HP proprietary performance tools such as *Glance* use both *pstat(2)* and the event traces described in the next section.

The following code illustrates one way of using *pstat* to obtain performance data:

```
#include <sys/pstat.h>
#include <sys/param.h>
{
#define BURST ((size_t) 10 )
    struct pst_pstatus pst[BURST];
    int i, count;
    int idx = 0; /* index within the process context */
    while ( count = pstat_getproc(pst,sizeof(pst[0],BURST,idx)) > 0) {
        for (i=0;i<count;i++) {
            (void) printf ("pid=%d, command=%s\n",
                pst[i].pst_ucomm);
            }
            idx = pst[i].pst_ucomm;
        }
    if (count == -1) perror ("pstat-getproc: ");
    }
```

See the *pstat(2)* manual (man) page for a description of the many ways to invoke *pstat(2)*. This *man* page is very complete, even showing example code for calling wrapper routines that make the calls easier and more self-documenting. Here are a few of the wrapper routines, and the data they return:

- *pstat_getdisk()*—per-disk information
- *pstat_getproc()*—process table entries
- *pstat_getprocessor()*—per-CPU statistics
- *pstat_getshm()*—shared memory information
- *pstat_getvminfo()*—virtual memory statistics

4.1.3.6   Advantages and Disadvantages of Counters

Here are the advantages and disadvantages of counters:

+ Easy to implement
+ Reasonably standard across Unix implementations
+ Low fixed CPU consumption to do the counting
+ Minimal memory consumption to maintain the counters
+ Interval of data collection is up to the tool
+ Volume of data depends upon sampling interval and counters requested

- Minimal information
- Medium CPU consumption to access all counters
- Time-stamping must be performed by the tool that reads the data
- Sampled counters are incremented synchronously with respect to the system clock

4.1.3.7   Event Traces

HP is currently unique in that it employs a second method for instrumenting the HP-UX kernel. The approach is to generate event traces that answer the following questions:

- Who? What process caused or initiated the event?
- What? What is the event? (for example, a disk read operation)
- When? When did the event occur? (a very accurate time-stamp)
- How much? How much or how many were requested? (for example, number of bytes read)

One can easily assume that such additional detail does not come free. Event traces generate a lot of data that must be read from the kernel and then analyzed and reduced into usable performance data. Event traces are similar to data generated by hardware monitors in terms of greater volume and the need to reduce the data.

Event traces also have advantages (+) and disadvantages (-):

+ Increased detail over counters shows the user of the resource
+ Chronological time-stamp is maintained by the kernel
+ Interval of data collection is up to the tool
+ Tracing can be turned on or off
+ Tracing is asynchronous with respect to the system clock

- Event trace buffers consume kernel memory
- Variable CPU consumption is required by the kernel to collect the information
- Event traces are more difficult to implement than counters
- There is a high volume of data which must be analyzed and reduced
- Events must be read quickly or data will be lost

Since event traces are asynchronous with respect to the system clock, they can be generated more frequently than every 10 milliseconds. This means that the measurements can be much more accurate than those from counters, because specific events initiate the traces. For example, a trace might be generated when a process is created and when it is terminated, so that we have a more accurate measurement of elapsed time.

4.2 Kernel Instrumentation and Measurement Interface

In HP-UX, event traces are generated by the kernel using a mechanism called Kernel Instrumentation (KI). They are written into a circular buffer in the kernel for each occurrence of events such as:

- System call (operating system intrinsic)
- Context switch (from one user process to another)

• Page outs

• I/O events

There are more than three hundred different system calls in HP-UX that normally occur at a rate of thousands of calls per second. Context switches occur quite often, sometimes hundreds or thousands of times per second. Therefore, HP-UX event traces can result in a large amount of data generated. The overhead associated with kernel-generated event traces, although larger than that of counters, provides so much additional detail that it is worth it. This overhead is a function of the workload on the system and cannot be measured directly, even though event traces are not always turned on.

The KI is turned on selectively by a user process called *midaemon*. Each instrumentation point in the kernel can be turned on or left off as necessary for collecting various types of data. Certain event traces are enabled and read by *midaemon*. This process runs at a real-time priority of 50, which gives it higher priority than normal time-share processes. (Process priorities will be discussed in the chapter on CPU.) *Midaemon* needs this higher priority so that it can read the circular event trace buffer written by the KI before it overflows. After the event trace buffer is read, it must then be analyzed to reduce the large volume of data. This task is also performed by *midaemon*, which summarizes the data and makes it available through a library called the *Measurement Interface* (MI). In fact, that is where the name *midaemon* originated. All of the optional HP performance tools such as *Glance* and *MeasureWare* use the MI to gather their data.

Since *midaemon* is a user process, the overhead associated with reading, analyzing, and reducing the event traces to manageable form can be directly measured. It is usually less than 3%, although the exact amount of overhead is workload dependent. Computer professionals who come from the mainframe environment see performance data collection as a "cost of doing business" and would generally consider anything less than 10% overhead acceptable.

4.2.1 Acceptable Overhead

What should you consider *acceptable overhead*? Here, you can apply **Rule #1**: "It depends." Specifically, what is acceptable changes based on the kind of system and the kind of application. The answer will vary for

• Workstations

• Servers

• Single-user systems

• Multi-user systems

• Systems running scientific or engineering applications

• Systems running business applications

Also recall **Rule #3**: "Performance cannot be measured without impacting the system being measured." Remember that it is impossible to collect performance data without consuming resources and thus changing the *system* that is being measured.

4.3 Performance Metrics Categories

Metrics can be categorized by their scope within the system being measured. They can also be viewed from the perspective of the type of data they provide.

4.3.1 Categories of Metrics by Scope

Instrumentation in the kernel provides metrics that fall into several categories:

- Global performance metrics
- Per-process performance metrics
- Application performance metrics
- Subsystem metrics
- Process profile metrics

Within each of these categories, data from the major kernel subsystems may be available. This data may include CPU utilization metrics, virtual memory utilization metrics, disk utilization metrics, network utilization metrics, and kernel resource utilization metrics.

4.3.1.1   Global Performance Metrics

These are the most basic types of metrics. They reveal what is happening on the system from a global perspective; that is, the *what* can be detected, but not the *who*. The particular process consuming the resource cannot be found using global data. Global metrics are reported by all of the *standard* Unix tools, as well as HP-written tools.

4.3.1.2   Per-Process Performance Metrics

These provide various levels of detail about individual processes. Thus, the *who* as well as the *what* can be determined. Per-process information takes more of the CPU resource to acquire, so **Rule #2** gets invoked: there is a trade-off between acquiring more information and using more of the CPU resource to get it. The *ps* command and System V Accounting are the only standard Unix commands that report per-process information. There are several HP-written tools that report per-process information.

4.3.1.3   Application Performance Metrics

These are an HP invention and are not generated by the kernel. Simply stated, application metrics are obtained by summing per-process metrics for an arbitrary grouping of processes, whereas the arbitrary grouping is defined by the performance manager. Only HP-written tools provide application metrics.

4.3.1.4   Subsystem Metrics

The choice of subsystem metrics will depend on the reason for making the measurement. Whereas global and application CPU, memory, and disk utilization measurements may be sufficient for performance characterization and forecasting, per-process CPU, memory, and disk utilization are most useful in performance problem diagnosis. Remember that if the purpose of the measurement is performance problem diagnosis, more metrics and more detailed metrics are necessary.

4.3.1.5   Process Profile Metrics

Both counting and sampling methods are used for application profiling at the procedure level. Procedure calls are counted by caller and procedure called, and the time spent in each procedure is sampled as described above. Profiling will be discussed in greater detail in Chapter 14, "Application Profiling" on page 437.

4.3.2   Categories of Metrics by Type of Data

Three types of data can be gathered for all the subsystems and categories mentioned above. They are saturation metrics, queue metrics, and rates.

4.3.2.1   Saturation Metrics

Saturation metrics indicate how much of a resource is being utilized. An example would be the percentage of global or per-process CPU utilization.

4.3.2.2   Queue Metrics

Queue metrics show the amount of "waiting for a resource" by processes. Examples include the CPU run queue and the disk I/O queue.

4.3.2.3   Resource Rates

Rates are the requests for a resource per unit of time. They indicate how often an event is occurring. Examples include I/Os per second, context switches per second, and interrupts per second.

4.4 Summary

It is impossible to carry out performance management unless system performance can be measured. Measuring system performance requires some method of instrumentation. Software instrumentation is the most practical method for measuring system performance, even though it is invasive to the operating system; that is, it will often affect the performance of the system being measured. The amount of effect is called the overhead of the measurement. The smaller the overhead of the measurement, the more accurate it will be.

An important goal of performance tools is to minimize the overhead of the tool so that the performance data presented accurately reflects the state of the system. Different tools have different amounts of overhead. The state of the system will determine the real impact that the tool imposes on the system. As the system becomes busier, the chance that the tool will impact the system that is being measured increases.

The instrumentation in the various kernel subsystems provides different categories of data. Tool selection must be made based on the purpose of the measurement and the data presented by the tool. Information about which performance tool shows which type of data, and which metrics, will be presented in Chapter 5, "Survey of Unix Performance Tools" on page 51.

Survey of Unix Performance Tools

T here are many different performance tools available for Unix systems in general and for HP-UX in particular. This chapter presents a broad overview of system performance tools by type. These tools provide information on the system's utilization of the major resources (CPU, memory, I/O, etc.), which is called global utilization. They also provide information on each process's utilization of these same system resources, and this is called per-process utilization. Certain tools provide additional capabilities as described in each section.

It is important to recall that any major application software package includes performance monitoring tools specific to that application. Since application tuning usually results in the greatest performance improvement, one should always use application-specific performance tools when they are available. Since these tools are so varied and so application-specific, it is not in the scope of this book to discuss individual application performance tools. Although one may not start with these tools, it is often useful to use them in conjunction with system performance tools to correlate the information and better determine the cause of a given performance problem.

The goal of this chapter is to familiarize the reader with how the system performance tools are used and the metrics that they display; however, we will not go into the meaning of each of the metrics. Metrics will be discussed in the chapter on the bottleneck to which they apply. The following topics are presented:

- Choosing the Right Tools
- Multi Purpose Diagnostic Tools
- CPU Diagnostic Tools
- Disk Diagnostic Tools

- Memory Diagnostic Tools
- Performance Characterization Tools
- Performance Prediction Tools
- Process Accounting Tools
- Application Optimization Tools
- Network Diagnostic Tools
- Resource Management Tools
- Capacity Planning Tools

These tools have come from a variety of sources. Appendix A "Performance Tools Alphabetical Reference" on page 471 contains tables listing all the available tools discussed in this book, with information about their origins.

Some of the tools are available only on certain versions of HP-UX. Appendix B, "HP-UX Version Naming Reference" on page 507 lists both the marketing name of the operating system version (such as HP-UX 11i version 2) and the version number reported by the *uname -r* command (such as 11.23).

When performing tuning of the system, one often needs to change the value of tuneable parameters in the OS. Each bottleneck chapter will explain the tuneable parameters that are important to that particular system resource. Some tuneable parameters are now dynamically tuneable; i.e., the value of the parameter can be set in the currently running kernel, thus obviating the need to generate a new kernel and reboot the system. Some tuneable parameters are even tuned automatically by the kernel itself as resource utilization changes.

See Appendix C, "Dynamically Tuneable Parameters" on page 509 for a list of which tuneable parameters are dynamically tuneable and which ones are automatically tuned. If any tuneable parameters are changed dynamically and the changes are expected to be permanent, make sure to reconfigure the kernel in */stand/vmunix* so that the new values take effect when the system is rebooted.

5.1 Choosing the Right Tools

Deciding which tools to use under which conditions probably seems difficult at this point. We will demonstrate that some tools are better than others under certain circumstances and depending upon particular needs. Recall **Rule #4** on page 11: "No single performance tool will provide all the data needed to solve performance problems." The major performance tools and their relationship to the data sources are shown in Figure 5-1. These tools provide most of the information that is available about the system and processes running on it.

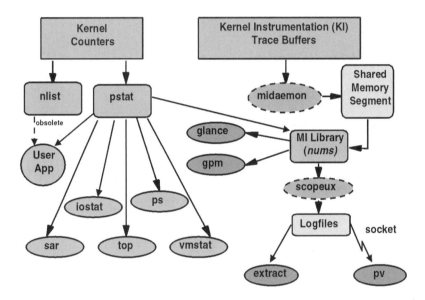

Figure 5-1　Performance Tools and Data Sources

Most of the tools in Figure 5-1 use data that is provided by two basic Unix elements: the kernel counters, and the kernel instrumentation trace buffers monitored by *midaemon*. In general, tools can be grouped into categories based on the kinds of questions they help to answer:

- Diagnostic: "What is going on now?"
- Performance Characterization: "What happened last month compared with this month?"
- Performance Prediction: "When will I run out of CPU?"
- Application Optimization: "Why is this process so slow?"
- Network Diagnostic: "Which system is heavily loaded?"
- Capacity Planning: "What will happen if I add twenty users?"

Each category is described below together with the most useful tools for addressing the problem. Note that because some tools fit into more than one category, they may be described more than once.

5.2 Multipurpose Diagnostic Tools

Diagnostic tools provide a snapshot of system or subsystem behavior at particular moments. Although data from diagnostic tools can also be used to compare system activity over longer periods, the tools are designed primarily to provide current data.

Diagnostic tools are of many different types, some offering a general, multipurpose set of metrics covering many subsystems, others with more specialized uses. The most important multipurpose tools are *GlancePlus/UX*, *GlancePlus/Motif*, *PerfView* and *sar*. Also included in this group are time-related tools, such as *uptime*, *time*, and *timex*.

It is important to emphasize that the Measurement Interface (MI) based tools such as *Glance, MeasureWare* and *PerfView* have access to the most accurate metrics and data available from the system. Since many of these metrics are based on event traces, the data are absolutely accurate. For instance, when measuring per-process CPU utilization, event traces (time stamps) are generated as the process moves from one state to another. Therefore, MI-based tools report very accurate data such as user mode, system mode, and context switching times, etc.

For multi-threaded applications, *glance* and *gpm* are the tools of choice. One can easily show all of the threads associated with a given process, and drill down on resource utilization by each thread.

When investigating system performance issues, it is often useful to measure the utilization of the various system calls. This measurement can result in reliable clues about the actual cause of the bottleneck. Although *sar* reports on the utilization of several system calls, only *glance* and *gpm* report on the utilization of all system calls. *Glance* and *gpm* provide system call utilization information on a global and per-process basis.

5.2.1 *GlancePlus/UX*

GlancePlus/UX is an interactive performance tool that displays numerous metrics organized on a number of different screens. *Glance* is available for HP-UX, Solaris, and AIX, and comes in two versions: character-mode and *Motif*. The *Motif* version is called *gpm* and will be discussed separately, since it has a number of additional features.

Due to the number of metrics and features provided, *glance* occupies more memory than the standard Unix tools. Following the adage that nothing worth anything comes without cost, *glance* is not included with the OS and must be purchased separately.

Glance displays both process and global information, a great advantage over the standard Unix tools. When process information is displayed, multiple criteria are available to limit the output to processes of interest, such as those that correspond to particular CPU, memory and disk thresholds. In addition, filters are available to restrict the output to a particular user, terminal device name (tty), or process name. *Glance* is generally invoked without parameters. However, it does have some command-line options and is invoked in the following way:

glance [-j interval] [-p dest] [-f dest] [-maxpages n] [-command]
[-nice n] [-nosort] [-lock] [<midaemon control parameters>]

The command line parameters are:

- *-j <interval>*—specifies the data refresh interval
- *-p <dest>*—enables printing to the print spooler printer destination
- *-f <dest>*—enables printing to a file
- *-maxpages <n>*—limits the number of pages to be printed
- *-command*—selects the initial metric screen
- *-nice <n>*—nice value at which *glance* runs
- *-nosort*—don't sort processes on the process screen
- *-lock*—locks *glance* into memory

For quicker *glance* startup, *midaemon* or *scopeux* should be run from the */sbin/rc*d/mwa* script. Alternatively, create the */sbin/rc*d/mwa/midaemon* file so that *midaemon* starts up at boot time. *Glance* resides in */opt/perf/bin* on HP-UX versions 10.0 or later, versions 11.x or later, and Solaris 2.X.

5.2.1.1   *Glance* Screens of Metrics

Glance has the following screens of metrics, which may be selected by pressing the labeled softkey or by typing the single letter shown below:

- *a*—All CPU detail (for SMP systems)
- *B*—Global Wait states
- *c*—CPU detail
- *d*—Disk detail
- *f*—Single process open file detail
- *g*—Global process list
- *G*—Process threads (see also *Z*)
- *h*—Online help
- *i*—Disk I/O by file system
- *I*—Per-thread resource utilization
- *j*—Adjust data refresh interval
- *J*—Thread Wait states
- *l*—LAN detail
- *L*—Per-process system call utilization
- *m*—Memory detail
- *M*—Single process memory regions detail

- *N*—Global NFS activity
- *n*—NFS detail by system
- *o*—Change process list filtering (thresholds)
- *s*—Single process detail
- *t*—System table utilization
- *u*—Disk queue lengths
- *v*—Disk LVM detail
- *w*—Swap detail
- *W*—Single process wait states detail
- *y*—Renice a process
- *Y*—Global system call utilization
- *Z*—Global threads
- *?*—Display a list of the single character shortcut commands and the screen that each invokes

Since it is desirable to present performance data in a timely manner, *glance* is "nastied" by default with a nice value of -10, so that it has a higher priority than most time-share processes. Bear in mind, however, that there are times on a very busy system when *glance* may be delayed in its report of the data. You should resist the temptation to run *glance* with a real-time priority, because doing so would have a severely negative impact on system performance. Interactive processes should usually not be given a real-time priority.

Glance is meant to run interactively to diagnose performance problems. Although it is possible to print a particular screen of metrics, either once or continuously, it is recommended that screen printing be done continuously only when the refresh interval is 60 seconds or longer, since the printing may have an impact on system performance. (Remember **Rule #3** on page 5: "Performance cannot be measured without impacting the system being measured.") Additionally, the Adviser can be used to print a customized set of metrics to a file.

The overhead that *glance* imposes on the system is as follows:

- CPU—depends on the data refresh interval and the number of running processes
- Memory—depends on the number of running processes

5.2.1.2   Per-Process Information in *glance*

One important advantages of *glance* is its wealth of per-process information. Not only can one determine what is happening on the system, one can also determine who is using it. Detailed process information includes the following:

- CPU utilization
- System call rate
- Context switch rate (voluntary and involuntary)
- Paging and swapping rates

- Some particular system call rates
- I/O rates, amounts, and types
- Detailed global information on CPU, memory, disk, Local Area Network (LAN), Network File System (NFS)

CPU utilization is further broken down into:

- User (normal)
- User (niced or nastied)
- User (real-time priority)
- System (system calls)
- System (context switch)
- System (interrupt processing)
- System call rates
- Context switch rates
- Load averages
- The bar graphs for CPU, memory, disk, and swap

At a glance (pun intended), the CPU, memory, disk, and swap utilization may be seen. CPU utilization is broken down into System (S) and User (U), Nice (N) and RealTime (R). It should be noted that *glance*'s concept of Nice CPU utilization differs from that of other performance tools in that it reports both the "nasty" and "nice" forms of *nice* as Nice (N) CPU utilization and (A) Negative Nice ("nasty"). The performance tools *sar, iostat,* and *top* use the kernel's concept of Nice CPU utilization, which considers only those processes that have used the "nice" form of *nice* to degrade their process priority.

Memory utilization is broken down into the amount of memory consumed by the System (S), Users (U), and the Buffer Cache (B). The Buffer Cache portion of the bar is most useful on those systems that support a Dynamic Buffer Cache, since the amount of memory consumed by it will fluctuate.

The disk bar shows peak disk utilization of the busiest disk during the interval, broken down into File System I/O (F) and disk I/O due to Virtual Memory System operations (V).

Rather than display paging or swapping activity, the swap bar shows the amount of space that is Reserved (R) or Used (U) on each of the swap devices. Many Unix operating systems allocate swap space immediately when the process is *exec*'d or when it grows in size. This paradigm wastes CPU time by allocating space on the swap device even if it is never used. HP-UX allocates space on the swap device only when it needs to page or swap the process out. Therefore, in order to follow the standard Unix paradigm of making sure that swap will be available if it is ever needed, HP-UX reserves the swap space at *exec* time, or at the time of process growth (*malloc(3)* or *sbrk(2)*) merely by decrementing a global counter that represents the total amount of swap space available.

5.2.1.3   Advantages and Disadvantages of *glance*

Advantages (+) of *glance* include:

+ Filters for the process list. The process list may be sorted alphabetically by name, by
  CPU utilization, or by disk utilization. Additionally, the process list may be limited by
  user name, tty name, and thresholds for CPU, disk, and memory utilization by the individual process.

+ Extensive online help. Although a manual is available for *glance*, there is little need for it
  because all the necessary information is available on-line. Understanding the meaning of
  a particular metric or screen is as simple as invoking the on-line help facility.

+ Availability for HP-UX, AIX, and Solaris. The *Motif* version of *glance*, called *gpm*, is
  available on all of these Operating Systems. The character-mode version is available only
  for HP-UX.

The disadvantages (-) of *glance* include:

- More overhead than traditional simple tools. This point is an example of **Rule #2**— "Performance tuning always involves a trade-off." You can't collect detailed performance data
  without cost. *Glance* collects and displays much more detailed information than is available from the standard performance tools. In doing this, however, it consumes more CPU
  and memory than the simpler tools.

- Limited logging of data. *Glance* will optionally log the current screen data for each interval to a spooled printer or to a disk file. Because of the overhead, logging should only be
  invoked when the screen-refresh interval is 60 seconds or longer.

- Relatively slow startup. If *midaemon* is not running, *glance* must first start it up. *Glance*
  then checks its on-disk databases to see if the information is still compatible with the currently running kernel; if not, it must recreate the databases. All this activity results in a
  clearly perceptible startup time.

The CPU overhead associated with running *glance* depends on the refresh interval and the
number of running processes. Longer intervals use less overhead. Memory overhead depends
on the number of running processes, because *glance* keeps information about all running processes in its user memory to reduce CPU overhead. The counters and other metrics accessed by
glance are collected by *midaemon*; some of them are turned on only when *midaemon* is running.

Figure 5-2 shows the *GlancePlus* report screen for Resources used by the process *init*, PID 1.

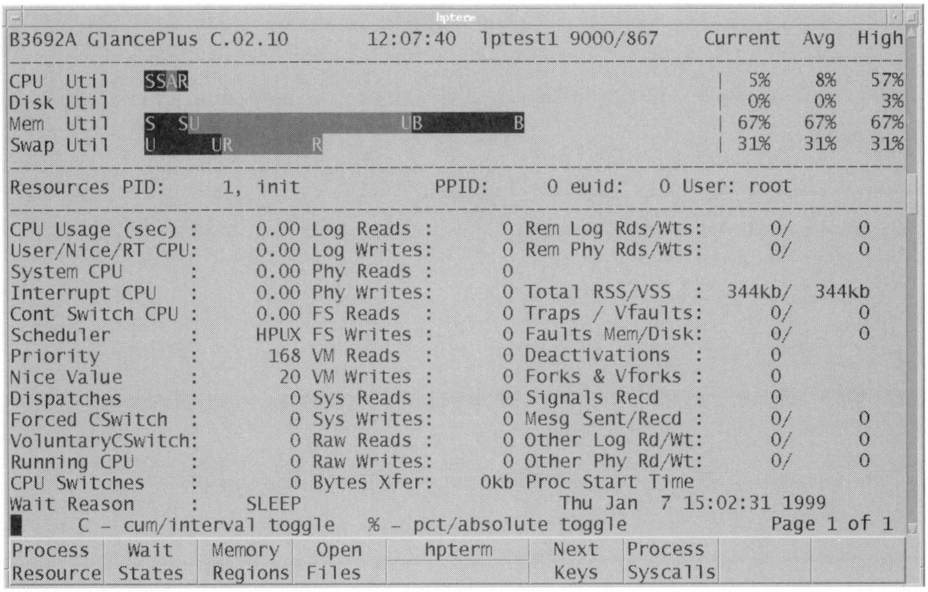

```
 -                                         hpterm                                    |▾| ▢
B3692A GlancePlus C.02.10        12:07:40  1ptest1 9000/867     Current  Avg  High
-------------------------------------------------------------------------------------
CPU   Util  SSAR                                              |   5%    8%   57%
Disk  Util                                                    |   0%    0%    3%
Mem   Util  S  SU                    UB            B          |  67%   67%   67%
Swap  Util  U      UR            R                            |  31%   31%   31%
-------------------------------------------------------------------------------------
Resources PID:      1, init             PPID:     0 euid:   0 User: root
-------------------------------------------------------------------------------------
CPU Usage (sec) :      0.00 Log Reads :     0 Rem Log Rds/Wts:    0/       0
User/Nice/RT CPU:      0.00 Log Writes:     0 Rem Phy Rds/Wts:    0/       0
System CPU      :      0.00 Phy Reads :     0
Interrupt CPU   :      0.00 Phy Writes:     0 Total RSS/VSS  : 344kb/   344kb
Cont Switch CPU :      0.00 FS Reads  :     0 Traps / Vfaults:    0/       0
Scheduler       :      HPUX FS Writes :     0 Faults Mem/Disk:    0/       0
Priority        :       168 VM Reads  :     0 Deactivations  :    0
Nice Value      :        20 VM Writes :     0 Forks & Vforks :    0
Dispatches      :         0 Sys Reads :     0 Signals Recd   :    0
Forced CSwitch  :         0 Sys Writes:     0 Mesg Sent/Recd :    0/       0
VoluntaryCSwitch:         0 Raw Reads :     0 Other Log Rd/Wt:    0/       0
Running CPU     :         0 Raw Writes:     0 Other Phy Rd/Wt:    0/       0
CPU Switches    :         0 Bytes Xfer:   0kb Proc Start Time
Wait Reason     :     SLEEP                   Thu Jan  7 15:02:31 1999
█      C - cum/interval toggle   % - pct/absolute toggle              Page 1 of 1
-------------------------------------------------------------------------------------
Process  Wait   Memory  Open    hpterm     Next  Process
Resource States Regions Files              Keys  Syscalls
```

Figure 5-2   *GlancePlus* Resources by PID—Report Screen

5.2.2   *GlancePlus Motif*

Gpm is the *Motif* version of *glance*. It is bundled with *glance* and provides more features than the character-mode version. Although *glance* and *gpm* use the same data source (the MI), *glance* provides a much larger number of metrics for reporting.

Not all of these metrics are available in the standard screens. Some of the screens may be easily customized to report data from any of the metrics that one desires to investigate. Becoming familiar with the *Configure/Choose Metrics* menu selection will enable one to customize the screens and reports according to the needs of each performance analysis. There are over 250 metrics to choose from, and experience will help one to quickly determine which ones are of use for a given situation. One can also customize the reports available through the *Reports* menu selection.

Gpm uses color to indicate severity and signal alarms, and provides a short-term history in graphical format. Also, some new metrics and screens are shown by *gpm*. Since *gpm* is a *Motif*

application, the DISPLAY environment variable must be set before invoking *gpm*. It is invoked with the following syntax:

gpm [-nosave] [-rpt <name>] [-sharedclr] [-nice <nicevalue>][-lock]
[<midaemon control parameters>]

The command line parameters are:

- *-nosave*—Do not save configuration changes at exit.
- *-rpt <name>*—Display one or more report windows at startup.
- *-sharedclr*—Have *gpm* use a shared color scheme in case of color shortage at the cost of disabling user color configurability.
- *-nice <nicevalue>*—Change the *nice* value at which *gpm* runs (default -10).
- *-lock*—Lock *gpm* into memory.

Figure 5-3 shows the *GlancePlus Motif* main screen.

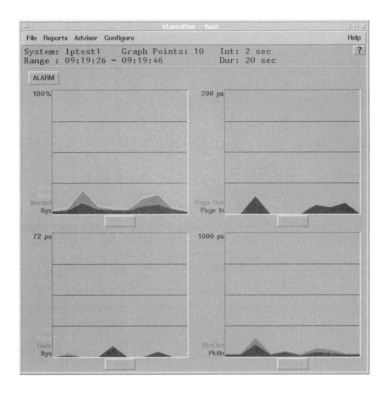

Figure 5-3 *GlancePlus Motif*—Main Screen

For quicker *gpm* startup, *midaemon* or *scopeux* should be run from the */sbin/init.d/mwa* script. Alternatively, create the */sbin/init.d/midaemon* file so that it starts up at boot time. *Gpm* resides in *opt/perf/bin* on HP-UX versions 10.0 or later, versions 11.x or later, and Solaris 2.X.

Since *gpm* is a *Motif* application, its functions are selected from a menu bar at the top of the main control window. This control window displays four graphs that show the utilization of the major system resources of CPU, memory, disk, and network. Notice that the fourth graph shows different data than the fourth bar shown at the top of each *glance* screen; *glance* shows swap utilization, whereas *gpm* shows network data. Figure 5-3 shows the main screen of *Glance-Plus Motif*.

Gpm displays metrics on the following screens, which are called *report windows*. They may be selected from the menu bar on the control window, and are shown as the menu items to be selected with the mouse.

5.2.2.1   Reports / Resource History

This window contains four line graphs, by default, showing CPU, memory, disk, and network utilization over the last 'n' samples. The look of this window can be changed with *Configure*. Each graph has several lines representing types of each resource; that is, the CPU graph shows Normal, System, Real-Time, and Nice CPU utilization.

5.2.2.2   Reports / CPU / CPU Graph

This graph shows a history of the one-minute Load Average metric, which is one measure of a CPU bottleneck.

5.2.2.3   Reports / CPU / CPU Report

The CPU report is a table of the various global CPU metrics, such as the seven types of CPU utilization, the one-minute Load Average, and the system call rate. This report, shown in Figure 5-4, is identical to the *glance* CPU (c) screen. The CPU report is most useful in a Uniprocessor environment.

```
                    GlancePlus - CPU Report
 File  Reports                                              Help

 System: 1ptest1     Last Update: 09:20:45     Int: 2 sec    ?

 Top CPU User: gpm                   PID: 17685

 State            Current    Avg.    High     Time    Cum Time

 Normal             0.5%     1.5%    10.4%     0.0       1.47
 Nice Nice          0.0%     0.0%     0.0%     0.0       0.00
 Negative Nice      1.5%     3.0%    29.1%     0.0       2.84
 RealTime           1.5%     1.6%     4.5%     0.0       1.56
 System             1.5%     3.3%    32.4%     0.0       3.18
 Interrupt          1.0%     1.2%     2.7%     0.0       1.17
 Context Switch     0.0%     0.4%     1.2%     0.0       0.36
 V Fault            0.0%     0.3%     2.4%     0.0       0.31
 Trap               0.0%     0.0%     0.5%     0.0       0.01
 Idle              94.0%    88.6%    95.0%     1.9      84.39

 Activity          Rate    C Rate     High

 Syscalls         246.0    448.3    3648.7
 Interrupts       356.5    353.2     516.5
 Cont Switches     44.0     52.5     144.2

 Queues          Length     Avg.     High

 Load Average      10.1     10.1     10.1
```

Figure 5-4   *GlancePlus Motif*—CPU Report

5.2.2.4 Reports / CPU / CPU by Processor

This report is most useful in a Symmetric Multi-Processor (SMP) environment because it contains metrics that do not appear on the CPU Report. It shows CPU utilization; the one-minute; five-minute; and fifteen-minute load averages; the context switch rate; fork rate; and last PID; all by processor number. It is the same as the *glance* All CPU screen (a).

5.2.2.5 Reports / Memory Info / Memory Graph

This window graphs the three most important indicators of a memory bottleneck: Page-outs, Swapouts, and the number of processes blocked on Virtual Memory (Wait Queue).

5.2.2.6 Reports / Memory Info / Memory Report

Similar to the *glance* Memory (m) screen, this report displays the important global memory metrics. The Buffer Cache Read Hit Ratio, a disk metric, is also shown in this report. The metrics are shown as current, cumulative since *gpm* started up, and percent.

5.2.2.7 Reports / Disk Info / Disk Graph

This window contains a graph of the percent utilization of the busiest disks. Chapter 9, "Disk Bottlenecks" on page 253 will demonstrate that the Disk Queue metric is more useful than the data presented here.

5.2.2.8 Reports / Disk Info / Disk Report

This report is like the *glance* Disk (d) screen. It shows global disk metrics including Logical I/O rates, Physical I/O rates, and User and System I/O rates.

5.2.2.9 Reports / Disk Info / I/O by Disk

This window lists metrics such as Disk Queue Length and utilization, along with Physical, Logical, Virtual Memory, File System, System, and Raw I/O rates. Although similar to the *glance* Disk Queue (u) screen, this screen shows several new metrics as well.

5.2.2.10 Reports / Disk Info / I/O by File System

Like the *glance* I/O by File System (i) screen, this report indicates the I/Os that are associated with each mounted file system.

5.2.2.11 Reports / Disk Info / I/O by Logical Volume

Since the Logical Volume Manager (LVM) feature of HP-UX can result in a File System or Raw Volume being split or striped across multiple physical disks, disk metrics related to each Logical Volume are useful to monitor in conjunction with the Physical Disk rates. This report is like the *glance* Disk by Logical Volume (v) screen.

5.2.2.12 Reports / Network Info / LAN Graph

The LAN graph window shows the LAN packet I/O rates, percent LAN Errors and percent LAN Collisions. Collisions are a measure of Network saturation, and Errors are a measure of Network quality. Both cause degradation in network throughput.

5.2.2.13   Reports / Network Info / Network by LAN

In the presence of multiple LAN cards on the system, it is useful to determine the distribution of I/Os, collisions, and errors across each LAN when looking at network loading.   The *glance* LAN (l) screen shows similar information.

5.2.2.14   Reports / Network / NFS Global Activity

This report shows Network File System (NFS) global activity from *this system's* perspective, as well as metrics such as Read and Write Queues, Idle Biods, and response time. It is similar to the *glance* global NFS (N) screen.

5.2.2.15   Reports / Network / NFS by System

Since it is useful to display the amount of NFS activity generated by particular systems, this report shows the NFS I/O rates for each system with an NFS-mounted file system. It is important to distinguish whether these rates are generated as an NFS client or an NFS server. This information can be seen on the *glance* NFS by system (n) screen.

5.2.2.16   Reports / Network / NFS by Operation

NFS uses various access methods, including remote file access and remote procedure calls. NFS activity is shown by particular NFS operation in this report.

5.2.2.17   Reports / System Table Info / System Tables Graph

One of the system-tuning functions involves monitoring the utilization of the various system tables whose size is tuneable. This report graphs the percent utilization, over time, of the process, system file, shared memory-identifier, message-identifier, semaphore-identifier, file lock, and pseudo-terminal tables. It also graphs the utilization of the global swap space.

5.2.2.18   Reports / System Table Info / System Tables Report

Along with the metrics shown in the System Tables Graph, this report displays utilization of the inode table, maximum shared memory, message buffer memory, and the file system buffer cache. It is similar to the *glance* System Tables (t) screen.

5.2.2.19   Reports / Swap Space

The amount of swap space available and used by swap device or swap file system is shown in this report. It is similar to the *glance* Swap (w) screen.

5.2.2.20   Reports / Application List

MeasureWare has a feature that aggregates certain metrics for user-defined collections of processes, which are called Applications. The application definition list is shown in this report.

5.2.2.21   Reports / Process List

If you know a resource bottleneck exists, you want to determine which process or processes are causing it. The process list is the first step in making this determination. This screen is similar to the Global (g) screen in *glance*, but drilling down to the Single Process (s) screen works differently.

Since *gpm* is a *Motif* application, double-clicking with the mouse on the line showing a particular process will display the Single Process window. Single-clicking the mouse on one or more lines of individual processes will highlight these processes and lock them onto the Process List. This makes important processes much easier to follow.

The arrangement of the columns can be changed to suit the preference of the user or the needs of the performance problem. Sorting and filtering processes in this list is discussed under "Reports / Process List / Configure" in later sections.

5.2.2.22   Reports / Process List / Admin / Renice

The superuser or owner of the process can easily change the nice value of individual processes after selecting the process from the Process List. Changing the nice value of a running process will directly impact the priority of the running process, and indirectly impact the amount of CPU that the process receives. Only the superuser can assign a "nasty" nice value that will improve the priority of the process, thus increasing its opportunity to use the CPU.

5.2.2.23   Reports / Process List / Admin / Kill

A runaway process can be killed by highlighting it in the Process List and selecting Admin / Kill.

5.2.2.24   Reports / Process List / Reports / Process Resources

This report window is like the Single Process (s) screen in *glance*. It lists the per-process CPU, memory, and disk performance metrics for the selected process.

5.2.2.25   Reports / Process List / Reports / Process Open Files

It is sometimes desirable to see which files are being accessed by a process. This report window, like the *glance* open file (F) screen, shows all the files that a process currently has open. It also shows the current file offset position, which can be watched to see random or sequential file activity.

5.2.2.26   Reports / Process List / Reports / Process Wait States

The various wait states for a process can help identify the reason why a process is running slower than expected. For instance, if a process is blocked waiting for Semaphores, the reason might be a locking or serialization problem with the application. This information can be seen in *glance* by selecting the Process Wait States (W) screen. The wait states are shown as the percent of time during the interval in which the process was waiting in that particular state.

5.2.2.27   Reports / Process List / Reports / Process Memory Regions

Finally, the sizes and locking status of the various memory regions for a process can be seen in this report window. This information can be used to determine which kinds of memory pages in use by the process are included in the Resident Set Size (RSS) and Virtual Set Size (VSS) of the process. *Glance* shows this same information in the Process Memory Regions (M) screen. An important metric in this screen is the amount of memory locked. This can be used to see what processing may be causing memory bottlenecks.

5.2.2.28   Reports / Process List / Configure / Column Arrangement

All the columns shown in the Process List report window can be rearranged to suit the user. You can also choose columns to be locked at the left of the screen when the display is scrolled horizontally.

5.2.2.29   Reports / Process List / Configure / Sort Fields

This screen lets you define how to sort the processes in the Process List based on the values in one or more columns.

5.2.2.30   Reports / Process List / Configure / Filters

Filters can be used to determine which processes are to be listed in the Process List. Filters are based on comparison of the individual column metrics to threshold values. Comparisons include "equal to," "less than," "less than or equal to," and the like. Processes that exceed a particular threshold can be highlighted with the color of your choice. This screen provides a powerful way of limiting the potentially hundreds of processes that would normally show up in the process list.

5.2.2.31   Configure / Colors

The colors used on the various graphs as well as the colors for the alert levels may be chosen by the user if there are enough colors available in the X/Server. This might depend upon how many other windows are open and the number of colors used in those windows.

5.2.2.32   Configure / Measurement

The interval associated with data refresh can be set in minutes and seconds.

5.2.2.33   Configure / Icon

When *gpm* is iconified, the icon is an active representation of the four major resource measurements. The contents of the icon can be changed from line graph to bar graph or kiveat (radar) plot.

5.2.2.34   Configure / Main Graph / Horizontal, Vertical, Pie, History

The graphs displayed in the initial control window can be changed from the Resource History line graph to a horizontal or vertical bar chart, or a pie chart.

5.2.3   *GlancePlus Motif* Adviser

Gpm has a feature called the Adviser that is unique among performance tools. The Adviser is a customizable set of rules that determines when and if a performance problem exists. The Adviser bases its decisions on user-specified *symptoms* that are defined in terms of the *interval* time period, and *alarms* that are defined for longer periods of time. Symptoms and alarms can ease the performance management of complex systems by warning operators of impending performance problems by sending *alerts*. The Adviser can be accessed and configured through the following menu items:

5.2.3.1   Adviser / Symptom Status

This window shows the status of all symptoms during the current interval.

5.2.3.2   Adviser / Alarm History

This window shows a textual list of alarms that have been generated since startup or rest time.

5.2.3.3   Adviser / Adviser Syntax

The actual syntax of the alarms is shown and may be edited in this window. If you prefer, the syntax can be saved to a file, edited with the editor of choice, and then reloaded into *gpm*. Alarm syntax consists of a symptom name, a probability value, a time period, an alert for a major resource, and a reset value. The following is an example of how to code an alarm based on the size of the run queue:

```
if runqueue > 74 for 5 minutes {
    start YELLOW ALERT CPU
    reset
    }
```

The variable *runqueue* is defined as a symptom in the Symptom Window.

5.2.3.4   Adviser / Adviser Syntax / Window / Symptom Window

The rule-based symptoms are displayed and can be edited in this window or edited with an editor by saving the rules to a file. Symptoms are named, and consist of a collection of rules that are based on specific metrics. The exact metric names can be found by using the on-line help facility, or you can create your own variable names. For example, to create a rule based on the size of the CPU Run Queue, one would define a new symptom variable called *runqueue* and set it to a probability of 75 if the length of the CPU run queue exceeds 10:

```
SYMPTOM runqueue
RULE gbl_pri_queue > 10 probability 75
```

5.2.4   Advantages and Disadvantages of *GlancePlus Motif*

The advantages (+) and disadvantages (-) of *gpm* include those of *glance* as well as the following:

+ Colors and color graphical presentation. Color is used by *gpm* to indicate the severity of an alert (*red* for alert, *yellow* for warning, *green* for OK) and for showing types of resource utilization. Color improves the readability of the data and the detectibility of problems. Color graphics are much easier to assimilate than tabular data. One can quickly get an idea of health of the system, and in some cases view critical historical information (last 'n' intervals).

+ Extensive process list filtering and sorting. The process list can be filtered by <u>any</u> of the metrics displayed in the window, based on mathematical comparisons. The process can be highlighted by configurable color. Also, the process list can be sorted by any of the window metrics.

+ Customizable alarms and advice. Alarms can be generated based on default and user-defined rules that can be customized for the particular system environment.

- Significant memory consumption. Since *gpm* is a *Motif* application, it must allocate memory for each of the windows that are being displayed, resulting in a minimum Resident Set Size of 2.5 MB and a Virtual Set Size of 6.5 MB. So **Rule #3** applies here: "Performance cannot be measured without impacting the system being measured." You probably should not use *gpm* to diagnose a severe memory bottleneck.

- Very limited logging capability. Data presented by *gpm* cannot be logged, by default, to the disk or to a printer. By creating new Adviser syntax, individual metrics can be printed to standard out (which can be redirected to a file) or to the alert window.

As with *glance*, the CPU overhead associated with running *gpm* depends on the refresh interval and the number of running processes. Longer intervals use less overhead. Additional CPU overhead is generated by the *Motif* calls in displaying the windows and graphics, as with any *Motif*-based application.

Memory overhead depends on the number of running processes because *gpm* keeps information about all running processes in its user memory to reduce CPU overhead. Additional memory is consumed for each currently displayed window. The counters and other metrics accessed by *gpm* are collected by *midaemon,* and certain ones are turned on only when *midaemon* is running.

5.2.5   sar (System Activity Reporter)

Sar originated in System V Unix. It is now available as part of many Unix systems, including some Berkeley-based Unix systems. *Sar* retrieves all of its metrics via the */dev/kmem* or *pstat(2)* interface, although in HP-UX some of the counters are specific only to *sar*. As with most of the counter-based performance tools, overhead is minimal as long as the sampling interval is 5 seconds or more.

Sar was designed to log data in the background to a binary-format disk file using the program */usr/lib/sa/sadc*. Therefore, *sar* and *sadc* are useful when collecting data over long periods of time, for purposes such as baselines or general performance characterization.

5.2.5.1   Running *sar* Interactively

In interactive mode, to report current metrics, *sar* must be invoked with command-line parameters:

sar [-AabcdMmPqSuvwy] <interval in seconds> [number of iterations]

Forgetting to supply these parameters results in a cryptic error message:

```
can't open /usr/adm/sa/saxx
```

In this message, *xx* is a two-digit number that is the same as the number of the month. This message means that *sar* expects a daily system activity file to exist in the directory */usr/adm/sa*. Optionally, a different file to be analyzed can be specified with the *-f* option. By default, data for CPU utilization (the *-u* parameter) will be displayed interactively, storing the data to a binary output file:

sar -o <filename> <interval in seconds> [number of iterations]

Note that the results are also listed to the standard output while the data is being logged to the binary-format file interactively, displaying previously recorded data:

sar [-AabcdMmquvwy] [-s starttime] [-e endtime]
[-i interval in seconds to report] <-f binary data file>

5.2.5.2   Running *sar* in the background

Sar may be invoked in the background only through the program */usr/lib/sa/sadc*. By default, binary output is written to the daily system activity file */usr/adm/sa/saxx* where *xx* is the date of the month, with no output to the *standard output*. This mode is most often invoked in the superuser's *crontab* file to run at midnight every day. The data in this file is then displayed by invoking *sar* in the interactive mode.

WARNING: There are two problems with *sadc* log files: First, the data files will grow without bound, and therefore may be quite large. Sufficient disk space on the */usr* file system must be available to accomodate these files. Second, each month, the *sadc* files are overwritten since the names include only the day of the month. Procedures must be in place to archive these files to tape before they are overwritten.

The command-line parameters for *sadc* are different from those for *sar*. *Sadc* is invoked as follows:

sadc <interval in seconds> [number of iterations] [output file name]

Note that there are no metric parameters for *sadc* because it collects *all* of the various metrics. Additionally, two shell scripts, *sa1* and *sa2*, can be found in the directory */usr/lbin/sa*. These shell scripts may be modified and are supplied to invoke *sadc* in the most common way.

The following is the code in */usr/lbin/sa/sa1*:

```
#! /usr/bin/sh
# @(#) $Revision: 72.3 $
#        sa1.sh

DATE=`date +%d`
ENDIR=/usr/lbin/sa
DFILE=/var/adm/sa/sa$DATE
cd $ENDIR
if [ $# = 0 ]
then
      exec $ENDIR/sadc 1 1 $DFILE
else
      exec $ENDIR/sadc $* $DFILE
fi
```

Here is the code in */usr/lbin/sa/sa2*:

```
#! /usr/bin/sh
# @(#) $Revision: 72.1 $
#    sa2.sh

DATE=`date +%d`
RPT=/var/adm/sa/sar$DATE
DFILE=/var/adm/sa/sa$DATE
ENDIR=/usr/sbin
cd $ENDIR
$ENDIR/sar $* -f $DFILE > $RPT
find /var/adm/sa \
    -name `sar*' -o -name `sa*' \
    -mtime +7 -exec rm {} \;
```

5.2.5.3   Command Line Options
The various metrics are displayed based on command-line parameters. Any combination of command-line metric parameters is permitted. These command-line parameters are:
- *-A*—All metrics
- *-a*—File system lookups
- *-b*—Disk logical, physical & raw reads/writes; buffer cache hit ratios

- -*c*—System call rates
- -*d*—Disk I/Os and queue lengths by disk drive
- -*M*—CPU utilization by CPU in an HP-UX SMP environment (used with -*u* or -*q*)
- -*m*—Message and semaphore operations
- -P— Processor set information (must be used with -*M* and -*u* or -*q*)
- -*q*—Run queue
- -S—Select system call rate (must be used with the -*m*)
- -*u*—CPU utilization
- -*v*—Kernel table utilization
- -*w*—Swapping and context switching
- -*y*—Terminal I/O

Although *sar* can collect data in intervals as small as one second, for reasons of volume of output and system overhead it is recommended that the interval be reduced according to purpose. If the purpose is performance characterization, intervals of 5 minutes (300 seconds) or even 1 hour (3600 seconds) may be satisfactory. Intervals of 5 to 30 seconds are recommended for problem diagnosis.

The following is a listing of basic sample output from *sar*:

```
HP-UX lptest1 B.10.20 A 9000/867    01/13/99

16:12:13    %usr    %sys    %wio    %idle
            device  %busy   avque   r+w/s  blks/s  avwait  avserv
         runq-sz %runocc swpq-sz %swpocc
         bread/s lread/s %rcache bwrit/s lwrit/s %wcache pread/s pwrit/s
         swpin/s bswin/s swpot/s bswot/s pswch/s
         scall/s sread/s swrit/s   fork/s   exec/s  rchar/s  wchar/s
          iget/s namei/s dirbk/s
         rawch/s canch/s outch/s rcvin/s xmtin/s mdmin/s
         text-sz  ov proc-sz  ov  inod-sz  ov  file-sz  ov
           msg/s  sema/s
16:12:14      1       1       0       98

            1.0      99     0.0       0
              0      87     100       0       0       0       0       0
           0.00     0.0    0.00     0.0      71
            627      14      23    0.00    0.00  540388       0
              0       8       0
              0       0       0       0       0       0
            N/A     N/A 112/276       0 476/476       0 237/800       0
           0.00    0.00
```

5.2.5.4   Advantages (+) of *sar*

The biggest advantage of *sar* is familiarity. Many people have used it to diagnose system performance because it was the only tool available. Many scripts (*awk, sed,* and *shell*) have been written to analyze and summarize data from *sar*. Another important advantage is that among all the performance tools, *sar* provides several unique metrics, described in the next few sections (the command line options are shown in parentheses).

Table Overflow Information (-v)   In addition to showing the number of entries currently being used for the process (proc), text, system file (file), and inode tables, *sar* also indicates the number of times that an entry was requested but was unavailable because the table was full. This information is given in the "ov" column in the output. An application receives an error and an error message is written to the console when one of the tables overflows. These messages may include:

- *Cannot fork* (the process table is full)
- *File table overflow* (the system file table is full)
- *Inode table overflow* (the inode table is full)

Sar counts the number of occurrences of table overflow during the measurement interval.

Warning on Inode Table Overflow: The inode table is a cache. Recently used entries for files that have already been closed may remain in the table until an entry is needed to open another file. Therefore, this metric may *always* show the table as full. There are three ways to determine if you need to increase the inode table size:

1. Look at the "ov" column in the output.
2. Look for system console messages saying "inode table overflow."
3. Look for application errors related to an inability to open files.

Read and Write Buffer Cache Hit Ratios (-b)   Several of the tools report read buffer cache hit ratio. Only *sar* reports the read and write buffer cache hit ratios separately.

Semaphore and Message Queue (IPC) Operation Rates (-m and -S)   The IPC operation rates are often important to know, especially for relational databases, which make frequent use of these CPU-consuming system services. The rates show the frequency of system call invocation and do not refer to the number of semaphores or message queues that are currently allocated. The *-S* option can be used to view the *select* system call rates in addition to the semop and message queue rates.

5.2.5.5   Disadvantages (-) of *sar*

The major disadvantages of *sar* include:

- No per-process information. *Sar* collects only global metrics. Therefore, it is possible to determine *what* is occurring, but not *who* is causing it.
- There is little virtual memory information. Only global paging-in and paging-out rates and swapping-in and swapping-out rates are shown by *sar*. Currently, the HP-UX version of

sar reports only swapping rates. *Sar* is limited in its ability to diagnose memory bottle-necks.

- The output produced by *sar* is difficult to analyze and parse. Its output is command-line parameter-specific, so that analysis depends on the options chosen. In addition, *sar* writes a blank in a field rather than a zero, which makes it difficult to look for data in fields. The output can be improved by using the *sar -o* option, which places all the data in columns. However, very long lines can be generated.

- Graphics and tabulation require other tools. *Sar* does not offer any graphics features. It merely produces output with so many lines per interval chosen. Other tools must be used to change the data into more suitable forms. There is also no per-process information.

- The binary output file format can have different versions. *Sar* must match *sadc* in revisions.

- The *sar* data must be analyzed on the system where it was acquired, because it needs information from */stand/vmunix* and must be analyzed on the same running OS instance as the one contained in */stand/vmunix*.

- The CPU breakdown between user, system, wio, and idle may not always be accurate. The problem is that these values are sample-based and interrupt activity can cause problems with how these values are collected. *Glance* is the best tool for obtaining CPU usage information because it uses more accurate data collected by the MI.

The CPU overhead consumed by *sar* is only dependent upon the interval. This is because all the data is collected all the time, even if it isn't being displayed. Longer intervals consume less CPU, and memory consumption is fixed. The counters used by *sar* are always turned on, so that overhead is not measureable and is constant.

5.2.5.6   Minimizing Overhead When Using *sar*

Using *sar* and *sadc* on a system can consume an unacceptable CPU time just to collect the data, resulting in a high amount of overhead. Here is a simple trick for minimizing the overhead while collecting data for a particular application, assuming that one can control what activity is occuring on the system under analysis.

Use the following command to place a single snapshot of the performance counters into a user-defined file:

/usr/lib/sa/sadc 1 1 <filename>

After the command is invoked, one can then run the application whose performance is to be analyzed. When the application has terminated, or when it is felt that enough time has elapsed for the data to reflect a characteristic period of application use, take another snapshot with the following command:

sar -Af <filename>

The data reported will pertain to the time beginning with the snapshot taken before the application was run for analysis. This way, there is no overhead generated by the use of *sar* or *sadc* while the application was running.

5.2.6   *time*

Time reports on the time required for the execution of a command. Output includes real time, user time, and system time. *Time* is either an external command or a built-in function within some of the shells. The external command */usr/bin/time* may be invoked by full path name, and it is the version used by the obsolete Bourne shell. The Posix, Korn, and C shells use a built-in function that is a variation of */usr/bin/time*. Unfortunately, none of the output formats are the same. But the built-in functions consume less resources because they do not fork another process. Typical output is shown below for an execution of the MC/ServiceGuard *cmviewcl* command. The output of the ServiceGuard command is shown first, followed by the timing data.

```
lptest1 B.10.20 # time cmviewcl
```

CLUSTER	STATUS			
cluster3	up			*ServiceGuard*
				Command
NODE	STATUS	STATE		*Output*
lptest1	up	running		
PACKAGE	STATUS	STATE	PKG_SWITCH	NODE
xclock	up	running	enabled	lptest1
xmeditor	up	running	enabled	lptest1
NODE	STATUS	STATE		
lptest2	up	running		

```
real        0.49
user        0.10                              time data
sys         0.04
lptest1 B.10.20 #
```

5.2.7 *timex*

Like *time, timex* reports on the time required for the execution of a command, but has additional options that provide more information. Option *-s* prints *sar* data for the interval in which the program ran, and *-p* prints process accounting information for the interval in which the program ran. The following example shows *time* data and the *sar* data as provided through use of the *-s* option.

```
lptest1 B.10.20 # timex -s cmviewcl

CLUSTER       STATUS
cluster3      up

   NODE          STATUS        STATE
   lptest1       up            running

      PACKAGE       STATUS        STATE         PKG_SWITCH    NODE
      xclock        up            running       enabled       lptest1
      xmeditor      up            running       enabled       lptest1

   NODE          STATUS        STATE
   lptest2       up            running

real          0.49
user          0.10
sys           0.04
```

ServiceGuard Command Output

timex data

Another example shows the use of the *-p* option. (Note that for the *-p* option to work with the *timex* command, the command */usr/sbin/acct/turnacct on* must first be used to enable process accounting.)

```
timex -p cmviewcl

CLUSTER        STATUS
cluster3       down

  NODE          STATUS        STATE
  lptest1       down          unknown
  lptest2       down          unknown

UNOWNED_PACKAGES

    PACKAGE        STATUS        STATE        PKG_SWITCH      NODE
    xclock         down                                      unowned
    xmeditor       down                                      unowned


real          2.75
user          0.16
sys           0.04


START AFT: Fri May 14 14:07:57 1999
END BEFOR: Fri May 14 14:07:59 1999
COMMAND                        START   END        REAL    CPU     CHARS   BLOCKS
NAME          USER   TTYNAME  TIME    TIME       (SECS)  (SECS)  TRNSFD   R/W
#cmviewcl  root      ttyp1    14:07:57 14:07:59   2.74    0.19    61656        0
lptest1 B.10.20 #
```

5.2.8   *uptime*

Uptime is most useful for quickly displaying load average metrics. It shows the current time, the length of time the system has been up, the number of users logged on to the system, and the average number of jobs in the run queue over the last 1, 5, and 15 minutes.

Uptime has very low overhead. Partial sample output is shown below; load average data is shown in larger italic type.

```
$ uptime -lw
  3:52pm  up 265 days,  4:55,  81 users,  load average: 1.03, 1.27, 2.07
User      tty           login@  idle   JCPU   PCPU   what
dts       ttyrc         10:16am  2:58                -ksh
sganesh   ttyp1          6:51pm 21:00                -ksh
john ttyp2             12:41pm 24:59                -ksh
barb ttyp3              5:28pm190:24    1:18   1:18  /usr/local/lib/synchronize/HP
800/bin/synchronize -server hps
annasu    ttyp4          7:39am  8:13                -ksh
whine     ttyp6         11:12am  4:34                -ksh
```

5.3 CPU Diagnostic Tools

Many tools provide data about currently executing processes and CPU load. Some important examples are *ps, xload*, and *top*. *Glance* and *sar* also supply CPU-related metrics. The *machinfo* tool (described in more detail in "Machinfo" on page 79) provides information about the processors installed in an IPF system.

5.3.1   *ps*

Used for process status display, *ps* is perhaps the best known and most commonly used of all the performance tools. Its many options (see the man page on *ps*) allow for very specific display of process information. The following is an example showing output of *ps -ef* on a workstation. This display is limited to processes owned by UID *peterw*:

```
  UID    PID  PPID  C    STIME TTY      TIME COMMAND
peterw 14336 14335  0   Jan  8 ttyp2    0:00 rlogin lptest1 -l root
peterw 14323 14322  0   Jan  8 ttyp2    0:00 -ksh
peterw 13146 13145  0   Jan  8 ?        0:06 /usr/bin/X11/hpterm -ls -sl 255
peterw  4743  3825  2 12:16:51 ttyp4    0:00 ps -ef
peterw 13147 13146  0   Jan  8 ttyp1    0:00 -ksh
peterw  2239     1  0 09:03:41 ?        2:21 /opt/adobe/fmsgml55/bin/makersgml
peterw  3824  3823  0 11:04:59 ?        0:01 /usr/bin/X11/hpterm -ls -sl 255
peterw 14271 13147  0   Jan  8 ttyp1    0:00 rlogin lptest1 -l root
peterw 13140 13106  0   Jan  8 ?        0:15 dtwm
peterw 13106 13092  0   Jan  8 ?        0:00 /usr/dt/bin/dtsession
```

Ps also shows information about Process Resource Manager (PRM) groups.

5.3.2 *top*

Top displays the top processes on the system and periodically updates the information. It also provides global information, including:

- The number of processes in particular states.
- Global CPU utilization by type (one line for each CPU in an SMP system).

It then lists the running processes ordered by CPU utilization. On an SMP system, *top* shows the CPU number to which the process is currently assigned. *Top* uses the *vi* commands **j** and **k** to navigate between screens.

Top's display includes system data, memory data, and process data. Raw CPU percentage is used to rank the processes. The following example shows the top ten processes on a workstation:

```
$ top -n 10

System: hpmfac89 Mon Jan 11 11:08:28 1999
Load averages: 0.14, 0.14, 0.12
124 processes: 122 sleeping, 1 running, 1 stopped
CPU states:
  LOAD    USER    NICE    SYS    IDLE   BLOCK   SWAIT    INTR    SSYS
  0.14    0.2%    0.0%    0.0%   99.8%   0.0%    0.0%    0.0%    0.0%


 Memory: 32672K (8116K) real, 55592K (28060K) virtual, 7708K free   Page# 1/9

TTY    PID USERNAME PRI NI    SIZE    RES STATE     TIME %WCPU   %CPU COMMAND
  ?   1226 root     154 20    692K   180K sleep   105:16  0.17   0.17 dtgreet
  ?  13140 peterw   154 20   1528K  1532K sleep     0:15  0.14   0.14 dtwm
  ?   3859 peterw   154 20    616K   784K sleep     0:00  0.14   0.13 hpterm
 p5   3911 peterw   178 20    388K   268K run       0:00  0.45   0.12 top
  ?    930 root     154 20   6100K   932K sleep    66:28  0.10   0.10 rpcd
  ?   1178 root     154 20    868K   468K sleep    56:27  0.08   0.08 opcle
  ?   1210 daemon   154 20   2436K   232K sleep    24:36  0.07   0.07 X
  ?      3 root     128 20      0K     0K sleep    25:24  0.07   0.07 statdaemon
  ?   1176 root     154 20   2576K   284K sleep    25:41  0.05   0.05 opcmsga
  ?    993 root     120 20    236K   116K sleep     7:52  0.05   0.04 xntpd
```

> **NOTE:** On SMP systems with many CPUs, the global per-CPU list takes up more of the display with fewer lines of process information. The *-h* option can be used to display only a summary of the CPU information, thus providing several more lines of process information.

5.3.3 *xload*

An X-Windows graphical display of CPU load over time appears in *xload*. The information is updated once a minute. An example is shown in Figure 5-5. The values shown are the load average rather than CPU utilization. See Section 7.5.2, "Global CPU Queue Metrics: Run Queue vs. Load Average" on page 195 for an explanation.

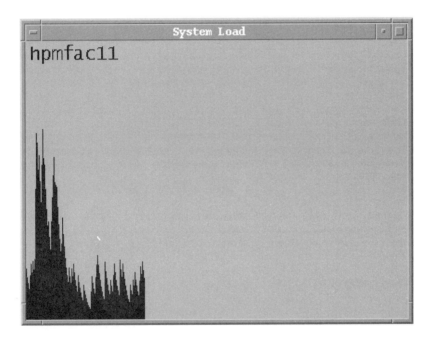

Figure 5-5   Graphic Display of CPU by *xload*

5.3.4 *Machinfo*

The *machinfo* command displays information regarding some of the important system characteristics of IPF-based systems. In particular, it displays the CPU quantity, type, speed, and cache configuration. This may be the only way of determining this information for a specific system other than reviewing HP datasheets and tables in this book.

This command is very useful when verifying the actual hardware configuration of a system. Knowing that a system which is performing well has 3 MB caches while the one that is not performing well has 1.5 MB caches can be useful information in debugging performance issues.

The following shows an example of the *machinfo* output.

```
# machinfo
CPU info:
   Number of CPUs = 4
   Clock speed = 1000 MHz
   CPUID registers
       vendor information =        "GenuineIntel"
       processor serial number =  0x0000000000000000
       processor version info =   0x000000001f000604
           architecture revision:     0
           processor family:          31   Intel(R) Itanium 2 Family  Processors
           processor model:           0    Intel(R) Itanium 2 processor
           processor revision:        6    stepping B2
           largest CPUID reg:         4
       processor capabilities =   0x0000000000000001
           implements long branch:    1
   Bus features
       implemented =  0xbdf0000060000000
       selected    =  0x0000000040000000
           Bus Lock Signal masked

Cache info:
   L1 Instruction: size =   16 KB, associativity = 4
   L1 Data:        size =   16 KB, associativity = 4
   L2 Unified:     size =  256 KB, associativity = 8
   L3 Unified:     size = 3072 KB, associativity = 12

Memory = 12281 MB (11.993164 GB)

Firmware info:
   Firmware revision = tjg2.view.01.41-0
   FP SWA driver revision: 1.9
   BMC version: v01.20
   BMC version: v01.20

Platform info:
   model string =         "ia64 hp server rx5670"
   machine id number =    ffffffff-ffff-ffff-ffff-ffffffffffff
   machine serial number =
OS info:
   sysname  = HP-UX
   nodename = gunnison
   release  = B.11.23
   version  = A (two-user license)
   machine  = ia64
   idnumber = 4294967295
   vmunix _release_version:
@(#) $Revision: vmunix:    vw: ruemmler_tpcc_0428    selectors:
CUPI80_BL2003_0428 'cup2_ruemmler_tpcc_0428' FLAVOR=perf Tue Apr 29  10:30:10
PDT 2003 $
```

5.4 Disk Diagnostic Tools

Disk diagnostics include *bdf*, *df, ioscan,* and *iostat,* which also provides data on terminal I/
O. *Glance* and *sar* also provide disk-related data. Some of the tools report on inode utilization.
An inode is a data structure used by the kernel and the file system metadata associated with each
file open in the kernel and each file that exists on the disk. There are in-core inodes and on-disk
indoes, each of which have a particular format.

5.4.1 *bdf and df*

Bdf is the name given to the Berkeley version of the *df* (disk free) command in HP-UX. It
is listed as a performance metric for its resource consumption metrics of on-disk inodes and file
system disk space.

Because it reports disk space consumption in KB rather than blocks (512 bytes), *bdf* is
often preferred over *df*. It can be used to manage file system capacity for two reasons: to avoid
running out of space, and to prevent file system block allocation performance degradation,
which occurs when the file system is more than 90% full.

The *-i* option to *bdf* displays HFS on-disk inode utilization as well as file system data
space utilization. An inode is the data structure on disk and in memory which describes the location and number of blocks required for each file in an HFS file system. By default, one HFS
inode is created for every 6 KB of disk space in the file system (HP-UX 10.X and later; earlier
systems used an inode for every 2 KB). This default worked well when disks were small and
there were typically many small files. With today's larger disks and larger files, the default
causes a lot of disk space to be wasted.

Each on-disk inode consumes 128 bytes of space, which seems small; however, on a 2 GB
volume, over 333,000 inodes are created by default. On a 2 GB volume, this translates to 42 MB
that is allocated specifically for inodes and cannot be used as data space. Very seldom are there
333,000 files in a file system. Even if there were 33,000 files (10% of the inodes allocated, but
still a large amount) in a file system, over 38 MB of disk space would still be unused and
unavailable for data.

This space consumption is particularly wasteful when large files consume most of the
disk, because very few inodes are actually needed to describe the few large files. The way to
tune these situations will be described in Section 9.7.1.4, "HFS Tuneable Parameters" on
page 289.

Here is an example of output from the *bdf -i* command:

```
Filesystem          kbytes     used   avail %used   iused   ifree %iuse Mounted on
/dev/vg00/lvol3      83733    71263    4096   95%    4232    9208   31% /
/dev/vg00/lvol1      95701    17997   68133   21%      21   15339    0% /stand
/dev/vg00/lvol8     307421   113513  163165   41%    2693  142011    2% /var
/dev/vg00/lvol7     331093   240790   57193   81%   13617   39375   26% /usr
/dev/vg00/lvol6      30597     7969   19568   29%     114   15118    1% /tmp
/dev/vg00/lvol5     247157   220125    2316   99%    4048   35504   10% /opt
/dev/vg00/lvol4      19861       53   17821    0%       6    3450    0% /home
```

NOTE: In-core and on-disk inodes for a JFS (VxFS) file system are dynamically allocated. JFS inode utilization is not shown by *bdf*.

5.4.2   *ioscan*

Ioscan is an HP-UX tool that displays the complete I/O configuration of a system. It shows how I/O adapter cards are mapped to hardware paths, and for mass storage it shows what external devices are attached to the adapters. It also shows the software drivers assigned to handle work for each of the adapters. The following is an example of ioscan output:

```
Class        I   H/W Path       Driver     S/W State    H/W Type      Description
=================================================================== =====
root         0                  root       CLAIMED      BUS_NEXUS
ioa          0   0              sba        CLAIMED      BUS_NEXUS     System  Bus Adapter (1229)
ba           0   0/0            lba        CLAIMED      BUS_NEXUS     Local   PCI-X Bus Adapter (122e)
tty          0   0/0/1/0        asio0      CLAIMED      INTERFACE     PCI   SimpleComm (103c1290)
                                /dev/diag/mux0   /dev/mux0        /dev/tty0p0
tty          1   0/0/1/1        asio0      CLAIMED      INTERFACE     PCI   Serial (103c1048)
                                /dev/MPdiag1     /dev/mux1        /dev/tty1p2
                                /dev/diag/mux1   /dev/tty1p0      /dev/tty1p4
ext_bus      0   0/0/2/0        c8xx       CLAIMED      INTERFACE     SCSI  C896 Ultra Wide Single-Ended
target       0   0/0/2/0.0      tgt        CLAIMED      DEVICE
disk         0   0/0/2/0.0.0    sdisk      CLAIMED      DEVICE        SEAGATE ST318404LC
                                /dev/dsk/c0t0d0       /dev/rdsk/c0t0d0
                                /dev/dsk/c0t0d0s1     /dev/rdsk/c0t0d0s1
                                /dev/dsk/c0t0d0s2     /dev/rdsk/c0t0d0s2
target       4   0/0/2/0.7      tgt        CLAIMED      DEVICE
ctl          0   0/0/2/0.7.0    sctl       CLAIMED      DEVICE        Initiator
                                /dev/rscsi/c0t7d0
ext_bus      1   0/0/2/1        c8xx       CLAIMED      INTERFACE     SCSI  C896 Ultra Wide Single-Ended
target       3   0/0/2/1.2      tgt        CLAIMED      DEVICE
disk         3   0/0/2/1.2.0    sdisk      CLAIMED      DEVICE        HP        DVD-ROM 305
                                /dev/dsk/c1t2d0   /dev/rdsk/c1t2d0
target       5   0/0/2/1.7      tgt        CLAIMED      DEVICE
ctl          1   0/0/2/1.7.0    sctl       CLAIMED      DEVICE        Initiator
                                /dev/rscsi/c1t7d0
ba           1   0/1            lba        CLAIMED      BUS_NEXUS     Local   PCI-X Bus Adapter (122e)
ba           2   0/1/1/0        PCItoPCI   CLAIMED      BUS_NEXUS     PCItoPCI Bridge
ext_bus      2   0/1/1/0/1/0    c8xx       CLAIMED      INTERFACE     SCSI  C1010 Ultra160 Wide LVD A6794-
60001
target       7   0/1/1/0/1/0.7  tgt        CLAIMED      DEVICE
ctl          3   0/1/1/0/1/0.7.0        sctl    CLAIMED      DEVICE        Initiator
                                /dev/rscsi/c2t7d0
```

```
ext_bus      3  0/1/1/0/1/1    c8xx      CLAIMED    INTERFACE    SCSI  C1010 Ultra Wide Single-Ended
A6794-60001
target       6  0/1/1/0/1/1.7  tgt       CLAIMED    DEVICE
ctl          2  0/1/1/0/1/1.7.0sctl      CLAIMED    DEVICE          Initiator
                              /dev/rscsi/c3t7d0
lan          0  0/1/1/0/4/0    igelan    CLAIMED    INTERFACE    HP  A6794-60001PCI 1000Base-T
ba           3  0/2            lba       CLAIMED    BUS_NEXUS    Local  PCI-X Bus Adapter (122e)
fc           0  0/2/1/0        td        CLAIMED    INTERFACE    HP  Tachyon XL2 Fibre Channel Mass
Storage Adapter
/dev/td0
fcp          0  0/2/1/0.8      fcp       CLAIMED    INTERFACE    FCP  Protocol Adapter
ext_bus      4  0/2/1/0.8.0.108.0       fcparray CLAIMED  INTERFACE    FCP Array Interface
target       8  0/2/1/0.8.0.108.0.0     tgt       CLAIMED    DEVICE
disk         4  0/2/1/0.8.0.108.0.0.0   sdisk     CLAIMED    DEVICE          HP A6189A
                              /dev/dsk/c4t0d0    /dev/rdsk/c4t0d0
ext_bus      5  0/2/1/0.8.0.255.6       fcpdev    CLAIMED    INTERFACE    FCP Device Interface
target       9  0/2/1/0.8.0.255.6.12    tgt       CLAIMED    DEVICE
ctl          4  0/2/1/0.8.0.255.6.12.0  sctl      CLAIMED    DEVICE          HP A6189A
                              /dev/rscsi/c5t12d0
ba           4  0/3            lba       CLAIMED    BUS_NEXUS    Local  PCI-X Bus Adapter (122e)
ba           5  0/4            lba       CLAIMED    BUS_NEXUS    Local  PCI-X Bus Adapter (122e)
ba           6  0/5            lba       CLAIMED    BUS_NEXUS    Local  PCI-X Bus Adapter (122e)
ba           7  0/6            lba       CLAIMED    BUS_NEXUS    Local  PCI-X Bus Adapter (122e)
lan          1  0/6/2/0        intl100   CLAIMED    INTERFACE    Intel  PCI Pro 10/100Tx Server Adapter
ba           8  0/7            lba       CLAIMED    BUS_NEXUS    Local  PCI-X Bus Adapter (122e)
processor    0  120            processor CLAIMED    PROCESSOR    Processor
processor    1  121            processor CLAIMED    PROCESSOR    Processor
processor    2  122            processor CLAIMED    PROCESSOR    Processor
processor    3  123            processor CLAIMED    PROCESSOR    Processor
ba           9  250            pdh       CLAIMED    BUS_NEXUS    Core  I/O Adapter
ipmi         0  250/0          ipmi      CLAIMED    INTERFACE    IPMI  Controller
                              /dev/ipmi
acpi_node    0  250/1          acpi_node CLAIMED    INTERFACE    Acpi  Hardware
```

When using ioscan, always use the *-k* option to get a quick response unless ioscan is being used to identify a newly added device. If the *-k* option is not used, a full scan of the I/O subsystem is performed to collect information. This full scan can take several seconds to minutes depending on how many devices are attached to the server.

5.4.3 *iostat*

Iostat is a Berkeley Unix-based tool that displays disk and terminal I/O statistics. Like its counterpart, *vmstat*, *iostat* displays no per-process information. Instead, it displays global information on per-spindle disk I/O rates by default and terminal I/O rates optionally. *Iostat* is invoked as follows:

• Interactively:

iostat [-t] [interval in seconds] [number of iterations]

• By saving data to a file:

iostat [-t] [interval in seconds] [number of iterations] > output-file-name

The -*t* parameter means list terminal I/O (hardwired terminal devices and pseudo-terminals) and CPU utilization.

By default, *iostat* reports the results every second. Except in a few cases, one second is too frequent. Even for the purpose of diagnosing problems, 5 seconds or 30 seconds are much more reasonable intervals, and use less CPU overhead.

For terminal I/O, *iostat* reports the number of characters input and the number of characters output during the last interval, as well as user, system, and *nice* CPU utilization. Note that *nice* CPU utilization counts CPU time for those processes which have used the "nice" version of *nice*; this differs from the way MI-based tools like *glance* report nice CPU utilization.

For disk I/O, *iostat* reports the following data by disk spindle:

- *bps*—Kbytes transferred per second.

- *sps*—Seeks per second which should be the same as I/Os per second.

- *msps*—Milliseconds per seek. On modern disks that have features such as command queueing, *msps* no longer makes sense as a performance metric. This metric is hard-coded to a value of 1.

The disk I/O metrics are reported horizontally for all disks, making the report line quite long; it may be so long that it exceeds the maximum 256-byte line length, and therefore might be truncated on large systems with many disks. Other tools that provide a greater volume of similar information are now available. This has dramatically decreased the usefulness of *iostat*.

Because *iostat* is not controlled by any Unix standard, its output may change from one operating system release to the next.

5.5 Memory Diagnostic Tools

Memory data are provided by memory diagnostic tools including *size*, *vmstat* and *ipcs*, as well as by *glance* and *sar*.

5.5.1 *size*

Size produces section size information for each section in the object files. The size of the text, data and BSS (uninitialized data) sections are printed along with the total size of the object file. Two examples of output from the *size* command are shown below; the first provides a summary, and the second, using the -*v* option, provides the information in more detail.

The output of the *size* command may be misleading for executables that use shared libraries or shared memory, and have large heap and/or stack sizes. The text and data metrics reported by *size* do not include any of these areas.

```
hpgsyha9/B.11.00:size scopeux
443507 + 92120 + 11305 = 546932

hpgsyha9/B.11.00:size -v scopeux

        Subspace                 Size      Physical Address      Virtual Address

        $SHLIB_INFO$            86167              4096                 4096
        $MILLICODE$              9016             90264                90264
        $CODE$                 132772             99284                99284
        $CODE$                 132884            232056               232056
        $CODE$                  30784            364944               364944
        $LIT$                     448            395728               395728
        $UNWIND_START$          41440            396176               396176
        $UNWIND_END$             9992            437616               437616
        $RECOVER_END$               4            447608               447608
        $PFA_COUNTER$               8            450560           1073745920
        $DATA$                  75508            450568           1073745928
        $SHORTDATA$              1404            526080           1073821440
        $PLT$                    9816            527488           1073822848
        $DLT$                    5368            537304           1073832664
        $GLOBAL$                   16            542672           1073838032
        $SHORTBSS$               1025                0           1073838048
        $BSS$                   10280                0           1073839080

        Total                  546932
```

5.5.2   *swapinfo*

Swapinfo prints information about device and file system paging space. The word "swap" is a misnomer, since HP-UX actually implements virtual memory through paging, not swapping. Using the *-t* switch with *swapinfo* will add a totals line that sums all of the lines above it. This total may not be the system-wide total if other switches are used to produce specific output.

Sample output from the *swapinfo* command is shown below:

```
hpgsyha9/B.11.00:swapinfo
             Kb        Kb       Kb    PCT  START/      Kb
TYPE       AVAIL     USED     FREE   USED  LIMIT RESERVE  PRI  NAME
dev       307200        0   307200    0%      0       -    1  /dev/vg00/lvol2
reserve        -    81696   -81696
memory    196360    29172   167188   15%
```

5.5.3   *vmstat*

Vmstat is a tool that is familiar to people using BSD-based Unix systems. It produces output of one line of information per interval and includes CPU and virtual memory metrics. *Vmstat* is invoked as follows:

- Interactively:

vmstat [-dS] [interval in seconds] [number of iterations]

- By saving data to a file:

vmstat [-dS] [interval in seconds] [number of iterations] > output-file-name

- With special non-interval options:

vmstat [-fsz]

The command line parameters for *vmstat* are as follows:

- *-d*—Per-disk information
- *-f*—Forks and pages of virtual memory since boot-up
- *-S*—Display swap information as well as paging
- *-s*—Display the total count of paging-related events
- *-z*—Zero out the counters

By default, *vmstat* reports the results every second. Except in a few cases, one second is too frequent. Even for the purpose of diagnosing problems, 5 seconds or 30 seconds are much more reasonable intervals, and use less CPU overhead.

The major advantage of *vmstat* is that it produces a great deal of data in a single line of columnar output. This data is organized into the following groupings of metrics:

- Queues (run, blocked, and runnable but swapped out)
- Virtual memory metrics (page faults, paging and swapping rates)
- Scheduler metrics (context switches and interrupts)
- CPU utilization metrics (user, system, and idle)

Although it is quite useful in monitoring virtual memory, *vmstat* is limited in that it does not display process information. Therefore, one can determine that memory is a potential problem, but not which processes might be causing the problem.

A typical output from *vmstat* is shown below:

```
$ vmstat -dS
          procs                  memory                    page
    faults          cpu
    r    b    w      avm     free   re   at    pi   po    fr   de    sr    in
    sy    cs   us sy id
    0   41    0     5832      985    4    4     0    0     0    0     0   140
    315   32    0  0 99

Disk Transfers
  device     xfer/sec
  c0t6d0        0
```

The first line of output from *vmstat* (except when invoked with the *-f, -s,* or *-z* options) shows the various metrics as an average since boot-up or reset time. This information is generally ignored when diagnosing problems.

You should be careful in interpreting the data from *vmstat* because the headings are cryptic one-, two-, three-, or four-letter mnemonics and are very poorly documented. For instance, someone who is familiar with CPU hardware might conclude that the column *at*, which is documented as the number of address translation faults, might give a rate of Translation Lookaside Buffer (TLB) faults, because address translation is the function of the TLB. The number of TLB faults would provide a very useful measure of the efficiency of a critical system component. Unfortunately, that is not what *vmstat* is reporting; instead, it is reporting the number of page faults.

Another example is the *avm* column. Because it is a memory metric and is placed next to *free*, one might conclude that *avm* stands for available memory, but in fact, *avm* stands for active virtual memory. It takes looking at the *vmstat* source code to determine that *avm* is the sum of text, data, and stack pages in use for all processes, not including shared library or shared memory pages! Also note that two columns are labeled identically: the first *sy* is the number of system calls, and the second *sy* is the percent of system CPU utilization.

The most important data obtained from *vmstat* are:

- *r*—The number of processes in the run queue
- *b*—The number of processes blocked for any reason
- *w*—The number of processes swapped out but runnable
- *free*—The number of free memory pages
- *re*—The number of virtual memory page reclaims
- *at*—The number of virtual memory page faults
- *pi/po*—The number of pages paged in and out

- *si/so*—The number of pages swapped in and out (in HP-UX 10.0 and later, these refer to deactivations and reactivations)

- *in*—The number of interrupts

- *cs*—The number of context switches

- *us*—Percentage of user CPU utilization

- *sy*—Percentage of system CPU utilization

In general, the output produced by *vmstat* is easily parsed by *awk* for use with spreadsheets or other programs for summarizing and averaging the data over long periods of time. Sometimes, however, the numbers exceed the number of columns allotted and will use up the space between columns; this can make it difficult to parse the output.

The CPU overhead associated with running *vmstat* is relatively small, but depends on the interval. The counters used by *vmstat* are always turned on, so that overhead is not measurable and is fixed. Longer intervals use less overhead; memory overhead is constant.

5.5.4 *ipcs*

Both *ipcs* and *ipcrm* are tools that let you manage inter-process communication, although *ipcrm* is not a measurement tool. *Ipcrm* lets you delete an IPC object. *Ipcs* provides a report on semaphores, message queues, and shared memory. Sample *ipcs* output is shown below:

```
$ ipcs
IPC status from /dev/kmem as of Wed Jan 13 15:44:06 1999
T       ID   KEY        MODE         OWNER     GROUP
Message Queues:
q        0 0x3c1c0234 -Rrw--w--w-    root      root
q        1 0x3e1c0234 --rw-r--r--    root      root
Shared Memory:
m        0 0x2f180002 --rw-------    root      sys
m        1 0x411c0209 --rw-rw-rw-    root      root
m        2 0x4e0c0002 --rw-rw-rw-    root      root
m        3 0x41201041 --rw-rw-rw-    root      root
m        4 0x00000000 --rw-------    root      sys
m      205 0x431c1b43 --rw-rw-rw-    daemon    daemon
Semaphores:
s        0 0x2f180002 --ra-ra-ra-    root      sys
s        1 0x411c0209 --ra-ra-ra-    root      root
s        2 0x4e0c0002 --ra-ra-ra-    root      root
s        3 0x41201041 --ra-ra-ra-    root      root
s        4 0x00446f6e --ra-r--r--    root      root
s        5 0x00446f6d --ra-r--r--    root      root
s        6 0x01090522 --ra-r--r--    root      root
s      519 0x4c1c1b43 --ra-r--r--    daemon    daemon
```

5.5.5   chatr

The *chatr* command allows one to modify various load-time attributes of an executable, including attributes that affect memory. Not all *chatr* options are available for all applications on all versions of the operating system. Refer to the *chatr(1)* man page for the specific options for a given operating system revision and architecture. The following sections describe some of the more useful options to *chatr*.

5.5.5.1   +pd/+pi

The +*pd* and +*pi* options allow up to the maximum virtual memory page size to be chosen for the data and text segments respectively. These options can be used to dramatically reduce TLB misses, which are discussed in Section 6.1.5, "Translation Lookaside Buffers" on page 109. Page size should be chosen carefully based on the access characterization of the program code and/or data.

5.5.5.2   +r

The +*r* option can be used to enable and disable static branch prediction on PA-RISC 2.0 processors. However, the option can cause a performance degradation if set for PA-8000 and PA-8200 processors and Profile Based Optimization (described in Section 11.6, "Profile-based Optimization" on page 391) is not used. For this reason, this *chatr* option should not be used to direclty enable static branch prediction. Instead, use the compiler option +*Ostaticprediction* to enable static branch prediction.

5.5.5.3   +k

The +*k* option requests that kernel-assisted branch prediction be enabled or disabled. When enabled for a binary running on a PA-RISC 2.0 processor, the kernel will attempt to modify code dynamically to improve branch prediction. This feature only works with applications that have enabled static branch prediction. In addition, it is only useful for PA-8000 and PA-8200 processors since later PA-RISC processors have adequate branch prediction hardware.

This *chatr* option can be tried if an application is using static branch prediction and running on a PA-8000 or PA-8200 processor. It will not hurt performance, but may significantly help performance. Usually, it greatly helps performance in cases where the profile-based optimization performed was not optimal or does not correspond well to a specific workload. Almost all of the database vendors ship their applications using static branch prediction, so enabling this feature may be beneficial for these applications. Note, however, that it can only be enabled before an application starts to execute.

5.5.5.4   +mergeseg

When enabled, all data segments of all shared libraries loaded at program startup are merged into a single block. This allows the system to make better use of virtual memory large pages and reduces TLB pressure. It may be very useful for programs that access several different shared libraries during program execution. Given that the data segment of each shared library is merged, there is no impact on other processes also using the shared libraries.

5.5.5.5   +z

The +*z* flag enables or disables lazy swap for all of the segments in the executable.

5.6 Performance Characterization and Prediction Tools

The goal of performance characterization is to obtain a baseline of activity for a system or subsystem, and then compare it with activity at various times. The emphasis is placed on making comparisons rather than on taking snapshots. Prediction takes the process one step further by extrapolating future performance out of the data from past runs.

5.6.1 *MeasureWare*

MeasureWare lets you obtain data relating to performance characterization, performance trending, capacity planning, workload estimation, and chargeback accounting. Data is obtained over time, and data from different periods can be compared. *MeasureWare* is configured by editing the */var/opt/perf/parm* file.

MeasureWare consists of four programs: *midaemon, scopeux, utility,* and *extract*. *Midaemon* accesses data from the kernel, massages it, and stores the results in a shared memory segment that is accessed by *scopeux*. *Scopeux* retrieves the data from the shared memory segment, rejects "uninteresting" data, averages the rest, and stores the results in a circular binary log file.

Utility reports on and can resize the binary log file. *Extract* pulls data from the circular log file and saves it in a binary or ASCII log file. ASCII data can be analyzed via spreadsheet or statistical analysis programs. Binary data is used by the *PerfView* tools, which are described in the next section.

It is very important that the *parm* file be customized appropriately for each system and application environment. The parm file in the directory */var/opt/perf* is the active configuration file used by *scopeux*. It contains a minimally defined configuration, by default. Other example parm files may be found in */opt/perf/newconfig*. The following customizations should be considered.

5.6.1.1   Customizing the ID of the Binary Data File

The ID in the binary data files will default to the official hostname of the system where the data is being collected. You can choose a different name by setting the *id* parameter. Setting a recognizable name for this field is especially important when data is being collected on multiple systems. The reports and graphs will be labeled with this name.

5.6.1.2   Customizing the Log Parameter

Set the *log* parameter to the type(s) of data that are to be collected. The default setting

```
log global application process device=disk,lvm
```

should be sufficient on most systems since it collects all of the available data. However, on busy systems, collecting all of the data will cause the binary files to be overwritten quickly. To minimize the overhead of data collection and storage, *scopeux* averages and saves global and application data every 5 minutes.

Process data is averaged and recorded on disk every minute. Disk and LVM data contains detailed device file names and should always be logged. Otherwise, you may not be able to correlate the per-disk drive data with actual disk devices.

5.6.1.3   Customizing the Data File Size

It is very important to set the *size* parameter appropriately. *MeasureWare* data is collected in a set of binary files of fixed size that are accessed in a wrap-around manner. The files should be large enough to contain a minimum of one week's worth of data and optimally one to two months worth of data. You may have to set the size by trial and error.

Use the *utility* command to show the current utilization of the files, including the dates that the data covers. As the system grows busier, monitor the utilization so that the files are large enough to accomodate the minimum requirements that you have determined.

The default sizes, in MB, are:

```
size global=5.0, application=5.0, process=10.0, device=5.0
```

The *process* file typically fills the fastest; therefore, it should be sized bigger than the other files. The binary data files are very compact and are stored in the directory */var/opt/perf/datafiles* and are given the names *logappl, logdev, logglob, logindx,* and *logproc.* The file called RUN in this same directory is periodically monitored by the *scopeux* process. If you remove this file, *scopeux* will cleanly terminate.

Procedures should be established for extracting and archiving data from these circular binary files so that long-term trends can be analyzed. These files may also be used for performance problem diagnosis to look at the performance of the system before the problem manifested itself.

Use the *extract* command with the *extract* function to save the data for a desired range of dates to another disk file in compact binary format. These extracted files should be archived to tape on a weekly or monthly basis. Make sure that you extract the data before the circular file has wrapped around and overwritten some of the data you need to save.

The *extract* program can also be used to produce textual reports that can be analyzed if you like to look at columnar data. These reports can be customized by selecting the desired metrics that are listed in several sample report files, *reptall, reptfile, repthead,* and *repthist* in the directory */var/opt/perf.* Metrics are selected by removing the asterisk at the beginning of the line.

5.6.1.4   Customizing Thresholds

To reduce overhead associated with data collection and disk space utilization, *Measure-Ware* records process data only on what it considers to be interesting processes, as configured in the parm file. By default, the line

```
threshold cpu = 5.0, disk = 5.0
```

causes process data to be recorded for any process that uses at least 5% of CPU utilization *or* does at least five disk I/Os per second. Additionally, *MeasureWare* records process data for all process creations and terminations.

You can use process data for performance problem diagnosis or for security auditing purposes, since it records every process that runs on the system. However, it may not produce a record every minute for every process since the threshold parameter limits those processes for which it records data.

See the *MeasureWare* documentation for information on other thresholds that can be defined.

5.6.1.5   Assigning Applications and Users to Application Groups

Each major application and/or group of users should be assigned to a user-defined application group. The group name is arbitrary, but it should be recognizable. Applications can be defined based on a combination of:

- Executable program names (not the full path name). Note that an asterisk can be used as a wild card character for the program name.
- User login names.

Otherwise, most of the application data will be placed in the OTHER application group. When too much utilization shows up as the application OTHER, the application data is not useful for either chargeback accounting, or for performance management and diagnosis.

The order of applications listed in the parm file is very important. When a process record is analyzed by the scopeux *MeasureWare* process, it scans the parm file from the top looking for the first appropriate application definition. Once it finds a matching application definition, it includes that process data in that application metric. You must carefully look at the application definitions to ensure that if a process can fit into more than one application because of the combination of wild card application names and user names, it will be counted in the application where you really want it counted.

The number of applications listed in the parm file has a direct effect on *MeasureWare* overhead. The more applications listed, the higher the overhead. Make sure that you list the applications in the order of most commonly expected to least expected. That way, *scopeux* will find the correct application sooner, reducing its overhead for searching the parm file.

5.6.1.6   Limitations of Metrics in *MeasureWare*

MeasureWare does not acquire and record all of the same metrics that are available with *glance* and *gpm*. In some cases, there are additional metrics in *MeasureWare*. However, *MeasureWare* does not acquire and record a very important class of per-processor metrics associated with multiple CPUs on an SMP system. The following is an example.

From Bob's Consulting Log—A client once asked me to help him review some performance data from a system being benchmarked. There did not seem to be any bottlenecks based on simple interactive access. The response time criteria for the benchmark were being met. However, graphs of data from the system showed the following:

- 100% CPU utilization

- Load average of ten

- Multiple processes running as part of the application

The client was perplexed. A load average of ten coupled with 100% CPU utilization would normally indicate a rather busy system. I looked at the data and asked a few questions to confirm that the benchmark was running properly and getting appropriate results.

Next, I asked whether the system was an SMP system, which it was. I asked further how many CPUs were on the system, and he answered ten. The interpretation of the data now fell into place. A global load average of ten spread across ten CPUs (processors) leads to a load average of one *per processor*, which is much more reasonable, given the satisfactory response times.

Also beware of the metric *gbl_run_queue*. This is misnamed, since in fact it refers to the one-minute load average (described further in Section 7.5.2, "Global CPU Queue Metrics: Run Queue vs. Load Average" on page 195), not to the run queue. The actual run queue metric is *gbl_pri_queue*.

5.6.2   *PerfView*

PerfView is a set of Unix performance management tools that accesses the data collected by *MeasureWare*, which runs on many vendors' platforms. For general-purpose monitoring of HP-UX, the ultimate source of data is the set of counters reported on by *midaemon*, which provides the data through *scopeux*. Data is displayed on the *PerfView* management console, which has a single interface for displaying, analyzing, comparing, and predicting future trends in performance data. Specific *PerfView* components are *PerfView/Analyzer*, *PerfView/Monitor*, and

PerfView/Planner. The *Analyzer* is the central general-purpose display shown in Figure 5-6. A specific example of the graphic display of global disk usage is shown in Figure 5-7.

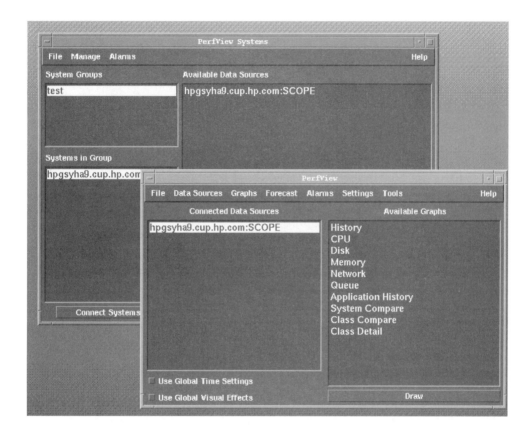

Figure 5-6   *PerfView/Analyzer* Display

The *MeasureWare* agent takes more than a single system view. Because *PerfView*'s tools operate in a networked environment, they permit comparison of data from a multitude of data sources among distributed systems and from different platforms. Additionally, specialized modules are available for collecting performance data from a variety of major databases. Other modules obtain health and performance data from network operating systems including *Novell NetWare* and *Windows NT*.

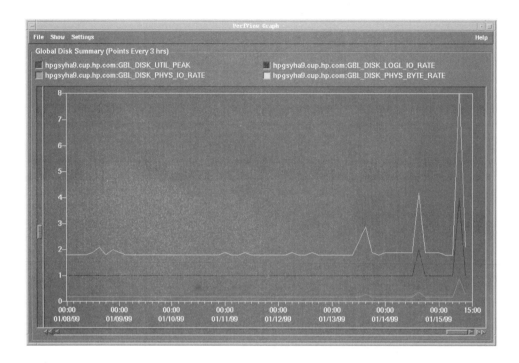

Figure 5-7   Global Disk Usage in *PerfView*

5.6.3   PerfView/Analyzer

The detailed information provided by *PerfView/Analyzer* is useful for obtaining a solid baseline of performance at three levels: process, application, and global resources. *Analyzer* is a *Motif*-based program that can produce standard and custom graphs from the data of one or more systems. It is used to analyze *MeasureWare* data in non-real-time.

Recall that *MeasureWare* records process data every minute and global and application data every five minutes. Therefore, you must wait at least that long after starting *MeasureWare*, or after an event of interest occurs, before that data is accessible by *PerfView/Analyzer*.

Analyzer can access the data from the log files in the */var/opt/perf/ datafiles* directory from one or more systems. It can access these files locally, on the same system where it is running, or remotely via NFS mounts.

Be very careful when analyzing data that is averaged over long periods of time such as one or more hours. Averages tend to flatten out spikes and dips in the data, and important events or trends can be missed if the "Points every" setting is too long.

Analyzer is an extremely flexible tool that will allow you to create graphs of performance metric data. Standard graphs are predefined, and the user can create custom graphs that include any of the supported performance metrics. You can even compare similar data from multiple systems on a single graph.

A very big advantage of *PerfView/Analyzer* and its partners *PerfView/Monitor* and *PerfView/Planner* is the on-line help system. Not only does the help system give information about using the tool, it also gives detailed information about the meaning of each of the metrics that is available.

5.6.4 *PerfView/Monitor*

PerfView/Monitor is a *Motif*-based management tool that receives performance alarms from one or more systems running *MeasureWare*. The emphasis is on getting the information to operators who can take action. Setting the trigger points for alarms depends on your understanding what is normal and what is abnormal performance in a process, application, or system. Alarm thresholds are defined in the */var/opt/perf/alarmdefs* file. Alarms are sent to the central monitoring system, where an operator can receive the alert, analyze the cause, and take appropriate action.

When an alarm is received by the central performance monitoring workstation, *PerfView/Monitor* can easily access detailed data stored in the *MeasureWare* binary log files for all the systems for which it is configured to monitor. It accesses these log files via a socket connection over the network. No NFS mount of the remote file systems is necessary. *Monitor* can also easily invoke an instance of *glance* or *gpm* that runs on the remote system where the alarm occurred, but is displayed on the central performance monitoring workstation.

5.6.5 *PerfView/Planner*

PerfView/Planner is a *Motif*-based add-on module that can be used to predict when a system resource is expected to be exhausted. Requiring at least three months of historical data, it creates a forecast using one of several statistical methods. Data from the forecast may be used to plan for hardware upgrades to the system.

Planner lets you project future performance trends based on the kinds of data displayed above in *PerfView/Analyzer*. Their displays use graphs that are similar to each other.

5.6.6 *sar* and *sadc*

As mentioned above, *sar* was designed to log data in the background to a binary-format disk file using the program */usr/lib/sa/sadc*. Therefore, *sar* and *sadc* are useful when collecting data over long periods of time for baselines or general performance characterization.

5.7 Process Accounting Tools

There are various system programs that provide accounting data. Among these are *acct* and *diskusg*.

5.7.1 *acct*

/usr/sbin/acct (HP-UX 10.0 and later systems) contains the accounting data that is generated after accounting is enabled with the command.

```
turnacct on
```

The man page for *acctsh* describes a number of accounting commands and procedures.

5.7.2 *diskusg*

A second process accounting tool, *diskusg,* generates disk accounting information and outputs one line per user in the following format:

```
uid login #blocks
```

5.8 Application Optimization Tools

The following tools are available for optimizing applications. More information about several of these tools is available in Chapter "Application Profiling" on page 437."

5.8.1 *Caliper*

Caliper is a performance analysis tool that can be used for applications running on HP-UX versions based on the Itanium Processor Family (IPF). This is a very good tool to use for performance analysis of programs on IPF-based systems. It replaces the *Puma* and *CXperf* tools. *Caliper* allows one to measure various low-level details of a program such as cache misses, branch mispredictions, and total cycles. A full description of this tool is found in Chapter 13 "Application Profiling" in Section 14.1, "Caliper" on page 438.

5.8.2 *CXperf*

CXperf is an interactive run-time performance analyzer for programs compiled with Hewlett-Packard Fortran 90, ANSI C++, and ANSI C compilers. It allows low level performance issues such as cache misses, TLB misses, and context switches to be attributed to instructions in a profile. This tool is no longer supported as of March 31, 2003 and was removed from distribution as of December 1, 2001. The *Caliper* tool should be used instead on IPF platforms. There is no real replacement on PA-RISC platforms.

5.8.3 *dpat* (Distributed Performance Analysis Tool)

Dpat is an interactive, X/Windows-based utility for profiling application programs. Ported to HP-UX from the Apollo Domain Operating System, *dpat* has been replaced (since HP-UX 10.20) with *puma* which itself has been replaced by *Caliper.*

5.8.4 *hpc* (Histogram Program Counter)

Ported to HP-UX from the Apollo Domain Operating System, *hpc* is a real-time character-mode utility for profiling application programs. *Hpc* has been replaced (since HP-UX 10.20) with *puma*.

5.8.5 *gprof/gprof++*

Gprof is the Berkeley Unix version of *prof*, an application profiling tool. *Gprof++* is used for programs written in C++. On HP-UX, *gprof* is part of the Programming Environment and *gprof++* comes with the C++ compiler. *Gprof* performs all the functions that *prof* performs, and then adds call-graph functionality.

5.8.6 *prof*

Used as the basic System V profiling tool, *prof* produces the same output as *gprof* (above), but does not produce the call graph. Since *gprof* is the more useful of the two, the authors do not recommend the use of *prof*.

5.8.7 *Puma*

Available in the HP Performance Analysis Kit (HP PAK), *Puma* monitors the program counter, the call/return stack, and other performance statistics. Data are stored in a file that can be viewed in a number of ways. *Puma* replaces *dpat* and *hpc* at HP-UX 10.20. *Puma* has been replaced by *Caliper*.

5.8.8 *TTV* (Thread Trace Visualizer)

TTV is a tool for threaded applications. It uses a graphical format to display trace files produced by the instrumented thread library (*libpthread_tr.sl*). *TTV* lets you see how threads are interacting, and discover threads that are blocked on resources.

5.9 Network Diagnostic Tools

The following diagnostic tools are available to help answer your questions about network performance.

5.9.1 *netstat*

Netstat provides a wealth of metrics on network activity. It reports packet in-and-out metrics, collisions (Ethernet only), and errors, as well as memory consumed by the network portion of the kernel for network buffers.

Providing statistics for network interfaces and protocols, *netstat* also reports the contents of various network-related data structures. The output format varies according to the options selected. The following is a partial example of the output for *netstat -aAn*, which displays a list of active sockets. Internet connections are listed first, followed by Unix domain connections:

```
Active Internet connections (including servers)
PCB       Proto Recv-Q Send-Q  Local Address         Foreign Address     (state)
114af00 tcp        0      0  127.0.0.1.1383        127.0.0.1.5304      TIME_WAIT
11c2000 tcp        0      0  127.0.0.1.1382        127.0.0.1.5304      TIME_WAIT
1141800 tcp        0      0  127.0.0.1.1381        127.0.0.1.5304      TIME_WAIT
 e39a00 tcp        0      0  127.0.0.1.1380        127.0.0.1.5304      TIME_WAIT
10bb300 tcp        0      0  127.0.0.1.1379        127.0.0.1.5304      TIME_WAIT
11c2c00 tcp        0      0  127.0.0.1.1378        127.0.0.1.5304      TIME_WAIT
 d51e00 tcp        0      0  127.0.0.1.1377        127.0.0.1.5304      TIME_WAIT
1240a00 tcp        0      0  127.0.0.1.1376        127.0.0.1.5304      TIME_WAIT
11c2700 tcp        0      0  127.0.0.1.1373        127.0.0.1.5304      TIME_WAIT
1140a80 udp        0      0  192.3.0.1.5301        *.*
1140a00 udp        0      0  15.13.172.229.5301    *.*
1123780 udp        0      0  192.3.0.1.5300        *.*
 10da80 udp        0      0  15.13.172.229.5300    *.*
 126880 udp        0      0  *.4760                *.*
 126800 udp        0      0  127.0.0.1.4755        *.*
10c1c80 udp        0      0  *.177                 *.*
110d780 udp        0      0  *.*                   *.*
110d700 udp        0      0  *.*                   *.* (Continued Next Page)
```

```
Active Unix domain sockets
Address Type   Recv-Q Send-Q   Inode    Conn    Refs  Nextref Addr
10ca400 stream      0      0        0  fa05c0       0        0
 f12e00 stream      0      0   87c64c       0       0        0 /etc/vx/vold_diag/socket
 f12f00 stream      0      0   87ca3c       0       0        0 /etc/vx/vold_requ/socket
108a800 stream      0      0        0  fa0300       0        0
105f700 stream      0      0        0  fa0140       0        0 /tmp/.AgentSockets/A
105c700 stream      0      0        0  fa0340       0        0
108a900 stream      0      0        0  fa02c0       0        0 /tmp/.AgentSockets/A
```

5.9.2   *nettune* (HP-UX 10.x) and *ndd* (HP-UX 11.0 and Later)

The *nettune* and *ndd* commands permit examination and modification of several items that affect networking. The following example gets the value of the *tcp_send* object (socket send buffer size):

```
$ nettune tcp_send
32768
```

5.9.3   *nfsstat*

The *nfsstat* command reports information about the Network File System (NFS) and Remote Procedure Call (RPC) interfaces to the kernel, and can also reinitialize this information. If no options are given, the default is

```
nfsstat -cnrs /stand/vmunix
```

which means: display everything but modify nothing. Typical output appears as follows:

```
/opt/IRuser from irma:/opt/IRuser (Addr 15.0.69.57)
 Flags:     hard,int,dynamic, read size=8192, write size=8192,  count = 4
 Lookups: srtt=  8 ( 20ms), dev=  4 ( 20ms), cur=  3 ( 60ms)
 Reads:     srtt=  6 ( 15ms), dev=  3 ( 15ms), cur=  2 ( 40ms)
 All:       srtt=  8 ( 20ms), dev=  4 ( 20ms), cur=  3 ( 60ms)

/opt/acrobat3 from hoffman:/opt/acrobat3 (Addr 15.13.169.233)
 Flags:     soft,int, read size=8192, write size=8192,  count = 4
 Lookups: srtt= 10 ( 25ms), dev=  6 ( 30ms), cur=  4 ( 80ms)
 Reads:     srtt=  7 ( 17ms), dev=  3 ( 15ms), cur=  2 ( 40ms)
 All:       srtt= 10 ( 25ms), dev=  6 ( 30ms), cur=  4 ( 80ms)

/opt/acrordr3 from hoffman:/opt/acrordr3 (Addr 15.13.169.233)
 Flags:     soft,int, read size=8192, write size=8192,  count = 4
 Lookups: srtt=  7 ( 17ms), dev=  4 ( 20ms), cur=  2 ( 40ms)
 Reads:     srtt= 23 ( 57ms), dev=  3 ( 15ms), cur=  4 ( 80ms)
 All:       srtt= 10 ( 25ms), dev=  5 ( 25ms), cur=  3 ( 60ms)
```

GlancePlus and *gpm* provide these and additional metrics, and present them in a much more usable way.

5.10 Resource Management Tools

Resource management tools use performance measurement dynamically in the process of reallocating resources on a system. The tools in this category are Process Resource Manager (PRM) and Workload Manager (WLM).

Resource management tools implement Service Level Objectives (SLOs) that are defined by the organization. These SLOs are usually part of an agreement called the Service Level Agreement (SLA) that is negotiated between the user department (or Line of Business) and the IT organization.

SLOs may include various measures such as:

• Application criticality
• Acceptable planned and unplanned downtime
• Acceptable duration of outages
• Average monthly or annual availability
• Expected hours of availability
• Number of users to access the application
• Expected resource availability or allocation
• Acceptable response time and/or throughput
• Contracted costs (payments)
• Penalties to be assessed if contracted SLOs are not met

Traditionally IT departments have purchased computing equipment for either a specific application or for use by a specific Line of Business (LOB). Recently, some organizations have adopted a process called Server Consolidation in which multiple applications are hosted on the same server or group of servers. It is in the Server Consolidation environment that resource management tools offer the biggest advantages. By using these tools, the IT department can make more productive use of the available computing equipment while guaranteeing the LOB its fair share use of the equipment and computing resources for which it is paying.

Resource management tools discussed in the next section use the concept of a process group which provides a means of defining which of the various LOBs or applications are given a certain amount of a computing resource. Often, the resource management tools will provide for various means of allocating resources to a process group and for defining what processes or applications get assigned to a process group. For instance, CPU utilization can be allocated based on models such as:

• The relative importance of the application.
• The relative share of funding that the LOB provides for the computing equipment and application services.
• The relative number of users that access the application.

The particular model employed is chosen by the organization and mapped into the structure provided for by the tools. The shares are then assigned on a percentage basis. The HP resource management tools provide for control over the utilization of the major system resources: CPU, memory and disk. The capability exists to cap resource utilization even if there is excess resource availability.

Resource management can be implemented in either kernel space or user space. Implementation in kernel space is more complex and requires kernel modification; however, the result of this implementation is much greater accuracy. The first version of memory resource management was implemented in user space, and provided only limited control over actual memory utilization by the groups. Later versions were implemented in the kernel and now provide very accurate control of memory utilization.

5.10.1 Process Resource Manager (PRM)

HP Process Resource Manager (HP PRM) is a resource management tool used to control the amount of resources that groups of processes use during peak system load. HP PRM can manage maximum-allowed utilization of CPU, memory, and disk. Processes can be grouped by name, by user id, or by process id (PID). The maximum number of groups varies according to the exact version of HP-UX.

5.10.1.1 CPU

PRM can ensure a minimum allocation of CPU for an application, and if desired, no more than a capped amount of CPU. You can place applications in an FSS PRM group with a higher relative number of CPU shares than other groups. To assign dedicated CPU access to an application, you can put the application in a PSET PRM group. Control of the CPU by PRM is further discussed in Chapter 7 "CPU Bottlenecks" in Section 7.2.3, "Process Resource Manager (PRM) and CPU Resource Allocation" on page 179.

5.10.1.2 Memory

PRM can ensure a minimum allocation of physical memory and (optionally) a soft upper bound. PRM provides two memory managers:
- /opt/prm/bin/prm0d
- /opt/prm/bin/prm2d

Prm0d, the original PRM memory manager, is the default on HP-UX versions prior to 11i. When *prm0d* is used, available memory is apportioned to active processes using the standard HP-UX method. *Prm0d* then attempts from user space to influence which processes are more susceptible to having their memory pages paged out. This memory manager is most successful when there is significant memory pressure present on the system.

With *prm2d* (the PRM memory manager that is available starting with HP-UX 11i), memory can be apportioned on a percentage basis to PRM process groups. *Prm2d* has an in-kernel module that partitions memory so that each PRM group will get a partition equivalent to the process group's entitled percentage of the available memory. Each partition is subject to paging separately.

5.10.1.3 Disk

PRM can enforce a minimum allocation of disk bandwidth for LVM volume groups. Working in conjunction with Logical Volume Manager, PRM reorders volume group I/O requests to delay requests coming from low-priority processes and to accelerate requests from higher-priority processes.

5.10.1.4   Commands and Utilities Used with PRM

/opt/prm/bin/prmanalyze   The *prmanalyze* utility scans accounting files for information on the desired resource type (disk, memory, or CPU) and orders the accounting records by the requested sort key (user, Unix group, command name, or PRMID). Use *prmanalyze* to find patterns in resource usage, then change your PRM configurations accordingly.

/opt/prm/bin/prmconfig   This command updates the PRM configuration based on a configuration file. The command can be issued by an interactive user directly or by a program like Workload Manager, which uses the command to perform a dynamic PRM reconfiguration of the allocations given to PRM groups.

/opt/prm/bin/prmmonitor   This   command   displays   current   configuration   and resource usage information.

/opt/prm/bin/xprm   *xprm* is a graphical user interface that allows you to create PRM configuration files and update the PRM configuration.

5.10.2   Workload Manager (WLM)

The WLM product works in conjunction with PRM to allocate system resources (primarily CPU) in order to maintain application performance even during changing system conditions and fluctuations in workload demand. In order for WLM to determine the appropriate resource allocation, the system administrator places applications in **workloads**, then creates one or more **service level objectives** (SLOs) for each workload. Among other things, an SLO includes a PRM group name, a priority, and an optional metric goal (a desired level of system behavior) or usage goal (CPU share).

Figure 5-8 shows the basic flow of data in Workload Manager.

WLM starts by reading the configuration file, then determines if an application is overperforming or underperforming compared to its configuration. If necessary, WLM requests an adjustment to the CPU entitlement of the application. Requests can be for fixed entitlements or for shares-per-metric entitlements.

The *arbiter*, an internal module of WLM, collects all the requests for CPU entitlements and tries to satisfy them based on priority. If there are not enough resources, the arbiter satisfies the highest priority requests first. Optionally, WLM determines how much memory to distribute to meet the minimum memory requests and then, if any memory remains, divides it among the groups with active SLOs. Periodically, WLM creates a new PRM configuration that applies the new CPU and (optional) memory entitlements.

If the system is configured for virtual partitions, the WLM instance in each partition continuously requests a certain number of CPUs for its virtual partition. Based on these requests, the WLM global arbiter dynamically allocates CPUs to the partitions.

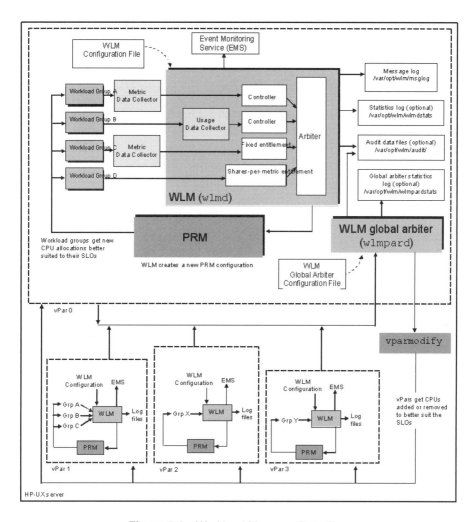

Figure 5-8 Workload Manager Data Flow

The status of the SLOs and information about the performance of WLM are sent to the Event Monitoring Service (EMS). Using an EMS client such as System Administration Manager (SAM), a system administrator can choose from a number of notification methods (such as email, SNMP traps, TCP, UDP, and OPC Messaging) for receiving events of specific interest.

WLM is integrated with and has knowledge of Serviceguard clustered environments. In a Serviceguard cluster, WLM can be invoked to automatically change resource allocations when a failover occurs. For example, when systems are available for use, the "normal" resource allocation is used. Then, after a system failure occurs that causes an application to be started on a backup server that may already be running one or more other important applications, WLM can reallocate the resources according to relative application importance. When desired, WLM can shutdown the least important application so that more resources are available to the most important applications. Finally, when the failed system is repaired and restored to service, WLM can restore the resource allocations back to the "normal" allocation values.

WLM does not currently perform its functions across multiple servers or hard partitions within a server. Instead, it controls resource utilization solely within a server or partition. It is expected that a future version of WLM may provide some additional capabilities in multi-server and multi-partition environments.

5.10.2.1   Commands, Utilities, and Files Used with WLM

/opt/wlm/bin/wlmaudit   Displays information from the */var/opt/wlm/audit* file about usage. Format can be in plain text or HTML.

/opt/wlm/bin/wlminfo   Displays information about SLOs, metrics, workload groups, and vPars (virtual or soft partitions) that have been configured on the current host.

/opt/wlm/toolkits/apache/bin/wlm_watch.cgi   This CGI script allows you to monitor WLM using a web interface to *prmmonitor, prmlist*, and other monitoring tools.

/var/opt/wlm/audit   TA log file containing data about currently configured SLOs. This file is created when you start the WLM daemon *wlmd* with the *-t* option.

/var/opt/wlm/wlmdstats   TA log file containing data about currently configured SLOs.

/var/opt/wlm/wlmpardstats   TA log file containing data about SLOs that operate across virtual partitions.

5.10.3 Capacity Planning Tools

Capacity planning deals with "What if" questions, such as: "Will I have enough capacity to add an additional twenty users?" or "What will happen to response time if I add 16 GB of memory?" or "What will happen to throughput if I upgrade from a D580 to a Superdome?" A capacity plan is based on one or more characteristic workloads, each of which yields data for short time periods. For example, you might do separate capacity plans for OLTP 9-5, for end-of-month, and for overnight batch processing.

Various vendors offer capacity planning tools and solutions. Further explanation of capacity planning is outside the scope of this book.

Hardware Performance Issues

The hardware components of Unix systems may be the source of major performance issues. Processor speed is certainly not the only significant variable. Cache size and organization, TLB size and organization, bus structure and speed, I/O characteristics—all these and other variables are also very important.

This chapter will discuss some performance-related aspects of the major hardware units. Certain terms will be defined, and the architecture of several HP-UX systems will be presented in some detail. Topics are as follows:

- Terminology
- Processor Characteristics
- Multi-Processing
- Cache Memory Performance Issues
- Main Memory Performance Issues
- Physical and Virtual Address Space
- I/O Performance Issues
- PA-RISC Systems
- Itanium® Systems

6.1 Terminology

Like other fields, the computer industry has spawned its own special terminology. Knowing some of this terminology is essential to understanding how the design of the computer hardware may affect system performance.

6.1.1   Central Processing Unit

The *Central Processing Unit (CPU)* or *processor* is the component within the computer that performs all of the main processing or calculation. A processor consists of one or more chips; there may be anywhere from one to several hundred processors in a computer system. Systems that contain more than one processor are said to be *multi-processor* systems. Processors execute a series of *instructions* to perform computations. Groups of instructions are combined to form *applications* or *programs*.

6.1.2   Main Memory

Main memory or *physical memory* is the location where data and executable software reside while the computer is operating. Processors carry out computation by copying instructions and data from main memory into several *registers*, special locations within the processor that hold data while it is being manipulated. The function of copying data and instructions is known as *fetching objects from main memory*.

Main memory is usually physically separate from the CPU. Today, it is common to have anywhere from hundreds of megabytes to several gigabytes of main memory. The size and allocation of physical memory usually have a strong impact on system performance and may affect other system resource utilization as well.

The *latency* of main memory access (that is, the time delay in fetching an object from main memory) can vary greatly from system to system. Typically, a smaller system with one or two processors will be able to access main memory with lower latency than a larger system, such as a 64-processor system. This means that for tasks that need to access main memory, the data can probably be processed more quickly on a small system than on a larger system.

6.1.3   Virtual Memory

Virtual memory is a way to address large amounts of memory without needing to have an equivalent large amount of physical memory present. This is accomplished by allowing a virtual address to map to a location on disk (called the *backing store*) or a location in main memory. Virtual memory is organized into chunks known as the *page size*. HP-UX supports various page sizes in the range of 4 KB to 4 GB. The operating system can map a given virtual page to different physical memory pages on the system.

6.1.4   Cache Memory

Cache memory is a form of high-speed memory that is used for storing recently used data and instructions in the hope that they will be accessed again soon. Cache size, speed, and organization directly affect performance. Cache memory may be internal and/or external to the CPU chip, but it is always in close proximity to this chip. Caches typically range anywhere in size from 16 KB to 8 MB, and may be even larger in some high-end systems. There may be one or several levels of cache in a processor's memory hierarchy. Each cache is typically referred to as the "level N" cache where "N" corresponds to the order in which the cache is accessed. For example, the first-level cache in a processor is typically referred to as the *level 1* cache, although for some systems it can also be referred to as the *level 0* cache.

Caches are made from chips that are much faster and more expensive than those used for main memory. Therefore, caches are much smaller than main memory, but they run much closer to the speed of the CPU itself. Caches may be *unified* (that is, data and instructions may share a single cache) or *split* (data and instruction are in separate caches). Instructions and data are moved in blocks between the caches and main memory; more is moved in than is immediately requested in the hope that future references will exhibit "spatial locality," the tendency of addresses to cluster around those of earlier references. The amount of data moved is called the *cache line size* and typical sizes are 32, 64, or 128 bytes.

The cache lines are organized into sets within the cache. Set sizes can range from one, which is called a *direct-mapped* cache, to several. When a cache set contains four cache lines, it is said to be *four-way set associative*. A cache with all of its lines contained in one set is said to be *fully associative*. Fully associative caches are very rare given that more cycles and complex logic are needed to select a given line. In order to choose which set a given cache line should reside within, an index function is used to map either a physical address or virtual address to a given cache set. For cache sets that contain more than one cache line, a selection algorithm is then used to choose a location in the set for a given cache line. Some common selection algorithms are *random* and *least-recently-used* (LRU). Finally, a cache that uses the virtual address to choose a set is referred to as a *virtually indexed cache* while one that uses a physical address is referred to as a *physically indexed cache*. Figure 6-1 on page 110 shows some examples of instruction and data caches.

6.1.5   Translation Lookaside Buffers

To quickly determine the mapping from a virtual to a physical address, the processor keeps a small cache of virtual to physical translations that is known as the *translation lookaside buffer* or *TLB*. TLBs are organized like caches, anywhere from direct-mapped to fully associative. In addition, TLBs can either combine translations for data and instructions into one *unified* cache or *split* these into separate caches. More recent processor designs tend to have small but fully associative TLBs that are either split or unified. A processor may contain multiple levels of TLB caches.

Early processors, as well as some current processors, only allowed a single page size to be mapped in the TLB. Typically, this page size is very small, such as 4 KB. Some newer processors allow for different page sizes to be mapped simultaneously in at least one level of the TLB hierarchy. Allowing larger TLB page mappings decreases the chance of not finding a mapping and thus reduces TLB misses because more memory can be mapped with the same number of entries. System performance is improved by reducing TLB misses because it is faster to fetch memory if the translation is found in the TLB. Figure 6-2 on page 111 shows generically how a virtual address is converted to a physical address by a processor with a TLB.

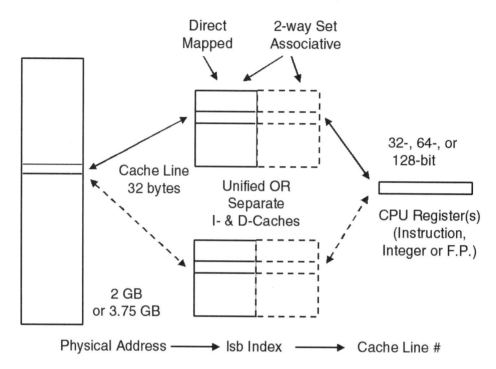

Figure 6-1   Instruction and Data Caches

6.1.6   Branch Prediction

As a processor executes instructions it will often have to change program control flow to execute different instructions based on the current state of the program. Branch instructions indicate to the processor when it should change program control flow. Branches can be either direct or conditional.

There are different types of direct branch instructions. *Calling direct branches* save the current program location before branching to a new location. These are used for calling subroutines in a program. The calling direct branches are usually matched with *return direct branches* that return to the location immediately following the saved location from a calling direct branch. Finally, there are some direct branches that simply alter program flow to another location in the program.

Conditional branch instructions indicate to the processor where to start executing if a given condition holds, such as equality, inequality, greater than, less than, etc. If the condition does not hold, then conditional branches will not branch. An example of a conditional branch is:

If x <= y then goto label300

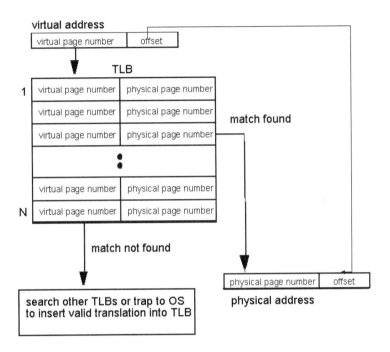

Figure 6-2 TLB Translation

Both direct and conditional branches can be either *PC (Program Counter) relative,* which means the new execution location is based on a distance from the current execution point, or they can be *absolute,* which means the exact address is specified. An absolute address may be accessed via a register in a branch instruction; this type of absolute branch is often referred to an an *indirect branch.* Most PC-relative offsets are actually embedded in the branch instruction. The offset is also usually much smaller than the size of a register, so PC-relative branches tend to have less ability to branch over long distances in the program, unlike indirect branches, which can branch anywhere in the program space. In most programs, however, the majority of the branches are PC-relative because control flow is usually over short distances. Also, PC-relative target addresses are easier for processors to calculate, so the compiler prefers to generate them over indirect branches whenever possible.

In most processors, neither the information indicating whether or not a conditional branch will be taken nor the actual branch location is known when the processor needs to actually fetch new instructions. This lack of information is because most modern processors are pipelined (see Section 6.2.4 on page 120) and instructions are fetched from memory before earlier instructions have fully completed. Therefore, most processors predict whether or not to take the branch and predict the branch location, sometimes well before the actual outcome is known. When the processor uses characteristics of the instructions themselves to predict whether or not a branch is taken, this is referred to as *static branch prediction*. If the processor uses some sort of stored history of branches to predict future branches, then this is referred to as *dynamic branch prediction*.

Being able to predict branches accurately is important because the penalty for mispredicting a branch can be high in some cases. The mispredict penalty often results in several wasted cycles and results in lower overall performance for an application.

6.1.6.1   Static Branch Prediction

Static branch prediction can be implemented in different ways. One common method is to predict if the conditional branch is taken or not based on whether a PC-relative branch is going to go forward or backward in the instruction stream. The usual strategy is to predict that forward branches are not taken and backward branches are taken. This logic comes from noticing that loops in programs tend to have a frequently executed backward branch to resume execution at the top of the loop. All PA-RISC chips use this type of static branch prediction.

Another method for statically predicting the direction of a branch is to have the compiler put a hint in the instruction. For instance, a hint could be added to each branch indicating if the processor should use the default static heuristic or some other heuristic (such as reversing the way the default works). The HP-UX compilers include static hints when compiling code for PA-RISC version 2.0 processors and all Itanium® processors.

Hewlett-Packard's 64-bit PA-RISC processors provide a static hint via an interesting method. The processor will statically predict a conditional branch as taken or not based on the register numbers used in the *cmpb* PC-relative branch instruction. The heuristic is:

1. If the first register number in the instruction is numerically less than the second, then the branch is predicted as taken if it is backward and as not taken if it is forward.

2. If the first register number is numerically greater than or equal to the second, then backward branches are predicted as not taken and forward branches are predicted as taken.

This gives the compiler complete control over specifying how the processor should predict a given PC-relative branch. For instance, if the compiler believes a given forward branch should be taken, then it makes sure the first register number used in the *cmpb* instruction is greater than or equal to the second register number. If the compiler believes a forward branch should not be taken then it makes sure the first register number used is less than the second register number. The following code example shows this behavior:

```
top:
.....CMPB,= R1,R2,end ; forward branch predicted as not taken
.....ADD R1, R2, R3
.....CMPB,< R2,R1,end ; forward branch predicted as taken
.....ADD R1, R3, R3
.....CMPB,> R10,R2,top ; backward branch predicted as not taken
.....NOP
end:
.....ADD R2,R2,R3
```

One problem with pure static branch prediction is that it does not work well or at all for indirect branches. The problem is that even if the processor could predict if the branch is taken or not, it will not be able to readily form the target address because the branch target is stored in a register and thus is typically not available when branch prediction occurs. Therefore, the processor has to stall until the branch target can be determined.

6.1.6.2 Dynamic Branch Prediction

Processors that implement dynamic branch prediction use many different and elaborate hardware techniques. In fact, dynamic branch prediction is an area of processor design that is highly patented. In general, however, a processor will keep a global history table that stores past branch history for executed branch instructions. This table is often referred to as the *branch history table* (BHT). Each time a branch is executed, the actual branch direction will be used to update prediction information in the table. When the processor subsequently fetches a branch, it will look in the table to predict which direction to go. The way this table is maintained to determine the branch direction is very processor-specific.

There are several factors that affect how well the dynamic branch prediction works. First, the size of the BHT controls how many branches can be tracked at one time. A small table will most likely result in less reliable branch prediction than a larger table because less information on the executed branches can be stored. For instance, the PA-8000 has a relatively small BHT of 256 entries, while the PA-8500 and later PA processors have a BHT table size of 2048 entries. So, the PA-8500 can keep track of eight times as many branches as the PA-8000. Due to its small BHT size, the PA-8000 relies more heavily on static branch prediction than dynamic prediction for performance.

Most systems probably have hundreds of different processes running, and each process may have hundreds or thousands of branch instructions. So, a big problem with a small history table is that multiple different branches (from different processes or the same process) may all hash to the same entry in the table, causing a collision. If these colliding branches have different taken or not taken characteristics, then the history becomes corrupt and not very useful. The actual information recorded in the BHT can also affect the overall prediction. Just recording the last branch direction may not always be a good indication of what direction the branch will take next. However, recording a small history of the last "N" branches might be better. For instance, most PA-8XXX chips use a two-bit history to determine the branch direction.

Some of Hewlett-Packard's 64-bit PA-RISC chips use an "agrees" mode of dynamic branch prediction, where the history information stored tells whether the last branch agreed with what the static branch heuristics would predict. If the history claims that the branch agrees with the static branch prediction, then the static branch prediction is used; otherwise, the opposite of the static branch prediction is used. This attempts to combine the aspects of static branch prediction with those of dynamic branch prediction. It has the benefit that two branches can collide in the branch history table, but if they both agree or disagree with their given static hint, then they will end up not polluting the history table. The end result is that a smaller BHT can actually hold as much useful information as a larger table not using "agrees".

6.1.6.3   Branch Target Addresses

A structure like the branch history table works well for predicting if conditional branches are taken or not, but additional structures are usually needed to determine where to branch. To determine the branch target address, another small hardware cache is typically used that contains the last branch target for a particular taken branch. This cache is sometimes referred to as the *branch target address cache* (BTAC). The cache is maintained completely by the hardware on PA-RISC systems. As the processor executes taken branches, it stores the address where it branched in the BTAC along with the address of the actual branch instruction. Every time the processor predicts a given branch will be taken, it looks up the instruction address of the branch in the BTAC and sees if a match is found. If so, it uses the branch target address found for the branch instruction to change the control flow. If there is no match, then the processor may need to wait several cycles to calculate the branch address, therefore reducing the overall performance. If a match was found but the branch address was not correct, then a mispredicted branch occurs. The larger this cache, the more addresses that can be held while minimizing collisions. Due to the large number of bits that need to be stored in this cache (potentially 64 bits or more for both the branch address and branch instruction address) and the need for high-speed lookup of the address, it tends to be small in size (32-128 entries). To maximize the available cache space, the compiler tries to minimize the number of taken branches that may occur in the instruction stream by rearranging branches it feels should not be taken as not taken branches. Branches that are taken often tend to be flow control branches to the top of loops, so having a small structure is not detrimental, given that computation loops tend to have few taken branches in them other than the branch to the beginning of the loop.

In addition to the BTAC, some processors may implement a stack of subroutine call addresses that is used to predict subroutine returns. As calling-type direct branches are made, the return address is pushed onto a small stack of addresses. When a return-type direct branch is encountered, the processor pops the top return address from this stack and predicts that as the return branch location. If the predicted location does not match the real return location, then a mispredicted branch occurs. PA-RISC processors prior to the PA-8500 did not have this hardware structure, so all subroutine returns were always mispredicted. This made optimizations like subroutine inlining (described in Section 11.2.4.1 on page 365) more important on processors such as the PA-8000 and PA-8200. The PA-8500 and later processors have a one-entry stack, so only non-nested subroutine call returns can be predicted correctly. Itanium® processors may have eight or more entries for their subroutine return stacks, allowing multiple levels of subroutine returns to be predicted correctly.

6.1.7   Input/Output Devices (I/O Devices)

Input/Output devices or *I/O devices* are components that provide an external interface for the computer. Typical devices include disks, monitors, tape and CD drives, and networking hardware. Each I/O device has its own performance characteristics, and the link to which it is attached has distinct attributes that affect performance.

One important class of I/O devices is called *peripherals.* This is because they frequently stand apart from the computer chassis itself, and they often operate at the periphery of the flow of data—that is, they provide the first input to the computer or receive the last output (a disk write or a display update, for example).

6.1.8   Buses

A *bus* is a data conduit through which data moves as it goes from memory to a processor's registers or from memory to an external device like a disk or printer. Buses are of various types and speeds, and their speed is a fundamental aspect of performance.

Buses are used for intercommunication among the major components of the computer: between the processors and memory, between memory and I/O devices, and so forth. Occasionally a computer system can use different buses running at different speeds. In these cases, a *bus converter* or *adapter* is used to connect different buses.

Buses are typically classified as *memory, I/O,* or *peripheral* buses. Memory buses usually connect CPUs and memory, while I/O buses connect memory and I/O cards, and peripheral buses connect I/O cards and peripheral devices. Buses may be proprietary, or they may conform to various standards. The peripheral SCSI bus used for I/O devices, for example, uses the ISO standard SCSI protocol. This bus is said to be compliant with SCSI standards, including SCSI II and Fast/Wide SCSI.

6.1.9   Graphics Devices

Graphics devices deserve special mention because they often require large quantities of memory and processor activity to provide the needed functionality for an application, including transformation and conversion of bitmap data. The high-resolution graphics display needed for CAD applications frequently requires specialized supporting hardware within the computer, as well as additional memory and high-speed transmission of data.

As more and more applications follow the client/server model, and as graphics-intensive applications on the Internet become the norm rather than the exceptional case, these performance issues will increase in frequency and importance.

6.2 Processor Characteristics

Processors can be implemented in several different ways. Many current Unix systems, including those of Hewlett-Packard, use processors that are classified as *RISC* (Reduced Instruction Set Computing) processors. RISC processors tend to have simple, fixed-length instructions that are executed in as few cycles as possible. Hewlett-Packard's RISC processors all are based on the *Precision Architecture* and are classified as PA-RISC chips. Another common processor classification is *CISC*, which stands for Complex Instruction Set Computing. The Intel® x86 family of processors are all considered CISC, although recent versions behave very much like RISC processors internally. CISC processors execute variable-sized instructions of variable complexity. Some CISC instructions could take several cycles to complete. Finally, Intel® and Hewlett-Packard have recently teamed up to create a new paradigm for high performance computing called *EPIC* (Explicitly Parallel Instruction Computing). EPIC processors group multiple simple instructions together into a larger, fixed-size instruction called a *bundle*. The EPIC processor then potentially executes all instructions in a bundle at one time. The EPIC paradigm allows the compiler to provide some information regarding potential parallelism to the processor. Intel® has developed the *Itanium® Processor Family* (IPF) architecture that specifies the instruction set and system specifications for their EPIC processors. Currently, the Intel® Itanium® and Itanium® 2 processors implement the IPF architecture.

The following sections describe features of processors that effect the performance of the system. In particular, the RISC and EPIC types of processors will be discussed.

6.2.1 Instruction Types

The CPU evaluates various *instruction types* by using one or more *functional units*. Instructions are usually defined into major classifications: *integer, load/store, branch, multimedia,* and *floating point*. Integer instructions can include operations such as addition, subtraction, shift, rotate, and bit manipulation. Load/store instructions handle moving all data from the caches or main memory into high-speed registers on the chip. Branch instructions handle changing the flow of control of a program's execution. Multimedia instructions usually allow for some parallel computation to be performed on data such as parallel additions, comparisons, merges, etc. These multimedia instructions are often classified as *SIMD* (Single Instruction, Multiple Data). Multimedia instructions are useful when dealing with graphics and sound applications. Finally, floating point instructions include the following:

  • Floating point addition, subtraction, multiplication, and conversion. These may require anywhere from two to six CPU cycles to complete, and are executed on a floating point arithmetic logical unit (ALU). Special multiply-accumulate instructions also will execute on these units.

- Divisions and square root operations may require up to twenty cycles for single precision (32-bit) or thirty cycles or more for double precision (64-bit). They are typically executed on a complex floating point unit.

Processors are implemented with multiple *functional units*, each one of which can execute independently. Functional units may be specialized, capable of executing only some of the processor's instructions. Therefore, different classes of instructions may execute concurrently. This is especially important for engineering and scientific applications. Since the organization of functional units may differ from one processor implementation to another, these types of applications typically must be recompiled to take full advantage of a particular architecture. Business-oriented applications, however, do not benefit as much from this type of recompilation because the mix of instruction types is not nearly as great as for technical applications.

The types of instructions available to a processor may make it perform some applications better than other processors. For instance, having an instruction that multiplies two 64-bit integer values together may provide a large performance advantage over a processor that does not have this type of instruction. Both the PA-RISC and IPF instruction sets are very extensive and contain many useful instructions for efficiently executing programs.

Not all processors that implement an instruction set will implement all instructions natively in hardware. Sometimes instructions will be emulated and the processor must trap to the operating system when encountering these non-native instructions. Trapping to the operating system can typically take several hundred cycles, so emulating frequently accessed instructions is not a high performance design.

The instructions executed by a processor execute at a certain rate. This execution rate is referred to as the *processor frequency*. The higher the frequency of a processor, the more instructions it can potentially execute in a given amount of time. Current processors execute with frequencies anywhere from several hundred megahertz (millions of cycles per second) to a few gigahertz (billions of cycles per second). Frequency is only one of several factors that determine overall processor speed. Processors executing at lower frequencies can outperform higher frequency processors. For instance, PA-RISC and Itanium® processors currently operate at frequencies that would be considered average to below-average, but these processors tend to be some of the fastest in the industry.

6.2.2   Out-of-Order versus In-Order Execution

Many recent processor designs execute instructions *out-of-order*. Out-of-order processors are able to start instructions in a different order than specified in the program. However, all instructions will complete (retire) in program order. A processor that does not execute out-of-order is said to execute instructions *in-order*. Early PA-RISC processors executed instruction in-order while all recent PA-RISC processors execute out-of-order. All current IPF processors execute in-order.

With out-of-order execution, the compiler tries to organize non-dependent instructions into instruction groups that can be executed by the hardware in whatever order is most efficient. The CPU executes the instructions on the various functional units that are available. Instructions are then retired (completed) in the same order as specified in the program code. This preserves the sequential execution order of the application. If an instruction traps, any instructions following the trapping instruction that have been started but not completed are flushed and subsequently restarted after the trap completes; this may involve as many as fifty-six instructions on the PA 8XXX line of processors.

One advantage of using out-of-order execution is that functional unit and scheduling differences among processors do not necessarily require recompilation of the application to improve efficiency. Instead, the CPU executes the instructions in the most beneficial way according to its particular design.

With in-order execution, the compiler has to work much harder to try and schedule instructions such that they will not cause the processor to stall. This means potentially scheduling long latency instructions (such as a memory load) several cycles before the output of the instruction is needed. The compiler also needs to schedule instructions such that the processors' functional units do not become oversubscribed. With in-order processors, more of the burden on execution speed is placed on the compiler. If the instruction latency or number of functional units dramatically change, a recompilation may be needed with in-order processors to achieve optimal performance. Even though more work may be required by the compiler for an in-order processor, the compiler still needs to perform many of these same techniques on out-of-order processors to achieve optimal performance.

6.2.3   Scalar and Superscalar Processors

Scalar processors have the ability to start one instruction per cycle; *superscalar* processors can start multiple instructions per cycle. Superscalar processing depends on having a wide enough instruction path to fetch two or more instructions from the instruction cache in one cycle. For example, if an instruction is 46 bits in size, then the bus that connects the instruction cache to the CPU must be a multiple of two or more times the instruction width to be superscalar.

Applications should be recompiled to take full advantage of a particular in-order superscalar architecture, meaning that you must have a different version of the executable for each different processor architecture. The reason for this is that the bundling of instructions that can be executed together may change from processor to processor. If the bundling changes dramatically between two different processors, then the ability to execute instructions together may diminish if the code is not recompiled with a compiler that is familiar with the new bundling. Out-of-order processors typically don't benefit as much from recompiling because they can dynamically look at instructions in the code stream and schedule them according to what resources are available.

Business applications execute integer, load/store, and branch instructions almost exclusively, and may not benefit greatly from recompilation because these instructions can typically be executed in parallel among different superscalar implementations. Engineering and scientific applications, however, generally see significantly improved performance from recompilation for a specific superscalar architecture for both integer and floating point instructions.

Hewlett-Packard Precision Architecture (PA-RISC) systems have incorporated different designs over the years. Early versions executed a single instruction every other cycle. The newest versions can initiate four RISC instructions per cycle and can execute as many as twenty or more instructions concurrently. Table 6-1 shows the characteristics for a variety of PA-RISC processors over the years.

Table 6-1   PA-RISC Scalar and Superscalar CPUs

PA-RISC Architecture Version	Models	Characteristics
PA 1.0	PN5, PN10, PCX	• Scalar implementation
PA 1.1a	PA-7000	• Scalar implementation
PA 1.1b	PA-7100, PA-7150	• Limited 2-way in-order superscalar implementation • One integer *and* one floating point instruction per cycle for floating point; ALU and MPY instructions alternate
PA 1.1c	PA-7100LC	• Limited 2-way in-order superscalar implementation • Two integer *or* one integer and one floating point instruction per cycle
PA 1.1d	PA-7200	• Limited 2-way in-order superscalar implementation • Two integer or one integer and one floating point instruction per cycle
PA 1.1e	PA-7300LC	• Limited 2-way in-order superscalar implementation • One integer and one of any other instruction; one load/store and any instruction except a load/store; one floating point instruction and any other instruction except a floating point instruction.
PA 2.0	PA-8000, PA-8200, PA-8500, PA-8600, PA-8700	• 4-way superscalar implementation with out-of-order execution • Two load/store instructions and two of any other type except for branches • 64-bit extensions

All of the IPF processors developed to date are in-order superscalar processors. Table 6-2 shows the characteristics of IPF processors.

Table 6-2   IPF Superscalar CPUs

IPF Processor	Characteristics
Itanium®	• EPIC (see Section 6.2) superscalar implementation, two bundles per cycle, three instructions per bundle • Has two integer, two floating point, three branch, two multimedia, and two load/store units (some integer operations can be performed on these as well) • Unfortunately, fewer than six instructions are usually issued simultaneously in most cases, due to the logic design.
Itanium® 2	• EPIC superscalar implementation, two bundles per cycle, three instructions per bundle • Has two integer, two floating point, three branch, one multimedia, and four load/store units (some integer operations can be performed on these as well) • Two loads and two stores can be executed simultaneously. • It can often issue six instructions per cycle and has very few limitations as to the types of bundles that can be issued at once.

6.2.4   CPU Pipelines

In modern processors, the *CPU pipeline* is employed to execute instructions in steps or stages. Multiple instructions may be overlapped in the same processor, each in a different stage of execution, thus operating in parallel on that processor. This is not the same as the superscalar architecture, where multiple instructions are started at the same time. The goal in a pipelined design is to reduce cycle time and thus increase the rate of instruction execution by making each pipeline stage as short as possible. Cycle time is the reciprocal of the clock speed (often measured in megahertz (MHz) or gigahertz (GHz)) of a CPU chip, and the number of stages corresponds to the number of instructions that must be executed before the CPU is operating at full efficiency.

Processors that have many pipeline stages are often said to be *super-pipelined* designs. The Intel® Pentium® 4 processor, which has a twenty-stage pipeline and runs at over 3000 MHz (3.0 GHz) would be considered a super-pipelined processor. None of the PA-RISC processors are super-pipelined. Super-pipelined designs are extremely complex, and the penalty for missed branch prediction increases greatly as the pipeline depth increases.

Figure 6-3 shows a simple CPU pipeline with three stages. As soon as three instructions are exe-

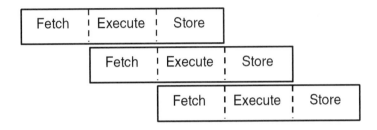

Figure 6-3 Simple CPU Pipeline

cuting concurrently, the processor has reached its most efficient operation, starting a new instruction with every CPU cycle. "Fetch" means "go get the instruction"; "execute" means "perform the operation specified by the instruction"; and "store" means "complete the intent of the instruction."

Figure 6-4 shows a more complex CPU pipeline with five stages. In this example, the Execute phase can be either an ALU operation or the computation of the effective address of a branch. In this case, as soon as five instructions are executing concurrently, the processor has reached its most efficient operation.

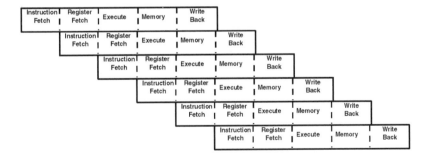

Figure 6-4 More Complex CPU Pipeline

Table 6-3 shows how pipeline length has evolved with PA-RISC and IPF processors. Notice that the pipeline depths have gotten deeper with successive designs but are nowhere near the twenty-stage pipeline of the Intel® Pentium® 4.

Table 6-3   Pipeline Length

Architecture	Stages
PA-RISC 1.0	3 stages
PA-RISC 1.X	5+ stages. (This means 5 stages plus some additional operations.)
PA-RISC 2.0 and later	Variable, because of out-of-order execution with a completion queue. Main pipeline is 6 stages.
IPF	8-10 stages

6.2.5   Problems with Pipelined Architectures

Several categories of problems peculiar to pipelined architectures may occur during instruction execution. The optimization phase of program compilation attempts to make these problems happen less frequently.

6.2.5.1   Register Interlock

Register interlock occurs within a pipelined machine because certain instructions such as loads and stores may be multi-cycle, requiring several cycles to complete execution. When register interlock occurs, the CPU is forced to wait on an instruction that takes more than one cycle to complete when a subsequent instruction references the same register. In in-order systems, this can result in CPU stalls; the situation becomes more serious if there is a cache miss; that is, if necessary data or instructions are not in cache memory. In out-of-order systems, there can still be a stall, but the processor will try and execute other non-dependent instructions first before stalling the entire pipeline.

Here is an example in simplified assembly code (LDW = Load Word, STW = Store Word):

```
        LDW R1
        LDW R2
        ADD R1, R2, R3    --- Probable Interlock with R1 and R2
        STW R3            --- Possible Interlock with R3
        LDW R5
        LDW R6
```

Compiler optimization attempts to prevent these situations by re-ordering instructions so that multi-cycle instructions that reference the same register are separated. After optimization, the code could look like the following if the compiler can determine that R3, R5, and R6 contain the contents of different memory locations:

```
LDW R1
LDW R2
LDW R5
ADD R1,R2,R3
LDW R6
STW R3
```

To properly account for interlock issues, the optimizer must know how many cycles instructions for a given architecture take to complete.

6.2.5.2 Branching

When a processor executes a branch instruction, it must determine from where to fetch new instructions. With a pipelined design, however, branching is the source of additional problems. Branches on PA-RISC and on many other processors always take two instruction cycles. The instruction immediately following the branch is called the "delay slot," which is executed while the branch is completing. If the application is not optimized, the delay slot is filled with a no-op instruction, thus wasting an entire instruction cycle. Compiler optimization can make use of the delay slot to reduce the impact by placing a non-dependent instruction after the branch. For IPF processors, there is no notion of a delay slot, so the compiler does not need to worry about placing instructions after a branch instruction.

Branching also can result in flushing the pipeline if the processor does not implement branch prediction or if the branch target is not predicted correctly. In pipelining, the next instruction will be started as soon as the current one is underway. However, if the current instruction results in a branch that the processor had not predicted correctly, then the next several instructions that were already in the pipeline must be flushed, since the sequence of instruction execution has changed. Flushing the pipeline can waste several machine cycles. The number of wasted cycles is proportional to the size of the pipeline, thus longer pipelines, such as those used in super-pipelined processors, result in a higher *branch mispredict* penalty. Here is an example (COMBT = Compare and Branch if True):

```
LDW R1
COMBT <,R1,R0,<somewhere>
STW R5 --- Delay Slot
ADD R1,R9,R10 --- Flushed from the pipeline if branch taken
```

The larger the pipeline, the more information gets lost in this branching situation. There-fore, it is important for processors with long pipelines to have very good branch prediction. Pro-cessors with shorter pipelines can get by with less accurate branch prediction because the penalty for each misprediction is not as high.

6.2.6   EPIC Features

The EPIC paradigm is similar to *very large instruction word* (VLIW) designs that predated RISC technology. However, it has key improvements over early VLIW designs. In VLIW pro-cessors, an instruction field requiring multiple bits is encoded for each functional unit in the CPU. When CPUs are built with many functional units, more than 32 bits may be needed to fully encode the instruction. In addition, the size of the instruction word may increase as more func-tional units are added. The fixed mapping in a VLIW instruction between the instruction and a functional unit made it difficult to run VLIW programs on newer implementations that contained more functional units.

The EPIC architecture is like VLIW in that it contains more than one sub-instruction per instruction word, but it does not contain an instruction per functional unit. IPF implementations of the EPIC architecture contain three sub-instructions per 128-bit word. Each instruction is 41 bits in size, leaving 5 bits for a template description field. The template description field tells the processor to which type of functional units each of the three instructions should be sent. The IPF architecture also provides an arithmetic function type that can be handled by either the load/store unit or the integer units. Figure 6-5 shows a conceptual view of an IPF bundle.

127   87 86   46 45   5 4   0

| Instruction 2 | Instruction 1 | Instruction 0 | template |

Figure 6-5   IPF Bundle

The EPIC paradigm has several different features that allow more parallelism in the com-piled program codes that result in the possibility of achieving higher performance. To optimize branches, EPIC provides *predication*. To reduce memory latency, EPIC provides *speculation* and a large register set that is automatically saved and restored using a *register save engine* (RSE). Finally, to fully utilize all functional units in tight loops, the architecture provides the concept of *rotating registers*.

6.2.6.1   Predication

Predication is a method to help improve branch prediction by eliminating the need to exe-cute branch instructions. Almost every instruction in the IPF implementation of the EPIC archi-tecture can have a predicate register associated with it. IPF processors provide sixty-four predicate registers. The predicate registers are set via a multitude of compare instructions. Based on the results of a compare instruction, one or two predicate registers can be set to true or false. These predicates can then be associated with instructions to disable or enable execution of any number of instructions based on the value of the predicate. False predicates will not execute instructions, while true predicates will. The predicate *p0* always returns true, so it can be used to always enable an instruction. In fact, if no predicate is specified in front of an IPF instruction, then it is assumed to use predicate *p0*. Below is a simple example of how predication works.

```
         cmp.ne p1,p2 = r2, r3 ;; // compare if r2 != r3
(p1)  sub r4 = r2, r3 // r2 != r3 so subtract
(p2)  add r4 = r2, r3 // r2 == r3 so add
```

Here the *cmp.ne* instruction compares to see if register *r2* and *r3* are not equal. If they are not equal, then predicate *p1* is set to true and predicate *p2* is set to false. If they are equal, then predicate *p1* is set to false and predicate *p2* is set to true. Of the two instructions following the cmp.ne instruction, only one will execute given that only *p1* or *p2* can be true but not both.

6.2.6.2   Speculation

Speculation is a method by which load instructions can be fetched before they would normally be in a traditional in-order processor. This is done to try and eliminate the latency associated with loading data from main memory or the slower caches. The speculation explicitly performs what an out-of-order processor might do as it reorders instructions. Speculation, however, provides much more control than is provided in out-of-order processors. IPF provides both control speculation and data speculation.

Control Speculation

Control speculation allows load instructions and any instructions that are dependent on the loads to be moved above branches. There are special *NaT* (Not a Thing) bits for the integer registers and *NatVals* (Not a thing Value) for floating point registers that allow control speculation to work. Although *NaT* is only one bit and *NatVal* is a full floating point value, both are used to indicate that the contents of the associated register is not a valid number. For floating point, the values for infinity and other invalid numbers are defined by the IEEE Floating Point standard.

If a load is moved above a branch and it generates an exception, the *NaT* bit is set for integer registers or the *NatVal* is set for a floating point register. This *NaT* bit or *NatVal* is then propagated through dependent instructions and later checked with a special "check" instruction. If the check instruction detects a *NaT* or *NatVal*, then it branches to recovery code to redo the operations non-speculatively. The following shows an example of a control speculation:

```
ld4.s r4 = [r10] ;; // Speculatively load value at [r10]

// Execute other instructions
     cmp.ne p1 = r2, r3 // compare if r2 != r3
(p1) br.cond some_other_code ;; // r2 != r3 so branch
     chk.s r4,recovery_code // Is r4 valid?
     add r4 = r4, r3 // Use r4 given it is ok now
```

The "chk.s" instruction goes where the non-speculative load would have normally been placed in the instruction stream had speculation not occurred. The speculation allows the latency of the load to be hidden by executing other instructions after the load and before the load's use. In the case where the speculation fails, the net result is a performance loss due to the extra recovery instructions that need to be executed. Therefore, the compiler only tries to speculate things that it feels have a good chance of not failing.

Data Speculation

Data speculation is where loads are executed before other memory operations that may potentially be to the same (or conflicting) address. In most instances, loads and stores are independent, but in some programming languages such as *C*, it is possible to have two variables alias each other, in which case what look like independent loads and stores are really not. The purpose of data speculation is to execute a load well before it is actually needed to help reduce any stalls that may occur while waiting to load the value from cache or memory. A special *advanced load* qualifier is added to a load instruction to perform a data speculation and a special *check* qualifier is used to check if the speculation worked or not. The following shows a data speculation example:

```
ld4.a r4 = [r10] ;; // Advance load value at [r10]

// Execute other instructions
     st4 [r11] = r5 // store r5 at [r11]
     ld4.c r4 = [r10] // check if r4 valid?
     add r4 = r4, r5 // Use r4 given it is ok now
```

In this example, the load from what is at *r10* was speculatively moved well above a store of what appeared to be a different address at *r11*. If *r10* and *r11* happen to be the same address, then moving the load above the store would not be functionally correct because the value fetched would be the value of what resides at address *r10* instead of the value of *r5*. The *ld4.c* instruction verifies that what was loaded earlier did not overlap with the store to r11. If there was no collision with any stores, then the *ld4.c* does nothing. However, if the fetched value did collide with the store, then the *ld4.c* instruction executes the load again in time for the new value to be available for the *add* instruction that follows.

There is special hardware on Itanium® processors called *ALAT* (Advanced Load Address Table) that indicates whether advanced loads collided with any subsequent store instructions. The *ld4.c* instruction accesses the ALAT to determine if the load needs to be reissued or not. The ALAT is not infinite in size, so it can be oversubscribed and then provide false positives regarding the status of advanced loads. This would result in excessive advance load failures and poor performance. The HP-UX compiler knows how to manage the ALAT so it does not become oversubscribed. This is yet another example of why it is so important to use current versions of the compilers and to recompile the program when running it on newer processors.

6.2.6.3   Register Save Engine

The IPF architecture contains many more visible registers than previous processor architectures. There are 128 integer registers and 128 floating point registers. Of the 128 integer and floating point registers, the first 32 registers are fixed. For the integer registers, the last 96 registers are stacked and virtual. The IPF processor will automatically spill these registers to memory when a program uses more of these than are physically available. In addition, as a program needs to access registers, the processor will also load them automatically from memory. The *alloc* instruction is used to allocate integer registers for use in a program at any point in time. All allocated registers are automatically freed when a program exits a function. The register save engine hardware on the IPF processor chips manages the automatic saving and restoring of the stacked integer registers.

By having so many registers and by having the processor automatically read and write these from memory as a program executes, the latency associated with loading up registers can be reduced. The CPU can access a register at CPU speed, whereas accessing cache memory is much slower, assuming that the needed element is already in the cache. In addition, having so many registers means cache memory is not needed as often to hold frequently accessed values, given that the frequently accessed values will be held in one of the several high-speed registers on the processor.

6.2.6.4   Rotating Registers

Rotating registers is a complex feature of the IPF architecture that allows for efficient software pipelining and results in efficient utilization of the processor's functional units in small loops. When a special loop branch instruction is executed, the specified rotating registers rotate one position upward. The integer registers from *r32* upward can all be rotated in multiples of eight. The predicate registers *p16* through *p63* and the floating point registers *f32* through *f127* also rotate, but they rotate in a group. The following is a small and incomplete example of how rotating registers work to pipeline a copy operation where the number one is added to each element copied.

```
copy_top:
(p16) ld4 r32 = [r10],4 // load value at [r10]
(p17) add r33 = r33, 1 // add one to r33
(p18) st4 [r11] = r34,4 // store value at [r11]
br.top copy_top ;;
```

In this example, the predicate registers *p16-p18* and the integer registers *r32-r34* all rotate, while the registers *r10* and *r11* don't rotate. The predicate registers are set up before the loop so *p16* has a value of one and the others are zero when the loop is entered. So, on the first loop iteration, only the *ld4* instruction is executed. On the second iteration, the next *ld4* is executed and the result of the first *ld4* has one added to it. Finally, on the third loop iteration, the third *ld4* is executed, the second addition is performed, and the value plus one read on the initial iteration is stored to memory. All three of these operations are done in parallel each loop iteration. Several other details regarding setting up rotating registers and the special branch instruction have been removed to simplify this already complex example.

6.2.7   Vectorization

Vectorization in a processor is a technique where a single instruction can operate on multiple registers at one time. For instance, an addition instruction may take several registers as inputs, add them together in parallel, and write several registers as output. Extreme bandwidth is needed in the register file to be able to do this on several registers at one time. This technique has been used on vector supercomputer processors from Cray. PA-RISC and IPF processors have similar functionality to this in their multimedia (audio/video) instructions. These instructions allow a register to be split into multiple pieces, and these pieces can then be operated on in parallel. So, a *multimedia add* of two 64-bit registers may add all four 16-bit sub-words in parallel and concatenate the 16-bit results to a 64-bit result register.

6.2.8   Summary of processors

The following tables show the evolution of processor technology over the years in HP-UX systems. First, the early processors are shown in Table 6-4.

Table 6-4   Summary of early PA-RISC processors.

	Discrete TTL design	NS1	NS2	PCX
Processor Type	scalar	scalar	scalar	scalar
Clock Speed	8 MHz	12.5-13.75 MHz	27.5-30 MHz	40-60 MHz
Memory Bus	central bus	SMB, Midbus, NIO	SMB, NIO	SMB, Summit
Cache	L1-I: 64KB direct map L1-D: 64KB direct map	unified L1- I/D: 16KB 2-way or 128KB 2-way	L1-I: 128KB or 512KB 2-way set L1-D: 128KB or 512KB 2-way set	L1-I: 512KB or 2MB 2-way L1-D: 512KB or 2MB 2-way
Memory Bus Speed	32 MB/sec	NIO: 32 MB/sec	NIO: 32 MB/sec	SMB: 256 MB/sec Summit: 960 MB/sec
TLB	I-TLB: 1KB direct map D-TLB: 1KB direct map	I-TLB: 1KB direct map D-TLB: 1KB direct map	I-TLB: 1KB direct map D-TLB: 1KB direct map	On-chip: 64 entry ITLB 2-way, 64 entry DTLB 2-way Off-chip: ITLB: 4K or 16K direct map DTLB: 4K or 16K direct map
TLB miss handling	software	software	software	software
HW Page Size(s)	2 KB	2 KB	2 KB	2 KB
Block TLB	no	no	no	no
FP Registers	16	16	16	16

Of these early chips, the PCX design was the most impressive. With its huge TLBs and 2MB first-level instruction and data caches, it was able to process huge commercial workloads much more quickly than competing designs of the time.

These early CPU designs consisted of multiple chips to constitute the main processing unit. To simplify the overall design and cost, HP next consolidated several chips into a few chips in the PA-RISC 7000 series. Here, the processor consisted of either a single chip or a single processor and floating point co-processor. Table 6-5 shows the Series 7000 chips. To further reduce cost, highly integrated Series 7000 chips were developed that included the processor, floating point, some cache, I/O controller, and memory controller all on one chip. Table 6-6 shows attributes of these chips..

Table 6-5   Early PA-7000-based PA-RISC chips

	PA-7000	**PA-7100/7150**	**PA-7200**
CPU Type	scalar with limited floating point parallelism	limited 2-way superscalar	limited 2-way superscalar
Clock Speed	32-64 MHz	33-125 MHz	100-120 MHz
Processor Bus	SMB	PMB/SGC	runway
Bus Throughput	256 MB/sec	256 MB/sec	768 MB/sec
Cache Sizes	L1-I: 64-256 KB direct map L1-D: 64-256 KB direct map	L1-I: 64-1024 KB direct map L1-D: 64-1024 KB direct map	L1-I: 256-1024 KB direct map L1-D: 256-1024 KB direct map
Cache Line Size	32 bytes	32 bytes	32 bytes
TLB	96 entry fully associative and split	120 entry fully associative and unified	120 entry fully associative and unified
TLB Miss Handling	software	hardware and software	hardware and software
Block TLB	4 each	16	16
HW Page Sizes	4KB	4KB	4KB
FP Registers	32 double or 64 single precision	32 double or 64 single precision	32 double or 64 single precision

Table 6-6   Highly integrated PA-7X00-based chips

	PA-7100LC	**PA-7300LC**
CPU Type	limited 2-way superscalar	limited 2-way superscalar
Clock Speed	48-100 MHz	132-180 MHz
Processor Bus	GSC	PMB/SGC
Bus Throughput	128 MB/sec	256 MB/sec
Cache Sizes	unified 64 -1024 KB	L1-I: 64 KB 2-way set L1-D: 64 KB 2-way set L2: 1024 KB direct map
Cache Line Size	32 bytes	32 bytes
TLB	64-I/64-D entry fully associative and split	96 entry fully associative and unified
TLB Miss Handling	hardware and software	hardware and software
Block TLB	4 each	16
HW Page Sizes	4KB	4KB
FP Registers	32 double or 64 single precision	32 double or 64 single precision

Table 6-7   PA-8X00 processors

	PA-8000	PA-8200	PA-8500
CPU Type	4-way out-of-order superscalar	4-way out-of-order superscalar	4-way out-of-order superscalar
Clock Speed	160-180 MHz	200-240 MHz	300-440 MHz
Processor Bus	runway	runway	2x-runway
Bus Throughput	768 MB/sec	768 MB/sec	768-1534 MB/sec
Cache Sizes	L1-I: 1 MB direct map L1-D: 1 MB direct map	L1-I: 2 MB direct map L1-D: 2 MB direct map	L1-I: 512 KB 4-way set L1-D: 1 MB 4-way set
Cache Line Size	32 bytes	32 bytes	32 or 64 bytes
TLB	96 entry fully associative and unified	120 entry fully associative and unified	160 entry fully associative and unified
TLB Miss Handling	software	software	software
Block TLB	none	none	none
HW Page Sizes	4KB, 16KB, 64KB, 256KB, 1MB, 4MB, 16MB, 64MB	4KB, 16KB, 64KB, 256KB, 1MB, 4MB, 16MB, 64MB	4KB, 16KB, 64KB, 256KB, 1MB, 4MB, 16MB, 64MB
FP Registers	32 double or 64 single + rename	32 double or 64 single + rename	32 double or 64 single + rename

Table 6-7 and Table 6-8 show HP's next chip series, the PA-8X00, line which was its most aggressive PA-RISC design. This was a 4-way superscalar out-of-order design. The design continued the PA-RISC tradition of having very large first-level caches and relatively large TLBs. In addition, this series added support for using several different page sizes simultaneously and added support for 64-bit processes. Over the years, HP simply fine-tuned the original PA-8000 design when designing the other chips in the series.

Table 6-8 PA-8X00 processors (continued)

	PA-8600	**PA-8700**
CPU Type	4-way out-of-order superscalar	4-way out-of-order superscalar
Clock Speed	400-552 MHz	650-875 MHz
Processor Bus	2x-runway	2x-runway
Bus Throughput	768 - 1536 MB/sec	1536 MB/sec
Cache Sizes	L1-I: 512 KB 4-way set L1-D: 1 MB 4-way set	L1-I: 768 KB 4-way set L1-D: 1.5 MB 4-way set
Cache Line Size	32 or 64 bytes	64 bytes
TLB	160 entry fully associative and unified	240 entry fully associative and unified
TLB Miss Handling	software	software
Block TLB	none	none
HW Page Sizes	4KB, 16KB, 64KB, 256KB, 1MB, 4MB, 16MB, 64MB, 256MB, 1GB	4KB, 16KB, 64KB, 256KB, 1MB, 4MB, 16MB, 64MB, 256MB, 1GB
FP Registers	32 double or 64 single + rename	32 double or 64 single + rename

Finally, HP is transitioning to a new processor design, developed together with Intel®, that implements the EPIC architecture. The Intel® Itanium® line of processors will be used in future HP-UX systems. Table 6-9 shows the characteristics of these processors.

Table 6-9   Itanium® processors

	Itanium®	Itanium® 2
CPU Type	EPIC 2-bundle	EPIC 2-bundle
Clock Speed	733-800 MHz	900-1500 MHz
Processor Bus	Itanium®	Itanium® 2
Bus Throughput	2.1 GB/sec	6.4 GB/sec
Cache Sizes	L0-I: 16 KB 4-way set L0-D: 16 KB 4-way set L1: 96 KB 6-way set L2: 2-4 MB 4-way set	L0-I: 16 KB 4-way set L0-D: 16 KB 4-way set L1: 256 KB 8-way set L2: 1.5MB-6MB 6-24 way set
Cache Line Size	64 bytes	128 bytes
TLB	L0-D: 32 entry fully associative L0-I: 64 entry fully associative L1-D: 96 entry fully associative	L0-D: 32 entry fully associative L0-I: 32 entry fully associative L1-D: 128 entry fully associative L1-I: 128 entry fully associative
TLB Miss Handling	hardware and software	hardware and software
Block TLB	48 data and 8 instruction	64 each
HW Page Sizes	4KB, 8KB, 16KB, 64KB, 256KB, 1MB, 4MB, 16MB, 64MB, 256MB	4KB, 8KB, 16KB, 64KB, 256KB, 1MB, 4MB, 16MB, 64MB, 256MB, 1GB, 4GB
FP Registers	128	128

6.3 Multi-Processing

Computer systems started out as *single processor systems* having a single Central Processing Unit (CPU). Single processor systems evolved into *multi-processor systems*. Today, typical multi-CPU systems can contain up to sixty-four or more processors. Various types of implementations have been created using multiple CPUs.

6.3.1　Master/Slave Implementation

The earliest multi-processor system used a *master/slave* implementation. In this type of system, the operating system (OS) ran on only one processor, the master processor. Other CPUs were reserved for user processes.

The master/slave arrangement made it easy for the writers of the operating system, because specialized multi-processing code was not required. Performance was usually very good for compute-bound applications. Applications that were I/O-intensive would compete for the operating system, which ran only on the master CPU. Adding CPUs usually would not improve performance for I/O-intensive applications.

6.3.2　Asymmetric Implementation

Like the master/slave multi-processor, the *asymmetric implementation* allowed the OS to run on a single CPU at a time, but it could be any of the CPUs in the system. This implementation was an improvement on the master/slave model, since the operating system could run on the same processor as the user process, therefore taking advantage of the built-up *context* (cached data) from the user process.

6.3.3　Symmetric Multi-Processing Implementation

The *symmetric multi-processing (SMP)* implementation allowed the OS to run on any processor, and now allowed different parts of the OS to run on different processors at the same time. To accomplish this, the operating system can be modified in either of two ways. First, different sections of code may be designated as able to run concurrently. For example, multiple I/O's can be processed using different device drivers. Alternatively, the data itself may be the differentiator. For example, multiple processors may be executing System V semaphore lock/unlock code, but acting only on different semaphore sets.

The HP-UX kernel has supported symmetric multi-processing beginning with HP-UX version 8.06. The OS uses several locking mechanisms–spinlocks and kernel semaphores–to ensure that multiple processes do not modify the same data at the same time.

Symmetric multi-processing also allows for various granularities in the unit of execution at either the process or the thread level. To take advantage of multi-threading, the operating system itself must be designed to run in a multi-threaded environment. The HP-UX operating system has been designed to support kernel threads beginning with HP-UX version 11.0.

6.3.4　Massively Parallel Processing Implementation

Systems that use a *massively parallel processing (MPP) implementation* typically include hundreds of processors, not tens of processors. The OS has to be different, and the application must be designed to take advantage of the MPP system. You can't just take an application off the shelf and implement in this environment without customization.

In an MPP machine, each processor may have its own memory, or multiple processors may share the same memory.

6.3.5   Parallelization

Parallelization is the attempt to make different pieces of a single process run on different CPUs. The application typically has to be designed for parallelization, and compiler technology can facilitate this somewhat. Kernel threads make this type of manipulation easier, because different threads can run on different processors, but *only if the application is designed with threads in mind.*

There can also be process-level parallelization if it is designed into the application. For example, a database might be designed with multiple back-end processes, each of which runs on a different CPU. These may or may not be able to do parallel work, depending on how users access the application.

Parallelization may also result in pieces of the application running on completely separate computer systems. For instance, an application may interact with the user on one system, use another system for the compute-bound portion, and display intensive graphical results on a third system.

6.4   Cache Memory Performance Issues

The processor caches used for data and instructions can greatly affect the performance of the system. Caches are used specifically to store information that is read in with the expectation that it will be needed again soon by the CPU. In a multitasking environment, the cache contains entries belonging to many different processes, in the hope that the processes will execute again before needed locations are flushed by other processes.

6.4.1   Cache Designs

Caches may be of varying size, speed, and organization. Since they are made from higher speed components than main memory, they are expensive. Designers, striving for an optimal solution, must always tradeoff cost and performance. The following sections describe various cache attributes and how they affect system performance.

6.4.1.1   Size

Larger caches can significantly improve system performance but also increase the cost of the system. Large caches can greatly improve the performance of commercial applications, because many recently accessed main memory locations belonging to different processes can be held at one time. Large instruction caches can be especially effective because of the large number of instructions that typically are required to execute a large commercial application. Larger caches can also improve the performance of scientific or engineering applications by holding more data that can be operated on without accessing main memory, or by holding the instructions that, for example, belong to a large loop and are executed many times.

6.4.1.2   Access Speed

The number of cycles spent accessing a cache is another critical factor in overall cache performance. Having a large and slow cache may not be better than a smaller but very fast cache. In general, caches should always be designed to be as fast as possible while not significantly affecting the size. Typical first-level cache access times are anywhere from one to three cycles. Access times for other cache levels typically range anywhere from five to sixty or more cycles. Out-of-order processors can usually handle longer cache latencies compared to in-order processors, given that other work can potentially be performed while waiting for a memory access. Some in-order processors, such as Itanium® processors, have special instructions that allow memory accesses to be launched well before their use, which helps to reduce the performance hit of longer latencies.

6.4.1.3   Organization

The organization of the cache can also greatly affect performance. Typically, first-level caches tend to be split designs because speed is of the utmost importance to keep the processor busy. Split caches, with their dedicated design (one cache for each instruction and data), can be made to operate faster than a unified cache, but usually with a higher overall cost. A unified cache, although less expensive to implement, can be a better design choice further down the cache hierarchy, where caches are larger and slower and absolute speed is not as critical. If the performance of a unified design becomes an issue, multiple ports to the cache may be added to allow more simultaneous access to the cache. Adding multiple access ports increases the cost and complexity but improves the performances.

Another organizational aspect of cache design is the associativity. The more associative the cache, the better it is able to handle multiple addresses that all map to the same set of the cache. Caches may be organized into sets, which are groups of instructions or data that are referred to by the same hash value, for example.

Direct-mapped caches can only map one line per cache set, so if two cache lines happen to map to the same set, one will always be flushed from the cache. However, with something like a 4-way set associative design, up to four different cache lines can map to the same set at the same time. When a cache line is evicted from the cache due to other cache lines mapping to the same set, this is referred to as a *conflict miss*. The higher the associativity of a cache, the fewer conflict misses that will occur. In general, higher cache associativity is better as long as the cache size and speed are not significantly affected due to the higher associativity.

6.4.1.4   Line Size

The width of the cache line is the amount of data or instructions that will be transferred from main memory into the cache at one time. The line size used in a cache can have an effect on performance, especially for applications that cluster memory accesses together. For example, many technical applications will stride sequentially through memory, accessing all data in a cache line before moving to the next line. The larger the cache line size, the more data is fetched from memory in one access and the fewer overall cache misses that occur for a sequential access pattern. Commercial applications, which tend to have more of a random memory access pattern, can also benefit from large cache line sizes if they have a high locality of access within each line.

On the negative side, a cache line that is too large can be harmful if an application does not use much of each cache line. In this case, a lot of the cache becomes wasted because only a small portion of each cache line is used.

Typical cache line sizes range from 32 to 128 bytes. Newer 64-bit processors tend to use both 64-byte and 128-byte cache lines. This allows between eight and sixteen doublewords to be retrieved from memory on each cache access. Later PA-RISC processors and the Itanium® processor use a 64-byte cache line, while the Itanium® 2 processor uses a 128-byte cache line size. These newer processors will exhibit increased performance when running those applications that often wait for cache lines to be loaded from main memory.

6.4.1.5   Cache Hashing

Caches use either the virtual or physical address to map a given cacheline to a set in the cache. Usually, a simplistic algorithm, such as selecting certain bits in the address, is used to select the cache set index. However, sometimes more advanced mapping/hashing algorithms can be used to improve cache performance. For instance, many PA-RISC processors implement a hash that includes both the base virtual address and the space identifier (described later in the chapter). This is done to help reduce conflict misses in the large, virtually-indexed caches used on several PA-RISC processors. Given that many bits of the virtual address for several different processes may all be identical, and given that PA-RISC first-level caches are all virtually indexed, adding the space identifier to the hashing algorithm helps to place virtual addresses from two separate processes in different places in the cache. By using the space identifier in the hash, the likelihood that two different processes containing similar virtual addresses will map to the same cache index is reduced.

6.4.1.6   Write-Through or Write-Back

When storing data to a cache, the data may be written either immediately to the next level in the cache hierarchy (a write-through design), or it may be just placed in the cache and marked as dirty (write-back). A write-through cache can potentially cause an excessive amount of traffic between cache levels. Often this activity can be reduced through various micro architecture optimizations. All PA-RISC caches are write-back, while IPF processors contain a combination of both write-back and write-through caches.

6.4.2   Visible Cache Problems

Cache problems become visible as overuse of user or system CPU resources. You can see this in CPU utilization metrics, or you can compare performance metrics on systems with different cache sizes or organizations. Unfortunately, it is very difficult to detect cache problems directly. One system taking millions of cache misses per second may actually be performing well while another taking several hundred thousand a second may not perform well. What really matters is how well the processor is able to overlap the miss time with useful work.

There are some tools that allow a user to directly measure cache misses on HP-UX systems. For PA-RISC systems, the *CXperf* tool can be used to collect cache miss statistics. Unfortunately, HP support for this tool has been dropped as of early 2003. Fortunately, for IPF systems, there is a tool called *Caliper* that allows cache misses to be tracked easily. In addition, other cache metrics such as latency per miss can be tracked. It is a very useful tool for analyzing cache behavior on IPF systems. See Chapter , "Application Profiling" on page 437 or a discussion of using *Caliper* and *CXperf* to get per-process cache utilization information.

Cache problems may be due to either data or instruction access patterns in a single process, or among multiple processes. How do you solve cache problems? The hardware solution is to switch to a system with:

- A larger cache
- A different cache organization
- A different hashing method (that is, using a different number of bits)

Software solutions include using compiler optimization to change how memory is used, and modifying the application itself to change memory access patterns. It is easy to demonstrate how performance may be dramatically affected by data access patterns.

The following code samples show two very similar calculations; the only difference between them is in the dimension of the array that is varied first in the loops. In Sample Code 1, the inner loop varies the first dimension, while the outer loop varies the second, whereas in Sample Code 2, the inner loop varies the second dimension, while the outer loop varies the first.

Sample Code 1

```
#define X 1024
#define Y 1024

main()
{

int a[X][Y];
int b,i,j;

for (j=0;j<Y;j++){
     for(i=0;i<X;i++){
          a[i][j]= i+j;
          }
     }
for (j=0;j<Y;j++){
     for(i=0;i<X;i++){
          b = a[i][j]*a[i][j];
          }
     }
}
```

Sample Code 2

```
#define X 1024
#define Y 1024

main()
{

int a[X][Y];
int b,i,j;

for (i=0;i<X;i++){
     for(j=0;j<Y;j++){
          a[i][j]= i+j;
          }
     }
for (i=0;i<X;i++){
     for(j=0;j<Y;j++){
          b = a[i][j]*a[i][j];
          }
     }
}
```

When these programs are compiled using only the *-O* option, and then executed using the *time* command, the results are as follows. (The execution environment was a lightly loaded HP 9000 workstation.)

Timings from Execution of Sample Code 1 and Sample Code 2

```
# time ./c1

real    0m1.37s
user    0m1.28s
sys     0m0.07s

# time ./c2

real    0m0.11s
user    0m0.05s
sys     0m0.06s
```

Why is *c2* so much faster? The reason is that *c2* accesses the data in the same order in which it is stored in physical memory, thereby taking advantage of transferring a cache line (32 bytes or more) from memory to the cache in a single transfer. It also benefits from efficient use of the TLB (discussed in the Section 6.5.2.2).

6.4.3   Cache Coherence

In a Symmetric Multi-Processing (SMP) system, each of the multiple CPUs has its own cache. Cache coherence is the requirement that executing programs behave as if there is only a single instance of any given memory location, regardless of the many copies that may exist in the system caches.

The main area where cache coherency comes into play is accessing shared data in an SMP environment. As multiple processes modify shared data, the system must keep the data uptodate. The system uses cache coherency protocols to make sure all processors see a consistent copy of the data. If a program shares a lot of data on an SMP system and modifies that data often, a performance hit can occur as data transfers back and forth among the caches in the system as data is shared. If the shared data is only read, then all processors can keep a copy of the same data. However, once the data is written, the processor modifying the data will keep a private copy which purges the other shared copies from the other processors. Subsequently, if a processor wants the modified data, it must take a cache miss to reload the cache line containing the modified data.

Another aspect of cache coherence that can affect an application's performance is *false sharing*. False sharing occurs when multiple different pieces of data are contained on a single cache line. Some of the data may be shared among processors and some may not. The shared and unshared data alike residing on the same cache line will move from cache to cache as the shared data is referenced by different CPUs. Extra cache misses will then occur when a processor wants to access the non-shared data because the data has been moved to another processor with the shared data. To prevent false sharing, disjoint pieces of data should not be allocated together. In addition, hot shared objects should always be allocated in cache line size chunks and then aligned on a cache line boundary. Finally, keeping read-only data separate from data that can be modified helps because read-only data can be kept simultaneously in multiple caches on a multi-processor system, while modified data may only reside in one cache at any one time.

The method in which cache coherency is implemented can be different on different systems. For instance, systems with a few processors may implement a "snoopy" protocol where the other processors in the system look at all of the memory traffic and grab the appropriate copy of the data. This is an efficient protocol for a small numbers of processors, but it does not scale well when many processors are configured in a system. Another mechanism is to use a directory-based scheme where the coherency information for each cache line is maintained in main memory. Each processor then looks up what the current state of the cache line is in the directory. This is the type of coherency scheme used in HP's mid- and high-end systems today, given that it allows for much better scaling over typical snoopy schemes.

6.5 Main Memory Performance Issues

Usually, not all data can be stored in the processor's caches. Some cache misses are inevitable for large applications. Therefore, the performance of a system's memory subsystem is the next area that can impact an application's performance. Both physical and virtual memory issues can cause problems.

6.5.1   Physical Memory

The amount of physical main memory available on a particular system depends on four criteria:
* The number of physical slots available for memory boards
* The density of RAM chips used to build the memory boards
* The number of bits used to address physical memory
* The amount of memory supported by the operating system

Today's HP systems may support anywhere from 128 MB to 512 GB of main memory. System performance may vary greatly depending on the amount of main memory, speed of accessing this memory, and memory organization.

6.5.1.1   Memory Capacity

Adding more memory to a system is often a very good way to increase performance. Adding memory is one of the most cost-effective ways to increase the overall performance of a system. The extra memory can always be used to cache more data so the system does not have to access slow disk or networked devices as often. As systems become faster and faster, reducing disk accesses becomes more and more important for performance.

Another benefit of adding more memory is that typically this is done via adding more physical memory modules to the system. Adding more modules usually increases the total bandwidth available to the memory subsystem and improves the overall system performance.

Memory capacity typically scales with the size of the system. Systems configured with many CPUs should usually be configured with much more main memory than smaller systems.

6.5.1.2 Memory Speed

The speed of the physical memory system can also greatly impact system performance. Often, a lot of the overall execution time of an application will be spent stalled, waiting on physical memory accesses. If the time to access physical memory is improved, then the application will go faster.

Typically, smaller one- to two-way systems are able to access main memory much quicker than large sixty-four way systems since there is much more complexity in a larger system's memory system. Thus, there is a trade-off of memory speed when designing a system with many processors.

6.5.1.3 Memory Organization

The way main memory is organized in a system can also affect performance. Some systems may come with multiple memory controllers. If it is an available option, configuring more than one memory controller may improve the overall system performance. Also, it is also very common for a system to have an optimal way to configure memory modules to achieve optimal memory throughput. For instance, the order in which memory modules are installed or the way modules are grouped together may affect performance. Unfortunately, there are no general rules, so one should consult the specific configuration guide for a given system to learn about the optimal way to organize memory.

6.5.2 Virtual Memory

The way the virtual address space is organized can have an impact on overall system and application performance. Virtual memory may be located within:

- Physical memory
- The swap area (raw or file system swap)
- Executable files
- A memory-mapped file

Any location other than physical memory is referred to as the *backing store*. To understand how virtual memory is used by the OS, one must first understand virtual address space.

6.5.2.1   Virtual Address Space

HP-UX's primary virtual address space implementation is referred to as a *global virtual address space* model. The global virtual address space is a system-wide representation of all virtual memory spaces for all processes. Depending on the HP-UX implementation, the system may use 32 or 64 bits to address memory, in addition to an address space identifier (referred to as a *space ID* on PA-RISC and a *region ID* on IPF). The address space identifiers are stored in one of eight registers on both PA-RISC and IPF. These registers are referred to as *space registers* on PA-RISC and *region registers* on IPF. Space registers can be anywhere from 16 bits to 64 bits in size depending on the implementation, while region registers are 24 bits in size.

To create a global virtual address, the process virtual address is combined with an address space identifier. The register containing the address space identifier is chosen implicitly via the top 3 bits of the virtual address for IPF systems and via the top 2 bits for PA-RISC systems. In addition, on PA-RISC, the identifier register can be chosen explicitly via some of the PA-RISC instructions.

The formation of the virtual address is slightly different for PA-RISC and IPF. Figure 6-6 shows how virtual addresses are created for each platform. For IPF platforms, the region register

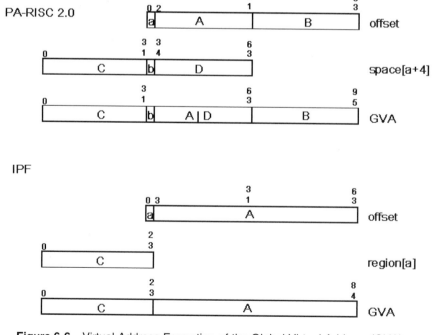

Figure 6-6   Virtual Address Formation of the Global Virtual Address (GVA)

and the lower 61 bits of the virtual address offset are combined to form a global 85-bit virtual address. For PA-RISC, the global address formation is a little more involved because part of the space identifier is bitwise OR'ed together with part of the virtual offset. To allow for larger virtual address ranges in each space, HP-UX currently sets the lower 10 bits of each space ID to zero when using PA-RISC 2.0 processors. This allows 42 bits, or 4 TB of the offset, to be used in each space for 64-bit processes while allowing for 2^{22} spaces (assuming 32-bit space ID registers). For 32-bit processes, zeroing of the lower bits of the space ID is not important, given that none of the 32-bit offset bits are OR'ed with the space ID.

The *page directory table* is an HP-specific data structure that contains one entry for each physical page of memory. It is located in the data space of the operating system, and it always resides in physical memory.

Figure 6-7 shows the basic addressing scheme. Pages in the global virtual address space

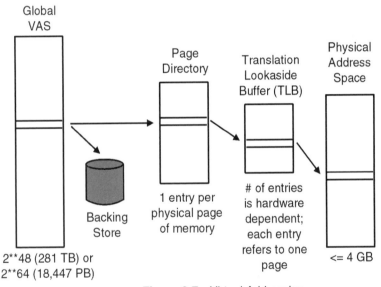

Figure 6-7   Virtual Addressing

are accessed with a virtual page address. This address may map to a location on disk or a location in main memory. If it refers to a location in main memory, an entry in the page directory table provides the translation from virtual to physical address. Recently referenced entries from this table are stored in the TLB on the CPU chip. Table 6-10 shows the maximum physical address space, global virtual address space, and per-process virtual address space for the PA-RISC and IPF architectures.

Table 6-10   Virtual and Physical Address Limits

Architecture	Maximum Global Physical Address	Maximum Global Virtual Address Space	Maximum Per-Process Virtual Address Space
PA-RISC 1.x	2^{32} bytes	2^{64} bytes	2^{32} bytes
PA-RISC 2.x	2^{44} bytes (PA-8700)	2^{64} bytes	2^{44} bytes
IPF	2^{50} bytes (Itanium® 2)	2^{85} bytes	2^{64} bytes

6.5.2.2   Page Directory and Translation Lookaside Buffer

The page directory contains one entry for every page in physical memory. Page directory and TLB entries contain the following on PA-RISC and IPF:

- Virtual page number
- Physical page number
- Page size (on PA-RISC 2.0 systems and IPF systems)
- Access rights: read, write, execute on this page
- Protection ID: who owns the page
- Recently referenced bit (in the page directory only)

There are some distinctive features of TLB management on HP-UX systems. First, ever since HP-UX 10.20, the operating system has used large page mappings on PA-RISC 2.0 and later processors to efficiently map memory. For Itanium® systems, HP-UX has been using large page mappings since the first IPF-based release–HP-UX 11.20. Pre-PA-RISC 2.0 systems used special TLB entries on the processor called *block TLB entries* to allow mapping of larger than a single page of memory with one entry. For instance, the entire graphics buffer for the display could be mapped with a single block TLB entry. These block TLB entries were used only for operating-system-specific data and not for user-level data. PA-RISC 2.0 processors use large pages to map important large areas of memory versus block TLB entries. For IPF processors, large pages are also used, but some TLB entries can be dedicated to important mappings.

HP-UX implements a global virtual address space, and a protection ID is assigned to each virtual memory region to guarantee access rights to the region to only those processes that are authorized to access it. Protection ID registers get loaded with the appropriate protection IDs when a process starts running on a processor. PA-RISC 1.x processors only have four protection ID registers, while PA-RISC 2.0 processors have eight and current IPF processors have sixteen.

Increasing the number of protection registers does increase CPU chip cost, but it may result in increased system and application performance. The protection ID registers serve as a cache for the most accessed protection IDs. If a process accesses more memory objects requiring different protection IDs than there are protection ID registers, register thrashing may occur, especially if the processes frequently switches among the memory objects. For this reason, an application will normally execute faster if it allocates and accesses a small number memory objects, such as shared memory segments or memory mapped files, rather than many of them.

Finally, due to the global virtual address space and the use of protection IDs, the TLB does not need to be flushed on a context switch for either PA-RISC or IPF systems. This allows HP-UX-based systems to be very efficient in environments where context switches occur frequently.

6.5.3   TLB Designs

Like caches, there are several aspects of how a TLB is designed that can affect performance. Such things as the size, organization, speed, replacement algorithm, and access patterns can all affect TLB performance.

6.5.3.1   Size

The size of the TLB can impact performance because every mapping not found in the TLB must be looked up using a method much slower than an actual TLB query. A larger TLB can hold more translations at one time than a smaller TLB. A general rule of thumb is, the larger the TLB, the better. However, TLBs are built from very high-speed components and larger TLBs can increase the cost of the CPU chip or even limit the speed at which the processor can execute. Therefore, as with so many things in computer design, TLB size involves several trade-offs.

6.5.3.2   Organization

A TLB can be organized as a single structure or a split structure (one for data translations and one for instruction translations). TLBs can also be arranged in configurations ranging anywhere from direct-mapped to fully associative. Finally, there can be several levels in the TLB hierarchy, much like the levels of the cache hierarchy. Typically, TLB access is on the critical path of many processors, so there will be a small and commensurately fast TLB at the first level backed by a larger and slower main TLB. This is especially true for instruction translation.

Like caches, split TLB designs tend to be higher-performing, given parallel paths to the translations. In addition, fully associative designs will perform better than direct-mapped or low-associative designs. Most fully associative designs will use some sort of recently used replacement algorithm.

6.5.3.3   Page Sizes

The ability to map multiple page sizes at the same time in a TLB is a real performance advantage. All PA-RISC 2.0 processors and IPF processors allow mapping fixed-sized pages in the range 4 KB to 4 GB. The exact page sizes implemented are processor, and operating-system-dependent. Having the ability to map large pages for translations can dramatically reduce the number of TLB faults that a program takes.

In fact, some programs can completely eliminate all TLB misses with proper use of large pages. "Sample Code 1" on page 140 is one such example. The amount of data being accessed in this case is 4 MB (1024*1024*4). Using 4 KB pages would require 1024 TLB entries to hold all of the translations for the two-dimensional array, which would not fit in most current TLBs. However, using large pages, a single 4 MB page could be used to hold the entire mapping and only a single TLB miss would occur to initially load the translation. How to do this will be discussed in Section 8.2.1 "Variable Page Sizes" on page 218.

6.5.3.4   Miss Handling

When a TLB miss does occur, the processor may handle it in two different ways. Some processors have the ability to automatically lookup the TLB translation in the page directory table. Processors that have this ability are said to have a *hardware page table walker*. Another method would be to trap to the OS and have the OS load the translation. The OS method is always going to be much slower than having hardware find the translation, because traps are very expensive in terms of CPU overhead. Traps interrupt the instruction flow and switches from user mode to kernel mode. Kernel software then must determine which page table entry to load into the TLB, and this may be a lengthy process for large page tables. However, a hardware-based design is always more complex and thus more costly. In addition, most hardware designs will only look at the first entry in the page directory table. If the translation is not contained in the first entry, then an OS trap will occur. Of course, if the number of misses can be dramatically reduced or eliminated, then the miss performance is not a huge issue.

Some of the PA-RISC 7X00 processors do implement a hardware page table walker. For instance, the PA-7100 and PA-7200 both have hardware walkers. None of the PA-RISC 8X00 processors implement a hardware page table walker. All of these processor rely heavily on the use of large pages to minimize the chance of a TLB miss. All IPF processors to date implement a hardware page table walker as well as make large page sizes available.

6.5.4   Visible TLB Performance Problems

TLB issues show up as CPU overhead caused by extra system traps and TLB maintenance. Problems may be visible through comparison with systems that have different TLB sizes or organizations. Hardware counters may also provide useful information, although currently only *Caliper* and *CXperf* have access to these counters. The next sections discuss several ways to reduce TLB misses.

6.5.4.1   Global Virtual Address Space

HP-UX's use of a global virtual address space helps to reduce pressure on the TLB. The reason TLB pressure is reduced is that several processes in a global virtual address space can share the same TLB entries because there is one and only one mapping from a given virtual address to a given physical address. Access rights protection is provided by the protection IDs assigned for a particular process. Most other operating systems use a multiple address space model that shares data via address aliasing, which creates a separate TLB mapping for each process accessing the shared piece of data. All of these different mappings to access the same physical data can quickly overwhelm a TLB in a multi-process environment.

6.5.4.2 Large Pages

Using large page mappings is a very good way to reduce TLB misses on HP-UX systems. HP-UX has a very powerful large page implementation compared to other operating systems. Any piece of memory on the system can use large pages. In addition, the size of a large page can be as large as 4 GB on Itanium® 2 processors. This allows a huge amount of memory to be potentially mapped at one time by the TLB, greatly reducing the chance of having a TLB miss. Other operating systems tend to limit large pages to shared memory only and exclude things like a process's private data and instructions. In addition, the selection of large pages is limited in most other operating systems where just two page sizes can typically be used. Section 8.2.1 "Variable Page Sizes" on page 218 describes how to manage large pages on HP-UX systems.

6.5.4.3 Protection ID Issues

Since HP-UX uses a global virtual address space, it needs to have protection IDs to manage access to the potentially shared TLB entries. To make checking a given process's protection ID quick, a fixed-size group of registers on each processor (see Section 6.5.2.2) holds a set of protection IDs. Protection register thrashing can occur if too many protection IDs are needed. Typically, there is one protection ID needed for the program's instructions and one needed for the program's private data.

Other protection keys may be used for shared memory segments and shared libraries. HP-UX allows all shared libraries to share the same protection ID if the library file is not marked as writable in the file system. Therefore, it is important to make sure all user-supplied shared libraries are marked for only reading and executing as part of their file attributes (see the *chmod* command). If shared libraries are marked for writing, then protection IDs will quickly be used up and excessive protection key faults may occur.

A similar issue occurs for shared memory segments. In general, as few shared memory segments as needed should be created on HP-UX systems, given that each shared memory segment uses its own protection ID. Creating several small shared memory segments can result in excessive protection ID faults. Like traps, faults increase overhead by interrupting the instruction flow and by causing a switch from user mode to kernel mode followed by execution of kernel routines to resolve the fault.

6.5.4.4 Code Practices to Avoid TLB Misses

Programmers can minimize TLB misses by carefully organizing data so that data accessed closely in time is placed close together in virtual memory. Even with large pages, modifying the application to reorganize the data can be an important way to reduce TLB misses.

Another code modification that can be helpful is to arrange array accesses such that the arrays are traversed sequentially in memory. Thus an entire TLB page will be accessed before continuing to the next page. Recall the code example shown in Section 6.4.2.

Finally, the compiler can help eliminate TLB misses as well. Profile-based optimizations rearrange code so that the hot instruction paths are accessed from a few TLB pages. The compiler may also try to position frequently accessed global data efficiently based on access patterns with profile-based optimization. See Section 11.6 "Profile-based Optimization" on page 391 for more information on profile-based optimization.

6.6 I/O Performance Issues

I/O performance is affected by the following factors:

* System bus speed
* I/O backplane bandwidth
* Number of I/O backplanes
* Number of host adapters
* Host adapter speed

I/O throughput is itself constrained by the speed of the system Main Bus, to which the CPU, memory and I/O backplanes are usually attached. I/O throughput is limited by the "weakest link" in the chain of components.

Backplane bandwidth is determined by the hardware design. This includes the length of the backplane, width (number of parallel lines), the speed of components, and the protocol employed in accessing the backplane. Hardware designers constantly strive to improve backplane bandwidth.

The number of I/O backplanes in a system determines how widely distributed the I/O can be. If there is only one backplane, all I/O is constrained by the bandwidth of that backplane. Multiple backplanes allow the administrator to spread out the I/Os for the same or different I/O types (SCSI, FibreChannel, Ethernet, for example), thus increasing total I/O throughput.

Finally, I/O throughput is constrained by the number and speed of individual host adapters, such as Fast/Wide SCSI or FibreChannel. For instance, an F/W SCSI host adapter supports up to fifteen disk targets. Although each disk may be able to transfer data at a sustained rate of 5 MB per second, the host adapter is limited to a peak aggregate rate of 20 MB per second. Therefore, adding disk drives may require additional host adapters and I/O backplanes to maintain adequate performance.

6.6.1 I/O Backplane Types

For HP-UX systems, there have been several different types of I/O backplanes used over the years. In the early HP-UX systems, most of the I/O backplanes used were HP-proprietary. These included HP-PB, HSC, and GSC buses. Later on, HP decided to use commodity buses such as EISA and PCI. Table 6-11 shows the features of various I/O backplanes used over the years.

Table 6-11   I/O backplane types used in HP-UX systems

Name	Speed	connector
HP-PB	32 MB/sec	end
GSC	160 MB/sec	end
HSC	160 MB/sec	end
EISA	32 MB/sec	side
PCI	132-528 MB/sec	side
PCI-X	1056 MB/sec	side

6.6.2   I/O card types

The type of I/O card used to connect peripherals and for networked communication can have a large effect on the overall performance of a system. Some cards perform better than others in terms of both bandwidth and CPU utilization used per transaction. For attaching disks to HP-UX, the most efficient cards are the newer 1 Gb and 2 Gb FibreChannel cards. For network interface cards (NICs), the gigabit Ethernet cards are the most efficient network attach. Finally, for a cluster interconnect, the HyperFabric cards should be used to achieve optimal performance with applications such as Oracle RAC that use the cluster interconnect for application purposes. HyperFabric cards can use an optional protocol called HyperMessaging Protocol (HMP) which is much lower latency and high throughput that is the normally used TCP/IP protocol.

6.6.3   I/O Problem Solving

How do I/O problems manifest? Due to a lack of tools that measure backplane and bus saturation, it is sometimes difficult to determine if slow I/O performance is caused by backplane, bus and host adapter saturation, or data distribution and layout. The I/O performance of disks and networks is of greatest concern. Performance can often be improved by distributing network or disk I/Os across multiple host adapters. However, adding host adapters will not improve performance if the I/O backplane is saturated. Deducing the source of the I/O problem is extremely difficult, and generally may be only inferred indirectly. Sometimes it is easiest to use a trial-and-error approach by adding host adapters. The best results occur only on systems that have multiple I/O backplanes.

6.7 PA-RISC Systems

The designs of specific systems using PA-RISC processors can have particular effects on performance. This section reviews major PA-RISC systems at a high level. For complete information, refer to the detailed documentation for a specific system.

6.7.1 Early Models

Figure 6-8 shows an early type of architecture: the HP-PB-based Series 800 Models F, G, H, and I servers. (HP-PB stands for HP Precision Bus architecture.)

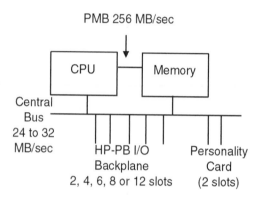

Figure 6-8 Early PA-RISC Systems

The original HP-PB systems used a single backplane to which everything was connected. Later HP-PB systems also included a private memory bus (PMB) between the CPU and memory, since the I/O backplane was relatively slow (32 MB/sec).

6.7.2 700 Series

Figure 6-9 shows some of the early 700 Series architectures. Note the existence of different types of buses; this variety allows for very flexible design, but applications may run differently when executed on systems with different buses.

6.7.3 890, T500, T520

Figure 6-10 shows 890 and T500 architecture. BIU stands for Bus Interface Unit; there is some inefficiency here because of sharing by CPUs. The main bus speed is fast (960 MB/sec), and the large number of I/O slots (112) and buses allows for wide distribution of the I/O. All three systems used only half of the 960 MB/sec of bandwidth on the BIU bus because only half of the bus pins were used. The 890 supported up to four PCX processors, the T500 supported twelve PA-7100 processors, and the T520 supported fourteen PA-7150 processors.

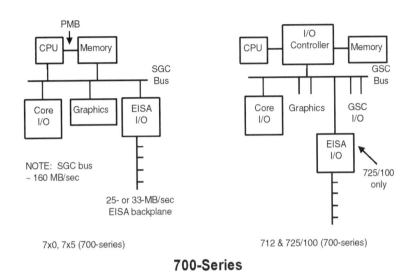

700-Series

Figure 6-9   700-Series Architecture

6.7.4   T600

Figure 6-11 shows T600 architecture. The T600 was the first T-class box to use the entire BIU bus bandwidth. The T-600 supported up to twelve 180 MHz PA-8000 processors and had a relatively large 8MB L2 (level two) cache per processor. The T-600 also added high-speed HSC I/O slots as optional I/O connectivity.

6.7.5   E-Series

Figure 6-12 shows E-Series architecture using the HP-PB bus with 20 MB/sec sustained speed and a 32 MB/sec peak. The E-series used PA-7100LC processors and was a low-cost server solution.

This more complex system uses bus adapters, which convert between protocols, and bus converters, which match speed. The GSC bus is much faster than the HP-PB bus.

6.7.6   K-Series

Figure 6-13 shows generic K-Series architecture. This was the first PA-RISC system to incorporate the high-speed runway bus. The runway bus has been the main processor to memory bus used in most PA-RISC systems to date. It is an asynchronous bus running at 120 MHz and it is 64-bits wide. The bus shares the same pins for both address and data. On any tick when the bus is available, either an address transaction or data transaction may occur. Address transac-

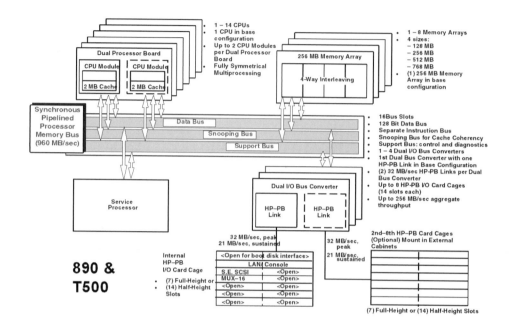

Figure 6-10   890 and T500 Architecture

tions require a single cycle, while data transactions require four cycles. Given that one tick is used for the address, the maximum data bandwidth in the K-class is 768 MB/sec. The K-series models with the 100 MHz PA-7200s and 200 MHz PA-8200 processors clock the runway bus at 100 MHz compared to 120 MHz for other models, so the overall system bandwidth on these models is only 640 MB/sec.

The I/O system in the K-class uses HSC buses, which run at 80–160 MB/second, and are much faster than PB buses (32 MB/second peak). Given the speed of the HSC I/O buses, four I/O cards can be connected to each bus. The HP-PB buses were included in the K-class to connect legacy I/O devices. A bus convertor is used to connect the HP-PB buses to the HSC bus.

The K-class was a very long-lived midrange solution for Hewlett-Packard. It was able to incorporate several different processors (PA-7200, PA-8000, and PA-8200) and was modified partway through its life to incorporate as many as six processors from the original design of only four processors. Figure 6-14 shows the final incarnation of the K-class, specifying which parts were available for which models.

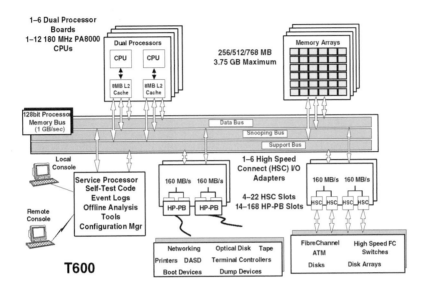

Figure 6-11   T600 Architecture

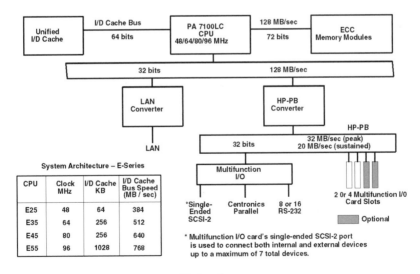

CPU	Clock MHz	I/D Cache KB	I/D Cache Bus Speed (MB / sec)
E25	48	64	384
E35	64	256	512
E45	80	256	640
E55	96	1028	768

E-Series

Figure 6-12   E-Series Architecture

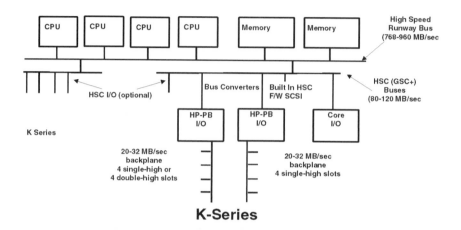

Figure 6-13   K-Series Architecture

6.7.7   V-Series

The V-series was built from a high-end system design obtained when Hewlett-Packard acquired Convex Corporation in the mid 1990s. It is a cross-bar design connecting multiple runway buses and processors to the memory and I/O system. It supported up to sixteen PA-8200 processors or up to thirty-two PA-8500 or PA-8600 processors. All systems used a 32-byte cache line to transfer data to and from main memory. The memory latency was almost double that of smaller boxes such as the K-class, but the overall memory throughput was much higher. Only 64-bit HP-UX 11.0 and later is supported on the V-series. Figure 6-15 shows V-Series architecture.

6.7.8   D-Series and R-Series

The D-series was the successor on low-end system to the E-class. The D-series contained several different processor families in the same box (PA-7100LC, PA-7300LC, PA-7200, PA-8000, and PA-8200). It was also one of the only PA-RISC servers that incorporated the EISA I/O bus. The form factor of the D-series was meant to be similar to the PC-AT form factor found in many PC designs. Unfortunately, this form factor did not lend itself to efficient rack mounting, so HP later repackaged the D-series boxes into an efficient rack design which became the R-series. Figure 6-16 shows a generic D-Series. Figure 6-17 shows the basic configuration of the PA-7100LC and PA-7300LC based D-Series systems, while Figure 6-18 shows the configuration of the runway-based models.

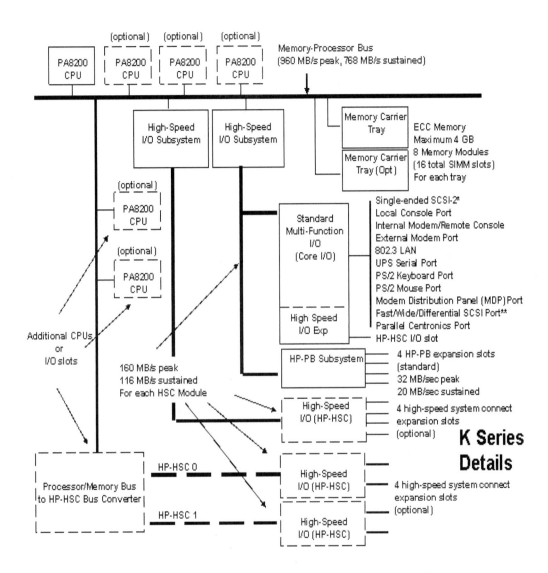

Figure 6-14 K-Series Detailed Architecture

6.7.9   N-Series (rp7400)

The N-series, now known as the rp7400, was the next generation of midrange servers after the K-class. This server contains two Itanium® buses running at 120-133 MHz attached to a central memory controller. A special bus converter connects a runway bus from each processor to one of the two Itanium® buses. The runway bus is "double pumped" in this design, which

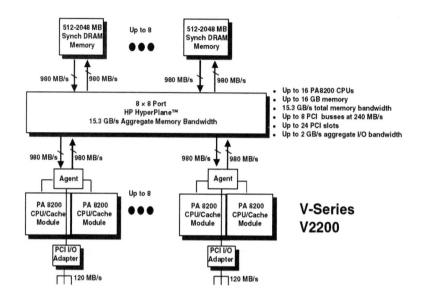

Figure 6-15   V2200 Architecture

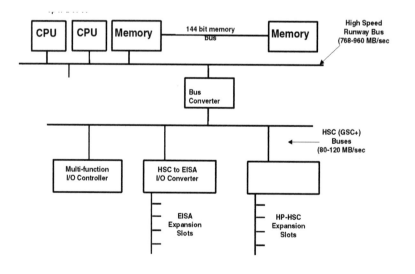

D-Series

Figure 6-16   D-Series Architecture

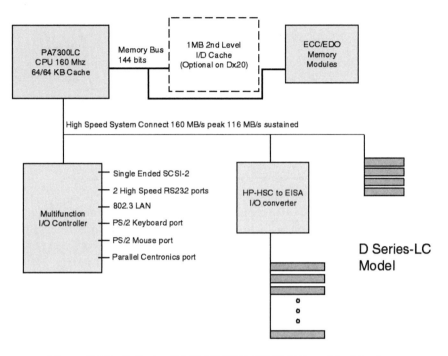

Figure 6-17 D-Series PA-7100LC/PA-7300LC Based Architecture

allows both the rising and falling edge of the clock to be used to transfer data. Therefore, the effective amount of data that could be transferred in the five runway ticks per transaction doubled to 1536 MB/sec. The processor cache line size also doubled to 64 bytes. As many as eight PA-8500, PA-8600, or PA-8700 processors are supported.

The N-class contains thirty-two DIMM (Dual In-line Memory Module) slots spread evenly among four memory carriers. Adding a memory carrier increased the overall memory bandwidth, so it is important for performance to have one carrier for every two processors installed in the box. With 1GB DIMMs, the N-class supports up to 32GB of memory.

For I/O, the N-class was the first Hewlett-Packard server to use an innovative I/O bus design called *ropes*. The *ropes* design allowed each PCI card to have a dedicated PCI bus. Each dedicated PCI bus connected to one of two I/O controllers. This design allowed for easy hot-plug of PCI I/O cards and gave each PCI card access to the full bandwidth of a PCI bus. By dedicating two ropes to a PCI card, 4x speed PCI card slots could be supported (HP called these *twin-turbo* slots with 2x PCI slots called simply *turbo*).

The N-series is only supported on 64-bit versions of HP-UX 11.0 and later. Figure 6-19 shows N-Series architecture.

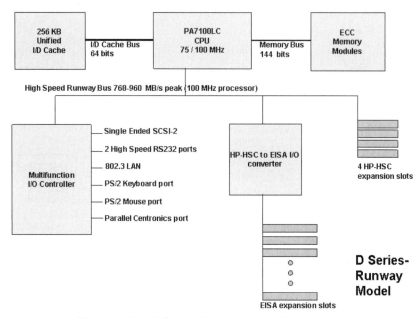

Figure 6-18   D-Series Runway Based Architecture

6.7.10   L-series (rp54xx)

The L-series, now known as the rp54xx series, is a 4-way design. The L1000 (rp5400) and L2000 (rp5450) servers are based on a low-cost single runway design.

The runway bus is "double pumped" as in the N-class, but it only runs at 80 MHz for an effective bandwidth of 1024 MB/sec. Given the slower bus throughput on the L1000 and L2000, they should be considered more low-end servers. The L3000 (rp5470), however, is based on the same dual Itanium® bus design as the N-class. Thus, a 4-way L3000 has as much bus bandwidth as an 8-way N-class. The newer rp5430 is also based on the dual Itanium® bus design. An rp5470 system is shown in Figure 6-20.

The L-series architecture supports various processors ranging from 440Mhz PA-8500s to 875 MHz PA-8700s. Not all L-series servers support the same processors. For I/O, the L-series uses the same *ropes* architecture as in the N-class. The L3000's architecture is very similar to the N-class architecture.

6.7.11   Superdome

The Superdome server has the first new HP-designed high-end Core Electronics Complex (CEC) since the 890. A CEC is very expensive to design and a given CEC is usually used for several generations of processor and server. The CEC links the CPU chip with the memory and I/O hardware subsystems in the server, and can have a large influence on overall system perfor-

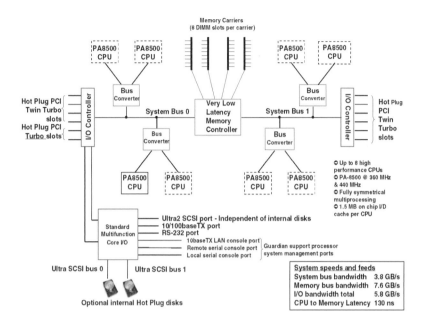

Figure 6-19   N-Series Architecture

mance. That is why the same CPU chip operating at the same clock rate can show quite different performance when used in different servers.

Superdome is based on a cell-based architecture where some of the system memory, CPUs, and I/O are connected together in a module called a *cell*. Several cell modules are then connected via a crossbar-based backplane to form a larger system. Each cell board contains thirty-two DIMM slots and four processors. One Superdome cabinet supports eight cell boards for thirty-two processors and up to 256 GB of memory (with 1 GB DIMMs). Two Superdome cabinets can be attached together via cables to support a 64-way system with up to 256 GB of memory.

The I/O subsystem on the Superdome is an enhancement of the N-class I/O subsystem. There are several *ropes* attached to *RIO* (Ring I/O) controllers. There is one RIO controller per cell board, for a total of sixteen RIOs in a 64-way system. Each RIO supports up to twelve PCI slots for 192 total I/O slots in a Superdome. Each Superdome cabinet comes with the capability to attach four I/O bays internally and four I/O bays externally.

The Superdome server was the first server that allowed for partitioning of the server hardware. The server allows different cellboards or groups of cellboards to be running different operating system instances at the same time. This allows one to partition the server into multiple pieces, each of which can be allocated for potentially different tasks. For instance, one partition could be running production software while another partition could be running test software.

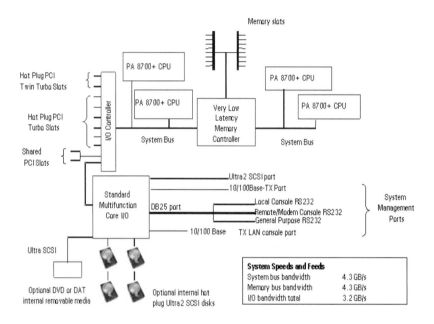

Figure 6-20   The L-Series (rp5400) Architecture

Each partition is electrically isolated from the other, so any crash in one partition will not cause others to fail; these partitions are called *hard partitions* (or *nPARs* for native partitions) since they are electrically isolated, and must be allocated in multiples of one or more cell modules. In fact, with high availability software such as Serviceguard, partitions can act as nodes and have failover among the partitions within a single Superdome as well as among partitions in other Superdomes or non-Superdome servers.

PA-RISC-based Superdomes currently support the PA-8600 and PA-8700 CPUs. Superdome servers require 64-bit HP-UX 11i and newer. Figure 6-21 shows the architecture of the Superdome server.

6.7.12 The rp8400 Server

The rp8400 server is a 16-way server based on the same cell architecture as the Superdome server. It physically occupies much less space than a Superdome. Two of these servers can

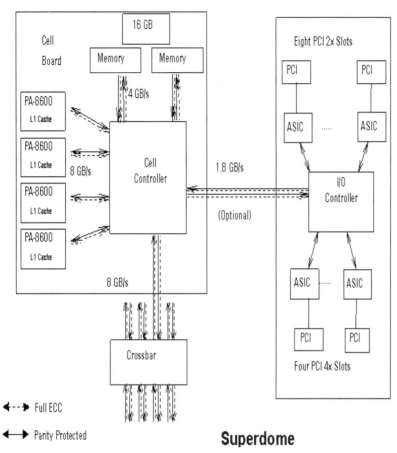

Superdome

Figure 6-21   Superdome Architecture

be racked in a standard 19-inch 2-meter rack. Each cell board on an rp8400 has half the total DIMM slots as a Superdome cell board, so the total memory supported with the same DIMM technology is half that of a Superdome. The rp8400 can be configured with two independent core I/O boards. This allows the server to be electronically split into two separate servers all the way down to the core I/O board.

The rp8400 currently supports only PA-8700 processors running from 750-875 MHz and runs only HP-UX 11i. Figure 6-22 shows the architecture of the rp8400.

6.7.13   The rp7405 and rp7410 Servers

The rp7405 and rp7410 servers are 8-way designs using the same cell boards as the rp8400. The rp7405 is a lower cost 8-way that uses 650 MHz PA-8700 processors, while the

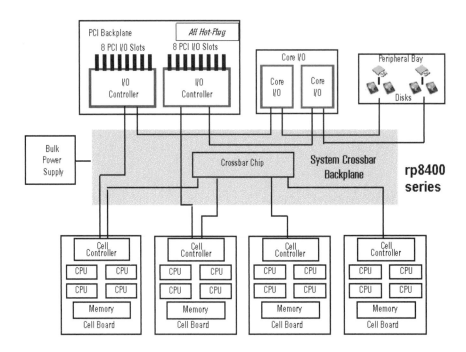

Figure 6-22   The rp8400 Architecture

rp7410 supports 750-875 MHz PA-8700s. Both servers contain two cell boards connected "back-to-back," with no intervening cross-bar element, thus saving space, power, cooling, and cost. Each server can be partitioned into two separate 1- to 4-way servers. Each server runs only HP-UX 11i. Figure 6-23 shows the architecture of the rp7410 and rp7405 servers.

6.8 Itanium® Systems

The Itanium® Processor Family (IPF) systems are the next generation of servers set to succeed the PA-RISC line of servers. These systems contain high performance 64-bit processors developed jointly between Intel® and HP. Most of these servers will also support the upcoming PA-8800 processor and its successors, because these newer PA-RISC processors have dropped the runway bus interface and adopted the Itanium2 bus interface. These processors provide a transitional product for customers wanting to migrate from PA-RISC to IPF.

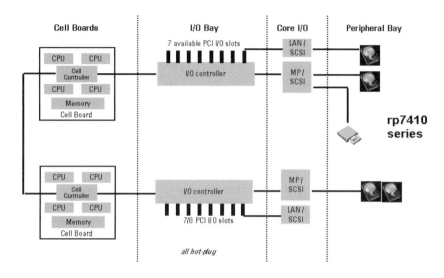

Figure 6-23   The rp7405 and rp7410 Architecture

6.8.1   rx4650 server

The rx4650 server was the first Itanium®-based system sold by Hewlett-Packard. It contained up to four 733 MHz or 800 MHz Itanium® processors. An interesting feature was that it provided up to 64 GB of main memory for a very high memory-to-CPU ratio of 16 GB. It has mainly served as a development platform for future Itanium® systems and is supported only on HP-UX 11i v 1.5 and v1.6.

6.8.2   rx5670 and rx2600

The HP Integrity Server rx5670 and rx2600 were the first Itanium® 2-based servers HP developed. They are both based on the HP Scalable Processor Chipset zx1. Each server is based on the Itanium® 2 bus, which is a 128-bit-wide 400 MHz bus capable of 6.4 GB/second of bandwidth. The rx5670 can be configured with up to four Itanium® 2 processors. It contains forty-eight DIMM slots for a total of 48 GB of main memory with 1 GB DIMMs and 96 GB of memory with 2 GB DIMMs. The rx2600 can be configured with up to two Itanium® 2 processors and contains twelve DIMM sites. In order to support the large number of DIMM slots in the rx5670 memory, extenders were used which slightly increased the memory latency compared to the rx2600. These servers continue HP's use of *ropes* for PCI devices. The rx5600 can contain ten

PCI cards while the rack optimized rx2600 can be configured with only four PCI cards. Figure

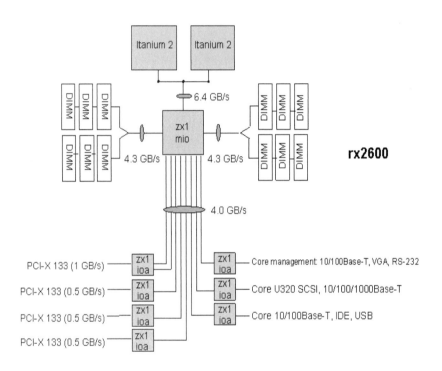

Figure 6-24   HP Integrity rx2600 Architecture

6-24 shows the architecture of the rx2600.

6.8.3   Integrity Superdome

The HP Integrity Superdome server is an IPF-version of the Superdome server that has been modified to support Itanium® 2 processors. A new cell board was developed for IPF processors that connects to existing Superdome systems. The cell board supports four Itanium® 2 processors attached with two Itanium® 2 buses. Each cell board contains the same number of DIMM slots as the PA-based Superdome; however, the Integrity version currently supports higher-capacity DIMMs and an overall memory capacity of 512 GB. With the new IPF-based Superdome, the Superdome server now supports both IPF and PA-RISC processors. The IPF version of Superdome supports HP-UX 11i v2 and later releases. For the IPF versions of Superdome, the internal cell memory bandwidth available to the processors tripled, while the bandwidth between cells stayed the same. The I/O buses on the IPF-based Superdome have also been upgraded to support PCI-X slots.

6.8.4   rx8620

The HP Integrity Server rx8620 is the same design as the PA-RISC rp8400 server, but it contains Itanium® 2 IPF cell boards. These cell boards are again identical to the HP Integrity Superdome boards in most functionality, except that they hold half the amount of memory. The PCI buses have been upgraded to support PCI-X. HP-UX 11i v2 and later releases run on the rx8620.

6.8.5   rx7620

The HP Integrity Server rx7620 is the same cell-based design as the PA-RISC rp7410, but it contains Itanium® 2 based IPF cell boards. These cell boards contain only sixteen DIMM sites per board, as in the rp7410. Support for PCI-X cards has also been added. The server supports HP-UX 11i v2 and later.

CPU Bottlenecks

This chapter describes major CPU bottlenecks, gives typical symptoms and techniques for diagnosis, and presents many of the metrics relating to CPU performance. It also describes some methods for tuning.

Topics covered in Chapter 7 are:

- Processes and Threads
- Scheduling
- System Partitioning
- Traps and Protection Violations
- Global CPU Metrics
- Typical Metric Values
- Symptoms of a CPU bottleneck
- CPU use and Performance Tools
- Tuning CPU bottlenecks

7.1 Processes and Threads

Process is the name given to a particular instance or context of an executable in the operating system. The processors of a system execute the instructions contained within a process context. There can be multiple processes in varying states of completion running on the processors of a system. Processes have been the basic executable unit of work since the beginning of Unix in the 1970s. Each process under HP-UX uses various types of memory regions, such as:

- text (executable code)
- data (private global data such as globals and BSS area, stack, heap, etc.)
- shared libraries (code)
- shared memory (data)
- memory-mapped files

See Chapter 8, "Memory Bottlenecks" on page 203 for additional information about how a process uses memory.

As of HP-UX 11.0, processes can be further divided into sub-tasks called *threads*. Threads, like processes, can independently execute on any processor in the system. Every process in HP-UX 11.00 and later is actually created with an initial thread. It is the thread that does all of the processing, just as the process did the processing prior to HP-UX 11.00. If only this initial thread is created in an HP-UX process, then the process is referred to as a *single-threaded process*. Once a process creates at least one additional thread, it is referred to as a *multi-threaded process*. In multi-threaded processes, two or more threads share access to the private data area of a process. Therefore, locking is needed when accessing data in this region to provide exclusive access to the data when it is being modified by one of the threads. This locking incurs additional overhead, and may cause the thread to block if the area is already locked by another thread. No locking is needed for this area for a single-threaded process.

When threads execute on the same processor, there are several performance advantages as compared to separate processes executing on the same processor. Since threads share the same process private memory regions, they also share the same cache, thus reducing cache misses and avoiding physical memory accesses to load the cache. Similarly, threads share TLB entries, which means they are less susceptible to TLB misses. Also, since process private memory regions are shared, the overall physical memory consumed by a multi-threaded process is usually lower than that consumed by several single-threaded processes.

Another advantage of threads is that the creation time for an additional thread is faster than creating a whole new process. The speed-up occurs because the private data area does not need to be replicated when a new thread is spawned, because all threads share this area. When a new process is created, however, the entire private area of the process is potentially replicated to the new process. Also, a small thread cache is maintained for each process to make spawning threads even faster by not having to reallocate common parts of a threads context. This trades off using a little additional memory to speed up thread creation time.

Threads can contain an additional *thread local storage* (TLS) area that is private to each thread and therefore does not require locking for access. This TLS area is allocated from part of the process private memory region, but is only associated with a single thread. The HP-UX C/C++ compilers have a special keyword _ _*thread* that specifies that a variable should be allocated from thread local storage compared to the default of process global storage. This keyword is used in the following example to force the variable "tls" to be thread-local rather than process-global:

```
struct thread_local_data {
     int var_a;
     int var_b;
     int var_c;
};

typedef struct thread_local_data thread_local_data_t;

/* Create the tls variable private to each thread */
_ _thread thread_local_data_t tls;

/* can call a function like this to access tls */
int add()
{
        return tls.var_a+ tls.var_b;
}
```

In addition, the POSIX call *pthread_key_create(3T)* can be used to create a key for accessing *thread-specific data* (TSD). The key that is created is shared by all threads in a process, but when the key is used in calls to the functions *pthread_getspecific(3T)* and *pthread_setspecific(3T)* (which are used to read and write thread-specific data respectively), data specific to each thread is accessed. The following partial example shows how these POSIX calls would be used to set up and access thread-specific data:

```
struct thread_local_data {
        int var_a;
        int var_b;
        int var_c;
};

typedef struct thread_local_data thread_local_data_t;

pthread_key_t thread_local_key;

/* Before creating any threads do the following to create a key */
(void) pthread_key_create(&thread_local_key, NULL);

/* within each thread do this to create the thread specific area */
void setup_local_storage(void) {
        void *ptr = malloc(sizeof(thread_local_data_t));
        (void) pthread_setspecific(thread_local_key, ptr);
}

/* can call a function like this after thread specific data is setup */
int add()
{
        thread_local_data_t *ptr;
        ptr = (thread_local_data_t *)pthread_getspecific(thread_local_key);
        return ptr->var_a + ptr->var_b;
}
```

This POSIX method for accessing thread-specific data is a standard, but the HP method of providing a keyword makes accessing thread-local data extremely efficient and is easy to use. In the POSIX model, a call to *pthread_getspecific(3T)* may be needed each time a thread-local variable is accessed. This can result in a lot of overhead. With the _ _*thread* keyword method, however, HP-UX and the compiler maintain a thread storage pointer that is kept in a dedicated register on the processor that always points to the running thread's local storage area. Accessing a variable in the thread-local area simply requires the compiler to add an offset to the thread storage pointer to calculate the thread-local variable's address. This is one *addition* computation compared to an entire procedure call which in turn may call other procedures or perform other time-consuming operations such as acquiring locks in the POSIX method. Any time that a program makes a function call, procedure-calling overhead is incurred to save and restore registers. Also, the control flow of the program changes, which slows down a pipelined system.

Writing a program with threads can offer benefits over writing one as a monolithic process:

- First, some people find programming in a multi-processor environment to be easier with threads than with processes. Processes typically require some sort of IPC mechanism to communicate among two or more cooperating processes. However, in a threads model, having multiple threads communicate can be much easier since all threads share the global private data space of the process.
- Secondly, the POSIX threads implementation provides mechanisms for locking and waiting on resources that often require special programming in a process model.
- Finally, threads tend to use less memory than processes when many threads are used. This is due to each thread context sharing all of the data in a process, compared to having separate data for each process. However, if thread-local storage is extensively used, then this memory advantage may not be as great.

More detailed information regarding how *pthreads* work and the ability to create and control threads can be obtained via the *pthread(5)* man page.

HP-UX provides two different thread models that an application can use. Both models adhere to the POSIX *pthread* standard. One model is called *1x1* threads and the other is called *MxN* threads. The next two sections describe these models in more detail.

7.1.1   1x1 Threads

The *1x1 threads* model was introduced in HP-UX 11.00. In this model, there is one instance of a kernel context assigned per user-level thread context. The kernel context contains information such as a pointer to the process where this thread is contained as well as things like the thread's stack. Given this one-to-one mapping, threads created with this model are often referred to as *bound threads*.

For small numbers of threads, this model works very well, because the kernel does not need to manipulate many contexts. When there are fewer contexts, processor cache pressure can be reduced due to fewer non-shared items, such as the thread stack, potentially colliding in the cache. In addition, resource contention is usually not as high when there are a smaller number of contexts, so SMP scaling can be better. The 1x1 model works well for computationally-bound threads because the number of context switches among the threads is usually low.

7.1.2   MxN Threads

Another thread model called *MxN threads* was introduced in HP-UX 11i v1.6. In an MxN model there are many user-thread contexts that can map onto a single kernel context, so there is no one-to-one mapping of contexts. Threads created with this model are often referred to as *unbound threads,* given the lack of a one-to-one mapping between the user thread and kernel context. By default, the value of "N" is chosen by HP-UX and will represent the number of vir-

tual processors that the "M" user-level threads are able to run upon. Usually, the number of kernel contexts created, "N", will equal the number of physical processors available for use. A user
program can specify the concurrency level directly via the *pthread_setconcurrrency(3T)* call.
The value passed to this call is a hint to HP-UX as to the number of concurrent threads that
might need to run at one time. HP-UX will create an appropriate number of kernel thread contexts to allow running the specified number of concurrent threads. Not all applications using the
MxN thread model may benefit from the default concurrency level provided by HP-UX. If there
is excessive idle CPU, then setting the maximum concurrency higher may improve performance.

There is a user-level scheduler in an MxN thread model that assigns "M" user-thread contexts to one of the "N" kernel-thread contexts. This user-level context switch is more lightweight
than a kernel-level context switch in a 1x1 model. The kernel still handles context switching
among the "N" kernel-thread contexts. One complication of this two-level scheduling configuration is that there is less control over how threads get scheduled. For instance, the user level-
scheduler may schedule a thread, but then the kernel scheduler may not schedule the kernel context where the user-level thread was scheduled as soon as the application may desire.

Because of the decreased context switch time of the MxN thread model and the huge
reduction in the number of thread contexts that are no longer managed by the kernel, the MxN
thread model usually performs better than the 1x1 model for applications that create thousands
of rapidly switching threads. For example, a simply written program might create a thread for
every user attached to the program. When thousands of users attach, the number of contexts
needed to be managed by the kernel can be enormous with the 1x1 model. However, with the
MxN model, the kernel only has to manage "N" contexts, which is usually on the order of the
number of processors versus the number of processes. Be aware also that programs that create
thousands of threads per process tend not to scale well due to contention issues for locking
resources and algorithms that might not scale as the number of threads are added.

Most other application usages of threads perform better with the 1x1 model. Well-written
multi-threaded applications tend to have a few threads that run constantly and use asynchronous
I/O methods, such as *select(2)* or *aio(5)*, to keep from blocking. For instance, many high-performance Web Servers will create a few threads and use asynchronous I/O to switch between input
and output streams. It is also recommended that computationally-bound threads also use the 1x1
model because they don't have many context switches and typically use few threads. Therefore,
this environment won't benefit from the improved context switch times and kernel thread context reduction of the MxN model.

Due to POSIX standards requirements, a program built on HP-UX 11i v1.6 and later versions will default to use MxN threads unless the program specifically requests 1x1 threads. For
backward compatibility, a program built prior to HP-UX 11i v1.6 will continue to use 1x1
threads when run on any HP-UX system. The *pthread_attr_setscope(3T)* function can be used to
specify   the   thread   model   to   use.   In   fact,   both   the   1x1   model   (using
PTHREAD_SCOPE_SYSTEM) and MxN model (using PTHREAD_SCOPE_PROCESS) can
be used within the same process by assigning different scheduling policies to each thread.

Finally, if code is compiled with the flag *-DPTHREAD_COMPAT_MODE*, then the 1x1 thread model will be used. Refer to the *pthread(3T)* man page for specifics regarding MxN threads.

7.1.3 Conclusions and recommendations

The choice between using processes, 1x1 threads, or MxN threads can sometimes be difficult. This is another "it depends" type of decision. In general, single-threaded processes using shared-memory suffice for most applications. One disadvantage of the single-threaded process model, however, is that programming in an SMP environment can be more difficult. Performance can also suffer when thousands of processes are needed to complete a task. For easier coding in an SMP environment, 1x1 threads work well, given the wealth of POSIX-supplied interfaces. Unfortunately, a lot of these interfaces are not as efficient as they could be for a specific application. The interfaces need to be flexible to handle a multitude of different configuration options. So, there is some inherent overhead associated with the POSIX interfaces. For applications that need many threads, the MxN model may work the best, because it provides a lighter-weight thread switch and provides fewer kernel contexts than would normally be needed in a 1x1 or single-threaded process model.

7.2 Scheduling

Scheduling is the assignment by the operating system of CPU resources to individual processes and/or threads.[1] HP-UX assigns a priority to each process, and the scheduler enforces this priority by giving the process the appropriate amount of CPU. When talking about process priorities, a high priority may not necessarily be numerically higher than a low priority. Three types of priorities are in use in HP-UX: the POSIX *rtsched* real-time priority; the HP-UX *rtprio* real-time priority; and the default HP-UX time-share priorities for normal system and user processes. The different types of priorities are shown in Figure 7-1.

7.2.1 Time-share Scheduling

The time-share scheduling policy is the default for most processes on HP-UX systems. Time-share priority is somewhat complicated because it is divided into system- and user-priorities, as well as signalable and non-signalable priorities. User processes occupy priorities 178—255, with 255 as the lowest priority. System priorities occupy 128—177. Two types of time-share schedulers are described in the following sections: the normal HP-UX time-share scheduler, and the fixed priority HP-UX time-share scheduler.

7.2.1.1 Normal Time-share Scheduler

The behavior of the normal time-share scheduler needs to be understood when determining whether priority is the cause of a bottleneck. Each CPU in an SMP system has a queue of

---

[1]For the sake of simplicity, from here on out the word *process* will be used to describe both processes and kernel threads. When talking about user-level threads (i.e., threads in an MxN model), the word *threads* will be explicitly used.

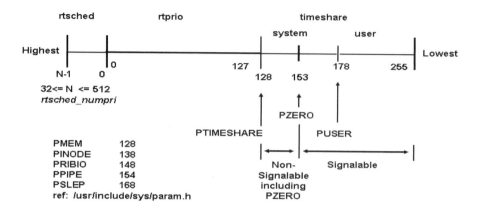

Figure 7-1 Process Priorities

runnable processes which are run and halted depending on the current priority that the operating system has assigned to them. The highest priority runnable process in each CPU's queue is dispatched. All the kernel threads of a particular process might not have the same priority because one thread may execute longer or more often than another thread. A new kernel thread's priority starts out with the same value as the initial process priority.

The scheduler assumes by default that all processes have equal importance, and that all recent CPU usage is remembered. As each process consumes CPU time, its priority degrades linearly. When another process's priority exceeds that of the process whose priority is degrading, the current process is switched out and the other process starts. As each process waits, its priority improves exponentially. Equal priority processes are time-sliced.

When ordinary user processes are blocked, awaiting system resources, they are not runnable. During this time, they are assigned a system priority. For example, if a process is set to sleep by calling the *sleep()* system call, it will be assigned a system priority of PSLEP, or 168. Blocked processes are assigned high priority at the system level so that they will get CPU time long enough to release critical system resources. They will then return to their user priority.

Processes are also categorized as *signalable* or *non-signalable*. During I/O operations, the operating system might change the priority of a process from signalable to non-signalable so that it cannot be interrupted until the I/O is finished.

NOTE: You may have tried to kill a process and found that it would not terminate. This was probably due to its being blocked on a resource that required a non-signalable priority. The *kill* signal would have resulted in the dealloca-tion of the pages assigned to the process. Therefore, the operating sys-tem prevents the process from being killed and having its pages deallocated during these asynchronous operations by giving the process a non-signalable priority.

Nice Values

One interesting feature of the normal time-share scheduler is that priorities can be influ-enced by assigning a value to them using the *nice(1)* command. All processes start by default with a nice value of 20. The nice command can then be used to change this value to somewhere in the range of 0 to 39. *Nice* values in the range 21 to 39 degrade priority, while *nice* values of 0 to 19 improve it. These latter *nice* values (sometimes called *nasty* values!) require superuser access. Starting in HP-UX 10.0, the *nice* value also affects the likelihood of a process's pages being selected for pageout under memory pressure.

NOTE: By default, some shells *"nice"* background processes. The korn shell, for example, sets the shell variable *bgnice* to 4 by default, which sets the *nice* value to 24.

Algorithms for Modifying Priority

Every clock tick (10 milliseconds), CPU time is accumulated for the currently running process whether or not it used the CPU for the entire tick. Every four clock ticks (40 millisec-onds), the priority of the currently running process is degraded based on the amount of CPU time consumed during the last four ticks. After a process has run for ten ticks (100 millisec-onds), a forced context switch may occur to run the highest-priority process if the currently run-ning process no longer has the highest priority.

NOTE: This 100-millisecond interval can be changed by setting the tuneable ker-nel parameter *timeslice*, which controls the number of clock ticks before a process may be switched out. The default value of *timeslice* is ten clock ticks.

Although processors have become much faster, the clock tick duration is still set at 10 mil-liseconds. Many processes may run, block, and run again within the tick period, which is why this method has become less accurate as a means of calculating CPU utilization.

Although global CPU utilization is still calculated based on what is happening at the time of the tick, per-process CPU utilization has been made much more accurate. A time-stamp is recorded when the process is dispatched and again when it is context-switched out. The difference is added to the current sum and is used to accumulate total CPU utilization for that process. Priority calculations are still based upon the old sampling method, however.

7.2.1.2   Fixed-Priority Time-share Scheduler (noage)

As of HP-UX 11i, a new scheduler called *sched noage* was added to HP-UX. This new scheduler has a scheduling policy that is similar to the default time-share policy with one difference: process priorities never get weaker or stronger over time. The *rtsched(1)* command can be used to run a process at a fixed *SCHED_NOAGE* priority between 178 (highest) and 255 (lowest). A user must either have superuser privileges or be part of the *RTSCHED* privilege group (see the *setprivgrp(1M)* command) to assign a process a *sched noage* priority.

The *sched noage* policy is very useful for running applications such as databases that are broken up into separate executable units (processes or threads) designed to communicate with each other and/or to run in a multi-processor environment. In general, poor interactions can occur among these executable units using the default time-share policy. For example, the normal time-share policy allows process priorities to dynamically get stronger and weaker over time. If a process becomes blocked on a resource, such as a disk I/O, its priority will become stronger so it is able to run once the disk I/O completes. If a process has been running a long time, its priority will get weaker to allow other processes to have a chance at running. Due to the time-share method of increasing and decreasing priorities, a process or thread that is holding a critical resource may be switched out involuntarily. This context switch can then cause resource contention if other running processes need the same resource held by the switched-out process. Such resource contention can lead to inefficient processor utilization and poor scaling when upgrading to a faster CPU or adding CPUs in a multi-processor system. By using the *sched noage* policy for a group of cooperating processes, however, the processes priorities stay fixed, so a process gets switched out only after a timeslice or when explicitly relinquishing the processor voluntarily. Therefore, such a process is less likely to be switched out while holding a critical resource, and performance can be improved.

7.2.2   Real-Time Scheduling

Real-time schedulers provide the means of establishing a category of higher precedence than the default for processes that need it. A well-behaved real-time process:

- Is important
- Consumes a small amount of memory
- Locks itself into memory to minimize startup overhead
- Executes quickly
- Passes heavy processing to a time-share process
- Has been thoroughly debugged
- Runs relatively infrequently
- Is linked with archive libraries

HP-UX employs its own real-time scheduler in addition to several POSIX-based real-time schedulers.

7.2.2.1   HP-UX Rtprio Real-Time Scheduler

The HP-UX real-time scheduler defines HP-UX real-time processes as those running with priority ranges from 0 (highest priority) to 127 (lowest priority). These processes have precedence over the HP-UX time-share priority processes. Moreover, priority does not degrade or improve as the process executes, but remains constant.

The HP-UX real-time scheduler has been available in HP-UX since 1986. A process can be assigned a real-time priority using the *rtprio* program. A user needs to either have superuser privileges or be part of a group that has the *rtprio* privilege (see *setprivgrp(1M)* manpage). Programs assigned an *rtprio* priority have precedence over all time-share processes, but have less precedence than programs with a POSIX real-time priority. Only processes at the same HP-UX real-time priority are timesliced. Otherwise, an HP-UX real-time process receives as much CPU as it requires unless it blocks on a resource such as an I/O request, or a process of a higher priority wants to run, including POSIX real-time processes.

7.2.2.2   POSIX Rtsched Real-Time Scheduler

The POSIX real-time scheduler uses three scheduling algorithms: SCHED_FIFO, in which the queue is ordered by the amount of time processes have been in the list; SCHED_RR, in which each priority queue is timesliced; and SCHED_RR2, in which the timeslice interval depends on priority. The *rtsched(2)* man page contains details about these algorithms.

The POSIX *rtsched* real-time priorities are defined by the POSIX 1003.4 standard. Priorities are assigned as positive numbers from 0 to 31; however, the priorities are actually presented in reports as negative numbers from -1 through -32. Also, the maximum real-time priority can be set as high as 511 by setting the tuneable kernel parameter *rtsched_numpri*.

One negative aspect of the POSIX real-time scheduler is that all POSIX real-time processes are placed on a single run queue because of POSIX standards requirements. In large SMP environments, this single run queue can become a severe contention point and result in a lack of system scalability if many processes are being placed on and off the global run queue. Given this fact, POSIX real-time processes will perform better on large SMP systems if there are only a few of them and if the time spent executing them is long before needing to block on a resource.

7.2.3   Process Resource Manager (PRM) and CPU Resource Allocation

HP's Process Resource Manager product (HP PRM) provides an alternative mechanism for scheduling. This product is based on the *Fair Share Scheduler* originally defined by AT&T, although it does not maintain a history of priorities. PRM gives the CPU to groups of processes based on percentage allocations assigned by the system administrator. PRM honors processor affinity (defined later) on SMP systems.

7.2.3.1   Advantages of Using PRM

PRM can be switched on and off, and replaces the standard scheduler when it is turned on. With PRM, processes are assigned to groups, which are guaranteed a minimum percentage of CPU time, and excess CPU is distributed according to the same allocations. Groups are configured by the system administrator, and group membership or percentage allocation can be changed by editing ASCII files. Within a process group, PRM behaves like the standard HP-UX scheduler. PRM gives the allocated share of the CPU to a process group, not necessarily to a specific process.

CPU allocations are enforced only when the CPU is saturated; that is, if there is no available CPU. Process groups may exceed their allocations unless the CPU cap is configured. PRM can be used to simulate a true batch queue, such as that found on mainframes. A batch process group can be allocated 1% of the CPU, and will receive a larger allocation only when other more important processes are not using the CPU.

7.2.3.2   Process Groups

PRM's process groups are dynamically loadable. You can define up to sixty-four process groups (16, in earlier versions). Note that the number of process groups is dependent on the actual kernel version. Process groups may be defined according to a user-defined model such as:

- Budget
- Number of users
- Application priority, including service-level agreement-based objectives

Membership in a process resource group is assigned by user name or by the absolute path name that is to be executed by *prmrun*. Users may belong to more than one process group, and a process may be moved to any group to which the user is assigned.

7.2.3.3   How PRM Works

In PRM, processes are scheduled into slots in an arrangement that resembles a carnival carousel. In HP-UX 11.0 and earlier releases, the "carousel" had one hundred slots, each representing 1 %. In HP-UX 11i and later, the carousel has 6400 slots, and for HP-UX 11i v2 this value is tuneable with the kernel parameter *fss_maxhorses*. When PRM is configured or reconfigured, process groups are distributed according to their percentage allocations. Figure 7-2 shows an example in which only three groups have been defined.

Once PRM has been enabled, every time the clock ticks, the scheduler chooses the highest-priority runnable process in the process group of the current slot. If none of the processes in the process group is runnable, the carousel turns to the next slot. In any case, the carousel turns to the next slot at every clock tick (10 msec). The PRM carousel is shown in Figure 7-2.

On an SMP system, each CPU has its own carousel, and the runnable processes in the selected group are distributed across the CPUs. If a selected process is locked by affinity to a

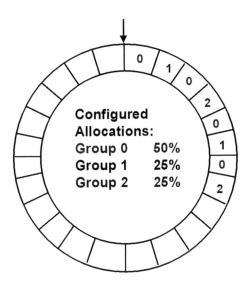

Figure 7-2   PRM Carousel

particular processor, that processor is skipped for the non-locked processes during that pass of the distribution.

7.2.3.4   Side Effects of PRM

PRM has numerous side effects that derive from its methods of operation. A number of these are described here.

- Processes that bypass login–such as socket applications–are not initially assigned to a user's resource group, but are assigned to the SYSTEM group. This makes PRM less useful for client/server applications such as database systems in which clients access the database across the network.

- Real-time processes can exceed the PRM allocations and can prevent other processes in the same group from ever running at all. In effect, this starves all other processes in a process group.

- High allocations result in short latencies. Applications that need deterministic latencies should be given a higher allocation than they might otherwise need. On the other hand, low allocations might result in long latencies.

- Although a process group may be allocated only one of several percentages, that may not be desirable, since processes in that group may wait for relatively long periods for CPU time.

- PRM distributes processes in a process group across CPUs in an SMP system. This *might* result in a greater or smaller number of CPU switches (discussed below), depending on the nature of the processes.

- A process group will receive a smaller amount of CPU than its allocation if there are more CPUs than active processes in a process group. Therefore, groups should be defined so that they typically have at least as many runnable processes as there are CPUs.

- Context switches can occur at every clock tick rather than every timeslice, which is the usual case.

- The user of *su* can cause undesirable effects, such as a process running in a different group than expected. Only when *su-* is used will the process be assigned to the *new* user's group.

- Absolute path name definitions are effective only when the process is run with the *prmrun* command.

7.2.4   Workload Manager (WLM)

Workload Manager (WLM) is discussed in Section 5.10.2, "Workload Manager (WLM)" on page 104. Since WLM uses PRM to perform its CPU-controlling functions, the discussion on PRM above applies to WLM as well. WLM has the advantages of a graphical user interface (GUI) and the ability to monitor and control CPU allocations among a group of servers.

7.2.5   Context Switches

A context switch is an event that takes place as a CPU begins work on a new process. A **voluntary** context switch occurs when a process sleeps, exits, or waits for an event, such as I/O. A **forced** context switch occurs in the following cases:

- At the end of a timeslice when a process with an equal or higher priority is runnable
- When a process returns from a system call or trap and a higher-priority process is runnable
- At a clock tick when a higher-priority real-time process is runnable
- When a process is stopped with *ptrace(2)*
- When a kernel thread is stopped with *ttrace(2)*

With PRM, a forced context switch most likely occurs at every clock tick (10 milliseconds).

Context switches consume roughly 10,000 CPU cycles needed by the kernel. It follows that a large number of context switches will result in excessive system CPU utilization and poor application performance. In addition, as a new process begins execution, it can potentially remove cache lines associated with the previous process from the processor's caches as it accesses its own data. Therefore, as context switches increase, less reuse of cache lines can occur, causing more cache misses and slowing down performance.

7.2.6   SMP Scheduling Issues

Before discussing SMP scheduling issues, it is necessary to define some terms. A *parent process* is defined as a higher-level process that spawns one or more *child processes*. For example, when a user types a command from a *shell* prompt (e.g., the Korn Shell, C-Shell or POSIX Shell), the *shell* is the parent process, and the command (or program or application) that it starts (spawns) is called the *child process*. Unless the *child process* disconnects itself from the parent, it remains connected until either it or the parent terminates. When the *child process* terminates, the parent process is notified by a signal from the kernel. If the *parent process* terminates first, the *child process* is inherited by the process *init*.

Traditionally, SMP systems have implemented a scheduling policy with the guiding rule that simplicity produces lower overhead. Here is the general algorithm that is used (this is subject to change in any release of HP-UX):

- A child process, including a *shell*, is always initially assigned to the same CPU as the parent process. This can be changed by adjusting the launch policy from the parent process.

- Once every second, if the difference in load averages among the CPUs is considered significant, the scheduler moves *at most one* process from the most heavily loaded processor to the least heavily loaded processor.

- When a process resumes from a blocked state, the scheduler tries to assign it to the same processor on which it was running before it blocked.

- When a processor becomes idle (i.e., it is not assigned any processes to run), it will search other processors' run queues for work.

- Processor affinity algorithms, described below, modify the above policies.

For cell-based systems such as Superdome, the scheduling algorithm is modified slightly to optimize for issues related to cell local memory, which is described in Chapter 8. The cell-based scheduling modifications include:

- Child processes may not launch on the same CPU as the parent. Instead, a cell with the lowest load may be chosen. This may hurt fork performance because private data will need to be copied from the parent to the child across cells, but this helps to make sure cell-local memory is not oversubscribed if a lot of children are created by a process. The benefits of this are described in much more detail in Section 8.2.2, "Cell Local Memory" on page 222.

- The once-a-second balancing of processes is done only within a cell. There is a second balancing algorithm that works every five seconds that balances processes among cells.

- When an idle processor looks for processes to run from other processor's run queues, it will prefer to take a process from a processor in its own cell rather than one in another cell.

The SMP scheduling policies just discussed provide an opportunity for additional types of bottlenecks. These bottlenecks may include resource contention, overhead for maintaining cache coherency, TLB misses, run queue priorities, assumptions about order of execution, and serialization.

7.2.6.1   Resource Contention

The kernel uses locks to protect kernel data and/or code from being modified or executed at exactly the same moment on different CPUs. These locks are either spinlocks, which are non-blocking, or kernel semaphores, which cause blocking. Spinlocks consume system CPU and may result in poor application performance when there is contention for the same resources among processors. Spinlocks are used when it is expected that resources will be held for relatively short periods of time.

Kernel semaphores are used when resources are expected to be held for long periods of time. However, locking a kernel semaphore is an expensive operation, since it results in a context switch of the user process requesting an unavailable resource. Contention on a kernel semaphore may show up as idle time that can't be consumed.

7.2.6.2   Cache Coherency and CPU Switches

In SMP systems, each CPU has its own hardware cache, and these must be synchronized. This can be a significant problem when a process moves from one CPU to another during the course of execution. A running process builds up a context in the cache of the CPU on which it is running. If a process is switched to another CPU, its cache content may need to be copied to another cache and flushed to main memory. Copying cache data or flushing caches to main memory are expensive operations, because the CPU remains stalled (due to cache misses) while this is occurring.

7.2.6.3   Run Queue Priorities

Because each CPU has its own run queue, not all the highest-priority processes *system wide* may be running. Example:

CPU 1: priorities 181, 183, 221
CPU 2: priorities 185, 208

One would normally expect processes with priorities 181 and 183 to be dispatched. In this example, the priority 183 process was unluckily assigned to the wrong CPU. The process with priority 185 was dispatched instead, because it was the highest-priority runnable process on its CPU.

The POSIX real-time scheduler, however, does maintain a global queue of requests for each priority. This allows the highest-priority process to run on any processor. However, this global queue design can cause kernel contention issues as multiple processors search the queue for something to run. If the context switch rate is high, multiple processors may contend heavily on locks that protect the global queues.

7.2.6.4   Order of Execution

On a uni-processor system, it may be safely assumed that a real-time priority process will execute before a time-share process. On an SMP system, however, both processes may run concurrently, which may result in unexpected behavior if the programmer did not plan for it. Here is an example:

Process A has a real-time priority. Process B has a time-share priority. On a uni-processor system, process A is guaranteed to use as much of the CPU as it wants before process B can run. On an SMP system, they may run concurrently on different processors. If they are cooperating processes, it is likely there will be a data synchronization problem on the SMP system.

7.2.6.5   Serialization

Another type of problem may occur when processes executing on different CPUs are serialized on a shared resource. Serialization problems could occur on a uni-processor system; however, this is fairly unlikely. The impact of a serialization problem is much greater on an SMP system. So is the probability of its occurrence. Example:

Processes A and B both lock semaphore S before doing certain critical work. If process A holds the lock, process B will sleep when it tries to acquire the lock. On a uni-processor system, this is normally not a problem since process A will be doing useful work on the only CPU in the system. On a two-CPU SMP system, if there are no other processes wanting to use the CPU, one CPU will remain idle since process B cannot run because it is blocked waiting to lock the semaphore which has been locked by process A. Therefore, less work will be done than what was expected. This is a major reason that some applications do not scale well in an SMP system.

7.2.6.6   Deadlocks

Deadlocks (also called *deadly embraces*) occur when multiple processes try to access resources at the same time but probably in a different order. Although deadlocks can occur on a uniprocessor system, they are much more likely to occur on an SMP system where multiple processes can execute concurrently on different CPUs. Here is an example:

Process A, which is currently executing on CPU 0, locks semaphore S1. Process B, which is currently executing on CPU 1, locks semaphore S2. Process A tries to lock semaphore S2 but blocks, since this semaphore is already locked by Process B. Process B attempts to lock semaphore S1 but blocks, since that semaphore is already locked by process A. One possible solution to this problem is to require programmers to lock semaphores only in a pre-defined order.

7.2.6.7   Interrupt Handling

When an I/O event finishes from a peripheral device or network, an *interrupt* is sent to a processor allowing that processor to start executing kernel code to handle what ever processing is needed to finish processing the I/O. Whatever process may have been running on the interrupted processor at the time of the interrupt is temporarily suspended until the interrupt completes. No other processor can schedule the interrupted process until all pending interrupts for the processor are complete.

This interrupt processing can cause a processor bottleneck because interrupts for a particular interface card are usually assigned to a particular processor. For HP-UX 10.0 and later releases, interrupts from I/O cards are assigned to different processors in a round-robin manner. Prior to HP-UX 10.0, however, all interrupts were assigned to processor 0 in an SMP system. This obviously led to bottlenecks for systems that performed a lot of I/O. See Section 7.3.4.4 for a discussion on how the default interrupt assignment can be changed.

7.3 System Partitioning

HP-UX systems provide extensive mechanisms for partitioning large servers into more workable pieces. Partitioning has become more important as large servers can be configured with increasing numbers of processors (CPUs). Partitioning has many benefits:

- It allows a single server to be used by potentially different groups and for different tasks.
- The resources in the server can be reconfigured to match the needs of the various users.
- Having a single large server can help with maintenance costs compared to several small independent servers.

By using partitioning, applications with radically different patterns of CPU utilization can be isolated from each other by allocating a unique set of hardware to each application. At a gross level, partitioning also provides a capability to allocate and cap a level of processing power to a particular application or set of applications. This is in contrast to using Process Resource Manager (PRM) to perform a similar function using software within an operating system instance.

HP-UX systems provide several different levels of partitioning. Some of the newer servers, such as Superdome, can be physically partitioned into several independent servers. HP-UX 11i also provides the ability to virtually partition a server into several HP-UX instances. Each HP-UX instance can then further divide their processors into sets of processing elements. Finally, individual processes can be assigned to particular processors and interrupts can be manually assigned to processors.

7.3.1   Hardware Partitioning

Hardware partitioning allows a single large server to be split logically into multiple smaller servers, each with its own set of CPUs, memory, and I/O cards. HP refers to a hardware partition as an *nPartition* or *nPar* or *hard partition*. Each hardware partition is isolated from the others so if a hardware component were to fail within one partition, the other partitions would continue to run. Each partition can run its own instance of HP-UX and each instance can be independent of the others and even be a different release.

Currently, *nPartitions* need to be rebooted after the partition definition is modified. Hardware partitions are created using a hardware *cell* as a building block. Cells are hardware modules in Superdome and other servers that group processors, memory, and I/O together. See Section 6.7.11, "Superdome" on page 160, for more information on cells. HP-UX uses the term *locality domain* when describing a group of processors that has uniform *access latency* to a part of memory. All processors in a given cell therefore constitute a locality domain because they can all access the local memory in the cell uniformly.

See the *partition(1)*, *parcreate(1M)*, *parmodify(1M)*, and *parstatus(1)* man pages for more information on managing hardware partitions. The *parmgr* command provides a graphical interface for easily managing *nPartitions*.

When configuring *nPartitions*, care must be taken to follow the configuration guidelines provided by HP for each hardware platform. If cells in a partition are not chosen properly, different performance problems can occur. For instance, selecting cells in an *nPartition* that are not "near" each other can lead to high memory latency, which leads to performance issues. The problem is that accessing memory on another cell is not uniform, that is, some cells have higher latencies than others relative to a given base cell. Another factor to consider is that if the memory configured on each cell in an *nPartition* is not equivalent, then the interleaving of memory among cells may not be uniform, causing additional memory latency and bandwidth issues.

7.3.2 Virtual Partitions (vPars)

With virtual partitions (*vPars*), an entire HP-UX server or an *nPartition* within a server can be subdivided into several virtual HP-UX servers, each with its own dedicated memory, I/O cards, and processors. However, these groupings of CPUs, memory, and I/O cards are not electrically isolated from each other as are *nPars*.

For example, an 8-way *rp7400* server could be subdivided into four 2-way servers with each virtual server running a different configuration or version of HP-UX 11i. Each server may be initially configured with a different number of processors, amount of memory, or I/O connectivity. In addition, the number of CPUs within a *vPar* can be modified dynamically without a reboot. Changing the memory or I/O configuration requires a reboot of the *vPar*.

The dynamic flexibility of CPUs provides efficient means for a system administrator to efficiently manage the server hardware. For instance, the number of CPUs in a given partition could be increased at night when batch processing is done and then decreased in the morning when batch processing has completed.

Virtual partitions work by having a monitor program that controls the partitioning of hardware resources within a server. The monitor program is what gets initially booted, before the HP-UX instance is booted, on a server configured with *vPars*. This monitor then handles the booting of the actual HP-UX instance for each individual *vPar*. Each *vPar* is independent of the others on the system, and an individual partition can be rebooted or can crash without affecting the other partitions. Also, because the monitor continues to execute while a *vPar* is rebooted, no system hardware diagnostics are reexecuted during the OS reboot. Thus, the reboot time for a *vPar* is much faster than booting a non-*vPar* instance of HP-UX. The *vparmgr* program can be used to manage the *vPars* on a server.

Vpars, like *nPartitions*, can be used to separate different applications into different HP-UX environments. This can often be a performance win because each HP-UX virtual server can be configured to optimally handle the workload it is assigned to run. For instance, a single *rp7400* server could be divided into two pieces with some processors handling the user interface aspect of a client/server application and the other processors running the back-end database. Given that each application is running on a different instance of HP-UX, each may be tuned individually by adjusting HP-UX tuneable parameters. In addition, the number of CPUs assigned to each job can be dynamically fine-tuned to reach an optimal balance for the particular application. Resource utilization can therefore be better when using *vPars* than when running everything on one server.

One performance disadvantage of *vPars* is that two different *vPars* can potentially negatively interact with each other due to the sharing of some common server components such as the buses and memory controller. For instance, if four *vPars* were configured on a *rp7400* system, each containing two processors, a memory intensive application could potentially cause memory references for the other *vPars* to take longer than normal by creating a heavy traffic load on the shared memory controller. This means that the performance of an individual *vPar* may be somewhat non-deterministic depending on what other *vPars* in the system happen to be doing. Hardware *nPartitions* don't have this problem since all hardware in one *nPar* is isolated from hardware assigned to other *nPars* on the system.

Virtual partitions are available in HP-UX 11i and later releases only. In addition, only a small subset of HP-UX servers, such as Superdome, *rp8400*, and *rp74xx* support virtual partitions. In particular, as of HP-UX 11i v2.0, virtual partitions are not currently supported on any IPF server. Please refer to HP-UX configuration guides to determine if a particular server supports virtual partitions.

7.3.3   Processor Sets

In addition to virtual partitions, HP-UX 11i supports *processor sets*. Processor sets allow processors within an HP-UX instance to be partitioned into groups or sets. The processor set then corresponds to a scheduling domain and any process assigned to the set will only be scheduled on the processors in the set. Processor sets can be created dynamically without needing to reboot the operating system. Processors can also be added and removed from sets dynamically. The *psrset(1M)* command is used by the administrator to manipulate and assign processes to processor sets. Processes can be assigned to processor sets by process ID (PID), at execution time, or via process group ID (PGID). There is a set of system calls to allow programs to have access to the processor set functionality. The APIs include *pset_create(2)*, *pset_destroy(2)*, *pset_assign(2)*, *pset_bind(2)*, *pset_getattr(2)*, *pset_setattr(2)*, and *pset_ctl(2)*.

Processor sets also allow for greater control over interactions between processes and interrupts. For instance, a processor set can be set up using *psrset -F* where processor interrupts from I/O devices are excluded. This allows processes executing in the processor set to execute without the possibility of being interrupted asynchronously by an I/O completion or some other interrupt. These interrupts would be handled by the kernel running on different CPUs.

This functionality is especially useful for processes that need a more deterministic result for when they are able to obtain processing resources. This feature can also be useful in large SMP configurations to help reduce lock contention when processes are interrupted and switched out while holding locks on a resource. Real-time extensions have also been added for processor sets where kernel *daemons* as well as interrupts can be excluded from executing on a processor set. The *psrset -R* option can be used to create this special real-time processor set.

Processor sets provide similar performance advantages as virtual partitions. One big advantage of processor sets over virtual partitions is that faster IPC mechanisms can be used to communicate between processes in different processor sets, whereas with virtual partitions a network-based IPC mechanism must be used to talk between virtual partitions. Some of the weaknesses of processor sets are that only process scheduling can be manipulated and all processor sets run under the same instance of HP-UX. The negative interactions that can occur between processor sets can also occur for virtual partitions.

From Chris's Consulting Log—A client/server application was being benchmarked on a 64-way Superdome server where both the client program and the Oracle backend program were allowed to run on any processor. The performance of the box was not good. Measurements from some internal tools showed that the cache miss rates on the processors were high. It was theorized that the client program and Oracle processes were colliding in the cache. So, two processor sets were configured, one for the Oracle back-end processes and one for the client processes. Each got its own dedicated number of CPUs. This reduced the cache misses and solved the problem.

Processor set definitions do not survive across a reboot of HP-UX. This means they have to be recreated on each reboot of the operating system. The *psrset* command can be used in a startup script to automatically recreate a given partition on reboot. In addition, the process resource manager (PRM) can be used to create processor sets, and it will make sure the sets are redefined on each reboot. If the *psrset* command is used while PRM is enabled, then the *-f* option must be used to manipulate processor sets.

7.3.4   Processor Affinity

Processor affinity is a method used on SMP systems to lock a process to a particular CPU or locality domain. It is usually used with processes that communicate with each other by some IPC mechanism to minimize cache coherency problems. It can also be used to eliminate potential processor-to-processor migration of important processes and therefore eliminate the cache refill that may occur as a process moves between processors in an SMP system.

While processor affinity can lock a process to a CPU or group of processors, it *cannot* do the following:

- Exclude processes from processors
- Reserve processors for locked processes only
- Flag processes to be moved as a group

See the next section for a discussion of the *gang scheduler,* available on HP-UX 11.0 (9812) and later. The gang scheduler allows a group of processes to be assigned to a group of processors. All processes in the gang are scheduled to run simultaneously on each processor in the gang set.

Care should be taken when using processor affinity to lock different threads to different CPUs. The same is true for different processes that use inter-process communication, because these techniques can result in cache coherency problems. In addition, the advantage of processor affinity where a process can be assigned to run on a particular processor can also be its biggest disadvantage: a process could be bound to a processor that is saturated even though there are other idle CPUs in the system.

A type of application that may benefit from processor affinity is one in which multiple processes are spawned to take advantage of multiple CPUs. One such example is the Sybase ASE database, where typically one process per processor is launched. In this case, each process should be locked to its own CPU using processor affinity. Performance is improved by reducing context switches, cache coherency problems, and TLB misses.

7.3.4.1   Gang Scheduling

The gang scheduler allows a set of processes or threads within a process to be run simultaneously on several processors. This set of processes or threads must be written to use the Message Passing Interface (MPI) for inter-process communication. Since synchronization (inter-process communication) among execution units of a parallel application cannot occur if one or more of the execution units is blocked from running by higher-priority processes, using the *Gang Scheduler* to group these execution units on a set of processors can result in better performance. The kernel will assign each process in a gang to its own processor, creating an affinity between the thread and a processor. This helps improve cache utilization and makes sure each thread in the gang can run at the same time.

To enable gang scheduling, the MP_GANG environment variable needs to be set to a value of ON. If this environment variable is not set or is set to a value of OFF, then gang scheduling is not enabled.

Typically, it is best if the size of the gang is less than or equal to the number of processors on the system. If more processes or threads than there are processors are made part of the gang, then these other processes and threads are executed independently, outside of the gang. Only time-share processes can be gang scheduled. Since all processes in the gang are scheduled simultaneously, a ganged process may end up preempting a time-share process of higher priority. For a complete description of gang scheduling and its limitations, see the man page *gang_sched(7)*.

7.3.4.2 *mpsched* Command

The *mpsched* command allows the user to bind processes at startup or that are currently running to a given CPU or locality domain. It also can be used to control gang scheduling and specify the launch policy (the processor or locality domain where a process and its children are first created; this will be discussed more in "CLM Launch Policies" on page 225). The affinity of a process may be changed dynamically with this command as the process is running. An affinitized process may also be *unbound* using this command. The following shows how to bind a process to processor 0 with the *-p* and *-c* options:

```
# mpsched -p 1234 -c 0
Pid 1234: bound to processor 0 using the default process launch policy
```

To bind a process that is not owned by the user executing the *mpsched* command, the user must either be logged in as *root* or have the PRIV_MPCTL access privilege. Unfortunately, the *mpsched* command only works for processes. Binding individual threads is not supported. If a multithreaded process is bound to a particular processor using this command, then all future threads created will be bound to that processor as well.

The *-s* option is very useful in showing the current configuration of the system. It shows locality domains and the processors assigned to each domain. The *-q* option will show all current bindings.

7.3.4.3 Affinity-Related System Calls

In addition to the *mpsched* program, there are system calls that allow a program to control process and thread placement on processors. The *mpctl* system call allows a program to assign processes and lightweight processes (kernel threads within the process) to processors and locality domains. In addition, useful information like the number of processors or locality domains configured in the system can be returned. The launch policy for new processes and lightweight processes can also be set. The header file *<sys/mpctl.h>* contains the information needed for this system call. The call is supported in HP-UX 10.20 and later and is documented in the *mpctl(2)* man page.

Here is an example of a piece of code that will lock the calling process to CPU #3:

```
#include <sys/mpctl.h>
err = mpctl(MPC_SETPROCESS_FORCE,(sput)3,MPC_SELFPID);
```

A similar call can be used to lock a process other than the calling process.

To unlock a process, code similar to the following can be used:

```
#include <sys/mctl.h>
err = mpctl(MPC_SETPROCESS,MPC_SPUFLOAT,MPC_SELFPID);
```

The *pthread* library includes different routines for implementing processor affinity in a threaded application. See the man page for *pthread_processor_bind_np(3T)* for more information. Muli-threaded applications should use these system calls rather than the *mpctl* system call.

7.3.4.4   Interrupt Binding

HP-UX 11i allows the superuser to change the assignment of interrupt processing for specific I/O cards to different processors. By default, HP-UX 11i will assign interrupt handling to all CPUs in the system in a round-robin manner. However, it may be beneficial for performance reasons to isolate the interrupt activity of some heavily used I/O cards to their own dedicated processor or to group several card interrupts together on a single processor to utilize the processor cache more efficiently. Recall that interrupts cause an asynchronous transition from the currently running process to the kernel and then back to the currently running process.

The *intctl* command can be used to display the current interrupt binding and to bind interrupts to specific processors. The process of changing the interrupt binding is only supported on certain hardware platforms and with certain I/O cards. The man page *intctl(1M)* provides specifics on how to use this command and on-line documentation describes specific limitations.

In most instances, the HP-UX operating system will do a good job of distributing interrupts among the processors. However, if there are a lot more I/O cards in a system than CPUs, more than one I/O card may have its interrupts assigned to the same CPU at boot time. If the I/O load is heavy for the cards bound to the same CPU, then the CPU assigned to handle the interrupts could become saturated, resulting in a CPU bottleneck. The *intctl*(1m) command can be used to dynamically move the assignment of interrupt handling for one or more I/O cards to a different CPU to relieve the bottleneck without rebooting the system.

In other instances, however, it might be beneficial to combine interrupt processing from multiple cards onto one or more CPUs. For instance, when using processor sets, a set of processors could be dedicated to handle interrupt processing for all of the I/O cards. This would then allow other processors to run processes without being interrupted. This separated configuration has several performance benefits.

- First, by having dedicated "interrupt" processors, the cache behavior of both the processors handling the interrupts and the processors not handling interrupts may be improved. The cache improvement can occur because the operating system and application no longer share the same processor cache(s).
- Second, in a large multi-processor environment, processes holding critical resources now will not be interrupted due to I/O processing. This can help to improve scalability.

7.4 Traps and Protection Violations

Another important category of CPU bottleneck is caused by traps. Traps are software interrupts that are caused by:

- Page faults
- Page protection violations
- Floating point emulation
- Integer and floating point overflow and underflow

Traps are costly in CPU utilization because whatever is executing is interrupted. A trap requires a switch to kernel mode, a save of state, and processing time to determine the cause of the trap and then take the appropriate action. A trap may also cause a context switch if the action causes an I/O such as a page-in, or if a higher priority process is ready to run.

Protection violations occur when a process attempts to access a page of memory for which the protection ID is *not* loaded into a control register. *Control registers* are a special type of register that are set by the kernel for an executing process. *Protection IDs* are used to define ownership of a section of the virtual address space. Only processes whose protection IDs match the protection ID set on a page of memory are allowed to access that page. Figure 7-3 shows some examples of protection IDs for a PA-RISC 1.1-based system. In the figure, Protection IDs 1 and 2 are both fixed for the life of the process and therefore would not cause violations. Protection IDs 3 and 4, however, are subject to change as a process accesses different memory segments.

NOTE: Shared libraries use the public protection ID if the file permission is 555 on the shared library. In this case, the shared library does not require a protection ID register. Any shared library used on HP-UX platforms should use the 555 file permission to avoid oversubscribing the protection ID registers.

Protection registers are needed for each non-locked shared memory segment, non-global shared library, and memory-mapped file accessed by the process. Locking shared memory seg-

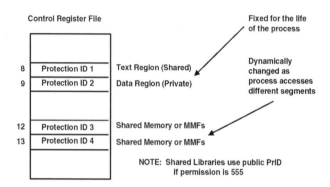

Figure 7-3 Protection Violations

ments into memory uses only one protection ID for all locked shared memory segments. PA 1.x systems have four protection ID control registers, PA 2.x systems have eight, and Itanium processors have sixteen. Given the relatively small number of protection ID registers, care should be taken not to allocate many shared memory regions and *mmap* regions that are actively used by an individual process. If the number of actively used regions exceeds the number of protection ID registers minus two, then protection ID faults will occur. Extensive protection ID faulting can cause serious performance degradations.

7.5 Global CPU Metrics

A variety of global metrics are available for identifying potential bottlenecks in the CPU.

7.5.1 Global CPU Saturation Metrics

The following metrics are useful in determining if the CPU is saturated and in what areas saturation is taking place. They are expressed as percentages of total CPU; that is, they add up to 100%. Abnormally high values may indicate potential problems. Most metrics are easily visible with *glance*.

- *% User*—percentage of CPU consumed by processes in user mode
- *% Nice*—percentage of CPU consumed by *nice*'d processes in user mode
- *% Nasty*—percentage of CPU consumed by processes assigned a negative *nice* value
- *% Real-time*—percentage of CPU consumed by real-time processes running in user mode
- *% System*—percentage of CPU consumed by processes in kernel mode (system calls)
- *% Interrupt*—percentage of CPU consumed by kernel interrupt processing
- *% Context Switch*—percentage of CPU consumed by kernel scheduling

- *% V Fault*—percentage of CPU consumed by kernel memory management
- *% Traps*—percentage of CPU consumed by kernel trap handling
- *% Idle*—percentage of idle CPU

7.5.2 Global CPU Queue Metrics: Run Queue vs. Load Average

The global CPU queue metrics include the run queue and the load average. These metrics capture different aspects of the CPU load; together they provide a more complete picture. The *run queue* is the current instantaneous number of processes waiting to use the CPU (that is, they are in the SRUN or TSRUN state). The value is provided per CPU in an SMP system. Different tools may or may not count the current running process.

The *load average*, on the other hand, shows 1-minute, 5-minute, and 15-minute averages of CPU use. The load average is the count of processes in the run queue plus fast sleepers (that is, the processes in the SRUN or TSRUN state and some in the SSLEP or TSSLP state). These values are also per CPU in an SMP system.

Also significant is the global priority queue, which shows the number of processes blocked on PRIORITY. The global priority queue, available only from *glance*, *gpm* and *MeasureWare*, is analogous to the run queue but is calculated differently.

7.5.3 Other Global CPU Metrics

Other important global CPU metrics include the system call rate (global and per system call), the context switch rate, and the kernel profile. The global system call rate is an important metric because it reflects the rate of invocation of system services. It is related to system CPU utilization. The context switch rate is an indicator of application contention and kernel contention on SMP systems.

7.5.4 Per-Process CPU Metrics

Some metrics are also available to indicate CPU usage on a *per-process* basis. Saturation metrics include *% User*, *% System*, and user, system, and elapsed times. Per-process CPU queue metrics include *% Blocked on PRIORITY* (runnable). Other per-process CPU metrics include per-process system call rate (total and per system call), context switch rate (forced and voluntary), CPU switch rate (for SMP systems), and the process profile.

7.6 Typical Metric Values

What, then, would be considered *normal* or *typical* values for these metrics? Of course, the best answer is given by **Rule #1**: "It depends." Run-queue and load-average metrics have values that depend on the following, and it is not useful to provide a single rule of thumb for the values of these metrics.

- Whether the application is interactive or batch

• Whether the application is compute- or I/O-intensive

• Whether the application is a server or client application

• Speed of the CPU

• Time in queue (the *glance* metric *% Blocked on Pri* is a measure of this)

One heuristic can be provided for the global system call rate. A rate of 3,000 syscalls per second per CPU may be indicative of a CPU bottleneck, although this heuristic will increase as processors become faster. Context switch rates have a heuristic threshold of one-third of the system call rate. A system's exceeding these heuristic thresholds may be either an indicator of possible poor performance, or the cause of poor performance. The types of system calls may also be signficant.

Figure 7-4 shows some ratios of values for system versus user CPU utilization.

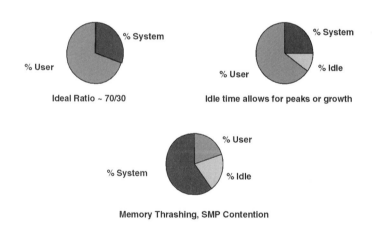

Figure 7-4   Ratios of System and User CPU Utilization in Unix

These ratios can be helpful in judging whether a given metric reflects a problem. An ideal ratio is 70% user to 30% system usage for a typical OLTP environment. Compute-bound environments may see ratios of 90% user to 10% system usage or more. Allowing a small percentage of idle CPU helps to provide for peaks or for expected growth in usage. The ratio at the bottom of the figure might indicate such problems as memory thrashing or SMP contention.

The ideal ratio shown above would not be the same for other operating systems. In Unix, system CPU utilization includes time spent in system calls on behalf of the user process. This is why the percentage of system usage (30%) is so high. Higher numbers do not necessarily indicate a performance problem. It may merely be that the application utilizes a lot of system calls.

7.7 Symptoms of a CPU Bottleneck

What are the symptoms of a CPU bottleneck? The four major areas are:

• Saturation of CPU
• Large queues
• Resource starvation
• User dissatisfaction with the system

7.7.1 Saturation

Saturation may be indicated by the following:

• Zero idle CPU
• A high percentage of user CPU usage
• A high percentage of system CPU usage

In the case of high system CPU usage, memory management, I/O management, and SMP kernel contention involving spinlocks may cause false symptoms of saturation. Real causes of CPU saturation from heavy system CPU usage are:

• A heavy IPC system call rate
• Heavy *termio* load
• Evidence of process creation
• Heavy network traffic
• An SMP kernel contention, but only if caused by a user process

7.7.2 Expensive CPU Utilization

The factors that cause high levels of user CPU usage–normal, *nice*, or real-time, are:

• Computation
• Cache misses resulting from CPU switches or from the application
• Maintaining cache coherency after CPU switches or IPC activity

The factors that cause high levels of system CPU usage are:

• Time spent in system calls
• SMP contention involving spinlocks
• Cache misses

Context switching caused by process scheduling or SMP contention from kernel semaphores is expensive. Also expensive are processing hardware interrupts, processing page faults
and TLB miss handling, processing traps (protection, emulation, computation), and spinning
while waiting for DBMS latches to release.

7.7.3   Expensive System Calls

The most expensive types of system calls are *fork(2)* and *exec(2)* for process management,
select(2) for I/O processing, and *semop(2)* (System V semaphores) and *msgop(2)* (System V
message queues) for inter-process communication (IPC).

Figure 7-5 shows the expensive parts of a *fork(2)* call. Data structures must be copied at
the time of the fork, and data pages must also be copied when accessed or written.

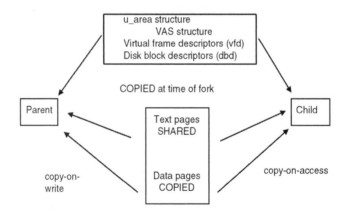

Figure 7-5   Expensive Parts of a *fork()* Call

NOTE: On PA-RISC and IPF systems, there are no instructions for a direct mem-
ory-to-memory copy operation. Copying items from one location to
another in memory is done using a series of loads and stores, which can
use many machine cycles. Later PA-RISC 2.x processors and all Itanium
processors provide prefetch instructions to help efficiently copy memory
using load and store instructions.

Figure 7-6 shows some of the costs of the *exec( )* call. In this call, nothing is actually copied. Instead, pages for the new process must be created or loaded from disk.

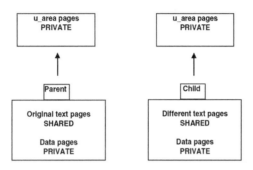

Figure 7-6 Elements Copied by the *exec()* Call

7.8 CPU Use and Performance Tools

Many tools provide useful data for dealing with CPU bottlenecks. Table 7-1 provides a summary.

Table 7-1 Tools That Provide Data on CPU Use

	glance/gpm	MeasureWare	sar	top	vmstat	iostat
user	X	X	X	X	X	X
nice	X	X		X		X
nasty	X					
real-time	X	X				
system	X	X	X	X	X	X
interrupt	X	X		X		
context switch	X	X		SSYS		
vfault	X					

Table 7-1   Tools That Provide Data on CPU Use (Continued)

	glance/gpm	MeasureWare	sar	top	vmstat	iostat
trap	X				X	
wait I/O			X			
idle						
Run Queue	*	*	X	X	X	X
Load Average	X	X		X		

* Not shown by default; may be accessed through the Adviser.

Not all of these tools always provide accurate values for the various CPU data. In particular, *sar*, *top*, *vmstat*, and *iostat* don't always accurately account for interrupt time. In fact, they may count interrupt time as user time, idle time, or system time, depending on when the interrupt arrived. This results in the overall CPU utilization breakdown to be wrong. For instance, if interrupts are counted as idle time, then one may think that the system is idle when viewing *sar*'s CPU statistics when in reality the system is not. *Glance* and *MeasureWare* are the preferred tools for accurately displaying the breakdown of CPU utilization.

7.9 Tuning CPU Bottlenecks

There are several ways to tune a CPU bottleneck:

- Hardware solutions
- Software solutions
- Application optimization
- Adjusting CPU-related operating system tuneable parameters

7.9.1   Hardware Solutions

The simplest solution may be to move to a faster CPU. This solution will help most but not all applications with CPU bottlenecks. Another strategy is to move work to other systems or create an *nPartition* by creating a client/server environment or by moving monolithic applications.

If the bottleneck is caused by increasing workload, the following strategies may help:

- Upgrade to a CPU with a larger cache
- Upgrade to a CPU with a larger TLB
- Upgrade to an SMP system
- Add a CPU in an SMP system
- Remove CPUs to use *fewer* processors

- Use *nPars* to isolate applications and OS instances from each other

---

WARNING: Not all applications benefit from an SMP system, and some applications may not scale well when another CPU is added. In the extreme case, an application may actually get slower as more cpus are added.

7.9.2   Software Solutions

The following software solutions may be used to address CPU bottlenecks:

- Use PRM, *vPars*, or processor sets to control CPU allocation.
- Use processor sets to isolate applications and/or interrupts.
- Use the gang scheduler to group the scheduling of cooperating processes.
- Use WLM in a distributed environment.
- Use *serialize()* if large processes thrash memory (to be discussed in Section 8.3.8, "Serialization" on page 231).
- Use the *nice* command to assign lower priority to less important processes.
- Consider using real-time priorities for processes, where appropriate.
- Restrict the RTPRIO and RTSCHED privilege groups.
- Use *sched noage* priorities to help keep important processes from being preempted while holding locks.
- Change the time-slice value.
- Move work to other time periods; for example, use batch jobs.
- On SMP systems, use processor affinity with processes that communicate with each other.

7.9.3   Application Optimization

The following strategies are suggested for application development:

- Use compiler optimization.
- Minimize the use of expensive system calls. Specifically, switch from System V Semaphores to memory-mapped Semaphores (see *msem_init(2)*); switch from *fork(2)* to *vfork(2)*, if appropriate; switch from System V message queues to shared memory.
- If using *malloc(3)*, consider changing default behavior with *mallopt(3)*.
- Parallelize the application. Use threads or create a distributed architecture.
- Profile the application and rewrite routines that show a high CPU utilization.
- Minimize traps, including legal protection violations due to the number of shared segments.

From Bob's Consulting Log—I was called in to assess an X-windows application that drew maps with various data filled in, such as topology, structures, vegetation, etc. Performance was 50% of expectation for this application, based on comparison with others. I found that the application was making 15,000 *ioctl()* calls per second. Further investigation showed that the application would check for keyboard input between drawing each vector on the map to see if the user wanted to abort. It was certainly not necessary to check for this user request 15,000 times per second! Changing the code to once per second doubled performance.

7.9.4   Tuning CPU-Related Parameters

The following CPU-related parameters may be tuned. In HP-UX 10.0 and later systems, they are in */etc./conf/master.d/**.

- *acctresume*—pertains only to System V process accounting and has little overall effect on performance.
- *acctsuspend*—pertains only to System V process accounting and has little overall effect on performance.
- *netisr_priority*—refers to the priority of the network interrupt service routine. Its value should not normally be changed, because it is not applicable to all releases of HP-UX.
- *rtsched_numpri*—affects only the number of POSIX real-time priorities.
- *streampipes*—refers to whether the original HP-UX implementation or the streams implementation is used for the pipe pseudo-driver. The HP-UX implementation is much more efficient but does not conform to the new desirable implementation paradigm.
- *timeslice*—It is not usually recommended to change the *timeslice* value. However, certain compute-bound workloads can benefit by disabling timeslicing. This is done by setting *timeslice* to -1.

NOTE: Disabling timeslicing is usually not a good idea with OLTP applications, due to added pressure on the scheduling resources.

Memory Bottlenecks

This chapter describes major memory bottlenecks, starting with a review of some important concepts in the area of memory management. This is followed by a description of typical bottleneck symptoms and some techniques for diagnosing and tuning them. Chapter 8 covers the following topics:

- Virtual Address Space Layouts
- Adaptive Address Space
- Variable-Sized Pages
- Cell Local Memory Allocation
- Paging, Swapping, and Deactivation
- Dynamic Buffer Cache
- Memory-Mapped Files and Semaphores
- Process and Thread Execution using Fork() and Vfork()
- Sticky Bit
- Malloc()
- Shared Memory
- Shared Libraries
- Memory Management Policies
- Sizing Memory and the Swap Area
- Memory Metrics
- Types of Memory Management Bottlenecks
- Expensive System Calls
- Tuning Memory Bottlenecks
- Memory-Related Tuneable Parameters

8.1 Virtual Address Space

While the amount of physical memory available for HP-UX is determined by the number of memory chips installed on the computer, the system can make a much larger amount of space available to each process through the use of *virtual memory*. Virtual addressing is used to access the virtual memory on the system. In order to understand the major bottlenecks that affect memory, it is necessary to know how virtual addressing works on Precision Architecture and IPF machines. Section 6.1.3, "Virtual Memory" on page 108 describes the virtual addressing mechanism at the hardware level in some detail for PA-RISC and IPF. This section will describe how HP-UX uses the hardware virtual addressing features to provide a virtual address space configuration for applications.

HP-UX provides a global virtual address space layout, which has fundamental performance benefits. In particular, the global layout provides for more sharing of virtual addresses, which results in fewer TLB entries, fewer OS data structures, and less memory used for maintaining virtual mappings. A strict global layout, however, also imposes a static layout of virtual memory, which can be restrictive at times, especially for 32-bit applications. HP-UX works around these restrictions by providing multiple static layouts, which allows for flexibility when running different application types.

In general, HP-UX partitions the global virtual address space into several regions of memory that contain particular memory objects. For instance, one region always holds the virtual memory of the operating system itself. Other regions hold memory objects that can be shared among multiple processes. Finally, some regions hold private memory objects for an application.

In general, the amount of virtual memory directly available to an application virtual is as follows in HP-UX:

- For 32-bit processes, the virtual address space available to each process is 4 GB, spread over four 1 GB quadrants that are used for various kinds of memory objects.
- For 64-bit programs (running under HP-UX 11.0 or later), the process address space is 16 TB for PA-RISC, spread over four 4 TB quadrants, whereas for 64-bit IPF processes, the architected user level address space is enormous: seven regions of 2^{61} bytes each.

The actual limit on virtual memory is based on the CPU and memory system implementation, including the size of registers and TLB entries. Thus, the upper bound on the size of virtual memory for a given system is often less than the absolute limit of the overall architecture.

The next sections describe the general and specific address space layouts used in HP-UX for both PA-RISC and IPF platforms. The performance aspects of each layout are also discussed.

8.1.1 PA-RISC Virtual Address Space Layout

In HP-UX systems utilizing PA-RISC processors, processes will have different virtual memory layouts depending on whether the 32-bit or 64-bit process model is used. Different levels of HP PA provide different amounts of virtual address space (VAS), as shown in Table 8-1.

Table 8-1   PA-RISC Virtual Address Space Levels

Level	Virtual Addressing
0	32-bit physical addressing only (Note: HP has never made a Level 0 system)
1	48-bit virtual addressing 2^{48} total VAS (272 TB) 2^{16} (32768) spaces of 4 GB each
2	64-bit virtual addressing 2^{64} total VAS 2^{32} spaces of 4 GB each
3	96-bit virtual addressing 2^{96} total VAS up to 2^{64} spaces of 4 GB to 2^{62} bytes each

8.1.1.1   PA-RISC 32-bit Virtual Space Layout

The 32-bit virtual layout for PA-RISC systems consists of four 1 GB quadrants. These quadrants will hold different memory objects depending on which 32-bit virtual layout is used by an application. The quadrant used is usually implicitly selected by the top two bits of the virtual address. The contents of the space register associated with the quadrant are used to form the complete global virtual address. Figure 8-1 shows the default 32-bit virtual address organization, while the other 32-bit layouts will be described later in the chapter. The *chatr(1)* command can be used to determine the type of 32-bit executable. If the *chatr(1)* output has "shared executable" in the description, then the executable queried has the default virtual address layout, which is referred to as the SHARE_MAGIC layout.

In the SHARE_MAGIC layout, each quadrant has a specific purpose such as text, data, or shared objects. *Shared text*, which is code that can be used by many processes, is located in Quadrant 1. *Private data* is in Quadrant 2. This data includes:

• Initialized data

• Uninitialized data (BSS)

• Dynamically allocated memory

• u_areas

• Kernel stack

• User stacks

• All data from shared libraries

• Private memory-mapped files

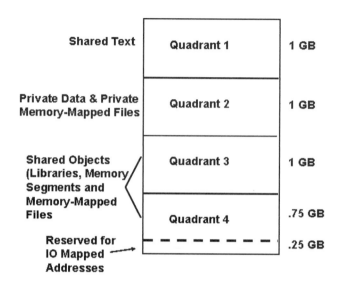

Figure 8-1 HP-UX VAS SHARE_MAGIC Format for 32-Bit HP-UX

Originally in HP-UX, shared library text occupied Quadrant 3, while Quadrant 4 was for shared memory. This layout limited the amount of shared memory in the system to only 1 GB. Therefore, in HP-UX 10.0 and beyond, the third and fourth quadrants are globally allocated. Shared library text, shared memory-mapped files, and shared memory can go anywhere within the third or fourth quadrants, but no single segment can cross the boundary between them. This limits any one segment size to a 1 GB maximum. Note that because shared objects are mapped globally, the total size of all shared objects in the system must fit within the third and fourth quadrants. Finally, the last 256 MB of the fourth quadrant is reserved for hard and soft physical address space (I/O space), which is used for addressing hardware devices based on slot number. This limits the fourth quadrant to only 756 MB of shared data.

Note the following characteristics with the 32-bit SHARE_MAGIC format:

- Text is limited to 1 GB
- Private Data is limited to 1 GB
- Text is shared
- Text is read-only
- Text and data are demand paged in
- Swap space is reserved only for the data

The use of four fixed-size quadrants can be a limitation to the amount of virtual address space that a 32-bit application can access, since each quadrant is used for different memory objects. Loosely speaking, if a particular memory object does not occupy the entire quadrant, then the process will not be able to consume the entire 4 GB virtual address space. This is an artifact of HP-UX's global virtual address space. For most applications, the default SHARE_MAGIC layout provides a good compromise for distributing the configurable memory for private and shared data objects. However, some applications may require more shared space or more private space than is provided by the default layout. Therefore, other static layouts for 32-bit applications are described later that allow different amounts of private and shared memory to be allocated.

8.1.1.2   PA-RISC 64-bit Virtual Space Layout

The sole virtual space layout for 64-bit PA-RISC applications is slightly different from the default 32-bit layout. The biggest difference is that the quadrants are 4 TB in size compared to the 1 GB 32-bit quadrants. With 64-bit PA-RISC applications, the large quadrant size makes private versus shared memory space configuration a non-issue since a single 4 TB quadrant is much larger than physical memory available today, and most applications are still far away from consuming the entire 4 TB virtual address space.

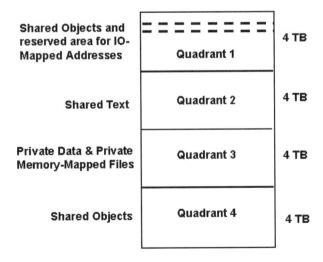

Figure 8-2   HP-UX PA-RISC SHARE_MAGIC Format for 64-Bit executables

The quadrant size is only 4 TB (42-bits worth of offset) for 64-bit PA-RISC applications, due to a trade-off in HP-UX between the number of spaces supported and the size of each quadrant. Recall from Section 6.5.2.1, "Virtual Address Space" on page 144, that PA-RISC processors form the global virtual address by bitwise ORing the lower 32 bits of the space register with the upper 32 bits of the virtual offset. To keep from generating duplicate addresses due to the ORing function, HP-UX makes sure the lower 10 bits of each space identifier that it creates contains all zeros. Since all current PA-RISC processors contain at most 32-bit space registers, this leaves 22 bits for specifying space identifiers, or approximately four million space identifiers. HP-UX also makes sure that it does not create an offset with more than the lower 42-bits, thus creating the current 4 TB limit.

The second biggest difference with the 64-bit virtual layout is that the quadrants contain different data than the 32-bit layout. Quadrant 1 contains shared 64-bit objects, plus a portion of which is for shared 32-bit objects. The 2-4 GB address range of Quadrant 1 is for shared access with the third and fourth quadrants for 32-bit objects. This allows 64-bit applications and 32-bit applications to share up to 2 GB of data with each other. This 2-4 GB range also includes the 256 MB of 32-bit I/O space that is at the end of Quadrant 4 for 32-bit applications. The 64-bit I/O space is also configured into Quadrant 1 from 4 - 68 GB making this unavailable for user data. Quadrant 2 contains the shared text and Quadrant 3 contains the private data. Finally, Quadrant 4 is fully allocated to globally shared objects. Figure 8-2 shows the 64-bit SHARE_MAGIC organization.

While 64-bit layout allows a far greater number of addresses, only a subset of the possible addresses within the 4 TB is normally used. The actual number of addresses used is constrained by the total swap space available.

8.1.2   IPF Virtual Address Space Layout

The IPF virtual address space layout is different from the PA-RISC layout and is also different between 32-bit and 64-bit processes. For IPF machines, the address space is a flat 64-bit address range. However, the OS divides this address space into eight 2^{61}-byte (2 exabyte) regions with the top three bits of each virtual address selecting a region register (RR) to use. The region register is analogous to the PA-RISC space register. The region register is 24 bits in size and it is combined with the 61-bit offset of the virtual address to form an 85-bit global virtual address that is used by the hardware and OS. The following sections describe the 32-bit and 64-bit layouts for the Itanium® Processor Family.

8.1.2.1   32-bit Virtual Space Layout

The default 32-bit IPF virtual memory layout is similar in many ways to the PA-RISC 32-bit layout. There are four 1 GB regions that make up the user space virtual address layout. The first octant contains shared text, the second contains private data, and the third and fourth octants contain shared data. Unlike PA-RISC, the u_areas for the 32-bit applications are stored in the fifth octant instead of being allocated with the private data. (Note: a u_area is a process-specific data structure called the "user area". It is pointed to from the process table entry for a specific

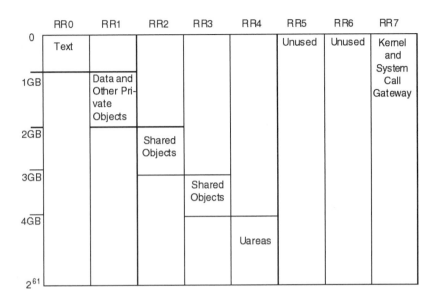

Figure 8-3 Default IPF Per-Process Virtual Address Space (32 Bits)

process.) Also, the fourth octant does not have a missing 256 MB for I/O space as the fourth quadrant in PA-RISC does. Figure 8-3 shows the default virtual address layout for 32-bit IPF processes, which is referred to as the SHARE_MAGIC configuration, as in PA-RISC.

All pointers used to reference memory on IPF platforms are 64 bits in size, even for 32-bit executables. However, pointers in 32-bit executables are stored using only 32 bits. In order to create a 64-bit pointer that can be used to reference memory from the 32 bits of stored address, the IPF architecture provides the instructions *addp4* and *shladdp4* to convert 32-bit addresses into 64-bit addresses. This conversion process is known as *swizzling*. The swizzling process zeros the upper 32 bits of the new 64-bit address and copies bits 31 and 30 of the 32-bit address to bits 62 and 61 (higher order bits) of the new 64-bit address (see Figure 8-4). For example, for the 32-bit virtual address 0x40005200, the swizzled 64-bit address would be 0x2000000040005200.

Because only two bits of the 32-bit address are used to select the region register, 32-bit IPF executables have direct access only to region registers 0 through 3. Region registers 4 through 7 are either unused by 32-bit processes or are used by the HP-UX kernel.

8.1.2.2   64-bit Virtual Space Layout

The 64-bit IPF virtual address layout is somewhat different than the PA-RISC layout. First, the 64-bit IPF layout has a much larger virtual address range than PA-RISC. For instance, there are almost eight exabytes of virtual address space available for shared 64-bit objects, compared to the eight terabytes in PA-RISC versions of HP-UX. In addition, there are four exabytes

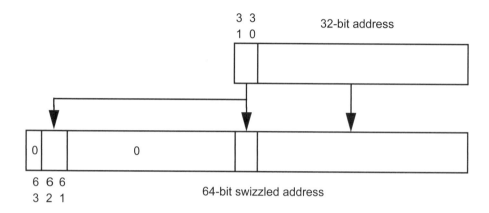

Figure 8-4   Swizzling a 32-bit Pointer

of private data versus the four terabytes in the PA-RISC layout. The IPF 64-bit virtual address space layout is shown in Figure 8-5.

	RR0	RR1	RR2	RR3	RR4	RR5	RR6	RR7
0	Null Deref	64-bit Shared Objects	Text	Data	More Heap	64-bit Shared Objects	64-bit Shared Objects	Kernel and System Call Gateway
1GB	64-bit Shared Objects							
2GB	Objects shared with							
3GB	32-bit apps							
4GB	64-bit Shared Objects			Heap	Uareas and Private Memory Mapped Files			
2^{61}								

Figure 8-5   IPF Per-Process Virtual Address Space (64 Bits)

As in PA-RISC, the 64-bit virtual address layout for IPF binaries was designed to allow efficient interaction with 32-bit binaries. In particular, the layout allows the 2 GB shared region of the 32-bit layout to be shared with 64-bit applications. This is accomplished by mapping the shared area referenced by the 32-bit process into the first octant of the 64-bit process, and then making sure that the region identifier used for the first octant for the 64-bit application is identical to the region identifier used for the third and fourth octant in the 32-bit application. If a 64-bit application wants to access data in the 32-bit shared memory area it can actually load the 32-bit pointer and cast this to a 64-bit pointer. The compiler will zero-extend the 32-bit pointer, thus creating a virtual address that ends up selecting the first octant for the region ID. Since the first octant region identifier is identical on all 64-bit processes and also identical to the third and fourth octant for all 32-bit processes, the resulting global virtual address is identical between a 32-bit and 64-bit access of the pointer.

8.1.3   Modifying the Default Virtual Address Space Layout

The default virtual address space layouts for PA-RISC and IPF applications under HP-UX were previously shown. However, these default layouts don't necessarily work well for all applications. In particular, the 32-bit layouts can be overly restrictive for applications that access very little shared data but need to access a lot of private data or applications that access lots of shared data but have little private data.

Executable programs compiled for HP-UX include a *magic number* in their *a.out* file. This number tells the operating system what type of virtual memory layout to use for an application. Based on the virtual memory layout, the kernel changes how it interprets references in the code to either the four quadrants for PA-RISC or the eight octants for IPF, as described in the previous section. The default virtual address layout has a magic type that is called SHARE_MAGIC. Other magic types include EXEC_MAGIC and SHMEM_MAGIC. Additionally, there are modifications to these three layouts which are referred to as the Q3 private/Q4 private layouts. Note that for 64-bit executables, only the SHARE_MAGIC type is used. All of the other magic types are available for 32-bit executables only.

8.1.3.1   EXEC_MAGIC

The EXEC_MAGIC format was introduced with HP-UX 10.0 on the Series 800 and with HP-UX 9.01 on the Series 700. In this format, the private data objects and text objects are allowed to share quadrants 1 and 2 for PA-RISC and octants 1 and 2 for IPF. The objects can exceed 1 GB in size, but must be less than approximately 2 GB. This layout doubles the amount of private data that a 32-bit application can access and therefore may improve performance for applications that need to access more than 1 GB of private data, such as multi-threaded or technical applications.

One potential drawback of EXEC_MAGIC executables is that the text (code) is private versus shared. Having private text means there can be multiple virtual copies in memory compared to one shared copy. Having multiple virtual copies of the text means that there will be separate sets of instruction TLB entries needed for each copy and the separate instantiations of the program will not share cache lines in the upper level instruction caches, which are virtually indexed on both PA-RISC and IPF processors. HP-UX does use virtual aliasing of the text pages in an EXEC_MAGIC executable to allocate only one set of physical pages when multiple processes are created, so this allows the physical memory usage to stay the same as with a SHARE_MAGIC executable.

The lack of virtual address sharing for the text may cause severe performance problems if multiple copies of the same program are run at the same time. This is especially true for PA-RISC processors if the application has a large text "footprint," such as is the case for many commercial applications. The problem is that separate cache lines will need to be allocated in the cache for each text copy and this can cause severe cache pressure. Normally with a SHARE_MAGIC executable, many processes all share the same virtual mapping so only a single copy resides in the instruction cache. For IPF processors, private text is not so much of a problem because the virtually indexed first level caches are relatively small, so these caches most likely don't hold the required data on a context switch anyway. TLB pressure can still be an issue for IPF machines with private text regions and multiple copies of an application.

For a multi-threaded application, however, having private text is usually not a performance loss because all threads within the process share the private text just like they share the private data. Only if many of the same multiply-threaded processes are executed at the same time will a multi-threaded application potentially have performance issues with an EXEC_MAGIC layout.

Text is writable with EXEC_MAGIC even though text is not modified during its execution. Since it is writeable, swap space must be reserved for the text segment, although a lazy swap allocation scheme is used in which swap space is allocated only for text pages that are modifiable. Even this lazy swap is wasteful, since virtually no modern application uses modifiable code.

For 32-bit IPF applications, the EXEC_MAGIC type is only supported in HP-UX 11i v2 and later releases. The HP-UX 11i v1.5 and v1.6 releases have no support for the EXEC_MAGIC layout. The EXEC_MAGIC layout is enabled by linking an application with the -N linker flag.

Due to the potential performance problems, it is recommended that this form of magic only be used for programs that really need the extra private data storage, are multi-threaded, or use at most one process per processor. In most non-threaded applications, it may be more efficient to convert a 32-bit application to a 64-bit application rather than using EXEC_MAGIC, unless you are constrained to run the application on a system that supports only 32-bit applications.

8.1.3.2   SHMEM_MAGIC

SHMEM_MAGIC is similar to EXEC_MAGIC, but instead of extending the private data area, it increases the virtual address space available to global shared objects. SHMEM_MAGIC achieves this goal at the expense of the virtual address space available for process text and private data, which is limited to 1 GB together when using this option. The total amount of area available for shared objects is 2.75 GB under this layout for PA-RISC and 3 GB for IPF. In this layout, the first quadrant or octant is used for private text and data. The other three quadrants or octants are for shared data, with the second quadrant or octant available for System V shared memory only.

This layout has all of the same performance problems as the EXEC_MAGIC layout because text is no longer shared among multiple processes. However, for 32-bit applications that need a lot of shared memory, this layout can help increase the amount of shared memory available and, potentially, improve performance. For instance, a multi-threaded database application could use a SHMEM_MAGIC layout to increase the amount of its shared cache for data read from the database.

From Chris's Consulting Log—An application developer insisted on using the SHMEM_MAGIC virtual memory layout to increase the amount of shared memory available to a 32-bit application from 1.75 GB to 2.75 GB on HP-UX. Unfortunately, the application was written as a multi-process application and it had a very large text footprint. When the developer switched from the standard SHARED_MAGIC layout to SHMEM_MAGIC, performance dropped by a factor of two even though they were now using much more memory for the internal buffer cache. The problem was that a huge number of TLB misses and instruction cache misses resulted from the lack of shared text, and this overwhelmed any reduction in I/O from disk that was obtained by the increased shared memory. This developer quickly reverted to the default SHARE_MAGIC layout for the 32-bit application and eagerly awaited the arrival of 64-bit computing.

The SHMEM_MAGIC layout has been available for PA-RISC-based machines since HP-UX 10.20 and has been available for IPF-based machines since HP-UX 11i v2. The *-N* linker option must be used to first enable the application to be an EXEC_MAGIC application, and then the *chatr(1)* command must be used with the *-M* option for PA-RISC and the *+as shmem_magic* option for IPF, to convert the EXEC_MAGIC executable to a SHMEM_MAGIC executable.

8.1.3.3   Q3/Q4 Private Data

Some 32-bit applications need more than the 1.9 GB of memory provided by the EXEC_MAGIC virtual layout in PA-RISC, so starting with HP-UX 11i, *chatr(1)* options were created to modify the meaning of the third and fourth quadrants for any of the 32-bit virtual layouts. When the *chatr(1)* *+q3p enable* option is used, the third quadrant is used for private data and when the *chatr(1)* *+q4p enable* option is used, the fourth quadrant is used for private data. If the fourth quadrant is chosen to use private data, then the third quadrant is automatically set to use private data as well. For an EXEC_MAGIC executable, enabling *+q4p* will allow up to 3.8 GB of private data for a 32-bit PA-RISC application. Enabling *+q3p* will enable up to 2.85 GB of private data over the default of 1.9 GB for an EXEC_MAGIC layout.

These *chatr(1)* options can greatly increase the amount of private data available to a 32-bit application and potentially provide a performance improvement by having this extra memory available. When using these options with EXEC_MAGIC and SHMEM_MAGIC executables, all of the same negative performance aspects surrounding private text still exist with these options as exist with the generic EXEC_MAGIC or SHMEM_MAGIC layout. However, using these options with the standard SHARE_MAGIC layout allows more private data at the cost of shared data while still maintaining the good properties of shared text. These *chatr(1)* options are not available for 32-bit IPF applications. Instead, an adaptive address space model is used.

8.1.4   Adaptive Address Space

Traditionally, HP-UX provides a global address space (GAS) for all processes running on the system. The GAS design provides advantages in TLB design and OS memory management codes. However, some application designers like to write their applications using address aliasing, which provides some programming conveniences. Address aliasing is not supported with a GAS operating system.

Starting in the HP-UX 11i v2 release, with IPF systems only, the HP-UX operating system allows a process to allocate memory similar to how a multiple address space (MAS) operating system like Linux would. HP refers to this ability as an adaptive address space because it allows an application running under HP-UX to choose between a global address space layout or a more private address space layout. This functionality is only available on IPF-based servers for both 32-bit and 64-bit applications.

Application writers using a multiple address space system often take advantage of programming shortcuts by using features such as address aliasing. The adaptive address space functionality was added to make it easier when porting programs from a multiple address space OS like Linux to HP-UX and to remove some of the global address space restrictions for 32-bit applications that require a large amount of private data. The *chatr(1)* command can be used to mark an application as using the multiple address space layout using the *+as mpas* option. MPAS stands for *mostly private address space* as compared to the standard mostly global address space normally found in HP-UX. A 32-bit application must have been first compiled with the *-N* linker option in order to apply the *+as mpas* option.

Thirty-two bit processes can allocate any combination of private and shared objects up to the 4 GB 32-bit virtual address space limit under the MPAS model. This allows great flexibility for an application compared to the various other global virtual memory layouts. For instance, with the 32-bit global address layout, the 1 GB octants can cause limitations in the total amount of memory available to an application, given that each octant must be used for a particular type, like text, private data, or shared objects. An MPAS layout does not have this restriction. For 64-bit applications, however, memory limitations are not really an issue, so there is no real memory allocation advantage for the MPAS layout over the standard global address space layout. The 64-bit MPAS layout is shown in Figure 8-6. Octant 7, which contains the global shared objects, can only be accessed by using the MAP_GLOBAL flag to *mmap(2)* calls, or by using the IPC_GLOBAL flag for *shmget(2)* calls.

Application writers may like the MPAS layout because it provides more flexibility compared to the standard global address space layouts. For instance, for 32-bit applications, a shared object can now be greater than 1 GB in size. In addition, more control over *mmap(2)* operations,

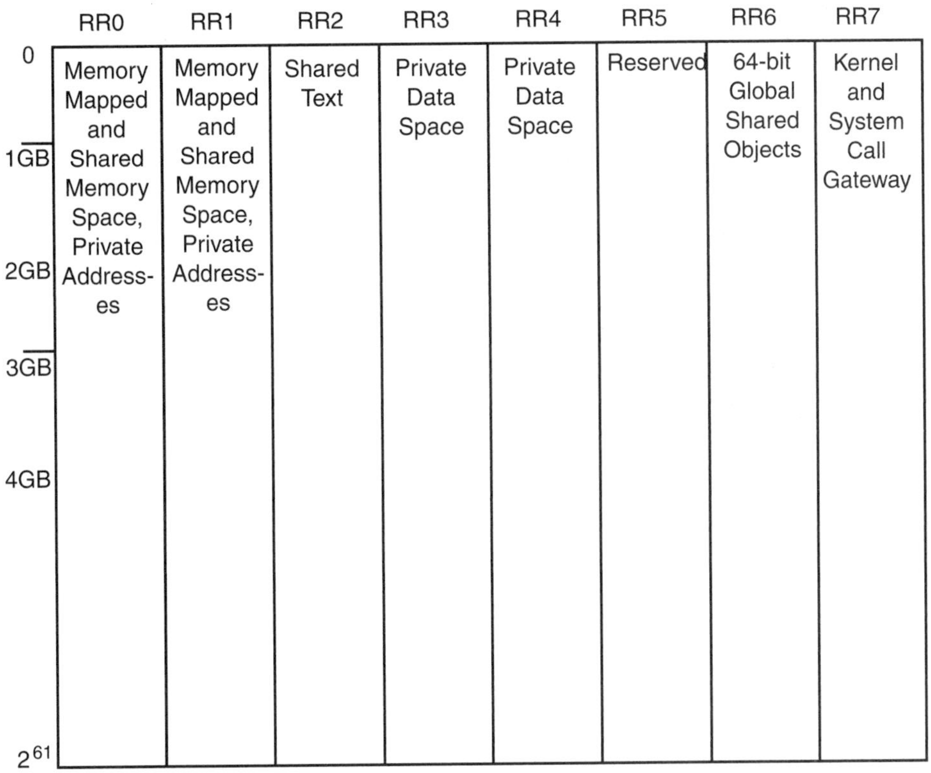

RR0	RR1	RR2	RR3	RR4	RR5	RR6	RR7
Memory Mapped and Shared Memory Space, Private Addresses	Memory Mapped and Shared Memory Space, Private Addresses	Shared Text	Private Data Space	Private Data Space	Reserved	64-bit Global Shared Objects	Kernel and System Call Gateway

0
1GB
2GB
3GB
4GB
2^{61}

Figure 8-6 IPF Mostly Private Virtual Address Space (64 Bits)

such as being able to map part of a shared file multiple times with a single process, is allowed using the MPAS model, With the MPAS model, an application can also map certain shared objects at a different virtual address in separate processes. Sharing is provided through virtual aliasing, where two separate virtual addresses can map to the same physical address. This allows a process to use the same virtual address for a shared object on each invocation of a given program. Most applications, however, don't have a need to map objects at a particular address.

MPAS applications may not run as efficiently as the normal global address space executables, particularly if the application shares a lot of data. The problem with multiple address space executables is that they use TLB mappings to provide protection between processes instead of the protection IDs used by the global address space layout. This means there will be increased TLB pressure when multiple MPAS-type processes are executing. In addition, running multiple MAS-type executables may also affect the overall system performance by requiring more page table entries and thus causing even global address space processes to spend more time in TLB misses. Finally, the 32-bit MPAS model will have the same performance issues with private text as the EXEC_MAGIC layout. The 64-bit MPAS model uses shared text versus private, so it does not have the text-side TLB or cache issues.

Variable page allocation, described later in the chapter, may be worse using the MAS layout because each virtual address chosen for a shared object needs to be aligned the same. If all mappings for a shared object can't be aligned the same, the page size currently allocated will be demoted to the smallest page size that aligns properly for all mappings. A global address space layout does not have this issue because all shared addresses use the same virtual address.

In general, the increased flexibility and private memory available with the MPAS model may outweigh any potential negative performance aspects for 32-bit executables, especially multi-threaded ones. Applications that share a lot of data between processes may want to consider not using the MPAS model, given the potential TLB performance hits and the potential for not being able to allocate large pages. In any event, testing should be done if possible to verify that the MPAS model is not causing performance problems compared to a global address space layout. For 64-bit executables, the MAS virtual layout it is not recommended unless a simple port of an application is needed. For 64-bit applications, there are no 1 GB octant restrictions on memory objects, so the memory allocation flexibility of the MPAS layout is not needed.

8.1.5   Shared Memory Windows

Shared memory is normally a globally visible resource to all applications. With HP-UX's global virtual address space, all applications use the same virtual address to access shared data. For 32-bit applications, all shared objects must be placed in memory quadrants 3 and 4 with the default SHARE_MAGIC layout; therefore, the total size of all shared objects that 32-bit applications can access is 1.75 GB. This may be acceptable on smaller systems or with smaller applications. On large systems, however, where the total size of shared memory segments for different applications exceeds 1.75 GB, this can be severely limiting for 32-bit applications.

For HP-UX 11.0, extension media has been released that will allow 32-bit applications to access shared memory in windows that are visible only to the group of processes that are authorized through the use of a unique key. This feature is standard starting with HP-UX 11i. Each shared memory window provides up to 2 GB of shared object space, which is visible only to the group of 32-bit processes configured to access it with the *setmemwindow(1m)* command. The total amount of shared memory in a shared memory window depends on the magic number of the executable. SHARE_MAGIC and EXEC_MAGIC executables can use a shared window of up to 1 GB, whereas SHMEM_MAGIC executables can use a shared window of up to 2 GB.

The per-process virtual address space for SHARE_MAGIC and EXEC_MAGIC virtual layouts using shared memory windows is identical to the normal layouts for these magic types with the exception that the third quadrant contains the shared memory window. For SHMEM_MAGIC layouts, both the second and third quadrants contain the memory window. In addition, using the *-b* option of the *setmemwindow(1m)* command with SHMEM_MAGIC layouts will cause the second and third quadrants to use the same space identifier so a single contiguous shared memory segment can be created. Applications that have been *chatr*'ed to use Q3 or

Q4 private data don't work in a windowed environment, given that their third quadrant will be private data versus being able to be used for the shared memory window.

Use of shared memory windows constrains the globally accessible shared object virtual address space to 768 MB on PA-RISC and 1 GB on IPF for 32-bit applications. This means that all shared libraries, memory-mapped files, and shared memory segments that must be accessible to all processes on the system must fit into Quadrant 4. Therefore, use shared memory windows with care.

The number of shared memory windows is configurable with the tunable parameter *max_mem_window*. Each group of applications can access its own private memory window. The shared objects placed in Quadrant 4 remain globally visible. Therefore, HP-UX tries to load all shared libraries into Quadrant 4 when shared memory windows are used. Shared objects placed into Quadrant 3 are not globally visible. Rather, these objects are visible only to the set of applications that attach to a particular shared memory window.

Using memory windows has several side effects:

* Shared libraries that cannot be placed into Quadrant 4 are placed in Quadrant 3 and must be mapped into each shared memory window, consuming extra memory for each window.
* The IPC_GLOBAL attribute must be used to force a shared memory segment into the globally-shared fourth quadrant using *shmat(2)*.
* The MAP_GLOBAL attribute must be used to force a memory-mapped file into the globally-shared fourth quadrant using *mmap(2)*.
* Processes must be in the same memory window to share data in a window. Processes can always share data in the globally-shared fourth quadrant.
* Child processes inherit the shared memory window ID.
* The shared memory window ID may be shared among a group of processes by inheritance or by use of a unique key referred to by the processes.

Shared memory windows are not needed for 64-bit applications given the huge amount of virtual address space available in the 64-bit model.

8.1.6   Page Protection

Pages of memory in PA-RISC and IPF can have two types of protection assigned to them: authorization, which is granted with a Protection ID, and access rights (read/write/execute), which are the same as the actual file permissions for shared libraries and memory-mapped files. Note that, in general, for HP-UX, text does not normally have write permission, which means that code cannot be modified in memory.

If many different memory objects are accessed within a process in HP-UX, protection ID thrashing can occur and cause a performance degradation. As mentioned in Section 6.5.4.3, "Protection ID Issues" on page 149, there is a cache of protection IDs stored in the chip of each PA-RISC and IPF processor. This cache is not large, and a protection ID entry is needed for each separate memory object accessed. For instance, each shared memory segment created requires a separate protection ID, the text segment requires an ID, and the private data segment requires an ID. HP-UX maps shared libraries using a global protection ID, so a separate ID is not needed for each shared library. Applications can easily experience protection ID thrashing or even run out of protection IDs by allocating several shared memory-mapped objects, so care needs to be taken when creating memory maps or shared memory segments in HP-UX. The mostly private address space virtual layout under IPF servers running HP-UX 11i v2 and later don't use as many protection IDs, so these protection ID issues are not as relevant.

The *mprotect(2)* system call can be used to change or check access rights on pieces of memory that have been allocated via *mmap(2)*.

8.2 Memory Organization

The way in which both virtual and physical memory is organized can affect the overall performance of the system. Some of the hardware organizations of memory were discussed in Section 6.5, "Main Memory Performance Issues" on page 142. This section discusses how HP-UX organizes the virtual memory into different page sizes to make better use of the processor's TLBs and how it chooses to allocate memory on cell-based machines to improve the memory latency and overall system throughput.

8.2.1 Variable Page Sizes

PA-RISC 2.0 and IPF-based systems typically have smaller TLBs than early PA-RISC systems that had very large off-chip TLBs. The small TLBs are a necessity for newer processors, since the CPU chip is a very expensive component, CPU chip area is a scarce resource, and TLB access time can limit the processor's frequency. compared to large TLBs, small TLBs consume less space on the CPU chip and can be accessed quickly. A small TLB, however, means that fewer virtual to physical address mappings can be held at one time, which could increase TLB misses.

To complicate matters, PA-RISC 2.0 chips don't have a block TLB and also don't have a hardware TLB walker, so TLB misses are especially costly on these chips. To offset the loss in TLB entries for PA-RISC 2.0 and IPF processors, each entry was allowed to reference different size pages (see Table 8-2), whereas in earlier designs, only a fixed-size page size could be used. Being able to map different sized pages is referred to as *variable pagesize* mapping.

In HP-UX revisions 10.20 and later, the operating system takes advantage of the variable pagesize feature when creating memory objects. Using variable pages allows for more efficient use of the processor's TLB and thus better performance due to reduced TLB misses. In addition, the use of variable-sized pages allows the operating system to represent memory more compactly. Table 8-2 shows the pagesizes allowed for various PA-RISC and IPF processors. Given the very large mappings (up to 4 GB on Itanium® 2-based systems), even a small number of

TLB entries can map huge amounts of virtual address space. HP-UX supports all of the processor pagesizes except for the 8KB page sizes on the IPF processors.

Table 8-2   TLB Pagesizes Supported on PA-RISC and IPF Processors

Processor	Pagesizes
PA-8000 *PA-8200* *PA-8500*	4 KB, 16 KB, 64 KB, 256 KB, 1 MB, 4 MB, 16 MB, 64 MB
PA-8600 *PA-8700*	4 KB, 16 KB, 64 KB, 256 KB, 1 MB, 4 MB, 16 MB, 64 MB, 256 MB, 1 GB
Itanium®	4 KB, 8 KB, 16 KB, 64 KB, 256 KB, 1 MB, 4 MB, 16 MB, 64 MB, 256 MB
Itanium® 2	4 KB, 8 KB, 16 KB, 64 KB, 256 KB, 1 MB, 4 MB, 16 MB, 64 MB, 256 MB, 1 GB, 4 GB

The ability of HP-UX to handle mapping variable-sized pages has evolved over the years. Starting with HP-UX 10.20, variable-sized pages were only used for shared memory that was locked into main memory, or for text regions that were locked into main memory. These restrictions were applied due to the complexities in modifying HP-UX to handle paging variable-sized pages from memory to disk. Most databases, however, had the ability to lock both their shared memory segments and text segments, so large performance gains could be achieved in HP-UX 10.20 even with this limited model.

In HP-UX 11.00, the variable page implementation became much more elaborate. Variable-sized pages can now be used for almost any area of memory and there are no restrictions that require pages to be locked into memory (although locking pages in memory results in HP-UX using the largest pages available on a given system, which may provide further performance advantage over default HP-UX variable page size settings). Variable-sized pages are used in the kernel, for the process's text regions, data regions, stacks, *u_area*, shared memory, and anonymous memory-mapped regions. Only for HP-UX 11i v1.6 and later are lazy swap memory objects able to use variable-sized pages. Variable pages are not used for the buffer cache or for regular memory-mapped files due to complexities involving remapping I/O. HP-UX has the most advanced variable page implementation of all commercial UNIX™ operating systems.

In general, variable-sized pages only help improve performance, given the large time penalty that TLB misses can entail. However, variable-sized pages are not without a disadvantage. Because physical memory is allocated and assigned to a process in pagesize units, overuse of variable-sized pages can result in *internal* memory fragmentation within a page. Internal fragmentation can happen when the operating system allocates a larger page, but the application only references part of the page, whether it is code or data. Had a smaller page been used, the application may have more fully utilized the entire page. This internal page fragmentation can result in under-utilization of memory, and thus more physical memory is needed to perform a specific task. This problem can be more pronounced for systems that create thousands of processes. For systems running a single large process (such as engineering and scientific applications), internal memory fragmentation is usually less of an issue.

In addition to internal fragmentation, there can also be *external* memory fragmentation caused by many processes allocating several small pages. When several smaller pages are allocated, the free memory can become fragmented, creating few large contiguous memory regions from which larger pages can be allocated.

HP-UX provides several ways to adjust how it uses variable-sized pages. By default, HP-UX will only use pages up to 16 KB in size. The default behavior can be modified globally via kernel-tuneable parameters and on a per-program basis via the *chatr(1)* command.

8.2.1.1   HP-UX Tuneables To Control Pagesizes

• The *vps_ceiling* tuneable parameter can be set to adjust the <u>maximum</u> pagesize used to anywhere from 4 KB to the maximum supported pagesize for the given platform (see Table 8-2). The default for this value is 16 KB. The *vps_pagesize* tuneable parameter can be used to set the <u>minimum</u> pagesize that HP-UX will use. The default for this tuneable is 4 KB. HP-UX will choose pages in the range *vps_pagesize* to *vps_ceiling* that are based on the memory object size.

• The default value of *vps_ceiling* is set conservatively to minimize memory fragmentation. However, with large memory setups (more than 1 GB of memory), setting this value to 1024 (1 MB) or larger may result in significant speed up of many applications while not greatly increasing memory usage.

• In general, the *vps_pagesize* tuneable should probably not be modified. Setting the *vps_pagesize* parameter larger than the default of 16 KB may result in significant internal page fragmentation. For instance, if the *vps_pagesize* was set to 256 KB, but only 64 KB of data needed to be allocated, the operating system would still use a 256 KB page to allocate the 64 KB of data, wasting 192 KB of memory. Even setting *vps_pagesize* to something like 16 KB can result in wasted memory due to the page fragmentation issue. However, for systems with multiple gigabytes of memory and lots of processes, setting *vps_pagesize* to 16 KB may improve overall performance due to potentially using fewer TLB entries, but most likely this will increase the amount of memory needed to run all of the applications. Unfortunately, experimentation is the only way to determine if there is a significant performance increase with an acceptable memory usage increase.

• Finally, the *vps_chatr_ceiling* tuneable parameter limits the maximum pagesize allowed by any individual program that may have specified a maximum pagesize via the *chatr(1)* command. This is a system resource management tuneable parameter that is intended to limit the ability of individual programs to set their own maximum pagesize above a specific value. In general, this tuneable should not be lowered from its default value of the maximum available pagesize on a given platform. The reason this value should not be lowered is that many important database and technical applications will specify large maximum pagesizes via the *chatr(1)* command, and lowering *vps_chatr_ceiling* would make these programs run slower.

8.2.1.2   Setting Pagesize With *Chatr* or the Linker

The maximum pagesize allowed for a specific executable can be modified via the *chatr(1)* command or via equivalent linker options. The maximum pagesize for both the text segment and data segment can be manipulated individually.

The *+pi chatr(1)* option (and linker option) sets the text segment maximum pagesize, while the *+pd chatr(1)* option (and linker option) sets the data segment maximum pagesize. The value used with the *+pd* option also controls the pagesize for the stack, shared memory segments, and memory-mapped regions that are directly created by the executable.

For applications that typically access gigabytes of data via shared memory, memory mapped files, or directly via the heap, we recommend that you set the data segment's maximum pagesize to the value of "L," which will instruct the operating system to use up to the largest available pagesize supported on the given hardware. One caveat with using "L" is that additional memory consumption may occur when performing something like a processor upgrade if the newer processor supports a larger pagesize than the previous processor due to fragmentation issues.

For the text page size, typically a value between 1 MB and 16 MB works well depending on the size of the executable's text segment. The *chatr(1)* size used for text should be the largest page equal to the text size or just smaller than the text size. For example, an executable with a 12 MB text segment could use the *+pi 4 MB* option to *chatr(1)* to set the maximum text pagesize to 4 MB. This would most likely result in the operating system choosing to map the text segment using three 4 MB pages, which would be very efficient and waste little memory, given that the text segment is normally a shared memory object in HP-UX.

Depending on what is being allocated and the process's access pattern, the operating system will choose page sizes up to the limits allowed by the system and *chatr(1)* tunables. The *chatr(1)* tuneables will have precedence over the system tuneable *vps_ceiling*, so an individual executable can obtain pages larger than *vps_ceiling* if it has individual segments *chatr*'ed to a pagesize larger than *vps_ceiling*. Maximum *chatr(1)* pagesizes are limited, however, by the system tuneable *vps_chatr_ceiling*.

8.2.1.3   General Pagesize Information

The size of memory allocated has a large effect on the number and size of pages allocated by the operating system. For example, if a 1 MB shared memory segment is created, the operating system will attempt to allocate a single 1 MB page for this segment if values of the tunable parameters allow. However, if a 1020 KB (4 KB less than 1 MB) segment is allocated instead, then the operating system would probably allocate three 256 KB pages, three 64 KB pages, three 16 KB pages, and three 4 KB pages for a total of twelve pages. So, rounding up memory allocation to a larger multiple pagesize value can help reduce the total number of pages that the operating system must allocate, but it will create some amount of internal fragmentation.

For dynamic memory allocation such as from the heap or stack, HP-UX uses algorithms to gradually increase the pagesize used based on the amount of activity seen in the recent past, as well as based on the size requested. When there is severe memory pressure, the memory management system may be forced to use smaller pages due to a lack of free large pages. The memory management system will tend to page-out smaller pages to make room for new memory requests versus larger pages, given that larger pages may tend to be referenced more often than smaller pages because of the larger amount of data contained in a large page.

Internal memory fragmentation for a particular executable can be controlled via the *chatr(1)* command to explicitly set a given application's maximum pagesize to something smaller than the system default. For example, setting the +*pi* and +*pd* options to both 4 KB will cause an application to use only 4 KB pages, which will minimize the memory usage, but probably cause severe TLB pressure. System memory fragmentation in general can be controlled via the *vps_pagesize* and *vps_ceiling* parameters. Keeping these at the system defaults will help reduce memory fragmentation. In general, however, systems are now configured with larger amounts of physical memory. The cost of this additional physical memory compared to the cost of taking TLB misses and significantly slowing the performance of the application is usually worth the extra price paid for the additional memory. So, using large pagesizes and potentially increasing the cost of the system due to the need for additional memory is usually not a bad trade-off.

8.2.2   Cell Local Memory

As described in Section 6.7.11, "Superdome" on page 160, several HP-UX servers (such as Superdome) are configured using a cell architecture. These cell-based systems distribute memory among all of the cells in the system, compared to locating memory in one central location. When a processor must access memory residing in a remote cell, the latency to access the memory is longer than accessing memory located in the local cell.

Before HP-UX 11i v2 (11.23), all of the memory on these systems was cache-line-interleaved among the cells. Cache line interleaving places the first cache line of a memory page on one cell, the second cache line on the next cell, and so on until all cells contain one cache line, and then the process repeats. This interleaving has the effect of scattering memory accesses among all cells. This scattering makes the overall memory latency look uniform even though accessing memory on distant cells takes longer than accessing memory on a local cell.

In the global sense, for general purpose systems, it is a good design to scatter the cache lines across the cells, because processes may migrate from processor to processor and cell to cell for load balancing purposes. This has the effect of evening out the time spent in accessing memory among all of the processes on the system. For those system administrators who cannot or do not wish to tune memory accesses by processes, this is probably a good compromise.

With the release of HP-UX 11i v2 and the IPF versions of the cell-based servers, the concept of *cell local memory (CLM)* was introduced. All of the processors, memory, and I/O residing on a given cell constitute a *locality domain*. The firmware on the IPF cell-based servers was modified to allow part of the memory to be interleaved between cells, as before, and part of the memory to stay local to each cell. The HP-UX virtual memory system was then modified in HP-UX 11i v2 to allocate memory from either the interleaved pool or the cell local pool, depending on what type of memory needed to be allocated, or based on parameters passed to various system calls.

8.2.2.1   Performance Aspects of CLM

Using CLM can result in significant performance improvements for two reasons. First, accessing CLM typically can be up to twice as fast as accessing the farthest remote memory. If memory requests can be serviced faster, then the CPU has to wait less on memory misses and can be utilized more efficiently. Second, the aggregate memory bandwidth within the individual cells is typically much higher than the overall system bandwidth achievable when communicating between cells. This means memory-intensive applications can simultaneously access CLM at a much higher rate than if they all accessed memory interleaved among the cells. This typically leads to much higher scalability for memory-intensive applications on systems with large numbers of cells. This increased bandwidth and decreased latency associated with CLM can result in large performance gains (up to 2-3 times) depending on the application. In particular, applications that access a lot of memory benefit the most from CLM because these applications tend to have more cache misses, given the huge amounts of data being accessed. Many technical applications benefit from CLM, as do database applications such as Oracle.

Using CLM, however, can also negatively affect system performance if it is not used properly. For instance, if all memory for a process was allocated locally from a particular cell and the process migrated to another cell, the resulting memory accesses would always be remote, and the overall memory latency could be worse than the default of cell-interleaved memory. In addition, if some piece of memory is shared among multiple processes residing in multiple cells, but the memory was allocated local to a single cell, a bottleneck can form on the cell containing the memory, as all misses for the piece of memory need to be serviced from a single cell. HP-UX is not able to help out in these situations because it currently purposely does not migrate memory pages between cells once the memory is allocated, so CLM will mostly reside in one cell for the life of a process. One exception to this, however, is that if a piece of memory is paged out due to memory pressure, it may be paged back in on a different cell.

8.2.2.2   Configuring CLM

Currently, CLM is not enabled by default in HP-UX. This a conservative default, since not all applications may see a benefit, and choosing too much cell-local memory may actually result in worse performance than using all interleaved memory (the default), considering the negative performance aspects described above.

To specify how memory should be distributed between the cell-interleaved memory and cell local memory, the *parmgr* utility, *parcreate(1)*, or *parmodify(1)* commands can be used. A good starting point is probably 20% of memory in each cell should be cell local. Depending on the application, one may want more or less than this amount. Highly parallel technical applications may benefit from more cell local memory because they tend to have large amounts of private data with high numbers of cache misses. Applications that make extensive use of shared memory may benefit less from cell local memory because shared memory is allocated from the interleaved pool by default.

Note that not all memory can be made cell local. There needs to be some memory that is interleaved on the system for use by the operating system. However, not all cells need to use interleaved memory, so a few cells could use interleaved memory, while others could use cell local only. There is one performance aspect, however, of allocating too few cells for the interleaved pool. Most of the kernel memory is allocated from the interleaved pool, so having too few cells allocated to interleaved memory can result in memory bottlenecks for applications that spend a significant amount of time in the operating system, such as databases.

8.2.2.3   Using CLM

Once some amount of CLM has been configured, the operating system will start using it. By default, process private data, such as the stack and heap, will always be allocated from cell local memory, while shared data, such as text or shared memory, will be allocated from interleaved memory. Cell local memory is used for process private data because typically this data is not shared among other processes. A multi-threaded application, however, will share the heap memory and therefore a mechanism is provided to override the default cell local memory placement. For shared data, the interleaved pool works better to prevent a single cell from being saturated with memory requests. If a single cell were used for shared data, processes sharing the data in other cells would send requests to the single cell, causing a system bottleneck.

Overriding Private Data Placement

For multi-threaded processes, the private data allocated from the heap is shared among all threads in a process. Under CLM, this can potentially result in very poor performance if the heap is allocated from a single cell, or even just a few cells. Given this problem, HP-UX has a way to specify that a given process should allocate its private heap data from the interleaved memory area instead of from CLM. The *chatr(1)* command can be used with the *+id enable* option to specify that a given process should use the interleaved pool for private heap memory. The default behavior is to use CLM for private heap memory. The allocation behavior is inherited across process *forks* but not across a process *exec*.

Overriding Shared Memory Placement

To override the default behavior of shared memory allocation, HP-UX has modified some memory allocation system calls to accept hints indicating where memory should be allocated. For instance, the *shmget* system call can be called using the IPC_MEM_LOCAL flag to create the shared memory segment from cell local memory, or it can be called with the IPC_MEM_FIRST_TOUCH option to allow the memory to be allocated in the cell where the first process accesses it. Additionally, the *mmap* call can use the MAP_MEM_LOCAL flag to specify that memory should be mapped as cell local or it can use the MAP_MEM_FIRST_TOUCH to specify that the first process touching the memory should map it as cell local. Applications that are "cell aware" may benefit from creating a shared memory region per cell. This could greatly reduce memory access latency if the application could partition large pieces of its memory such that processes and threads local to a particular cell used data from the shared memory segment on the given cell.

CLM Launch Policies

Given that HP-UX does not currently migrate cell local pages once they have been allocated in a locality domain, initial launch placement of processes is usually critical to achieving good performance with CLM. The *mpsched(1)* command can be used to specify where processes launch after being forked from a parent process. The launch policy is important because the process private data and stack memory, which are allocated from CLM, may be allocated shortly after a process is launched, depending on the application. Therefore, having a good initial placement of processes is important for evenly allocating local memory among the cells. Table 8-3 describes the per-process launch policies supported. The launch policies are inherited

Table 8-3 *mpsched* Process Launch Policies

Policy	Description
RR	Round Robin. Under this policy, direct child processes are launched one per locality domain in a round robin manner. Once each locality domain has launched a process, the initial domain is chosen again.
LL	Least Loaded. Under this policy, processes are launched on the locality domain that is least loaded with other active processes. This is a non-deterministic algorithm, given that it is based on the load of the system, which may change dynamically at any time.
FILL	Fill a domain. Under this policy, direct child processes are launched on every processor in a locality domain before moving to the next locality domain. Once all domains have been filled, the initial domain is selected again.
RR_TREE	This is similar to RR, but all descendents of a process participate in the RR algorithm versus just the direct children. The behavior of this algorithm is non-deterministic, given that processes launched from the children of the initiating process may launch in a different order from one invocation to the next.
FILL_TREE	This is similar to FILL, but all descendents of a process participate in the FILL algorithm versus just the direct children. The behavior of this algorithm is non-deterministic, given that processes launched from the children of the initiating process may launch in a different order from one invocation to the next.
PACKED	Pack a domain. Under this policy, all processes forked from a process are launched in the same locality domain as the parent process.

Table 8-3   *mpsched* **Process Launch Policies**

Policy	Description
NONE	The default HP-UX launch policy is used. (NOTE: the default can be subject to change from release to release.)

among all descendents created by a process. When using the *mpsched(1)* command, the resulting processes that get created will stay bound to the initial locality domain where they were launched. The processes will then only be allowed to run on other processors within that locality domain. This is done given that HP-UX does not support page migration between locality domains. Therefore, if a process was moved to another locality domain, excessive cross cell traffic would result as the process accessed its cell local memory residing on its launch locality domain.

The following is an example of how to launch a process named "clm_test" that will create four worker processes using the *mpsched(1)* round robin launch policy on a system with four locality domains:

```
# mpsched -P RR clm_test
Pid 1234: bound to locality domain 0 using the round-robin process
launch policy
```

Performing the *mpsched -q* command shows the resulting bindings for the processes created:

```
# mpsched -q
Pid 1234: bound to locality domain 0 using the round-robin process
launch policy
Pid 1235: bound to locality domain 1 using the round-robin process
launch policy
Pid 1236: bound to locality domain 2 using the round-robin process
launch policy
Pid 1237: bound to locality domain 3 using the round-robin process
launch policy
Pid 1238: bound to locality domain 0 using the round-robin process
launch policy
```

Notice that each child process (processes 1235-1238) was placed on its own locality domain, allowing it to allocate private memory and use CPUs associated with that domain.

The launch policy one chooses will usually be dependent on the workload. Most workloads, however, work well with the round robin (RR) policy, so this should be used as a first attempt. FILL should be used as a second attempt. Note that the RR and FILL policies are preferred for typical applications, while the RR_TREE and FILL_TREE policies are intended for special situations where the application may benefit from a whole-tree launch policy.

For complete control over launch policies in an application, HP-UX also provides all of these launch policies via the *mpctl(2)* system call. See the *mpctl(2)* man page for specific usage. By using the *mpctl(2)* system call, a program can have complete control over how subprocesses (and threads) are launched. Some could potentially use round robin, while others could use FILL or PACKED. The behavior of the child processes and threads would dictate which policies to choose.

Finally, processor sets (see Section 7.3.3, "Processor Sets" on page 188) can be used to configure processors such that all of the processors for a given cell reside in the same processor set. Then any processes allocated to the processor set would be cell local without needing to use *mpsched(1)*.

8.3 Paging Control

HP-UX systems use a variety of strategies for handling high demand on memory resources. These include paging, swapping, deactivation, memory management, and locking.

8.3.1   Paging

Paging is the process by which memory pages are brought into memory and removed from memory. Various algorithms for paging have been used in different HP-UX systems. *Page-ins* occur when a process starts up, when a process requests dynamic memory, and during page faults after a page-out, a swap-in, or a reactivation. Page-ins are always performed as needed. Code that is never executed never gets paged in.

Page-outs and *page-frees* occur when memory is scarce. The pager daemon *vhand* (further described below) does page-outs only for dirty data pages; text (code) pages and unmodified data pages are simply freed.

It is important to note that with modern computer systems, excessive paging can have a very adverse effect on overall performance. Performance can be severely hit with paging because computer processors are so much faster than disks. Having to wait for memory to be paged-in and out to disks can be very time-consuming. Another negative aspect of paging is that it can cause external fragmentation of the memory. This fragmentation will cause fewer large pages to be available for use by applications. Fragmentation occurs because as the operating system frees large pages under memory pressure, the large pages will tend to be broken up into smaller pages to satisfy the new memory requests. Then, when the large page that was paged out is ready to be brought back in, there may be few large pages available and small pages must be chosen instead.

8.3.2   Operation of *vhand*

Vhand, also known as the page daemon, is the system process that manages the paging out and freeing of data pages in a dynamic buffer cache. The name *vhand* was suggested by the two parts ("hands") of the daemon. The *age hand* cycles through memory structures, clearing the "Recently Referenced" bit in the PDIR (page directory) and flushing the TLB entry. The *steal hand* follows, freeing or paging out those pages that the age hand has cleared and which the application has not accessed since the time the "Recently Referenced" bit was cleared. See Figure 8-7.

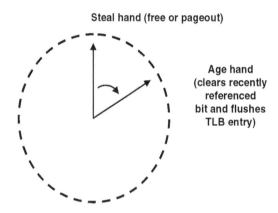

Figure 8-7   Two-Handed Clock Algorithm of *vhand*, the HP-UX Page Daemon

The TLB must be flushed to force a page fault, even though the page may still be in memory. Memory pressure has a negative impact on CPU utilization, because the CPU must deal with more TLB misses, page faults, and other memory-management housekeeping.

8.3.3   Swapping

Swapping is an event that occurred with user processes in HP-UX systems earlier than 10.0 when memory was very scarce or when the virtual memory system was thrashing. The algorithm for swapping depended on paging rates and on the amount of free memory in the system. In *swapping out*, the entire process, including private data, the *u_area*, and the *vfd/dbd* data structures, were written to the swap space in a series of large (up to 256 K) I/O operations. Shared text (code) was not swapped, but freed, and the process was not removed from the run queue. The opposite process, *swapping in*, required a large number of page faults to bring back code and data as the process started executing again.

Since a swapped process remains on the run queue, its priority will soon be improved to the point where it is the highest priority process again, and then it will be swapped back in. This

potentially starts the severe memory pressure again as the process that was swapped (and probably had a very large RSS) executes again, page-faulting in its pages.

The swap area is used for both paging and swapping (pre-10.0). It is the backing store for
private data, pageable process structures, shared memory, private text (executables with the
EXEC_MAGIC format), and shared text (where the sticky bit is set and the executable is remotely
accessed). *Swapper* was the process responsible for swapping processes out. Swapping is no
longer implemented as all-or-nothing, but deactivated processes are the first to be paged out.

8.3.4   Deactivation

Swapping out has a tremendous negative impact on the system. Because of this, "swapping" has been implemented through *deactivation*, starting with HP-UX 10.0. Deactivation
occurs when memory is very scarce, or when the virtual memory system is thrashing. The algorithm determines when deactivation is needed based on paging rates, the number of running processes, the amount of CPU idleness, and the amount of free memory.

In deactivation, a user process may be removed from the run queue for up to twenty minutes. Process structures (*u_area*) are written to the swap area after all the pages have been paged
out. A candidate for deactivation is chosen based on the process size, priority, and time in memory, as well as on whether or not the process is interactive, whether or not it is serialized, and
whether it is running or sleeping. *Glance* shows deactivation and reactivation statistics, but there
is no utility that can give a list of processes that are currently deactivated. *Sar* and *vmstat* continue to refer to "swapping," although the term now means "deactivation". The process *swapper*
is now responsible for deactivating processes rather than for swapping them out.

The biggest advantages (+) of deactivation over swapping, from a system perspective, are:

+ Deactivation causes pages to be trickled out to the disk by *vhand* rather than all at once
  with multiple large I/Os.
+ With deactivation, the process stops executing for a while, so it does not immediately
  cause its pages to be brought in again.

Of course, the user of the deactivated process may not like having to wait up to twenty minutes
before forward progress continues.

8.3.5   Memory Allocation Management with PRM

On HP-UX 10.20 and later systems, Process Resource Manager (PRM), working with the
standard memory manager, lets you allocate memory amounts or percentages independent of
CPU allocations. Process groups are guaranteed a minimum percentage of memory and, optionally, a maximum percentage. This guarantees a fair share to a process group, but not necessarily
to a given process. Shares are enforced when paging is occurring; processes in an oversubscribed PRM group are suppressed, and the suppressed processes return memory to the free
pool. You can choose to suppress all the processes in a process group, or just the largest. In addi-

tion, processes can be specified to be restricted from suppression by listing them in the
/opt/prm/exempt file.

Starting with HP-UX 11i v1.0, there is a second memory manager that is used by PRM
called the *prm2d* manager. The original PRM manager is referred to as the *prm0d* manager. The
prm2d manager is the default in HP-UX 11i and later releases. This manager works with HP-UX
to actually partition physical memory into different memory partitions that are used by the configured groups. Each memory partition pages separately compared to the global paging scheme
with the *prm0d* manager. Using *prm2d*, a PRM group's memory can be marked as *isolated*,
which will not allow other groups to use its memory and will not allow the isolated group to use
other groups' memory. The memory for a group can also be capped so that if a process in a
group requests more memory than is available to the group, other processes in the group will be
forced to swap to free-up memory. With the *prm0d* policy, the memory cap is a soft limit, not a
hard limit like with *prm2d*. Exceeding the cap with *prm0d* simply causes other processes in the
PRM group to be suppressed before processes in uncapped groups.

In general, under the *prm2d* policy, when a group oversubscribes its memory use, it can
borrow memory from other groups as long as its memory use is not capped or it is using isolated
memory. Once memory pressure begins, borrowed pages are reclaimed from the groups which
borrowed the memory.

Some side effects of using PRM for memory allocation are:

• PRM reports available memory—the maximum amount of memory that is available for
  allocation to user processes.

• PRM does not suppress a process that locks memory; however, use of locked memory will
  affect other processes in the process group because the locked memory counts as memory
  used by the group.

• Allocations may interact with CPU allocations in such a way that a process group may not
  use all of the CPU it is allocated if it cannot use any more memory.

• If the PRM memory daemon dies unexpectedly, processes will remain suppressed until
  prmrecover is used.

• Process groups will exceed their allocations, even with a cap (except for *prm2d*-managed
  groups), in the absence of memory pressure.

Using PRM can be a powerful way to partition memory on an HP-UX system, especially
when using the *prm2d* memory manager. The ability to have separate resource groups contend
for memory only within their group gives an administrator much more control over the critical
memory resource. Critical applications, such as database servers, can be assigned memory pools
that can be dedicated to their use to prevent unwanted swapping of the application's memory.

8.3.6   Locking Memory

HP-UX provides the ability to lock memory objects into memory using the *mlock(2)* and *plock(2)* system calls. By locking memory objects, you can guarantee that the locked memory object will not be paged to disk. Locking also provides an additional hint to the operating system that large pages can be used because the OS does not have to worry about potential issues with needing to break apart the large pages later for a page-out event. A process requesting locking must either have super-user privileges, or be a member of a group having the MLOCK privilege (see *setprivgrp(1M)*).

The *mlock(2)* system call is used by simply specifying a memory address and length to lock. Any pages within this range will be locked if the calling process has the MLOCK privilege and valid access to all of the pages. The *plock(2)* system call, on the other hand, locks specific memory objects within a process. For example, the TXTLOCK option can be used to lock the process text into memory, and the DATLOCK option can be used to lock the data segment. It is not recommended to mix using the *plock(2)* and *mlock(2)* calls in the same application, as they can interact with each other in unexpected ways.

8.3.7   Sticky Bit

The *sticky bit* is a mode setting on executable files indicating that shared code is to be paged or swapped out to the swap area due to memory pressure instead of being discarded and paged back in from the original *a.out* file, since text is not normally modifiable. Under these circumstances, star-up of the executable may be faster from the swap area than from the *a.out* file itself, which is beneficial for frequently executed programs like *vi*. However, text pages are almost always shared, non-modifiable, and merely deallocated when memory pressure occurs. The sticky bit is set on an executable using the *chmod(2)* command. In current implementations of the sticky bit (10.0 and later), the bit is honored when *a.out* is remote (for example, when it is mounted across an NFS mount) and when a local swap area is present. In addition, if the *page_text_to_local* kernel parameter is set to 1, then all executables behave as if the sticky bit is set. This may be useful in distributed environments where programs are executed remotely.

8.3.8   Serialization

Serialize() is a system call and command that was introduced with HP-UX 10.0. It can improve performance when the overhead for paging in and out would be excessive. The use of the *serialize()* call provides a hint to the memory management system that the process is large, and that throughput will probably increase if the process is run serially with respect to other "serialized" processes. Serialization has no effect on processes that are not serialized.

Serialize() lets a process run for up to one hour before another serialized process is allowed to run; it is effective only when there is a shortfall of memory and when there are several serialized processes. There is no tool that shows you whether or not a process has been serialized.

The following is an example of using *serialize()*.

From Bob's Consulting Log—Five engineers were running a compute-bound application that used as its input a very large data set, with each engineer supplying a different data set. I/O was only done at the end to write out the results. Normally, the five copies of the application would run concurrently and be timesliced, causing forced context switches. Accessing five very large data sets caused such severe memory pressure that the applications actually ran for longer than 5 X the average time for one copy because of this additional overhead.

Each user saw consistent slow performance and roughly the same execution time. After serializing these processes, the users saw inconsistent performance and total execution times. The first process would execute in one-fifth the average time; the last process would execute in 5 X the average time. The important thing is that *overhead on the system had been significantly reduced*.

8.4 File Access

8.4.1 Dynamic Buffer Cache

The use of the file system buffer cache is another important area where memory bottlenecks can be observed. The storage of pages in buffers means quicker access to the data on the second and successive reads, because they do not have to be read in again from disk or across the network. It is possible to set the size of the file system buffer cache, and the cache can be set up as either dynamic or static.

A dynamic buffer cache is enabled when the system parameters *bufpages* and *nbuf* are both set to zero; this is the default for HP-UX 10.0 and later. The buffer cache grows as the buffer page faults occur, which in turn results in pages being added. The cache shrinks as the page daemon *vhand* reclaims pages and *syncer* trickles out dirty buffers. Trickling is a process by which the *syncer* process attempts to avoid large spikes of I/O by writing out pages in small groups.

An advantage of the dynamic buffer cache is the fact that when buffers are not in use, the memory they occupy can be reclaimed for other purposes. The use of dynamic caches makes the most sense in scientific and engineering applications, which may alternate between intensive I/O and intensive virtual memory demands.

A big disadvantage with the dynamic buffer cache, however, is that large memory pages can become easily fragmented due to the use of only 4 KB virtual memory pages for the buffer cache. As the buffer cache dynamically grows, it will tend to split larger virtual pages into small 4 KB pages for its use. When the buffer cache shrinks, the 4 KB pages that get returned to the main memory pool most likely will not be contiguous in memory. Not having contiguous 4 KB pages will result in the operating system not being able to allocate large pages (those greater than 4 KB) for future memory allocations.

Dynamic caches are not always the best strategy: most database environments and many other applications will run better with a fixed cache size. Growth and shrinkage of the cache may in fact cause performance degradation due to issues such as external large page fragmentation. Finally, given the dynamic aspect of the dynamic buffer cache, application performance can be less predictable.

8.4.2 Memory-Mapped Files

An alternative to the use of the file system buffer cache for file I/O is the use of memory-mapped files. The *mmap(2)* system call creates a mapping of the contents of a file to the process's virtual address space. Private memory-mapped files are mapped into the Private Data space; shared memory-mapped files are mapped into shared quadrants. With memory mapping, I/O is not buffered through the buffer cache but is page-faulted in and paged out. The backing store is the original file, and *vhand* writes the pages to the original file for shared memory-mapped files. For private mappings, the swap area is used.

The *madvise()* system call can be used to specify random or sequential access to a memory-mapped file; sequential access results in clustered reads. Starting in HP-UX 10.0, the kernel clusters the reads if sequential access is detected.

Advantages (+) of using memory-mapped files include the following:

+ After setup, data is accessed by pointer, so no system calls (such as *read()* and *write()*) are used to access the data; thus there may be fewer context switches.
+ Dirty data can be flushed by request. Reads cause page faults unless they are already in memory, and page-outs of dirty data directly to the file are initiated by *vhand*.
+ The data is not double buffered (meaning that it is stored only once in memory, in the process address space), and no swap space is allocated for the pages associated with the memory-mapped files. When memory-mapped files are not being used, data is stored in both the process VAS and in the buffer cache.

The use of memory-mapped files does not necessarily mean better performance. Here are some of their disadvantages (-):

- They require significant coding changes to the application. The most appropriate use is when you have a lot of data and do not want the swap area to be too large.
- Memory-mapped pages are not trickled out to the disk by *syncer* as is the case with the buffer cache. Instead, they are either written out a page at a time by the *vhand* daemon or written out over a range specified by the *msync(2)* system call.
- The *mmap* files are only partially synchronized with the buffer cache, so modifying an *mmap* file at the same time as modifying a copy in the buffer cache can cause corruption.
- Accessing the memory-mapped file may not result in a reduction in system overhead because a system trap is needed to access each unreferenced portion of the memory-mapped file. The number of traps executed depends on the page size used for the memory-mapped region.

- There may be protection ID fault thrashing.

Table 8-4 shows the maximum file size that can be mapped as well as the maximum combined size of all shared mapped files, all shared memory, and all shared libraries.

Table 8-4   Memory-Mapped File Size Limits

	32-bit applications	64-bit applications (PA-RISC)	64-bit applications (IPF)
Maximum memory-mapped file size	1 GB	4 TB	~2^{63} bytes
Combined maximum size for shared mapped files, all shared memory, and all shared libraries without shared memory windows	1.75 GB	~8 TB	~2^{63} bytes

Use of memory-mapped files requires considerable care. Concurrent access to the same file by traditional file system calls and by memory-mapping can produce corrupted data. The user cannot always specify the mapped address range, and only one fixed contiguous mapping of a shared mapped file can exist; no address aliasing is possible. Even if more than one process is accessing the file, both processes must map the file in the same way. Separate calls to *mmap(2)* for the same file might result in non-contiguous virtual addresses, depending on what occurred on the system between calls; this may cause application problems. Extending a memory-mapped file might result in an ENOMEM error to the application if global shared memory space is full. Variable-sized pages are only used for anonymous memory mappings (not backed by a file). Furthermore, using the MAP_NORESERVE flag on HP-UX 11i v1.0 and earlier operating systems will result in only fixed 4 KB pages being used for the memory-mapped region. Given the MAP_NORESERVE limitation on some versions of the operating system care should be taken to not specify this flag if performance matters to the application.

8.4.3   Memory-Mapped Semaphores

Memory-mapped semaphores may be used with memory-mapped files or with an anonymous memory object created with *mmap()*. These semaphores require additional memory (at least one page), although multiple semaphores may be located on the same page. Memory-mapped semaphores are binary (set or clear) instead of counting. They are managed with the *msem_init()*, *msem_lock()*, *msem_unlock()*, and *msem_remove()* system calls. Although memory-mapped semaphores consume more memory than do traditional System V semaphores, they are much more efficient. Their use will usually improve both application and system performance.

Memory-mapped semaphores are mentioned here for consistency and completeness since they are implemented as part of the memory-mapped file implementation. Their employment in a user process is really an application design or optimization choice that may improve CPU utilization. Application design is discussed in Chapter 13, "Designing Applications for Performance" on page 419. See especially "System V Semaphores" on page 424 and "Memory-Mapped Semaphores" on page 425.

8.5 Process and Thread Execution

As a process or thread begins execution, the operating system looks at its magic type and other attributes that may have been specified at link time or with the *chatr(1)* command. Based on the attributes, the operating system will use a specific allocation scheme when allocating virtual memory. Processes are created via *fork(2)/vfork(2)* system calls, while threads are created with the *pthread_create(3T)* call.

8.5.1 *fork* and *vfork*

Virtual memory bottlenecks may also occur as the result of the *fork(2)* system call, which creates a new process derived from a currently running one. With *fork(2)*, the VAS data structures—virtual frame descriptors (VFDs) and disk block descriptors (DBDs)—are copied for use by the child process; this may even require page-outs to provide enough additional memory. Full swap space reservation is made for the child process. Furthermore, copy-on-write is implemented for the parent—that is, the child process receives a copy of the data page before the parent writes. Moreover, copy-on-access is implemented for the child, which means that a fresh copy of data is created whenever the child writes or reads data.

Vfork(2) creates a new process like *fork(2)*, but instead of copying VAS structures, it temporarily borrows the virtual address space and thread of control of the parent process, which makes it much more efficient than *fork(2)*. No swap space reservation is necessary for the child. When using *vfork(2)*, the parent waits, suspending execution, and the child must be coded to call *exec(2)* or *exit(2)* immediately; these calling conventions must be used. *Vfork(2)* saves the resources of CPU time and required memory for copying the VAS structures. The larger the process, the greater the amount of overhead that is saved.

From Bob's Consulting Log—I was called in to diagnose a workstation performance problem. The customer was running a large engineering design application. The application ran well until the engineer used a feature that allowed a shell escape to type a system command. Performance suddenly degraded significantly: the disk drive could be heard performing I/Os for about 90 seconds, and then, finally, the shell prompt appeared.

What I found was that the system had only 128 MB of memory, and the engineer was calling up a model of a satellite that took over 150 MB of data space. This resulted in physical memory being totally filled, plus some of the data being written to the swap area.

When the engineer did a shell escape, the application called *fork(2)*, which copied all of the VAS structures associated with the application. These VAS structures were quite large because of the 150 MB of data space. The copying not only took some time, but it also caused paging out to occur to make room for the new copy of the VAS structures. However, to do the shell escape, the application now called *exec(2)* to start up the shell. The *exec(2)* threw away the VAS structures that were just copied and created new ones for the shell process!

The solution was to convince the third party software supplier to change the *fork(2)* call to a *vfork(2)* call. When they made this change, the large VAS structures were no longer copied, and the shell prompt appeared in less than a second.

8.5.2   pthread_create

The *pthread_create(3T)* system call is made to create a new thread of execution within a process. Threads share the memory objects of the process where they are created, so there is little if any virtual address space setup that needs to take place when creating a new thread. This the main reason why threads can be created much faster than an entire process.

8.6 *Malloc*'ed Memory

For the "C" language, process private and thread global memory can be allocated via the *malloc()* library call. HP-UX will allocate the requested memory using the largest pages possible based on the general large page parameters set up in the kernel or via the process's large page parameters. HP-UX provides the *mallopt()* call and environment variables to control the performance of the *malloc()* routine.

8.6.1   Mallopt

The *mallopt* call allows the application to modify the way the *malloc()* function works. The important options that can be set via *mallopt()* are M_MXFAST, M_NMBLKS, and M_GRAIN, which control a feature known as *small block allocation*.

- Setting the M_MXFAST option indicates that all requests below M_MXFAST bytes in size should be allocated in M_NMBLKS chunks. The default for this is 0 for PA-RISC, which effectively disables the feature by default. For IPF, the default is 512 so it enables the feature by default.

- The M_NMBLKS parameter specifies the number of M_MXFAST blocks that get allocated at one time. The default value for M_NMBLKS is 100, and any value specified for M_NMBLKS must be greater than 1.

- The M_GRAIN option specifies the value in bytes that all requests below M_MXFAST in size should be rounded up to. For instance, if M_GRAIN were set to 32, then all requests smaller than M_MXFAST would be rounded up to a multiple of 32 bytes.

In general, the default values used for these parameters are satisfactory for most programs. However, if many small pieces of memory are being allocated and freed by an application, then setting these parameters may be beneficial. For instance, if an application always allocates 128-byte quantities, then it might want to set M_MXFAST to 129. Only via experimentation can any individual application determine what works best for it. Also, be aware that once these values have been set and the first allocation takes place, the values can no longer be adjusted within that process.

8.6.2 Environment Options

HP-UX also provides a few environment options to control the *malloc()* implementation. The _M_ARENA_OPTS and _M_SBA_OPTS environment variables control the number of *malloc()* arenas used for threaded applications and the small buffer allocator options, respectively.

8.6.2.1 _M_ARENA_OPTS

The _M_ARENA_OPTS environment variable allows the user to configure the number of *malloc* arenas allocated and the number of 4 KB pages that are used to fill each arena when it becomes depleted. *Malloc* arenas allow different threads in a multi-threaded environment to simultaneously allocate memory via *malloc()* at the same time. If arenas were not used, different threads *malloc*'ing memory would probably block on locks protecting the *malloc* pools. Arenas allow different threads to potentially access different arenas at the same time and therefore bypass lock contention during memory allocation. The more threads an application has, the more arenas that should be allocated. The default number of arenas created for a multi-threaded application is eight. The number that can be allocated is in the range from 1 to 64.

In addition to the number of arenas, this environment variable specifies the number of 4 KB pages allocated each time a given arena becomes depleted of memory. The default value is 32 or 128 KB. The valid range for the refill size is from 1 to 4096. If a lot of memory is being allocated or the number of arenas is small, then larger refill values should be used. Smaller values can be used for light memory allocation or when many arenas are used.

The format of the environment variable is *arenas:fill pages*.

8.6.2.2 _M_SBA_OPTS

The _M_SBA_OPTS control how the small block allocator works. The small block allocator tries to optimize small *malloc* requests, given that applications making small requests tend to make a lot of them compared to applications *malloc*'ing large pieces of memory. The format of the small block allocator option is *maxfast:numlblks:grain*. These values work identically to the M_MXFAST, M_NMBLKS, and M_GRAIN *mallopt* options described earlier. HP-UX provides the _M_SBA_OPTS environment variable to set these values because *mallopt* can't be used early enough for C++ and Java applications. Thus programs compiled with C++ or using Java can use the environment variable to make sure the small block allocator is set up when it needs to be.

In addition to the _M_SBA_OPTS environment variable, there are three global variables that can be set to manipulate the *maxfast*, *nmblks*, and *grain* values on IPF platforms. These globals are *__hp_malloc_maxfast*, *__hp_malloc_num_smallblocks*, and *__hp_malloc_grain*. Setting these globals can override the _M_SBA_OPTS environment variable. Setting *__hp_malloc_maxfast* to -1 will disable the small block allocator. The small block allocator is disabled by default for PA-RISC and enabled by default for IPF.

8.6.3   General *Malloc* Issues

It is important to note that when using *malloc()*, the memory that is allocated and later freed is only returned to the operating system when the process exits. This means that if a process allocates a lot of memory and frees it, from the standpoint of the operating system and other processes, that process will still be using all of the initially allocated memory. Subsequent memory accesses from a process, however, will use any free memory that may be available before requesting new memory from the operating system.

Finally, be aware that the memory pools used by *malloc()* may become fragmented over time. Therefore, the amount of contiguous memory available may not match the amount requested. For instance, a program may request a 1 MB chunk of memory, but even if there is 1 MB of memory that has been previously *free*'d, the *malloc* library may have to request a new 1 MB piece of memory from the operating system to satisfy the request, because the 1 MB of memory available may not be contiguous. The *malloc* code does make attempts to coalesce memory when it is *free*'d, but depending on the *malloc* and *free* patterns, fragmentation of the memory can still occur.

8.7   System V Shared Memory

In addition to memory-mapped files, HP-UX provides support for shared memory through the System V Shared memory API. This API consists of the *shmget(2)* call to allocate a memory object, the *shmat(2)* call to attach to an allocated region, *shmdt(2)* to detach from a region, and *shmctl(2)* for controlling attributes of the shared memory region. There are also three HP-UX tunable parameters, *shmmax*, *shmmni*, and *shmseg,* that control the shared memory system behavior.

8.7.1   Allocating Shared Memory

To allocate a shared memory region of a specific size, the *shmget(2)* system call is made. This returns a shared memory identifier that can be used to later attach to the shared memory segment. Be aware that the size of the shared memory segment created may be limited by the value set for the *shmmax* tuneable parameter as well as the type of application, 32-bit or 64-bit. 64-bit bit PA-RISC applications can have a 4 TB maximum shared memory segment size, 64-bit IPF applications can have a 2^{61}-byte maximum segment size, and 32-bit applications can have only a 1 GB maximum segment size. The *shmmax* tuneable parameter can be used to reduce the maximum segment size supported.

When sharing a memory segment between an adaptive address space application with a global address space application on IPF versions of HP-UX, the IPC_GLOBAL flag should be used to eliminate the cost of aliasing. See Section 8.1.4, "Adaptive Address Space" on page 214 for more information on the use of the adaptive address space.

When using shared memory windows with 32-bit applications (see Section 8.1.5, "Shared Memory Windows" on page 216), using the IPC_GLOBAL key will force the shared memory to be allocated from the global shared memory quadrant (Quadrant 4) compared to the local shared memory window quadrant (Quadrant 3).

Finally, the size of the memory segment can have an affect on overall performance. It is best to choose a segment size that is a multiple of a large page (see Table 8-2, "TLB Pagesizes Supported on PA-RISC and IPF Processors" on page 219). For instance, if a 1 GB shared memory segment were created, the operating system may choose to map this with a single 1 GB page if large pages were enabled for the application. If instead, a 1020 MB region (4 MB less than 1 GB) was created, then the operating system would map the region using multiple pagesizes such as three 256 MB, three 64 MB, three 16 MB, and three 4 MB pages, since the requested size did not fit evenly into a larger page.

8.7.2   Attaching to a Shared Memory Segment

After a shared memory segment is created with *shmget(2)*, it can be accessed via attaching to it with the *shmat(2)* system call. For global address space applications, an address of zero should always be used for the attach address to *shmat(2)*. This is because the OS will manage the address allocation globally for all of the processes running on the system.

However, for adaptive address space processes, a specified attach address can be passed into the *shmat(2)* call and the OS will attempt to map the region at the given address. In addition, an adaptive address space process may attach multiple times to the same shared memory region at separate addresses; however, not all attaches are guaranteed to succeed. Any failed attaches will return SHM_FAILED. Finally, adaptive address space applications should pass in IPC_GLOBAL to the *shmat(2)* call to reduce aliasing overhead costs.

8.7.3   Modifying Shared Memory Attributes

The *shmctl(2)* command can be used to modify some of the shared memory region attributes. In particular, a shared memory region can be locked into memory using the SHM_LOCK command to *shmctl(2)*. The process doing the locking needs to either have root privileges or be part of a group that has PRIV_MLOCK privileges (see *privgrp(4)*). To unlock the shared memory segment from memory, use the SHM_UNLOCK. For shared memory regions that always need to be accessed quickly, locking the shared memory into memory guarantees the operating system will not page it out if memory pressure builds up. In addition, a side effect of locking shared memory is that the operating system will choose the largest pagesizes available for mapping the region, resulting in more optimal TLB behavior.

8.7.4   Kernel Tuneable Parameters for Shared Memory

The most important tuneable parameter for shared memory is *shmmax*. This tuneable controls the maximum amount of shared memory allowed in one segment. If it is set too low, applications will not be able to create large memory segments and may run suboptimally or not at all. Applications may run poorly with a small *shmmax* value because they may have to create many small shared memory segments, and this can result in protection ID thrashing in HP-UX as described in Section 6.5.4.3, "Protection ID Issues" on page 149. Therefore, it is recommended that this tuneable parameter be set to the maximum amount of physical memory available in the system. So, for a machine with 128 GB of physical memory, *shmmax* should be set to 137438953472 which is 128 GB. Be aware that some 32-bit applications may not run with this value set to anything larger than 1 GB because they may always try to allocate at least *shmmax* worth of memory and 32-bit applications can't allocate more than 1 GB per shared memory segment.

The other two shared memory kernel tuneable parameters, *shmmni* and *shmseg*, are simply sizing parameters which control the total number of shared memory segments in the system and per process, respectively.

8.8 Shared Libraries

Shared libraries are used by default on HP-UX systems. With the use of shared libraries, the library on the disk is not made a part of the *a.out* file, and disk space is saved as a result. However, shared libraries may consume more CPU, consume more memory, and require more I/O activity.

With shared libraries, deferred binding is the default. Binding is done upon the first call to a procedure in the library. This means that unresolved symbols may not be detected until *exec( )* time. Shared libraries are compiled as position-independent code (PIC), which results in reduced performance compared with executables linked with archive libraries. PIC code is bigger and uses more instructions to do equivalent work. Also, shared libraries cannot be locked in memory, and swap space is reserved for data required by every procedure in the library, even those that are not called.

Shared libraries are favored by software vendors because updates to the shared library do not require relinking of the *a.out* file. They are favored from a system perspective only because they consume less disk space; however, they consume more CPU and usually more memory. Performance trade-offs with shared libraries are discussed further in the chapter on "Application Optimization."

8.9 Memory Management Policies

The memory management system within HP-UX uses a variety of thresholds to enforce a consistent policy for memory management. Some of these thresholds–*lotsfree, desfree,* and *gpgslim*–are used in relation to *freemem*, the amount of memory currently free on the system.

A description of the basic HP-UX memory management parameters is in Table 8-5. Table 8-6 shows how the default values of the variable parameters are calculated.

Table 8-5   HP-UX Parameters for Memory Management

Parameter	Tuneable	Description	Comment
lotsfree	Yes	Upper bound where paging starts and the threshold at which paging stops.	The default is a variable number of pages based on physical memory size.
desfree	Yes	Lower bound where paging starts.	The default is a variable number of pages based on physical memory size.
gpgslim	No–dynamic	The current threshold between *lotsfree* and *desfree* where paging actually occurs.	Default = (*lotsfree* + 3**desfree*). Recalculated every time *vhand* runs based on how often *freemem* = 0.
minfree	Yes	Threshold where deactivation occurs. Any process is chosen. VM system is thrashing and cannot keep up to provide enough free pages.	The default is a variable number of pages based on physical memory size.

8.9.1   *Regions* and *Pregions*

The memory management policy of HP-UX version 10.0 and later has positive effects on the handling of *region*s and *pregion*s. A *region* is a collection of pages belonging to all processes that are all of a certain type–for example, text, private data, stack, heap, shared library text, and shared memory segments. A *pregion* is a collection of pages belonging to a particular process that are all of a certain type. In HP-UX since version 10.0, the following policies are used:

• All regions are treated equally no matter the size.
• Shared regions are not more likely to be aged.
• All pages of a pregion are eventually scanned.

Pages belonging to lower priority ("niced") processes are more likely to be aged and stolen; pages belonging to higher-priority processes are less likely to be aged and stolen. Processes blocked for memory are awakened in CPU priority order rather than in FIFO order, with interactive processes usually being favored. Page-ins are clustered unless too little memory is available. Page-ins cause process blocking as available memory approaches zero (amount depends on process priority). Finally, the buffer cache can shrink as well as expand.

8.9.2   Thresholds and Policies

Memory management thresholds vary based on the amount of physical memory and CPU speed and are set at boot time. The value of *gpgslim* floats between *lotsfree* and *desfree*, depending upon demands on memory. When *freemem* < *gpgslim*, *vhand* runs eight times per second and scans a set number of pages (depending on need and swap device bandwidth) and uses no more than one-sixteenth of a particular pregion at a time and no more than 10% of the CPU cycles for that interval. Each time *vhand* scans a pregion, it starts scanning pages at the point where it left off the previous time. The *nice* value affects the probability that a page will be aged. When *freemem* < *minfree*, *swapper* runs to free up large blocks of memory by deactivating processes. (Although the name is still *swapper*, HP-UX no longer swaps.)

Starting with HP-UX 10.20, *lotsfree, desfree,* and *minfree* are tuneable. However, unless you really understand the needs of the application and how it is affected by these parameters, it is highly recommended that you accept the default values. In 11.x and later versions, the default values for *lotsfree, desfree,* and *minfree* have been adjusted, especially for systems with large amounts of physical memory (> 2 GB). This was done because it is much better to start paging sooner on such systems, so that the paging process can meet demands more effectively.

8.9.3   Values for Memory Management Parameters

In these sample calculations for the default values of the memory management parameters, "N" is the number of non-kernel free pages at boot time.

Table 8-6   Calculations for Default Values of Memory Management Parameters

Parameter	N <= 8K and physical memory size is 32 MB	8K < N <= 500K and physical memory size is 2 GB	N > 500K and physical memory size is 2 GB
lotsfree	MAX (N/8, 256)	MAX (N/16, 8192)	16384 [64 MB]
desfree	MAX (N/16, 60)	MAX (N/64, 1024)	3072 [12 MB]
minfree	MAX (*desfree*/2, 25)	MAX (*desfree*/4, 256)	1280 [5 MB]

8.10 Sizing Memory and the Swap Area

Choosing the right memory size and configuring the right swap area size can contribute to good memory performance. Only experience can determine the right values for any particular installation, but some initial guidelines are provided in the next paragraphs.

8.10.1 Sizing the Swap Area

For the swap area, the old rule of thumb was to use two to three times the size of physical memory, with a minimum of one times the size of physical memory. However, this may not always be realistic. For large memory configurations, the use of *pseudo-swap* in addition to normal swap allows up to 75% of available memory to be used once the swap devices are full, without the need to reserve physical swap space. Pseudo-swap is enabled by setting the kernel tuneable parameter *swapmem_on* to 1.

When physical memory size is greater than 16 GB, a more realistic guideline is to use 25% of physical memory as a minimum, plus the following:

- The sum of all shared memory requirements (not including text, memory-mapped files, and shared libraries) minus the amount of locked memory. (Note: if the shared memory segment is locked into memory, do *not* count it.)
- "N" times the private virtual memory requirements for each application (private VSS) where "N" = the number of users; use *glance* (Memory Regions screen) to calculate this for each process.
- The sum of shared text VSS requirements when accessing remotely with the sticky bit set.
- 10% overhead for a fudge factor.

Beyond this, pseudo-swap should allow for peak periods. Note that using pseudo-swap limits the amount of lockable memory on the system to seven-eighths of the total size of memory, compared to almost all of it when not using pseudo-swap. For large database configurations that push the memory to the limits, using pseudo-swap may artificially limit the amount of memory that can be locked and therefore, the rule of thumb of equivalent swap as physical memory should be used.

8.10.2 Sizing Memory

The following determine physical memory size:

- The sum of all resident shared memory requirements (text, shared libraries, shared memory, memory-mapped files), including the amount of locked memory (shared RSS).
- "N" times the private resident memory requirements for each application (private RSS) where "N"= the number of users.
- 10% of physical memory for the kernel and static tables.
- The size of the fixed-buffer cache, if applicable.
- Initial allocation for the dynamic buffer cache, if applicable (a minimum of 10% of physical memory is required; 20% is recommended).
- An estimate for networking needs (10% of physical memory).
- Additional memory for NFS.

8.11 Memory Metrics

A variety of global and per-process metrics are available for identifying potential bottlenecks in memory.

8.11.1 Global Memory Saturation Metrics

Global memory saturation metrics (provided by *glance*, *gpm*, and *vmstat*) tell whether the memory system as a whole is saturated. These include:

- Free memory in KB or pages
- Active virtual memory (avm) in the last twenty seconds
- Available memory (physical memory, kernel memory, fixed-buffer cache memory)

The most useful global saturation metric is free memory.

8.11.2 Global Memory Queue Metrics

The only queue relating to memory is the number of processes blocked on VM. *Measure-Ware* gives this as a count; *glance* and *gpm* show this as a percentage of time blocked on VM.

8.11.3 Other Global Memory Metrics

Other global metrics include:

- Page-in/page-out rate
- Page-in/page-out quantity
- Swap-in/page-out rate (before 10.0)
- Swap-in/page-out quantity (before 10.0)
- Deactivation/reactivation rate (10.0 and greater)
- Deactivation/reactivation quantity (10.0 and greater)
- Number of page faults and paging requests
- Number of VM reads and VM writes (clustered)

The following global metrics are the most useful in diagnosing memory bottlenecks:

- Page-out rate. Page-ins are normal, even when there is no memory pressure. Page-outs occur only when memory pressure exists.
- Deactivations. Deactivations only occur as a last resort when there is severe memory pressure, and when the paging system cannot keep up with demands.

8.11.4 Per-Process Memory Metrics

Per-process memory saturation metrics (provided by *top*, *glance*, and *gpm*) include Resident Set Size (RSS) and Virtual Set Size (VSS). Per-process memory queue metrics include the percentage blocked on VM. Other per-process memory metrics are:

• Number of VM reads and VM writes

• Number of page faults from memory

• Number of page faults from disk

• Number of swaps (before 10.0)

• Number of deactivations (10.0 and later)

• Number of each variable page size used (10.20 and later)

Looking at the RSS will show you how much of a process tends to occupy memory. VSS shows you how large the process is, including:

• Text in memory as well as text not yet referenced from the *a.out* file (error routines may never be paged in if not needed)

• Data in memory and data not yet paged in from the *a.out* file

• Shared libraries in memory and not yet paged in from the *.sl* file

• Shared memory

• Memory-mapped files in memory and not yet paged in from the original file

• Private data that has been paged out to the swap area

• Shared memory that was not locked, and that was paged out to the swap area

The VSS size on IPF versions of HP-UX will tend to be much larger compared with what is seen on PA-RISC systems. On IPF systems, HP-UX reserves the entire stack virtual area since IPF chips have two stacks that grow toward each other (the normal stack and the register save stack). This reserved virtual area is marked lazy, so swap space is not needed for the amount not used. The main drawback is that the VSS size increased dramatically from PA-RISC-based systems. The size increase does not have any negative performance impacts other than requiring more entries in the process's VAS data structures and therefore increasing the size of the process's *u_area*.

8.11.5 Typical Metric Values

Page-ins occur normally, and thus do not indicate memory pressure. However, page-outs are an indicator of memory pressure. Page-outs of the following can cause pressure:

- Process data pages
- Process text pages for EXEC_MAGIC format executables
- Shared memory pages
- Writes to memory-mapped files (MMFs)
- Shrinkage of the dynamic buffer cache

Swapping or deactivation is an indicator of severe memory pressure.

8.12 Types of Memory Management Bottlenecks

What are the symptoms of a memory bottleneck? The four major ones are:

- Saturation of memory
- A large VM queue of disk traffic (*glance* will show this)
- Resource starvation
- User dissatisfaction with response time

Saturation is indicated by low free memory and by process deactivation (swapping in systems before 10.0). A large VM queue sustained over time is also indicated by a high percentage of processes blocked on VM, as well as by large disk queues on swap devices. Resource starvation occurs when a high percentage of CPU utilization is used for VM activity or when the disk subsystem is consumed by VM activity. User dissatisfaction with the system results from poor transaction response time.

Lack of memory often results in other problems with the CPU and disk systems, and these problems tend to mask the true cause, which lies inside the memory-management subsystem.

From Bob's Consulting Log—One client had recently added 20% more users to an OLTP system, and performance degraded significantly compared to the state before adding the users. I was asked to recommend a CPU upgrade. On investigation, we found that the degradation of performance was much more severe than what you would expect for the number of users being added. I looked at how much memory each new user needed and found that the new users increased the memory beyond what was physically in the system. Memory was thrashing, and performance was degrading much more than expected. The actual solution to the problem–a memory upgrade–turned out to be a lot less expensive than the CPU upgrade the client thought he needed.

8.13 Expensive System Calls

The most expensive system calls from the standpoint of memory are *fork(2)* and *exec(2)*, *malloc(2)*, and *mmap(2)*. *Fork(2)* and *exec(2)* require extensive new memory allocation for VAS/pregion structures; *vfork(2)* offers a partial remedy (see Section 8.5.1, "fork and vfork" on page 235).

Malloc(2) and *mmap(2)* also are expensive calls because they have a high amount of over-head per invocation, so calling them frequently can result in high CPU overhead.

8.14 Tuning Memory Bottlenecks

There are several bottlenecks that can occur in a computer system due to the memory sub-system. In particular, there can be memory capacity bottlenecks where not enough memory is available for use, there can be memory latency and bandwidth issues, and there can be memory allocation problems such as not allocating large enough pages, which can cause memory bottle-necks. There are several different ways of tuning these memory bottlenecks:

- Hardware solutions
- Software solutions
- Application optimization
- Adjusting memory-related operating system tuneable parameters

8.14.1 Hardware Solutions

For capacity-based memory bottlenecks, the simplest hardware solution may be to increase the amount of physical memory. Another strategy is to use multiple swap devices that are striped together by the volume manager if not enough physical memory can be installed to prevent page-outs.

When using cell-based machines such as Superdome, cell-local memory can be enabled to tune latency related memory bottlenecks. Enabling cell-local memory will usually increase the performance of the memory subsystem.

For dealing with memory bandwidth bottlenecks, adding more memory controllers (if physically possible) may help improve the throughput of the memory system.

8.14.2 Software Solutions

There are several software solutions that can be attempted to relieve memory bottlenecks. For instance, to alleviate memory-capacity bottlenecks, the following can be done:

- On small systems, reduce the size of the kernel (subsystems and tables) by tuning kernel parameters.
- Carefully reduce the size of the fixed-buffer cache.
- Use a dynamic buffer cache, and tune it carefully.
- Reduce and/or restrict the use of memory locking by defining the system parameter *unlockable_mem*.
- Use privileges (see *setprivgrp(1m)*) to regulate user access to memory.
    - Use the MLOCK privilege to lock processes into memory.

- Use the SERIALIZE privilege on large processes and batch processes.
- Nice less important, large, or batch processes.
- Move work to other time periods, or run them as batch jobs.
- Reduce the number of workspaces in a VUE environment.
- Restrict maximum process size by setting the following parameters:
    - *maxdsiz*
    - *maxssiz*
    - *maxtsiz*

Keep in mind that setting these values affects all processes on the system.

- Switch from using *hpterm*s to using *xterm* or *dterm*, since they use significantly less memory.
- Use the sticky bit for NFS-mounted executables (doing this requires setting the PAGE_TEXT_TO_LOCAL parameter).
- Use *setrlimit(2)* starting in HP-UX 10.10.

For dealing with memory bottlenecks where a lot of time may be spent handling TLB misses, the variable-page-size tuneable parameters can be used to increase the use of larger pages. Finally, when dealing with memory-latency bottlenecks, the following can be done:

- Enable cell-local memory.
- Use the *mpsched(1)* command to distribute processes among cells evenly when using cell-local memory.

It is recommended that a database's shared memory segments be locked into memory. These segments are caches, and it makes no sense to allow a portion of a cache to be paged out. As a side effect of locking the segments into memory, the HP-UX kernel will use the largest pages possible for these regions which will improve the TLB behavior of the database.

8.14.3 Application Optimization

When tuning memory bottlenecks in application programs, the following suggestions will reduce the amount of CPU used to access and manipulate memory:

- Minimize the use of expensive system calls:
    - Switch from *fork( )* to *vfork( )* if appropriate.
    - Minimize the use of *mmap( )*.
- Use the *chatr(1)* command to specifically set the largest page size allowed for particular applications.
- Minimize the number of *malloc( )* calls made.

When trying to fix memory capacity bottlenecks, the following can be used:

- Use memory leak analysis software (for example, *Purify* from Rational Software).
- Use *malloc()* carefully, because it allocates memory in such a way that the virtual space cannot be returned to the system until the process exits. Using free() releases memory only at the process level; such memory is still considered to be in use by the system. Also, watch for malloc pool fragmentation.
- Minimize the use of resources that consume memory indirectly, such as user-space threads and semaphores.

Finally, when fixing memory-latency bottlenecks, the following application modifications can be tried:

- Use the *chatr(1)* command for multi-threaded processes to allocate private heap memory in the interleaved space on cell-based systems.
- Use the *mpctl(2)* command to explicitly launch worker processes for an application in a certain manner.
- Use software prefetch and other compiler optimizations to allow the compiler to more efficiently access memory. Explicit methods of doing this are discussed in Section 11.4.4, "Memory Latency Optimizations" on page 376.

8.15 Memory-Related Tuneable Parameters

The following memory-related parameters may be tuned. These are found in the file */usr/conf/master.d/** on systems prior to HP-UX 11i v2. Starting with HP-UX 11i v2, this directory no longer exists and the *kctune* command is used to modify the parameters. Items marked with an asterisk (*) are discussed in more detail in Chapter 9, "Disk Bottlenecks" on page 253.

- *bufpages* *
- *dbc_max_pct* *
- *dbc_min_pct* *
- *desfree*
- *lotsfree*
- *maxdsiz, maxdsiz_64bit*
- *maxssiz, maxssiz_64bit*
- *maxtsiz, maxtsiz_64bit*
- *maxswapchunks*
- *maxusers*
- *minfree*
- *msgmax, msgmnb*
- *nbuf* *
- *nclist*
- *netmemmax*
- *nfile* *
- *ninode* *
- *nproc*
- *page_text_to_local*
- *shmmax*
- *strmsgsz*
- *swapmem_on.* Can be enabled to reduce the amount of swap space required for large memory systems (greater than 8 GB). The total amount of lockable memory will be reduced to seven-eighths of the total memory when this tuneable is set.
- *unlockable_mem.* Can be used to limit the amount of memory that can be locked by processes.
- *vps_pagesize*
- *vps_ceiling*
- *vps_chatr_ceiling*

While most of these parameters have only a small effect on memory utilization, system tables should not be sized arbitrarily large.

It is highly recommended that *desfree*, *lotsfree*, and *minfree* not be tuned unless HP support specifically tells you to do so.

For the buffer cache, use either *bufpages* to create a fixed-size buffer or *dbc_max_pct* and *dbc_min_pct* to create a dynamic (variable size) buffer cache. These parameters will be discussed further in Section 9.13.1, "bufpages and nbuf" on page 310 and Section 9.13.2, "dbc_max_pct and dbc_min_pct" on page 311.

8.15.1 Logical View of Physical Memory Utilization

Figure 8-8 shows a logical summary of the components of physical memory that must be managed in performance tuning.

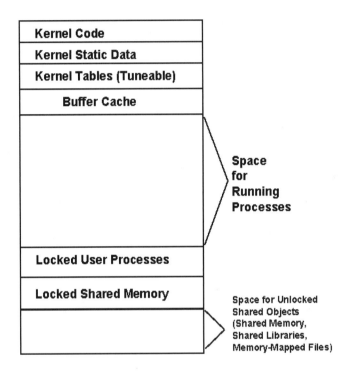

Figure 8-8 Logical View of Physical Memory Utilization in HP-UX

## CHAPTER 9

Disk Bottlenecks

This chapter describes major bottlenecks related to the HP-UX disk I/O subsystem. A review of some of the basic concepts of disk I/O for HP-UX is followed by a description of typical symptoms, techniques for diagnosing them, and methods for tuning. Here are the topics:

- Review of Disk Hardware and I/O concepts
- Disks and Disk arrays
- Logical Volume Manager (LVM) Concepts
- VxVM Volume Manager Concepts
- Shared-Bus Access Considerations
- File Systems and the Kernel
- File System Types
- Disk Metrics
- Types of Disk Bottlenecks
- Expensive System Calls
- Tuning Disk Bottlenecks
- Database Issues
- Disk-Related Tuneable Parameters

Dealing with I/O often involves many choices. The wisdom of **Rule #2** is especially good to remember in this arena: "Performance tuning always involves a trade-off."

9.1   Disk Hardware Descriptions

The disk subsystem of an HP-UX computer system is composed of interface cards connecting disk and tape peripherals to the system. The choice of I/O interfaces, number of interfaces, peripheral types, number of devices, and the distribution of devices and interfaces can have a very large impact on the overall system. The next sections describe various peripherals and their interface to the system.

9.1.1   Interface Cards (Host Bus Adapters or HBAs)

There are several different ways to attach peripherals to an HP-UX system. Some of the older methods included the HP-IB and Fibre Link buses. These were both HP-proprietary buses that were used on early HP-UX systems. Later, HP switched to standardized interfaces such as SCSI and Fibre Channel for attaching disks.

9.1.1.1   SCSI

By far the most popular of all the server peripheral interconnects over the years has been SCSI (Small Computer System Interface). SCSI started out as an 8-bit, 5 MB/second bus that allowed seven devices. It went through various enhancements over the years and now comes in a 16-bit, 320 MB/sec flavor that allows up to fifteen devices on the bus. Table 9-1 shows the various SCSI standards over the years.

The early SCSI devices were attached via thick cables that had a large low density 50-pin connector and were very thick and stiff. With the Ultra SCSI enhancement, the cable and connector were changed to a somewhat more manageable compact design called high-density with a 68-pin connector. At 320 MB/second, SCSI actually provides the highest bandwidth of any of the current peripheral attachments. In addition, the Ultra640 SCSI standard is just now being deployed.

One of the disadvantages of SCSI is that the cable lengths are fairly short. As the speed has gotten faster, the maximum cable length for each standard has gotten shorter depending on the number of devices and the speed of each device on the bus. Please refer to configuration guides to determine the maximum cable length and number of supported buses for a specific configuration.

Cable length is particularly a problem for clusters where multiple nodes must be physically attached to the same disks. The larger the cluster, the more cables are needed. In fact, special "V" cables must be used so that multiple servers can connect to the same SCSI disks.

9.1.1.2   Fibre Channel

Fibre Channel is an optical bi-directional interconnect. It was originally designed as a universal link that could handle both networking and disk I/O requests on a single cable. However, its use as a network attachment device was short-lived and it is now used solely for peripheral attachment on HP-UX systems. Fibre Channel currently comes in two types: 1Gbit/second and 2 Gb/second. The 1 Gb/second version uses a connector of approximately one inch, while the 2 Gb/second version uses a smaller half inch micro-connector. The micro-connector allows multi-

Table 9-1 SCSI Evolution

Common Name(s)	Maximum Speed (MB/second)	Signaling	Maximum Devices	Cable Lengths
SCSI-1	5	single-ended	7	up to 6m
SCSI-2 Fast SCSI	10	single-ended, high-voltage differential	7 15	up to 6m single-ended up to 25m differential
SCSI-3 Fast & Wide SCSI	20	single-ended, high-voltage differential	7 15	up to 6m single-ended up to 25m differential
Ultra SCSI	40	single-ended, high-voltage differential	7 15	up to 6m single-ended up to 25m differential
Ultra2 SCSI	80	low-voltage differential	15	up to 25m point-to-point up to 12m for multiple devices
Ultra3 SCSI or Ultra160 SCSI	160	low-voltage differential	15	up to 25m point-to-point up to 12m for multiple devices
Ultra320 SCSI	320	low-voltage differential	15	up to 25m point-to-point up to 12m for multiple devices

ple connections to be placed on a single adapter card or array controller. Fibre Channel is very reliable and scalable.

Fibre Channel has become the connection of choice for attaching storage to enterprise-level servers. Several of its properties make it superior to SCSI as a storage interconnect. For instance, Fibre Channel can connect devices as far as 2 km apart, unlike SCSI, which has a maximum connection limit of 25 meters. Switches or hubs with long-wave transceivers can be used to extend Fibre Channel to a maximum of 10 km, and dense-wave-division multiplexing (DWDM) can be used to extend the link to a distance of 100 km or more.

Fibre Channel also allows for different connection topologies unlike the simple bus topology of SCSI. With Fibre Channel, you can connect devices in a loop configuration (called Fibre Channel Arbitrated Loop, or FCAL) which is analogous to the SCSI bus. In addition, switches can be used to attach Fibre Channel devices, which allows for a more network-like configuration and much greater total bandwidth than with other configurations. The switch topology also allows multiple servers to attach to the same storage, allowing for configurations not possible with SCSI storage. Finally, Fibre Channel allows for many more devices to be attached to a single adapter than SCSI, allowing for very large configurations to be developed. However, due to protocol issues, attaching more than twenty-five devices in a Fibre Channel Arbitrated Loop configuration can result in performance degradation, so connecting more than twenty-five devices on a single loop is not recommended.

For HP-UX systems, the Fibre Channel driver has been highly optimized and is very efficient in the amount of CPU used per I/O transaction. Thus, for the same I/O rate, Fibre Channel attached storage will use less CPU than SCSI on HP-UX systems; therefore, it is also the attachment of choice for high-performance applications.

9.1.2   Disk Mechanisms

Disk mechanisms have evolved enormously over the years. Back in the late 80s, a server-attached drive may have been as large as a washing machine and had a capacity of only 300MB. Today, individual mechanisms are approaching several hundred gigabytes in capacity in small 3-1/2" sizes. With current disk mechanisms, there are a few factors that can affect the performance of the devices: rotational speed, seek time, data density, and cache behavior.

9.1.2.1   Rotational Speed

Disk devices spin around and around like a vinyl record, but at a much higher rate of speed. They spin to allow arms that move from the outside to the inside of the disk platter to read data on any part of the platters that constitute the device. Early disks spun at speeds of around 2400 RPM. Current high-performance drives spin at a top speed of 15,000 RPM. The higher the rotational speed, the quicker the drive is able to position the read/write head under the desired location on disk. At a speed of 15,000 RPM it will take 4 milliseconds (ms) to perform a complete trip around the platter. This means on average, the rotational latency component of performing a disk I/O will only be one half or 2 ms.

Rotational speed is very critical to achieving high random I/O rates. Applications heavily affected by random I/O latency should be configured to use disks with high rotational speeds. For applications that require high bandwidth from the disks, rotational speed may not be as critical. Other factors such as data density on the disk and efficient caching or read ahead may be just as important for achieving high bandwidth.

9.1.2.2   Seek Time

The *seek time* of a disk mechanism is the time that it takes to move the disk arm from its current location to the location of the next requested piece of data. Unfortunately, the average seek time is usually not specified as part of a disk description like the rotational speed is. However, some manufacturers will provide the average seek time as a metric that one can use for comparison. Lower average seek times are always better.

Low average seek times are very important for random I/O applications. For sequential workloads, the average seek time is not important.

9.1.2.3 Data Density

The density of the data stored on disk has been getting higher and higher over the years. Disk drives have stayed the same size or gotten smaller over the years, yet the overall drive capacity doubles almost every year. A disk drive with a high density will be able to transfer more data in one revolution of the disk than one with a lower drive density. If more data per revolution of the disk can be transferred, then a higher throughput rate can be achieved. The data density mainly effects the sequential throughput a disk can achieve but can also affect random performance as well because more data may be able to be placed in a smaller area of the disk. The detailed technical documentation on a disk drive usually contains information regarding the drive density.

9.1.2.4 Cache and Queue Behavior

Most modern disk drives provide some sort of buffer or cache on the drive itself that allows the drive to match the incoming or outgoing data rate with the speed of the disk. If a cache were not present, any interruptions on the bus during a transfer might cause the drive to interrupt its transfer and potentially wait a full revolution before continuing to transfer data. The size of the cache or buffer needs to be large enough to stream data to or from the disk. Usually, a one- to eight-megabyte cache is sufficient to keep even the fastest drives streaming at full data rate.

Many modern disk drives can be configured to report write completion either when the data has reached the cache of the disk (this is called immediate report) or only after the data is actually written to the disk spindle. Choosing which way to report involves a trade-off of data integrity versus faster overall performance. See Section 9.5.4 for further discussion of using immediate reporting.

In addition to the cache, modern drives are able to handle multiple outstanding requests at one time. The maximum number of requests that a drive can handle simultaneously is called the *command queue depth*. Many drives perform advanced sorting algorithms on the entries in their queue in order to reduce the overall latency for each I/O. A common technique is to do a two-dimensional sort by both seek distance and rotational distance to a given location on disk. The better drives will also make sure that forward progress is made so that no individual disk request gets starved. The disk drives' sorting algorithms are usually far superior to anything the operating system can do, because much more information is available to the drive than to the operating system. Therefore, HP-UX by default will send down a maximum of eight requests at one time for the disk to potentially sort. This maximum can be increased by tuneable parameters, which will be described later.

Reading the detailed technical documents for individual disk mechanisms will usually give more details on how the caching and queuing work within a particular drive.

9.1.3   Disk Arrays

Disk arrays group multiple individual disks together to provide significantly larger capacity than that of a single mechanism. These multiple disks can be grouped together into addressable sets called logical units (*LUNs*). Each LUN can typically be configured in a different mode, such as a RAID mode, described in the next section. The LUN is what is accessed by the computer rather than the individual disk mechanisms.

Arrays also provide a variety of options that facilitate high availability and multi-system access. Most of the features of disk arrays have performance implications.

9.1.3.1   RAID Modes

The acronym RAID stands for "redundant array of inexpensive disks." A RAID device consists of a group of disks that can be configured in many ways, either as a single unit or in various combinations of striped and mirrored configurations. The different types of configurations are classified into RAID levels:

- RAID 0: Disk striping
- RAID 1: Disk mirroring
- RAID 0/1: Combination of mirroring and striping. Also called RAID 1/0 or RAID 10
- RAID 2: Multiple check-disks using Hamming code
- RAID 3: Bit/Byte-striped, single check-disk using parity
- RAID 4: Block-striped, single check-disk using parity
- RAID 5: Block-striped, data and parity spread over all disks
- RAID 5 DP: RAID 5 with two parity segments spread over all disks instead of one
- RAID S: Block-striped with a stripe group of four and a stripe depth of one (a special case of RAID 5 used on EMC Symmetrix disk arrays)
- AutoRAID: HP's term for an adaptive RAID system that migrates data automatically between RAID 1/0 and RAID 5 or RAID 5 DP

The various RAID levels can be implemented in either hardware or software. Hardware RAID and software mirroring are most often used as the data redundancy solution. One-way data redundancy is possible using RAID 1, 3, or 5.

RAID 0

RAID 0 arrays don't provide protection against disk failures. All data is block-striped across the disks in the array (or a LUN in the array). In some arrays, the size of the block used for striping can be chosen. Typical values are 1 KB to 64 KB in size. Reads and writes to RAID 0 arrays are theoretically "N" times faster than a single disk, where "N" is the number of disks in the RAID 0 group. Actual transfer rates will be constrained by the controller and the link bandwidth. Unfortunately, the chance of losing data in a RAID 0 group becomes larger as more and more disks are added to the group. This is because the overall reliability of a RAID 0 group drops as a function of the number of disks in the group. RAID 0 is only recommended for data that is unimportant, such as temporary files. Even then, the downtime incurred due to a disk failure in a RAID 0 array may be too large to effectively use a large RAID 0 array.

RAID 1

RAID 1 arrays store a copy of all data on two separate disk mechanisms. If any disk fails, a copy is always available on another drive in the system. RAID 1 performance implications include the following:

- With a hardware solution, mirroring is done in the array, so that only one write occurs from the CPU. CPU utilization is decreased and thus improves performance in comparison to software mirroring where the CPU must perform multiple independent writes, one to each mirror copy.
- Multiple reads can be distributed by the software or the controller to both sides of the mirror to increase performance.
- The benefit that might be obtained by doing reads from a pair of software mirrors attached to separate SCSI buses might be lost in a hardware solution, unless dual controllers are used.

RAID 1 requires 100% additional disk mechanisms for each mirror copy desired and thus costs significantly more than other configurations.

RAID 1/0

RAID 1/0 arrays combine both mirroring and disk striping to form a high performance and highly available RAID solution. This level provides the high-performance benefits of a RAID 0 solution with the availability benefits of a RAID 1 solution. In this configuration, RAID 1 disk pairs have data block striped among them. A RAID 1/0 configuration can be configured with as few as three disks, as long as any block of data is always written to two separate disks in the RAID 1/0 group. RAID 1/0 requires an additional 100% disk mechanisms for the data redundancy, but this configuration is recommended when high-performance I/O is needed, whether it is random or sequential.

RAID 3

A RAID 3 array maintains consistency when a disk is lost in the group via a parity disk. The parity disk can be thought of as containing the sum of all of the data from the data disks. If any disk is lost, it can be reconstructed from the data on the remaining disks and the parity disk. The disks in a RAID 3 system are typically synchronized such that writing data to each disk will take equivalent time. Since data is bit- or byte-striped across all of the disks, performance degrades for small reads or writes (less than 64 KB).

The decreased performance is due to the array controller needing to read or write all disks in the stripe set for any size access. RAID 3 random performance is typically 20% of that of stand-alone mirrored disks. Sequential read and write performance, however, is usually quite good for a RAID 3 system. RAID 3 systems therefore can make good log devices for databases. RAID 3 usually requires 20% or 25% more disk mechanisms for the parity information.

RAID 5

A RAID 5 system also maintains a parity disk to reconstruct data in the event of a disk failure, but unlike RAID 3, the parity is spread among all disks in the stripe set. This is done so the parity disk does not become a bottleneck. In addition, data is striped in blocks versus bytes across all of the disks. A RAID 5 block could be anywhere from 1 KB in size to 64 KB or more.

For RAID 5, performance degrades for small writes (2 KB, for example), but random small read performance (2 KB) can be equivalent to RAID 0 striping. Although you cannot control the placement of data for tuning purposes, a large write cache on the array may reduce the small write penalty by allowing the array controller to coalesce multiple small writes into a few larger ones. Figure 9-1 shows how RAID 5 striping is done.

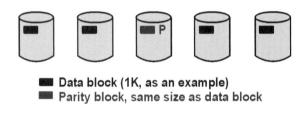

■ **Data block (1K, as an example)**
■ **Parity block, same size as data block**

Figure 9-1   RAID 5 Block Striping with Parity

The use of RAID 5 for small I/Os can cause the array controller to perform several read-modify-write operations in order to properly update the parity information. In the RAID 5 configuration in Figure 9-1, for example, a 2 KB write would require the array to read the original 2 KB of data (two 1 KB reads from two separate disks) and read the original 1 KB of parity (from a third disk). The new parity would then be calculated based on the original 2 KB of data, old parity, and new 2 KB of data. Finally, the new 2 KB of data (two 1 KB writes to two separate disks) and the new 1 KB of parity would be written back to disk. In all, six 1 KB I/O operations (three read and three write) are performed to write out 2 KB of data.

By enlarging the block size from 1 KB to something like 4 KB or 8 KB, a write smaller than or equal to the block size would then potentially only require four I/O operations because only the parity drive and a single data drive would be involved in the update. For I/O writes that consume an entire stripe, i.e. 4 KB in the setup in Figure 9-1, then no read operations are needed, only writes to each of the drives and the parity. RAID 5 usually requires 20% additional mechanisms to store the parity information, assuming five disks are used in the stripe group.

RAID 5 DP

With RAID 5 DP, everything works as in RAID 5 except that there are now two parity blocks to update instead of a single parity block. This allows two drives in the stripe set to fail and still retain all data. RAID 5 DP is used in some more recent HP arrays such as the VA 7400. It is needed when the number of drives that a RAID 5 group is striped over becomes large (ten disks or more). The problem with RAID 5 and large stripe sets is that the probability of losing a second mechanism in the stripe set before the initial failed mechanism can be recovered increases as the number of disks in the stripe set increases. The double parity in RAID 5 DP allows a second mechanism to fail in the stripe set while the array still retains all data. The extra parity block, of course, has a performance impact for writes as well, given that two parity blocks need to be updated on each write compared to just one with RAID 5. The number of extra mechanisms needed for RAID 5 DP depends on the size of the stripe set. Usually RAID 5 DP arrays use stripe sets of ten or more disks, so the extra space needed would be 20% or less.

RAID S

RAID S (an EMC Symmetrix variant on RAID 5) provides a stripe group of four, but blocks are sequentially laid out rather than striped. This provides good performance for both sequential and random reads (Note: you are likely to have multiple concurrent random reads). There may be degraded performance for small (less than 32 KB) writes, but the write cache should provide insulation against this for the application. Figure 9-2 shows the striping for RAID S.

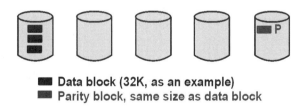

■ **Data block (32K, as an example)**
■ **Parity block, same size as data block**

Figure 9-2   RAID S Block Striping with Parity

The use of RAID S may cause the Symmetrix controller to perform a read-modify-write operation. For a write, for example, the controller would read 32 KB blocks of data and 32 KB parity blocks, modify the appropriate amount, compute XOR parity at the level of the individual mechanism controller, and then write out 32 KB blocks of data and parity. RAID S requires 25% additional storage.

AutoRAID

AutoRAID is the term used for an array management system that moves data automatically between RAID 1/0 and RAID 5 or RAID 5 DP. AutoRAID has been used in the HP arrays by the same name (such as the AutoRAID Model 12H) as well as the VA 71xx and VA 74xx families of arrays. In an AutoRAID system, the array determines if a given write should reside in the RAID 1/0 space on the array or the RAID 5 area on the array. It does this based on heuristics and access patterns to individual blocks. AutoRAID systems are completely virtual, so a particular block on the device may be physically placed at any location within the array and can be moved at any time to any other location in the array.

AutoRAID systems try to keep data that is randomly written with a high frequency in the RAID 1/0 space and data that is mainly read in the RAID 5 space. If space is needed in the RAID 1/0 space for more data, the AutoRAID system may migrate less frequently accessed data from RAID 1/0 to RAID 5. In addition, if data in RAID 5 is found to be written more than it used to be, it may be migrated to RAID 1/0. The AutoRAID system is designed to take a lot of the headache out of creating specific LUNs at a specific RAID level and then trying to guess how a particular file will be accessed. It also adapts to changing workloads over time, unlike a static RAID configuration. Given its dynamic nature, however, an AutoRAID array may also experience periods of slow behavior if the access pattern for a given block changes rapidly. Additional storage requirements range from 20% to 100%, depending on the ratio of RAID 1 to RAID 5 storage.

9.1.3.2   Caching and Queuing

Unlike an individual disk, a disk array is subject to large performance effects from the size of the cache and the choice of caching algorithms. The cache on a disk array serves two purposes. One is to allow scattered writes to be potentially coalesced together to eliminate possible RAID 5 penalties or to make writes to the backend drives more efficient. A second is to allow potentially hundreds of outstanding read requests to complete independently and then send responses back to the host in the most optimal order. In general, the amount of cache available for reading does not need to be as large as the amount for write buffering. Caches on high-end disk arrays can be very large, up to 16 GB or more.

Just as in an individual disk, an array can queue up multiple requests at one time and then process these requests out of order in an optimal manner. Enabling a larger queue depth is very important with disk arrays. The queue depth is specified on a per-LUN (logical unit number) basis in a disk array. The default queue depth of eight provided by HP-UX is usually not enough to allow an array LUN to be saturated with I/O. A general rule of thumb is that at least two entries in the queue should be allocated for every disk configured in a LUN, so a LUN configured with fifteen disks should have a queue depth of at least thirty.

Some arrays, such as the AutoRAID arrays, allow all drives in the array to be used for different LUNs at the same time. For these types of arrays, the sum of the queue depths for all LUNs should be at least twice the number of disks. If the LUNs are not evenly accessed, then the LUNs with more activity should have a higher queue depth. In general, the queue depth should be set to a large enough value to provide the best performance, but not so large that there are an unreasonably high number of I/O requests outstanding for a given disk array.

9.1.3.3   Controllers

The controller on a disk array is analogous to a computer server. It will have a central processor that handles distributing requests to the internal disk drives and will potentially have multiple I/O channels to connect to the disks. The speed at which the controllers can access the disks in the array affects the overall array performance. An array with a slow controller will not be able to saturate all of its disks. It is often difficult and costly to make a controller fast enough to handle hundreds of disk drives. Therefore, it is often better from a performance standpoint to use multiple small arrays compared to one very large array. Some large arrays, however, do scale the number of controllers with the number of disks, so as long as the ratio of controllers to disks is not too large, then large arrays can also perform well.

Many arrays provide multiple controllers for redundancy. However, not all arrays will provide symmetric access across the controllers. Some arrays work in an active/passive configuration where the second controller is there mainly to take over control if the primary controller should fail. Other arrays allow both controllers to actively participate in I/O. This is referred to as an active/active configuration. Even though some arrays may allow activity on both controllers, some of these may not allow even access to a given logical unit from both controllers. For instance, when configuring logical units (LUNs) on a VA7410 array, a redundancy group is specified for each LUN. Each redundancy group is tied to a particular controller. Accessing a LUN via the "wrong" controller will result in poor performance, but both controllers can be used to simultaneously access the particular LUNs assigned to them, resulting in good performance.

9.1.3.4   Virtual Array Issues

Virtual Arrays, such as the VA71xx and VA74xx series, can have strange performance characteristics in some instances due to the nature in which they operate. In a virtual array, there is no fixed mapping between a piece of data and where it is stored in the array. The array may choose to move a given block of data from one physical location to another at any time. In order to do this, virtual arrays contain a "map" of logical block addresses (which are specified by the operating system) to physical block locations in the array. Since the array has a map of all locations on disk, it also knows which locations actually have valid data and which are "empty."

This last issue can make doing performance testing on virtual arrays challenging. For instance, if an empty file is created on a virtual array and then immediately read, the performance may be much different than if the block had already been written. This performance difference is because for the read of "never written data," the array will know that there is no data actually on the disk and will simply return a fixed pattern as data for each request. Once data is actually written once, the array will return real data.

A similar issue occurs when the data are written for the first time for a given disk block of a file. The virtual arrays usually store data in 64 KB blocks on disk. So, if a random piece of data that is smaller than 64 KB is written to an "unused" block, the array will fill in the other bytes in the 64 KB block with a fixed pattern of data. This extra "fill" operation will take longer than just writing out the smaller piece of data. However, on subsequent writes to anywhere in the same 64 KB range, the fill will not need to be done and the write will be much faster.

9.1.4   HP StorageWorks Disk Array XP-series

Enterprise class storage includes the high-end XP-series of disk arrays. These disk arrays combine very high performance with very high capacity. Currently at the top of the family, the XP1024 supports up to 129 TB of usable storage capacity and up to 32 I/O channels. One can choose between 10,000 RPM 146 GB disk mechanisms and 15,000 RPM 73 GB disk mechanisms. Choosing the right mechanism size involves a trade-off of capacity versus performance.

Software is available for these disk arrays to help in the configuration of LUNs and I/O channels. Tuning such a large disk array involves many trade-offs and is really beyond the scope of this book. However, these disk arrays provide the potential for absolutely the highest level of disk I/O performance with HP-UX systems.

9.1.5   Tape Drives

Tape devices are mainly used to back up the online storage of a system. The performance of the tape subsystem needs to be matched with the amount of storage that needs to be backed up. Having a slow tape system on a system with lots of storage can cause long backup times. The longer the backup period, the more chance things can change during the backup. Current HP-UX backup solutions include DDS, DLT, and LTO Ultrium tape.

9.1.5.1   DDS

DDS stands for *digital data storage*. It is a data storage format developed by HP and Sony that was derived from DAT (*digital audio tape*), thus DDS drives are sometimes referred to generically as DAT drives. DDS media is a 4 mm-wide tape contained in a small cassette format. The tapes hold between 2 GB and 36 GB of uncompressed data, depending on the format (DDS-1 to DDS-5). Backup speeds are not extremely fast (183 KB/second to 3 MB/second) and therefore DDS backup solutions are mainly for small systems. SCSI is the main driver interface.

9.1.5.2   DLT

DLT stands for *digital linear tape*. This is a format that was developed by Digital Equipment Corporation and later sold to Quantum. DLT devices can be read and written much more quickly than DDS (currently up to 16 MB/sec native, 32 MB/sec compressed). DLT tapes also have a much higher capacity than DSS: up to 160 GB uncompressed and 320 GB compressed. The actual tape size is much larger than DDS tapes, but this is one of the reasons for the much higher capacity. Many high-end systems will include DLT backup devices to rapidly backup and restore gigabytes or terabytes of data. DLT supports compressing data on the fly and is very reliable.

Future plans are for capacities of over 1 TB per tape and uncompressed backup speeds of 100 MB/sec. SCSI is again the interface of choice for DLT, although future plans call for Fibre Channel interfaces as well.

9.1.5.3   LTO Ultrium

LTO Ultrium tape drives feature high capacities and high transfer rates. The linear tape technology behind Ultrium drives was developed by HP, IBM, and Seagate as an "open format" technology to allow for multiple sources for tapes and tape drives. In fact, the LTO stands for *Linear Tape-Open*. The first generation of tapes and drives support up to 200 GB of compressed data at a transfer rate of 20-40 MB/sec. The second generation of tapes support up to 400 GB of compressed data at transfer rates of 40-80 MB/sec. Future plans call for tape capacities of 1.6 TB and speeds of 320 MB/sec. Currently, HP-supported Ultrium tape drives all run under the SCSI interface.

A unique feature of the Ultrium drives is that they can detect already-compressed data and will not compress data that is already compressed. In addition, the HP drives have the unique ability to dynamically slow down and speed up to match the input rate of data being sent to the drive. This allows the drive to stream the data to tape and prevents the drive from having to rewind while waiting for new data. This improves the overall performance and reduces wear on the tape and drive.

9.2   Review of Disk I/O Concepts

The Unix operating system sees all input to and output from the CPU as a matter of reading from or writing to files. Disk files are one specific type of I/O governed by the same rules and using the same I/O stack as all the I/O operations. This stack, as it applies to disk devices, is shown in Figure 9-3.

The application code makes system calls to the I/O subsystem, specifying what is to be opened, closed, read, or written as a *filename*. The filename determines the type of object that is opened and accessed. Object types include whole disks, disk sections, or LVM volumes. I/O types used to access the data include raw (unbuffered) I/O, buffered file-I/O, and direct file-I/O. Access methods can be either synchronous or asynchronous. Depending on the object type and I/O type, different *system calls* and different *device drivers* are used to access data. Each call or driver has characteristics that affect performance. The following sections describe the most important of these calls and drivers.

9.2.1   Disk Access Methods

Disk data may be accessed through a variety of methods. In HP-UX, these methods have evolved over time from the early use of disk sections, down to the current methods employed by

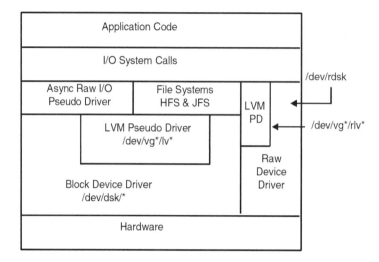

Figure 9-3   I/O Stack

specialized volume management software–for example, Logical Volume Manager (LVM). The following disk access methods are possible:

- Whole disk. This is accessed by a device file specifying section 0. Example:
    - */dev/[r]dsk/c#t#d0* (HP-UX 10.0 and later).
- Sections. Each brand of hard disk formerly had a set of fixed definitions contained in the file */etc/disktab,* which described sixteen potentially overlapping partitions of the disk. No support is provided for disks or arrays that have been introduced since HP-UX 9.04, though a pseudo-driver allows the continued use of the disk section access method.
- LVM. Logical Volume Manager replaces the use of disk sections beginning with HP-UX version 10.0. The additional overhead could result in a 3-5% performance degradation for the worst case. More typically, applications may experience degradation in the 0-2% range. This may be an acceptable price to pay for the added functionality provided by LVM.

Any of the access methods mentioned here may be used with each of the various I/O types described in the next sections.

9.2.2   Unbuffered (Raw) I/O

Unbuffered I/O does not use HP-UX file system buffers to pass data to and from applications. This means that raw I/O does not use a file system, but depends on the user's application to manage the organization of the data on the disk device. Raw I/O is performed by accessing the character (raw) device file associated with the disk on which the data resides. A typical example is */dev/rdsk/c0t0d0*. Two varieties of raw I/O are the basic and asynchronous types. A logical view of basic raw I/O is shown in Figure 9-4.

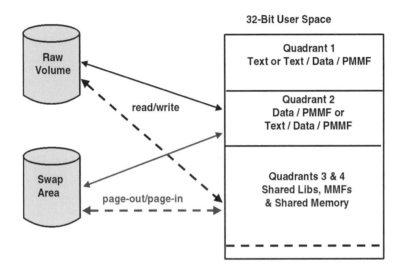

Figure 9-4   Logical Diagram of Basic Raw I/O Blocking

9.2.2.1   Basic Raw I/O

With basic raw I/O, data is transferred directly to or from the user's buffer. Only synchronous reads and writes are allowed. The process blocks until the I/O is complete, regardless of whether the application is performing a read or a write operation on the device. For this reason, raw I/O can actually be slower than buffered I/O in some circumstances.

9.2.2.2   Asynchronous Raw I/O

In asynchronous raw I/O, data is transferred to and from user data buffers without blocking. In HP-UX there are two methods to achieve asynchronous disk I/O, via the /dev/async driver and via the POSIX async interfaces.

Async Device Driver (/dev/async)

The async driver (/dev/async) is used by the majority of the database vendors to transfer data to and from disk. Before HP-UX 11i, all transfers had to be to and from shared memory. As of HP-UX 11i, however, transfers can also be made to and from a program's heap or stack. Once an I/O is launched asynchronously, the process can continue to do other things. The process then checks back via one of several methods to determine if the I/O has complete. The /dev/async driver allows the user to check through:

- a *select(2)* system call,
- issuing a blocking read call to check status from the driver,
- a polling a flag set up in shared memory.

The async driver interface allows a program to send multiple read and write requests to the driver simultaneously. The driver can then be set up to return a completion notice when one or many I/O requests have finished processing. Individual error status is available for each I/O request.

The async driver requires special *ioctl(2)* calls to configure the shared memory segment and other properties; therefore, the application must be rewritten to take advantage of it. Asynchronous raw I/O can use either the block device driver or character device driver. In addition, LVM can be used in conjunction with the async driver. Finally, since the process is not blocked, it is possible to queue up multiple I/Os, and this improves performance.

The database vendors that use the async driver will open the /dev/async device for each disk device they need to use in asynchronous mode. Some properties of the driver can be configured by creating the /dev/async special device in certain ways. Normally, the minor number for this device should be zero when making the device with the *mknod(2)* command. By using the minor number of 0x1 (hexadecimal), however, the async driver will enable immediate report for all disk drives that it accesses. This is sometimes needed to enable a disk array to cache writes. In particular, the older FC60 array does not cache writes unless this minor number is enabled even when mirrored and battery-backed caches are used on the array. As long as all of the devices being accessed are on a UPS (uninterruptible power supply) or have battery backed-up write caches, then enabling the minor number of 0x1 is perfectly safe. To do this, the following command would be used:

```
# mknod /dev/async c 101 0x1
```

The use of asynchronous raw I/O in the major relational database management software packages has resulted in substantial performance increases. Databases almost always benefit by using raw volumes in conjunction with asynchronous access rather than using a file system (either HFS or JFS), even when the file system offers a *direct* I/O feature.

POSIX *async I/O*

With the addition of threads in HP-UX 11.0, HP-UX added the POSIX async I/O (*aio(7)*) interfaces. The POSIX *async I/O* allows a process or thread to asynchronously issue I/O requests to both raw- and filesystem-based devices. Asynchronous reads are issued via the *aio_read()* system call, and asynchronous writes are issued via an *aio_write()*. Multiple read and write requests can be issued at one time with the *aio_listio()* system call. One problem with the

POSIX *async I/O* interface is how the completion status of the I/O is determined. The main way to determine if an I/O request is done is via a polling *aio_return()* system call. If the I/O is complete, *aio_return()* will return the same status as a read or write call would have for a synchronous request. However, if the I/O is still in progress, then *aio_return()* returns a -1 with *errno* set to EINPROGRESS.

There is a lot of overhead in performing any system call, but this is especially true for calls that check the completion status of an I/O request. In addition to the I/O call itself, an invocation of *aio_return()* is needed for every I/O issued, whereas the *async* driver is able to read completion status for several I/Os at once with a single system call. As of the HP-UX 11i v2 release, however, the POSIX implementation on HP-UX has been modified to include the *aio_reap()* call, which will allow multiple requests to be retrieved at one time much like the async driver. POSIX *aio* also implements the *aio_suspend()* system call to block until any I/O is complete, but this is also much less efficient than the async driver method of blocking for completion.

Another issue with POSIX *async I/O* on HP-UX is that one kernel thread is spawned for every I/O request. On systems that have heavy I/O activity, the spawning of a thread for every I/O can cause excessive context switches. Cache pressure can also occur due to having more thread context contend for the processor caches. This implementation issue has been fixed somewhat with HP-UX 11i v2, where a thread is only spawned for filesystem I/O. For raw I/O, a thread is no longer spawned, but instead a simple context is maintained for each request.

9.2.3   Buffered I/O

Buffered I/O (Figure 9-5) makes use of the Unix file system buffers. Synchronous reads are done from disk or from the buffer cache while the process blocks. Asynchronous read-ahead places additional pages of data from the file system into the buffer cache to speed up subsequent accesses. When the O_SYNC flag is used as part of the *open* system call, synchronous writing blocks the process while data is copied to the cache from application data space and written to disk. When O_SYNC is not used, the default write on HP 9000 workstations is an asynchronous copy-to-cache and write-to-disk without blocking the process if the last byte in the block has been written. (This is also known as *write-behind.*) Otherwise, the data is written in a delayed fashion by *syncer.* On HP servers, when O_SYNC is not used, the default is an asynchronous copy to cache without blocking the process, followed by a delayed write to disk by *syncer.* Buffered I/O requires a copy of data between the kernel and the user spaces, and this impacts performance.

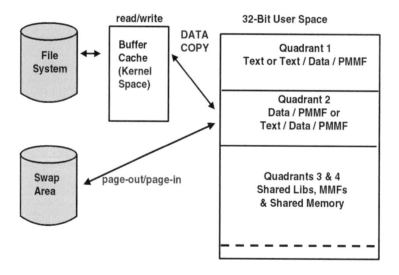

Figure 9-5   Buffered File I/O Blocking

9.2.4   Direct Files and Memory-Mapped Files

Direct file I/O (Figure 9-6) is possible only for JFS file systems. It is possible to have synchronous reads and writes, during which the process blocks. The performance advantage is that there is no copying of data between the kernel space and the user space, and data is unbuffered.

This type of I/O is good when the application does relatively large I/Os and does not reference the data again for a long time, meaning that the buffer cache performs no useful function. For instance, a scientific application that writes a very large output file when it completes may benefit from direct I/O. JFS direct I/O, because it has the properties of raw I/O but the manageability of a filesystem, can also be useful for databases, which usually maintain their own buffer caches.

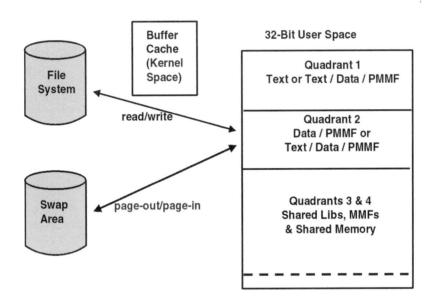

Figure 9-6 Direct File I/O Blocking

9.2.5   Memory-Mapped I/O

Memory-mapped I/O (Figure 9-7) provides unbuffered transfer of data in a file system to and from quadrants of user address space. Reading is done by page faults, and there are clustered page-ins (read-aheads) if the file is sequentially accessed. Writing is done via the *vhand* daemon or through the *msync(2)* and *close(2)* system calls.

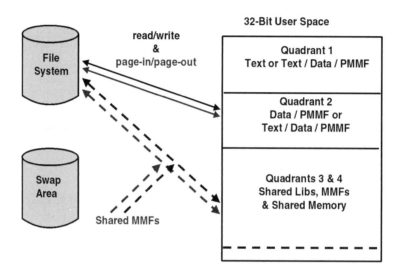

Figure 9-7   Memory-Mapped File I/O

9.3   Logical Volume Manager Concepts

Since HP-UX 9.0, Logical Volume Manager (LVM) has become the most common tool for creating and managing disk storage. LVM provides the capability to group multiple physical disks into a single volume group composed of one or more logical volumes. Logical volumes can contain file systems, or they can be accessed like raw files.

Although non-default naming is possible, LVM objects usually have device file names beginning with */dev/vg* (for example, */dev/vg00* for a volume group, and */dev/vg03/lvol9* for a logical volume). These objects are accessed via the LVM pseudo-driver, which in turn accesses either the block or character-mode driver to perform actual I/O to the disk.

Volume groups offer a great deal more flexibility than the historical disk section access method. You can configure up to 256 volume groups (the default is 10), up to 255 physical volumes (disks or LUN's) per volume group, and up to 255 logical volumes per volume group. .

Table 9-2   Maximum Logical Volume Sizes by Release

HP-UX release	Maximum logical volume size (GB)
HP-UX 9.04, HP-UX 10.0, HP-UX 10.01	4
HP-UX 10.10, HP-UX 10.20	128
HP-UX 11.00, HP-UX 11i	2048

Table 9-2 shows the maximum logical volume sizes by release. Volumes can be striped or mirrored to enhance performance, and in HP-UX 11.0, volumes can be striped and mirrored at the same time.

9.3.1   LVM Striping

LVM striping is a software technique in which data is written to disks in a volume group in a manner that allows parallel reads and writes to speed up performance. The I/O is split into equal pieces, each of which is written to a different disk. The *stripe size* is the amount written to one disk. Logical volumes can be quickly created with stripe sizes of 4, 8, 16, 32, or 64 KB in HP-UX 10.x and earlier. The allowed stripe sizes increased to any power of two between 4KB and 32 MB with HP-UX 11.0 and later releases. Striping is done by the LVM pseudo-driver; no additional system calls are needed. LVM striping is the software equivalent of RAID 0 for hardware arrays.

How does striping affect performance? It improves large sequential write performance by involving multiple disk drives in the I/O. Striping should improve small random read and write performance, because statistically the I/Os will be spread across multiple drives. Yet striping may reduce the performance gains expected from the I/O merging feature of HP-UX 10.0 and later, where multiple I/Os that are physically contiguous are merged into a single I/O. The fewer I/Os made possible by merging may yield better performance than the larger number required for striping; fewer I/Os are almost always better than more I/Os. However, if an I/O operation spans multiple stripes, the I/Os to all of the LUNs involved in the operation are initiated in parallel, thus potentially increasing performance.

9.3.1.1   LVM Striping Recommendations

The author uses the philosophy of not striping everything everywhere. Instead, place a large file or file system on a separate striped group of disks. This philosophy increases the likelihood of detecting "hot" files, and lets you control their placement to get better performance. The use of smaller separate volume groups can also reduce the time needed to restore data in case of a mechanism failure. This is because you must restore the entire volume, not just the part that was on the failed disk.

Set the stripe size according to I/O size and access patterns. This is more difficult to do when you are using JFS, where the I/O size is variable. On HFS, the I/O size is equal to the block size, which is 8K by default. Typically, match the stripe size to the file system I/O size: the block size on an HFS file system, and the average extent size on a JFS file system.

It may be easier from a management perspective to use the philosophy of striping everything over all of the available drives in a volume group. This may be especially true if you do not have the luxury of investigating disk I/O bottlenecks, rearranging the data placement on the disks, and then hoping for improved performance. Very large databases may perform well enough with this stripe philosophy that it is not worth the time and effort of deciding what data to place on which stripe group.

9.3.1.2   LVM Extent-Based Striping

An older, "manual" way to stripe using LVM is *extent-based striping*. In this method, the administrator must issue a large sequence of *vgextend* commands, alternating among the physical volumes in the volume group. This method of striping is usually less effective than the built-in striping discussed earlier, because the minimum stripe size is the same as the minimum extent size, which is 1 MB.

9.3.1.3   LVM Distributed Allocation Policy

The new, automatic way to stripe using LVM is by using the Distributed Allocation Policy. By enabling this policy with the *lvcreate -D* command and by using PVG-strict allocation with the */etc/lvmpvg* file, extents are automatically allocated in a distributed manner across all of the physical volumes in a volume group. It is therefore no longer necessary to manually create extents with a sequence of *vgextend* commands.

9.3.2   LVM Mirroring

LVM mirroring in HP-UX is provided by the optional add-on product Mirror Disk/UX. LVM mirroring provides RAID 1 mirroring in software, and allows two-way or three-way mirroring (that is, one or two levels of redundancy), in addition to split/merge capabilities.

LVM mirroring gives better performance than application mirroring, which requires multiple write system calls. Mirroring is done by the LVM pseudo-driver, so that no additional system calls are necessary. Reads are done from the mirror with the shortest queue, resulting in a read performance improvement of up to 100%. (You may only notice this when the disks are very busy.) Writes cause multiple I/O requests to the driver, thus potentially decreasing write performance by as much as 50% since there are now double the number of writes. In typical cases, where the read rate is much higher than the write rate, mirroring will usually improve overall system and application performance.

Hardware mirroring may provide better performance, but this depends on the hardware implementation (remember Rule #1). Also, hardware mirroring does not usually provide three-way mirroring and split/merge, except for the EMC Symmetrix with the Symmetrix Multi-Mirror Facility (SMMF). In addition, the SureStore XP disk arrays have the ability to create two or more mirror copies.

9.3.2.1 Mirror Scheduling Policy

You can select either a parallel or serial write policy with mirrored logical volumes. Parallel write (the default) is faster for raw access and for JFS file systems. A serial write policy may be faster for HFS in HP-UX 10.01 and later versions because of I/O merging.

9.3.2.2 Mirror Consistency

If you create a mirrored logical volume with the *-c y* option of *lvcreate(1M)*, LVM guarantees that mirror copies will be consistent with one another, even following a crash. In the event of a system crash, LVM must recover mirror copies to a consistent state.

To speed up the recovery process, LVM provides a *mirror write cache* (MWC), which keeps track of the changes in the logical track groups (LTGs) on each disk. An LTG is a region of the volume consisting of 256 MB of data space. You enable the mirror-write cache by using the *-M y* option of *lvcreate(1M)* at the time you create a mirrored logical volume. When the mirror-write cache is enabled and when the status of any LTG changes, time-stamped mirror consistency records are written to the volume group data area (VGDA) of one of the disks where the logical volume resides.

Maintaining the *mirror write cache* has definite performance implications. There is a trade-off between degraded on-line performance and fast recovery following a system crash. On-line performance suffers because:

- In order to write MCRs, the disk heads can potentially move from the outer tracks (where the VGDA is written) to the inner tracks, where user data resides.
- Additional writes occur to post the MCRs to each physical volume in the volume group.
- Delays are possible when the *mirror write cache* is full and there are I/Os in the queues pending for all entries in the logical track group.

The advantage of the MWC is that the synchronization of logical volume mirrors on reboot after a crash is very fast.

To check for MWC contention with *GlancePlus* or *gpm*:

- Choose I/O by Logical Volume ("v").
- Select a volume ("S"). Pick a logical volume, not the volume group or group file.
- Look at statistics for MWC hits/misses. Hits are good; misses are bad. Look at the metric "MWC Misses." For good performance, there should be few MWC misses.

You can help reduce contention by creating a larger number of smaller volume groups rather than a few large volume groups. In HP-UX 11.0, the MWC has been increased in size from 32 to 120 cache entries, so there should be less contention.

9.3.2.3   Mirrors and Volume Group Size

If you are using mirroring, the number of volume groups versus the number of logical volumes can be an important decision point. For most configurations, it is better to use more volume groups with fewer logical volumes in each.

The mirror-write cache has less impact on performance with a large number of smaller volume groups than with a smaller number of larger volume groups, because there is less contention for LTG entries in the mirror-write cache. (This is because each volume group has its own mirror-write cache.)

Smaller volume groups will normally result in shorter recovery times after a system crash. This is because logical volume resynchronization is done serially within a volume group, but in parallel among volume groups.

Fewer volume groups are easier to administer in most instances.

9.3.2.4   Disabling the Mirror-Write Cache

You can disable the mirror-write cache for a mirrored logical volume by using the *-M n* option with *lvcreate(1M)* when creating the volume. This will not result in on-line performance degradation, but rather in a slow recovery following a system crash. In this scenario, one side of the mirror is chosen as current and is copied fully to the other side(s) of the mirror upon volume group activation after a crash; this can take in the tens of minutes. All of the mirrored logical volumes within the volume group are resynchronized serially. On the positive side, volume groups are accessible during resynchronization. Once they are resynchronized, on-line performance is not affected.

NOTE: Although it is possible to disable mirror consistency by using the *-c n* option with *lvcreate(1M)* when creating mirrored logical volumes, this is never a safe alternative for anything other than a swap device, because it may result in inconsistent mirrors after a system crash.

9.3.3   Bad Block Relocation

Every so often a disk block may go bad. LVM has the ability to keep track of these bad blocks. By default, when LVM detects that a block on disk has gone bad on a write, it will attempt to remap that block to a different location on disk. If it does remap the block, it records the new location in a Bad Block Directory. If it can't remap the block, it will return an I/O and attempt to remap the block again on the next I/O to the block.

Unfortunately, bad block relocation can cause a slight performance degradation under high I/O loads due to locking issues. In addition, disk arrays often have extensive mechanisms to remap bad blocks, so using LVM bad block remapping with disk arrays is redundant. Therefore, it is recommend that logical volumes be configured without bad block relocation when disk arrays are used as the components in the volume group. This can be done by specifying the *-r N* option to the *lvcreate* command. If single disk mechanisms are used, then bad block relocation can be used, but even some of these drives can do their own bad block management, which again makes the LVM functionality redundant.

9.3.4   Read-Only Volume Groups

LVM lets you configure read-only volume groups, which allow on-line read-only access to a split-off mirror of a mirrored logical volume by another SPU. This feature is designed to work only with mirrored logical volumes; a snapshot of the data is obtained when one mirror is split.

This feature is not meant to improve performance, and must be used only with a dormant logical volume such as a split-off mirror. If used on an active logical volume with a file system, a panic will occur on the read-only SPU as soon as a change is made to the file system by the read-write SPU. If used on a non-split raw logical volume, there will be data consistency issues.

9.3.5   Note on Mixing RAID Parity Hardware Striping and LVM Striping

LVM striping is not recommended with the use of disk arrays without taking into consideration the block stripe size used by LVM and the array. The problem is that all I/Os to and from disk arrays are via the array cache, and all I/Os between the cache and the disks are usually in some fixed block size. Writing data that is less than the array's cache block size with parity protected RAID such as RAID 5 can cause a read-modify-write penalty and performance degradation. Setting the LVM stripe size to something smaller than the array's cache block size will cause this behavior and may actually slow down performance.

An array's cache block size may be quite large. For instance, most AutoRAID arrays have a stripe size of 64 KB. It is often better to configure logical volumes contiguously on large arrays that use large internal block sizes and stripe over many disks. If LVM striping is used in conjunction with disk arrays that stripe internally, the stripe size should be chosen very carefully. A good rule of thumb is to choose the stripe size that is at least as big as the block size used by the array. Thus, for an AutoRAID array, you would not want to LVM stripe any smaller than 64 KB.

LVM striping can also interact negatively with arrays that perform RAID 0 or RAID 1/0 striping. Often, performance degrades when too small a stripe size is chosen. A small stripe size may cause lots of small I/Os to be sent to the arrays which then will not be able to optimize the requests to minimize accesses to the disks.

Finally, hardware striping in arrays is not always superior to LVM striping. On HP Model 10 and 20 disk arrays in RAID 5, for example, the segment size is 128 KB. Each time data is modified, the array recomputes the *checksum* and writes out the corrected data. This is expensive, especially for database applications with many small writes. When comparing hardware and software striping, be sure to remember **Rule #1**: "It depends." With RAID 5, if the write I/O size is smaller than the stripe size multiplied by the number of disks in the stripe set, there is a condition in which a read/modify/write operation is done in the array, and this can dramatically degrade performance.

9.3.6   PV Links

Physical Volume (PV) links are provided with LVM in HP-UX 10.0 and later as a way to provide a redundant path to a disk hardware unit. Using PV links, you attach different buses to a multi-controller disk array so that access to the data is maintained even when the primary path fails. PV links are *not* used for concurrent access to the same logical device or LUN. However, if the disk device supports it, PV links can be used to increase potential performance by providing two separate I/O paths from the LUNs on the disk device to the computer. This behavior is supported with most current disk arrays as long as the I/Os are to different logical devices. You must carefully define the volumes, however, in order to achieve this potential performance improvement.

Product-specific software, such as AutoPath for the XP/VA arrays and PowerPath for the EMC Symmetrix, actually replaces the PV links' functionality. Each of these software solutions provides load balancing among the multiple links in addition to failover in case of link failure. The VxVM volume manager also provides a load balancing feature in addition to failover.

The operation of PV links is illustrated in Figure 9-8. When the volume group is created,

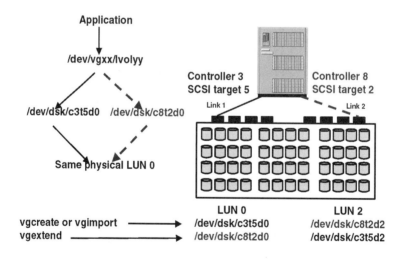

Figure 9-8   PV Links

two separate physical volume device files (representing paths to the disk array from two different SCSI controllers) are used for each LUN. This provides an alternate path to the data. In this example, link #1 is the primary link for LUN 0 and the secondary link for LUN 1, as determined by the device names specified in the *vgcreate* command (primary link) and *vgextend* command (secondary link). The order is reversed for LUN 2, therefore ensuring that both links are used for I/Os under normal circumstances.

9.4   VxVM Volume Manager

The VxVM Volume Manager from Veritas is an alternative disk management system that is provided on HP-UX 11i systems. It provides almost all of the features of LVM, plus additional features that mainly help with availability and manageability. For instance, the VxVM product provides a graphical user interface for creating logical volumes on the system. It also allows both striping and mirroring to be done simultaneously (RAID 10 support) and provides RAID 5 support. VxVM can also provide up to thirty-two mirrored copies of data. The multiple mirror support allows VxVM to provide a snapshot copy of a volume group for backup and then to automatically resync the snapshot copy with any changes that may have occurred during the backup. Note that most of the VxVM features that are different from LVM don't come standard with the system. Features such as the RAID 10, RAID 5, multiple mirrors, and snapshot are sold separately with the "full" VxVM add-on product.

There are only a few features from LVM that VxVM does not support. One is bad block relocation, but since most modern arrays and disk drives do their own bad block relocation, this is not a huge loss of functionality. The other area where VxVM differs from LVM is that LVM will automatically recover from a disk power failure where the disk may go away for some period of time and then reappear, whereas with VxVM a configuration tool needs to be run manually after a powerfail event.

The next few sections describe some of the performance aspects of VxVM. For general information on VxVM, please consult on-line documentation at www.docs.hp.com or the *vxintro(1M)* man page.

9.4.1   Performance Features

There are a few performance enhancements to VxVM over LVM that should be considered. VxVM has the ability to dynamically adjust the stripe size or layout while keeping all data in the volume group available.

Second, VxVM provides for dynamic multipathing for arrays that have dual active controllers such as the high-end HP XP disk arrays. This feature evenly distributes I/O requests among multiple paths to the array. Be aware that not all arrays with dual active controllers may benefit from having a LUN accessed on each controller. For instance, the VA7410 array experiences a performance hit when accessing a LUN via a controller that is not the controller where the LUN was initially created.

9.4.2   Performance Problems

One major issue to be aware of is that any software RAID 5 solution is going to perform extremely poorly if there are more than just a few writes. Many expensive operations are done to maintain the RAID 5 parity information each time a write occurs, which consumes many resources in a computer system including the CPUs, buses, and disks. Writing to a RAID 5 volume in less than full block increments (the block size as defined by the RAID 5 software, in this case) incurs a "read/modify/write" operation sequence, which is very slow. So, unless performance is of no concern or a volume is read-only, RAID 5 volumes should not be used with VxVM.

9.4.3   Performance Measurement

The VxVM package provides its own measurement interface via the *vxstat(1M)* command. This command provides total read/write counts, read/write block counts, and average access times for both volumes and disks. The statistics provided are from the view of the VxVM software layer, so things like the average disk response time may not match exactly to counters such as *sar*'s average disk response time. Refer to the *vxstat(1M)* man page for specifics on using the command.

9.5   Shared-Bus Access to Disks

The use of SCSI buses or Fibre Channel allows for configuration of data storage with access by more than one system at a time. The type and number of buses used, particularly in mirrored configurations, can affect performance considerably.

9.5.1   Single-Initiator Configurations

A single-initiator configuration is one in which a single SPU initiates access to a disk. An example is shown in Figure 9-9. This figure shows two configurations. At the top is a configuration with disks for two applications attached to the same SCSI bus, and the mirrors on a separate bus for high availability. At the bottom is a better performing configuration, in which the disks for the different applications are separated from each other. The cost is, of course, more card slots and buses.

9.5.2   Multi-Initiator Configurations

In a multi-initiator configuration, more than one SPU accesses the disks from the same bus. A sample is shown in Figure 9-10. Again, two configurations are shown. The one at the bottom performs better for two reasons: each application's disks are accessed on a different bus, and each SPU will normally access data for one application.

9.5.3   Performance Load on Multi-Initiator Buses

SCSI buses can easily become overloaded, especially in a multi-initiator environment. It is important to set SCSI priorities (determined by SCSI address) so that no device is starved for access to the bus. SCSI controllers (on the interface card attached to the SPU) should have the highest priority. Large disk queues or long service times on low-priority devices indicate performance issues.

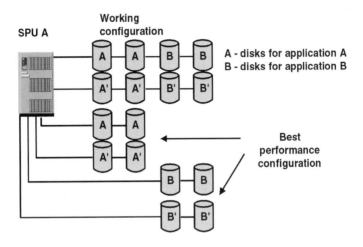

Figure 9-9 Single Initiator Disk Configurations

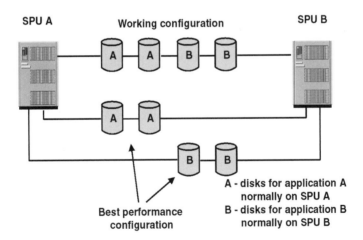

Figure 9-10 Multi-Initiator Disk Configurations

Table 9-3 gives a performance load factor (PLF) for typical devices attached to a Fast/Wide SCSI bus. The values are based on peak transfer rates associated with devices and interfaces. For best results, the maximum PLF on a multi-initiator F/W SCSI bus is 11.5. The sum of the values for all active F/W SCSI interfaces on a single bus must not exceed this value, or severe performance degradation will result.

Table 9-3   Performance Load Factors for SCSI Devices

Device or Interface	PLF
F/W SCSI Host Adapter	1.5
Stand-alone Disk Drive (JBOD)	1.0
Disk Array with one Controller (Storage Processor) attached to the bus	2.0

9.5.4   Disk Drive Write Caches

Most modern disk drives and arrays contain RAM for a read and/or write cache that can be enabled or disabled. The read cache is usually enabled by default. Enabling the write cache is also called "turning immediate report on," and signals I/O completion when the data is written into the RAM cache. Enabling the write cache is especially good for sequential writes.

On some disk arrays (Models 10 & 20, for example), the cache can be split between read cache and write cache. This has some implications for performance:

- Cache sizes must be carefully chosen according to I/O patterns.
- The read cache is redundant if the application also caches.
- The write cache is less useful in read-mostly applications.

On the workstations, the kernel enables the write cache by default on all stand-alone disk drives and arrays since users of these systems usually rank raw performance higher than data integrity. On servers, the kernel disables the write cache by default on all stand-alone disk drives. The default behavior can be modified with the HP-UX tuneable parameter default_disk_ir. Setting this to one enables write caching while setting it to zero disables write caching. Behavior on a per disk basis can be modified with the following utility:

/usr/sbin/scsictl -m immediate_report= <0 | 1>, where 0=disabled and 1=enabled

Most large, modern disk arrays will ignore the value specified for write caching because they will automatically cache writes if the array provides a mirrored and battery-backed cache. Some arrays, however, may abide by the write cache setting and not cache writes if write caching is not enabled. In this case, write caching should be enabled as long as the array is guaranteed to provide redundancy and battery backup in its cache.

WARNING: You must make a trade-off between loss of data integrity in case of power failure or device reset, and gain in performance from disabling the write cache for individual disk mechanisms. For mission-critical environments, it is recommended that immediate report be *disabled* unless there is battery backup for the disk caches and the servers attached to the disks.

9.6   File Systems and the Kernel

The Unix virtual file system (VFS) supplies a standard interface to various physical file systems. On HP-UX, supported file systems include *hfs* (hierarchal UNIX file system, also called *ufs* or Unix File System), *JFS* (Journaled File System, which is the Veritas VxFS), *lofs* (loopback file system), *cdfs* (Compact Disc File System), *dosfs* (FAT file system for floppy disks), and *NFS* (Network File System). NFS performance issues are discussed in detail in Chapter 10, "Network Bottlenecks" on page 317. Tuning recommendations will be presented later in this chapter for HFS and JFS file systems only.

9.6.1   I/O-Related Kernel Tables

Figure 9-11 shows the kernel tables that describe files and file systems.

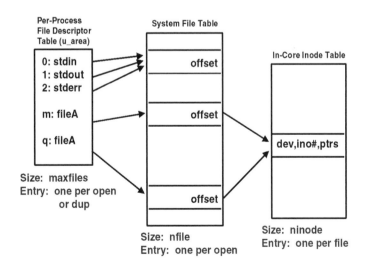

Figure 9-11   Kernel Tables for I/O

The user process has a table of file descriptors that points to entries in the system file table. This in turn points to the in-core inode table, which contains one entry per open file. One entry in the per-process file descriptor table is used for each file *open(2)* or *dup(2)*. Its size is determined by the tuneable parameter *maxfiles,* which defaults to sixty. Larger sizes can result in wasted space, fragmentation, and slower performance. Instead of increasing the size of this table for all processes, use *getrlimit(2)* and *setrlimit(2)* within the application, if possible, to increase the size of the file descriptor table for only that application rather than all applications.

An entry in the system file table is used for each *open(2)*. It contains the current file offset for the particular file descriptor used by a process. It may safely be sized arbitrarily large: each entry is small, and access to the table is very efficient.

The in-core inode table is used only for HFS file systems. Only one entry is used for a given file, no matter how many times it has been opened. This table often appears to be full. This is deceptive, however, since it is really a cache that contains both active and previously used entries. It should *not* be sized arbitrarily large, since the algorithm used for accessing the table is most efficient for table sizes of 4096 or smaller. Inode tables may need to be sized above 4096 entries according to real application needs. The inode table used by the JFS is initially sized at 50% of *ninode* and will grow dynamically to 150% of *ninode*.

9.6.2   File System Limits

Files and file systems are limited in size by system architecture, file system type, and other considerations such as having a 64-bit operating system. For instance, if you are not using LVM, then the maximum size of a raw boot disk is 2 GB (prior to HP-UX 11i v1.5), which means that the file system is also limited to 2 GB. It follows that an individual file cannot exceed 2 GB.

Table 9-4   HFS File System Size Limits

HP-UX Version	File Size Limit	File System Size Limit
10.01	2 GB	4 GB
10.10	2 GB	128 GB
10.20, 11.00, 11i	128 GB*	128 GB

For HFS file systems, Table 9-4 shows the maximum supported file and file system limits, while Table 9-5 shows the maximum supported file and file system limits for JFS.

Table 9-5 JFS File System Size Limits

HP-UX Version	File Size Limit	File System Size Limit
10.01	2 GB	4 GB
10.10	2 GB	128 GB
10.20	version 2 layout: 2 GB version 3 layout: 128 GB*	128 GB
11.00	version 2 layout: 2 GB version 3 layout: 1 TB version 4 layout: 1 TB	version 2 layout: 128 GB version 3 layout: 1 TB version 4 layout: 1 TB
11i v1-v1.6	version 2 layout: 2 GB version 3 layout: 2 TB version 4 layout: 2 TB	version 2 layout: 128 GB version 3 layout: 2 TB version 4 layout: 2 TB
11i v2	version 2 layout: 2 GB version 3 layout: 2 TB version 4 layout: 2 TB version 5 layout: 2 TB	version 2 layout: 128 GB version 3 layout: 2 TB version 4 layout: 2 TB version 5 layout: 4 TB (using VxVM only)

* When accessing files greater than 2 GB in size, 32-bit applications must be modified to use 64-bit pointers and to call *create64(2)*, *open64(2)*, *lseek64(2)*, etc.

9.6.3 Buffer Cache

The buffer cache is used to buffer file system I/O between the application and the disk. It supports the following patterns of reading and writing data from disk files:

- Synchronous reads: When data is not in the buffer cache, the process blocks until the data is read from the disk.
- Immediate reads from cache (does not involve I/O): When data is already in the buffer cache, it is copied to the process without blocking unless the inode or buffer are "busy."
- Synchronous writes: When the O_SYNC flag is specified, the process blocks until data is written to the disk.
- Asynchronous writes (write-behind): Queue the block to be written, but do not block the process.

• Delayed writes: The block is written by the *syncer* process some time in the future.

On typical large memory systems, the larger the size of physical memory, the larger the buffer cache that is desired. Buffer caches more than 500 MB in size may cause performance degradation, however, due to VAS allocation and overall management of the large number of buffers.

The cache can be no larger than 1 GB (one quadrant) for HP-UX version 10.0 and 10.10 systems; it can be as large as 3.75 GB in HP-UX 10.20 and later 32-bit operating systems. With 64-bit HP-UX 11.x, it can be multiple terabytes in size. You should reduce *dbc_max_pct* from the default of 50% on large memory systems if a dynamic buffer cache is used.

9.6.4   Fixed Buffer Cache

The cache was of fixed size only prior to 9.0 for Workstations and prior to 10.0 on Servers. The default size equals 10% of physical memory if *nbuf=bufpages*=0.

In 10.0 and later, you can fix the size of the buffer cache by setting *nbuf* and/or *bufpages* to non-zero values in the system file. A good default for *bufpages* is

sizeof(physmem) * 10% / 4096

if you don't know where to start. Note that there is usually no need to change the value of *nbuf* from its default value of zero.

9.6.4.1   Performance Implications

A fixed-size buffer cache often improves performance for commercial applications, or in cases where the environment is static. Buffer caches that are too large waste memory and can cause memory bottlenecks. Buffer caches that are too small can cause disk bottlenecks. A fixed buffer cache does not adapt to changing conditions. The balance between VM and I/O can be controlled, however, by adjusting the fixed size of the buffer cache.

Fixing the size of the buffer cache is also useful for commercial database applications where the database itself is maintaining a large internal cache. It is not advisable to have two separate and large buffer caches, one in the kernel and the other in the application.

9.6.5   Dynamic Buffer Cache

A dynamic buffer cache became the default in HP-UX 9.0 for Workstations and in HP-UX 10.0 for Servers. The starting size equals 5% of physical memory, and the maximum is 50% by default. The dynamic buffer cache grows in size by allocating new pages when VM demands are low and I/O demands are high. The cache shrinks in size when VM demands are high and I/O demands are low. The use of the dynamic buffer cache is enabled when *nbuf* = *bufpages* = 0.

9.6.5.1 Performance Implications

Dynamic buffer caches often improve performance for technical (CAD/CAM) applications or in cases where the environment is dynamic. With a dynamic cache, the size of the buffer cache changes according to demand, and additional overhead occurs for page allocation and freeing. Note that the system administrator cannot control the balance between VM and I/O.

A 50% maximum size is often too much. You should reduce the maximum size by setting *dbc_max_pct* to a value between 20% and 30% for most applications and setting *dbc_min_pct* to something lower than *dbc_max_pct*.

9.6.6 Maxusers, Maxfiles and Other Kernel Parameters

Maxusers is employed in formulas to size other parameters, including *nproc*, *nfile,* and *ninode*. Removing the dependency on *maxusers* from the definitions of these other parameters is recommended. You can hardcode the values of *nproc*, *nfile*, and *ninode* as needed. *Maxusers* does not have anything to do with the user license level of the system. It is merely a convenience parameter for sizing several other parameters at once. *Maxusers* is no longer a tuneable parameter starting with HP-UX 11i version 2.

9.7 File System Types

This section describes several of the most common file system types along with some of the tuneable parameters that relate to the creation and mounting of file systems.

9.7.1 HFS

The High Performance File System (HFS) is known by at least four names:

• HFS
• *ufs* (Unix File System)
• Berkeley File System
• McKusick File System

HFS is not the same as the System V File System, although some System V Release 4 variants may offer both. HFS was designed for environments with many small files; users of large files in HFS are deliberately penalized from a performance perspective, as will be seen in following sections.

9.7.1.1 HFS Layout

HFS file systems use the layout on disk shown in Figure 9-12. An HFS file system is composed of a primary and a secondary superblock containing structural metadata describing the layout, and one or more cylinder groups that contain both inodes (metadata for individual files) and data blocks. Note that kernel tables in memory also contain inode data for open files.

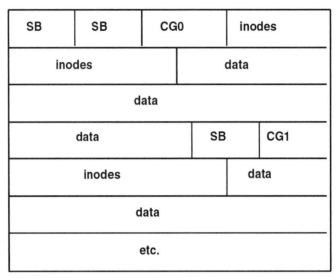

Figure 9-12   HFS File System Layout

The design of the HFS file system allows the inode for a file and the data blocks of the file to be located in close proximity, to improve performance. The inode is written when the file is created and any time data blocks are added to the file.

Figure 9-13 shows how pointers to the data blocks operate when the default block size of 8 KB is used. There are always twelve direct pointers, each of which points to an 8 KB data block. This results in very good performance for files of 96 KB or less. As the file grows above 96 KB, the indirect pointers are used. The single indirect pointer refers to an 8 KB block of pointers (2048 pointers), which in turn point to data blocks. Two I/Os are necessary to access the next 16 MB of the file in the worst case scenario, in which the block of pointers does not remain cached. The use of double and triple indirect pointers further degrades performance for the largest files.

9.7.1.2   Disktab File

Prior to HP-UX 10.0, disk geometry for HFS was determined by the */etc/disktab* file, which contains the number of cylinders, tracks, sectors, rotational speed, size of the file system, block size, and fragment size for a particular model of disk drive. In HP-UX 10.0, section definitions other than section 0 (whole disk) were removed. Information in the disktab file is used to figure "optimal" block placement on the disk, not necessarily contiguous placement.

NOTE: By default, */etc/disktab* is no longer used by *newfs*. See the *newfs* man page for default geometries used. While the default geometries *may* cause performance degradation as compared to their use on pre-10.0 systems, disk geometries usually have little impact on the performance of modern disks.

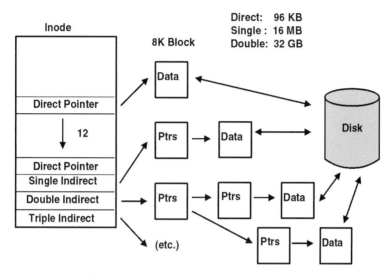

Figure 9-13 HFS Inodes (8 KB Blocks)

9.7.1.3 HFS Block Allocation Policies

With HFS, the system attempts to allocate the first blocks of the file in the same cylinder group as the directory. When the file size exceeds that which is pointed to by direct pointers, the system places new blocks in a different cylinder group. Therefore, large files are deliberately scattered among multiple cylinder groups. By default, a single file is not allowed to occupy more than 25% of a cylinder group. As the file system becomes full, a block may be placed in any free location.

9.7.1.4 HFS Tuneable Parameters

An HFS file system is created with either the *mkfs* command or the *newfs* command, although *newfs* is easier to use. The following can be chosen at creation time:

- Block size (minimum I/O size): default = 8 KB, choose from 4 KB, 8 KB, 16 KB, 32 KB, 64 KB. Larger block sizes improve sequential I/O performance at the cost of consuming buffer cache pages faster, and time to complete I/O. Smaller block sizes improve random I/O performance for small I/Os.

- Fragment size (minimum file size): default = 1 KB, choose from block size divided by 1, 2, 4, or 8. Larger fragments waste disk space for small files, but improve performance during large file creation. Smaller fragments use less disk space for small files, but degrade performance during file creation when the file size is < (block size * 12).

- Cylinders per cylinder group: default = 16, minimum 1, maximum 32. There is little benefit in changing this, except where the file system contains only large files. In this case, increase to 32.
- Bytes per on-disk inode: default = 6144 (10.0), maximum 65536. This determines the maximum number of files per file system. Use of ACLs halves the maximum number of files per file system. Too many inodes wastes disk space. Change this value to 65536 for file systems that contain only a few large files, such as file systems used with databases.
- *Minfree* (minimum free space): default = 10%. New block allocation performance degrades as file system capacity exceeds 90%. Reserved space can be used only by the super-user. *Minfree* often wastes disk space for file systems containing databases because the space is preallocated, and the free space goes unused. For file systems containing only large, preallocated files, set *minfree* to zero.

You can also use the *tunefs* command to adjust the following:

- *Minfree* (see previous list).
- *Maxbpg* (maximum blocks per group): default = 25% of total blocks in CG, maximum 100%. Determines amount of scattering of large files. Increase to 100% for file systems with mostly large files by following these steps:

    - Step 1. Use *tunefs -v* to report the structural values of the file system.
    - Step 2. Look for the parameter *bpg*. This is the number of blocks in the cylinder group.
    - Step 3. Change *maxbpg* by using *tunefs -e <number>*, where *<number>* is the value found in Step 2.

- *Rotdelay* (rotational delay): default = 0 ms in 10.0 and later releases, driver-dependent in previous releases. Determines sequential block placement by using disk rotational speed and an estimate of the time delay for the OS to issue multiple sequential I/O requests. *Rotdelay* should be kept at zero so that files may be allocated contiguously on the disk. For today's disks, there is no longer a need to change the value.

9.7.1.5   HFS Inode Posting Behavior

The HP-UX HFS is more reliable than those provided with other Unix variants. Inodes are posted synchronously to the disk when an important field in the inode is modified (access times, file size, or pointers), causing the file to be inaccessible until the inode is written to disk. This can be seen in *glance/gpm* when processes block on "inode," virtually ensuring the structural integrity of the file system even if the system crashes.

Default posting behavior can be modified by using the file system mount option *fs_async* or by setting the kernel tuneable parameter *fs_async* = 1. Although using this option *may* significantly improve performance, it is risky. If the system crashes, *fsck* may be unable to repair the file system, or, at a minimum, some data will be lost. Since changing this parameter affects all file systems system-wide, it is recommended that the *mount* option be used instead, and only for those file systems where the risk is acceptable, such as a temporary file system.

9.7.1.6 HFS Mount Options

The following options may be used with the *mount* command to control the behavior of some aspects of HFS file systems:

- *-o behind*: Enables asynchronous write behavior for blocks in which the last byte has been written (default on Workstations). This is useful when buffers will not be modified again soon.

- *-o delayed*: Enables delayed write behavior for all dirty blocks unless the file is opened with O_SYNC (default on Servers). This is useful when buffers are frequently modified.

- *-o fs_async*: Enables delayed posting of modified inodes. There is a trade-off between improved performance and potential data integrity problems if the system crashes. This option is useful for temporary file systems, in cases where files grow, or when files are modified rapidly. This is a **high-risk** option.

- *-o no_fs_async*: Enables synchronous posting of modified inodes (default). There is a trade-off between increased writes and possible loss of structural integrity. This is the **lowest risk** option.

NOTE: Neither *fs_async* nor *no_fs_async* affects how data are written; these options only affect how file system metadata (*inodes* and *Superblocks*) are written.

9.7.1.7 HFS syncer

Syncer is the daemon responsible for flushing dirty buffer cache pages to the disk. Its default scheduling of thirty seconds is divided into five intervals. Every six seconds, *syncer* flushes 20% of the dirty pages that are "older" than thirty seconds to disk, attempting to spread the I/Os and to age the buffers sufficiently to ensure that they are finished with.

The scheduling intervals can be adjusted by editing */sbin/init.d/syncer* to change the default. It is possible to reduce the scheduling interval when buffers will not be written to more than once and increase the scheduling interval when buffers will be modified many times. The trade-off is between the risk of data loss and the possible occurrence of disk bottleneck problems.

NOTE: *syncer* calls *sync(2)*, which initiates a *sync* of all virtual file systems.

9.7.2   JFS

The Journaled File System (JFS) is a newer alternative to HFS. JFS has the following characteristics:

- *Fsck* is faster due to the use of an intent log.

- Intent log contains recently committed file system metadata (*indoes, Superblocks*, etc.) and optionally, actual data.

- Size of intent log is configurable.

- Performance of JFS varies with the application and may differ from HFS performance.

- It can't be used for the */stand* file system on any PA-RISC server; however, for IPF servers, JFS can be used for the */stand* file system.

9.7.2.1   JFS Structures

JFS uses allocation units, extents, and blocks. An allocation unit is similar to an HFS cylinder group. Extents are groups of blocks occupying contiguous space on the disk; they default to *variable* length. (OnLine JFS offers a fixed length option.) Indirect extents default to eight blocks, but may be up to 32 MB with a Version 2 layout or larger with a Version 3 layout. Blocks are similar to HFS fragments. They default to 1 KB, and can be up to 64 KB in size. Block size determines the smallest file size, but the extent size determines the size of the I/O up to a maximum I/O size of 1 MB.

9.7.2.2   JFS File System Layout

The layout consists of primary and redundant superblocks, the intent log, allocation units, maps, extents, and inodes and data blocks. For more information, see the man pages on *fs_vxfs(4), inode_vxfs(4),* and *mkfs_vxfs(1m)*. Figure 9-14 shows the layout graphically.

Allocation units are similar to cylinder groups; extents are contiguous groups of data blocks.

NOTE: The Version 3 layout differs slightly from what is shown in Figure 9-14, but the differences are not important to this discussion.

JFS inodes are shown in Figure 9-15. The figure shows how pointers to the data blocks are used with the JFS file system. Ten direct pointers each point to one direct data extent whose size varies from one file to another depending on access patterns, I/O size, and file system. Indirect pointers always point to 8 KB extents containing 2048 pointers, which point to data blocks. Indirect data extents default to 64 KB in size and may be increased. Thus, with a JFS, there is a potential for placing large files in large extents and for fewer I/Os needed to access data.

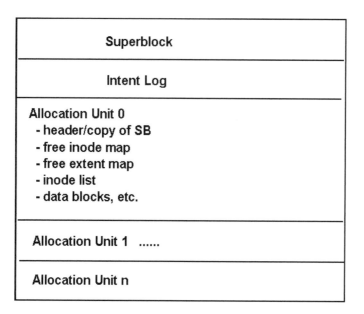

Figure 9-14   JFS File System Layout (Version 2)

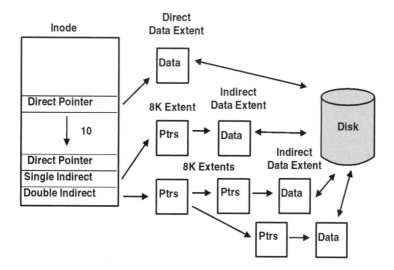

Figure 9-15   JFS Inodes

9.7.2.3   Creating a JFS File System

You can create a JFS file system with either *mkfs* or *newfs*. The use of *mkfs* is recommended, however, since it lets you specify a much greater number of the following options:

- *-o inosize=n* (on-disk inode size). Default = 256 bytes, maximum 512. No known reason to change from default.
- *-o bsize=n* (block size [minimum file size]). Default = 1K; choose from 1, 2, 4, or 8K. Larger blocks waste disk space for small files but improve performance during large file creation.
- *-o ninode=n* (inodes per file system). Default = total # of blocks in FS/4. Increase if average file size < 4 blocks; decrease if average file size > 4 blocks
- *-o nau=n* (number of allocation units–AUs–per FS). Default <= 8; it is suggested not to exceed 10 for overhead reasons. More AUs should improve file locality; fewer AUs should improve performance for large files. This option is not supported in all versions.
- *-o ausize=n* (size in blocks of AU). Alternative way to specify number of AUs. This option is not supported in all versions.
- *-o aufirst* and *-o aupad*. Esoteric options for attempting to improve performance by aligning AUs and data blocks on cylinder boundaries. These options are not supported in all versions.
- *-o logsize=n* (intent log size). Default = 512 blocks; range 32 to 1024. No reason to reduce size of intent log unless very short on space. Increase intent log size if metadata modification rate is too high for posting routine to keep up. For example, an NFS workload might perform better with a larger log. The maximum logsize is 16 MB in Versions 4 and 5 layouts.

9.7.2.4   JFS Mount Options

The following mount options are used with the *mount -F vxfs* command:

- *-o log*. Enables synchronous posting of modified inodes to the intent log (default prior to version VxFS version 3.5). The trade-off is that logging means additional writes to disk (immediate write to the intent log, followed by the inode itself, later); not logging means longer recovery after a system crash. This is the **lowest-risk** option.
- *-o delaylog*. Intent log writes are asynchronous (default in version VxFS 3.5 and later). "Double" writes will still occur, but the process does not block while the intent log is being written to; there is a potential performance increase at small additional risk. This is a **low-risk** option.
- *-o tmplog*. Intent log writes are delayed; recent changes will be lost if the system crashes; *fsck* is still quick. This option is recommended for temporary file systems. There is **medium risk**. This option is similar to enabling *fs_async* for an HFS file system.

- *-o nolog*. Disables intent log; full *fsck* required after system crash. The trade-off is potential data integrity problems if the system crashes versus improved performance. This is a **high-risk** option.

- *-o blkclear*. Clears all data extents before allocation. The trade-off here is between increased security preventing access to deleted data versus the loss of performance due to an increased number of writes to clear the extents.

- *-o snapof*. Specifies snapped file system name. Here there is a trade-off between the ability of one process to access data as of a point in time while other processes are updating the data, versus the performance cost of the additional writes needed to copy the original data to the snapshot FS.

- *-o mincache=direct*. All reads and non-O_SYNC writes are unbuffered and do not occur through the HP-UX buffer cache. This possibly *degrades* performance, since the process blocks until the I/O completes. The trade-off is reduced need for pages in buffer cache versus process not blocking. Useful for large I/Os direct from the application and/or when the application performs its own I/O buffering.

- *-o mincache=dsync*. Converts non-O_SYNC and non-VX_DIRECT writes to data synchronous. Data is posted synchronously but inodes are delayed if only the access times are being changed. This option *degrades* performance. The trade-off is increased data integrity when source code is not available versus performance.

- *-o mincache=tmpcache*. Disables delayed writes and extent clears when file is extended; explicit *fsync(2)* required to post changes. The trade-off is data integrity versus performance. This option is useful for temporary files.

- *-o mincache=closesync*. Enables automatic *fsync(2)* upon file close. The trade-off: risk of compromised file integrity and flurry of writes upon close versus the performance cost of waiting for the writes to be done by *syncer*.

- *-o mincache=unbuffered*. All reads and non-O_SYNC writes are unbuffered and do not go through the HP-UX buffer cache. This differs from the *direct* method in that when a file is extended or space is allocated to the file, the inode is not synchronously written to disk. This option is slightly better from a performance standpoint than the direct method.

- *-o convosync=direct*. Converts O_SYNC or O_DSYNC reads and writes to unbuffered reads and writes, and thus, I/Os do not go through the HP-UX buffer cache. Possibly *improves* performance. The trade-off is a reduced need for pages in the buffer cache versus the process always blocking. This option is useful for large I/Os direct from the application since it does not perform a data copy.

- *-o convosync=closesync*. Converts O_SYNC or O_DSYNC writes to delayed with *fsync* at close. The trade-off is between increased performance when source code is not available versus a possible loss of data integrity. This is a **high-risk** option if application robustness depends upon synchronous writes.

- *-o convosync=dsync*. Converts O_SYNC writes to data synchronous. Data is posted synchronously, but inodes are delayed if only access times are being changed. This option improves performance. It is an excellent **low-risk** choice for database and other file systems where files are preallocated; otherwise, it is **medium risk** if access times are not critical.

- *-o convosync=delay*. Converts O_SYNC or O_DSYNC writes to delayed writes. *Improves* performance. The trade-off is increased performance when source code is not available versus a possible loss of data integrity; *high risk* if application robustness depends upon synchronous writes.

- *-o convosync=unbuffered*. Converts O_SYNC or O_DSYNC reads and writes to be sent unbuffered to disk. This differs from the direct method in that when a file is extended or space is allocated to the file, the inode is not synchronously written to disk. This option is slightly more risky than the direct method.

- *-o datainlog*. Posts O_SYNC or O_DSYNC writes to the intent log, as well as inode changes involving access times (default). The trade-off is that the disk heads stay over intent log longer versus potential increased performance by writing data only once with higher potential head movement (inodes to intent log, data directly to extents).

- *-o nodatainlog*. Posts O_SYNC writes of the data directly to the file. This is analogous to HFS behavior. *Improves* performance. The trade-off: fewer writes with possibly increased head movement versus double writes with less head moves.

- *-o logiosize=1024|2048|4096*. This option controls the size of each intent log write. It is useful to be able to change the size because some disk arrays that implement a read-modify-write for certain block sizes may see increased performance by changing the intent log size. The intent log writes are issued in one or more multiples of the specified size.

- *-o noatime*. This option ignores file access time updates unless the file is written or created. This option can reduce overhead and inode update activity on file systems where the access time may not be necessary (such as read-only file systems or for database files).

- *-o qio|noqio*. This option enables or disables quick I/O on a file system. Quick I/O is an optional Veritas option for improving database performance. It requires a separate license. If a system has a license installed, then quick I/O is enabled for all file systems by default unless the *noqio* mount option is specified.

- *-o qlog[=<special device file>]*. This option enables the Veritas Quicklog functionality, where the intent log for multiple file systems can be moved to a dedicated intent logging device. If no device is specified, then a quicklog special device is selected. This option can greatly improve performance when logging is needed. It keeps the disk arm from moving back and forth between the log- and the data-areas on the disk and has the potential for significantly improving disk I/O performance for write-intensive applications.

NOTE: It is very important to understand that any use of the *convosync* option overrides the desire of the original application designer. This override may result in data corruption under certain failure scenarios such as a server power failure. The use of these options should occur only after careful consideration of the consequences and the design of the application. For instance, unless the database vendor specifically allows the use of these options, these options should never be used, especially with database logs and indices.

9.7.2.5 Tuning a JFS File System

The *vxtunefs(1M)* command allows some JFS file system parameters to be tuned dynamically. This command can also be used to view the current parameters for a given file system by only specifying a given file system for the command. The */etc/vx/tunefstab* file contains a list of tunes that are applied to specified file systems each time they are mounted. One can also specify global tunes that should be applied to all file systems in this file and these tuneables take preference over any file system-specific tuneables that were specified. The format of the file can be found by reading the *tunefstab(4)* man page.

The following list describes some of the more important tuneables for performance. For all tuneables that take a size parameter, the size can be specified in bytes, kilobytes (append a *k* or *K*), megabytes (append an *m* or *M*), or sectors (1024 bytes in a sector, append an *s* or *S*).

- *-o discovered_direct_iosz=*. Specifies the size of an I/O request where the file system will copy the data directly into the user buffer versus keeping a copy in the file system buffer cache. This option is helpful to keep large I/Os from polluting the buffer cache. The default size is 256KB.
- *-o max_buf_data_size=*. This specifies the maximum file system buffer size allocated for file data. Only 8KB and 64KB are accepted values. The default is 8KB. 64KB can be used to improve performance when sequentially accessing large files. Use 8KB when doing random I/O or doing I/O in small chunks.
- *-o max_direct_iosz=*. The maximum I/O size that the file system will send to the disk subsystem. Any I/O request larger than this size will be broken up into *max_direct_iosz* chunks. The default value should be sufficient for the majority of applications.
- *-o max_diskq=*. This limits the number of bytes that any one file can have outstanding at one time. The default value is one megabyte. This parameter helps to keeps file flushes from consuming huge amounts of disk bandwidth and locking out other I/O requests. Setting this value higher may increase throughput and decrease responsiveness. Decreasing it may decrease throughput and potentially increase responsiveness for other accesses to the file system.
- *-o read_ahead=*. This is a VxFS version 3.5 option only. It allows the read-ahead behavior of the file system to be modified. Specifying 0 turns off read-ahead. Specifying 1 (the default) enables the standard sequential read-ahead. Finally, specifying 2 enables a more elaborate read-ahead that can detect forward/backward patterns and multi-threaded sequential reads to the same file in addition to simple sequential reads. For completely random workloads, read-ahead can be disabled. For sequential workloads, the level 2 read-

ahead may be needed to achieve optimal performance. By default the level 2 read-ahead can track 5 threads at once. To change this value, the *vx_era_nthreads* parameter in the */etc/system* file can be modified to another value.

- *-o read_nstream=* and *-o read_pref_io=*. These two tuneables work in conjunction to control the amount of read-ahead performed. *Read_pref_io* is the preferred I/O size to use when performing read-ahead (default is 64 KB). The *read_nstream* tuneable controls the total number of read-ahead requests that can be outstanding at one time (default is 1). The total amount of read-ahead performed is the product of *read_nstream* and *read_pref_io*. To increase the amount of read-ahead, either value can be increased. For fast devices, it may be more desirable to increase read_pref_io up to the point of about 256 KB and then start to increase *read_pref_io* if more read-ahead is needed. Measurement on actual workloads is the best way to tune these parameters.

- *-o write_nstream=* and *-o write_pref_io=*. These two tuneables work in conjunction to control the amount of write behind done for a file system. The product of *write_nstream* and *write_pref_io* controls when the file system does its flushing. The *write_nstream* controls the number of *write_pref_io* requests that can be outstanding at one time, while the *write_pref_io* specifies the maximum size of each request. The default value for *write_nstream* is 1 and the default for *write_pref_io* is 64 KB.

- *-o write_throttle=*. This tuneable helps control the write rate to disk. It is primarily intended for systems with lots of memory and slow disks. What can happen in this situation is that many buffers containing recently written data can build up in memory and these buffers then cause a huge I/O bottleneck as they are flushed from memory to a slow disk subsystem. The *write_throttle* tuneable controls the number of buffers that can be written before the file system will start flushing them to disk. The default value is 0, which specifies that only a lack of space causes the buffers to be flushed. This tuneable should only be modified if a slow I/O subsystem is making the system appear to hang as many buffers are flushed to disk.

When using some of the read-ahead or write-behind parameters above with LVM, VxVM, or array striping, the stripe size should be considered when determining good values for the tuneable parameters. In particular, the value for *read_pref_io* and *write_pref_io* sizes should match the block stripe size and the values for *read_nstream* and *write_nstream* should match the number of stripes. If a RAID 5 array is used, then the *write_pref_io* size should match the product of the block stripe size and number of stripes so that full stripes are written, therefore reducing the RAID 5 write penalty.

For applications doing large sequential reads, the I/O request sizes issued should be greater than or equal to multiples of the product of *read_nstream* and *read_pref_io*. For large sequential writes, the I/O requests should be greater than or equal to multiples of the product of *write_nstream* and *write_pref_io*. Finally, when doing large sequential I/O, if the I/O size is greater than the value of *discovered_direct_iosz* as well, the requests will be more efficient by having the data sent directly to the user buffer.

9.7.2.6   JFS System Processes

The following system processes handle the flushing of buffers and other activities for JFS file systems in HP-UX 10.x:

- vx_sched_thread
- vx_iflush_thread
- vx_inactive_cache_thread
- vx_delxwri_thread
- vx_logflush_thread
- vx_attrsync_thread
- vx_inactive_thread

In HP-UX 11.x, there is a single process, *vxfsd*, that is composed of many threads which perform the various file system management operations like the processes listed above.

9.7.3   OnlineJFS

OnlineJFS is an optional product starting with HP-UX 10.01. OnlineJFS requires a JFS file system. OnlineJFS gives the capability of on-line dynamic file system resizing without unmounting. It lets you create a snapshot file system for on-line backup by keeping a copy of the original data when modifications occur. There is also a file system defragmentation utility.

OnlineJFS also allows users to define additional *file advisories* that are attributes of the file or the way that the application accesses the file. These advisories instruct the file system to behave in particular ways. Advisories permit tuning at the level of the individual file, rather than an entire file system all at once.

9.7.3.1   OnlineJFS File Advisories

File advisories pertain to individual files, not to the file system as a whole. They must be set by the use of *ioctl* calls from an application, and they can be backed up only by JFS backup utilities. Here are the advisories:

- `VX_SETCACHE VX_RANDOM`. Do not perform read-ahead. Should improve performance for randomly accessed files and conserve space in the buffer cache.
- `VX_SETCACHE VX_SEQ`. Perform maximum read-ahead. Should improve performance for sequentially accessed files.
- `VX_SETCACHE VX_DIRECT`. Bypass the buffer cache if it is page aligned and I/O size is a multiple of block size; otherwise default to `VX_DSYNC`. Should improve performance for large I/O sizes but process blocks.

- VX_SETCACHE VX_NOREUSE. Do not retain buffer pages in anticipation of future reuse. Should free up buffers in the buffer cache more quickly.
- VX_SETCACHE VX_DSYNC. Write data blocks synchronously and do *not* write the inode synchronously if only access times have changed. Should improve performance because the inode is not posted to disk synchronously if only the access time has changed. Will *degrade* performance if file was not originally opened with O_SYNC.
- VX_SETEXT VX_CONTIGUOUS. Allocate current file size contiguously and fix the extent size. Should improve performance for large files, and for all files that are accessed sequentially.

In addition to the above, there are other file advisories that do not affect performance.

9.7.3.2   OnlineJFS *fsadm* Utility

The *fsadm* utility features on-line file system resizing (note that it will not shrink below currently allocated space); reporting on directory and extent fragmentation; and reorganization of directories and extents to reduce fragmentation.

Defragmentation reorganizes directories by placing all subdirectories first, by ordering regular files by decreasing time of last access, and by compacting to remove free space. Defragmentation reorganizes extents by:

- Moving aged files to the end of the Allocation Unit (AU)
- Reorganizing non-aged files by minimizing number of extents
- Placing small files together in one contiguous extent
- Placing large files into large extents of at least 64 blocks
- Placing individual files into the same AU to improve locality of reference
- Migrating small files and directories to the front of the AU
- Migrating large files and inactive files to the back of the AU

It is recommended that defragmentation be performed once a day to once a month depending on the volatility of the file system. The trade-off is as follows: a severely fragmented file system will degrade performance, but defragmentation *may take a long time* and will definitely degrade on-line performance.

9.7.4   Quick I/O

The Veritas Quick I/O option allows databases to access preallocated file system files much like raw devices. The overhead of going through Quick I/O is almost as low as using raw I/O directly, while providing easier manageability of the files. A special naming convention provided by Quick I/O allows files to be accessed as raw devices while still being accessible as regular files and provides the following performance benefits over regular file system files:

- Support for asynchronous I/O using either the HP async driver or POSIX async I/O

- Support for direct I/O to and from a user buffer, which eliminates double buffering
- Removal of kernel lock contention for file sytem data structures

If Quick I/O is enabled on a system, then accessing a file through the "raw" interface can be done by appending the *::dev:vxfs* string to the end of the file name in the *open(2)* system call. For instance, if the file:

/dbs/account1

needed to be accessed via Quick I/O, it could be opened as

/dbs/account1::dev:vxfs

which would then make accessing the file almost identical to accessing a raw device. Restrictions when using Quick I/O include:

- If the file is being accessed with memory-mapped I/O, it can't be accessed via Quick I/O.
- If the file used for Quick I/O is not contiguous (i.e., it has a hole), then any I/O done in the hole will fail.
- The file cannot be extended by writing to the file through Quick I/O. Quick I/O only supports writing to preallocated file space.

To easily create flat database files, the *qiomkfile* command is provided. It creates a flat file and a link that can be used to the Quick I/O name for the flat file. For instance, specifying:

```
# qiomkfile -s 2000m account1
```

will create two files in the current directory: *.account1,* which is the file system file, and *account1,* which is a link to *.account1::dev:vxfs.* Since the file system file is created with a leading ".", it will be hidden in most listings via *ls* and only the *account1* file will be seen. The command *qiomkfile* will take into account adding extra storage space for Oracle header information to each flat file created if the *-h* option is used.

The Quick I/O feature is enabled by default on all file systems if the Quick I/O package has been purchased. To explicitly disable Quick I/O, the *-o noqio* mount option can be used. There should be no reason to need to disable Quick I/O for a given file system.

9.7.5   QuickLog

The Veritas QuickLog feature is a separate Veritas product that allows the intent logs from separate file systems to be placed on one or more dedicated log devices. This functionality helps to improve performance for metadata-intensive workloads such as NFS and software development environments. Normally, the intent log for a JFS file system is contained on the same device as the actual file system. This can result in seeking back and forth between the intent log region of the device and the data region of the device, causing extra overhead and reduced I/O throughput. By placing the intent log data on a dedicated device, higher performance can be obtained because the intent log can be written more efficiently and the data does not have extra intent log I/Os mixed in with the normal I/O requests. When using high-performance disk arrays and striping among disks, it may not be as important to have the QuickLog feature, since I/Os will be spread among the many disks in the array or stripe anyway. Simply adding more arrays and increasing the striping can help to eliminate I/O bottlenecks.

Up to thirty-two JFS filesystems can have their intent logs redirected to a QuickLog device. There can be up to thirty-one QuickLog devices on a system. The root file system intent log cannot be moved to a QuickLog device. The *qlogstat(1M)* command gives basic I/O statistics such as the number of reads and writes per second, bytes read/written per second, and average service times for the QuickLog devices. Such statistics could also be determined easily by *sar* or *glance*.

9.7.6   Comparison of HFS and JFS

Table 9-6 shows a summary of the two types of file systems, along with some of their advantages and disadvantages.

9.8   Disk Metrics

A variety of global and per-process disk metrics are available for identifying potential bottlenecks in disk I/O. The tools *glance*, *gpm*, and *sar* all provide methods for accessing some disk metrics.

9.8.1   Global Disk Saturation Metrics

The only global disk saturation metric is the per-disk utilization metric provided by *glance*, *gpm,* and *sar*. Unfortunately, this is an unreliable metric for the following reasons:

- The metric refers only to the busiest disk.

- 100% utilization does *not* mean that more I/Os are not possible. 100% utilization means that each time the disk queue length is inspected, there are one or more I/Os in the queue. There could be one I/O or a hundred. It does *not* mean that the disk is fully saturated, merely that it is busy.

- The metric does not reflect the size of the queue. It merely means that there is always at least one I/O pending for the busiest disk.

Table 9-6 HFS and JFS Characteristics

HFS	JFS
syncer flushes data buffers	*syncer* flushes inodes and data buffers
Metadata is written to the inode synchronously	Metadata is written first to the intent log and later to the inode
Data is written directly to blocks	By default, O_SYNC data is written to the intent log first and later to the extent
Enabling *fs_async* causes metadata to be posted by *syncer* (mount-time option or kernel parameter)	There are many mount-time options to control JFS behavior
High performance for small files	Equal performance for any size file
Low performance for large files (> 96 KB and > 16 MB)	Better performance with large files than HFS
Poor performance with database applications	Very good database application performance using Quick I/O
Limited set of features	Complete set of features

9.8.2 Global Disk Queue Metrics

Disk queue metrics are provided in *glance*, *gpm*, and *sar* as a per-disk I/O queue length. In addition, *glance* and *gpm* provide further information that describes the number of processes blocked on Disk, I/O, Buffer Cache, and Inodes.

9.8.3 Other Global Disk Metrics

A variety of other global metrics reported by *GlancePlus* include:

- All disks (Disk Report-d), which includes:
    - Logical and physical read and write rates
    - User, VM, system, and raw I/O rates
    - Remote logical and physical read and write rates
    - Read and write cache hit rates
    - Directory name lookup cache hit rates

- I/O by File System Report (i), including:
  - Logical and physical I/O rates
  - For selected file systems
    a. Logical and physical read and write rates
    b. Logical and physical read and write bytes
    c. Mapping information
- I/O by Disk Report (u)
  - Utilization
  - Queue length
  - KB/second
  - Logical and physical read and write rates
  - I/O rates
  - For selected disk drives
    a. Logical and physical read and write rates
    b. Logical and physical read and write bytes
    c. Queue length and utilization
    d. Mapping information
- I/O by Logical Volume Report (v)
  - LV read and write rates
  - For selected file systems
    a. Read and write rates
    b. Read and write bytes
    c. MWC hits and misses
    d. Mapping information

Sar also provides global disk metrics including:

- All disks (-b option), which includes:
  - Logical and physical read and write rates
  - Character device I/O rates (i.e., raw I/O)
  - Read and write cache hit rates
- I/O by Disk Report (-d option)
  - Utilization
  - Queue length
  - KB/second
  - physical I/O rates
  - Average queue latency
  - Average response time from disk

NOTE: On some versions of HP-UX, the average queue latency and utilization metrics reported by *sar* are not correct. For the queue latency, the reported value may be anywhere from 5- to 15-milliseconds even when there is no I/O queued up (it should be reported as 0 milliseconds). The utilization metric may be overly conservative and report 100% busy even if the device is as low as 10 % busy. These problems were both fixed in HP-UX 11i v2. The queue latency issue is not necessarily broken in all previous releases, but the utilization metric is. *Glance* is not affected by these problems.

9.8.4 Per-Process Disk Metrics

The following per-process disk metrics are available. The amount of information is much more limited than the information available in the global metrics.

- Logical and physical read and write rates
- File system read and write rates
- VM read and write rates
- System read and write rates
- Raw read and write rates
- Byte transfer rate
- Remote logical and physical read/write rate

9.8.5 Typical Metric Values

Disk utilization metrics are misleading because the graph shows only the busiest disk, and displaying it does not mean that it is incapable of more I/O. The physical disk queue is the most meaningful metric: consistent queue lengths as reported by *sar* or *glance* that are greater than four are indicators of bottlenecks. Note that queue lengths reported by these tools are the operating system disk queue lengths, not the length of the queue on each individual disk or array. For instance, if the command queue depth of a disk is set to eight and *sar* reports a disk queue length of four, then there are actually twelve requests waiting to be serviced by the disk.

Use logical and physical rates and buffer cache hit rates to check for the lack of repeated accesses, indicated by a read cache hit ratio < 90%, or a write cache hit ratio < 70%. Then use other metrics to drill down to the causes of physical I/O.

To determine whether the inode table or the buffer cache may be the problem, look at global and process wait states. Note that the cause of a problem may be usage (for example, O_SYNC) rather than too small a size.

Core dumps show up as physical I/O, user I/O, and system CPU, but the file does not show up as open. Remember that memory-mapped file I/O shows up as *virtual memory* I/O.

9.9   Types of Disk Bottlenecks

As with other types of bottlenecks, the four types are:

- Saturation—indicated by 100% disk utilization on one or more disks
- Queue—indicated by *large* per-disk queues *sustained over time* or a high percentage of processes blocked on disk, cache, or inode
- Starvation—less than 100% CPU utilization, and memory bottlenecks
- User satisfaction—poor transaction response time

9.10   Expensive System Calls

This section contains a list of some of the expensive system calls when performing disk I/O. Here are the expensive system calls for basic I/O:

- fsync()
- open
- stat
- sync

9.11   Tuning Disk Bottlenecks

The three ways of tuning disk bottlenecks include hardware solutions, configuration solutions, and application solutions.

9.11.1   Hardware Solutions

There are a variety of hardware solutions, all of which can be thought of as "spending money" solutions. Here are a few common approaches:

- Add disks drives and rebalance the I/O load.
- Add disk adapters and rebalance the I/O load.
- Use faster disks.
- Use faster disk links (e.g., Fibre Channel versus F/W SCSI).
- Use more device controllers, if applicable.
- Switch from disk arrays to stand-alone disks or from stand-alone disks to disk arrays.
- Use mirroring (stand-alone or arrays) to improve read performance. This may, of course, hurt write performance due to the extra writes involved with mirroring.

9.11.2   Configuration Solutions

This set of solutions requires additional study of the existing configuration, as well as some trial and error to obtain the right results.

- Rebalance the I/O load across available disks and adapters.
- Use LVM or VxVM disk striping if the I/O pattern warrants.
- Dedicate disks to a single application.
- Switch from file system to raw I/O.
- Use the *async* disk pseudo-driver for raw I/O, if appropriate.
- Switch from JFS to HFS or vice versa.
- Tune the file system.
- Increase the size of the fixed-size buffer cache.
- Increase the size of the database's internal buffer cache.
- Adjust the mount options.
- Change block size and other tuneables.
- Change OnLineJFS file advisories.
- Minimize the use of symbolic links.
- Start with a clean, empty file system.
- Stop using *ksh* or Posix shell history files for large, script-driven applications or bench-marks. For each line in the shell script, a synchronous write occurs to the history file, since the user may be logged in multiple times. This causes a significant bottleneck on the file system and disk drive containing the user's home directory.

9.11.3 File System Solutions

Another set of approaches to tuning depends on the type of file system you are using. For HFS file systems, you can:

- Defragment the file system by backing it up, recreating it, and then restoring it.
- Use *newfs* and *tunefs* to set block size, cylinder group size, and *maxbpg*.
- Use *newfs* to reduce the number of inodes.

For JFS file systems:

- Use *fsadm* to defragment the file system.
- Try switching to direct I/O.
- Try switching O_SYNC to data synchronous if risk is acceptable.
- Try using QuickLog for metadata-update-intensive applications.
- Try mounting temporary file systems with *-o tmplog*.

9.11.4 Application Solutions

Finally, there are application solutions:

- Review application I/O sizes and access patterns.
- Use relative path names.

• Preallocate files.

• Do not use O_SYNC if application integrity can be maintained.

9.12 Database Issues

The following tuning suggestions apply to databases and database applications, which have somewhat unique features and performance needs.

9.12.1 Use Raw Volumes

It is often recommended to use raw volumes with the async disk pseudo-driver rather than file systems. File systems have the following disadvantages that are troublesome for databases:

• I/Os are double buffered due to the buffer cache causing more CPU utilization and bus consumption.

• I/O size mismatches can cause read-modify-write penalties for RAID 5 type devices.

• Large file fragmentation or scattering frequently occurs.

• Indirect pointers are used.

• There is additional OS overhead.

• File system recovery time is required after a system crash.

• Files can be inadvertently removed.

• Critical database files are opened with the O_SYNC flag. Every time a write occurs to such a file, the file is locked, preventing all other reads and writes to that file.

There are disadvantages to raw volumes as well. These are relatively minor in comparison, but are often "emotional" issues rather than technical ones:

• Raw volumes require special backup tools.

• Moving objects to different disks requires deletion and recreation.

• Objects may not be visible through simple Unix commands. Using raw LVM can reduce this concern, since logical volumes can be given specific names much like a file can.

If you are using the file system, use a large buffer cache and possibly smaller shared-memory segment. However, rule #1 applies here. One must also consider that caching the disk blocks in a large internal application cache may be more efficient since no system calls are invoked to access those blocks. For a database application that was extremely read-intensive and where the same blocks are accessed multiple times, a large internal application would be better than a large file system buffer cache. However, where the application is more write-intensive, a larger file system buffer cache would be better. A large file system buffer cache is also better for times when tape backups are occurring.

In addition, with JFS, the Quick I/O feature should be considered when using the file system to obtain performance equivalent to raw I/O while still maintaining file system semantics. If using raw volumes, use a small buffer cache and large shared-memory segment.

9.12.2 Data Placement Recommendations

The following are some recommendations for placing database elements on disk:

• Place tables and indices on different disks.
• Place logfiles on a separate group of disks and preferably on high-speed disk arrays with write caches.
• Place tables that are accessed concurrently on different disks.
• Place temporary disk areas (used for sorting) on separate disks.
• Stripe large tables across multiple disks.
• Avoid RAID 5 for any data that is modified often, such as tables with frequent updates.
• Don't stripe indiscriminately and don't overdo striping. For instance, don't use LVM or hardware striping *and* database striping together.

From Chris's Consulting Log— Don't assume that striping, or that striping across all of the disks in a Volume Group, will always improve performance. Once, when configuring a very large Sybase database, Chris used LVM to stripe a large table over seventy-two VA7100 arrays in an attempt to spread heavy insert traffic to the table over all arrays. A stripe size of 64 KB was used. However, this created a disk bottleneck on nine of the seventy-two arrays! It ended up that Sybase was placing hot data at multiples of 512 KB within its table. Given a stripe size of 64 KB, every eighth array had hot data on it (512 KB/64 KB = 8). Now, seventy-two arrays divided by eight equals exactly nine, so that is why nine out of the seventy-two arrays were extremely busy. Reconfiguring the logical volume to stripe over only seventy-one of the seventy-two disks at any one time solved the problem.

9.12.3 Review and Tune Database Parameters

Here are a few more general suggestions for tuning the database:

• Tune the database parameters.
• Use the database performance monitors.
• Review locking methods (database, table, page, row).
• LVM mirroring is typically much more efficient than database mirroring (reduced system calls), and hardware based mirroring is typically better than LVM mirroring.
• Database striping features *may* be better than LVM striping, because the database "knows" where the data and holes are.
• The JFS intent log provides no benefit to databases, because database size and structure seldom change, and the database does its own logging anyway.

When changing the file system so that the intent log is not used, make sure that you separate database files (tables, logs, indices) from non-database files, such as error logs and other flat files, onto separate file systems. Disable the intent log only on those file systems that contain pure database files such as the tables, logs, and indices.

9.13   Disk-Related Tuneable Parameters

The following disk-related parameters may be tuned. For HP-UX 10.x systems, these can be adjusted via sam or via the */stand/system* file. For HP-UX 11.x systems, the *kmtune* can also be used for tuning these parameters. Finally, for HP-UX 11i v2 and later releases, the *kctune* command replaces the *kmtune* command for changing kernel-based tuneable parameters. The *kmtune* and *kctune* commands allow some tuneables to be changed dynamically without rebooting the system. See Appendix C, "Dynamically Tuneable Parameters" on page 509, for a list of dynamically tuneable parameters.

- *bufpages*
- *create_fastlinks*
- *dbc_max_pct*
- *dbc_min_pct*
- *default_disk_ir* (10.X and later)
- *max_async_ports*
- *maxfiles*
- *maxfiles_lim*
- *maxvgs*
- *nbuf*
- *nfile*
- *ninode* (keep < 4096)
- *no_lvm_disks* (10.X only)
- *scsi_max_qdepth* (11.0 and later)

9.13.1   *bufpages* and *nbuf*

Bufpages and *nbuf* are used together to control whether a file system is of fixed size or is dynamically sized. When *bufpages* = *nbuf* = 0, the buffer cache is dynamically sized, subject to the limits specified in *dbc_max_pct* and *dbc_min_pct*. The performance of commercial applications is often improved by fixing the size of the buffer cache to an optimal value. It is easiest to set *bufpages* equal to the number of 4KB buffers in the buffer cache. If you don't know what size to pick, a good starting point would be 10%–20% of physical memory. Use the formula:

$$bufpages = n*physmem/4096$$

where *physmem* is the size of physical memory in bytes and *n* is between .10 and .20.

9.13.2 *dbc_max_pct* and *dbc_min_pct*

If you choose a dynamic buffer cache, by leaving *bufpages* = *nbuf* = 0, the kernel starts with a size of *dbc_min_pct* (default 5%) of physical memory, and can grow to *dbc_max_pct* (default 50%) of physical memory. On large memory systems (512 MB or more), setting *dbc_max_pct* to 50% may cause excessive VM paging and, possibly, deactivations. It is better to set *dbc_max_pct* to 20% on large memory systems until there is a clear need for a larger value.

9.13.3 *create_fastlinks*

The *create_fastlinks* parameter is used to control whether symbolic link names less than sixty characters in length are stored in the inode, in place of the pointers, thus saving a disk I/O when the link is referenced.

9.13.4 *nfile*

The size of *nfile* should be increased as necessary to support the needs of the application to open many files. Use *sar*, *glance*, or *gpm* to determine when to increase this value.

9.13.5 *ninode*

The value of *ninode* should be increased only when absolutely necessary. It is used to size the in-core HFS inode table and, indirectly, the in-core JFS inode table, which starts at a size of *ninode*/2 but grows dynamically as needed. The algorithm used to access the HFS in-core inode table degrades in performance when the table has more than 4096 entries. Remember that this table is a cache of the inodes of currently- and previously-opened HFS files. Even when it appears full, it may not be necessary to increase its size because the inodes of closed files are flushed to make room for newly opened files. Increase the size if:

• You see application errors
• Applications often repeatedly open and close a large number of files
• There is a console error message "inode table overflow"
• You see overflows for the inode table in the output of *sar -v*

9.13.6 *max_async_ports*

The *max_async_ports* tuneable controls the maximum number of asynchronous I/O ports available in the system. Database applications such as Oracle and Sybase will open up ports when performing asynchronous I/O. For Oracle, the number of async ports needed is one per process, the sum of which includes parallel query slaves and shadow processes. For Sybase, the number of ports needed is equivalent to the maximum number of processors on the system, so on a sixteen-way system, *max_async_ports* should be at least sixteen. There is a fair amount of memory associated with each port, so if many more are configured than needed, memory could be wasted. The default value is fifty, which will almost always not be enough for running Oracle and will not be enough for running Sybase on a system with more than fifty CPUs.

9.13.7 maxvgs

You will need to increase *maxvgs* if you want to create more than ten LVM volume groups.

9.13.8 maxfiles

The *maxfiles* parameter controls the maximum size of the per-process file descriptor table and defaults to sixty. Some applications require more than sixty file descriptors. Since the algorithm for accessing the table is inefficient when the table gets large, it is better, if possible, to increase the size of the table only for those applications that need it. You do this by modifying the application code to call *getrlimit(2)* and *setrlimit(2)*.

9.13.9 maxfiles_lim, and no_lvm_disks

It should not be necessary and it is not recommended to change the values of these parameters.

9.13.9.1 default_disk_ir

As mentioned earlier, this enables or disables write caching on all disks in the system. Unless it is known that all disks on the system contain a nonvolatile cache or are on a uninterruptible power supply (UPS), this option should not be enabled, thus reducing the chance of any data loss due to power failure or device reset. Instead, it is recommended that the *scsictl* command be used to enable write caching on those disks or arrays that are known to have a nonvolatile cache or have an UPS attached.

9.13.10 scsi_max_qdepth

This tuneable parameter available on HP-UX 11.x systems allows the default queue depth for any SCSI- or Fibre Channel-based device to be set. It is important to understand that although this tuneable parameter is named SCSI, it applies equally to Fibre Channel storage. For HP-UX 11i, the tuneable can be dynamically set without rebooting using the *kmtune* or *kctune* commands.

When a SCSI or Fibre Channel device is opened, the *scsi_max_qdepth* value is used to set the command queue depth of the device. The command queue depth indicates how many I/O operations at one time a given device can handle.

The default value of eight is appropriate for individual disks as well as very small disk arrays (only four to five disks maximum). However, for large disk arrays, the value should be adjusted. A general rule of thumb is the minimum value should be equal to twice the number of disks that an array stripes over. So, for a device such as the VA7100 which stripes over fifteen disks, the value should be set to thirty.

If either this value or a disk's individual value are not set appropriately, disk bottlenecks may appear in the form of idle CPU. Dynamically setting the queue depth on I/O devices using the *scsictl* command can then be done to see if the bottleneck subsides. Note that even though dynamically setting *scsi_max_qdepth* is available in HP-UX 11i, the new value is used when a device is first opened, thus for any devices currently open, the value will be ignored. Therefore, *scsictl* is recommended to change the value on the fly when troubleshooting disk-queuing issues.

9.13.11 HFS-Specific Tuneable Parameters

Prior to HP-UX 11i, there was only one HFS-specific tuneable parameter, *fs_async*. This is a frequently misunderstood parameter. People often think it controls whether data from an HFS file system in the buffer cache is written synchronously or asynchronously. In fact, it refers to how HFS metadata (*superblocks* and *inodes*) are written.

By default, when *fs_async* is set to 0, HFS metadata is written synchronously; that is, any time metadata changes, it is written synchronously to the disk, thus blocking any other I/Os to that file (*inode*) or file system (*superblock*) until the physical I/O completes. This default behavior is intended to ensure structural integrity of the HFS file system in case of a system crash. However, it does so at the expense of diminished system and application performance.

Setting *fs_async* to 1 is generally very risky, although it can substantially improve performance. It is recommended that you leave this parameter at 0. If you are willing to accept the increase in risk that file system structural integrity cannot be repaired by *fsck(1m)* after a system crash, you should change this value on a per-file system basis, using the *-o fsasync* option with the *mount* command.

In HP-UX 11i, several read-ahead tuneable parameters were introduced for HFS. Read-ahead is an optimization where the operating system will speculatively read blocks adjacent to the blocks requested in anticipation that these blocks will be needed in the near future. This optimization allows sequential reads to achieve higher throughput by overlapping the read latency with the request for the actual blocks to be read. The new HFS read-ahead tuneables are:

- *hfs_max_ra_blocks*—This tuneable limits the total number of read-ahead blocks that the operating system may have in flight for any particular HFS file system. The default is eight and the maximum is 128.

- *hfs_max_revra_blocks*—This tunable limits the maximum number of reverse read-ahead blocks that the operating system may have in flight for any particular HFS file system. Reverse read-ahead occurs for a file when it is being read backward instead of by the frequent method of accessing a file from beginning to end. This tuneable should be modified only by HP field engineers because changing it from the default of eight can cause severe performance problems due to excessive read-ahead.

- *hfs_ra_per_disk*—The maximum amount of read-ahead in kilobytes that should be performed on each disk. If multiple disks are contained in a logical volume, then the amount of read-ahead performed for the logical volume is *hfs_ra_per_disk* * number of disks in the logical volume. The default is 64 KB.

- *hfs_revra_per_disk*—The maximum amount of reverse read-ahead in kilobytes that should be performed on each disk. The default is 64 KB. Only HP field engineers should modify this parameter.

- *hp_hfs_mtra_enabled*—This enables (if set to 1) or disables (if set to 0) HP's multi-threaded read-ahead algorithm. By default, this is enabled. The algorithm tries to detect multiple read-ahead streams in a file and perform read-ahead on all streams. Multiple read-ahead streams can occur in a multi-threaded application where each thread is reading a different part of the file sequentially.

9.13.12 JFS-Specific Tuneable Parameters

In HP-UX 10.x, there are no JFS-specific tuneable parameters. However, recent 11.0 and 11i extension media have added some new tuneable parameters:

- *vx_ncsize*—This is used to size the kernel file system directory name lookup cache (DNLC), which improves performance for frequently accessed directories. Default is 1024. This parameter was added because the structure was originally sized based on *ninode*, which is the size of the HFS in-core inode table. The DNLC is now sized based on both HFS and JFS needs. Usually, this parameter does not need to be changed. This parameter is no longer used for JFS version 3.5; instead the *vx_ninode* tuneable is used to size the DNLC for a JFS file system.

- vx_ninode—Controls the size of the internal inode cache for VxFS. The default value of 0 instructs the file system to calculate the size of the table based on the available memory in the system. Setting this value to some other value creates an inode cache of the given number of entries. The default value should be sufficient for most systems. This inode cache can consume memory, so adjusting it lower can help to reclaim system memory. Setting the value lower than *nfile* may result in performance problems, so this should not be done.

- *vx_bc_bufhwm*—Controls the maximum amount of data that can be cached in an internal metadata cache in VxFS. The default value is 0, which allows the system to calculate the size. This should be satisfactory for most systems. However, if a small buffer cache is configured, such as when a database is running on the system, more memory can be reclaimed by setting this value low. On the other hand, if a system has a lot of metadata traffic from file creation/deletions or directory searches, then setting this value higher may help improve performance. The value specified is in kilobytes and the lowest possible value is 6144 KB. This is a JFS version 3.5 tuneable parameter.

- *vxfs_ra_per_disk*—Controls the maximum number of read-aheads on a given disk with JFS file systems. The default is 1024. Usually, this parameter does not need to be changed. This tuneable is obsolete starting with JFS version 3.5; use the *read_nstream*, *write_nstream*, *read_pref_io*, and *write_pref_io vxtunefs* tuneable parameters instead.

- *vx_fancyra_enable*—Enables HP's read-ahead optimizations for JFS. With fancy reada-head enabled, the OS will perform read-ahead operations for both forward and backward streams. This tuneable is obsolete starting with JFS version 3.5; use the read-ahead *vxtunefs* tuneable instead.

- *vxfs_max_ra_kbytes*—Controls the maximum bytes for a read-ahead operation during sequential access of a file. The default is 1024. For applications or systems where there are many large sequential I/Os, it may be useful to increase this value to 65536 (64 KB). This tuneable parameter is obsolete starting with JFS version 3.5; use the *read_nstream*, *write_nstream*, *read_pref_io*, and *write_pref_io vxtunefs* tuneables instead.

To determine if the *vx_ninode* and *vx_bc_bufhwm* values are too large, the *vxfsstat(1M)* command can be run on a file system to show the size and hit rates for these caches. For instance:

```
# vxfsstat /

14:22:10.180 Wed Aug 27 2003 -- absolute sample

Lookup, DNLC & Directory Cache Statistics
    296960 maximum entries in dnlc
 59939952 total lookups              98.43% fast lookup
 59977158 total dnlc lookup          99.94% dnlc hit rate
4652728129444380672 total enter          99.94  hit per enter
         0 total dircache setup       0.00  calls per setup
     70744 total directory scan      26.94% fast directory scan

inode cache statistics
      2918 inodes current       2918 peak              296890 maximum
     23483 lookups            78.54% hit rate
      2918 inodes alloced          0 freed
    220806 sec recycle age [not limited by maximum]
   3600000 sec free age
```

This shows that the inode cache size is configured to be 296,890, but only 2,918 have ever been used. Therefore, on this system, the value for *vx_ninode* could be adjusted to reclaim some memory.

## CHAPTER 10

Network Bottlenecks

$\mathbf{T}$his chapter describes major bottlenecks related to networking in HP-UX. A review of some of the basic concepts of networking for HP-UX is followed by a description of typical symptoms, techniques for diagnosing them, and methods for tuning. Here are the topics:

- Network Hardware Descriptions
- Review of Network Concepts
- Network Access Methods
- Networked File Systems
- Clusters
- Network Metrics
- Types of Network Bottlenecks
- Expensive System Calls
- Tuning Network Bottlenecks
- Network-Related Tuneable Parameters
- Web Server Issues
- Database Server Issues

Dealing with network I/O often involves many choices. The wisdom of **Rule #2**, "Performance tuning always involves a trade-off," is good to remember in this arena.

10.1 Networking Hardware Descriptions

The network subsystem of an HP-UX computer system is composed of network interface cards (NICs) connecting external network devices, including other computers and client workstations to the system. The choice of and number of network interface cards can have a large effect on overall system design. The next sections describe various network interface types and other components of a network infrastructure.

10.1.1 Networking Infrastructure Devices

In order to connect multiple servers together, *hubs*, *switches*, and/or *routers* are almost always required. Early network solutions would connect multiple machines together on a single cable using T-style connectors, but today almost all networking interfaces attach via point-to-point connections to either a hub, switch, or router, which in turn can connect to other hubs, switches, and/or routers.

A hub connects multiple nodes together on the same network via point-to-point connections in a star configuration. A hub has several ports. All nodes sharing a hub share the bandwidth available on the hub and the network traffic from all other nodes attached to the hub is visible to that node. Addresses called MAC (Media Access Control) addresses determine the source and destination nodes. Hubs can be a good choice for connectivity at a low cost, but oversubscribed hubs can quickly become a network bottleneck if not managed properly.

A switch is similar to a hub, but each point-to-point connection is independent and sees only the traffic for the source and destination MAC addresses associated with that point-to-point connection. Exceptions are broadcast and multicast frames, which are passed by the switch to all connections. A switch is a high-speed device that can usually handle the full network bandwidth of all attached networks. Networks linked by a switch can be of the same variety (e.g., Ethernet 10BaseT, or 100BaseT, or GigE, or FDDI, etc.), or the switch can link different network types matching the speed and/or protocols (e.g., joining an FDDI network with an Ethernet network). Since each port on a switch acts independently, two different sets of nodes could transfer data at the full network bandwidth simultaneously. Switches only become a bottleneck if the internal switch bandwidth can't handle the aggregate bandwidth of all of its ports. Switches are a more high-performance solution compared to hubs, but usually cost more money.

A router is a special network switch that quickly moves or routes data from one network to another based on Internet Protocol (IP) addresses. It is more advanced than a general switch because it looks up a destination address via an internal routing table (using what is known as *level 3* protocols), whereas general switches typically use only *level 2* protocols that route requests locally based on the *MAC* address specific to a given node. Routers provide broadcast isolation by sending broadcast requests to only the nodes that should receive the request. Routers tend to be used at higher levels of the networking hierarchy given their ability to route to any address. Finally, routers are a good way to segregate collections of nodes into subnetworks so that the nodes on a given subnetwork can achieve full network bandwidth without being affected by traffic from nodes or other sub-networks, unless data is being exchanged between the subnetworks.

10.1.2 Ethernet

By far the most popular and widely used networking protocol is Ethernet. It is an IEEE standard labeled 802.3. The initial speed of Ethernet was 1 or 3 megabits per second (Mbps), while the first mainstream versions reached 10 Mbps. Ethernet transfers all data across the network in packets that are slightly larger than 1500 bytes in size. The initial Ethernet LANs (Local Area Networks) were mainly constructed with a bus-type structure where multiple nodes attached to a single wire. Any failure in the bus would result in the entire section of LAN being unusable.

The Ethernet protocol allows multiple nodes to share the fabric using an algorithm called Carrier-Sense Multiple-Access Collision Detection (the CSMA/CD protocol). When two nodes happen to transmit simultaneously, both detect a collision and then wait some random amount of time before trying to transmit again. Later, a point-to-point connection was implemented using hubs and switches that allowed multiple nodes to connect to the same Ethernet segment, but any failure in any one LAN segment would affect only nodes on that single segment. A hub or switch failure would still affect all nodes. The use of switches eliminates collision issues, given that only one node per port talks on a dedicated segment between the node and the switch.

In 1995, the 802.3u standard, or Fast Ethernet, was established. This added *full duplex* operation, where a node could both send and receive information at the same time. All connections were also point-to-point using copper cabling. The point-to-point and full-duplex operation eliminates the need for the CSMA/CD protocol. In addition, the one-way bandwidth was greatly increased to 100 Mbps, or 200 Mbps for the aggregate bandwidth with full duplex.

Today, 802.3z, or Gigabit Ethernet, is the fastest mainstream Ethernet standard. This standard allows up to 1 Gbps of bandwidth on the network (2 Gbps in full-duplex mode). Gigabit Ethernet can be implemented with both copper wires and glass fiber connections. As with Fast Ethernet, all connections are point-to-point through hubs, switches, and routers.

Recently, the 10-Gigabit standard was finalized. Products based on the standard will be available for HP-UX. Ten-Gigabit Ethernet is a point-to-point fiber optic solution and is only full duplex. The maximum length of a 10-Gigabit connection is now 40 km versus the 5 km for Gigabit Ethernet, allowing its use in wider area network applications. This larger distance is obtained without using repeaters or extenders, and allows 10-Gigabit Ethernet to be used in more wide area network applications.

10.1.3 FDDI

FDDI (Fibre-Distributed Data Interface) is a fiber-based networking interface that operates at 100 Mbps. It was the high-speed network of choice for server environments before the advent of Fast Ethernet (100 BaseT). FDDI is full duplex and rotates two tokens in opposite directions in a ring configuration. It does not have the collision issues of Ethernet because a node must possess the token before being able to send or receive data.

FDDI networks are limited to a 100 km distance (200 km including the second ring). Nodes can be attached to the FDDI network using single-attach station (SAS) connections via concentrators, or directly via dual-attach station (DAS) connections. FDDI networks usually use an IP Media Transmission Unit (MTU) of 4500 bytes. This large frame has advantages for transfers of large amounts of data among nodes.

10.1.4 ATM

ATM (Asynchronous Transfer Mode) networks are used primarily in the telecommunications industry. ATM networks initially came in speed specifications of 25 Mbps, 155 Mbps, and 622 Mbps. Today, it can reach speeds of 10 Gbps. ATM uses very small, fixed-size cells of 53 bytes, where five of the bytes are for header information and 48 of the bytes are for data. These cells can be easily and quickly switched allowing different streams to be easily intermixed on the same network.

ATM is preferred for telecommunications due to its ability to easily intermix voice and data on the same network. ATM networks usually provide Quality of Service (QoS) features, where some protocols and/or users get a higher priority for network bandwidth than do other protocols or users. This QoS capability is used heavily by networks transferring video, since interruptions in the video stream due to network congestion are usually not tolerated well by the users. ATM is not generally used for general purpose computer networks, especially when all nodes are within a short distance of each other.

Some network service providers (NSPs) have constructed ring networks around cities using ATM. In the United States, these ring networks are called SONET networks. SONET networks can provide high-speed connectivity among sites within a metropolitan area.

ATM networks can also be used for Ethernet traffic by using an encapsulation method called Ethernet over ATM. However, because of the various data types usually transferred over an ATM network (voice, video, TCP/IP, etc.), Ethernet over ATM does not typically provide a consistent or deterministic latency that Ethernet users have come to expect.

10.1.5 Hyperfabric

Hyperfabric is a high-bandwidth, low-latency, proprietary networking interface for HP-UX servers. First generation Hyperfabric systems used copper to transmit at speeds up to 2.56 Gbps, while second generation Hyperfabric systems utilize fibre or copper and can transmit at speeds up to 4.0 Gbps. Hyperfabric is often used in cluster solutions due to its low latency and low operating system overhead. Hyperfabric supports the standard TCP/IP protocols and a specialized Hyper Messaging Protocol (HMP). The TCP and UDP protocols are discussed in detail in Section 10.2.

Hyperfabric can use the HMP protocol to greatly reduce the operating system overhead associated with each network packet. Latency for the second generation Hyperfabric adapter card is less than 42 microseconds using TCP and is less than 22 microseconds using MPI (message passing interface) calls with HMP. Unlike older networking protocols, which are receiver-oriented, HMP uses a Remote Direct Memory Access (RDMA) algorithm that prenegotiates a destination buffer address in the receiving node, and the data is transferred directly from the host bus adapter into the application's buffer in memory. This algorithm was developed at HP Labs in Palo Alto, California.

HMP was developed in conjunction with Oracle to provide much better performance for Oracle's Real Application Cluster™ (RAC) (previously known as Oracle Parallel Server™, or OPS) solutions. Users may be connected to different nodes in the RAC cluster. When multiple users try to write to the same region of the database from different nodes, RAC uses locks to prevent different users from colliding. These locks are then passed across the network when a user or a different node needs to modify the same database region. A RAC cluster using HMP for passing the locks scales much better performance-wise when adding nodes to the cluster as the number of users increases. See Section 10.5.3 for a discussion about choosing the right protocol for use with RAC.

Technical computing clusters, large distributed-data warehousing solutions, and general high-performance clusters can all benefit from Hyperfabric networking.

10.2 Review of Networking Concepts

Networking in HP-UX is composed of several different layers. Figure 10-1 shows the streams-based networking stack for HP-UX 11.00 and later. For HP-UX 10.20 and earlier, the HP-UX networking stack was a monolithic Berkeley-based Unix stack. Unlike the disk subsystem, which uses mainly *read* and *write* system calls, networking can use *read* and *write* as well as *send(2)/recv(2)*, *sendmsg(2)/recvmsg(2)*, *sendto(2)/recvfrom(2)*, and *t_rcv(3)/t_snd(3)* for accessing the network. To create a file descriptor for talking across the network, the *socket(2)* system call can be invoked for the sockets interface and the *t_open(3)* call can be used for the *XTI* interface (X/Open Transport Interface).

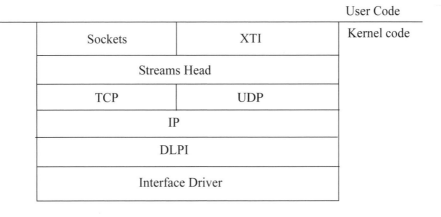

Figure 10-1 Streams Stack

Networking accesses can be either synchronous or asynchronous. Depending on the object type and I/O type, different *system calls* and different *networking layers* are used to access data. The following sections describe the various parts of the networking stack in HP-UX.

10.2.1 Interface Driver and DLPI

This level of the networking stack contains the interface driver code that manipulates the interface card attached to a network. Its main job is to move data to and from the network and pass this data up to the other layers of the networking stack for processing. The interface driver sends data to the upper layers through the *DLPI* (Data Link Provider Interface) layer. The DLPI layer is provided to allow interface drivers to communicate with the other layers without the other layers needing to know specifically the details of how the interface driver's protocols work. For instance, an Ethernet driver and FDDI driver can both talk to the same DLPI layer to communicate to other layers of the network stack.

10.2.2 IP

IP (Internet protocol) is the layer of the networking stack that handles resolving network addresses and routing requests to the proper location. The IP protocol is probably the most wide-spread network protocol used today. It is used to connect hundreds of thousands or more nodes to various disparate physical networks. All nodes in an IP network are given a unique address that describes their logical location within the network. The original *IP Version 4 address* was a 4-byte address (the IP number). When displayed, each byte of the address is typically displayed in decimal and separated by a period. Given the large number of new devices that are able to attach to the Internet, a 4-byte address was starting to limit the number of devices that could be connected. Recently, *IPv6* was introduced, which increased the IP address size to 16 bytes. HP-UX supports the IPv6 standard as an extension to HP-UX 11i v1 and built-in as part of HP-UX 11i v2. HP-UX supports IPv6 via a dual-stack implementation, where both the classic IPv4 and IPv6 stacks are in the kernel simultaneously.

When configuring IP addresses, a *netmask* is used to specify which parts of the address are specific to the network or subnetwork (subnet) and which parts specify the host. A common IPv4 network mask might look like 255.255.255.0. This specifies that the first 3 bytes of the network address identifies the network, while the last byte identifies a node on the network. The network is obtained by bitwise *AND*ing the netmask with the IP address, while the host is obtained by *AND*ing the twos-complemented netmask with the IP address.

The IP address is a network-level address associated with each node in a network. There is also an address associated with each network interface card, or NIC. This hardware address for Ethernet is 48 bits in size and is referred to as the *MAC* address. The *ARP* protocol (Address Resolution Protocol) maps logical IP addresses to actual physical addresses.

IP addresses can be assigned statically or dynamically at boot. Dynamic addresses are assigned via the *DHCP* protocol (Dynamic Host Configuration Protocol).

The IP layer is also responsible for packaging data passed down from the upper layers of the networking stack into *datagrams* that are then sent out across the network. If the amount of data passed in from the upper levels does not fit within one datagram, then the IP layer splits or *fragments* the data into multiple datagram fragments. This is known as *IP fragmentation* and is generally not considered a good thing for performance. Once a sequence of bytes has been fragmented, it needs to be reassembled by IP on the receiving end of the connection. The size of the datagram is generally determined by the *MTU* (maximum transmission unit) of the interface being used to transfer data. For example, Ethernet interfaces typically have an MTU of 1500 bytes, so the IP datagram size used over an Ethernet card with an MTU of 1500 bytes would be no more than 1500 bytes.

10.2.3 TCP

TCP (Transmission Control Protocol) is a reliable full-duplex protocol that guarantees the in-order arrival of a byte stream with built-in retry algorithms when one or more network packets get lost due to network glitches. It is an end-to-end protocol that eliminates the need for an application to deal with putting the pieces of the byte stream back together after it was broken up into pieces for transmission on a particular network. The application also does not have to worry about lost packets, since the protocol itself includes automatic retry algorithms. These capabilities of TCP do not come without a price: TCP is not always a low-latency, high-bandwidth protocol.

When sending a byte stream to a location on the network, TCP will disassemble the data into smaller pieces, called *segments* in proper TCP nomenclature, that are then addressed and put into datagrams via the IP layer for transmission across the network. The *maximum segment size* (MSS) used for each connection depends on the MTU of the interface being used. The MSS will be no larger than the MTU less the size of the TCP and IP headers (which are used to keep track of information about the data). For an Ethernet interface, this typically results in an MSS of 1460 bytes.

To insure that data transferred across the network is not corrupted, the TCP protocol *checksums* all data and transmits this checksum along with the data. A checksum is a summation of all of the bytes contained within a segment. On the receiving end, a checksum of the received segment is also performed and the new checksum value is compared to the checksum value sent. If the values don't match, the packet is considered corrupt and discarded, eventually resulting in a retransmission of the packet. To recover from server or network failures, TCP also allows for automatic retransmitting of data. To prevent a fast sender of data from overwhelming a receiver with data, TCP implements flow-control protocols to pace the rate at which data is sent on a connection.

On the receiving end of a TCP connection, the byte stream is reassembled from the arriving segments. Segments arrive in a different order than originally sent and the TCP layer will make sure the data is ordered correctly. Receiving segments out-of-order, however, can be bad for performance. If too many segments arrive out-of-order, it can cause spurious retransmissions. On well-configured networks, this should not happen. At times, there can be segment reordering on wide-area networks (WANs), however even then, a well-designed and well-run WAN will not reorder segments on a regular basis.

When TCP transfers data across the network, a TCP header is attached to each packet sent. This header contains useful information about each segment, such as the source and destination port, a sequence byte number, the acknowledgement byte number (for acknowledgements), the current receive window size, and a checksum value. There are also some flags that indicate if the segment contains a special TCP-control operation. Figure 10-2 shows the layout of this header. The use and meaning of these fields will be discussed in the next few sections.

16-bit Source Port			16-bit Destination Port	
32-bit Sequence Number				
32-bit Acknowledgement Number				
offset	reserved	flags	16-bit window	
16-bit checksum			16-bit urgent pointer	

Figure 10-2   TCP header

10.2.3.1   Establishing a TCP Connection

The TCP protocol is a point-to-point protocol where a connection is set up and maintained between two machines on the network while communicating. Higher-level protocols are built on top of TCP/IP. In addition, interfaces such as *sockets(7)* or *XTI* are used to communicate with the TCP layer from applications. For instance, the file transfer protocol (FTP) for transferring data between two machines is built on top of TCP and sockets. A well-known *port* is assigned to FTP and an *ftp* daemon *listens* on that port for incoming requests. Incoming requests *connect(2)* to the port where the *ftp* daemon is listening via a TCP SYN control segment to *synchronize* the connection. As part of the synchronization, a starting *sequence number* is specified by the connecting machine. This sequence number will be used for further communications on the connection. After receiving the SYN segment, an acknowledgement segment is sent back to the connecting machine to indicate the SYN was received. In addition, a SYN segment is sent by the receiving machine to communicate its own starting sequence number to the connecting machine. The acknowledgement and SYN can be sent together in one segment. Finally, the connecting machine sends back an acknowledgement segment to fully establish the connection. Once the

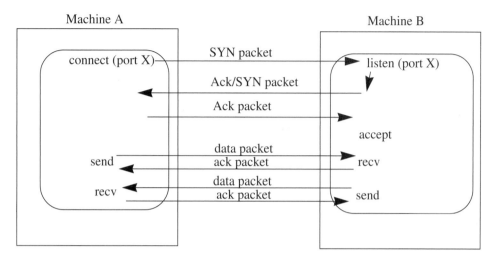

Figure 10-3   TCP Communications

connection is established, the daemon can do an *accept(2)* to start using the connection. A generic picture of a TCP connection establishment is shown in Figure 10-3.

10.2.3.2   Transferring Data

Once the connection is established, *send(2)* and *recv(2)* commands could be used to transfer data between the two machines. After sending each segment, the sending TCP connection waits for an acknowledgement that the receiving TCP connection has successfully received the data. During this time, the sending TCP connection must keep all information about the sent segments in case they need to be retransmitted. When the receiving side of the connection successfully receives data, it sends back an acknowledgement, which allows the sending TCP connection to free resources for the given segment.

This general mechanism for how TCP transfers data would result in a lot of overhead on the network if individual acknowledgement segments needed to be sent for each data segment received, especially for small segments. In addition, if the machine producing data is much faster than the machine receiving data, overflows could occur if the sending TCP connection is allowed to send without any control-flow. Finally, sending very small amounts of data could quickly swamp a system if a segment were to be sent for each piece of data. Fortunately, TCP has several algorithms for handling these situations, which are discussed below.

Sliding Window Algorithm

To allow for efficient flow of control, TCP maintains the quantity of bytes available that a receiving connection can accept before filling its receive buffer. This is referred to as the *receive window size*. The current receive window size is adjusted or *advertised* potentially as often as every transfer. However, in most cases, the window update is sent along with data or acknowledgements back to the sender in the TCP header (see Figure 10-2). The size of the receive window field in the header is only 16 bits, which would indicate a maximum window size of 64 KB - 1. However, with TCP RFC 1323 and later, a "window scaling" option is allowed during the connection synchronization sequence (passed in the SYN segments) that provides a shift factor for the window size. This shift factor is then applied to the window size value to allow for window sizes much greater than 64 KB - 1.

If the window reaches zero, no more data can be sent until a window update is received from the receiving side. If the window goes to zero and the receiving TCP does not send a window update for some period of time, the sending side will send a window probe segment to get a window update.

Whenever the receiving window size reaches zero, this indicates that the receiving application has stopped processing the incoming data for some reason. Any number of events could cause this. For instance, the receiving side application may not be getting enough CPU cycles to process the incoming data. Also, the receiving application may actually be waiting on some other resource, such as a disk, and can't get to the network queue.

Handling Acknowledgement Segments

Sending a separate acknowledgement segment for every data segment could become quite costly. This would effectively double the number of segments on the network. In order to reduce the number of separate acknowledgement segments, there is an algorithm in TCP to "piggyback" acknowledgements on *data segments* or *window update* segments. This is referred to as the *delayed acknowledgment* behavior. When a TCP connection receives data, it will delay sending the acknowledgement for a period of time defined by the *standalone ACK timer*. If during this delay the TCP connection needs to send data back, it will simply piggy-back an acknowledgement for data it received on the segment it sends. It will also piggy-back an acknowledgement on *window update* segments. If the acknowledgement can't be combined with some other segment being sent before the standalone ACK timer expires, then a separate acknowledgement segment will be sent out. For HP-UX, the default time for the acknowledgement timer is 50ms for HP-UX 11.00 and 11i and 200ms for HP-UX 10.20.

Nagle Algorithm

For interactive network connections such as a *telnet* connection, the network traffic would be tremendous if a segment were sent for every character typed. Therefore, the Nagle algorithm was developed that works as follows:

- If data is requested to be sent and the connection is idle (no outstanding acknowledgements) or the amount of the request plus any unsent data in the send queue is greater than the MSS, then send the request and all the unsent data now.

- Otherwise, queue the data and wait for more data to come down via a send request. If the connection becomes idle again (i.e., all outstanding segments get acknowledged), then data is sent out.

This algorithm greatly helps bundle multiple small sends together into larger segments on the network. However, the algorithm can cause strange interactions in some instances with the delayed acknowledgement algorithm. What can happen is that an application that manages to send out a message in two sends may end up waiting a full delayed acknowledgement time-out before all of its data is sent. The following example shows this situation:

1. Send (10 bytes). Connection is idle, so this gets sent immediately. The receiving application receives the data, but does not know what to do because this is only a partial message.
2. Send (15 bytes). This data is not sent since no acknowledgement has been received from the first send.
3. 50 ms passes and delayed acknowledgment timer expires on the receiving side.
4. Receiver sends an acknowledgement for the first 10 bytes sent.
5. The second send (15 bytes) is sent on the now-idle connection.
6. The receiving application receives the rest of the message and now knows what needs to be sent, so it sends back data as its reply piggy-backed with the acknowledgement for the 15 bytes received.
7. Initial node receives data and the 15-byte acknowledgement.
8. 50 ms passes and the delayed acknowledgement timer expires (on the initial node).
9. Initial node sends back an acknowledgement for the data it received.

Interactions with Nagle and the delayed acknowledgement algorithm introduced a 50 ms delay at Step 3. Had the initial message been given to TCP at one time, as properly written applications will do, it would not have been delayed.

10.2.3.3   Handling Time-outs

As part of the reliability feature of TCP, it verifies that all segments reach the remote TCP connection. This is done via the acknowledgement mechanism. Everything works fine as long as the receiving side always returns acknowledgements, but what if an acknowledgement is never returned due to a failing machine or lost segment? TCP handles the possibility of not receiving an acknowledgement by using timers that will expire if a certain amount of time has elapsed before an acknowledgement for sent data has arrived. Each time a segment is sent, TCP sets a *retransmission* timer that expires after some fixed amount of time. The wait time due to the retransmission timer can be different for each TCP connection. The time set is based on a round-trip time (RTT) estimation with the minimum wait time in HP-UX being 500 ms. The round-trip time is simply the time between when a segment was sent and when an acknowledgement for the segment was received. The round-trip time estimate is calculated dynamically as acknowledgements are received. A weighted average of the round-trip times for each segment sent is used to estimate how long the retransmission time-out should be. Basing the retransmission time-out on RTT is done because some transfers, such as one traveling across the world, may take much longer than others, so one retransmission time-out will not suffice for all connections. Having too long of a retransmission time-out would cause a connection to idle longer than necessary.

When a retransmission timer does expire, the sending side will retransmit the data and set a new retransmission time value. The new retransmission time is adjusted to twice the old value to allow for the possibility that the network was just slow and the segment was not really lost. If the time-out were not adjusted, then every segment sent may experience another time-out and forward progress would not be made. There is a limit in HP-UX as to the amount of time that can be set for the retransmission time-out–this is 60 seconds by default.

Additionally, TCP provides for a *fast retransmission* mechanism to help detect lost segments. The fast retransmission algorithm works because the receiver returns an acknowledgement when an out-of-order segment is received. As long as the receiver does not receive the segment it was expecting, it continues to send out immediate acknowledgements for that segment for every other segment it receives. For instance, if the sender sends segments 1, 2, 3, 4, 5, and 6 but segment 3 gets lost, then the receiver would return an acknowledgement for segment 3 when receiving segment 4, an acknowledgement for segment 3 when receiving segment 5, and an acknowledgement for segment 3 when receiving segment 6. If three such duplicate acknowledgements are received in a row, then the sender assumes segment 3 was lost and issues a retransmission of that segment. If segment 3 was simply reordered slightly by the network, the acknowledgements might be segment 3, segment 3, then segment 7, which indicates the receiving end found segment 3 and now expects to receive segment 7. In this case, a retransmission would not occur, given that the receiver now indicates it is expecting segment 7. This fast retransmission algorithm allows for quickly retransmitting data when segments are lost and eliminates having to wait potentially 500 ms or more for the retransmission timer to expire.

10.2.4 UDP

UDP (the User Datagram Protocol) is a raw protocol for sending information across the network. UDP is an unreliable protocol that does not guarantee either that messages arrive in order or that they arrive at all. It is completely up to the application to reorder messages, and to respond to lost messages. UDP, however, does provide checksum protection to ensure that data is not corrupted during transit.

UDP is a connectionless protocol. A connectionless protocol differs from a connection protocol like TCP in that it can obtain data from any host at any time on an endpoint. It can also send data to any host without setting up a connection.

10.2.5 Sockets

Sockets are the interface that allow a programmer to access the TCP/IP and UDP layers of the networking stack. Currently, sockets in HP-UX are Berkeley-based, but may become X/Open-based in the future.

10.2.6 Auto Port Aggregation

Auto Port Aggregation (APA) is an optional software subsystem that is available from HP in HP-UX revisions 10.20 and 11.x. APA works with Ethernet, FDDI, and Token Ring and provides two major features:

- Aggregation of multiple network host bus adapters (NICs) into a single logical network represented by a single network IP address.
- Failover of network connections from a failed NIC to any of the surviving NICs without loss of the connection.

Aggregating multiple NICs onto a single network backbone can significantly improve network performance in and out of the node running APA, especially when a single host bus adapter is slower than the network's bandwidth or cannot transfer enough data to make full use of the bandwidth of the network.

10.2.7 Streams

Streams are a mechanism that allows networking components to be connected together in a pipeline fashion. Multiple streams drivers can be connected in different order in a pipeline to perform networking tasks. For instance, an encryption stream module could be added to the standard networking stack such that data is encrypted before being sent out over the network. Streams support has been in HP-UX since HP-UX 10.30.

10.2.8 Checksum Offload

Some network interface cards have the ability to checksum the data on the adapter card versus having the operating system do the checksum. This functionality is referred to as checksum offload. In particular, HP's Gigabit Ethernet cards automatically provide for checksum offload. Performance is improved by not using CPU cycles on the server to perform the checksum operation.

10.3 Networking Access

There are various ways to access data remotely over the network. All methods are built upon the basic networking described earlier.

10.3.1 Ports

When communicating over a network to a host machine with TCP or UDP, a port address is used to specify the application that should receive the network request. Port numbers 0 through 1024 are reserved ports that are identical among all hosts and available only to applications with root-level privileges. There are 65536 total ports available. The */etc/services* file in HP-UX describes all of the assigned networking ports.

10.3.2 FTP

FTP (file transfer protocol) is commonly used on UNIX system to transfer file data between machines. On HP-UX, the *ftpd* daemon handles listening on the ftp port and accepting new ftp connections.

10.3.3 Telnet

Telnet is a protocol used to establish an interactive session on a remote machine. The *telnetd* daemon in HP-UX listens for new telnet connections. It will fork a new process for each new telnet connection.

10.3.4 Rlogin

The *rlogin* (remote login) program is used to establish a new network session on a remote machine. The *rlogind* daemon listens for new *rlogin* connections and forks off a new *rlogind* process for each new connection. A *.rhosts* file can be set up to bypass the login prompt allowing quick logins. Having a *.rhosts* file for the root user can be a security issue and is not recommended.

10.3.5 Name Resolution

All network transactions are via the numeric IP address. Unfortunately, humans deal with names better than with numbers. Therefore, various ways exist to translate a machine name into its IP address. There are both static and dynamic ways of managing these mappings. Efficient name resolution can be very important for applications that need to know addresses often, such as Web-based applications. The following describes the different methods for resolving names in HP-UX.

10.3.5.1 */etc/hosts* File

The */etc/hosts* file on each system provides a static mapping of machine names to IP addresses. It is simply a flat file that is read to find a particular IP address for a given server name. This is a fast and efficient way to manage address mappings when there are very few of them, such as fifty to one hundred, and when the address mappings don't change often. The */etc/hosts* file is parsed on each query, so it should just contain hostnames and addresses with comments minimized or eliminated. The addresses should also be organized from most-frequently accessed to least-frequently accessed.

Having an */etc/hosts* file is very important for name resolution performance in situations where a small group of remote machines are highly accessed. This removes pressure from dynamic name resolution methods, described below, that use a nameserver to resolve names. For NFS-mounted filesystems, it may be beneficial to add the NFS servers name resolutions in the */etc/hosts* file to improve the name resolution performance.

10.3.5.2   DNS

DNS (Domain Name System) provides a dynamic mechanism for translating a symbolic server name, such as www.hp.com, into an IP address. This system is actually a distributed collection of many servers around the world that propagate and cache mappings of symbolic names to IP addresses. To enable DNS for system name lookup, the */etc/resolv.conf* file, which contains IP addresses of *nameservers* that should be used to resolve system names, needs to be added. Usually a primary DNS server is specified as well as one or more backup servers. The backup servers are specified in case the primary server is unreachable due to a crash or network failure. For more detailed information regarding the format of the */etc/resolv.conf* file, refer to the *resolver(4)* or manpage.

The actual nameserver systems may need to be quite powerful, depending on the number of client systems that resolve addresses to each host or the rate at which name resolutions occur. Name resolution performance can be quite important for Web-based applications and NFS, so making sure that the nameserver systems are free of bottlenecks is important. The *named(1M)* process handles the requests for name resolutions on the nameserver systems.

10.3.5.3   NIS and NIS+

The *NIS* (Network Information Service) and *NIS+* (Network Information Service Plus) services developed by Sun Microsystems allow certain configuration files for several machines to be managed in a central location on a network. Files such as */etc/hosts*, */etc/password*, */etc/group*, */etc/services*, and others can be centralized on a server machine so individual copies don't need to be maintained on all machines in a network.

When NIS and NIS+ are used to centrally manage these files, the speed of the NIS/NIS+ server is important for the overall performance of the network. Small groups of systems (say, 30-50) should be managed by one NIS/NIS+ server. In addition, this server needs to be very reliable or else backup servers should be used, because losing an NIS/NIS+ server will cause the clients it is serving to no longer allow certain operations such as login. NIS and NIS+ is a convenience feature and it can add overhead to operations such as login where the server manages the needed information (i.e., the */etc/password* file). Both NIS and NIS+ provide name resolution as well as maintaining a centralized view of important files. For more detailed information regarding NIS and NIS+, please refer to man pages and on-line documentation.

10.3.5.4   */etc/nsswitch.conf* File

The */etc/nsswitch.conf* file is important for tuning name resolution performance on servers. This file lets an administrator specify the order in which the various name resolution methods are executed to resolve names. If this file is not present when trying to resolve host names, then by default, HP-UX will try DNS first, followed by NIS, and then followed by the */etc/hosts* file. This default behavior may not always be the most optimal for performance. For instance, even under the default behavior, resolving the name of the local machine will require going to a nameserver! The following shows output from the *nslookup(1)* command on a machine configured without an */etc/nsswitch.conf* file:

```
hpperf1-100> nslookup hpperf1
Name Server:  pal-resolver.americas.hp.net
Address:  15.243.160.51

Trying DNS
Name:     hpperf1.cup.hp.com
Address:  15.13.168.63
Aliases:  zebra.cup.hp.com
```

Notice that looking up the address of the host machine results in a DNS name lookup request to the nameserver. Copying the */etc/nsswitch.hp_defaults* file to */etc/nsswitch.conf* and changing the line with "hosts" on it as follows:

```
hosts: files [NOTFOUND=continue] dns
```

will result in the */etc/hosts* file being searched first, and then the DNS server, for a name. The */etc/hosts* file should always contain the address resolution for the host system and any highly accessed systems. After making the above modification to *nsswitch.conf*, an *nslookup(1)* to the host system looks like:

```
hpperf1-100> nslookup hpperf1
Using /etc/hosts on:  hpperf1

looking up FILES
Name:     hpperf1
Address:  15.13.168.63
Aliases:  hpperf1.cup.hp.com, zebra, webperf
```

Here the *FILES* method, which uses */etc/hosts,* was used for name resolution. Remember that the size of the */etc/hosts* file should be kept to a minimum because the entire file may be parsed on each lookup.

10.3.6 World Wide Web

Clients accessing the World Wide Web (WWW) use the HTTP (Hypertext Transfer Protocol) protocol to connect to a server. A Web server will usually listen on port 80 for incoming HTTP connections and reply with data based on the request. WWW servers need good name resolution performance due to the large number of short-lived connections that happen on a Web server. Each Web transaction can be a very short-lived connection, which requires a name resolution lookup each time.

10.4   Networked File System

The Networked File System (NFS) was developed by Sun Microsystems and is licensed by almost every operating system vendor. It provides a mechanism for sharing files across a network. There have been three revisions of NFS. The first version was a Sun proprietary version that was never available to other vendors. The second version was released in 1984 and available for use by other vendors. Finally, a third version was released in 1994 that tried to address some of the performance issues in earlier versions.

10.4.1   General NFS issues

NFS is a client/server architecture, so obtaining good overall performance requires tuning both the client side and the server side. NFS is also very network-, filesystem-, and disk-intensive, so making sure these are all tuned properly will help NFS performance. A lot of the NFS infrastructure depends on efficient name resolution, so making sure that the name resolution server is fast is important for good NFS performance.

10.4.1.1   NFS Version 2 Description

Version 2 of NFS was the first one available for non-Sun customers and is available on HP-UX versions 7.x onward. This version was initially supported only using the UDP, but is now also supported using the TCP. An HP-UX extension allows asynchronous writes to the server (synchronous writes are the default) via an export option. Asynchronous writes are faster than synchronous writes but are not totally safe, given that data could be lost if a server crashes before the asynchronous data has been written to disk. Transfers are up to 8 KB in size for both reads and writes. The maximum supported file system size is only 2 GB.

When accessing data attributes (such as permissions), Version 2 of NFS uses the *LOOKUP* and *GETATTR* requests. These requests can be a fairly high percentage of the overall requests to an NFS server. In addition, the *READDIR* and *LOOKUP* requests are used to access directories.

10.4.1.2   NFS Version 3 Description

Version 3 of NFS comes standard with HP-UX 11i and as a patch to HP-UX 11.00. It implements a safer form of asynchronous writes that is enabled by default, but may not perform as well as HP-UX's Version 2 asynchronous write implementation. It allows NFS to use the TCP, which allows for better performance over wide-area networks. It increases the read and write buffer transfer sizes to 32 KB maximum. Also, the maximum file system size supported is much larger with Version 3, since it uses unsigned 64-bit values for offsets compared to the signed 32-bit offsets used in Version 2. With HP-UX 11.00, one can mount 1 TB file systems, while with HP-UX 11i one can mount 2 TB file systems.

When accessing file attributes, Version 3 of NFS returns this information in every reply, so usually, explicit attribute requests are not needed, which reduces network overhead. For directory accesses, the *READDIRPLUS* request was added to combine *READDIR* with *LOOKUP*. This request can be slower, however, if file attributes are not needed.

10.4.2 Client-Side Issues

The client is where NFS file systems are mounted. The client is the one that actually reads and writes files that result in NFS requests being sent to the NFS server. On the client, *biod* processes can be used to help speed up reads and writes. The number of *biod*s used are tuned by adjusting the value NUM_NFSIOD in */etc/rc.config.d/nfsconf*.

If no *biod* processes are configured, then each process requesting a read or write operation from an NFS-mounted file system will block until the data is read or written from the server. If *biod*s are used, then an initial read for sequential data will block the application, but the *biod* will asynchronously read-ahead other blocks in anticipation that they will be needed. When using an asynchronous write mount option, a *biod* will let a process return as soon as it receives the written data and the *biod* will lazily flush written data to the NFS server in a write-behind manner.

The default number of *biod*s configured is four on HP-UX 11.00 and earlier releases, while it is sixteen on HP-UX 11i. Due to kernel contention issues in HP-UX 11.00, setting the number of *biod* daemons high, especially when the client uses large numbers of processors, can result in poor performance. For HP-UX 11.00 systems, it is recommended to keep the number of *biod*s low. The kernel contention issue was fixed in HP-UX 11i, so setting the number of *biod*s higher is not a real performance issue.

One might actually get the best performance by not configuring any *biod* processes at all. The reason for this is that when using *biod*s, the number of outstanding requests to the server is limited by the number of *biod* processes. Therefore, if the client has many different processes all issuing NFS requests, the total number of outstanding requests may actually be higher than the number of configured *biod* processes. Also, if *biod*s are used, an unavailable NFS server can make all *biod*s hang, causing accesses to available NFS servers to also not be serviced. Random read requests also don't benefit from *biod* processing since the *biod*s are only providing read-ahead in the read case. Finally, if the file system is mounted without using asynchronous writes, or if file locking is used, then the *biod*s don't help in the write case either, since all writes must block until the NFS server replies with success.

10.4.3 NFS Server-Side Issues

The server side of an NFS environment handles all of the file requests from the clients. On the server, the *nfsd* daemons service the NFS requests from the clients for UDP connections and they manage the TCP connections. The number of daemons can be adjusted by tuning the NUM_NFSD variable in */etc/rc.config.d/nfsconf*. The default is four for HP-UX 11.00 and earlier, but is sixteen for HP-UX 11i; there is no large disadvantage for configuring too many, other than causing the *nproc* limit to be reached. The *nfsd* daemons can also be initiated by using the */usr/sbin/nfsd* command.

When *nfsd* daemons are requested by setting NUM_NFSD or by running the *nfsd(1M)* command, the actual number of *nfsd* daemons started will be greater than the number specified. The number actually created will be an even multiple of the number of processors in the system, plus one. So, specifying fifteen for NUM_NFSD on a 4-way system will create seventeen *nfsd* processes. The reason more *nfsd* daemons are created than requested is that HP-UX will assign an *nfsd* to each active processor in the system, and there must be a whole number of *nfsd*s per processor. HP-UX does this to improve NFS performance by keeping *nfsd* daemons from migrating from processor to processor and thus reducing processor cache misses.

The *nfsd* processes handle read requests via looking in the local buffer cache and returning any found data. If the data is not found in the local buffer cache, then the daemon issues a disk read request and blocks waiting for the data to return from disk. Once the data returns, the data is sent to the client. For writes, synchronous NFS connections will block until the data is written all of the way to disk. Thus, for synchronous connections, it is important to have very fast disks to reduce the waiting on synchronous writes. Disk arrays with non-volatile write caches usually make very good disks for NFS servers, given that writes to the arrays return immediately after the data is written to the array cache (usually well under one millisecond). For asynchronous writes, the server returns acknowledgement to the client as soon as the data is written to the buffer cache. Then for Version 2 of NFS, the server tries to write out this data before the server may crash, to minimize any data loss. For Version 3 of NFS, the server tries to write out the request before receiving a *COMMIT* request to flush dirty data to disk.

In addition to *nfsd* processes, the system will create one multi-threaded *nfsktcpd* daemon if TCP connections were specified. TCP connections can be specified by setting the environment variable NFS_TCP in */etc/rc.config.d/nfsconf* to one. The *nfsktcpd* daemons handle servicing the TCP NFS requests. A maximum of ten threads per connection will be spawned to handle TCP requests. This can be an issue because one connection is set up for a client for all file systems it mounts from a given server. For a client with many processors, having only ten threads servicing its requests can be a performance issue. Of course, if there are several clients all accessing the server, then the ten-thread limit is not as big of an issue, since there will be ten threads per client. The threads assigned for a TCP connection only handle requests for that connection.

Finally, the *nfskd* daemon does nothing in HP-UX. It was designed to handle UDP requests, but those are handled by the *nfsd* daemons in HP-UX.

10.4.4 UDP Versus TCP Issues for NFS

The choice to use UDP or TCP for NFS connections can sometimes be a difficult one. There are various factors that make one protocol better the other; this is another example of Rule # 2. In general, using TCP will result in the best performance when mounting NFS file systems over wide-area networks. This is due to TCP's ability to better handle network problems, which can occur more often as more networking layers are involved. Also, some network switches may not provide as much buffering memory for UDP requests, since UDP is not usually as commonly used as TCP and thus these switches may drop UDP packets under load while not dropping TCP packets. In general, UDP can be used for small local area networks where the number of network retransmissions are small.

Another factor that may influence the choice of using TCP or UDP is the efficiency of each protocol on the systems involved with the NFS transactions. If a particular system can process TCP requests much faster than UDP requests, then it may benefit from using TCP for NFS instead of using UDP.

10.4.5 NFS Options

You can configure export options on the NFS server and mount options on the NFS client. Some of these have performance implications.

10.4.5.1   NFS Export Options on the Server

The *async* option, when set in the */etc/exports* file, enables asynchronous writes. The *biod* process waits only until the data has been written to the buffer cache on the server by the *nfsd* process. The trade-off is potential data integrity problems if the server crashes after it has replied to the client, versus improvement of write performance. This is a **medium-risk** option, depending on application needs.

The default is synchronous writes. The *biod* process waits until the data has been written to the disk by the *nfsd* process and file system. Note that the process does not wait while the *biod* sends the write to the server.

10.4.5.2   NFS Mount Options on the Client

The following options to the *mount* command have performance implications:

- *-o acdirmax* or *-o acregmax*—Retain directory cache and inodes on the client for a maximum of 60 seconds (the default) if not modified. The trade-off is potential data integrity problems versus the frequency of inode reads from the server.
- *-o acdirmin* or *-o acregmin*—Retain directory cache and inodes on the client for a minimum of 30 seconds for directories and 3 seconds for inodes if not modified.
- *-o noac* or *-o nocto*—Suppress inode and name-lookup caching. Suppress inode rereads upon file open. The trade-off is the risk of stale information versus quick file reopens and I/Os.
- *-o rsize*—Set NFS read-buffer size (default set by kernel). The largest possible should be used for NFS Version 3 (32768).
- *-o wsize*—Set NFS write-buffer size (default set by kernel) When buffers are smaller than block size, multiple I/Os are required. Make sure that wsize is >= the file system block size. For NFS Version 3, a value of 32768 is recommended.
- *-o vers*—Set the NFS version (2 or 3). By default, HP-UX will choose the highest version supported by both the client and server.
- *-o proto*—Use a specified network transport protocol (either TCP or UDP). By default, in HP-UX 11i, a TCP connection will try to be established. If this can't be established, then a UDP connection will be used. For HP-UX 11.00 and lower, the default is to use UDP.
- *-o timeo*—Set NFS time-out (.7 second default). Decreasing the time-out increases network traffic.

10.4.6 Measuring NFS Performance

Because the performance of the NFS filesystem involves the network, local file systems, and disk subsystem performance, bottlenecks can occur at any of these places and affect NFS performance. To directly count the number of NFS transactions, one can use the *nfsstat(1M)* command. This command provides static counts of both NFS Version 2 and Version 3 transactions for both server and client sides. For instance, it will display the number of NFS read and write requests handled by a server with *-s* option. Since only cumulative counts are provided, one needs to run the *nfsstat(1M)* twice with a delay in between to determine rates at which certain types of NFS transactions are occurring. The *-c* option gives statistics for the client side of NFS. Finally, the *-m* option provides useful information describing all of the mount options used for each NFS file system, such as the version used, protocol used, and read/write buffer sizes used.

10.4.7 Local File System Usage With NFS

The layout of a file system exported with NFS can make a different for performance. In general it is better to have a flat directory structure compared to a very deep structure with lots of subdirectories. The reason for this is due to NFS needing to issue LOOKUP/READDIR calls (Version 2) or READDIRPLUS calls (Version 3) for directories. Less directory depth means fewer of these calls will need to be made. However, making the directory structure too flat, with too many files in one directory, can also cause problems. There is an *rnode* structure maintained for every file in a directory and there are only a fixed number of these. So, if a large directory is searched, these entries may need to be reused. Reusing entries in HP-UX 11.00 causes the buffer cache to be purged of buffer pages matching the *rnode* values. If there is a large buffer cache, this operation can then take a while. The number of *rnodes* is sized indirectly via the *ninode* or *ncsize* tundables. This performance problem was fixed in HP-UX 11i.

In general, it is recommended that VxFS be used for file systems that will be exported via NFS. VxFS is able to invalidate files from the buffer cache quicker than HFS, since VxFS organizes the cache on a file-by-file basis versus a block basis. So, for HFS, a file invalidation requires searching the entire cache to find all related blocks. However, for VxFS, all of the blocks are organized with the file, so they can be quickly found and purged. When using VxFS, an 8 KB block size should be used with a 16MB intent log. The delay mount option should also be used if possible.

10.4.8 Other NFS-Related Processes

There are several other processes that participate in NFS activity on an HP-UX system. This section describes some of those processes and their effect on performance.

10.4.8.1 *Rpc.mountd*

The *rpc.mountd* process is a single-threaded process in charge of mounting file systems on NFS servers. It is started automatically when NFS_SERVER is set to 1 in */etc/rc.config.d/nfsconf*.

The performance of this process depends on the speed of hostname resolution. In addition, when using NIS, nested netgroups can take a long time to access, so making netgroups flat can help *mountd(1M)* performance. Problems with long startup times for the *rpc.mountd* daemon can sometimes be resolved by cleaning the */etc/rmtab* file, because this file is read every time the *mountd(1M)* daemon is started, and a large one can take several minutes to read.

10.4.8.2   *Rpc.lockd* and *rpc.statd*

The *rpc.lockd* and *rpc.statd* work in conjunction to handle file locking in NFS. The *rpc.lockd* handles the actual file lock requests, while the *rpc.statd* monitors the system to recover locks on failures. These two daemons the state which is needed for locking on top of NFS which is stateless. Name resolution performance has a big impact on locking performance. In general, however, file locking will slow down NFS accesses, so it should not be used unless absolutely needed.

10.4.8.3   *Automount* and *AutoFS*

The *automountd(1M)* daemon automatically mounts and unmounts NFS file systems. There are two different versions of this daemon in some versions of HP-UX–either the original *automount* style or the new *AutoFS* style. The two versions differ greatly in how they work.

The *automount(1M)* daemon was the original method for automatically mounting and unmounting NFS file systems. It only supports NFS Version 2 using UDP. It is single threaded and acts as a pseudo-NFS server. When mounting an NFS file system, it mounts the file system under a location in */tmp_mnt* and then creates a symbolic link from the specified mount location to the place where it mounted the file system under */tmp_mnt*.

The *AutoFS* automounter, however, works much differently because it is implemented on top of a real file system. It is multi-threaded and mounts the NFS file system directly to the location requested without using symbolic links. It works with NFS Version 3, using both UDP and TCP. It also works with the *CDFS* and *CacheFS* file systems. *AutoFS* is standard in HP-UX 11i and is available via a patch to HP-UX 10.20 and 11.00.

The original automounter will typically add overhead on the client for NFS. It also typically does not perform well since it is not a native file system and due to its single-threaded implementation. This automounter may also issue unnecessary unmount requests, causing more mounting and unmounting as a file system is accessed. The original automounter is enabled by setting the AUTOMOUNT variable to 1 in */etc/rc.config.d/nfsconf*.

The *AutoFS* version of the automounter is typically a better performing solution, given its native file system implementation. To enable the *AutoFS* automounter, set the AUTOFS variable to 1 in addition to setting the AUTOMOUNT variable to 1 in the */etc/rc.config.d/nfsconf* file.

Be aware that unmounting a file system requires that all associated pages and buffers be flushed from the file system caches. This happens even for unsuccessful unmounts. Depending on the amount of data cached from the file system, the unmount may take a long time. Therefore, one may need to set the time-out value for automatically unmounting high in order to reduce unneeded unmounts. The time-out value can be changed via editing the */etc/rc.con-*

fig.d/nfsconf file and adding a *-t* option (time-out value in seconds) to the AUTOMOUNT_OPTIONS variable for *AutoFS* and adding a *-tl* option (time-out value in seconds) to the AUTO_OPTIONS variable for the original automount. The default time-out for both of these is five minutes, which is probably too short.

10.4.8.4   CacheFS

The *CacheFS* driver is an NFS-caching mechanism provided only in HP-UX 11i and later revisions. It will store data read from an NFS server on a local client's file system to help reduce network traffic. It is meant to be used for read-only data, such as executables and documentation that don't change often. The *cachefsd* threads manage the cache in a least-recently used manner. The driver does not maintain frequent synchronization with the NFS server, thus the need to use read-only data. The cached files can only be loaded in thirty-two or fewer non-contiguous chunks. This can be a problem under UNIX due to 'demand paging' of executables–the OS may load an executable in a series of chunks as needed versus one contiguous piece. Using large pages for executables can help to keep the 'demand paging' feature of the OS from allocating too many text pieces. Also, the *rpages* option instructs the operating system to load all text pages at one time, which eliminates the problem.

A separate cache should be created for each NFS mount point since the kernel maintains data on a per-cache basis. One can use the *cachefsstat(1M)* command to measure how well the cache is performing.

10.5   Clusters

Networks are an essential part of a cluster architecture. On HP-UX, clusters are either Serviceguard or Serviceguard Extension for RAC (SGeRAC) clusters. SGeRAC clusters support the Oracle Real Application Cluster™ (RAC) parallel database software.

There can be three kinds of networks used in a cluster:

- Redundant networks connect the member nodes of the cluster together and are used to pass heartbeat messages between the member nodes and the cluster coordinator node
- Networks (usually redundant) are used for clients to connect to the applications running on servers in the cluster
- Special networks are used in an SGeRAC cluster that pass locks for data blocks among the nodes in the cluster

10.5.1   Heartbeat Networks in a Cluster

Although heartbeat networks are not required to be dedicated, it is highly recommended that at least one of the heartbeat networks is dedicated to intra-cluster communication only. Heartbeat messages are used to determine the health of each node in the cluster. If network congestion prevents the heartbeat message from getting through, then it will falsely appear that a node has failed. By default, heartbeat messages are sent once per second per node, although the message itself is relatively small.

Heartbeat problems can also be caused by broadcast or other network storms. A broadcast storm occurs when many thousands of messages are sent to many nodes at a time. These messages must each be inspected by each node, if only to see if it is destined for the node, or if the node needs to take action on it. Network storms can consume considerable CPU resources and prevent the cluster daemon from running. The cluster daemon sends and receives heartbeat messages among other tasks. On a multi-CPU system, the interrupts for network cards can be assigned to a set of CPUs with the PSETs feature or by using the *intctl(1M)* command (see Section 7.3.3, "Processor Sets" on page 188).

During cluster discovery, formation, and reformation, the Serviceguard software uses DLPI to discover which network connections are active. DLPI is also used by the Serviceguard network sensor to monitor heartbeat and client networks to make sure that they are in working order.

10.5.2 Client Networks in a Cluster

DLPI calls are used to monitor the health of most client networks, including all Ethernet networks and FDDI and Token Ring networks. EMS-based network monitor programs are used to track the health of other networks like ATM. Serviceguard tests the health of client networks to do one of two things in case of a network failure:

- If redundant networks are available, the Serviceguard network sensor or the ATM network monitor will switch all active connections to the redundant network. In this case, open socket connections are moved from the failed network NIC to the redundant network NIC without disconnection.

- If redundant networks are not available, or if they have all failed, the Serviceguard network sensor of the ATM network monitor will cause the application package to be moved to another node in the cluster with an active client network connection.

Auto Port Aggregation (APA) software can be used in place of the Serviceguard network sensor to provide both failover and load balancing capabilities as discussed in Section 10.2.6.

10.5.3 SGeRAC Lock Networks

Oracle RAC running in an SGeRAC cluster uses networks for the special purpose of passing database buffer locks among the nodes in the cluster to prevent more than one node from modifying a particular region of the database at the same time, which would result in data corruption. SGeRAC lock networks can be Ethernet or HyperFabric networks.

By its design, HyperFabric networks are high throughput, low-latency networks. Low latency means that it takes very few computer cycles to pass a message from one node to another. At a very rough estimate, HyperFabric should provide at least 20% better performance than an Ethernet network for SGeRAC lock purposes.

When using HyperFabric, there are multiple protocols to choose from. HyperFabric supports TCP, UDP, and HMP protocols. By default, Oracle RAC uses UDP for lock transfers; optionally, it can be relinked (see the Oracle administrators manual) to use HMP instead. Oracle RAC does not use TCP for lock transfers.

It is sometimes sufficient to just choose to use HMP because it is higher throughput and lower latency than UDP, even when using the same HyperFabric physical network. HMP does not currently support HyperFabric NIC failover; however, even when there are redundant NICs available. HMP does support load balancing among the multiple NICs. Thus, it is necessary to make a business decision as to which is more important: network failover or network throughput. If network failover is more important, then UDP should be used. Otherwise, HMP provides better throughput in very high-transaction environments when users from multiple nodes modify the same region of the database.

10.6 Network Metrics

A variety of global and per-process network metrics are available for identifying potential bottlenecks in network I/O. The tools *glance(1)*, *gpm(1)*, *lanadmin(1M)*, and *netstat(1)* all provide methods for accessing network metrics.

10.6.1 Global Network Saturation Metrics

There are no direct metrics available to indicate that a network device is saturated. Instead, there are metrics such as bytes received/sent per second, the network device speed, and outbound queue depth that can be used to determine if a network may possibly be saturated. For instance, if 8-10 MB/second of traffic is being transferred on a 100 Mbit/second (approximately 12.5 MB/second max bandwidth) network interface, then that particular network link is fairly saturated. However, given that network bandwidth can be shared when using some network connections, a transfer rate from a given server of only 1 MB/second on a 100 Mbit/second network may also be saturated, since other systems on the same network may be consuming part of the overall bandwidth. Finally, there is an outbound queue associated with each network card that should normally be zero in length on an unsaturated system. Sustained outbound queue values much larger than zero can indicate saturation of a given network.

The *glance(1)*, *gpm(1)*, *lanadmin(1M)*, and *netstat(1)* tools can all be used to determine network packet transfer rates and collision rates. *Glance(1)*, *gpm(1)*, and *landadmin(1M)* also provide data regarding the outbound queue depth for a given network adapter. The *glance(1)* and *gpm(1)* tools provide a good presentation of these metrics, while the *netstat(1)* and *lanadmin(1M)* commands are simpler but more cryptic.

10.6.2 Other Global Network Metrics

The list of global network metrics reported by *GlancePlus* includes:

- Input packets/second
- Output packets/second
- Collisions/second
- Errors/second

In general, global network metrics of this type are not extremely useful. This is because network bottlenecks usually happen on a per-network adapter basis and not on a system-wide basis. The more detailed descriptions found in the per-network adapter statistics are more useful.

The *netstat(1)* command does provide some useful global network metrics that relate to how well the various levels of the network stack, such as TCP and IP, are performing. These metrics will be described when describing the *netstat(1)* command in more detail further on in the chapter.

10.6.3 Network Adapter Metrics

The performance metrics found per network adapter card are very useful for tracking down networking bottlenecks. *Glance* provides the following per network adapter metrics:

- Input packets/second
- Output packets/second
- Input bytes/second
- Output bytes/second
- Collisions/second
- Errors/second
- Outbound queue size
- Network MTU size
- Interface speed

The *lanadmin(1M)* command also provides these same metrics, but as raw counts and not as rates. All of these statistics can all be used to track down how well an individual network adapter is performing and help to indicate whether or not the adapter may potentially be saturated.

10.6.4 Per-Process Network Metrics

There is no easy way to determine the network traffic an individual process is generating. One can track system call rates for individual processes in *glance* and then observe the number of calls to network-specific system calls such as *send(2)*, *recv(2)*, *sendfile(2)*, etc. There is no direct command for determining the network traffic generated by an individual process.

10.6.5 *netstat* Command

The *netstat(1)* command provides a wealth of information regarding the status of the network stack. It provides information for the various network protocols such as TCP and IP and provides some data for adapter cards. The following sections describe what can be obtained via the various options to *netstat(1)*.

10.6.5.1 Displaying Connections

Just issuing the *netstat(1)* command without any options will display all active Internet connections and all active UNIX domain sockets. This is useful for tracking down what connections are being used on the system at any point in time. Using the *-a* option will show the state of all sockets, active or not.

10.6.5.2 *-i* and *-I* options

The *-i* and *-I* options show statistics for all network interfaces or just a particular IP interface respectively. Both options show the number of inbound and outbound packets processed, the number of inbound and outbound packet errors, the number of collisions, and the MTU size for each network. All of the values are cumulative, so to find the rate (i.e., inbound packets per second) for any of the values, the *netstat -i* or *-I* command needs to run twice and the interval between invocations needs to be recorded. Having errors or collisions on a network connection can indicate networking problems. Excessive collisions may mean too many devices are directly attached to the same network.

10.6.5.3 Quick Interval Statistics

If a number is specified after the *netstat(1)* command, such as *netstat 1*, then *netstat(1)* prints out the total number of input and output packets. If the *-I* option is added, it prints out these statistics for the specified interface. For HP-UX 11.00 and earlier, the values printed out are cumulative counts since the last reboot, while for HP-UX 11i and later, the values are counts per interval except for the very first interval, which prints out the cumulative counts since reboot. Therefore, to obtain rates, the time of each interval needs to be taken into account.

10.6.5.4 Protocol Statistics

The *-p* option to *netstat(1)* displays statistics for a particular network protocol. Valid protocols are *tcp*, *udp*, *ip*, *icmp*, *igmp*, *ipv6*, and *icmpv6*. The *-s* option will display statistics for all of the protocols. The counts displayed are the cumulative counts since the system was last rebooted. Depending on what event is being counted, the event occurrence rate, and the size of the counter, the counter may overflow and wrap back around to 0 at some point. Wrapping of this value can occur for a system that has been running for a long time or on one with lots of TCP/IP network activity.

Therefore, it may not be possible to directly compare different counters, because some of them may have wrapped around one or more times. In addition, there is no way to zero the counters, so there is no way to get them all into a known state. Therefore, the best way to use the counters is to run *netstat(1)* twice and delay a fixed amount of time between each execution of *netstat(1)*. The rate of increase of each counter can then be obtained by subtracting the values in the second execution by those in the first and dividing by the delay between executions of the command. Table 10-1 describes the important TCP statistics.

Table 10-1   TCP Protocol Statistics from *netstat(1)*

Statistic	Description
packets sent	The total number of packets (data and control) sent out via TCP. Control packets include acknowledgements (acks), window updates, synchronize packets (SYN), finished packets (FIN), and reset packets (RST).
sent data packets and bytes	The number of data packets sent along with the total number of bytes sent. Dividing the bytes by the number of data packets gives the average number of bytes per packet. Be aware that due to wrap-around issues, the bytes and data packet counts may not be directly comparable.
retransmitted data packets and bytes	The number of data packets and bytes that have been retransmitted. The lower the better for this value. High retransmission rates may indicate a saturated network or other network problems.
sent ack only packets and delayed acks	The number of standalone acknowledgements sent for data received along with the number that were delayed. Delayed acknowledgements occur if no data was sent back on the TCP connection before the acknowledgement timer pops (a 50ms timer by default tuned via *tcp_deferred_ack_interval* with *ndd(1M)*). As described in the TCP section, send acknowledgements are normally piggy-backed on the data returned for the matching reply as long as the reply is within 50ms of the send.
other sent packets (urg, window, and control)	All other packet types that were sent on the network. Urg packets are for urgent data which is rarely used in TCP. Window probes are sent when an application receiving data appears to stop receiving data–i.e., it advertizes a zero byte window for a period of time. A window update is sent as a response to a window probe.
packets received	The total number of packets received via TCP.
received acks and bytes	The total number of acknowledgements received, either standalone or piggy-backing on some data packet, as well as the total number of bytes being acknowledged.

Table 10-1   TCP Protocol Statistics from *netstat(1)*

Statistic	Description
duplicate acks	The number of duplicate acknowledgements that were received for all packets sent. Duplicate acks are part of the "fast retransmission" mechanism for TCP when it receives out-of-order packets. This value should be small relative to the total number of acknowledgements.
packets received in sequence	The total number of data packets received in order along with the number of bytes.
out-of-order packets received	The total number of packets received out of order. Out-of-order packets cause more work to be done in the TCP layer and indicate that the network is either reordering or dropping packets. The lower this value, the better.
checksum errors	The total number of packets received that had checksum errors. This value should be close to zero, especially for private networks.
connection requests	The total number of connections that were requested to a remote system. These are the active connections initiated via a *connect( )* call.
connection accepts	The total number of connections accepted from a remote system. These are the passive connections initiated via an *accept( )* call.
connections established	The total number of connections (inbound and outbound).
connections closed and dropped	The total number of connections closed gracefully and non-gracefully (drops).
embryonic connections dropped	The number of connections dropped before they could be established. High number of these could be due to a denial of service attack, trying to establish a connection to an overloaded Windows™ system, or trying to establish a connection to a machine that is not listening for connections on a given port.
retransmit time-outs	The total number of times a retransmit time-out occurred. This value should be low on a well-running system.
keepalive time-outs	The total number of times the keepalive timer popped on a connection that requests keepalives.

Table 10-1   TCP Protocol Statistics from *netstat(1)*

Statistic	Description
connects dropped due to full queue	The total number of connections dropped because of a full listen queue. This value should be low or zero on a well-performing system.
connects dropped due to no listener	The total number of connections dropped because no listener was present. This value should also be low on a well-performing system.

Table 10-2 describes the important IP statistics.

Table 10-2   IP Protocol Statistics from *netstat(1)*

Statistic	Description
packets received	The total number of network packets received by IP.
packets forwarded	The total number of network packets forwarded to another machine. This should usually be zero unless the system is set up to forward IP requests.
fragments received	The total number of IP fragments that were received.
fragments dropped due to dup or out-of-space	The total number of fragments that were dropped because they were duplicates or there was no more space left to reassemble a fragment.
fragments dropped after a time-out	The total number of fragments that were dropped due to time-outs. This counter will only be incremented if there is packet loss in the network and therefore should be close to zero.

Table 10-3 describes the important UDP statistics.

Table 10-3   UDP Protocol Statistics from *netstat(1)*

Statistic	Description
bad checksums	The number of times the checksum was bad on a packet. This value should be very low or zero.
socket overflows	The number of times a socket buffer overflowed, dropping work. This value should also be low or zero. A high value here may indicate on an NFS server that not enough *nfsd* processes are configured.

10.7 Types of Network Bottlenecks

- Saturation—indicated by 100% utilization on one or more network interfaces
- Starvation—less than 100% CPU utilization, and memory bottlenecks
- User satisfaction—poor transaction response time

10.8 Expensive System Calls

This section contains a list of some of the potentially expensive system calls when performing network I/O. Here are the expensive system calls:

- *select(2)*
- *poll(2)*

As described earlier, select/poll should be avoided for large lists of file descriptors. Instead, the *event port* driver should be used (see the man page *poll(7)*). Using the *event port* driver is described in Section 13.5.2, "Event Port Driver" on page 430.

NFS:

- *open(2)*
- *sync(2)*
- *read(2)* and *write(2)* due to accessing data across the network

The sync system call should be avoided when using NFS, as it will cause excessive network traffic to sync potentially dirty buffers.

10.9 Tuning Network Bottlenecks

The three ways of tuning network bottlenecks include hardware solutions, configuration solutions, and application solutions.

10.9.1 Hardware Solutions

There are a variety of hardware solutions, all of which can be thought of as "spending money" solutions. Here are a few common approaches:

- Add more network adapters and rebalance the network load, say with *Autoport Aggregation*.
- Use faster network adapters (e.g., Gigabit Ethernet versus Fast Ethernet).
- Use switches instead of hubs.
- Use higher-performing switches.
- Use network adapters with checksum offloading to perform the checksum operation in hardware versus software.
- Use Auto Port Aggregation (APA) software to load balance multiple NICs onto a single logical network.

10.9.2 Configuration Solutions

This set of solutions requires additional study of the existing configuration, as well as some trial and error to obtain the right results.

- Rebalance the network load across the available adapters.
- Dedicate networks to a single application.
- Adjust the network tuning options.
- Change the network transfer size and other tuneable parameters.

10.9.3 NFS File System Solutions

- Increase the # of *nfsd* and/or *biod* daemons.
- Try switching to *async* writes on the server if risk is acceptable.
- Use TCP versus UDP for accessing NFS devices.

10.9.4 Application Solutions

Improper usage of some of the HP-UX system calls can often result in poor networking performance. In particular, the *select(2)* and *poll(2)* system calls can often be misused. Many of these traditional UNIX™ interfaces were not designed for the needs of today's networking applications. Also, for some specialized networking applications, sockets and other network structures may need to be configured differently from the default methods. Below are some of the things that can be done to improve networking performance for applications developed to run under HP-UX. Section 13.5.1 "Select and Poll System Calls" on page 430 describes these in more detail.

- Review application network I/O sizes and access patterns.
- Use the *event port* interface (/dev/poll) versus *select(2)/poll(2)* system calls.
- Increase socket send and receive buffer sizes.
- Use the *sendfile(2)* system call instead of *send(2)* for transferring data from a file.

10.10 Network-Related Tuneable Parameters

There are various ways to tune networking in HP-UX. There are general kernel parameters, specific network protocol parameters, and interface-card-specific parameters. Each of these parameters are tuned using different methods. The networking-specific protocol parameters can be modified using the *ndd(1M)* command on HP-UX 10.x and later. Finally, the *lanadmin(1M)* command can be used to manipulate adapter-specific parameters.

10.10.1 Kernel Tuneable Parameters for Networking

For HP-UX 10.x systems, kernel parameters can be adjusted via sam or via the */stand/system* file. For HP-UX 11.x systems, the *kmtune(1M) command* can also be used for tuning these parameters. Finally, for HP-UX 11i v2 and later releases, the *kctune(1M)* command can be used to tune these parameters. The following kernel tuneable parameters are available for tuning network-related issues:

- *npty*—This parameter, which defaults to 60, determines the maximum number of pseudo-terminal devices that may be opened. Some benchmark applications (e.g., the AIM benchmark) require a huge number of pseudo-terminal devices to simulate a large number of users. This tuneable parameter may need to be adjusted based on the needs of the applications. Note that you may also have to run *ioscan(1m)* or *insf(1m)* after increasing the value of this tuneable parameter so that the pseudo-terminal special device files get created.

- *tcphashsz*—Changes the size of internal networking hash tables. The default value is 2048 and acceptable values are 256 to 65536. Setting this value higher than the default may result in better performance on systems with many long-lived connections. More memory is used when this value is raised because it increases the size of internal tables, but this should be an acceptable trade-off since the memory increase is small compared to the benefit in improved performance.

- *streampipes*—Setting this tuneable parameter to a value of 1 forces all pipes to be streams-based. Streams-based pipes allow streams modules to be pushed onto the pipe stream. The default for this value is 0, which disables streams-based pipes. Unless there is an application that needs streams-based pipes, this value should be kept at 0 since the standard pipe driver is much more efficient.

- *nstrpty*—Maximum number of streams-based *ptys* (pseudo teletype devices) that are allowed on the system. The default value for this tuneable is 10. It is not recommended setting this value to values much greater than the number of *ptys* actually used, as kernel memory is reserved based on the number declared. A very large number of *ptys* is usually required in large-scale benchmarks.

- *STRMSGSZ*—The maximum number of bytes that can be placed in the data portion of any stream on the system. For HP-UX 11i, this should be left at the default value of 0, which allows any number of bytes to be placed on the stream. However, if the network is down for a long period of time, the lack of a limit on this parameter can cause kernel memory to fill. For earlier versions of HP-UX, the default value is only 8192 bytes, so this value may need to be increased.

- *NSTRSCHED*—Maximum number of streams scheduler daemons that run at any time on the system. The default value of 0 allows the kernel to choose the proper value of daemons to run. It is not recommended to change this value from the default value.

- *NSTRPUSH*—This is the maximum number of stream modules that can be pushed on any stream in the system. There should be no need to modify this tuneable as the default value of sixteen should be sufficient for even the most demanding systems.

10.10.2 ndd

The *ndd(1M)* command is used to change all networking parameters related to the various networking protocols for parameters that cannot be tuned by changing the values when creating the kernel. In most cases, the networking parameters are set to default values that work well in most instances. Listed here are some of those parameters that may need to be modified from the default. The changed values do not survive a reboot of the system; therefore, the file */etc/rc.config.d/nddconf* can be modified to set the values of the parameters automatically on each reboot. The following are the most useful parameters to set from a performance standpoint:

- *tcp_conn_request_max*—Maximum number of outstanding inbound TCP connection requests at one time on one listen endpoint. This is also referred to sometimes as the maximum depth of the listen queue. For each *listen* system call invocation, the number of queued requests at one time is the minimum of this value and the value passed to the listen call for the *backlog* parameter. If the number of connection requests dropped (caused by the queue being full) as seen in the *netstat -p tcp* output is non-zero, then this parameter might need to be modified. In general, setting this to 1024 or larger for most network server applications is probably a good idea. The default is 20.

- *tcp_conn_strategy* (11.00, 11i v1, v1.5, and v1.6)—This controls socket structure caching for TCP sockets. This is also referred to as "stack caching." When TCP connections are established and released, quite a bit of state is created and destroyed. With stack caching, when a socket is released, the state is saved so subsequent socket creation is not as costly. This is a good option to enable in environments with lots of connection establishments, such as on a Web server. The default value is 0, which means stack caching is disabled. Setting the value to anything between 1 and 512 enables a 512 element stack cache. Setting the value larger than 512 enables a cache of the specified size. Enabling stack caching with the 512 entries is recommended for applications that establish and release many connections per second, such as Web servers. Setting the value larger than 512 entries will most likely consume more memory without much performance advantage in most situations.

- *socket_caching_tcp* (11i v2 and later)—This is a rename of the *tcp_conn_strategy*, or stack caching, a feature of previous 11i releases. By default, caching is enabled and set to 512 entries. This default value should be sufficient for most workloads. Only the most demanding Web applications using more than sixteen processors may benefit from setting the value higher.

- *tcp_recv_hiwater_def*—The default size of the TCP receive window when applications don't call *setsockopt(2)*. The default is 32768 bytes for most HP-UX versions. This is basically the default size of the receiving socket buffer for most connections. Since TCP can't send more than a window's worth of data before waiting for a window update from the receiving end, this parameter can limit the throughput rate for slower connections or connections with sporadic response times. Tuning this parameter appropriately can cause a dramatic improvement in the performance of the system and the network.

- *tcp_xmit_hiwater_def*—The amount of data that has not yet been sent (i.e., queued up waiting to be sent) that will trigger flow-control algorithms. This can also be considered the default for the send socket buffer size. The default value is 32768 bytes for most HP-UX versions. Setting this value higher than 32768 allows the sending connection to put more data on the network at one time and possibly increase throughput. Setting the value of this parameter too high may increase the risk of packet loss due to network congestion issues. Therefore, setting this value higher than the default on a permanent basis should be done only after careful measurement of the impact on overall network performance by monitoring packet loss.

10.10.3 lanadmin

The *lanadmin(1M)* command can be used to manipulate tuneable parameters on individual network adapters. *Lanadmin(1M)* is used in HP-UX 10.x and later releases. Before HP-UX 10.0, the *landiag(1M)* command was used for similar functionality. The -x option to *lanadmin(1M)* shows the available tuneable parameters for a given *PPA* (Physical Point of Attachment). The PPA number is simply an identifying number assigned to each network adapter card for identification purposes. The PPA number can be obtained using the *lanscan(1M)* command. In HP-UX, Ethernet LANs are identified logically by the word "lan" followed by a number. The number is the PPA for the LAN. To set a tuneable parameter for an adapter, the -X option is used. Refer to the man page or on-line documentation for more information on *lanadmin(1M)*.

10.11 Web Server Tuning Issues

Networking became mainstream with the advent of the World Wide Web. Practically everyone that connects to a network uses the Web to communicate with other systems. Web servers provide the pages that people view when visiting Web sites. Heavily visited Web sites need to have highly tuned Web servers and networking infrastructure to handle the traffic that can be generated via people browsing a Web site. The following sections describe tuning needed to optimize Web server accesses on HP-UX systems.

10.11.1 Hardware Configuration

For a Web server, it is important to cache lots of content in the memory of the server so that disk I/O does not need to be performed to lookup Web pages. This means a Web server should be configured with as much memory as needed to cache the majority of the content being provided. Usually, the more memory, the better.

Next, the performance of the networking host bus adapter is critical to Web performance. We recommend using Gigabit Ethernet for the networks handling the Web traffic. For high traffic Web servers, multiple Gigabit Ethernet cards may be needed. Since most content should be cached in memory, the disk subsystem is not as important as the networking system. However, if Web accesses are logged, then a good log device should be used. We recommend using a high-speed disk array attached via Fibre Channel (e.g., the VA 7110).

The use of optional Auto Port Aggregation (APA) software should be considered. This software can group multiple NIC cards together into a single logical IP address. APA will provide both load balancing and failover capabilities to maximize the throughput onto a single network.

10.11.2 *ndd* tuneables

Using *ndd(1M)*, one can tune the following network TCP protocol parameters to help improve Web server performance:

- tcp_xmit_hiwater_def = 2000000
- tcp_conn_request_max = 2048 (max simultaneous connections - inbound)
- tcp_conn_strategy = 512 (for HP-UX 11.00 to HP-UX 11i v1.6)
- socket_caching_tcp = 512 (for HP-UX 11i v2)

The *tcp_xmit_hiwater_def* controls the amount of unsent data that can be accumulated before TCP flow-control is initiated. This limits flow-control from being enabled too frequently on a busy Web server. Setting *tcp_conn_request_max* parameter to a large value is needed to allow large numbers of inbound connections to occur at once, which can happen frequently on busy Web servers. If *netstat -p tcp* shows many connections dropped due to "queue full", then this parameter should be made larger. The value of 2048 should serve well for most Web servers.

Finally, *tcp_conn_strategy/socket_caching_tcp* controls "stack caching," which was described under the *ndd(1M)* command earlier.

10.11.3 HP-UX Tuneables

When running a large Web server, the following HP-UX tunables should be modified:

- tcphashsz = 16384
- maxfiles = 60000
- maxfiles_lim = 60000
- dbc_max_pct = 80
- dbc_min_pct = 80
- nfile = 1000000
- ninode = NFILE
- vps_ceiling = 16384

The *tpchashsz* controls the size of many internal TCP structures. Setting this to 16384 helps to make these tables large enough to make looking up elements more efficient when a large number of connections are being processed.

Given that a Web server will have access to thousands or even millions of files, setting the buffer cache and file parameters to appropriate values is essential. The *dbc_max_pct* and *dbc_min_pct* variables set the buffer cache to a fixed 80% of memory (this assumes a dedicated Web server), *maxfiles* and *maxfiles_lim* set the maximum number of open files by any one process, *nfile* sets the total number of files open at one time in the system, and *ninode* controls the number of inodes for the file system. Finally, *vps_ceiling* is set to 16384 KB to increase the largest page that can be allocated by default to help reduce TLB misses on the server.

10.11.4 File System Tuning

For well-tuned Web servers, most of the page requests will come directly from the file system buffer cache, which should result in very little disk I/O activity. However, the logging of the Web page accesses, which is done on most Web servers, will result in significant I/O activity. Here, HFS actually provides the best overall log-writing performance. When configuring an HFS file system for use as a Web log, a 64 KB block size should be used. Also, the *write-behind* mount option should be used to enable each page to be flushed to disk as soon as it is filled. *Write-behind* is the best for a log device because once an entire buffer is filled, that buffer is not accessed again, so it is better to purge it from the cache immediately. In addition, make sure that the file system is configured to allow for large files, because the file size for the log can get quite large over time, as some data is usually logged for each Web request.

10.11.5 Networking Card Tuning

For HP-UX, the Gigabit Ethernet cards provide the best networking performance solution. There are some tuneables that can be applied to HP's Gigabit Ethernet cards to provide better throughput in a Web server environment. In particular, the following settings should work well to increase throughput of a Web server:

- send_max_bufs=32
- send_coal_ticks=1000
- recv_max_bufs=32
- recv_coal_ticks=100

These tuneables are set using *lanadmin -X* or via setting the parameters in either */etc/rc.config.d/hpigelan* or */etc/rc.config.d/hpgelan*. These parameters control how many packets are sent or received before an interrupt is generated by the card to HP-UX. The *bufs* parameters specify the number of buffers the card should send or receive before generating an interrupt. The *ticks* parameters are time-outs, where an interrupt will be generated even if the number of *bufs* specified have not been reached. The *ticks* value is microseconds, so 1000 ticks is 1 millisecond. Setting these parameters helps to reduce the number of interrupts the Gigabit Ethernet card will generate, which helps reduce the amount of CPU needed to process a given number of packets. For low-throughput applications, however, setting these values may slow responses given the 1 ms send delay and 100 us (microsecond) receive delay.

10.11.6 Zeus Web Server Parameters

Currently, the fastest Web server available on HP-UX is the Zeus Web Server. It is a very efficient Web server that has very little overhead. It is built on an "engine" model wherein a certain number of Zeus engine processes are created to handle network traffic. For optimal performance, Zeus engines can be bound to particular processors using the *mpsched* command. In addition, the network card that a Zeus engine is communicating with can be bound to the same processor as the Zeus engine using the *intctl(1M)* command. The following is a list of useful options to use when configuring Zeus:

- bind_any no
- cache_cooling_time 0
- cache_files (value depends on configuration)
- cache_flush_interval 86400
- cache_large_file (value depends on configuration)
- cache_max_bytes 0
- cache_small_file 0
- cache_stat_expire 86400
- cbuff_size 65536

- keepalive yes
- keepalive_timeout 1200
- keepalive_max -1
- listen_queue_size 8192
- maxaccept 1024
- multiple_accept yes
- sendfile yes
- sendfile_reservefd (value depends on configuration)
- sendfile_minsize 0
- sendfile_maxsize 1048576
- softservers no
- so_rbuff_size 0
- so_wbuff_size 1048576
- timeout 600
- unique_bind yes
- use_poll no
- modules!stats!enabled no

More information about the specifics of each parameter can be obtained via Zeus documentation. Detailed descriptions of each parameter is beyond the scope of this book.

10.12 Database Server Tuning Issues

Usually, in a well-written database application and well designed configuration, networking is not so much of a performance problem as disk I/O. However, if a database application is poorly written, networking can quickly become a bottleneck, especially in client/server applications. Figure 10-4 shows a client/server database configuration designed for high availability and performance. The configuration shows redundant network paths between each client and the server cluster. The server is clustered into two machines, each sharing the disks with redundant paths. There is a redundant dedicated network connection between the two server machines. High-speed networking connects all of the components.

The following should be done to make sure that networking delays and latency do not dominate the total time for queries to complete on a database server:

- An */etc/hosts* file should reside on each client and server in the configuration that contains the IP addresses of all of the machines in the configuration. */etc/nsswitch.conf* should then be set up to use files first when attempting name resolution.
- Stored procedures, collections of SQL statements, should be used to perform complex queries on the database rather than executing individual SQL statements from the client machines. Using stored procedures eliminates a lot of network traffic between the client and server that would be needed if simple SQL statements were used for each query.

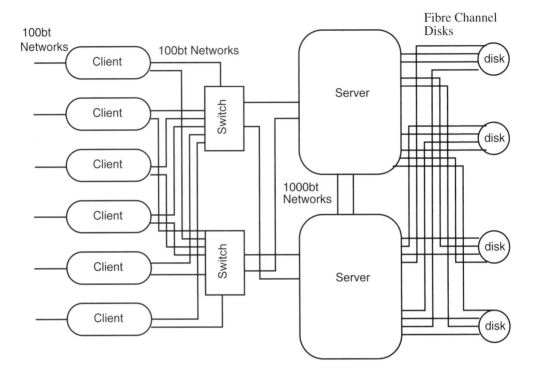

Figure 10-4   Highly Available Client/Server Database Configuration

- When performing large queries that may return a lot of data, be sure to filter the data on the server before transferring it to the client. This is particularly important in decision support systems (DSS), where queries can potentially return thousands of rows from a database.
- Make sure to always use high-speed networking (100bt Ethernet or faster) between the client and the server on a switched fabric. Between clustered servers, HyperFabric or Gigabit Ethernet should be used in a distributed database environment such as Oracle RAC™ and Informix XPS™.

Compiler Performance Tuning

 One technique for improving performance in executable code is optimization at compile and link time. Compiler optimization creates machine code that is more efficient for each source file compiled. A source file is often referred to as a *unit of compilation*. Link time optimization can create more efficient programs because the scope of optimization spans multiple compilation units. Here are the topics covered in this chapter:

- Compilers and Optimization
- Optimization Levels
- Compiling for a Target Environment
- Finer Control Over Optimization
- Trap Handling Options
- Linker Optimizations
- Profile-Based Optimization
- Specific Options for Fortran and COBOL
- Why Does Optimization "Break" Applications?
- Debugging Optimization Problems
- Porting Applications
- Code to Demonstrate Optimization Effects

Note that compiler optimization only fixes performance problems relating to CPU and memory. As with any kind of performance tuning, there are trade-offs, and these will be described in detail. The compiler options and features discussed in this chapter may vary from release to release of HP-UX; therefore, please refer to on-line manual pages or documentation at www.docs.hp.com for information regarding a specific release of HP-UX or specific compilers.

11.1 Compilers and Optimization

Compiler optimization uses compiler command options or directives to perform specific types of code modification as the compiler is building object code. For most compilers, the first step is the creation of low-level intermediate code, which the optimizer then modifies in specific ways. Depending on the optimization level you choose, the optimizer may create object code directly, or it may output intermediate code that can be further optimized at link time when the scope of the optimization is broader.

Figure 11-1 shows the relationship of various programming languages, compilers, and the linker.

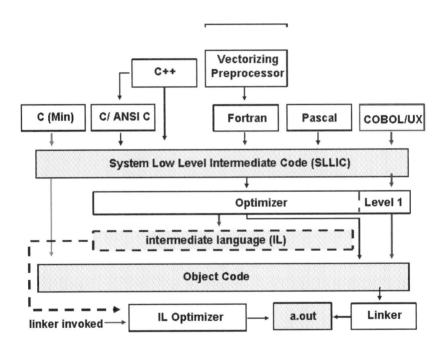

Figure 11-1   Languages, Compilers, and Optimization

Optimization is invoked with command line options or through the use of compiler pragmas embedded in the source code. A pragma is a language-specific directive used to instruct the compiler on what specific action to take, or what choice to make when there are multiple choices. Some pragmas specify which trade-off is more important during code compilation.

11.1.1 Advantages and Disadvantages of Optimization

The use of compiler optimization has many advantages (+):

+ Takes advantage of processor parallelism, tailoring the code to run with a specific pipeline, coprocessor architecture, or multiple computational units, if available. The goal is to achieve as much parallelism as possible.
+ Reduces memory accesses. Remember that loading from cache may require one or two cycles, whereas loading from memory may require as many as sixty cycles or more. This is a vital area of performance improvement. Keeping something in a register that will soon be accessed again can significantly improve performance.
+ Improves application performance as much as 200% to 300% for typical commercial and technical applications and by as much as 1000% for some scientific and engineering applications.

There are also disadvantages (-) to optimization:

- Optimizing may cause applications to break, especially at higher levels of optimization.
- Optimized code consumes significant resources during compilation. Optimization uses more CPU time, virtual memory, and disk bandwidth at compile time.
- Optimized code is more difficult to debug, because code is rearranged and/or removed and some higher levels of optimization are not compatible with symbolic debugging.

Note that the standard C compiler shipped with HP-UX does not optimize. This compiler is provided mainly to perform some simple compilation of files needed by the operating system. The optional ANSI C or C++ compiler should be used to optimize or compile any code for release on HP-UX platforms. Also, remember that when using these compilers, optimization is not the default behavior, therefore some option is needed to enable optimization.

11.2 Optimization Levels

Table 11-1 shows the basic optimization levels that are included in many compilers and indicates how they are invoked:.

Table 11-1   Compiler Optimization Levels

Level	Description	Command Line Option	C Directive	Fortran Directive
0	Very little optimization.	PA-RISC: the default, so no flag needed IPF: +O0	#pragma opt_level 0 #pragma optimize off	$Optimize off
1	Local optimization within block boundaries only.	PA-RISC: +O1 IPF: the default, so no flag needed	#pragma opt_level 1	$Optimize level 1 on
2	Global optimization within procedures only.	-O or +O2	#pragma opt_level 2	$Optimize level 2 on
3	Full optimization across all procedures within a single file.	+O3	#pragma opt_level 3	$Optimize level 3 on
4	Full optimization across the entire application program. This also involves linker optimization.	+O4	#pragma opt_level 4	$Optimize level 4 on

11.2.1 Level 0 Optimization

Level 0 optimization, the default on PA-RISC, only optimizes a little. The compiler just carries out constant folding and simple register allocation. Here is an example of constant folding that takes place when the compiler converts from source code to object code:

```
x = 3 * 5
```

is replaced by

```
x = 15
```

Since the value of the product of two constants does not vary as the program executes, the answer is a constant.

11.2.2 Level 1 Optimization (+O1)

Level 1 optimization is the default for IPF compilers and is an option with PA-RISC compilers. It is sometimes called *local* or *peephole optimization* because it can only be carried out on a small visible window of the application, namely, a basic block of code. In a typical piece of code having *if*, *then*, and *else* statements, each of these statements represents one block of code, resulting in a very narrow window. The following code shows examples of basic blocks inside boxes:

```
if ( i < 3 || i > 5 ) {

        j = i * 5;
        k = j + 6;
}
else {

        j = 3;
        k = 9;

}
```

Local optimization requires very little additional compile time and does result in better register allocation and branch optimization. It performs simple instruction scheduling and eliminates dead (impossible to execute) code. The IPF compilers also include faster register allocation and some branch optimizations. There is a low risk of breaking the application with Level 1 optimization.

11.2.3 Level 2 Optimization (-O or +O2)

Level 2 optimization is also known as global optimization. It requires longer compile times—twice as long or more compared to lower levels. The optimization occurs across block boundaries, but is limited to the procedure level only. Level 2 initializes uninitialized variables to zero and analyzes loops, expressions, data flow, and memory usage. It attempts to find ways to minimize memory references and to control how long a variable stays in a register. It may move loop invariant code from an inner loop to an outer loop or to a place outside the loop. It also performs advanced constant folding. On IPF platforms, it will attempt to insert prefetch instructions to help reduce main memory accesses and will take advantage of the IPF features of predication, control speculation, and data speculation. Two especially important techniques of optimization at Level 2 are loop unrolling and software pipelining.

11.2.3.1   Loop Unrolling

Loop unrolling changes the stride or increment in a loop and duplicates some code in an effort to reduce pipeline flushes due to top-of-loop branching. (Remember that pipeline flushes are inefficient; refer to Section 6.2.5, "Problems with Pipelined Architectures" on page 122.") This is most helpful for tight loops with few instructions and many iterations. The default loop unroll factor is 4 on PA-RISC and is chosen on a case-by-case basis for IPF; this default behavior can be changed on the command line with the option *+Oloop_unroll=<n>*. This technique, also used in the Fortran optimizing preprocessor, trades off increased memory consumption for reduced CPU utilization. The following example shows how a loop may be unrolled:

```
for (i=0;i<6000;i++) {
   x[i]=y[i]*z[i];
   }
```

becomes

```
for (i=0;i<6000;i=i+4;){
   x[i] = y[i] * z[i];
   x[i+1] = y[i+1] * z[i+1];
   x[i+2] = y[i+2] * z[i+2];
   x[i+3] = y[i+3] * z[i+3];
   }
```

11.2.3.2   Software Pipelining

Software pipelining optimizes loops by rearranging the order in which instructions are executed and by overlapping the execution latency of operations from different loop iterations. It is effective for instructions that take several cycles to execute, such as performing operations on floating point values or loading values from memory. The goal is to avoid CPU stalls due to memory or instruction latencies and more fully utilize a processor's functional units.

Pipelining may move a portion of the loop code to a position before the loop, and it may move a portion of the last iteration to a position after the loop. The loop is normally unrolled on PA-RISC platforms and may be unrolled on IPF platforms. Operations from different iterations are interleaved to maximize the utilization of the processor's functional units.

Software pipelining is used extensively by the compiler when compiling for the IPF architecture. There are specific features of the IPF architecture that allow for efficient software pipelining such as predication, rotating registers, and loop control instructions (see Section 6.2.6 "EPIC Features" for more detailed information on these features). The following is an example of a loop that could be software pipelined:

```
double x[100], y[100], z[100];
int i;
for (i = 0 ; i <= 100 ; i++) {
   z[i] = x[i] * y[i] + 4.0
}
```

This could be transformed into the following assembly using the IPF compilers:

```
        mov   ar.ec = 13                        // Setup epilogue count
        movl  r9 = 0x4010000000000000      ;; //
        setf.d f6 = r9                         // Setup 4.0
        add   r8 = 100, r0                 ;; // Setup loop count
        mov   pr.rot = 0                   ;; // clear rotating regs
        cmp.ne.or.andcm   p16, p0 = 42, r0     // set p16 to 1
        mov   ar.lc = r8                       // Set loop count
        nop.b                             ;;

..L5:
(p16)   ldfd  f32 = [r8], 8                    // load x[i]
(p16)   ldfd  f41 = [r11], 8                   // load y[i]
        nop.i
(p28)   stfd  [r10] = f54, 8                   // store z[i]
(p24)   fma.d.s0 f50 = f40, f49, f6            // z[i] = x[i]*y[i] + 4.0
        br.ctop.dptk.many ..L5            ;; // loop again
```

In the above assembly code, all of the instructions before the *L5* label are to set up the software pipelined loop, which begins after *L5*. The *ar.ec* value sets the epilogue count, which indicates how many iterations past the end of the program-specified loop count the loop should be executed in order to let the pipeline drain. In this particular case, 13 extra iterations are required after the 100 iterations of the loop have executed, for a total of 113 loop iterations.

In order to control which instructions in the loop get executed at each stage in the software pipeline, the rotating predicate registers are cleared, and the first rotating predicate (p16) is set to 1. This allows any instructions in the loop that are guarded by predicate p16 to execute on the first loop iteration. So, in the above example, the loading of x[i] and y[i] will happen on the first iteration of the loop. All of the other rotating predicates (p17-p63) will initially be zero, so any other instructions predicated in the loop with a predicate register greater than 16 will not execute on the first loop iteration.

After each iteration through the loop, the rotating predicate registers and rotating floating point registers (f32-f127) are "rotated" one register value upward, so the value in predicate register p16 is moved to p17, p17 to p18, and so forth. For the predicate registers, a value of 1 is also rotated into predicate register p16 on each loop iteration until the loop count is hit (in this case, 100). Once the loop count is hit, a zero is moved into p16 on each loop iteration until the epilogue count is hit (in this case, 13). Rotating a zero into a predicate register turns off instructions in the loop as the loop is drained and finishes the pipeline. In the above example, given that the

Cycle Number

1	2		9		13		101		110		113
x[0]	x[1]	···	x[8]	···	x[12]	···		···		···	
y[0]	y[1]	···	y[8]	···	y[12]	···		···		···	
		···	fma[0]	···	fma[4]	···	fma[92]	···		···	
		···		···	z[0]	···	z[88]	···	z[96]	···	z[99]
br	br	···	br	···	br	···	br	···	br	···	br

Figure 11-2   Software Pipeline Execution for Sample Code

fma.d.s0 instruction is predicated by predicate register p24, it does not execute until the ninth iteration of the loop because that is when the initial 1 that was in p16 at the first loop iteration is rotated into p24. The store of the first result does not occur until the thirteenth iteration. Once the thirteenth iteration is reached, six new instructions are started in parallel on every loop iteration, maximizing the issue bandwidth of the current IPF processors.

The floating point registers are also rotating in this example, so by the time the first *fma* instruction executes in the ninth loop iteration, the floating point values initially loaded into floating point registers f32 and f41 have been rotated to registers f40 and f49, respectively. Figure 11-2 shows which variables are accessed in some of the iterations of the software pipeline.

For IPF compilations, the compiler will favor software pipelining over loop unrolling because of the many features of the IPF architecture that make software pipelining a much better choice. As shown in the example, the compiler can use rotating registers in combination with predication (see Section 6.2.6.1, "Predication" on page 124) when software-pipelining a loop. This reduces the amount of code needed to be generated for the loop in contrast to the extra code inserted when unrolling the loop. The IPF compiler, however, may still loop unroll in addition to software pipelining to more fully utilize the functional units on each pipeline iteration.

11.2.3.3   Level 2 Min and Max with the Fortran Compiler

In Fortran, you can specify minimum and maximum optimization at Level 2. Minimum optimization turns off dangerous assumptions about the source code. Maximum optimization turns these assumptions on. There is a greater risk of breaking the application with Level 2 Maximum. Assumptions are further described later. See Section 11.8, "Why Does Optimization "Break" Applications?" on page 397.

11.2.4   Level 3 Optimization (+O3)

Level 3 optimization is also known as *inter-procedural optimization* because it does full optimization across all procedures within a single source file. Techniques used at Level 3 include transforming loops for improved cache access, procedure inlining, and procedure cloning. These transformations may result in code expansion, although the code should run faster.

11.2.4.1   Procedure Inlining

Inlining replaces a procedure call with the actual code, which results in code expansion. However, with procedure inlining, there is no longer any procedure-calling convention overhead, which may be significant, especially when the procedure is small or called frequently within a loop. The process uses more memory for the text region, but it decreases the use of CPU. It may also reduce the number of cache faults, page faults, and long branch operations. Inlining can be disabled by specifying the *+Onoinline* option.

The amount of inlining performed by the compiler can also be controlled. The *+Oinline_budget=val* option allows a way to tell the compiler how aggressive it should be at inlining. The *val* part of the option indicates the level of aggressiveness. The default value is 100. Specifying a larger value will cause the compiler to try to inline more. Choosing a smaller value will cause it to inline less. Choosing the value 1 will cause it to inline only if inlining reduces the code size.

11.2.4.2   Procedure Cloning

Instead of inlining the entire procedure at a call site, the compiler may instead make a *clone* of a procedure with constant parameters propagated through the source. For example, the following source:

```
void testit(int a, int b, int c)
{
    if (a + b > c) {
        return a+b;
    } else {
        return c;
    }
}

...
testit(3, 5, d);
```

might cause the compiler to clone the function *testit* and then redirect the *testit* call to the newly created clone as follows:

```
void testit_clone(int c)
{
      if (8 > c) {
            return 8;
      } else {
            return c;
      }
}

...

testit_clone(d);
```

Notice that the *a* and *b* parameters have been propagated through the source and the function has been renamed. The compiler may perform cloning rather than inlining if multiple sites all pass the same compile time constants as parameters. Cloning is enabled by default at *+O3* and *+O4* optimization levels. Cloning may be disabled with more recent compilers by specifying *+Ono-clone*.

11.2.5 Level 4 Optimization (+O4)

Level 4 provides all of the optimizations in Levels 3 and lower, plus full optimization across an entire application program. Level 4 transformations can result in an executable that consumes a large amount of virtual memory during compilation, since the linker must analyze across all files at once. However, it usually results in significantly faster execution.

Level 4 optimization causes the compiler to generate intermediate files instead of relocatable objects when each file is compiled. The linker then is responsible for compiling these intermediate files when a user tries to link them into an executable or shared library. This causes a Level 4 compilation to appear to compile each individual file quickly, but take potentially hours to link the resulting executable or shared library as the linker compiles each intermediate file one at a time. It is not uncommon to run out of virtual memory when performing a compilation with Level 4 optimization. If this happens, you can do the following:

- Compile only a subset of the files with Level 4 optimization. Typically, only a subset of files needs to be compiled at *+O4* to get the majority of benefit.
- Increase the HP-UX tuneable parameter *maxdsiz* to something high, such as 512 MB or 1 GB. This will allow the compiler to use more process data space for compilation. Make sure the system is also adequately configured with memory and swap.
- Use the *+Oselectivepercent* option with Profile-Based Optimization (see Section 11.6) to automatically have the compiler pick a subset of the files to compile at *+O4* (the rest will be compiled at *+O2*). This option is available only with the PA-RISC compilers.

- Increase the amount of swap space available to the system.
- It is recommended that Level 4 optimization be used only in conjunction with Profile-Based Optimization (PBO). In fact, the IPF compiler will automatically revert to Level 3 optimization if Level 4 optimization is specified without using PBO.

11.3 Compiling for a Target Runtime Environment

In designing applications, you may or may not know what kind of system will run them. On HP-UX systems, you can use specific compiler options to indicate a specific machine architecture, data model, or operating system revision where the resulting application will run. The particular options used in specifying the machine architecture are *+DA*, *+DD*, *+DS,* and *+DO*.

11.3.1 *+DA*

The *+DA* option lets you specify the instruction set architecture that should be used. It is important to set this option correctly, since code compiled for a later architecture will not execute on earlier architectures. Different levels generate different magic numbers in the *a.out* file. As a rule, you should choose the lowest level where code must execute. However, code will execute slower on newer systems if a lower level instruction set is chosen. Typical choices for PA-RISC architecture levels are *+DA1.0*, *+DA1.1*, and *+DA2.0*. You can also use *+DAportable*, which chooses a set of instructions that will run 32-bit programs fairly efficiently on both PA 1.1- and PA 2.0- based machines. Finally, for PA-RISC systems you can also specify the machine model number as returned from the *uname* command. For IPF systems, there is currently only one instruction set architecture, so this option is not supported when compiling code on an IPF system.

In addition to selecting the machine architecture, this option will define compiler pre-processor symbols depending on the architecture level chosen. For *+DA1.0*, the compiler enables *_PA_RISC1_0*; for *+DA1.1* it enables *_PA_RISC1_1*; and for *+DA2.0* it enables *_PA_RISC2_0*. An application can use these pre-processor definitions to generate machine-specific code for the given architecture.

If your application must run on PA 1.0, PA 1.1, and PA 2.0 systems, use *+DA1.0*. However, if the application will be used only with PA 2.0 systems, use *+DA2.0* so that it makes use of the extensive instructions available on PA 2.0 systems. In particular, choosing *+DA2.0* is especially important if the code makes use of 64-bit constructs even for 32-bit code, such as the *long long* keyword in the C language. Choosing the wrong architecture value will have one of two results:

- The code will not execute at all on certain systems; or
- The code will run less efficiently than it might otherwise.

The default value used by the compiler is the architecture of the system where the compilation is occurring; therefore, it is important to always explicitly set this option when compiling code that will run on machines other than the compilation system. Finally, programs compiled for PA-RISC will run on IPF processors, but much more slowly than native IPF programs. This is because PA-RISC programs are dynamically translated to IPF code as they execute, and the translated code is not nearly as efficient as the code the compiler can produce when it natively compiles a program for IPF. In addition, the dynamic translation process takes computation time that could be used for running a native program.

11.3.2 +DD

The *+DD* option specifies the data model to use—*32-bit* or *64-bit*. The default is to use the 32-bit ILP32 model. In this model, the size of the *int, long,* and *pointer* data types is 32 bits. If *+DD64* is specified, then the 64-bit LP64 data model is used. In this model, the size of the *int* data type is 32 bits, but the size of a *long* and *pointer* is 64 bits. For PA-RISC systems, if *+DD64* is specified, then the compiler automatically sets the architecture to PA-RISC 2.0 (i.e., *+DA2.0*). The compiler will also define the compiler pre-processor symbol *__LP64__* when *+DD64* is specified.

When compiling on IPF systems running HP-UX and using the default 32-bit data model, 32-bit IPF code is generated, not 32-bit IA-32 code. Be aware that Microsoft and Linux IPF compilation environments don't behave this way. Instead, these operating systems will generate IA-32 code when compiling a 32-bit application. These IA-32 binaries are then run through the legacy translation portion of the IPF chip, which causes the code to run much more slowly than native 32-bit IPF code. To generate native IPF code, these operating systems require a 64-bit compilation. The ability of the HP-UX compilers to generate 32-bit IPF code is a huge advantage for HP-UX because native 32-bit IPF binaries run much faster than 32-bit IA-32 binaries on IPF systems.

11.3.3 +DS

The *+DS* option lets you specify the instruction scheduling model. No matter what model is chosen, the resulting code will execute on all systems, although not optimally. Choose the scheduling model where the code will most commonly execute. For PA-RISC systems, one can specify the model number of the system (obtained via the *uname* command), PA-RISC processor name such as *PA7100* or *PA7200*, or the preferred method of specifying the architecture level: *1.0, 1.1, 1.1a, 1.1b, 1.1c, 1.1d, 1.1e,* or *2.0*. There are multiple 1.1 levels due to the different static scheduling policies for the different in-order PA-RISC 1.1 revision processors. The file */opt/langtools/lib/sched.models* maps processor names and machine models to PA-RISC version numbers.

For IPF systems, the choices are *itanium*, *itanium2*, *blended*, and *native*. The itanium option schedules based on the Itanium architecture, while the itanium2 option schedules based on the Itanium 2 architecture. The blended option chooses the set of scheduling options that results in the good overall performance on the current set of shipping processors. Currently, this results in the compiler scheduling in a manner that results in code that runs well on both Itanium and Itanium 2 processors, but not optimally on either. The native option chooses the scheduling option that corresponds to the system where the compilation is occuring.

Choosing the wrong value for *+DS* will only result in less efficient code. By default, the compiler will choose the scheduling policy that works best on the system compiling the code or a policy that makes sense based on the *+DA* option chosen. For instance, if just *+DA2.0* is specified, then the compiler will schedule as if *+DS2.0* was also specified. Given the large number of PA-RISC 2.0 systems deployed it is recommended that all PA-RISC code should be compiled with *+DS2.0*. For IPF-based systems, it is recommended that the *+DSitanium2* scheduling option be used due to the small number of original Itanium systems actually deployed compared to the large number of Itanium 2 systems that will be deployed.

11.3.4 +DO

The *+DO* option allows the target HP-UX operating system release to be specified. The compiler may be able to perform different optimizations if it knows on which version of the operating system the resulting application will run. When using this option, the resulting application is not guaranteed to run on versions of the operating system earlier than what was specified. For instance, if 11.23 is chosen as the operating system level, the resulting application will run only on HP-UX versions 11.23 (11i v2) and later. The value used for this option is usually the numeric operating system revision as returned by the *uname -r* command. Some compiler versions may use more elaborate names for the revision, so refer to on-line documentation for the supported values.

If this option is not specified, then the compiler uses the default value of the operating system used to compile the application. Since most applications should be compiled on the minimum operating system supported by the application, the default behavior should be sufficient for the majority of applications.

11.4 Finer Control Over Optimization

The HP compilers provide several options and pragmas to fine tune the optimizer's behavior. In general, most options are applicable between the C, C++, and Fortran compilers and between the IPF and PA-RISC compilers. However, some options may be available for only a particular compiler. Refer to the man page or on-line documentation for a specific compiler to see if a particular option is supported or not.

When combining multiple compiler options together on a command line, the options are applied from left to right on the command line. Therefore, options on the right may override options previously specified on the left. This feature of the compiler allows for greater flexibility in enabling and disabling options. For options that implicitly specify multiple other options, the behavior is as if all of the implicit options were specified immediately following the option specified. The following sections describe various individual optimizer flags that can improve application performance.

11.4.1 Storage Optimizations

The location where the compiler places data accessed by a program can make a difference to the overall program's performance. For instance, in HP-UX the TEXT region of a program is shared among all processes using that TEXT segment. So, placing read-only (constant) data in the TEXT segment helps to eliminate cache misses by keeping a single copy in the processor's cache, as compared to an individual copy of the identical data for every process. The following are useful options for managing storage with the compiler.

11.4.1.1   *+Olit= (+ESlit)*

The *+Olit* option (newer form of the older *+ESlit, +ESnolit,* and *+ESconstlit* options) informs the compiler to place read-only values in the TEXT segment of an executable. Read-only values can be string constants and variables declared with the C keyword *const.* The *+Olit* option has three amplifiers, *none, const,* and *all.*

When *none* is specified, no constant literals are placed in the TEXT. This is equivalent to the old *+ESnolit* option. When *const* is used, all string literals that are used in places where "const char *" would be valid and constant variables that do not require load-time or runtime initialization are placed in the TEXT segment. This is equivalent to the old *+ESconstlit* option. Finally, when the *all* amplifier is used, all string literals and all *const*-qualified variables that are initialized at compile time are placed in the TEXT segment. This is equivalent to the old *+ESlit* option. The default for the C compiler is the *const* option, while the default for C++ is *all.*

11.4.1.2   *+Oshortdata=*

The *+Oshortdata* option is IPF-specific. In the IPF runtime architecture specification, there is a 4 MB area of the DATA area that is addressable with a single address calculation. This area is referred to as the *short data* area. By default, the compiler will put all global variables that are 8 bytes and smaller in size in this area. All other variables will be placed into the regular data section and will potentially need multiple instructions, including expensive load instructions, to address data in this section.

The *+Oshortdata* option can be used to change the default behavior of what goes in the short data area. For instance, specifying *+Oshortdata=128* would put all globals that are 128 bytes or smaller in the short data area. If no value is specified after *+Oshortdata,* then all global data is placed in the short data area regardless of size. Finally, specifying a value of 0 for the shortdata value indicates that no data should be placed in the short data region.

If there happens to be more than 4 MB of short data in the application, then the linker will issue "GPREL22 relocation" errors when linking the application. For instance, the following error was generated when compiling an application with *+Oshortdata* that used more than 4 MB of short data:

```
ld: The value 0xfffffffffd80010 does not fit when applying the relocation
GPREL22 for symbol "a1" at offset 0x22 in section index 5 of the file test.c
```

If this linker error appears when using *+Oshortdata* without a size parameter, then most likely there is more than 4 MB of global data used by the application. If this error occurs, then using an explicit size parameter, such as 1024, may help to fit most of an application's data in the short data region without causing link errors. In general, most applications tend not to have more than 4 MB of global data unless large global arrays are created. For large uninitialized arrays, the compiler is often able to realize that the array should not be placed in the short data area and will ignore the directive if it does not make sense for a particular global array.

11.4.1.3   +Ofastaccess

The *+Ofastaccess* option is only used for 32-bit PA-RISC compilations. This option is both a compile-time and link-time option, so it should be used both for compiling each individual file and when linking the final executable. This option instructs the linker to order global data from smallest to largest in order to pack as much data as possible in a cache line. It also often helps to reduce the number of instructions needed to address each global by one.

11.4.1.4   +Odatalayout

The *+Odatalayout* option is a new option in HP-UX 11i v2 compilers that instructs the compiler to rearrange how global data is organized in the DATA section based on execution profile information (see "Profile-based Optimization" on page 390). The compiler will place frequently accessed globals together in the DATA section of an application to help reduce cache misses. The default behavior is to just arrange global data as it is encountered at link time. By rearranging the global data according to how often it is accessed and when it is accessed, both cache misses and TLB misses can be reduced. The default behavior is to not order the global data, and this option is ignored when PBO is not used. This option can potentially result in good performance gains for applications that access global variables frequently.

11.4.2   Standards-Related Options

The HP C and C++ provide several options that enable aspects of the various C and C++ standards. Table 11-2 describes the options for the C compiler. Table 11-3 describes the options for the C++ compiler. The more recent ANSI C and C++ standards allow the compiler to more

Table 11-2   Standards-Related Options for the C Compiler

Option	Description
-Aa	Use the ANSI dialect.
-Ac	Use K&R dialect (the original classic C-Language definition).
-Ae	Use HP's extended ANSI dialect. See compiler documentation for the specific options enabled. This is the default in recent C compilers.

Table 11-2   Standards-Related Options for the C Compiler (Continued)

Option	Description
-AOa	Use the ANSI dialect and assume the code adheres to the ANSI standard so certain optimization assumptions can be made.
-AOe	Use the extended ANSI dialect and assume the code adheres to the ANSI standards so certain optimization assumptions can be made.

Table 11-3   Standards-Related Options for the C++ Compiler

Option	Description
-Aa	Use newer ANSI C++ features. See compiler documentation for details.
-AA	User newer ANSI C++ features as well as newer headers and libraries. Objects are not compatible with -AP option.
-AP	Don't use newer ANSI C++ features and use older headers and libraries. Objects are not compatible with -AA option.
-Ae	Compile in C mode with the C++ compiler.
-AOe	Compile in C mode with the C++ compiler and enable optimizations that assume the compiled code is ANSI compliant.

easily compile complex pieces of code due to assertions made about how proper code should be written. Therefore, these options can potentially provide performance gains if an application is known to adhere to the ANSI standards.

11.4.3 Alias Options

It is actually very difficult to optimize C-language code due to the possibility of memory addresses aliasing through pointers. For example, in the following code:

```
void func(int *a, int *b)
{
     int c;

     c = *b;
     *a = 1;
     c += *b;
     return c;
}


func(&a, &b);
```

The compiler may not be able to determine that the parameters *a* and *b* to the function *func* don't point to the same value. Therefore, the compiler is forced to reload the value of *b* from memory after *a* is written in case *a* and *b* do point to the same value. The default behavior of the compiler is to assume that all pointers can alias with other data.

The compiler provides several options to control what it assumes regarding memory aliases. All of these options require that the user assert that the program has the desired properties.

11.4.3.1 +Onoptrs_to_globals

The *+Onoptrs_to_globals* option tells the compiler that none of the pointers in the code point to global variables. This keeps the compiler from having to reload global variables after stores to values through pointers. This can be a significant performance gain if a program makes extensive use of global variables and pointers. However, the program must not reference globals indirectly through pointers or else runtime errors could occur. The default behavior is to assume that all globals may have pointers (*+Optrs_to_globals* option). For some versions of the compiler, this option can take a list of globals that satisfy the condition versus applying the condition to all globals.

11.4.3.2 +Osignedpointers

The *+Osignedpointers* option tells the compiler that pointers should be considered signed quantities instead of the default of unsigned. This can improve the performance of some applications that do a lot of pointer comparisons in PA-RISC. However, applications that compare pointers in shared memory with data or stack memory may not run properly. Therefore, it is not recommended that this option be used.

11.4.3.3   +Otype_safety

The +*Otype_safety* option informs the compiler how aggressive it can be in assuming that memory references don't alias. If this option is used and the program's code does not adhere to the assumptions being made, then runtime errors can occur. This option has four modifiers—*off*, *limited*, *ansi*, and *strong*.

+Otype_safety=off

This is the default and tells the compiler to assume that all memory references may alias. With extensive use of pointers, this may cause the compiler to reload values over and over again to guard against aliasing.

+Otype_safety=limited

This option tells the compiler that the code follows the ANSI alias rules. Unnamed objects are treated as though they had an unknown type and thus could potentially alias with other memory references. The following is example of code that follows ANSI alias rules such that the compiler will assume the pointers can't alias when +*Otype_safety=limited* is used:

```
short b;

int func(int *a)
{
        int c = b;
        b = 3;
        /* Compiler can move load of *a above store to b because of ANSI
alias
        * rules
        */
        return *a + c;
}
```

In the above example, the compiler can assume that the global "b" does not alias with what "a" points to, given that a *short* and an *int* are of different types. This option is more risky than making no alias assumptions, but for code that follows the ANSI standard, it should usually provide increased performance. Many older applications have been written to alias variables of different data types for code-writing convenience, although doing so does violate the ANSI standard.

+Otype_safety=ansi

This option tells the compiler that the code follows the ANSI alias rules and, in addition, that unnamed objects are treated the same as named objects, so the compiler can eliminate potential reloads of memory for unnamed types. This option is similar to the deprecated option +*Optrs_ansi*. The following example shows code where the compiler will move a load above a store with *+Otype_safety=ansi* because under the ANSI-type safety rules, the pointers in the example are not supposed to alias:

```
void func(void **a, int **b)
{
        int *c = *b;
        *c = 3;

        /* Compiler may load *a before storing the value 3 into c above if
         * ansi aliasing is specified
         */
        c = *((int **)a);
        *c = 5;
}
```

Under the *limited* option, the compiler could not hoist the reading of *a before the first store to *c because it does not know if the two pointers are aliases or not, but under the *ansi* option it can. This option is more risky than the *limited* option, but can provide more speed up in most instances.

+Otype_safety=strong

This option tells the compiler that the code follows the ANSI alias rules with the following extensions–field addresses of structures cannot be taken and stores to a variable of a character type can't alias to any type other than character. This option is similar to the deprecated option *+Optrs_strongly_typed*. The following shows code where the compiler will move a load above a store if the *+Otype_safety=strong* is used, but will not for the *off*, *limited*, or *ansi* options:

```
int func(char *a, int *b)
{
        int d;
        int c = *a;

        *a = 3;

        /* With strong aliasing, the compiler may load b before the store
         * of 3 into a above
         */
        d = *b;
        return c + d;
}
```

To be able to use this aliasing option, the application cannot assign char * pointers to other pointer types, otherwise runtime errors will most likely occur. This is the most risky of the aliasing options, but can return the most performance gains.

11.4.4 Memory Latency Optimizations

As mentioned in Section 8.14.3, "Application Optimization" on page 248, the ability of the compiler to reduce the time to access main memory can have a large effect on overall performance. Most modern processors spend a lot of time waiting on memory accesses compared to actually processing data. In general, the compiler tries hard to optimize memory references without any special options. However, there are a few options that can be specified to help the compiler with this task.

11.4.4.1 +Odataprefetch

The *+Odataprefetch* option tells the compiler to use prefetch instructions to try to reduce main memory latency. When the compiler is able to insert effective prefetch instructions, this option can result in significant speed-ups–2x speed-ups are not uncommon. For the IPF compilers, *+Odataprefetch* is on by default.

For PA-RISC compilers, however, it is not the default because of several factors:

- PA-RISC 1.x chips don't have any software prefetching instructions, so software prefetching can only be enabled when the *+DA2.0* or *+DD64* compiler options are used.
- Prefetch instructions need to be added to the instruction stream and may consume instruction bandwidth, thereby slowing down performance if the prefetches are not necessary.
- PA-RISC 2.0 chips use out-of-order execution combined with large first-level caches, which may reduce the need to prefetch in some applications.
- The bus bandwidth for PA-RISC 2.0 chips is not huge, so issuing prefetches that end up not being needed can consume bus resources and potentially slow down the application.

Since prefetching is not on by default for PA-RISC 2.0 chips, this is often a very good option to try, especially for code that may contain large working sets, lots of loops, or a lot of floating point operations.

Sometimes prefetching can hurt performance, so specifying *+Onodataprefetch* or *+Odataprefetch=none* will turn prefetching off. Usually, prefetching hurts performance if the dataset being accessed fits entirely in cache. This is especially true for PA-RISC processors, given their extremely large first-level caches.

For IPF platforms, the first-level caches are small enough that prefetching can usually help, and thus is one reason for it being turned on by default. Other reasons why data prefetching is the default on IPF is that there is more instruction bandwidth to handle extra prefetch instructions, and the in-order nature of the processor makes prefetches more beneficial. The IPF platforms also allow for the type of prefetch to be specified–either *indirect* or *direct*. Indirect prefetching allows the compiler to prefetch data based on a mathematical calculation of a future address, while direct prefetching simply adds an offset to a given pointer for prefetching. By default, the IFP compiler uses indirect prefetching.

11.4.4.2   +Oentrysched

The *+Oentrysched* option only applies to PA-RISC compilations. It allows the compiler to schedule instructions that happen during entry of the function with the prologue instructions that save registers at function entry. This is not the default, because programs that handle asynchronous interrupts or perform error handling via signals may not perform correctly with this option. The overall speed-up that can be obtained by this option is usually small–no more than a percent or two.

11.4.4.3   +Oregionsched

The *+Oregionsched* option schedules instructions across branches in the code. Since instructions are moved across changes in control flow, the optimization is considered more risky and therefore is not the default for PA-RISC. Also, with out-of-order processing, the benefit of scheduling instructions across regions is less due to the processor's ability to schedule instructions across branches dynamically.

The IPF compiler, however, will schedule instructions across branches by default regardless if this option is specified or not. In fact, the IPF compiler simply ignores this option. The IPF architecture contains special instructions to allow scheduling instructions across branches to be performed much easier than on PA-RISC. In addition, the in-order nature of the IPF processors makes scheduling load instructions across branches necessary to hide latency.

11.4.5   Symbol Binding Options

HP-UX systems allow for extensive use of shared libraries. Shared libraries on HP-UX (and most UNIX implementations) provide for the ability to change the binding of functions and data symbols at runtime, depending on the order in which libraries are linked into an application. This functionality allows one to write their own version of a function, such as *malloc*, that can then be used instead of the *malloc* provided in *libc*.

Unfortunately, this symbol override ability can cause a performance degradation for code that does not need to override symbols due to the overhead in accessing symbols through the linkage table. In addition, the override ability is the default, so options need to be specified to disable this functionality. Furthermore, for Microsoft Windows platforms, the symbol override functionality is not the default, so porting applications from Microsoft platforms to UNIX can incur a performance hit if the symbol binding issue is not addressed.

The HP compilers provide extensive options to control how symbols are accessed in both shared libraries and executables. A combination of linker options and compiler options can be used to optimize the access of symbols in shared libraries and applications to potentially greatly improve overall performance.

11.4.5.1   Linker Binding Options

When building a shared library on HP-UX, the *-Bsymbolic* linker option should always be used unless symbol override is needed. This option will instruct the linker to directly call any function referenced within the shared library instead of going through stub code that is used for the function override ability. In addition to using *-Bsymbolic*, only those symbols that need to be shared by other applications or shared libraries should be exported.

By default, the HP-UX linker will export all symbols in the shared library. Using the *+e* linker option allows specific symbols to be marked for export. All symbols not marked will not be exported once any *+e* option is specified. If there are many symbols that need to be exported, then the *-c* option can be used to add the many *+e* options to a file that can be read by the linker.

The following code fragment shows a simple shared library example and how it might be compiled. Here is some simplistic C code that defines an unsigned addition routine and an unsigned multiply routine:

```
unsigned int sum(unsigned int a, unsigned int b)
{
     return a+b;
}
unsigned int umult(unsigned int a, unsigned int b)
{
     unsigned int j = 0;
     while(a--) {
          j = sum(j,b);
     }
     return j;
}
```

Now, each call to *sum* from *umult* will be potentially accessed through a call stub, which will load the address of the currently visible *sum* function via one or more load instructions and then branch indirectly to this routine. To eliminate this overhead, the following can be done to create a shared library using the above code:

```
# cc -O -c test.c
# ld -Bsymbolic +e umult -o libtest.sl test.o
```

This will cause the linker to resolve all calls to symbols within the shared library without using call stubs and only export (make accessible) the routine *umult* to other programs. No code outside of the shared library will be able to access the routine *sum* since it was not explicitly exported and some other symbol was. By limiting what is exported from the shared library to only what is needed, the size of the export table that gets created with each shared library is minimized. Having a smaller export table size means less memory is consumed by the shared library, which always helps performance.

When compiling shared libraries under PA-RISC, every attempt should be made to compile the shared library using *+DA2.0* to get the PA-RISC 2.0 instruction set. The PA-RISC 2.0 instruction set has a few critical instructions that are necessary for improving shared library call overhead. Of course, if the shared library needs to run on legacy PA-RISC 1.x boxes, then compiling the shared library as a PA-RISC 2.0 library is not an option, since PA-RISC 2.0 code will not run on PA-RISC 1.x processors.

11.4.5.2   Compiler Options for Symbol Binding

The linker binding options described above help inform the linker when and when not to use call stubs for function calls. However, if the compiler knows that a given symbol (global data or function) is going to be accessed locally to a program or remotely via a shared library, it can better optimize the access to a symbol.

By default, the C/C++ compiler will treat all symbols not defined within a *.c* file as being external and will use more costly indirect access methods to access the symbol. For function calls, this mainly just involves saving and restoring a register, which may not be too costly, but for global data this involves loading a linkage table pointer to find the address where the global is stored before accessing each global variable.

To help reduce the extra overhead associated with assuming that symbols are remote, the IPF C/C++ compilers provide extensive options for manipulating symbol binding and thus reducing the penalties for symbol override. Table 11-4 shows these options.

Table 11-4   Binding options for IPF C/C++ Compiler

Option	Description
-Bdefault	The default binding is used, which allows for symbols to be preempted.
-Bextern	Inlines import stubs for calls made to external symbols.
-Bprotected	Symbols are not allowed to be preempted by other modules.
-Bprotected_def	Same as -Bprotected, but only locally defined symbols are not allowed to be preempted.
-Bprotected_data	Same as -Bprotected, but only data symbols are not allowed to be preempted; functions can still be preempted.
-Bsymbolic	Same as -Bprotected and applied globally to all symbols.
-Bhidden	Symbols are not allowed to be preempted and symbol names are not exported for use by other modules. This means the hidden symbol can't preempt another symbol name in other shared libraries.

The *-Bdefault, -Bextern, -Bprotected,* and *-Bhidden* options can be specified in three different forms as follows:

1. As is, without any extra information. This syntax means that all symbols in the compiled file will be placed in the given binding class.
2. With a =*filename* extension where filename is a file containing a list of symbol names that should be assigned the binding class.

3. With a =*symbol* extension where *symbol* is a list of common separated symbols that should be assigned the given binding class.

The form of the binding options that specify that all symbols adhere to a given binding is useful when compiling certain applications. HP has provided additional options to make these blanket options even more useful.

For instance, the *-exec* option indicates that the compiled file will be used to create an executable. This option implies *-Bprotected_def* as well. Under *-exec*, the compiler will place any constants with hidden or protected status in the text segment and may use more efficient direct addressing to access globals on IPF.

Another useful combination option is the *-minshared* option. This option implies *-exec* with *-Bprotected*, so it allows all symbols to have the protected status. This is the option that most executables can use to provide optimal binding in an executable. The *-minshared* option assumes that the application will make minimal use of shared libraries and mainly use HP-provided shared libraries.

If non-HP supplied shared libraries are used, then the *+Oextern* option would be needed to specify the symbols that will be accessed externally to the executable.

The older *+Onoextern* and *+Oextern* options for the PA-RISC compilers correspond to the *-Bprotected* and *-Bextern* IPF options, respectively. Using these options for PA-RISC compilations is more involved since HP provides both archived and shared libraries for many of its PA-RISC libraries, so declaring that a given function will only be *external* in a header file does not work. Therefore, when using the blanket *+Onoextern* option with the PA-RISC compiler and when using shared libraries, the *+Oextern* option is usually needed to indicate those specific symbols that are declared in shared libraries.

Finally, IPF versions of HP-UX 11i use mainly shared libraries rather than archive libraries. To optimize the accessing of functions and data in the HP-supplied shared libraries, HP has put pragmas in the headers to indicate to the compiler that HP-supplied functions are *external* so the compiler can optimize access to these functions better. The compiler will then inline the external call sequence for these functions compared to branching to an import stub. It is important to note that if the proper HP header files are not included when using any of the blanket *-Bprotected* or *-Bhidden* binding types, link time errors will occur because the compiler will treat the HP library calls as being non-external, when in fact they are external. For example, the following simple "hello world" program:

```
int main(int argc, char ** argv)
{
        printf("hello world.\n");
}
```

will produce a linker error if compiled as:

```
cc -Bprotected -O -o hello hello.c
```

because the compiler will treat the call to *printf( )* as being protected, when in fact it is defined externally in *libc*. The message printed out will be something like:

```
ld: Unsatisfied protected symbol "printf" in file "hello.o"
```

If the source is modified to include the proper header for the *printf( )* function as follows:

```
#include <stdio.h>
int main(int argc, char ** argv)
{
        printf("hello world.\n");
}
```

then the program will link and run without errors when compiled as above.

11.4.6 Overhead Reduction Optimizations

One way for the compiler to speed up a program is to try to reduce overhead of common operations. The binding options discussed previously are one way to remove overhead when a program does not need the ability to override symbols. The HP compilers provide a few other options to reduce overhead.

11.4.6.1 *+Olibcalls*

The *+Olibcalls* option transforms some very popular *libc* and *libm* calls into inline assembly sequences. This can greatly reduce the overhead of making these calls.

For example, this option will convert a call to the function *sqrt* into the SQRT assembly instruction on PA-RISC platforms. It might also convert a *libc memset( )* call of fixed size and value to a sequence of inline store instructions.

For the IPF compilers, this option is not needed if the code includes the proper header files for the functions being called. This is because HP has decorated the header files with pragmas that indicate which library functions may be optimized by providing a faster inline version. Therefore, for IPF, *+Olibcalls* is on by default if a program includes the header files defining the functions used. If the user specifies *+Olibcalls* on more recent IPF compilers, a warning will be issued that this option has been deprecated and the user should instead include the proper header files.

11.4.6.2   +Opromote_indirect_calls

The *+Opromote_indirect_calls* option will convert calls through function pointers to direct calls to a function. The compiler will insert a comparison with the function pointer to see if the call is going to be made to a particular function. If it is, then that function will be called directly rather than going through an indirect branch. In the case where a particular indirect call is mainly to a particular function, this optimization can help eliminate call overhead and potentially eliminate mispredicted branches by the processor, since indirect branches are much harder to predict than direct branches.

This option is only enabled with Profile-Based Optimization, because without PBO, the compiler would not have any idea as to which function to call directly. PBO records which functions are called at each indirect call site and then can determine which, if any, are the most popular. If it finds a good candidate function, then it will insert the comparison and direct branch. The following code example:

```
int add(int a, int b)
{
     return a+b;
}

int   test(int *fptr())
{
     return fptr(1,2);
}
```

could get converted into:

```
int add(int a, int b)
{
     return a+b;
}

int   test(int *fptr())
{
     if (fptr == add) {
     return add(1,2);
     } else {
     return fptr(1,2);
     }
}
```

11.4.6.3   +Onorecovery

The *+Onorecovery* option informs the compiler that it should not use recovery code for fixing up mispredicted control speculations on an IPF system. By default, the compiler generates control speculation "recovery" code (*+Orecovery* option). The IPF architecture has the ability to move load instruction accesses before branches that may or may not execute by marking these loads with a special *.s* qualifier. The compiler can use the *ld.s* instructions to speculate that a given path will be taken by issuing these speculative loads before they normally would be executed in the program. This speculation is done to help hide memory latency.

With the default *+Orecovery* option, the compiler will generate a *chk.s* instruction at the location in the code where the speculative load normally would have happened without speculation. The *chk.s* instruction checks to make sure the speculation was valid. If so, then the code continues as normal past the *chk.s*. If not, the control flow is diverted to recovery code that re-executes the load in a non-speculative manner.

When recovery code is enabled, the processor will not perform a speculative load if the load would result in a TLB miss. This means that speculative loads that would have succeeded but did not have a proper TLB entry loaded will not be speculatively loaded when recovery code is enabled. Instead, the recovery path will be taken to execute the load.

When *+Onorecovery* is enabled, the compiler will not generate recovery code and will not generate *chk.s* instructions to check on the validity of the speculation. It also may not have to predicate as much to handle executing *chk.s* instructions properly. Removing all of these instructions can potentially reduce the number of instructions that need to be executed and improve performance.

Problems can arise, however, when using *+Onorecovery,* because when this option is enabled, each *ld.s* instruction will cause a TLB fault if the address is not found in the TLB. For bad speculations, this can result in an enormous amount of TLB miss activity. The HP-UX operating system tries to compensate for the most frequent speculation miss of loading something from address 0 by mapping a special page for address 0 that is shared among all applications. However, for speculative loads specifying some other invalid address, a TLB miss would be taken every time.

So, *+Onorecovery* can potentially speed up (by removing extra instructions) or slow down (by causing extra TLB misses) an application. The only way to determine if this option helps or hurts an application is by trying it and measuring the results.

11.4.7 Threaded Application Optimizations

If your application uses threads, then there are a few compiler features that can help to speed up performance. The following sections describe a few of these options.

11.4.7.1   *+tls*

The *+tls* option takes a modifier of either *static* or *dynamic*. This option indicates if the compiler should make the thread local storage (see Chapter 8) static to the program or dynamic. Static thread local storage is much more efficient than dynamic, but does not work for code that will be included in a dynamically loaded shared library. Therefore, the static modifier can only be used in executables or shared libraries that will be directly specified in an executable. The dynamic option allows thread local storage to be included in dynamically loaded shared libraries, but it has much more overhead. Since the dynamic modifier works in all cases, it is the default. For performance-sensitive applications, the static model for thread local storage should be strongly considered. It does not have as much flexibility as the dynamic model, but if thread local storage is accessed frequently, the reduced overhead of the static model can make a performance difference.

11.4.7.2   +Oparallel

The *+Oparallel* option informs the compiler to convert some loops into pieces of code that can be executed in parallel by multiple threads. This allows loops with very large iterations to be greatly sped up on multi-processor systems. For instance, the code example below:

```
void bigloop(double **b, int n)
{
    int i,j;

    for(i = 0; i < n; i++) {
        for(j = 0; j < 1000000; j++) {
            b[i][j] = 0.0;
        }
    }
}
```

might be broken up into multiple threads each calculating the inner most loop. For instance, one thread might perform the following inner-most loop:

```
    int j;

    for(j = 0; j < 1000000; j++) {
        b[2][j] = 0.0;
    }
```

The number of threads created would be a function of the number of processors in the system. No more threads than the number of processors would be created. However, if "n" were lower than the number of processors, only "n" threads would be created. Once all threads have finished their respective loops, then the procedure will return. The creation of the threads is completely transparent under the *+Oparallel* option.

Since the *+Oparallel* option works well for loops with large iterations, it is usually not useful for commercial-style applications that tend to have lots of branching and control flow and not many large loops. Technical applications, however, tend to have very large loops, and *+Oparallel* can be a good option to improve the performance of these applications.

11.4.7.3   +Oopenmp

The *+Oopenmp* option informs the compiler to honor any OpenMP directives in the source code. *OpenMP* is a standards-based application programming interface (API) for writing parallel technical applications. By default, any OpenMP directives are ignored unless this option is specified.

11.4.8 Floating Point Options

The compiler provides several optimization flags that relate strictly to optimizing floating point code. Since floating point instructions can take several cycles to execute, being able to optimize these instructions is critical to achieving good performance. The following sections briefly describe several of the more important optimizer flags controlling floating point code generation. A much more detailed description of these and other flags can be found in the "Parallel Programming Guide for HP-UX Systems" at www.docs.hp.com.

11.4.8.1   +Ofltacc

The +*Ofltacc* option lets the compiler know how accurate it needs to be when calculating floating point expressions. Floating point math has several issues in a binary-based computer, such as infinity, NaNs (not a number), and roundoff. The +*Ofltacc* option provides the *default*, *limited*, *relaxed*, and *strict* modifiers, which are described below.

+Ofltacc=default

The default level allows the compiler to used fused multiply-accumulate instructions for performing a combined multiply and add in one instruction, but does not allow any other optimization that may alter the precision of the results.

+Ofltacc=limited

The limited modifier adds on top of the default modifier. It allows everything as is done by default and also allows optimizations, which may affect the generation and propagation of NaNs, infinities, and the sign of zero (since there can be both a positive zero and a negative zero with IEEE floating point numbers).

+Ofltacc=relaxed

The relaxed modifier allows everything in limited, plus it allows for extensive reordering of expressions even if they are parenthesized. This level may affect the rounding of the results of arithmetic computations. This level is the same as specifying +*Onofltacc*. This option will result in the best overall floating point performance at the risk of not having results as precise as could occur without the option. Use this option when precision is not as important as performance.

+Ofltacc=strict

The strict modifier disallows any optimization that could result in numerical differences. This level does not even use fused multiply and add instructions, because the use of this instruction may result in numerical results that are different from what the IEEE standard specifies. In general, however, a fused multiply-and-add will produce more accurate results, since there is less round-off in a fuse operation than when doing each operation in sequence. This option is equivalent to +*Ofltacc*. Performance will be the worst with this option, but accuracy will be consistent with the IEEE standard. Use this option when standards-based accuracy is more important than performance.

11.4.8.2   +Onoparmsoverlap

The *+Onoparmsoverlap* option informs the compiler that the parameters to all functions in the unit of compilation don't overlap. This option is very useful when compiling C code that has been directly translated from Fortran. It allows the compiler to assume that parameters will not alias with each other and therefore allows the compiler to generate more efficient instructions for code within a function where the function parameters are used.

11.4.8.3   +Onorotating_fpregs

This is an IPF-only option. If specified, the compiler will not use any of the rotating floating point registers (f32-f127). With this option, the compiler will not be able to use software pipelining for loops that have floating point operations. This option can greatly reduce the amount of state that needs to be saved on a context switch. This is a good option to try if the application does not do many floating point operations and has a high context switch rate.

11.4.8.4   +Oloop_transform

The *+Oloop_transform* option will attempt to rearrange loops such that nested loops walk down arrays in a cache-friendly manner. For example, it will transform the sample code provided in Section 6.4.2, "Visible Cache Problems" on page 138, such that the two dimensional array is traversed in a cache-friendly manner. This option is the default at optimization levels *+O3* and higher.

11.4.8.5   +Oloop_block

The *+Oloop_block* option informs the compiler to arrange loops to be aware of the cache size on the processor. If the amount of data to access in a group of nested loops is more than can fit in the processor's cache, the compiler will "block" the accesses in the loop such that part of the data is accessed completely before moving onto the next part. This results in a high amount of cache reuse and can greatly improve overall performance.

11.4.8.6   +Oloop_unroll_jam

This option works by unrolling the outer-level loops in a nested loop configuration and then fusing (or "jamming") the unrolled portions back together. This is done to eliminate potentially redundant load operations that may occur in different iterations of a loop and create more values that can remain in registers for longer periods of time. It also helps to create more instances where high-performing multiply and add instructions can be used.

11.4.8.7   +Omoveflops

The *+Omoveflops* option is a PA-RISC-only option that instructs the compiler that it can move floating point operations out of loops. By moving the operation out of a loop, the number of times the operation gets executed should be greatly reduced. Be aware that the way floating point exceptions are handled may be changed by using this option.

11.4.8.8 Trap Handling Options

By default, the application is not notified of floating point traps; therefore, it may be producing incorrect results or performing poorly due to trap handling. The *+FP* compiler option can be used to provide floating point traps. The following options may be used at link or compile time, and may be changed at run-time by using *fpgetround(3M)*:

- *+FPV*—enable signal on invalid FO operations (IEEE FP)
- *+FPZ*—enable signal on divide-by-zero
- *+FPO*—enable signal on floating point overflow
- *+FPU*—enable signal on floating point underflow
- *+FPI*—enable signal on inexact results (e.g., 1./3.)
- *+FPD*—enable sudden underflow of denormalized values
    - Flushes denormalized values to zero in hardware
    - Eliminates software traps for denormalized calculations
    - Undefined on PA 1.0
    - May significantly improve computation performance
    - May produce inaccurate results when performing arithmetic operations on several very small numbers

Note that integer overflow does not generate an error in C; integer divide by zero generates a floating point exception (SIGFPE) in C. Integer overflow and divide by zero do not generate an error in Fortran unless enabled with the ON statement. For example:

```
ON integer div 0 abort
ON integer overflow abort
```

These examples also require the use of the $Check_overflow directive. The +FPD option can be very useful in greatly improving performance of applications that may experience denormaliized numbers but are not affected by rounding these to zero.

The trade-off for enabling trap handling is that you find out about application or data errors that cause invalid results at the cost of the application aborting when the trap occurs.

11.4.9 Trade-offs Between Memory Expansion and CPU Utilization

Additional compiler options allow you to specify your preference in the trade-off between memory and CPU:

- *+O[no]limit*—Suppresses optimizations that significantly increase compile time or consume a lot of memory. *+Olimit* is the default. Specifying the *no* modifier allows optimizations that may significantly increase compile time and/or consume a lot of memory, but performs optimizations that may not be performed otherwise. Usually *+Onolimit* is recommended unless it is found that compile time is greatly increased for no performance gain when using +*Onolimit*.

- +*O[no]size*—Suppresses optimizations that significantly increase code size. Specifying the *no* modifier allows optimizations that may increase code size such as loop unrolling and inlining. +*Onosize* is the default.

11.4.10 Bundled Convenience Options

The HP compilers provide several convenience options to allow ease of use. These options are discussed below.

11.4.10.1 +Ofast

The +*Ofast* (or -*fast* for portability convenience) groups several common optimizations under a single flag. This flag can be used for the majority of applications to achieve good overall application performance. The individual options enabled under this option vary from compiler to compiler and may change from one compiler release to another. As an example, the IPF compiler currently enables the following options with +*Ofast* – +*O2*, +*Olibcalls*, +*Ofltacc=relaxed*, +*Onolimit*, +*DSnative*, +*FPD*, "-*Wl,+pi,4M*," "-*Wl,+pd,4M*," and "-*Wl,+mergeseg*." There may be some applications that can't compile with all of the options provided by +*Ofast*. For instance, a program that needs more accurate floating point may not be able to use +*Ofltacc=relaxed*. However, options in the compiler are always applied left to right on the command line, so a fixup option can be used with +*Ofast* to override the default behavior. For instance, a program that needed the default floating point behavior could specify +*Ofast* +*Ofltacc=default*.

11.4.10.2 +Ofaster

This option simply raises the optimization level of +*Ofast* to either +*O4* or +*O3*. If Profile-Based Optimization is used, the +*O4* is used, otherwise the level is raised to +*O3*. This option is good for small programs that can handle full program optimizations. Very large programs would probably be better off specifying the specific option wanted with +*Ofast* on a per-file basis, such as specifying +*Ofast* +*O3*.

The legacy PA-RISC compilers have a similiar option called +*Oall*. This option compiles the code at +*O4* and enables several aggressive optimizations. It is a deprecated option and +*Ofast*/+*Ofaster* is preferred.

11.4.11 Informative Options

The HP compilers provide a few options that don't directly improve performance but can provide information that can be used to help the overall performance of an application. The +*Oinfo* option provides information on various optimizations the compiler performs such as loop transformations, inlining of functions, and cloning of functions. This option is extremely useful in determining if the compiler is doing a good job of inlining or if it is performing excessive inline operations. If excessive inlining is taking place, then the +*Oinline_budget* flag described earlier can be used to reduce the amount of inlining.

Another very useful informative option is the *-S* option, which produces an assembly output of what the compiler produces as code from the high-level language. Using the *-S* option, a user proficient in assembly language can determine how well the compiler is doing at compiling pieces of code. If the compiler is not doing a good job, one may be able to use different compiler options to help the compiler produce better code. Also, sometimes rewriting C code in a different manner can help the compiler generate better code.

11.5 Linker Optimizations

The linker (*ld* command) should rarely be called directly. For linking applications from a series of *.a*, *.o*, and *.sl/.so* files, the appropriate compiler should be used instead to do the linking. When using the compiler, it knows to provide certain runtime libraries for the linker based on the language. In most cases, the same compiler options used to compile the individual files can be used for the link step, but *.o*, *.a*, or shared libraries are specified instead of *.c* files. For linker specific options, the C or C++ compiler can be used to pass these options to the linker using the *-Wl* option.

11.5.1 Options When Linking Shared Libraries

The main linker option that should be used when compiling shared libraries is the *-Bsymbolic* option. This option allows the linker to bind uses of functions and data to any definitions within the shared library, instead of resolving these definitions in some other shared library.

This eliminates extra call stub code that would normally be needed to allow for function override in a shared library. The use of this option is recommended for all shared library links under HP-UX unless the function override capability is needed. See Section 11.4.5, "Symbol Binding Options" on page 377, for more detailed information about controlling symbol binding in shared libraries.

Another linker option that can help improve the performance of applications that include a lot of shared libraries is the *+mergeseg* option. This option sets a flag in the executable that informs the dynamic loader that data segments from all shared libraries loaded at startup time can be merged into one block. In addition, the data segments from dynamically loaded libraries will be merged with the data segments of their dependent libraries. This option allows the operating system to make better use of large pages, especially if several shared libraries are used that each contain relatively small data segments. By using larger pages, runtime performance may be improved via a reduction in TLB misses.

11.5.2 Options for Setting the Maximum Virtual Page Size

There are link time options that can be used to specify the virtual page size hints bound into the application. To specify the data page size hint, one uses the *+pd size* option where *size* is the maximum page size that the operating system may use for data allocated by the given application. The pagesize hint applies to all data that is allocated by the application–global data within the DATA/BSS section of the application, the stack, shared memory, memory-mapped files, and the heap (via *malloc*). Specifying "L" for the size will tell the operating system that it may use up to the largest page size available on a given processor.

To specify the instruction page size, the +*pi size* option is used where *size* is the maximum page size that the operating system can use for code. Again, specifying "L" for the size will inform the operating system that it may use up to the largest page possible for the platform.

Most large applications can benefit significantly from setting the maximum page size values. Choosing a proper value should be done carefully since a value that is too large may result in wasted memory and a value that is too small may result in poor performance due to taking too many TLB misses (see Chapter 8 for more detailed information regarding these issues).

The size to use for these parameters depends on how the application uses memory. In general, the size of the instruction page size should be the largest supported page that is greater than the TEXT segment of the application. The TEXT segment can be determined by using the *size* command. If the size command returns that the application is 970 KB in size, then one should use +*pi 1M* to let the operating system know it can use a page size up to 1 MB in size.

For the data page size, applications that allocate multiple gigabytes of memory should use the "L" option to allow the operating system choose the largest page size possible. Applications that allocate hundreds of MB of data may want to start with a page size of 4 MB or 16 MB. Finally, applications that allocate only several hundred kilobytes of memory may want to leave the data page size at the default value which generally allows the operating system to choose page sizes up to 16 KB in size.

11.6 Profile-based Optimization

Profile-based optimization (PBO) is a technique for building an application where information gathered about its run-time behavior is used to generate better code on subsequent compilations. You first build a special executable containing instrumentation and then run it with a training workload to create a profile database. Then you build again using the profile database. The "training" workload used with PBO is very important. It should be some workload that stresses the common paths through the code, not the error cases. For example, an error regression test suite would not work well as a training workload.

PBO rearranges the position of procedures in memory based on actual execution profiles. It attempts to place the code of called procedures on the same page of memory as the calling routine. Based on hot code paths, it rearranges branches or predicates not easily predictable control flow sequences, provides branch hints, performs prefetching, and may perform speculative loading of data for IPF implementations.

In general, the use of PBO should not be postponed to the end of application development. For environments where performance is tracked throughout a release, it is recommended that PBO be used throughout the development process. Using PBO early in the development process can be very beneficial because it can uncover coding bugs that regular optimization may not uncover. Also, due to the importance of having a good training workload, PBO should be incorporated early into the development process to work out any issues with the training set and over-all integration of PBO into the compilation process.

Here are the steps for using profile-based optimization:

1. Instrumentation. Compile the program with the *+Oprofile=collect* compiler option (*+I* is the legacy option). By default with most compilers, only arc counts are collected to tell the compiler the hot paths through the application. However, more recent compilers allow qualifiers to be added to the collect option, such as stride sizes when accessing data in a loop. Knowing a common stride size is helpful in performing prefetches of the data. To specify that stride sizes should be analyzed in addition to arcs, use *+Oprofile=collect:all* or *+Oprofile=collect:arc:stride*.

2. Data Collection. Execute the program with various characteristic input data. The input tests should stress the common paths and not the error cases, so don't use regression test suites to drive the PBO training. This step writes profile information to a database file named *flow.data*. If the application is a multi-process or multi-threaded application, then the training set should be run on a two-processor system and not a single-processor system. In general, no more than two processors are needed to train any workload and having more than two can sometimes result in an inaccurate profile due to contention introduced by the slowdown that occurs with the instrumented application.

3. Optimization. Relink or recompile the program with the *+Oprofile=use* option (*+P* is the legacy option), which uses the profile information in the file *flow.data*. A specific file can be specified as well as a qualifier to the option. For instance, if the profile data is in the file */src/profiles/profile.data*, then one could use *+Oprofile=use:/src/profiles/profile.data* (the legacy option would be *+df /src/profiles/profile.data*).

Figure 11-3 shows the steps involved in using PBO. There are several ways that PBO helps to improve run-time performance. First, since it knows which paths through the code will be executed more frequently, the optimizer can generate specific code to handle these paths more efficiently. In particular, it can rearrange branches so the hot paths are adjacent to each other in the text segment. This can help to reduce branch mispredictions as well as to reduce I-cache misses. PBO also allows the compiler to rearrange the functions within an executable to place all of the frequently accessed functions close to each other in the executable. More hot code is packed into a given page, therefore reducing TLB misses and I-cache misses.

For the IPF architecture, PBO can help the compiler determine which variables may be better suited to speculation and which branches may be better suited to predication. PBO can also guide the compiler to place hot global data next to each other which packs frequently accessed data into a fewer number of cache lines, which can reduce D-cache misses (using the *+Odataplacement* option). Typically, PBO helps commercial-style code with lots of error handling much more than technical-style (engineering and scientific) code, which tends to contain a few large loops. Typical speed-ups due to PBO are in the 15% range, with speed-ups of 30% or more possible.

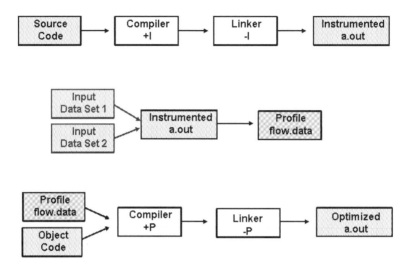

Figure 11-3   Steps in Using Profile-Based Optimization

11.6.1 PBO Issues

There are a few things to be aware of when using Profile-Based Optimization. First, the instrumented application will run considerably more slowly than a noninstrumented version. There is a large amount of extra code that gets executed in the instrumented case that causes this slowdown. Expect anywhere from a 2 to 5 time slowdown in the application. The slowdown for IPF-instrumented executables will be worse than for PA-RISC-instrumented executables.

Second, be aware that after a *flow.data* data set is collected, any changes to the source code will usually render the *flow.data* data useless for the particular procedure or file that was changed. This is much more likely to be the case if any flow-of-control changes were made to the code, such as adding an *if* statement in C.

When compiling with a *flow.data* file, the compiler will issue warnings if the code for a function has changed and state that the *flow.data* should probably be collected again. It is a very good idea to keep the *flow.data* as recent as possible to eliminate the possibility of code changes slowing down performance due to stale PBO information. The IPF compiler does a better job than the PA-RISC compiler at matching the *flow.data* information to the source code after the source code has been modified, so retraining may not be needed as often with the IPF compilers. In any event, the warning messages issued by the compiler regarding stale *flow.data* should always be used as an indication that a new *flow.data* should be collected.

11.6.2 Changing the Default flow.data File

In general, the *flow.data* file containing the profile information for an application is created in the directory in which the application was invoked. This default behavior may not always be desired. For instance, sometimes an application may be executed from multiple different locations, and a *flow.data* file would be created in each location under the default behavior. The FLOW_DATA environment variable can be used to specify a location for all *flow.data* files to be written. For instance, doing:

```
# export FLOW_DATA=/profiles/myapp.data
```

will cause any invocation of an instrumented application to write the *flow.data* information to the location /profiles/myapp.data.

11.6.3 PA-RISC and Itanium Differences When Using PBO

There are some subtle differences between the PBO implementation on PA-RISC systems and the one on IPF systems.

1. For Itanium systems, the Caliper program (described in Chapter 13) is used transparently to profile the application. The *+Oprofile=collect* option simply informs the compiler to compile the application in a way to allow Caliper to easily collect data. For PA-RISC, the compiler actually inserts profiling instrumentation into the executable.

2. On PA-RISC systems, the compiler produces an intermediate file, called an ISOM file, during both the instrumentation and use phases of PBO. The file created will be identical between the two stages; therefore, just a subsequent relink of the ISOM files created in the initial instrumentation phase is all that is needed to build the final executable.

   This process is sometimes referred to as the one and one-half step PBO process, since only a relink is necessary after collecting the flow.data. However, in reality, this one and one-half step process never really works for large applications since it can cause extremely long link times because the linker ends up compiling the entire application in a single-threaded manner.

   For the Itanium systems, this one and one-half step process was dropped, so a full recompile of all files is needed again after collecting the *flow.data* file. Although it may seem like more work, the individual files can all be compiled in parallel on multi-processor systems and will most likely finish much faster than a single-threaded compilation/link process would.

3. The *flow.data* file on PA-RISC systems can contain data for multiple different programs, while the *flow.data* file on Itanium systems contains information for only a single program, but can have data from multiple execution runs. The multiple-program profile feature of the PA-RISC compilers was rarely if ever used, so this feature was dropped from the Itanium implementation.

Due to the ability to have data from multiple programs in the *flow.data*, PA-RISC compilers have the *+pgm* option to specify which application (program) data to select from the *flow.data* file. This option is almost always necessary and therefore should be used all of the time. The value to use is the name of the application when the instrumented version was created. For example, if an instrumented application was linked with *-o myapp.instr*, then the *+pgm* option used for the *+P* phase of the PBO process would be *+pgm myapp.instr* regardless of the name of the final application.

4. For PA-RISC, the *+Ostaticprediction* option informs the compiler to mark the binary in a way such that a PA-RISC processor will use static branch prediction to predict if a branch is taken or not. When static branch prediction is used, the compiler generates hints that the processor uses to predict which way branches will go. The *+Ostaticprediction* option should almost always be used when using PBO on PA-RISC because it allows the PA-RISC processor to use the hints provided by the compiler and these hints are very accurate when using PBO. This option is currently not needed in the Itanium compilers because the IPF instruction set allows each branch to be individually marked as static or dynamic. Therefore, with PBO, the compiler can determine which hint is the most appropriate to use for each branch instruction.

11.6.4 Using PBO With Shared Libraries

Beginning with HP-UX 10.0, the ability to PBO-shared libraries was introduced. A shared library is compiled using the same PBO options as an application. The only difference is that an environment variable called *SHLIB_FLOW_DATA*, which contains the location of where the *flow.data* file will be written for the instrumented shared library, must be specified. If this environment variable is not set, then no profile information will be written out. For PA-RISC compilations, the name used for the shared library in the *flow.data* file will be the exact name used with the *-o* option when linking the instrumented shared library.

11.6.5 Speeding Up PA-RISC PBO Compilations

As mentioned earlier, the PA-RISC PBO process creates ISOM files for both the instrumentation and use phases of the PBO process. The linker then will compile any ISOM file when it performs a link. This works fine for small programs, but is effectively unusable for most large applications. To get around this feature of the PA-RISC PBO process, one can use the *ld* command with the -r option after every compilation of a file. This will compile each ISOM file into a relocatable object, which the linker will not subsequently compile. For instance, during the instrumentation phase, the following sequence could be used to create each *.o* file:

```
# cc +Oprofile=collect -O -c -o file.isom file.c
# ld -r -I -o file.o file.isom
# rm file.isom
```

Then, during the use phase, the following could be used:

```
# cc +Oprofile=use -O -c -o file.isom file.c
# ld -r -P -o file.o file.isom
# rm file.isom
```

This allows each file to be potentially compiled in parallel, therefore eliminating the long link time as the linker tries to compile all of the application's files. Two issues to be aware of with the above technique are:

1. The *-P/-I* linker options are necessary to keep the linker from merging all functions into a single relocation unit. The final link will not be able to move functions around if all of them in a particular file have been merged into one relocation unit.

2. If *+O4* optimization is desired, then the *ld -r* method above should not be used because it will effectively disable the *+O4* optimization, since *+O4* is a global optimization and the *-r* option of *ld* compiles each individual file into a relocatable object. When performing a final application link with relocatable objects (as opposed to ISOM files), the linker will not be able to optimize across all of the files because they will have already been compiled.

11.6.6   Execution Frequency Compiler Extensions

More recent compilers provide both compiler options and pragmas to help guide the compiler down the hot and cold parts of an application, much like PBO does. These options and pragmas, however, can be used without PBO.

11.6.6.1   Execution Frequency Options

PBO will automatically determine by profiling which functions are executed frequently and which are not. The compiler will then use this information to place frequently executed functions next to each other and nonfrequently accessed functions away from the frequently accessed ones.

The compiler option *+Ofrequently_called* can be used to specify a list of function names that are frequently called or a file name that contains a list of frequently called functions. The compiler will use this list when arranging the order of functions in the application.

The +*Orarely_called* option will allow either the infrequently called functions to be specified or a file containing a list of infrequently executed functions. Both of these options override any data found in a *flow.data* file via profiling, so be careful to make sure that the frequently-specified functions really are frequently-called and the rarely-specified ones really are infrequently-called.

11.6.6.2   Execution Frequency Pragmas

More recent compilers also provide pragmas to direct the compiler in a PBO manner without the profile information. The pragma *frequently_called* takes a list of symbols that are frequently executed in the application. The pragma *rarely_called* takes a list of symbols that are infrequently executed in the application These pragma must come before any definition or reference to the functions specified. Also, these pragmas override any data found in a *flow.data* file, so make sure the pragmas are accurate in their description of the frequent and infrequent calls.

To help the compiler determine where the hot and cold paths are through an application, the more recent compilers provide the *Estimated_Frequency* pragma that takes a value that is either between 0 and 1 when used for *if* statements and an integer value when used for loops. Here is an example of how this pragma could be used:

```
void myFunc(int a)
{
        if (a) {
           #pragma Estimated_Frequency 0.95
           . . .
           for(...) {
              #pragma Estimated_Frequency 10
              . . .
           }
        }else {
           . . .
        }
}
```

In the above example, the *if* part of the *if/else* is estimated to be executed 95% of the time, while the else part would be estimated at 5% (1-0.95). The *for* loop is estimated to execute ten times based on the pragma.

These pragmas can be used to help guide the compiler to make better optimizations much like PBO does. However, it is much better to use PBO for this type of optimization, since typing pragmas can be tedious, and they are prone to providing false information if not properly maintained as the code is modified. These pragmas should only be used for infrequently changing code or code that may not be easily profiled.

11.7 Specific Options for Fortran and COBOL

11.7.1 Fortran Optimizing Preprocessor

A special Fortran preprocessor performs source code optimization and vectorization. You use the *+OP* and *-WP* options to invoke *ftnopp* to preprocess the source code. The preprocessor is currently supported only for Fortran and must be invoked at initial compile time. It makes actual changes to the source code, including many special optimizer directives to control optimization. Changes also include the vectorization of DO loops by invoking vector libraries, and the substitution of procedure inlining and loop unrolling.

Performance of Fortran applications can be significantly improved by using the optimizing preprocessor.

11.7.2 Special COBOL Considerations

There are limitations on the degree to which you can optimize COBOL. The highest optimization level is Level 1 for compiled COBOL; interpreted COBOL cannot be optimized at all.

Various executable formats of COBOL have different performance characteristics:

- *<programname>.int*—Interpreted. This is the slowest form of COBOL, and it cannot be optimized. It needs the COBOL run-time environment. Symbolic debugging may be done with Animator.
- *<programname>.gnt*—Demand loadable generated native. This form also needs the COBOL run-time environment.
- *<programname>.snt*—Shareable *gnt*. This also needs the COBOL run-time environment. HP technology was incorporated into the *gnt* format by MicroFocus.
- *a.out*—HP-UX executable, including COBOL run-time-linked *int*. This is the fastest format, but it has the longest compile time.

Use the following commands and options to obtain the different types of COBOL executables:

To obtain *prog.int*, use *cob prog.cbl*

To obtain *prog.gnt*, use *cob -u prog.cbl*

To obtain *prog.snt*, use *cob +u prog.cbl*

To obtain *a.out* with shared libraries, use *cob -xo prog.cbl*

To obtain *a.out* with archive libraries, use *cob -xo prog.cbl -Q -aarchive*

To provide optimization for any of the above except *prog.int*, use *cob +O1*

11.8 Why Does Optimization "Break" Applications?

As indicated earlier in this chapter, optimization can sometimes break an application that executes correctly without optimization. Why does this happen? The most frequent reason is that the code violates the assumptions that the optimizer makes about the language. Sometimes the code does not conform to language standards. In other cases, code is poorly structured or expects architecture-dependent behavior that is not applicable. This problem is typical of old code that has not been modified to run on a newer machine. Other assumptions involve local variables appearing as static and the automatic zero initialization of variables.

Optimizer assumptions are language dependent as well as optimization-level dependent. A few generalizations are provided in the next sections. For details about which assumptions a compiler is making, refer to the appropriate language reference manual.

11.8.1 C and ANSI C Assumptions

These compilers assume knowledge of all variable references; however, this may be violated with shared memory or signal handlers. There is also an assumption that the application does not dereference a pointer with the & operator, or dereference a pointer outside object boundaries.

The compilers also assume that all functions *might* modify global variables; this assumption can be changed by using the statement:

```
#pragma no_side_effects function_name
```

This pragma should be used carefully, if at all. If a function calls another function, then it may indirectly modify global variables and the pragma would not be correct if used. To keep your code consistent with the compiler's assumptions, you should *avoid* the following programming practices:

- Referencing outside the bounds of an array.
- Referencing outside the bounds of an object (structure).
- Passing the incorrect number of arguments to a function (exception: VARARGS).
- Accessing an array in an array subscript. See the compiler manual or man page for clarification.
- Not including header files that provide function prototypes for the functions being used.
- Using variables that are accessed by external processes or are modified asynchronously unless protected via locks. The *volatile* keyword should be used if locks are not used to protect globally visible data. In general, *volatile* is not needed for the vast majority of code.
- Using local variables before they are initialized.
- Assigning pointers to integers or integers to pointers.
- Relying on a specific memory layout scheme when manipulating pointers.

On IPF machines, the assumptions above describing the use of uninitialized local variables and passing the wrong number of arguments to a function are especially important due to the way the architecture works. A *NaT* (Not-a-Thing) fault may occur on IPF if unitialized variables are accessed in the code, whereas on other architectures, accessing uninitialized variables may work fine and not cause problems. Therefore, when porting an application to IPF, definitely make sure that all local variables are initialized before use and that the correct number of arguments are passed to each function. The *+Oinitcheck* option can be used to have the compiler automatically initialize local variables that have at least one unitialized path to their use to the value 0. This option, however, could cause a performance degradation if the initialization is not needed, so it is better to fix the code to make sure all variables are initialized prior to being used.

11.8.2 Fortran Assumptions

The optimizer makes a number of assumptions about Fortran code. It assumes there are no parameter overlaps [as in `CALL SUBA (L, L, N)`, where the variable "L" is specified twice]. It assumes no side effects; in other words, it assumes that procedures modify only local variables. Further assumptions are that there are no parameter type mismatches, no external parameters, no shared parameters, no floating invariants, and no hidden pointer aliasing.

11.9 Debugging Optimization Problems

Optimizer bugs are usually a rare occurrence. However, if an optimizer bug does occur, tracking one down can be difficult. If an optimizer bug is suspected, then the first thing to do is to disable optimization for the entire program and try again. If the bug goes away, then an optimizer bug may be at fault; otherwise the bug is most likely due to a coding error.

If the problem disappeared with optimization off, the next step is to determine which file is causing the bug. If a debugger shows that the fault is in a particular routine, it is often best to start by turning off optimization on just the file that contains that routine. If the issue goes away, then some code within that file contains the problem.

If the problem does not go away, then a binary search should be done to figure out the file containing the problem by enabling optimization on some files and disabling it on others until a single file can be isolated. The particular piece of code within the file containing the bug can usually be determined by using pragmas to find the problem spot using binary search as follows:

1. Determine the level at which optimization is breaking the application. Most likely, it will be Level 2.
2. Coding with *#pragma OPT_LEVEL* statements, use the binary search method to find the portion of code that is responsible:
    - Compile half at the lower optimization level.
    - Compile half at the higher optimization level.
    - Keep splitting the problem source code in half, repeating the process until the problem is found.
3. Once you have found the problematic source procedures, decide whether to fix the source or compile only the problematic procedure at the lower optimization level.

Application profiling can help determine whether a given problem is worth fixing. If an application spends very little time in a procedure that breaks at optimization Level 2, then it is better to compile it at Level 1 than it is to spend time to fix the problem. On the other hand, optimization problems may actually point out underlying programming errors. Therefore, all optimization problems should at least be reviewed to determine whether the application is providing incorrect results even at the lower optimization level where the problem is not detected.

See Chapter 14, "Application Profiling" on page 435, for information about application profiling.

11.10 Porting Applications

When moving an application from one type of system to another, use the following procedure to phase in the types of optimization that are most effective:

1. Develop, port, and debug the application without optimization.

2. Use the migration and warning options to flag any potential source issues. The +*M* option will flag migration warnings. An option of 0 to +*M* flags K&R C to ANSI migration issues, a 1 option flags PA-RISC to Itanium migration issues, and a 2 option flags 64-bit migration issues. The +*w* option will turn on all compiler warnings, which can be very useful to detect subtle bugs that may occur in code.

3. Be aware that all HP-UX systems (PA-RISC and Itanium) are *big endian,* which means that numbers in memory are stored with the "big end" or higher bits of the number at the starting address of a value.

Other systems, such as IA-32- and Itanium-based Linux systems, are *little endian,* which means that numbers are stored with the "little end" or lower order bits at the starting address. This difference may require code modifications if some code makes assumptions regarding the order of bits or bytes within a word. Reading data files written in one endian format on a system that is a different endian format can also be problematic.

4. Look for warnings on uninitialized variables and lack of prototypes. For IPF platforms, HP-UX will report *NaT* faults that can occur from using uninitialized data as a SIGILL fault.

5. Test the code with test data sets to obtain a known set of outputs.

6. Use *lint* (C) or *lintfor* (Fortran) in addition to the compiler's built-in warnings to help discover problems.

7. In C, you might need to use the *-z* option, since it is usually incorrect to dereference a null pointer.

8. First use *-O*, which defaults to Level 2 optimization.

9. Next switch to *+Ofast,* which adds the most common finer tuning optimizations. Be aware that some of the options enabled by *+Ofast* may not be suitable for some particular applications, so specific features may need to be overridden with other options. Most applications, however, can use *+Ofast* without any concerns.

10. Next, add binding options that are specific to the usage (shared library or executable). For applications, the *-minshared* option should be tried. For shared libraries, *-Bsymbolic* should be used.

11. Next, use PBO to further optimize the executable.

12. Finally, increase the level of optimization (*+O3,* then *+O4*) if the application continues to execute correctly and with more performance gains.

13. If there are problems, back off to a lower optimization level, or turn off some or all of the optimizer assumptions.

14. Use the binary search technique to discover the areas where optimization does not work. Start by breaking the application into halves, with each part containing half of the procedures or files. Compile one half at one optimization level, and the other half at a lower compilation level. You should now be able to tell in which half optimization fails, and concentrate on refining the search by breaking the half that fails in half, again. Continue the binary search until you have located the routine(s) or file(s) where optimation fails. You can then choose to either fix the problem by changing the code, inserting specific compiler directives, or merely compiling that unit at a lower optimization level.

It is very important to make sure that all function calls have a proper prototype defined at their call sites. This means that the proper system header files should always be included in your code. Not including the proper system header files, and thus not including the proper function prototypes, can cause all sorts of problems that may appear to be compiler related. Using the *+w* or *+w1* option will cause the compiler to emit warnings when functions are called without a prototype defined.

One of the most common problems of not including a function prototype is that the compiler will assume all functions return an integer if it has no information about what the function may return. If the function is supposed to return a pointer, such as for the *malloc* function, then for 64-bit compiles, the compiler will chop off the top 32 bits of the 64-bit return value, thinking that the value should be an integer. This will result in program aborts when the modified pointer is used to access memory.

Finally, many HP-UX 11i releases have modified the system header files to give the compiler more information about the functions being called. In particular, when compiling for Itanium chips, the headers indicate that all *libc* functions are external to the compilation module because there is only a shared version of *libc* shipped with Itanium-based systems. This information allows the compiler to generate better code for calls to *libc* functions.

When choosing an optimization level, the *+Ofast* or *-O* optimization options are usually sufficient for commercial applications. However, programs with extensive use of small functions may benefit greatly from increasing the optimization to *+O3* or higher. Higher optimization levels are most useful for engineering and scientific applications.

11.10.1 Global and Static Variable Optimization

The goal of this technique is to reduce the number of instructions required for accessing global and static variables. Normally, two instructions are generated to reference a global variable. Depending on the locality of the global variables, it may be possible to use a single "load offset" instruction. The linker rearranges the storage location of global and static variables to increase the number of variables that can be accessed with a single instruction. When using this level of optimization, you should *avoid* some common though undesirable programming practices:

- Making assumptions about relative storage location of variables
- Relying on pointer or address comparisons between variables
- Making assumptions about the alignment of variables

11.10.2 Use of *Volatile*

In general, the *volatile* qualifier in C and C++ should not be needed in very many instances. For single-threaded applications that don't use shared memory to share data with other applications or processes, *volatile* should not be needed at all. For multi-threaded applications or multi-process applications that use shared memory, the *volatile* qualifier may be needed, but only in a few instances that are detailed below.

Any variable that is also a reference to a memory-mapped register on a piece of hardware, such as an I/O card, would also need to be declared as *volatile*. This is only an issue for operating system driver code that may be accessing an I/O device.

Any data structure protected via a lock (System V Semaphore, spinlock, etc.) should never need the *volatile* keyword. Only data structures that can be accessed by multiple threads or processes without holding a lock need to have the *volatile* keyword specified. In these cases, if the *volatile* keyword is not used, the compiler may load the variable into a register and not reload it on subsequent accesses, causing the application to not run properly. This may appear as a compiler bug, but is really an application bug.

For more recent C compilers, there is a *+Ovolatile=* option that can add qualifiers to how the compiler treats variables declared with the volatile keyword. The qualifiers available are:

- *_ _unordered*—the variable may be reordered with respect to other variables by the CPU. Variables marked as *_ _unordered* will not have the *.acq* or *.rel* qualifiers added to their load/store instructions, respectively.
- *_ _side_effect_free*—accessing the variable does not have any side effects. This is almost always a safe qualifier unless the code is accessing a register on an I/O device and reading or writing that register causes other events to happen as a result of the read or write.
- *_ _synchronous*—the variable is accessed synchronously, instead of the default of asynchronously. The compiler may delete some memory references or promote some accesses to a register. This is probably a uncommon *volatile* qualifier.
- *_ _non_sequential*—the variable may be reordered with respect to other variables by the compiler. This is most useful in combination with *_ _unordered*.

Each of the above qualifiers may also be added as qualifiers to the *volatile* keyword in the C code. For instance, one could declare a *volatile* variable as:

```
volatile _ _unordered _ _non_sequential _ _side_effect_free int my_global;
```

which informs the compiler it can move the accesses around, but it still must access the variable via a memory operation for each occurrence in the code.

Note that the *+Ovolatile* option can be specified without any qualifiers. Never use this form of the option. This form will declare all variables to be *volatile* whether they have a *volatile* keyword specified or not. This can dramatically slow down many applications.

11.11 Code to Demonstrate Optimization Effects

The following simple code can be used to observe the effects of optimization at the different levels and for different architectures:

```
main()
{
        int i,j,k,l,m,n;
        for (i=0; i<2; i++)
        {
        j=i*5;/* constant multiplication */
        k=j*1000;/* constant multiplication */
        l=i+1;
        m=l*j;/* variable multiplication */
        printf("loop=%d, j=%d, k=%d, m=%d\n",i,j,k,m);
        }
}
```

This code, when compiled with different options, results in quite a variety of performance characteristics. Some of this is revealed in the assembly language view of the compiled code. Using the command *cc +DA1.0 -go intnoopt int.c,* the code is compiled with no optimization. (The same output is obtained using *+DA1.1.*) The result is shown in the following listing:

Assembled Code for Source Program <u>Without</u> Optimization

1 :		00004130	main	STW	%r2,-20(%r30)
		00004134	main+0004	LDO	R'80(%r30),%r30
4 :		00004138	main+0008	STW	%r0,-120(%r30)
		0000413C	main+000c	LDW	-120(%r30),%r1
		00004140	main+0010	COMIBT,<=,N	2,%r1,main+009c
6 :	**i*5**	00004144	main+0014	LDW	-120(%r30),%r31
		00004148	main+0018	SH2ADD	%r31,%r31,%r19
		0000414C	main+001c	STW	%r19,-116(%r30)
7 :	**j*1000**	00004150	main+0020	LDW	-116(%r30),%r20
		00004154	main+0024	SH2ADD	%r20,%r20,%r21
		00004158	main+0028	SH2ADD	%r21,%r21,%r22
		0000415C	main+002c	SH2ADD	%r22,%r22,%r1
		00004160	main+0030	SH3ADD	%r1,%r0,%r31
		00004164	main+0034	STW	%r31,-112(%r30)
8 :		00004168	main+0038	LDW	-120(%r30),%r19
		0000416C	main+003c	LDO	R'1(%r19),%r20
	I*j	00004170	main+0040	STW	%r20,-108(%r30)
9 :		00004174	main+0044	LDW	-108(%r30),%r26
		00004178	main+0048	LDW	-116(%r30),%r25
		0000417C	main+004c	LDIL	L'2000,%r31
		00004180	main+0050	BLE**$$mulI**	R'430(%sr4,%r31)
→		00004184	main+0054	NOP	
		00004188	main+0058	STW	%r29,-104(%r30)
10 :		0000418C	main+005c	ADDIL	L'fffff800,%r27
		00004190	main+0060	LDO	R'730(%r1),%r26
		00004194	main+0064	LDW	-120(%r30),%r25
		00004198	main+0068	LDW	-116(%r30),%r24
		0000419C	main+006c	LDW	-112(%r30),%r23
		000041A0	main+0070	LDW	-104(%r30),%r21
		000041A4	main+0074	STW	%r21,-52(%r30)
		000041A8	main+0078	LDIL	L'4000,%r31
		000041AC	main+007c	BLE **printf**	R'118(%sr4,%r31)
		000041B0	main+0080	LDO	R'0(%r31),%r2
4 :		000041B4	main+0084	LDW	-120(%r30),%r22
		000041B8	main+0088	LDO	R'1(%r22),%r1
		000041BC	main+008c	STW	%r1,-120(%r30)
		000041C0	main+0090	LDW	-120(%r30),%r31
		000041C4	main+0094	COMIBF,<=	2,%r31,main+0014
→		000041C8	main+0098	NOP	
12 :		000041CC	main+009c	LDW	-148(%r30),%r2
		000041D0	main+00a0	BV	%r0(%r2)

Note the NOP instructions filling the branch delay slots at main+0054 and main+0098. This represents wasted cycles. Also note the branch instruction BLE at main+0050 in the code for multiplying l*j. The multiplication is done by branching to software routine $$mulI, which is expensive in processor time.

Using the +DA1.0 and -O options results in several improvements, which are shown below:

Assembled Code for Source Program <u>With</u> -O Optimization

```
 1 :              00004130   main        STW       %r2,-20(%r30)
                  00004134   main+0004   STWM      %r3,R'80(%r30)
                  00004138   main+0008   STW       %r4,-124(%r30)
 4 :              0000413C   main+000c   ADDIL     L'fffff800,%r27
     C: 4         00004140   main+0010   LDI       0,%r19
                  00004144   main+0014   LDO       R'0(%r1),%r3
 6 : C: 6         00004148   main+0018   SH2ADDL   %r19,%r19,%r24
 7 :              0000414C   main+001c   SH1ADDL   %r24,%r24,%r23
                  00004150   main+0020   SH3ADDL   %r23,%r24,%r31
     C: 8         00004154   main+0024   LDO       R'1(%r19),%r4
                  00004158   main+0028   SH2ADDL   %r31,%r31,%r20
                  0000415C   main+002c   LDO       R'0(%r24),%r26
                  00004160   main+0030   BL        $$mulI,%r31
                  00004164   main+0034   LDO       R'0(%r4),%r25
                  00004168   main+0038   STW       %r29,-52(%r30)
     C: 7         0000416C   main+003c   SH3ADDL   %r20,%r0,%r23
 8*:              00004170   main+0040   LDO       R'730(%r3),%r26
     C: 10        00004174   main+0044   BL        printf (hpux_imp
     C: 10        00004178   main+0048   LDO       R'0(%r19),%r25
 4 :              0000417C   main+004c   COMIBF,<=  2,%r4,main+0018
     C: 4         00004180   main+0050   LDO       R'0(%r4),%r19
12 :              00004184   main+0054   LDW       -148(%r30),%r2
                  00004188   main+0058   LDW       -124(%r30),%r4
                  0000418C   main+005c   BV        %r0(%r2)
     C: 12        00004190   main+0060   LDWM      -128(%r30),%r3
```

In this case, there is no NOP in the branch delay slot, and the BLE instruction has been converted to a BL. Both of these modifications result in major performance improvement.

Finally, using the +DA1.1 **and** -O options results in still more improvement due to the use of the multiply instruction (XMPYU), which is available on 1.1 systems.

Assembled Code for Source Program <u>With</u> +*DA1.1* and -*O* Optimization

```
 1 :                    00003000   main        STW       %r2,-20(%r30)
                        00003004   main+0004   STWM      %r3,R'c0(%r30)
                        00003008   main+0008   STW       %r4,-188(%r30)
 4 :                    0000300C   main+000c   ADDIL     L'fffff800,%r27   # A
        C: 4            00003010   main+0010   LDI       0,%r25            # A
                        00003014   main+0014   LDO       R'0(%r1),%r3      # A
 6 : C: 6              00003018   main+0018   SH2ADDL   %r25,%r25,%r24     # A
 7 :                    0000301C   main+001c   LDO       -168(%r30),%r31   # A
                        00003020   main+0020   STWS      %r24,-16(%r31)    # A
        C: 8            00003024   main+0024   LDO       R'1(%r25),%r4     # A
                        00003028   main+0028   STWS      %r4,-12(%r31)     # A
                        0000302C   main+002c   SH1ADDL   %r24,%r24,%r19    # A
                        00003030   main+0030   FLDWS     -16(%r31),%fr4L   # A
                        00003034   main+0034   FLDWS     -12(%r31),%fr5L   # A
                        00003038   main+0038   SH3ADDL   %r19,%r24,%r20    # A
                        0000303C   main+003c   LDO       -52(%r30),%r29    # A
                        00003040   main+0040   XMPYU,SGL %fr4L,%fr5L,%fr6L # :
                        00003044   main+0044   SH2ADDL   %r20,%r20,%r21    # A
                        00003048   main+0048   FSTWS     %fr6R,0(%r29)     # A
        C: 7            0000304C   main+004c   SH3ADDL   %r21,%r0,%r23     # A
 8*: C: 10             00003050   main+0050   BL        printf (hpux_import
        C: 10           00003054   main+0054   LDO       R'730(%r3),%r26   # A
 4 :                    00003058   main+0058   COMIBF,<= 2,%r4,main+0018   # A
        C: 4            0000305C   main+005c   LDO       R'0(%r4),%r25     # A
12 :                    00003060   main+0060   LDW       -212(%r30),%r2    # A
                        00003064   main+0064   LDW       -188(%r30),%r4    # A
                        00003068   main+0068   BV        %r0(%r2)          # A
        C: 12           0000306C   main+006c   LDWM      -192(%r30),%r3    # A
```

i*5

l*j

j*1000

Java Run-time Performance Tuning

Java is a portable, object-oriented programming language, set of libraries, and a run-time environment that was developed by Sun Microsystems and subsequently ported to many platforms, including HP-UX. On HP-UX, the Java 2 Standard Edition (J2SE) is included with the operating system and the latest version is available for download from www.hp.com/go/java. Java achieves high portability by using a bytecode object format that is interpreted by a Java Virtual Machine (JVM). The JVM can recognize frequently executed bytecode and use a dynamic run-time compiler that converts the bytecode to native instructions. Because Java bytecode does not have platform-dependent function calls, the same code in theory should run on any platform implementing a JVM, the associated set of libraries, and run-time environment. However, given the complexities of the JVM and the run-time environment, JVM configuration, bugs, or other system issues may cause a Java application to behave differently on different platforms.

In general, Java should be carefully considered for high-performance applications because of performance issues that will be discussed. The C, C++, and Fortran programming languages still provide a better solution from a performance standpoint for certain classes of high-performance applications. The next few sections describe common performance issues encountered with Java applications and methods of resolving the issues.

12.1 Overview

The Java Programming Language is an object-oriented language similar to C++. The Java source code is compiled into a bytecode format that is able to execute on a JVM on any platform. The JVM running on a platform interprets the bytecode to execute the program. The JVM may dynamically compile all or parts of the bytecode into native machine instructions that execute on that specific platform. The dynamic run-time compiler performs many of the same optimizations done by C and C++ compilers. Early versions of Java had a simple compiler that converted byte-code to native instructions without many optimizations. This simple compiler was called a *Just-In-Time* (JIT) compiler.

The Java language specification specifies automatic garbage collection of unused objects, so no explicit freeing of allocated memory is needed. All Java objects are stored in the Java heap. Automatic memory management eliminates *malloc*-type memory leaks, but can cause performance issues related to the length of the pauses that can occur during a garbage collection event.

Java also provides good support for creating multiple threads and support for atomically updating shared data structures via a *synchronized* keyword. The *synchronized* keyword is the only form of data protection provided among threads and can lead to performance issues, which will be described later.

Applications can be written to be entirely Java code or can mix Java code with some other programming language such as C by using the *Java Native Interface* (JNI). Applications that are entirely made up of Java code can run anywhere a JVM runs, but differences in the platform environment can influence the program's behavior at execution time. For instance, the initial amount of Java heap memory may not be the same on different JVM implementations and therefore an application may run very slowly or run into run-time errors on one platform and not another. We recommend that you verify that your Java program runs correctly and with the desired performance on all platforms where the code is intended to run.

There are two versions of Java–Java 1 and Java 2. Java 1 was the initial release of the Java language and run-time environment by Sun Microsystems. It contained application programming interfaces (APIs) for writing simple Web-based applications. Most Java 1 run-time environments were extremely slow, but were adequate for testing Java programs during development. The Java 2 version contains additional APIs which make programming in Java much easier. The JVMs available for Java 2 are very robust and the dynamic run-time compilers can produce very efficient native code.

The JVM provided by HP is based on the HotSpot JVM from Sun Microsystems. It contains a dynamic run-time compiler that compiles only the "HotSpots" or sections of Java code that get executed the most frequently. The dynamic run-time compiler is used to compile these hot spots as efficient native code. Only compiling the hot spots in the code results in very good performance because most programs spend 80% of their execution time in only around 20% of their code. The HotSpot JVM also contains advanced garbage collection mechanisms to help reduce slowdowns caused by garbage collection. Finally, the HotSpot JVM provides native support for the *synchronized* primitive that greatly reduces the overhead required to lock and unlock synchronized sections of code.

12.2 Performance Issues

There are a few aspects of Java and its execution environment that can cause severe performance problems if not recognized and corrected. In particular, too much time spent in automatic garbage collections of unused memory, synchronization issues, and the creation of large numbers of threads can cause serious performance problems in Java.

12.2.1 Garbage Collection Issues

The automatic garbage collection provided by Java is convenient, but it provides an environment that can have adverse impacts from a performance perspective. Garbage collection requires that at some point the unused objects in the Java heap need to be removed to find free space for newly created objects. As the number of live objects in the Java heap increases, the duration of this activity can increase. Garbage collection is usually costly because the collection process typically results in taking several cache misses, which stall processing. Since garbage collection is a feature of Java, there is no way to turn it off, so the only way to mitigate its effects is to control it. The following can be done to minimize the effects of garbage collection:

1. Ensure that the Java heap size is properly configured for your Java application. Having a heap that is too small can cause frequent garbage collection events and result in more program execution time spent in garbage collection than in the application code. It is best to accurately characterize the application under load and determine the best heap size for the application. If in doubt, it is best to err on having a heap that is too large instead of one that is too small. The *-Xms* and *-Xmx* options configure the starting and maximum heap sizes. If during the characterization of the application you find that the amount of space used by the application is close to the maximum, you can set the *-Xms* value to the same value as the *-Xmx* value.

   For Java 2, there is a *new generation* area of the heap that contains most newly created objects. As a starting point for your characterization, you should make certain that the *new generation* area is set to one-third the size of the maximum heap size. If it is not the default, you can set the size using the *-Xmn* Java option.

2. Never explicitly call the methods *System.gc()* or *Runtime.gc()* to force a garbage collection. The JVM knows when it is necessary to initiate garbage collection, and forcing one could just cause unneeded delays.

3. Minimize use of immutable objects (objects which don't allow inplace updates) because many short-lived objects can be created when manipulating these objects. The *String* object is an example of a frequently used immutable object. Use of the *StringBuffer* object can result in fewer short-lived objects when you are creating strings in your application.

Good options to use when trying to determine the frequency and length of each garbage collection are the *-Xverbosegc* and *-Xloggc* options. The *-Xverbosegc* option shows details about the type of garbage collection, for example, the "fast" scavenge, full, and concurrent garbage collections. Frequent full garbage collections can have a high negative impact on performance, and doing very frequent scavenges can also hurt performance. The overall throughput of the application is the most important measurement you can make to determine the impact of garbage collection on the application's performance. Again, characterization of the application under a load that simulates the load that you expect in production can help you to tune the Java heap and garbage collector so that you avoid garbage collection problems in the production environment. Use of visualization tools such as *HPjtune* can also help to analyze Java heap performance.

Garbage collection in Java 2 was improved by dividing the heap into multiple areas. The Java 2 heap contains three areas: "new," "old," and "permanent" area for objects. The "permanent" area is for class objects used by the Java run-time environment. The "new" and "old" areas are for the allocation of application objects. The "new" area is for the initial allocation of objects. The "new" area is further subdivided into the "Eden," "to," and "from" areas. The "to" and "from" areas together are the "survivor" area. Objects are initially allocated in the "Eden" area. When the "Eden" area fills, any live objects will move from the Eden area to the "to" area. Upon completion of the collection, the "to" area is renamed "from." At this point, the JVM has freed the space in the "Eden" area so that objects can again be allocated. On subsequent garbage collections, live objects will move between the "from" and "to" areas in the new region until a threshold is hit at which point the objects are moved to the "old" area (also called the "tenured" area). Eventually, the "old" area may also become full, requiring a garbage collection over the entire Java heap. A garbage collection that occurs predominantly to reclaim space in the "new" area is called a *Scavenge GC*. A garbage collection over the entire Java heap is a *Full GC*. Naturally, the length of time required for a GC will depend on the number of live objects considered during the garbage collection. This makes it advantageous to do scavenge-type garbage collections.

12.2.2 Synchronized Keyword

The *synchronized* keyword is used to provide synchronization when multiple threads could have access to a given Java object or variable at the same time. When a method or block of source code is marked as synchronized, the JVM will grab a lock before the region and release the lock after exiting the region. This prevents multiple Java threads from being in a region at the same time. However, grabbing and releasing a lock can incur excessive overhead if done too frequently. In addition, excessive contention can occur if synchronized regions that don't really need to be synchronized are declared, which can lead to performance problems.

In general, only use the *synchronized* keyword where it is absolutely necessary. It should also be used over the smallest region possible to minimize the amount of time a thread holds exclusive access to the region. In general, block synchronization should be used versus synchronizing an entire method. On HP-UX, you can use the *-Xeprof* option together with the *HPjmeter* tool to identify lock contention in your application. Again, simulation of a high load, as you might anticipate in production, is necessary to identify synchronization problems in your application.

12.2.3 Thread Management

When writing a Java application, it can be tempting to create many threads. However, as with any programming language, creating too many threads can cause performance problems. In particular, each thread needs to save some state particular to it and all of this state can cause processor cache pressure as threads are context-switched on the processor. Large number of threads can also cause increased contention on synchronized sections of Java code.

Finally, having short-lived threads is also a problem, even if there are only a few of them, because the creation and deletion of the threads takes time that could be better spent running the application. Therefore in Java applications, it is best to maximize the amount of work done by each thread and minimize the number of threads created. Program characterization under load using the *-Xeprof* option and *HPjmeter*, as well as the system tools *glance* and *Caliper*, can help you to determine the best configuration for your application. Remember that you also want to understand the impact of your application on others that might be running simultaneously on the same machine.

12.3 Versions on HP-UX

Java comes installed with most recent versions of HP-UX. All 11.00 and later versions of HP-UX will have the J2SE installed by default. The JVM installation should be located in the */opt* directory under one of the following directories:

- java–for versions 1.1.x (Java 1)
- java1.2–for versions 1.2.x (Java 2)
- java1.3–for versions 1.3.x (Java 2)
- java1.4–for versions 1.4.x (Java 2)

To determine the version of Java in use on a given system, type *java -version*. The various versions of Java 2 are supported only on HP-UX 11.00 and later. Java versions 1.1 through 1.2 are supported only on PA-RISC systems. Java 1.3, 1.4, and subsequent versions are also supported on Itanium systems. Java 1.4 and subsequent versions can run in 64-bit mode in addition to 32-bit mode. Finally, the Java 2 distributions for PA-RISC come in both a PA-RISC 2.0 version and a PA-RISC 1.1 version.

The PA-RISC 2.0 version of Java should always be used if the Java run-time environment is being executed on a PA-RISC 2.0 system, because it provides better performance and more heap space (see Section 12.5) than does the PA-RISC 1.1 version. For performance, functionality, and maintainability reasons, it is recommended that all Java applications run under Java 2 releases and preferably under the latest Java 2 releases.

Refer to www.hp.com/go/java for specifics regarding what versions of each Java release are supported on which versions of HP-UX. This same Web site will contain the most recent versions of Java from HP available for download as well as HP Java tools and documentation.

12.4 HP-UX Tuneable Parameters and Java

The default tuneable-parameters values for HP-UX are usually not sufficient to run server-side Java applications efficiently. Java applications make extensive use of kernel threads, socket connections, and file descriptors, and can use a large amount of heap memory per JVM instance. HP provides a tool called *Java out-of-box* (a *swinstall* package), which will modify system tuneables and scripts so that various HP-UX tuneables are set large enough for most server-side Java applications. There should be at least 512 MB of memory on a system where this script is run. The script will not lower the value of any tuneable parameter already set on the system where it is run.

Various HP-UX tuneables that may need to be increased on a Java system include:

- nproc
- max_thread_proc
- nkthread
- nfile
- maxfiles
- maxfiles_lim
- ncallout
- maxdsiz
- maxdsiz_64bit

The *ndd* tuneable *tcp_conn_request_max* might also need to be increased, depending on how many network connections the Java application maintains.

Finally, HP provides a tool called *HPjconfig* that is a 100% pure Java application that will suggest sizes for the above tuneable parameters based on the resources used by your Java application. It will also download a list of required patches for running Java on your HP-UX system and compare that list of patches with the list of patches installed on your machine. *HPjconfig* runs only on Java 2 version 1.2.2 or later, and requires HP-UX 11.00 or later. It will work on both Itanium and PA-RISC releases of HP-UX.

12.5 Using Large Java Heap Sizes

Since Java uses garbage collection to manage its memory usage, the amount of heap memory available can be critical to achieving respectable performance. Not having a large enough heap may cause the JVM to constantly perform garbage collections in an attempt to free memory required to allocate additional objects for the Java application. Too much time spent garbage collecting can dramatically reduce the application's response time and throughput. The amount of heap memory available in early Java 1 versions was limited.

Table 12-1 shows the maximum amount of heap available per release. The Java 2 releases

Table 12-1   Java Heap Sizes for Various Java Releases

Java Release	Maximum Heap
1.1.x	1.0 GB
1.2.x	1.0 GB for PA-RISC 1.1 1.7 GB for PA-RISC 2.0
1.3.x	1.0 GB for PA-RISC 1.1 3.8 GB for PA-RISC 2.0 3.8 GB for Itanium
1.4.x	1.0 GB for PA-RISC 1.1 3.8 GB for PA-RISC 2.0, 32-bit 3.8 GB for Itanium, 32-bit multiple TB in 64-bit mode

1.3 and 1.4 provide the most heap available for 32-bit applications, while Java 2 release 1.4 and subsequent releases can provide an enormous amount of heap using the 64-bit mode (*-d64* option to the JVM).

If an application is a 32-bit executable and needs to link in the Java library *libjvm.sl* to execute Java code from within a C program, then the application would need to link with the *-N* linker option to enable more than 1 GB of Java heap space. If the application is composed of multiple processes, rather than being a multi-threaded process, then linking with *-N* could hurt overall performance, even though it allows more Java heap space (see Section 8.1.3.1, "EXEC_MAGIC" on page 211). In addition, be aware that the Java heap area is allocated in the process's private memory region, so creating a very large Java heap area will reduce the amount of *malloc* heap memory available. Finally, for applications that need a very large Java heap, compile the application in 64-bit mode and attach it to the 64-bit JVM for the best performance.

For 100% pure Java applications, the 64-bit JVM can always be used to obtain as much heap as is necessary for an application. Be aware, however, that the 64-bit JVM may incur some performance loss compared to the 32-bit JVM, because all pointers maintained by the JVM will now be 8 bytes in size compared to 4-byte pointers in the 32-bit JVM. This change can result in more cache misses and slower performance. However, in most cases, the performance loss, if any, would be in the 10% or less range. Additional 64-bit-specific optimizations in the future may reduce this difference.

12.6 Performance Options

There are several different Java options that can be specified when running a Java application to improve the application's performance. Table 12-2 contains a list of the more helpful options for improving Java performance on HP-UX. Not all options are supported on all versions of the JVM, so consult the online documentation at www.hp.com/go/java or use the *-help* option with *java* to determine the available options for a given release. The release notes are par-

Table 12-2   Java Options for Improving Performance

Option Name	Description
-server	This option is the default for HP-UX JVMs. It specifies that the server-side JVM should be used that works best for long-running server-side applications. The dynamic run-time compiler uses a high-level optimizer that may take longer to execute, but generates highly optimized code. Additional configuration of the Java run-time environment also helps to maximize throughput for long-running applications.
-client	This option chooses the JVM that is best suited for short-lived GUI-type applications. If the Java application needs short response time to many events or does not run over long periods of time, then you might see better performance with this option.
-d64	Use the 64-bit JVM. This can help improve performance by enabling large amounts of heap memory. It can also decrease performance for applications that don't need the extra heap because object handles will be 8 bytes compared to 4 bytes in size for the 32-bit JVM.
-XX:+ServerApp	This enables a set of JVM optimizations that works best with long-running server applications.

ticularly useful for detailed information on options.

There are some other options that won't help performance, but will hurt performance if used. In particular, the *-Xint* option will disable all dynamic compilation of Java code and use the interpreter exclusively. This may make a Java application more stable and easier to debug, but will most likely dramatically reduce performance. As much as a 5-10X performance loss could occur when using only the interpreter, depending on the application.

Finally, when measuring Java performance, care needs to be taken to write benchmarks that measure what one wants to measure. In particular, simple tests that execute the same operation over and over again may not always generate optimal code in the length of time that the benchmark runs. This is particularly the case for benchmarks or sections of benchmarks that run for only a very short period of time. The problem is that the JVM and the dynamic run-time compiler may not translate the code into more efficient machine language instructions immediately. As a result, part or all of the benchmark could be either measuring interpreted code execution or measuring the actual compilation time. Therefore, it is typically better to test an application in its entirety rather than test individual components in isolation.

## CHAPTER 13

Designing Applications for Performance

Preceding chapters have dealt with *system* performance tuning, which is comparatively easy to accomplish. Designing the application with performance in mind is much more difficult, though doing so may have the largest impact on overall performance. You cannot always control every aspect of the design, especially if the application is already written or if the source code is unavailable. Unfortunately, too many application development organizations leave performance considerations until the end of the process. Features often have precedence over performance when development resources are assigned. However, designing an application for performance from the beginning of the development process will most often ensure that the application performs satisfactorily.

To design an application for performance, one must have a good understanding of the target operating system on which the application will run, including knowledge of the choices for various OS services such as inter-process communication (IPC). This requirement is a large reason why applications previously written to work with one OS that are quickly ported to another OS do not perform well.

This chapter gives some advice on designing the application to enhance performance. The recommendations all assume that you have access to the application source code. Topics are:

- Tips for Application Design
- Shared Versus Archive Libraries
- Choosing an Inter-Process Communication Model
- Shared Memory
- Berkeley Sockets
- Trade-offs with Network System Calls
- Instrumenting an Application for Performance Monitoring

13.1 Tips for Application Design

Here are some tips for good application design:

- Design the best possible algorithm first. Spending time up front to tune the algorithm so that it performs well often has the most impact on application performance. It is also more difficult to go back to analyze and tune the algorithm after it is written.
- Choose an IPC mechanism based on performance rather than ease of coding. This subject will be discussed more fully in the section on choosing IPC mechanisms.
- When large amounts of data must be shared among parts of the application, one should carefully evaluate relative performance differences among the following:

  - Using kernel threads
  - Employing user-space threads
  - Using child processes
  - Creating independent processes

Prototyping may be the best way to try these quite different designs.
- Data sharing can be accomplished via:

  - Structures in the private data segment
  - Structures in the shared data segment (shared memory)
  - Using IPC mechanisms that transfer rather than share data
  - Passing data via files

Each of these choices has an entirely different performance profile. Carry out evaluations to choose the best design based on frequency and volume of data, efficiency of the mechanism, and prototyping.
- When coding the application, do not always choose defaults for parameters to system calls and library routines. For instance, the behavior of the dynamic memory allocation routine *malloc(3C)* can be changed by calling *mallopt(3C)*.
- Specific tips for using *malloc(3C)* are:
  - Remember that *free(3C)* returns previously allocated memory only to the *malloc* pool, not back to the OS.
  - The *malloc* pool can easily become fragmented, and you can end up requesting much more memory from the OS than you expected. This may result in processes that are larger than they really need to be. Such processes hoard precious VM resources that are unavailable to other processes on the system.
  - An application that makes extensive use of *malloc(3C)* may benefit from the larger virtual memory page sizes available in HP-UX 11.0 and later.

- Use compiler optimization to improve application performance. Doing so can save a considerable amount of time.
- Analyze the application for memory leaks that consume precious system resources and degrade performance. Commercially available software can help greatly with this task.
- If the application is to be used on a symmetric multi-processing (SMP) system, extreme care must be taken to ensure that performance is not negatively impacted. As discussed in the chapter on "Hardware Performance Issues," cache coherency problems can be caused by the process's being switched among the CPUs by OS load balancing, or when various parts of an application communicate extensively by IPC mechanisms. Remember also that poor application design is often a source of kernel contention and/or application deadlocks when running on an SMP system.

The following tips benefit engineering and scientific applications the most:

- Understand how the programming language works, and code accordingly. For example, C stores multiply-dimensioned arrays in row-major order, while Fortran stores them in column-major order. Accessing the arrays in the wrong way will have a large detrimental impact on performance by causing unnecessary page faults, in addition to cache and TLB misses.
- Consider using the vector library for vector math operations.
- Use the Fortran optimizing preprocessor, *ftnopp*, if coding in Fortran.
- Use the higher compiler optimization levels (*+O2/+O3/+O4*).

13.2 Shared Versus Archive Libraries

Choosing between using shared libraries and archive libraries involves a classic memory-versus-CPU-utilization trade-off (Rule #2). Shared libraries, which are the default, are easier to use and consume less disk space. However, archive libraries consume less CPU while consuming more disk space. When deciding whether to use shared or archive libraries, consider their advantages and disadvantages, as described in the next sections.

13.2.1 Shared Libraries

Shared libraries have the following advantages (+) and disadvantages (-):

+ They are linked by default.
+ They use less disk space because they are not included in *a.out* and are shared among all processes in memory that invoke the same routines.
+ They make it easier to maintain the application without relinking it entirely.
+ They make it easier to add things dynamically, such as language support or support for different graphics devices.
+ There is a revision-control feature.

+ They can potentially improve the utilization of the virtual address space of a process because they are loaded into a different quadrant, leaving more room in other quadrants.

- There may be slow access on the first call of a procedure, depending on the binding rule used.
- They cannot be locked into memory.
- Data for shared libraries are private, requiring swap space reservation.
- They typically consume more system memory than archived libraries because data can be allocated for each shared library used regardless of whether or not the data is really needed. In addition, additional data is needed to maintain the ability to dynamically access the data in a shared library.
- They are incompatible with *prof(1)* and *gprof(1)* profilers for some versions of HP-UX.
- They are often slower because of the use of position-independent code (PIC) and cross-quadrant branching.
- Often an application can fail indirectly due to a modification made to a shared library it is using because the application was probably not tested against the changed shared library.
- They can cause protection register thrashing if the shared library permission is not read-execute for global, group, and user permissions. (See Section 6.5.4.3, "Protection ID Issues" on page 149.)

13.3 Archive Libraries

The use of archive libraries is optional, requiring one of the following options at compile or link time:

- *cc/f77 -Wl,-a,archive*
- *LDOPTS="a archive"*
- *ld -a archive*

For IPF applications on HP-UX 11i v1.5 and later, there are very few system libraries supplied by HP in archive form. In particular, the C library, *libc*, is only provided in shared form. Some frequently accessed routines from *libc*, such as *memcpy(3C)*, *memset*(3C), and *memcmp(3C)*, may be linked as *archived* by the compiler to improve performance. In addition, the math library, *libm*, is still provided in an archived form as well as shared form. Even on PA-RISC systems, not all system libraries are available in archive form.

Archive libraries have the following advantages (+) and disadvantages (-):

+ Faster process execution is typical.
+ All procedures are fully bound at link time, meaning that the application cannot be altered later via a modification to a shared library. This is especially an advantage because it pre-

vents the insertion of bugs that might be caused by placing a new version of a shared library on the system without testing it with the application.

+ Less system memory is typically used because the compiler will only link in the data used by an application from an archived library. Any data that can be determined as unused is not included in the *a.out*, saving memory when the application is run.

- A copy of the called routine is linked to each process, consuming more disk space.

- Modification of a library routine requires relinking the entire process.

13.4 Choosing an Inter-Process Communication (IPC) Mechanism

The use of different types of inter-process communication can have a significant impact on performance. Every application model naturally lends itself to using a certain IPC mechanism. For example:

- A producer/consumer application model with coarse-level synchronization would probably use pipes and messages.

- A database disk cache would be implemented with shared memory.

- An application requiring synchronization could use semaphores or shared memory (using spinlocks).

When considering which IPC mechanism is right for your application, recall that copying data on a RISC-architecture system consumes a lot of CPU, and may cause page faults and cache and TLB misses. Also remember that system calls cause execution to transfer to the OS, which interferes with the multi-tasking of user processes.

The following sections describe several types of IPC, each with its advantages (+) and disadvantages (-).

13.4.1 Pipes

+ They are universally available.

+ They are easy to code because they are accessed by a file descriptor in the same way a file is accessed.

- They are uni-directional.

- There is a limit of 8K bytes in the pipe at any one time (previously 5K).

- They are slow, since data is copied from user space to kernel space and back to user space.

- Named pipes cause inode accesses at *open(2)* time and *read(2)* or *write(2)* time.

13.4.2 Message Queues

+ They are easy to code, although special system calls are required–*msgsnd(2)* and *msgrcv(2)*.
+ They are bi-directional.
+ There can be multiple recipients of a message.
+ Queues can be blocking or non-blocking.
+ Synchronization and prioritization are done by the kernel.
+ Queues are persistent, even if a process terminates.

- They are optional in the kernel.
- One process can consume all available message queue space.
- They are limited to a total of *msgmax* bytes, and *msgmnb* bytes for any queue. The value of *msgmnb* prior to HP-UX 11i was capped at a maximum of only 64 KB. For HP-UX 11i and later releases, the maximum is 64 MB when an application is compiled using the *__BIGMSGQUEUE_ENABLED* preprocessor directive (enabled via *-D* compiler option or a *#define* in the C source before any *#include* statements). Programs compiled on releases prior to HP-UX 11i may interact improperly with programs using large queues (which need to be compiled on HP-UX 11i or later releases) if the large queue-enabled programs create the message queues.
- They are slow, since data is copied from user space to kernel space and back to user space. Thus, additional system calls cause more overhead.

Messages should be kept small and infrequent.

13.4.3 System V Semaphores

+ They are easy to code, although special system calls are required (*semget(2)*, *semctl(2)*, *semop(2)*).
+ They are bi-directional.
+ They can be blocking or nonblocking.
+ Synchronization and prioritization are done by the kernel.
+ They provide both binary and counting semaphore support.
+ Multiple semaphores within a set can be operated on at one time with a single system call.
+ They are persistent, even if a process terminates.

- They are optional in the kernel.
- One process can consume all available semaphores.
- System call utilization can be quite high.

It is recommended that you try memory-mapped semaphores if the application makes extensive use of semaphores and does not need features specific to System V semaphores. In addition, it is better for SMP scaling reasons to allocate multiple semaphore sets than to include all semaphores in one very large set. One kernel lock is allocated for each semaphore set, so placing all semaphores in one set means the kernel only uses a single lock to protect all of the semaphores (in the set).

13.4.4 Memory-Mapped Semaphores

Memory-mapped semaphores (*msem_init(2)*, *msem_lock(2)*, and *msem_unlock(2)*) are implemented on one or more pages of mapped memory in shared quadrants rather than in the OS. These semaphores are available with HP-UX 10.0 and later releases. The kernel code path is much shorter for these semaphores than the code path for System V semaphores. Memory-mapped semaphores therefore have less overhead. Here are the advantages (+) and disadvantages (-):

+ They are standard in the kernel.
+ They can be blocking or non-blocking.
+ Synchronization and prioritization are done by the kernel.
+ The number of semaphores is limited only by memory-mapped file limit.

- They are more difficult to code, mostly because of unfamiliarity.
- They only support binary semaphores, whereas System V semaphores support counting semaphores as well.

13.4.5 Shared Memory

Although shared memory segments require system call invocation for allocation and attachment, they are the most efficient IPC mechanism, having the least overhead. Access to the shared memory segment by either the writer or the reader is as easy as accessing a private variable or structure. However, extensive use of shared memory in an SMP environment may create cache coherency problems, depending on access patterns and CPU switching. (See Section 6.4.3, "Cache Coherence" on page 141) In spite of this potential problem, shared memory segments remain the best-choice IPC mechanism.

To provide for blocking access to shared memory objects, the application needs to provide some sort of locking mechanism, such as a spinlock. If no locking mechanism is provided, two different processes updating the same piece of shared memory may read and write the memory in random order.

If a piece of shared memory is not protected via a lock, then it should be marked as volatile (when using C or C++) to inform the compiler that some other context may modify the variable asynchronously. Doing so will help keep shared memory from being a reason that compiler optimization breaks the application. Be careful not to mark everything as volatile, as this will severely limit the optimization that can be performed by the compiler. Typically, for a well-written application that uses locks properly, very few variables need to be declared volatile. See further discussion on the use of the *volatile* qualifier, see Section 11.10.2, "Use of Volatile" on page 402.

Advantages (+) and disadvantages (-) of the use of shared memory segments for IPC are:

+ Setup and control are done via system calls–*shmget(2), shmat(2), shmctl(2), shmdt(2)*.

+ Access is by normal variable/pointer access–no system calls.

+ They are the most efficient IPC mechanism.

+ They are bi-directional.

+ They can be blocking or nonblocking.

+ They are persistent even if a process terminates.

- They are optional in the kernel.

- One process can consume all available shared memory space.

- They are more difficult to code due to synchronization requirements.

- They can cause protection register thrashing if too many shared memory segments are accessed by a single process. (See Section 6.5.4.3, "Protection ID Issues" on page 149.)

It is recommended that no more than two shared memory segments are heavily accessed per process for a PA-RISC 1.x-based system, no more than four for PA-RISC 2.x-based systems, and no more than fourteen for IPF-based systems, due to protection ID issues as discussed in Section 8.1.6, "Page Protection" on page 217 in the Memory Bottlenecks chapter.

Both spinlocks and semaphores can be used to provide synchronization for shared memory objects. Spinlocks will provide much lower overhead than semaphores. Figure 13-1 shows sample code for a simple spinlock implementation on PA-RISC 2.x-based systems, while Figure 13-2 and Figure 13-3 shows the similar code for IPF-based systems. The code works with both 64-bit and 32-bit compilations on both PA-RISC and IPF systems. In addition, it is very simple example code, so in the case of lock contention, the code merely spins on the lock.

A more elaborate and robust solution might be to spin for a while and then do something like a *sched_yield(2)* if the lock can't be obtained in a given amount of time. This would be done to allow any process holding the lock but unable to run on a processor due to other processes spinning access to a CPU to release the lock.

The routines assume a lock is simply a 32-bit word. The lock is free when the word is set to the value 1 and held when the lock is set to the value 0. The IPF example is broken into a C language portion and assembly language portion to make sure that the spinning part is optimal.

The performance while spinning can be a critical part of any spinlock solution, because the spinning code can potentially introduce many cache misses if not coded properly. For example, in Figure 13-3 the main spinning is done on a regular load instruction (*ld4*), instead of the *xchg4* instruction, which will modify memory and potentially cause a bus transaction each time it is executed in the spin loop. The *spinlock* and *spinunlock* routines each take a single argument, which is a pointer to the 32-bit lock word, and have no return value.

```
#define lock       arg0
#define one        ret0
#define lock_val   arg1

#ifdef __LP64__
    .level 2.0W
#else
    .level 2.0
#endif
    .code
    .export spinlock,entry,priv_lev=3,argw0=gr
spinlock
    .proc
    .callinfo frame=0,args_saved
    .entry
    .align 32

spinlock_try
    ldcws,co    0(lock),lock_val            ; try for lock
    cmpib,=,n   0, lock_val, spinlock_loop ; did we get it?
    bve (rp)                                ; Got lock, return
    nop
spinlock_loop
    cmpb,=,n   r0, lock_val, spinlock_loop ; loop while lock not
free
    ldw         0(lock),lock_val            ; look at lock value
    b spinlock_try
    nop
    .procend

    .exportspinunlock,entry,priv_lev=3,argw0=gr
spinunlock
    .proc
    .callinfo frame=0,args_saved
    .entry
    .align 32

    ldi  1, ret0
    bve  (rp)
    stw  ret0, (lock)
    .procend
    .end
```

Figure 13-1 PA-RISC Simple Spinlock Implementation in Assembly Language

```
typedef unsigned int spinlock_t;

#ifdef __ia64
#include <machine/sys/inline.h>
extern void spinlock_spin(spinlock_t *lock);

void spinlock(spinlock_t *lock)
{
    if (_Asm_xchg(_SZ_W, (void *)lock, 0, _LDHINT_NONE) == 0) {
        spinlock_spin(lock);
    }
}

void spinunlock(spinlock_t *lock)
{
    _Asm_sched_fence();
    *((volatile spinlock_t *)lock) = 1;
    _Asm_sched_fence();
}
#endif
```

Figure 13-2   IPF Simple Spinlock Implementation, C Language Portion

```
        .text
#ifdef __LP64__
    .psr    abi64
#else
    .psr    abi32
#endif
    .proc   spinlock_spin
spinlock_spin::
#ifndef __LP64__
        addp4   r32 = 0, r32        // M swizzle pointer if 32-bits
        nop.i                       // I
        nop.b                   ;;  // B
#endif
[loop:] ld4     r31 = [r32]     ;;  // M  Get lock value
        cmp4.eq p7, p6 = 0x0, r31    // M  Compare to zero
        nop.i                   ;;  // I

(p6)    xchg4   r31 = [r32], r0     // M Value good, try again
        nop.b   0x0
(p7)    br.sptk loop            ;;  // B Lock held, loop again

        cmp4.eq p7, p6 = 0x0, r31    // M Compare to zero
(p7)    br.spnt loop                // B Lock held, loop again
(p6)    br.ret.sptk.few b0      ;;  // B Got lock, return
        .endp
```

Figure 13-3   IPF Simple Spinlock Implementation, Assembly Language Portion

13.4.6 Berkeley Sockets

Here are some of the advantages (+) and disadvantages (-) of using Berkeley sockets:

+ They are a standard part of the kernel.

+ Setup, transfer, and control are done via system calls–*socket(2)*, *setsockopt(2)*, *accept(2)*, *connect(2)*, *send(2)*, *recv(2)*.

+ They are bi-directional.

+ They can be blocking or nonblocking.

+ Caching may be identical for both local and remote IPC.

+ Unix domain sockets are used when client and server are on the same system.

+ Internet domain sockets are used when client and server are on different systems.

- They are more difficult to code.

- The use of Internet domain sockets when client and server are on the same system causes unneeded overhead.

Recommendations: Code for both local and remote cases, and use *setsockopt(2)* (see Section 13.5.3) to appropriately size the send and receive socket buffers, to control the acknowledgement window size, and to improve network utilization and performance.

13.5 Trade-offs with Network System Calls

This section describes important networking performance issues that application writers need to be familiar with in HP-UX.

13.5.1 *Select and Poll* System Calls

The *select(2)* and *poll(2)* system calls provide a way to see if a file descriptor has available work ready for reading or is available for writing. Unfortunately, the interface for both *select* and *poll* does not scale well when the number of file descriptors is large. This can be a problem when these are used in applications where potentially thousands of connections could be open at one time. It is therefore recommended that neither *select* nor *poll* are used when more than thirty file descriptors need to be managed at one time. See Section 13.5.2 for a new method that can be used when there are more than thirty file descriptors.

The problem with the *poll* and *select* interfaces is that all file descriptors that need to be monitored are passed into the system call. Then, the operating system will mark which of the file descriptors have work. When the system call returns, every file descriptor needs to be queried to see if it was the one that had work. If there are thousands of file descriptors, all of them would need to be potentially queried to find which ones have work even if only one of them actually has work. Scanning the huge list of file descriptor structures can cause further complications due to processor cache misses that may occur as the huge list of file descriptors is scanned.

13.5.2 *Event Port* Driver

The */dev/poll* interface is used to access the *event port driver* in HP-UX. This driver is available in HP-UX 11i v1.6 and later versions, or via patches for earlier versions of HP-UX 11i. The event port driver allows one to efficiently manage hundreds to thousands of file descriptors at one time. The interface and performance of the event port driver is much better than that of *select(2)* and *poll(2)*, because it returns only those descriptors that are ready for processing. In contrast, *select* and *poll* return all of the descriptors in a sequential and potentially very large list; the descriptors that have data ready are marked, and the application must scan the entire list to find the ones with data ready. Therefore, with event ports, if only one descriptor has work, the entire list of descriptors does not need to be searched. Instead, the event port driver returns data for the single descriptor that has work. The event port driver supports file descriptors created via Internet Domain Sockets (AF_INET), Unix Domain Sockets (AF_UNIX), named FIFO files, pipes, XTI endpoints, and STREAMS devices.

To create an event port, the */dev/poll* device is opened as follows:

```
int eventp;

/* Open the /dev/poll event port */
int open_event_port()
{
    return open("/dev/poll", O_RDWR);
}}
```

If the event port was successfully created, then the file descriptor for the port is returned; otherwise a value of -1 is returned and *errno* is set to the given error. Currently, if *errno*=ENXIO is returned, then all of the required patches for event ports have not been installed.

Event ports for different groups of file descriptors can be created by opening */dev/poll* multiple times (once for each desired event port). Note, however, that only the process that creates the event port may manipulate it (other than closing it). This means that children that inherit the event port file descriptor can only close it. Therefore, each process that needs to query file descriptors needs to create and populate its own event port.

To register a file descriptor with the event port, the following code could be used:

```
/* Register a file descriptor with an event port for input access*/

    struct pollfd p[1];

    f[0].fd = fd;
    f[0].events = POLLIN;
    err = write(port, p, sizeof(p));
```

The above example only registers one file descriptor. To register a group of file descriptors, an array of more than 1 *pollfd* structures can be passed in the write call. Any of the poll events described in */usr/include/sys/poll.h* can be registered.

To query the event port for file descriptors with work, the following is done:

```
/* Access the event port to see what is available */
void query_port(int port, pollfd_t *entries, nfds_t num_entries)
{
    struct dvpoll p;
    p.dp_fds = entries;
    p.dp_nfds = num_entries;
    p.dp_timeout = -1;
    return ioctl(port, DP_POLL, &p);
}
```

In the above example, the *ioctl(2)* call will block until one of the file descriptors registered with the event port has work. Information about the file descriptor that has work will be copied to the entries array. If multiple file descriptors become active at one time, then information on all active descriptors will be returned up to the size of the array passed in (in the above example, the size of the entries array).

File descriptors can be deregistered from an event port by closing them or by performing the following code:

```
/* Unregister a file descriptor with an event port for input access*/

    struct pollfd p[1];

    f[0].fd = fd;
    f[0].events = POLLREMOVE;
    err = write(port, p, sizeof(p));
```

Using event ports when managing thousands of file descriptors can result in substantial performance gains compared to using *select* or *poll*. Performance improvements of over two times could be possible. Only in the case where almost all file descriptors have work does event ports not provide a significant speed-up over *poll* and *select*. We therefore recommend that event ports be used whenever the number of file descriptors to manage is large (say, more than thirty). More detailed information regarding the event port driver can be found in the *poll(7)* man page.

13.5.3 Configuring Berkeley Sockets for Performance

Sometimes it is important to configure sockets in special ways for performance. In particular, it may be necessary to set up an asynchronous operation on sockets or to set the socket buffer size to something large for better network throughput. The *getsockopt(2)* system call retrieves the current socket options, and the *setsockopt(2)* system call sets new socket options. The following are the important options that can affect performance:

- SO_SNDBUF—The size of the socket send buffer size. This controls the amount of data that can be sent before the application blocks. This value can be increased at any time, but can only be decreased before a connection is established.
- SO_RCVBUF—The size of the socket receive buffer size. This controls the amount of data that can be received before blocking further incoming requests. This value can be increased at any time, but can only be decreased before a connection is established.
- SO_KEEPALIVE—This is allowed for AF_INET sockets only and specifies that a given socket connection should not be allowed to be closed if it goes idle.

The SO_SNDBUF and SO_RCVBUF values may be increased from the default values to potentially increase throughput on a connection for large transfers or on socket connections that have many transfers over a short period of time. The default size of the buffer is dependent on the network protocol used. For TCP, the default is 32 KB for both SO_RCVBUF and SO_SNDBUF. For UDP, these defaults are 2 GB each.

13.5.4 *Sendfile* System Call

The *sendfile(2)* and *sendfile64(2)* system calls allow an application to transfer data in a file directly to another networked machine without copying the data into the application and then back out through the network. It also allows a single *sendfile* call to be made to transfer a file versus potentially having to use multiple *send(2)* calls.

Sendfile can have large performance advantages over the *send* system call because the extra copying involved with the *send* system call can be costly in terms of CPU and system bus usage. It is always advantageous to minimize the amount of copying needed to move data around.

The *sendfile64(2)* version of the system call allows large files (greater than 2 GB) to be sent from 32-bit applications. This version of the system call is only available for HP-UX 11.00 and later and when used in conjunction with large files. When using files smaller or equal to 2 GB for 32-bit applications, the *sendfile* command can be used in HP-UX 10.0 and later. Sixty-four bit applications should always use the *sendfile* system call and not the *sendfile64* system call.

13.6 Instrumenting an Application for Performance Monitoring

Hewlett-Packard has joined with other vendors and end-user customers to form the Application Response Measurement (ARM) Working Group. This working group has agreed on an application programming interface (API) specification that application developers can use to instrument their applications for performance monitoring. The ARM Software Developer's Kit (SDK) is available at no charge at the following URLs:

http://www.openview.hp.com/products/ovperf/index.html
http://www.tivoli.com/ (see "Downloads")

Additional information about the ARM Working Group is available at:

http://www.cmg.org/regions/cmgarmw

13.6.1 Metrics Available by Using the ARM API

Instrumenting the application with the ARM API can provide metrics that can be used to monitor:

- Application availability
- Application performance
    - Business transaction response time

- Workload throughput

- Service levels as seen by the user

• Application usage, including data for chargeback accounting

The transactions measurements may be correlated among multiple systems to measure end-to-end response time in a distributed and/or client/server environment.

13.6.2 Run-time libraries

API run-time libraries are available with *MeasureWare* on the following platforms:

• HP-UX 10.x and 11.x

• IBM AIX

• NCR MP RAS

• Sun Solaris

The ARM API is intended to work with various vendors' management applications, such as HP *MeasureWare*. The ARM agent (supplied by the management application vendor) receives metrics from the instrumented application when it calls the procedures in the run-time library, and sends the metrics to the management application.

13.6.3 Calls Available With the ARM API

The ARM API includes calls to:

• Identify a transaction with a label

• Indicate when a transaction starts

• Indicate when a transaction has completed

• Indicate the parent/child relations among pieces of transactions that may run on multiple systems in a distributed or client/server environment

Using the API is not difficult, but it does require access to the application source code and the ability to modify that source code. The benefits from instrumenting an application in this manner should provide the impetus necessary to convince the organization that the work should be done.

13.6.4 Using the ARM API to Measure Application Performance

The following steps are necessary to measure application performance using the ARM API:

1. Establish which business transactions are important from a measurement perspective. This may be done in conjunction with Service Level Agreement (SLA) creation.
2. Modify the application source code to include calls to the ARM API in appropriate places, to provide the data necessary to measure the business transactions defined in Step 1.
3. Link the application with the actual ARM library available from the management application vendor.
4. Run the instrumented application using various workloads over a suitable period of time.
5. Analyze the results with the management application, such as *MeasureWare* or *PerfView*.
6. Use the analyzed results to modify the application to improve its performance or to meet the established Service Level Objective (SLO).

Instrumenting an application with the ARM API is the most accurate way to actually determine how the application is performing. Only then can developers take knowledgeable actions to modify the application to improve its performance.

Application Profiling

A pplication profiling is a technique that uses a group of special tools to create executables that are designed to be analyzed for performance. This chapter describes the use of the following profiling tools:

- *Caliper*
- *CXperf*
- *gprof*
- *puma*
- *HPjmeter*

Profiling provides information on where the application spends its CPU time. *Caliper* provides extensive low-level processor information such as branch prediction data and cache and TLB misses on IPF based systems. *CXperf* and *puma* also provide information on virtual memory utilization. *HPjmeter* allows profile information from Java applications to be analyzed. You can use the results of an application profile to:

- Tune the algorithms used by the application
- Improve the overall performance of the application
- Decide whether or not it is worth spending time on tuning the application
- Decide which routines or procedures are worth tuning

After profiling an application, apply the following simple rule of thumb: it is worth tuning a single procedure if the profile shows that it consumes more than 5–10% of the CPU utilization *and/or* has significant virtual memory problems. If no single procedure consumes significant amounts of time, then whole-program-type optimizations such as function inlining or algorithm changes may be the only way to improve the performance of the application.

14.1 Caliper

Caliper is an extensive run-time performance analyzer for IPF applications running under IPF versions of HP-UX. It is available for HP-UX 11i v1.6 and later. *Caliper* allows a program developer to analyze a program to find performance bottlenecks. *Caliper* works with any IPF-based binary and does not necessarily need a special compilation of an application to provide useful feedback. It can even work on heavily-optimized applications. Caliper is provided as a free standalone product or is installed automatically when the HP ANSI C, ANSI C++, or Fortran compilers are installed.

Given *Caliper*'s general purpose framework, it is also used transparently by the compiler to collect profile-based compilation information when used with the compiler's profile-based-optimization feature. *Caliper* works with all multi-threaded processes (both 1x1 and MxN threads), programs optimized with or without debug information, 32-bit and 64-bit binaries, applications using any combination of shared and archived libraries, and applications that use *fork(2)*, *vfork(2)*, and *exec(2)*. It does not profile PA-RISC binaries, dynamically generated code, or any assembly code that does not follow the IPF calling conventions.

Caliper collects its data using a combination of dynamic instrumentation and using the performance monitoring unit (PMU) of the Itanium and Itanium2 chips. One or both methods are used, depending on what is being measured. *Caliper* always tries to use the least-intrusive measurement method possible to collect data, but be aware that some of its measurement methods may be very intrusive.

Caliper works with both preconfigured configuration files and user-generated configuration files. The preconfigured configuration files currently supported are described in Table 14-1. Any of these files can also be modified or new files can be created to generate personalized measurement configurations that measure any of the Itanium and Itanium2 PMU events. *Caliper* keeps a description of all of the PMU events in */opt/caliper/doc/text/itanium_cpu_counters.txt* and */opt/caliper/doc/text/itanium2_cpu_counters.txt*.

The main *Caliper* executable is **caliper**, which has the following syntax:

caliper [*config file*] [*--options*] [*executable*]

where *config_file* is either one of the standard *Caliper* configuration files mentioned above or a customized configuration file, *executable* is the optional program to profile, and *options* are any additional options to override default behavior.

14.1.1 Analyzing a Program With *Caliper*

The first step in analyzing the performance of an application with *Caliper* is to get a general profile of where all of the time is being spent within the application. The *fprof* configuration

Table 14-1 *Caliper* Configuration File Descriptions

Config File	Description
alat_miss	Reports exact counts of ALAT (Advanced Load Address Table) misses for the entire sample period as well as sampled places within the code containing ALAT misses. This configuration only works on Itanium2 and later processors.
arc_count	Reports all branch target address pairs and how often these branches are taken. This is a heavy weight profile.
branch_prediction	Reports exact and sampled counts of branch prediction for the program.
cgprof	Provides a call graph profile that shows both flat and call graph profiles of a program with output very similar to that of *gprof*. This is a heavy weight profile.
dcache_miss	Reports both exact and sampled data cache misses and average latencies.
dtlb_miss	Reports both exact and sampled data TLB misses for the program.
fprof	Reports a flat profile of the application as well as exact counts of CPU metrics for the program.
func_count	Reports the number of times functions were called in an application. This is a heavy weight profile.
icache_miss	Reports both exact and sampled data for instruction cache misses.
itlb_miss	Reports both exact and sampled instruction TLB misses for the application.
pbo	Provides branch profile information for use with the compiler's profile-based optimization. This configuration is usually not explicitly used, but happens automatically for programs compiled with the *+Oprofile=collect* compiler option. This is a heavy weight profile.
pmu_trace	Provides a trace of sampled cache misses, TLB misses, branch mispredictions, ALAT misses, and other CPU events. The trace includes things like the instruction address of the event and event metrics such as latency for cache misses.
total_cpu	Reports exact counts for various PMU metrics across a programs execution. The default is to measure information to calculate the CPI (cycle per instruction) of a program.

can be used for just this purpose. The small program shown in Figure 14-1 will be used as exam-

```
#include <stdio.h>
#include <stdlib.h>

#define SIZE 10000
unsigned long a[SIZE][SIZE];

void sum(unsigned long row, unsigned long column) {
        a[row][column] = row + column;
}

void multiply(unsigned long row, unsigned long column) {
        a[row][column] = a[row][column]*a[row][column];
}

void calculate_sum_values(unsigned long row, unsigned long column)
{
        unsigned long r,c;

        for(c = 0; c < column; c++) {
                for(r = 0; r < row; r++) {
                        sum(r, c);
                }
        }
}

void calculate_mult_values(unsigned long row, unsigned long column)
{
        unsigned long r,c;

        for(c = 0; c < column; c++) {
                for(r = 0; r < row; r++) {
                        multiply(r, c);
                }
        }
}

int main(int argc, char ** argv)
{
        /* Calculate the result */
        calculate_sum_values(SIZE, SIZE);
        calculate_mult_values(SIZE, SIZE);

        printf("a[%d][%d] = %ld\n",SIZE-1, SIZE-1, a[SIZE-1][SIZE-1]);
}
```

Figure 14-1   Sample Code Program, *test1*

ple code to show the various features of *Caliper.* This code is based off the "sample code 1" example given earlier in Section 6.4.2, "Visible Cache Problems" on page 138. The code was initially compiled as follows to create a 64-bit optimized binary:

```
# cc +DD64 -O -o test1 test1.c
```

Running the command:

```
# caliper fprof -o test1.fprof ./test1
```

will display an instruction pointer sample profile of where the instruction pointer happens to reside at random points in time. Using the *-o* (or *--output-file*) option will send the results to a specified file instead of standard output.

The *fprof* configuration is a low-overhead configuration script; it simply samples the value of the instruction pointer every so many cycles. The default is to sample every 500,000 cycles plus or minus about 5%. The default rate is set to keep the overhead of the caliper command to a minimum, but still allow for good sampling. The 5% adjustment is to make sure the sampling is randomized so that it does not always correspond with a particular part of the application.

It may be necessary, however, to adjust the sampling interval lower or adjust the randomness value. A lower sample value may be needed if not enough samples can be collected with the default value. Be aware, however, that a higher sample rate may interfere with the actual program execution time. Setting the randomness factor differently may be needed if the program appears to be running "in-sync" with the sampling period. For instance, say your program did something exactly every 500,000 CPU cycles. In this case, 100% of the samples may appear to be in a single place, when in reality, the application spends only a little amount of time in this code. The sampling rate and randomness factor can be changed via the *Caliper*'s *--sampling-counter* option. See the *Caliper* documentation for the exact syntax to use.

There are several sections to the *fprof* report. These sections are the system summary section, the list of modules included/excluded, the summary of your program, and finally, detailed information on each function in your program.

14.1.1.1   System Summary Section

The system summary section describes general information about your program and the system where it was run. For the sample program, this output is given in Figure 14-2. Important general system data that is shown include the number of processors on the system as well as the processor type and frequency. Important data about the application being measured include its memory model (LP64 in this case for a 64-bit application), the text page size used, and the invocation of the application that was performed. Finally, important information about the actual measurement taken includes the amount of time spent in user and system time, the number of samples collected, the sampling interval, and what exactly was sampled (in this case, the instruction pointer). To get a more precise profile, make sure the number of samples collected during the profile is more than one thousand. The number of samples that *Caliper* can collect is directly related to how long the profile period lasts and how often *Caliper* samples. If the profiling period can't be controlled, then the only way to increase the number of samples is to decrease the sample period.

```
================================================================================
HP Caliper Flat Profile Report
================================================================================

Target Application
  Program:                        /chris/caliper/test1
  Invocation:                     ./test1
  Process ID:                     5984 (started by Caliper)
  Start time:                     11:10:56 AM
  End time:                       11:11:15 AM
  Last modified:                  August 11, 2003 at 11:10 AM
  Memory model:                   LP64
  Main module text page size: default

Processor Information
  Machine name:          gunnison2
  Number of processors: 4
  Processor type:        Itanium2
  Processor speed:       1000 MHz

Run Information
  Date:     August 11, 2003
  Version: HP Caliper - HP-UX Itanium Version A.3.0.8 (6/19/2003) *stable*
  OS:       HP-UX B.11.23 U ia64

Target Execution Time
  Real time:   19.478 seconds
  User time:   18.027 seconds
  System time:  1.358 seconds

Sampling Specification
  Sampling event:             CPU_CYCLES
  Sampling rate:              500000 events
  Sampling rate variation:    25000 (5.00% of sampling rate)
  Sampling counter privilege: user_priv_level (user-space sampling)
  Data granularity:           16 bytes
  Number of samples:          35462
  Data sampled:               IP
```

Figure 14-2 *Caliper* System Summary Section

14.1.1.2   Important Modules Included and Excluded

Caliper has the ability to filter the results to include only data from specific modules of an application. For instance, any activity in HP-UX shared libraries can be ignored, if desired. The *--module-exclude* option allows a list of modules to exclude to be specified, while the *--module-include* allows a list of modules to be included to be specified. The default behavior depends on the configuration used, but usually includes the main application and all shared libraries touched by the application. When using the *--module-include* option, usually the *--module-default=none* option is specified first to turn off profiling for all default modules so only the modules specified are profiled.

Limiting the modules measured can help to speed-up some of *Caliper*'s measurements and reduce the amount of data that needs to be analyzed. For instance, it may not be useful to measure shared libraries that cannot be modified by the application. To measure only a main application and none of the shared libraries it may touch, the following caliper invocation can be used:

```
# caliper fprof --module-default=none --module-include=test1 ./test1 10000
```

14.1.1.3 Program Execution Summary

The program execution summary section displays an overall summary of the program's execution. Figure 14-3 shows an example from the *test1* program. The first part of this section

```
------------------------------------------------
Counter                 Priv. Mask        Count
------------------------------------------------
CPU_CYCLES              8  (USER)     17727687083
BACK_END_BUBBLE_ALL     8  (USER)     15626174680
BE_EXE_BUBBLE_GRALL     8  (USER)      5611854895
------------------------------------------------
% of Cycles lost due to stalls (lower is better):
  88.15 = 100 * (BACK_END_BUBBLE_ALL / CPU_CYCLES)

% of Cycles stalled due to GR/GR or GR/load dependency (lower is better):
  31.66 = 100 * (BE_EXE_BUBBLE_GRALL / CPU_CYCLES)
------------------------------------------------

Load Module Summary
------------------------------------------------
% Total  Cumulat
   IP      % of           IP
Samples   Total        Samples   Load Module
------------------------------------------------
 99.99    99.99         35457    test1
  0.01    99.99             3    *unattributed*
  0.01   100.00             2    dld.so
------------------------------------------------
100.00   100.00         35462    Total
------------------------------------------------

Function Summary
------------------------------------------------------------------
% Total  Cumulat
   IP      % of           IP
Samples   Total        Samples   Function                    File
------------------------------------------------------------------
 65.42    65.42         23199    test1::multiply             test1.c
 31.15    96.57         11045    test1::sum                  test1.c
  1.78    98.35           632    test1::calculate_mult_values test1.c
  1.64    99.99           581    test1::calculate_sum_values  test1.c
  0.01    99.99             3    *unknown_0xe000000000ffdf34*
------------------------------------------------------------------
```

Figure 14-3 Caliper Program Summary Section

shows the percentage of cycles wasted due to processor stalls. The processor may stall for any number of reasons, but the main reason is usually due to needing to wait on a memory access. In this particular case, the percentage of stalls is very high, indicating that there is a memory access bottleneck. The next statistic shows the percentage of cycles stalled due to instruction latency issues (GR/GR) or stalls due to not having a dependent load available for access (GR/load). The GR/GR latency can occur for instructions that take more than a cycle to execute and that are not separated in the instruction stream by more than their execution latency. The GR/load latencies can occur if a value loaded from memory is not available in time for use by an instruction. The percentage seen here is also high for the *test1* program, indicating that potential performance improvements are possible.

Next, the load module summary section shows how much time is spent in each load module that the application accesses. In this case, practically all of the time is spent in the *test1* application. Finally, the function summary section breaks down the execution time by function within each of the measured load modules. In this case, 65% of the time is being spent in the *multiply* function, and 31% is being spent in the *add* function, so 96% of all of the time in the program is coming from two functions.

14.1.1.4   Detailed Function Analysis

At the end of the report, *Caliper* will provide a detailed breakdown of where the sampled measurement events are occurring for each function. The *fprof* report shows the instructions that were executing when the sampling timer expired. Figure 14-4 shows the detailed output printed for the function *multiply* from the *test1* application. This output shows both the C instructions and assembly code generated. The IP Samples column shows the number of times the particular C statement was executing or particular instruction was executing when a sample was taken.

In this example, 100% of the time, the only C statement in the routine was executing (23199 samples of 23199 samples). For the assembly code, 56% of the time was spent on a single bundle containing a *setf.sig* instruction, which is used to convert a value in an integer register into a value in a floating point register. The next highest bundle is the bundle before the *setf.sig* bundle at 35.5%. So, over 91% of the total routine time is consumed in these two bundles. For the *Caliper* metrics that sample PMU events, such as *fprof*, the instructions that get marked as having high execution time may not be the actual instructions experiencing the high latencies. There is a delay associated between when the PMU event is captured and when the kernel records the IP address for that event. Given this delay, the PMU event configurations can closely approximate where the time is going, but may not precisely pinpoint the time.

14.1.2 Using *Caliper* to Track Down the Performance Issues

So now it is clear where the time in the hottest routine is being spent for the test program, but it is still not clear why. To determine where that time is actually being consumed, a second *Caliper* configuration file can be used to collect more data. In this particular case, given the large percentage of stalls, it is usually a good idea to run the *dcache_miss* configuration script that shows data cache misses. Data cache misses can be a large contributor to processor stall time. Running the *dcache_miss* configuration file results in the detailed output in Figure 14-5 for the multiply routine. Notice that the *ld8* instruction (loads 8 bytes of data from memory) has sam-

```
-----------------------------------------------------
% Total                       Line|
   IP              IP         Slot|  >Statement|
 Samples       Samples     Col,Offset  Instruction
-----------------------------------------------------
  65.42    [test1::multiply, 0x40000000000010c0, test1.c]
               23199                ~12  Function Totals
          ---------------------------------------------
          [/chris/caliper/test1.c]
               (23199)             ~12   >     a[row][column] = a[row][column]*
a[row][column];
                199       ~9,0x0000:0   shladd       r9=r32,1,r32
                          :1           dep.z        r8=r32,7,57
                          :2           addl         r10=32,r1 ;;
                414       ~9,0x0010:0   add          r10=r0,r10
                          :1           sub          r8=r8,r9 ;;
                          :2           shladd       r8=r8,2,r8 ;;
                409       ~9,0x0020:0   nop.m        0
                          :1           dep.z        r8=r8,7,57 ;;
                          :2           add          r8=r8,r10 ;;
               8263       ~9,0x0030:0   shladd       r8=r33,3,r8 ;;
                          :1           ld8          r9=[r8]
                          :2           nop.i        0 ;;
              13084       ~9,0x0040:0   setf.sig     f6=r9 ;;
                          :1           nop.m        0
                          :2           nop.i        0
                          ~9,0x0050:0   nop.m        0
                          :1           nop.m        0
                          :2           xma.l        f6=f6,f6,f0 ;;
                830       ~9,0x0060:0   stf8         [r8]=f6
                          :1           nop.m        0
                          :2           br.ret.sptk.many  rp ;;
```

Figure 14-4   Detailed Function Profile for the *Multiply* Function

```
-------------------------------------------------------------------
% Total                        Avg.        Line|
 Latency      Sampled    Latency  Laten.    Slot|   >Statement|
  Cycles       Misses     Cycles  Cycles  Col,Offset  Instruction
-------------------------------------------------------------------
 100.00    [test1::multiply, 0x40000000000010c0, test1.c]
             1248        58534    46.9       ~12  Function Totals
          ---------------------------------------------------------
          [/chris/caliper/test1.c]
             (1248)     (58534)   (46.9)      ~12  >  a[row][column] =
a[row][column]*a[row][column];
                                           ~9,0x0020:0 nop.m 0
                                              :1 dep.z r8=r8,7,57 ;;
                                              :2 add r8=r8,r10 ;;
                                           ~9,0x0030:0 shladd r8=r33,3,r8 ;;
                0          0                    :1 ld8 r9=[r8]
             1248       58534    46.9          :2 nop.i 0 ;;
                0          0                 ~9,0x0040:0 setf.sig f6=r9 ;;
                                              :1 nop.m 0
                                              :2 nop.i 0
```

Figure 14-5   Detailed Data Cache Miss Profile for the *Multiply* Function

pled misses, and the average latency is 46.9 cycles. This is quite long given the L2 cache latency for the 1 GHz Itanium2 processor used is around twelve cycles. Therefore, most of the misses that occur here are going to main memory.

So, why are most memory references going to main memory? The size of the data structure being accessed in the test program in Figure 14-1 is 10000*10000*8 bytes or approximately 763 MB which is much larger than the L2 cache size of 3 MB on a 1Ghz Itanium2 processor. However, the L2 cache line size is 128 bytes on an Itanium2 processor, so there should be sixteen 8-byte values in each cache line fetched from memory. So, if a cache miss to memory took 150 cycles and the level 0 cache hit took one cycle, then the average latency for each cache line would be (150 + 15*1) / 16 = 10.3 cycles. However, *Caliper* is reporting 46.9 cycles which is much larger.

The problem is due to the way the array is being accessed, as discussed in Section 6.4.2, "Visible Cache Problems" on page 138. The C language arranges two-dimensional arrays in rows (called "row-major" order), so all data from the first row appears sequentially in memory, followed by all data in the second row and so on. The code in Figure 14-1, however, traverses the two-dimensional array a column at a time (in "column-major" order), meaning that the first element of each row is accessed before going onto the next column.

Since the entire array does not fit into cache, most array accesses take a cache miss. So, what can be done is to calculate the values in row-major order first versus column-major order. This can be done by interchanging the two *for* loops in the *calculate_sum_values* and *calculate_mult_values* routines such that the <u>row</u> *for* loop comes first, followed by the <u>column</u> loop. Making this change and recompiling results in a run-time of 5.8 seconds, compared to the 19.5 seconds of the initial code.

Figure 14-6 shows the *fprof* function summary output and Figure 14-7 shows the *dcache_miss* output for the new code. Notice that the percentage of stalls went down after making the *for* loop changes: from 88.15% to 51.23% for the cycles lost due to stalls and from 31.66% to 25.30% for the cycles stalled on GR/GR or GR/load dependencies. This shows that the program has gotten more efficient, but actually is still wasting a large portion of time waiting for memory. Figure 14-7 shows that there are still misses for the *ld8* instruction in the function *multiply*, but notice that the average latency has now dropped to 11.7 cycles, which corresponds fairly well to the calculation done earlier that suggested 10.3 cycles for the average latency if the entire cache line was consumed on each miss.

Can this program be made to go faster? Given that 50% of the cycles are still stalled, the program can most likely be sped up even more. Notice in Figure 14-6 that 14.4% of the time is spent in the functions *calculate_mult_values* and *calculate_sum_values*. This result is much higher than before, considering that the memory bottleneck has been relieved. Notice also that these functions call *multiple* and *sum,* which end up doing very little work. These extra procedure calls can end up adding extra instructions, which can waste processor cycles. Also, the function calls are hiding from the compiler the fact that there is a memory access in the multiply and sum routines. If the compiler could see this memory access in the loop, it may be able to

```
------------------------------------------------
Counter              Priv. Mask        Count
------------------------------------------------
CPU_CYCLES              8 (USER)     4307230596
BACK_END_BUBBLE_ALL     8 (USER)     2206548293
BE_EXE_BUBBLE_GRALL     8 (USER)     1089913655
------------------------------------------------
% of Cycles lost due to stalls (lower is better):
  51.23 = 100 * (BACK_END_BUBBLE_ALL / CPU_CYCLES)

% of Cycles stalled due to GR/GR or GR/load dependency (lower is better):
  25.30 = 100 * (BE_EXE_BUBBLE_GRALL / CPU_CYCLES)
------------------------------------------------


Function Summary
-----------------------------------------------------------------------
% Total  Cumulat
   IP       % of              IP
Samples   Total           Samples  Function                      File
-----------------------------------------------------------------------
 69.13    69.13              5954   test2::multiply               test2.c
 16.39    85.52              1412   test2::sum                    test2.c
  7.34    92.86               632   test2::calculate_mult_values  test2.c
  7.11    99.97               612   test2::calculate_sum_values   test2.c
  0.01    99.98                 1   *unknown_0xe000000000ffdf34*
-----------------------------------------------------------------------
```

Figure 14-6   Caliper Program Summary Section After Code Change

```
                                    Avg.     Line|
% Total                            Laten.    Slot|  >Statement|
Latency       Sampled    Latency   Cycles  Col,Offset  Instruction
 Cycles        Misses     Cycles
---------------------------------------------------------------------
100.00    [test2::multiply, 0x40000000000010c0, test2.c]
              1251        14678      11.7            ~12  Function Totals
          ---------------------------------------------------------------------
          [/chris/caliper/test1.c]
              (1251)     (14678)    (11.7)          ~12  >  a[row][column] =
a[row][column]*a[row][column];
                                            ~9,0x0020:0 nop.m 0
                                                     :1 dep.z r8=r8,7,57 ;;
                                                     :2 add r8=r8,r10 ;;
                 0           0               ~9,0x0030:0 shladd r8=r33,3,r8 ;;
              1251        14678      11.7            :1 ld8 r9=[r8]
                 0           0                       :2 nop.i 0 ;;
                                            ~9,0x0040:0 setf.sig f6=r9 ;;
                                                     :1 nop.m 0
                                                     :2 nop.i 0
```

Figure 14-7   Detailed Data Cache Miss Profile for Multiply Function After Code Change

prefetch data, as described in Section 11.4.4, "Memory Latency Optimizations" on page 376, to overlap some processing with the cache misses. What we want to do then, is to inline the functions *multiply* and *sum* into the functions *calculate_mult_values* and *calculate_sum_values*, respectively. This can be done using the +O3 compiler option as follows:

```
# cc +DD64 +O3 -o test2.O3 test2.c
```

Making this compilation change now results in an execution time of only 2.1 seconds which is almost another tripling in the performance. The *fprof Caliper* data now shows the function summary output in Figure 14-8. Notice now that the cycles stalled due to GR/GR or

```
----------------------------------------------
Counter               Priv. Mask      Count
----------------------------------------------
CPU_CYCLES             8 (USER)     836159547
BACK_END_BUBBLE_ALL    8 (USER)     672816956
BE_EXE_BUBBLE_GRALL    8 (USER)        261368
----------------------------------------------
% of Cycles lost due to stalls (lower is better):
  80.47 = 100 * (BACK_END_BUBBLE_ALL / CPU_CYCLES)

% of Cycles stalled due to GR/GR or GR/load dependency (lower is better):
   0.03 = 100 * (BE_EXE_BUBBLE_GRALL / CPU_CYCLES)
----------------------------------------------

Function Summary
------------------------------------------------------------------------
% Total  Cumulat
   IP      % of            IP
Samples   Total        Samples  Function                              File
------------------------------------------------------------------------
 87.33    87.33          1461   test2.O3::T_1_6d8c_cl_calculate_mult_values  test2.c
 12.49    99.82           209   test2.O3::T_5_6d8c_cl_calculate_sum_values   test2.c
  0.06    99.88             1   libc.so.1::real_malloc              malloc.c
  0.06    99.94             1   *unknown_0xe000000000ffdf34*
------------------------------------------------------------------------
```

Figure 14-8 Caliper Program Summary Section After +O3 Compilation

GR/load dependency issues has gone to zero, which is very good. However, the lost cycles due to stalls in general has jumped back up to 80%. Most likely, by removing the function call overhead of the *multiply* and *add* functions, the code has again become memory-latency bound. The functions with the strange characters such as *T_1_6d8c_cl_* in front of them are routines that the compiler has "cloned" (see Section 11.2.4.2, "Procedure Cloning" on page 365, for details on cloning functions).

Figure 14-9 shows the full profile of the *calculate_mult_values* function, which includes the inlined *multiply* function. Notice the amount of code generated. This is a good example of several compiler optimizations in one place. The compiler performed software pipelining, loop unrolling, prefetching, inlining, and cloning all for these two routines (see Chapter 11, "Compiler Performance Tuning" on page 357, for details on all of these optimizations). Most of the ticks in the routine are coming on the last bundle of the function. This does not necessarily mean that the last bundle is responsible for those ticks. As mentioned earlier, the IP locations that get referenced don't necessarily correspond to the instruction executing when the sample occurs. The fact that one bundle has the majority of the ticks, however, does suggest a memory latency issue. Most likely, the code is still waiting on previous memory references to come from memory before being able to execute the *xma* (fixed point multiply-add) instructions at this point in the code. However, there probably is not much more that can be done at this point to improve the execution of this simple example other than improving the memory latency of the system to allow the loads to return from memory faster. However, doing so is out of the control of an application developer. The compiler is already doing what it can to prefetch these loads, but it still cannot fully overcome the latency, since not much processing is done between each cache miss.

14.1.3 Attaching to a Running Process

In addition to being able to monitor the full execution of a process, as was done in the previous section, *Caliper* can attach to a running process at any time to monitor events. This ability is useful for long running processes where one may not want to wait for the entire process to complete before seeing data. It is also useful for profiling a particular process out of a group of related processes. Finally, because *Caliper* can attach to any IPF binary, it also allows samples to be taking on applications where the source code may not be available, or for production applications. When using *Caliper* to profile a running application, the *--attach* and *--duration* options should be used. The *attach* option specifies which process ID (PID) to attach to, and the *duration* option specifies the time in seconds to profile the application. Currently, only a single process can be attached to at one time by *Caliper*.

Not all configuration files can be used in all instances to profile an already running application. In particular, any of the configuration files that require some sort of dynamic instrumentation of the application are more difficult to use dynamically. These configuration files include the *cgprof*, *func_count*, *pbo*, and *arc_count* configurations. For these, the application to attach to should have its dependent shared libraries loaded as private. Private mapping for the shared libraries of a process can be enabled by using the *chatr(1)* command with the *+dbg enable* option. Also, a side effect of profiling using the dynamic instrumentation configuration files is that *Caliper* will not exit until the program that it is monitoring exits, until Ctrl+C is typed on the *Shell* where *Caliper* was run, or until *Caliper* is sent an "INT" signal with the *kill* command. This means the *Caliper duration* option does not work when using these dynamic instrumentation configuration files.

14.1.4 Profiling Multiple Processes

By default, *Caliper* just profiles a single process via either attaching to it or executing it directly from *Caliper*. However, *Caliper* can profile processes that *fork()* or *exec()* other processes as well as processes that contain multiple threads when running multi-process and multi-threaded processes from *Caliper*. The *--process* option allows different behavior for tracing multi-process programs. If *--process=all* is specified, then all processes *fork*ed or *exec*ed

```
87.33 [test2.O3::T_1_6d8c_cl_calculate_mult_values, 0x4000000000000e80, test2.c]
                1461              ~26  Function Totals
            -----------------------------------------
                        ~2,0x0070:0      adds       r9=0,r8
                              :1         adds       r8=16,r8
                              :2         nop.b      0 ;;
         (1461)              ~12  *>     a[row][column] = a[row][column]*a[row][column];
                35      ~9,0x0080:0  (p16) ld8       r22=[r16],16
                              :1     (p16) ld8       r25=[r10],16
                              :2     (p17) xma.l     f41=f37,f37,f0
                        ~9,0x0090:0  (p18) stf8      [r9]=f47,24
                              :1     (p18) stf8      [r8]=f48,24
                              :2     (p17) xma.l     f44=f38,f38,f0 ;;
                33      ~9,0x00a0:0  (p16) ld8       r20=[r16],16
                              :1     (p16) ld8       r18=[r10],16
                              :2     (p17) xma.l     f45=f35,f35,f0
                        ~9,0x00b0:0  (p16) setf.sig  f39=r22
                              :1     (p16) setf.sig  f40=r25
                              :2     (p17) xma.l     f46=f36,f36,f0 ;;
                29      ~9,0x00c0:0  (p16) ld8       r25=[r16],16
                              :1     (p16) ld8       r22=[r10],16
                              :2     (p17) xma.l     f38=f33,f33,f0
                        ~9,0x00d0:0  (p16) setf.sig  f36=r20
                              :1     (p16) setf.sig  f37=r18
                              :2     (p17) xma.l     f47=f34,f34,f0 ;;
                26      ~9,0x00e0:0  (p16) ld8       r18=[r16],r14
                              :1     (p16) ld8       r20=[r10],16
                              :2           nop.i     0
                        ~9,0x00f0:0  (p16) setf.sig  f34=r25
                              :1     (p16) setf.sig  f35=r22
                              :2           nop.i     0 ;;
                44      ~9,0x0100:0  (p16) lfetch    [r16],r11
                              :1     (p16) setf.sig  f32=r18
                              :2           nop.i     0
                35      ~9,0x0110:0  (p16) setf.sig  f33=r20 ;;
                              :1     (p17) stf8      [r9]=f42,8
                              :2           nop.i     0
                40      ~9,0x0120:0  (p17) stf8      [r8]=f41,8 ;;
                              :1     (p17) stf8      [r9]=f43,24
                              :2           nop.i     0
                        ~9,0x0130:0  (p17) stf8      [r8]=f44,24
                              :1           nop.i     0
                              :2           nop.b     0 ;;
               1219     ~9,0x0140:0  (p17) stf8      [r9]=f45,8
                              :1     (p17) stf8      [r8]=f38,8
                              :2     (p16) xma.l     f41=f39,f39,f0
                        ~9,0x0150:0       nop.m      0
                              :1     (p16) xma.l     f42=f40,f40,f0
                              :2           br.ctop.dptk.many  .-0xd0 ;;
```

Figure 14-9 Detailed Data Cache Miss Profile for *calculate_mult_values* After +O3 Compilation

from the parent process and the parent process are profiled. If *--process=root-forks* is specified, then only the parent process and any process it *forks* are profiled. Finally, Caliper provides a very complex mechanism to selectively choose processes to measure. For instance, one can specify:

```
# caliper fprof --process="k*" program
```

to profile only those processes that begin with the letter *k* that are executed from the specified starting program. Please refer to *Caliper* documentation for a complete description of how to use the pattern matching mechanisms for process selection.

14.1.5 Making Your Own Configuration Files

In addition to the supplied configuration files in the */opt/caliper/config* directory, different configuration files can be created to measure any of the PMU events of the Itanium or Itanium2 processor. Usually, one of the configuration files already provided can be modified to use different PMU events. For example, the configuration file *total_cpu* records the total CPU activity for an application over the measurement period. Running this configuration file on the *+O3* optimized sample 1 code above gives the output in Figure 14-10.

The *total_cpu* configuration file is shown in Figure 14-11. The *global_counters* value in this particular configuration file controls which PMU counters are collected over the profiling period. Only four PMU counters can be measured at any one time. The files */opt/caliper/doc/text/itanium_cpu_counters.txt* and */opt/caliper/doc/text/itanium2_cpu_counters.txt* describe all of the counters available for the Itanium and Itanium2 processors, respectively.

So, if one wanted to count the L3 cache misses and the L3 cache accesses, two of the counters in the *total_cpu* script could be replaced with the *L3_MISSES* and *L3_REFERENCES* counters. If this is done, the default configuration files should be copied and renamed to reflect the new configuration file. Copying *total_cpu* to *total_l3_cache* and replacing the *NOPS_RETIRED* and *BACK_END_BUBBLE* with *L3_MISSES* and *L3_REFERENCES* results in the output in Figure 14-12 for the *+O3* compiled sample program. Notice that about one-half of the references result in a cache miss, which indicates that very few of the references are being found in the L3 cache. This is what one would expect from the sample program, since it does not fit in the processor's L3 cache.

The *Caliper* configuration files each provide instructions for how they can be modified with different PMU counters to collect different data. One can refer to these configurations to determine other ways to collect interesting data about an application.

14.1.6 Instrumenting Sections of an Application With *Caliper*

Caliper can also be used to analyze specific parts of a C/C++ application using the Itanium PMU via inserting start and stop points within your application. The supported configuration files for this include *alat_miss*, *branch_prediction*, *dcache_miss*, *dtlb_miss*, *fprof*,

```
Target Execution Time
   Real time:   2.083 seconds
   User time:   0.865 seconds
   System time: 1.216 seconds

Report Help
   Use the caliper option --info to append help to this report,
   or see /opt/caliper/doc/text/total_cpu.help.


-------------------------------------------
Counter                 Priv. Mask         Count
-------------------------------------------
IA64_INST_RETIRED        8 (USER)        826750324
NOPS_RETIRED             8 (USER)        162961539
CPU_CYCLES               8 (USER)        822213685
BACK_END_BUBBLE_ALL      8 (USER)        658879878
-------------------------------------------
% of Cycles lost due to stalls (lower is better):
   80.13 = 100 * BACK_END_BUBBLE_ALL / CPU_CYCLES

Effective CPI (lower is better):
   1.2387 = CPU_CYCLES / (IA64_INST_RETIRED - NOPS_RETIRED)

Effective CPI during unstalled execution (lower is better):
   0.2461 = (CPU_CYCLES - BACK_END_BUBBLE_ALL) / (IA64_INST_RETIRED - NOPS_RETIRED)
```

Figure 14-10   *Caliper total_cpu* Output After +O3 Compilation of Sample Program

icache_miss, *itlb_miss*, *pmu_trace*, and *total_cpu*. The *Caliper* header file */opt/caliper/include/caliper_control.h* needs to be included in each *.c* file that wants to use this functionality. Then, to enable the PMU at some point in your code, the macro:

CALIPER_PMU_ENABLE()

should be inserted at the location in the code where the measurement should start. If the PMU is already enabled, then this macro keeps the PMU enabled. To stop the measurement at a particular point, you insert the macro:

CALIPER_PMU_DISABLE()

which halts the measurement. If the PMU was already halted, then this keeps it halted.

Once these start/stop points have been compiled into the code, if the *--user-regions Caliper* option is specified with the *rum-sum* parameter, then *Caliper* will only enable the PMU counters when it hits the CALIPER_PMU_ENABLE() macro and will only disable them when it hits the CALIPER_PMU_DISABLE macro. With this option, the PMU counters are automatically disabled when the program first starts. If the *--user_region* option is not specified, then the macros have no effect, so they neither enable or disable the PMU.

```
# caliper      measure and report total cpu event counts

toolname = 'PMU'
pmu_report_type = TOTAL_COUNTS

# This config file is an example using caliper's global
# counters. These counters accumulate for the duration
# of the data collection period and are then read and
# reported.
#
if (pmu_type == itanium_pmu):
    global_counters = "CPU_CYCLES, UNSTALLED_BACKEND_CYCLE"
elif (pmu_type == itanium2_pmu):
    global_counters = "IA64_INST_RETIRED, NOPS_RETIRED, CPU_CYCLES, BACK_END_BUBBLE_ALL"

# Privilege level for the counters default to user level. You can explicitly set
# the privilege level to user_priv_level, kernel_priv_level, or all_priv_level.
# Pivilege levels can be abbreviated to as few characters as one. For example:
# global_counters = "IA64_INST_RETIRED:k, IA64_INST_RETIRED:u, NOPS_RETIRED:a,
CPU_CYCLES:a"

# The global_counters variable can be overriden on the command line.  For
# example:
#   caliper total_cpu --global-counters=FP_FLUSH_TO_ZERO,NOPS_RETIRED app
# note the use of '-' in place of '_' in the argument name.

# For a list with descriptions of available PMU events, see chapter 7 of the
# Intel Itanium Processor Reference Manual for Software Development
# or the online text files:
#    /opt/caliper/doc/text/itanium_cpu_counters.txt
#    /opt/caliper/doc/text/itanium2_cpu_counters.txt
```

Figure 14-11 *Caliper total_cpu* Configuration File

```
Target Execution Time
  Real time:   2.089 seconds
  User time:   0.866 seconds
  System time: 1.218 seconds

Report Help
  Use the caliper option --info to append help to this report,
  or see /opt/caliper/doc/text/total_cpu.help.


--------------------------------------------
Counter               Priv. Mask        Count
--------------------------------------------
IA64_INST_RETIRED     8 (USER)       826750324
L3_MISSES             8 (USER)         6351607
CPU_CYCLES            8 (USER)       822728183
L3_REFERENCES         8 (USER)        12609577
--------------------------------------------
```

Figure 14-12   *Caliper total_l3_cache* Configuration Output

14.1.7 Detailed Information on *Caliper* Configuration Files

For detailed information on the various included configuration files, the *Caliper* info options can be used. For instance, to find out more information about the *fprof* configuration, you could type the command:

```
# caliper info -r fprof
```

which will display a wealth of information about what all of the fields of output actually mean as well as potential caveats with each configuration.

14.1.8 *Caliper* and PBO

Caliper is the method used to collect profile-based optimization (PBO) data on IPF-based platforms when an application has been instrumented for PBO. The *+Oprofile=collect* option marks a file and program for profile-based optimization. When an instrumented PBO binary is run, *Caliper* will automatically start and collect detailed trace information regarding the control flow of the application. *Caliper* dynamically instruments the application to collect the PBO information. Given this dynamic instrumentation, the application will run much more slowly than normal while being profiled. Once the program ends, a *flow.data* file instead of a report will be produced by *Caliper*. This *flow.data* file can then be used with the compiler's *+Oprofile=use* option to produce a PBO optimized application. *Caliper* will also output a file called *flow.log* that contains diagnostic messages taken during the profile.

By default, the *flow.data* and *flow.log* files are stored in the same directory from which the program is executed. The location for these files can be overridden from the default by using the

FLOW_DATA and *FLOW_LOG* environment variables, respectively. If a *flow.data* file already exists at the location where *Caliper* will write the *flow.data* information, then the information collected is merged into the existing *flow.data* file. It is important to note that the *flow.data* file can contain information for only one program, but can be merged multiple times from different runs of the same program. This is a change from how the *flow.data* file worked on PA-RISC, where multiple programs could have data within a single *flow.data* file, and the data was not merged.

14.1.9 *Caliper* Output Options

All of the examples so far have been based on the standard text output of *Caliper*. However, *Caliper* also provides the option of outputting the results in HTML (HyperText Markup Language). The HTML output contains the same data as the textual output, but allows easier viewing of the data through links. The *--html=directory_name* option is used to specify the directory where the HTML output should be stored.

Finally, *Caliper* also provides a way to just store the profiling data after sampling a program in addition to outputting the textual analysis. This data file can then later be used to view the analysis. To save the output in a data file, the *--datafile=filename* option is used to specify the file where the data should be stored. Be aware that any previously existing file with the same name will be overwritten with the new data. At a later time, the data file can be analyzed using the *report* option. Saving a binary image of the data is useful in case some further data reduction is needed on a profile. If the data file is not saved, then the application would need to be run again under *Caliper* to produce a new reduction of the data. For instance, *Caliper* allows the data to be sorted in different ways and allows values below a certain amount not to be displayed, so being able to filter based on some of these parameters after collecting the data is much easier than having to take multiple runs of the application to collect different textual output files.

14.1.10 Advantages and Disadvantages of *Caliper*

Caliper is a very powerful tool for tracking down performance problems in IPF-based applications. It has the following advantages (+) and disadvantages (-):

+ No need to specially compile your application to profile it.
+ It can profile a wide range of applications–32-bit, 64-bit, C/C++, Fortran, Assembly, archived, shared libraries, single- and multi-threaded applications (including MxN), and applications that *fork(2)*, *vfork(2)*, or *exec(2)*.
+ All of the Itanium and Itanium2 PMU counters can be used to track down particular events in an application.
+ HTML output capability to easily view and traverse output results.
+ Can attach and detach dynamically from a running process.
+ PMU measurements can be restricted to particular parts of the application via code modifications to the application.

+ Most of the measurement scripts are lightweight and don't adversely affect the run-time of the application being measured.
+ Ability to profile multiple processes in a process tree.
+ Provides global, per-module, per-function, and per-bundle statistics.
+ Events can be correlated with source code in the application.

- It does not currently work with PA-RISC applications.
- There is no way to dynamically attach to more than one process at a time.
- Some of the configuration scripts may greatly slow down the application.
- It is supported only on HP-UX 11i v1.6 and later operating systems.
- Knowledge of IPF assembly language and the IPF architecture may be needed to fully understand the profiled data.

14.2 CXperf

CXperf is an interactive run-time performance analyzer for programs written in HP Fortran 77, Fortran 90, ANSI C, ANSI C++, and Assembler. *CXperf* also profiles multi-process (threaded) applications, message passing parallel programming models (including the Message Passing Interface, an API from HP), object files and archive libraries, and shared memory applications, including those that employ *pthreads* and user-specified parallel directives. *CXperf* can only be used on D-, K-, N- and V-Series HP 9000 systems because it requires special hardware instrumentation that is available only on these models. Additionally, *CXperf* runs only on HP-UX 11.0 (9806) or later. As of early 2003, *CXperf* has been discontinued and replaced with *Caliper*.

CXperf provides a powerful tool for application optimization by giving measurements of the following metrics on a procedure basis:

• Procedure execution count
• CPU time
• Wallclock time
• Instruction counts
• Instruction and data TLB misses
• Instruction and data cache hits and misses
• Context switches
• Thread CPU switches

CXperf also provides a complete call graph that shows the parent/child relationships of each of the procedures.

The main *CXperf* executable is **cxperf**, which has the following syntax:

cxperf [*executable*] [*pdf-filename*] [-options...]

where *executable* is the program to profile (the default is *a.out*) and *pdf-filename* is a performance data file (PDF) created by *CXperf* for analysis. The default is *<executable-program-name>.pdf*.

Both GUI and command line execution are available, and there is a batch mode. Man pages for *cxperf*, *cxoi*, and *cxmerge* contain detailed examples.

14.2.1 Steps in Using *CXperf*

There are five main steps for using *CXperf* to obtain data on an application's performance:

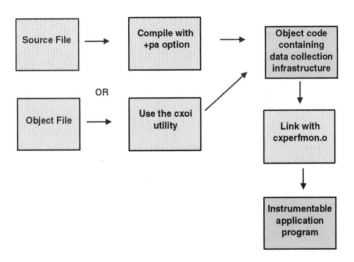

Figure 14-13 Preparing for Instrumentation with *CXperf*

1. Insert data collection "infrastructure" into the application using the *+pa* flag at compile time or by placing it directly into object files or archived libraries using the *cxoi* utility. You would use the *cxoi* utility if you don't want to recompile the program, or if you do not have access to the source code. However, without the source code, it may be very difficult to analyze the results or to decide how to improve the application design.
2. Link the resulting *.o* and *.a* files with *CXperf's* monitor routines (*cxperfmon.o*). The result of this second step is an *instrumentable* application. (This link step is usually automatic; after compilation, the *+pa* flag is also passed to the linker, which knows to link *cxperfmon.o*.) Steps 1 and 2 are both shown in Figure 14-13.

3. Instrument the application by specifying which functions and/or loops within functions to instrument for data collection. Also, choose which metrics you wish to obtain, bearing in mind that some metrics, such as call graph data, have a high overhead. This step can be done with the *CXperf* GUI, as shown in Figure 14-14.

4. Run the application, using what ever data inputs are normally used. You may want to run several profiles, because different data may cause different behavior in the application. On exit, a special data file is dumped that contains all the run-time performance data.

5. Analyze the resulting data file using any of several different report formats and queries. See the *CXperf* manual for more information on report formats and interactive commands.

A recommended method of using *CXperf* is as follows:

• First, get the CPU time for all routines in the application.

• Second, with a separate data collection run, get call graph information for all procedures.

• Third, focus further data collection on only those routines that consume most of the CPU time. For example, you might focus on only the top 10% of routines in CPU consumption, or just those routines using more than 5–10% of the total CPU.

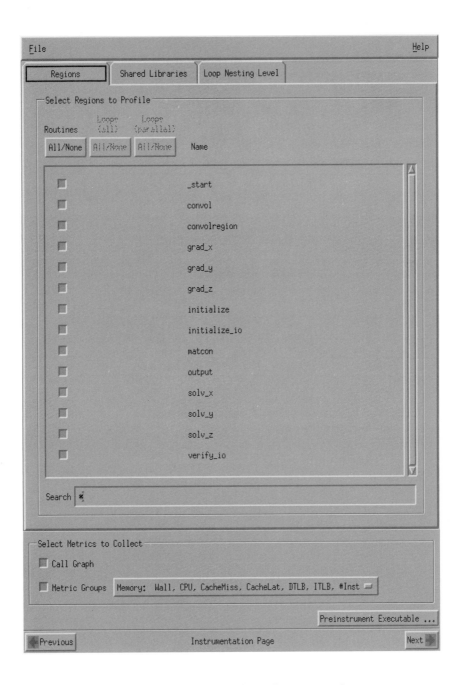

Figure 14-14 Choosing the *CXperf* Instrumentation

A summary screen showing call graph data from the *CXperf* GUI is shown in Figure 14-15. The GUI allows you to jump from the summary page to a page of detailed data (Figure 14-16) for a

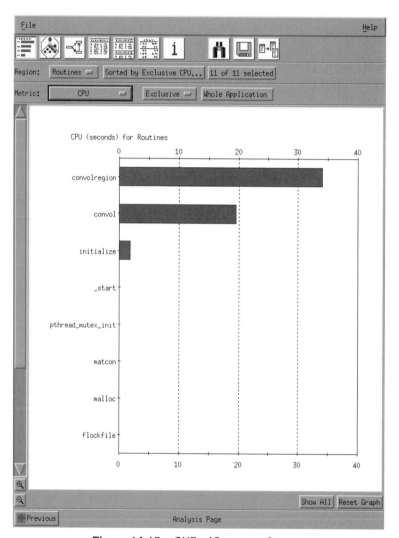

Figure 14-15   *CXPerf* Summary Screen

given metric. From the detail screen, you can jump to the source code (Figure 14-17) for which the data are displayed.

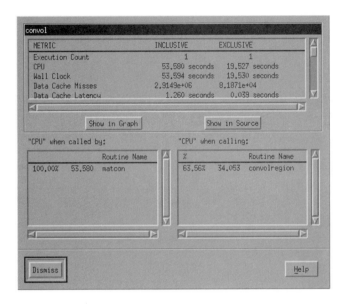

Figure 14-16 *CXPerf* Detail Metrics Screen

14.2.2 Metrics in *CXperf*

The following metrics are provided by *CXperf*:

- Wall-clock time
- CPU time
- Ratio of CPU/wall-clock time
- Execution count
- Instruction count
- MIPS
- TLB misses
- Context switches and thread migrations
- Cache misses

14.2.3 Advantages and Disadvantages of *CXperf*

A major advantage of *CXperf* is its ability to collect information on cache and TLB misses for PA-RISC platforms. No other profiling or system performance tool currently provides this information on PA-RISC. Disadvantages include the large instrumentation overhead needed for

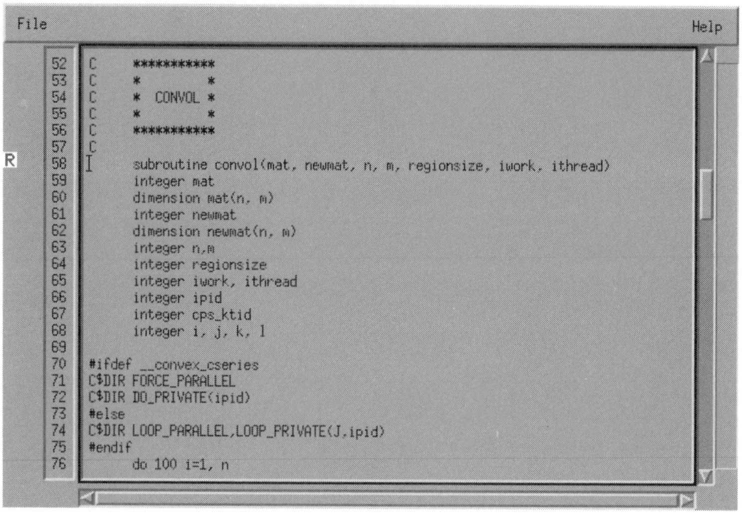

```
 File                                                                                      Help
    52  C     **********
    53  C     *        *
    54  C     * CONVOL *
    55  C     *        *
    56  C     **********
    57  C
 R  58  I     subroutine convol(mat, newmat, n, m, regionsize, iwork, ithread)
    59        integer mat
    60        dimension mat(n, m)
    61        integer newmat
    62        dimension newmat(n, m)
    63        integer n,m
    64        integer regionsize
    65        integer iwork, ithread
    66        integer ipid
    67        integer cps_ktid
    68        integer i, j, k, l
    69
    70  #ifdef __convex_cseries
    71  C$DIR FORCE_PARALLEL
    72  C$DIR DO_PRIVATE(ipid)
    73  #else
    74  C$DIR LOOP_PARALLEL,LOOP_PRIVATE(J,ipid)
    75  #endif
    76        do 100 i=1, n
```

Figure 14-17   *CXPerf* Source Code Screen

some metrics; this can create biased values for some metrics such as CPU time and wall-clock time; however, metrics such as TLB misses and execution counts will be accurate.

14.3 gprof

Gprof is the Berkeley application profiling tool. *Gprof* provides a superset of the functionality available with *prof*, the System V version. Therefore, it is recommended that *gprof* be used rather than *prof*. Profiling an application with *gprof* involves the following steps:

1. Special compilation and linking

2. Program execution

3. Profile generation

14.3.1 Step 1: Special Compilation and Linking

Application profiling is available for programs written in the C, C++, Fortran, and Pascal languages. The program must be specially compiled with the *-G* switch to prepare the application for profiling. This special compiler option causes calls to the procedure *_mcount()* to be inserted at the beginning of every procedure. In addition to recording the parent and child relationships of the procedure being monitored, *_mcount()* collects call count information and total procedure execution time. The program is also linked with the profiled version of several of the system libraries that are located in */lib/libp*. Only the system libraries *libc.a*, *libm.a*, and *libM.a* are supplied in profiled form. The compiling and link steps are shown in Figure 14-18.

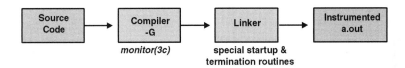

Figure 14-18   Compiling and Linking Steps with Gprof

Many versions of HP-UX don't support or have minimal support for profiling of shared libraries; therefore, a program should be linked with *archive libraries* using the one of the following sets of options to ensure that data can be profiled:

- At compilation: *Wl,-a,archive*
- At link time: *-a archive*
- Using an environment variable: *LDOPTS="-a archive"*

Link with archive libraries in order to get an accurate profile on versions of HP-UX that don't support profiling shared libraries. If shared libraries must be used, then the application must be profiled on HP-UX 11i and later. In HP-UX 11i v1, *gprof* supports profiling only a single 32-bit shared library, and you can't profile both a shared library and the application at the same time. To specify the shared library to profile, the *LD_PROFILE* environment variable is set to the full path of the shared library. There is also no need to compile the shared library with *-G*. Limitations for shared library profiling include not being able to profile shared libraries compiled with

-Bsymbolic (by which, unfortunately, most shared libraries should link) and local, static, and hidden functions are not profiled.

In HP-UX 11i v1.5 and later releases, support for profiling shared libraries was greatly improved. Both 32-bit and 64-bit shared libraries can be profiled, multiple shared libraries can be profiled at one time, and the main program can be profiled at the same time as the shared libraries. All you do is use the *-G* option on your main application and run normally. The resulting *gmon.out* file that is created will have information for all shared libraries invoked by the application as well as the main executable. To profile only specific modules, the modules to profile can be listed on the LD_PROFILE environment variable, and they are separated by a colon.

Finally, the application must be linked with the special start-up routine */lib/gcrt0.o* which causes *monitor(3c)* to be called before application start-up and after the application calls *exit(2)*. *Monitor(3c)* is an interface to the system call *profil(2)* that tells the kernel to record the application's program counter (*PC*) in a buffer at every clock tick.

Although no longer true, older versions of *monitor(3c)* limited the number of procedures that could be profiled. This limit may be increased by making an explicit call to *monitor(3c)*. Explicit calls to *monitor(3c)* may also be made to change the range of memory addresses that are profiled. Otherwise, it is recommended that *monitor(3c)* not be called directly. See the man page for *monitor(3c)* to learn the proper format of the calls.

14.3.2 Step 2: Program Execution

After special compilation and linking, the application is executed one or more times to generate profile data, as shown in Figure 14-19. Each execution must terminate normally by

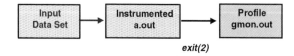

Figure 14-19 Executing the Application to Create Profile Data

calling *exit(2)* explicitly, or by returning from the *main* routine. Thus, programs in an infinite loop or those that are aborted will not produce a profile. A program which does not normally terminate could have a signal routine added to call *exit(2)*. Program termination calls *monitor(3c)*, which turns off profiling and causes the *gmon.out* file to be written to the disk.

14.3.3 Step 3: Profile Generation

After one or more profiling runs have been completed, the profile data is analyzed and printed with the utility *gprof*. *Gprof* reads one or more *gmon.out* files, and may read the summation file *gmon.sum*. Then it produces a printed profile that can be used to determine where the program is spending the most time. Figure 14-20 shows this graphically.

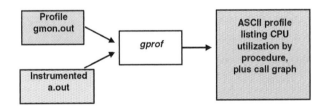

Figure 14-20   Creating the Profile

Procedures that are not profiled have the times of their profiled children propagated upward to them, but are shown as spontaneously invoked (the parent is shown as *<spontaneous>*), and the execution times are not propagated further upward. This results in the $START routine showing something less than 100% of the execution time.

Advantages (+) and disadvantages (-) of *gprof* are as follows:

+ It provides a call graph with parent and child relationships. *Gprof* tracks the number of times that a routine is called by specific callers, and also the number of times that it calls other routines; this is the parent/self/child relationship. *Prof* does not perform this function. This type of information helps determine where to spend time in optimizing the application.

+ It follows program execution into the system call code. The kernel keeps track of when a process is executing system call code and allocates this time appropriately in the profile. This helps to show how a program spends its time.

- It requires special compilation and linking. The source code of the application must be available in order to profile it, and special compilation options must be used.

- The application process must terminate normally. Long-running programs are difficult to profile; programs that never have a normal termination cannot be profiled.

- Accuracy is affected by multi-tasking. Results of the profile can vary by plus or minus 20 percent due to varying CPU cache hit ratios, because the cache is shared by other processes.

- *Gprof* does not work with shared libraries on some releases of HP-UX. The program must be linked with archive libraries in order to provide an accurate profile, because the profile tools require a contiguous instruction address space.

- Not all system libraries are available in profiled form. Because of disk space limitations, only a few system libraries are supplied in profiled format. Therefore, it is difficult to get full propagation when nonprofiled libraries are invoked.

14.4 Puma

Puma has been available in the HP Performance Analysis Kit (HP PAK) since the release of HP-UX 10.0. Written by HP, *puma* replaced *dpat* and *hpc* at HP-UX 10.20. As of HP-UX 11i, *puma* is no longer supported. It monitors the program counter, the call/return stack, and other performance statistics to show where a program is spending most of its time. Data is stored in a file that can subsequently be viewed in a number of ways. In the following example, *puma* is run from the command line with the *-invoke* option against the sample program *vanderbilt*.

```
hpgsyha9/B.11.00:/opt/langtools/bin/puma -monitor -invoke vanderbilt
Initializing image '/opt/langtools/hppak/examples/vanderbilt'...done.
Monitoring lasted 13 seconds.
Target ran 12 seconds and used 11 CPU seconds.
Monitoring stopped after 112 samples.
```

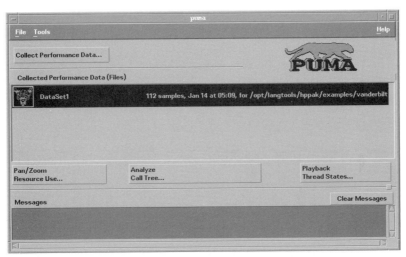

Figure 14-21   Graphic Display of Puma

The effect of this run is to generate a file (named *DataSet1* by default) containing performance data. *DataSet1* is displayed on the screen (shown in Figure 14-21) and may be selected for further analysis.

Puma supports different types of analyses. As an example of one type, *puma* generates a bar graph showing the calls in the program and the percentage of time the program spends in each routine. The call tree analysis is shown in Figure 14-22.

The advantages (+) and disadvantages (-) of *puma* are as follows:

+ It reports data on multi-threaded applications.
+ It produces a dynamic histogram of CPU time for each procedure as the process executes and a call graph.
+ It shows parent and child relationships with no special compilation (only if the *a.out* file has not been stripped).
+ Optionally, it shows a histogram of CPU time at the source-code line level (requires compilation with the *-g* option).

- Because of its sampling method, it is less accurate on a multi-user system.
- It seems to work best on compute-bound programs.

14.5 HPjmeter

The *HPjmeter* tool is a 100% Java tool developed by HP to help analyze profile information generated by the Java Virtual Machine (JVM). It works on HP-UX, Solaris, Linux, and Windows platforms and uses a graphical user interface to view and organize the profile information.

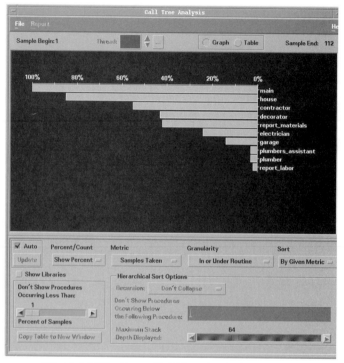

Figure 14-22   Puma Call Tree Analysis

Since *HPjmeter* is a post-processing tool, a Java profiling option is needed to collect a profile for *HPjmeter* to process. HP's Java supports the following profiling options: *-Xeprof* option for HP's Hotspot VM versions 1.2.2.05 or later, *-Xrunhprof* with Java 1.2.1 (Classic JVM) or Java 1.3.x or 1.4.x, *-prof* option for Java 1.1.x, and finally *-eprof* for Java 1.1, release 1.1.8 or later.

Some of the metrics that *HPjmeter* displays are:

- CPU time for threads and processes in list or tree form

- Clock time for threads and processes in list or tree form

- Call counts for threads and processes in list or tree form

- Object creation statistics

- Heap analysis

- Lock contention for threads and processes in a list or tree form

- Many thread-based metrics, including a breakdown of where each thread spent the majority of its time, such as waiting for I/O or in lock contention

It is important to note that not all metrics are available for all of the different profile collection strategies. Please refer to documentation for *HPjmeter* for specific restrictions as to what metrics can be displayed with which profiling methods.

HPjmeter provides a few unique features that make it very useful in tracking down Java bottlenecks. It has a "guess" area where it will make guesses or estimates about how performance of the application may be improved based on the data collected. For instance, it can suggest methods that might benefit from inlining. It may also suggest methods that appear to have excessive lock contention due to synchronization issues. Finally, *HPjmeter* has the ability to compare two different profile data files. This allows one to do before and after comparisons of modifications to an application to see how the various metrics changed due to a modification. One could also use this information to see how the behavior of an application varies over time by collecting different profiles at different parts of a program's execution.

Some of the advantages(+) and disadvantages(-) of *HPjmeter* are:

+ It is a 100% Java application, so it should work on any supported JVM.
+ It works with multiple different profile outputs.
+ It provides a graphical view of where the time is spent in Java code.
+ It can show lock contention profiles.
+ It can compare multiple profiles against each other.
+ It can provide information regarding memory usage to track down potential memory leaks.

- Not all features are supported with all profile types.
- It may run slowly due to being a Java application itself.
- The guess options may not be accurate and may even provide false positives, because the information provided is only a best guess at what may be wrong.

There is extensive documentation on-line at http://www.hp.com/go/java regarding *HPjmeter* and other issues for Java profiling.

Performance Tools Alphabetical Reference

T his appendix contains a complete alphabetized listing of all the performance tools discussed in this book. Each tool will be presented in a chart with a standard format that summarizes the major points about the tool and highlights unique metrics.

Unix performance tools come from many sources:

- **System V**. System V tools concentrate on the three major system resources: CPU, memory, and disk. While most provide only global performance information, several do provide limited per-process information.
- **BSD**. As with the System V tools, tools from Berkeley concentrate on CPU, memory, and disk resources, and display mostly global metrics.
- **Hewlett-Packard**. HP has provided a variety of tools for HP-UX and other Unix variants, including Solaris and AIX.
- **Other Sources**. Tools from other sources include *nfsstat* and *xload*. The purpose of these tools is very specific, and the information they provide is global in nature.

A.1 System V Tools

The System V tools include the following:

- *df*
- *ipcs*
- Process Accounting
- *prof*
- *ps*
- sar
- *size*
- *time* and *timex*

A.2 Berkeley Tools

Tools from Berkeley and related organizations include:

- *df* (called *bdf* on HP-UX systems)
- *gprof*
- *iostat*
- *netstat*
- *ps*
- *size*
- *time*
- *top*
- *uptime*
- *vmstat*

A.3 HP-UX Tools

HP tools include:

- *Caliper*
- *chatr*
- *CXperf*
- *dpat*
- *GlancePlus* (*glance* and *gpm*)
- *hpc*
- *ioscan*
- *machinfo*
- *MeasureWare*
- *midaemon*
- *Perf/RX*

- *PerfView*
- *Process Resource Manager (prm)*
- *scopeux*
- *swapinfo*
- *Workload Manager (WLM)*

A.4 Other Tools

The remaining tools discussed in this book come from various sources:

- *nettune* and *ndd*
- *nfsstat*
- *xload*

A.5 Headings in the Summary Chart

The summary chart for each tool is organized as follows:

- **Tool Source**. This lists the original author of the tool, such as System V Unix, BSD 4.X Unix, or Hewlett-Packard Company.
- **Documentation**. Documentation for the tool may come in the form of a man page, manual, on-line help, and/or kernel source code. Some tools are much better documented than others. In a few cases, it is necessary to review the kernel source code in order to understand the intent of a particular metric. The value of the tool increases with the quality of the documentation. In other words, if you don't understand what the metric means, you can't use it to decide when and how to tune the system.
- **Common Uses and Tasks**. The main purpose of the tool in managing performance is listed first: either Performance Management or Crisis Management. Some tools are better at making short-term, frequent measurements viewed in real-time for problem diagnosis. Others are better at making less frequent, long-term measurements for baseline or characterization purposes. Then, categories applicable to the tool are listed:

    - **Application Optimization** is of concern chiefly to application designers. These tools profile the application for CPU utilization or provide an indication of resource utilization by that application.
    - **Baseline measurements** are made when the system is running normally. They are compared with current measurements to highlight changes in system performance.
    - **Benchmarking** requires real-time measurement and analysis for short-duration benchmarks, or the ability to store measurements in a form that is easy to analyze. Tools that are commonly used or lend themselves to benchmarking are listed in this category.
    - **Capacity planning** requires long-term averages over weeks or months that measure

CPU, memory, disk, and network utilization and provide response time or through-put measurements. It does not require real-time measurements. A tool's ability to group resource utilization by various applications is advantageous for capacity planning.

- **Casual monitoring** is provided by a few tools that show limited information on a real-time basis; for example, the list of currently running processes.

- **Chargeback accounting** requires detailed listing of resource utilization by user or groups of users, and may include grouping by application or process.

- **Performance characterization** results in long-term measurements detailing major resource utilization and possible response-time measurements. Useful tools of this type provide an easy way to store and analyze large amounts of data.

- **Problem diagnosis** requires great detail and frequent, short-duration measurements. When the problem only happens occasionally, easy measurement storage and analysis are an advantage.

- **Resource utilization** is useful both to the System Administrator for system tuning, and to the Application Designer for sizing and utilization.

• **Interval of Presentation**. Measurements that can be displayed as frequently as every second are especially useful for Crisis Management at the cost of higher overhead. Performance Management tasks use measurements that are of longer duration than the measurements obtained in a crisis.

• **Data Source**. The source of the data–*/dev/kmem* or the Kernel Instrumentation and Measurement Interface–is important in determining data accuracy.

• **Kernel Data Collection**. Data collection may be continuous, or it may be turned on and off by a particular user process.

• **Type of Data**. This category lists whether or not the data is available at the Global, Application, Process, and/or Procedure levels.

• **Metrics**. The major categories of metrics are shown by kernel subsystem (such as CPU or Network) in this row of the table.

• **Summarization**. This category indicates what type of summary the tool provides. For example, some tools display an average of all of the samples at the end of the output. Other tools provide interval, average, and high values for certain metrics only.

• **Logging**. Some tools write only to the standard output, and can be redirected to a file. Other tools use screen addressing, and their output cannot be redirected to a file. These tools often provide a logging feature to log a screen of data to a file or to a printer.

• **Overhead Dependencies**. This category lists the factors that affect how much overhead is consumed by the tool.

• **Advantages**.

• **Disadvantages**.

A.6 Tool Reference Tables

The remainder of this chapter presents reference tables for the performance tools.

A.6.1 *bdf*

Tool Source	BSD 4.X Unix
Documentation	Man page
Common Uses and Tasks	Performance and crisis management
	• Problem diagnosis • Resource utilization
Interval of Presentation	On demand
Presentation Method	Tabular data
Data Source	On-disk file system
Kernel Data Collection	None
Type of Data	Global
Metrics	• File system utilization (capacity) • Inode utilization (capacity) • File system swap utilization
Summarization	By file system
Logging	Redirect standard out to a file
Overhead Dependencies	Number of file systems
Advantages	Shows on-disk HFS inode utilization
Disadvantages	• Does not show JFS inode utilization • Causes a sync of file systems, which can cause momentary performance degradation

A.6.2 *Caliper* (HP-UX 11i v 1.5 and later)

Tool Source	Hewlett-Packard
Documentation	User's manual, www.docs.hp.com, , /opt/caliper/doc/caliperug.pdf, and www.hp.com/go/hpcaliper.
Common Uses and Tasks	Performance management
	Application optimization
Interval of Presentation	
Presentation Method	Graphical data
Data Source	Kernel
Kernel Data Collection	Turned on by running the *Caliper* tool
Type of Data	Process
Metrics	• Procedure execution counts • Procedure coverage • CPU time • Instruction counts • Instruction and Data TLB misses • Instruction and data cache hits and misses • Branch prediction statistics • Customized statistics based on the IPF performance counters
Summarization	Detailed information by procedure
Logging	To data file
Overhead Dependencies	Particular metrics chosen for data collection
Advantages	• Works with applications in ANSI C, ANSI C++, Fortran 77 and 90, and Assembler • Works with threaded applications • Reports data on any of the IPF performance counters • Provides call graph information • Low overhead
Disadvantages	• Supported only on HP-UX 11i v 1.5 and later • Supported only on IPF systems

A.6.3 *chatr*

Tool Source	Hewlett-Packard
Documentation	Man page and www.docs.hp.com
Common Uses and Tasks	Performance enhancement
	Program attribute display
Interval of Presentation	On demand
Presentation Method	Multiple lines of output
Data Source	*a.out* file
Kernel Data Collection	None
Type of Data	Process
Metrics	• Shared libraries directly used • Set shared library binding type (immediate or deferred) • Enable/disable use of global hash table for symbol lookup • Enable extended or MAS virtual memory layout • Set lazy swap attribute • Control Large Page size hints • Control Branch hints
Summarization	None
Logging	None
Overhead Dependencies	None
Advantages	• Quick look at application attributes • Can also change some of the process attributes
Disadvantages	On some versions of HP-UX, may cause a running process to demote large pages if run

A.6.4 *CXperf* (HP-UX 11.0 (9806) and later)

Tool Source	Hewlett-Packard
Documentation	User's manual
Common Uses and Tasks	Performance management
	Application optimization
Interval of Presentation	
Presentation Method	Graphical data
Data Source	Kernel
Kernel Data Collection	Turned on by instrumenting the application and running the *CXperf* tool
Type of Data	Process
Metrics	• Procedure execution counts • CPU time • Wallclock time • Instruction counts • Instruction and data TLB misses • Instruction and data cache hits and misses • Context switches • Thread CPU switches
Summarization	Detailed information by procedure
Logging	To data file
Overhead Dependencies	Particular metrics chosen for data collection
Advantages	• Works with applications in ANSI C, ANSI C++, Fortran 77 and 90, and Assembler • Works with threaded applications • Is the only tool that reports TLB misses and hardware cache hits and misses • Provides call graph information
Disadvantages	• Supported only on HP-UX 11.0 • Supported only on D-, K-, N-, and V-class systems • Overhead can be quite large

A.6.5 *dpat* (replaced in later releases by *puma*)

Tool Source	Hewlett-Packard Company
Documentation	Manual, man page
Common Uses and Tasks	Performance Management
	Application Optimization
Interval of Presentation	One or more seconds
Presentation Method	Procedure histogram and flow graph to X/Window
Data Source	The individual process
Kernel Data Collection	None
Type of Data	Procedure
Metrics	CPU (by procedure) procedure flow
Summarization	Sample interval
Logging	None
Overhead Dependencies	Sampling frequency
Advantages	• Histogram presentation is easy to assimilate • Does not require special compilation • Provides playback of flow graph • Works well for compute-bound programs
Disadvantages	• Histogram presented only while process executes (cannot be saved or printed) • Sampling method does not capture system call time

A.6.6 *GlancePlus/UX*

Tool Source	Hewlett-Packard Company
Documentation	Man page, manual, online help
Common Uses and Tasks	Performance and crisis management
	• Problem diagnosis • Performance characterization • Benchmarking • Resource utilization
Interval of Presentation	Two or more seconds
Presentation Method	Tabular, multiscreen
Data Source	*pstat( )* and KI/MI
Kernel Data Collection	Turned on by *midaemon*
Type of Data	• Global • Process
Metrics	• CPU (global and process) • Memory (global and process) • Disk (global and process) • Kernel Resources (global) • Network (LAN - global) • Network (NFS - global)
Summarization	• Internal average • Average and high value since start-up
Logging	• Optional screen logging to a file • Optional screen print
Overhead Dependencies	• Number of processes • Presentation interval
Advantages	• Extensive per-process info • Extensive online help • Process filtering • Available for HP-UX, Solaris, AIX
Disadvantages	• Terminal version uses *curses* • Relatively slow start-up • Not bundled with OS

A.6.7 *gpm* (*GlancePlus/Motif*)

Tool Source	Hewlett-Packard Company
Documentation	Man page, manual, on-line help
Common Uses and Tasks	Performance and crisis management
	• Problem diagnosis • Performance characterization • Benchmarking • Resource utilization
Interval of Presentation	One or more seconds
Presentation Method	Tables & color graphs Tabular data with sortable columns
Data Source	*pstat( )* and KI/MI
Kernel Data Collection	Turned on by *midaemon*
Type of Data	• Global • Process
Metrics	• CPU (global and process) • Memory (global and process) • Disk (global and process) • Kernel Resources (global) • Network (LAN - global) • Network (NFS - global)
Summarization	• Interval average • Average and high value since start-up
Logging	Printing only through Adviser
Overhead Dependencies	• Number of processes • System call rate • Presentation interval
Advantages	• Color graphical presentation • Extensive per-process info • Extensive on-line help • Extensive process filtering • Customizable alarms and advice • Available for HP-UX, AIX, and Solaris
Disadvantages	• Relatively slow start-up • Not bundled with OS • Very limited logging capability

A.6.8 *gprof* / *gprof++*

Tool Source	BSD 4.X Unix
Documentation	Man page
Common Uses and Tasks	Performance Management
	Application Optimization
Interval of Presentation	Process completion
Presentation Method	Tabular data and call graph
Data Source	Individual process
Kernel Data Collection	Turned on when process starts
Type of Data	Procedure
Metrics	• CPU (by procedure) • Tabular procedure call graph • Call counts
Summarization	Process completion
Logging	Binary data file
Overhead Dependencies	None
Advantages	• Procedure call graph shows parent and child relationships • Shows where a process is spending the most time • Follows the program as it executes system calls
Disadvantages	• Requires special compilation (-G) • Process must terminate normally • Accuracy affected by multitasking • Does not work with shared libraries • Does not profile all system libraries

A.6.9 *hpc*—Histogram Program Counter (replaced in later releases by *puma*)

Tool Source	Hewlett-Packard Company
Documentation	Manual and man page
Common Uses and Tasks	Performance Management
	Application Optimization
Interval of Presentation	One or more seconds
Presentation Method	Tabular histogram
Data Source	Process
Kernel Data Collection	None
Type of Data	Procedure
Metrics	CPU (by procedure and source line within procedure)
Summarization	Interval and process completion
Logging	None
Overhead Dependencies	Debug information
Advantages	• Shows where a process is spending its time down to the source code line • Works well for compute-bound programs • Histogram is easy to assimilate
Disadvantages	• Requires special compilation (-G) • No call-graph information • Accuracy affected by multitasking • Sampling method does not capture system call time

A.6.10 ioscan

Tool Source	Hewlett-Packard
Documentation	Man page and www.docs.hp.com
Common Uses and Tasks	Performance and crisis management
	• Problem diagnosis • Resource allocation
Interval of Presentation	On demand
Presentation Method	Tabular data
Data Source	HP-UX kernel
Kernel Data Collection	None
Type of Data	Global
Metrics	• I/O configuration • Driver binding to adapter cards
Summarization	By card type, hardware path, driver type
Logging	Redirect standard out to a file
Overhead Dependencies	Number of devices configured in system
Advantages	Shows complete hardware I/O configuration
Disadvantages	Slow when actually scanning for I/O configuration

A.6.11 *iostat* (IO Statistics)

Tool Source	BSD 4.X Unix
Documentation	Man page and kernel source
Common Uses and Tasks	Crisis management
	Problem diagnosis
Interval of Presentation	One or more seconds
Presentation Method	Tabular data
Data Source	*pstat( )* counters
Kernel Data Collection	Always turned on
Type of Data	Global
Metrics	Disk (physical) Terminal I/O (optional)
Summarization	None
Logging	Redirect standard output to a file
Overhead Dependencies	Presentation interval
Advantages	• Statistics by disk drive • Fast start up
Disadvantages	• Many lines per interval • Limited statistics

A.6.12 *ipcs* and *ipcrm*

Tool Source	System V Unix
Documentation	Man pages
Common Uses and Tasks	Performance and crisis management
	• Problem diagnosis • Application optimization
Interval of Presentation	On demand
Presentation Method	Tabular data
Data Source	*/dev/kmem*
Kernel Data Collection	Always turned on
Type of Data	• Global • Process (limited)

Metrics	Kernel resource utilization for:
	    • Semaphores
	    • Message queues
	    • Shared memory

Summarization	None
Logging	Redirect standard out to a file
Overhead Dependencies	Number of IPC resources in use
Advantages	• Can detect and remove IPC entries flagged in use where the owners have terminated • Can detect current size of message queues and shared memory segments
Disadvantages	Process information limited to owner and last process to use the resource

A.6.13 *machinfo* (Machine information)

Tool Source	Hewlett-Packard Company
Documentation	Man page and www.docs.hp.com
Common Uses and Tasks	Performance and crisis management
	Problem diagnosis
Interval of Presentation	On demand
Presentation Method	Multiple lines of data
Data Source	*/dev/kmem*
Type of Data	Global
Metrics	Processor Type Processor Speed Processor Cache organization Number of processors Firmware revisions Memory information
Summarization	None
Logging	None
Overhead Dependencies	None
Advantages	Quick look at machine information
Disadvantages	• Limited information regarding complete machine configuration • Only available for HP-UX 11i v 1.5 and later

A.6.14 *MeasureWare*

Tool Source	Hewlett-Packard Company
Documentation	Man pages, manual, on-line help
Common Uses and Tasks	Performance management
	• Performance characterization • Performance trending • Capacity planning • Workload estimation • Chargeback accounting
Interval of Presentation	One minute and five minutes
Presentation Method	Tabular data suitable for import by another tool
Data Source	*pstat( )* and KI/MI
Kernel Data Collection	Turned on by *scopeux*
Type of Data	Global, process, and application
Metrics	• CPU (global, process, application) • Memory (global, process, application) • Disk (global, process) • Network (global)
Summarization	None
Logging	• To binary logfile • Converted to ASCII for export
Overhead Dependencies	• Number of processes • System call rate • Number and extent of application definitions
Advantages	• Compact logfiles • Extensive per-process information • Easy to maintain historical data • Easy to export data to other tools • Available for HP-UX, Solaris, AIX
Disadvantages	• Most useful in conjunction with another tool • Not bundled with OS

A.6.15 *midaemon* (Measurement Interface Daemon)

Tool Source	Hewlett-Packard Company
Documentation	Manual, man page
Common Uses and Tasks	Not applicable
Interval of Presentation	Not applicable
Presentation Method	Not applicable
Data Source	*pstat( )* and KI/MI
Kernel Data Collection	Turned on by *midaemon*
Type of Data	• Global • Process
Metrics	Numerous–used by *glance, gpm,* and *scopeux*
Summarization	Not applicable
Logging	To shared memory segment
Overhead Dependencies	• Number of running process • System call and context switch rates
Advantages	• Data is much more accurate than normal */dev/kmem* data • Consistent mechanism for data collection • Overhead of collection can be measured
Disadvantages	Additional overhead

A.6.16 PerfView

Tool Source	Hewlett-Packard Company
Documentation	Man page, manual, on-line help
Common Uses and Tasks	Performance and crisis management
	Problem diagnosis
Interval of Presentation	On demand
Presentation Method	Color graphics
Data Source	*pstat( )* & KI/MI
Kernel Data Collection	Turned on by *pv_alarmd*
Type of Data	• Global • Process
Metrics	• CPU (global and process) • Memory (global and process) • Disk (global) • Network (global LAN and NFS)
Summarization	One minute, five minutes and hourly
Logging	• To binary logfile • Alarms sent to central monitoring system
Overhead Dependencies	• Number of running processes • System call rate
Advantages	• Centralized and automated monitoring of the performance of a network of systems • Can be used with *GlancePlus/UX* and *PerfView/Analyzer* for more detailed investigation
Disadvantages	• Requires other tools for more detail • Minimum sample time is five minutes for some metrics and fifteen minutes for others

A.6.17 Process Accounting (System V)

Tool Source	System V Unix
Documentation	Man pages, manual
Common Uses and Tasks	Performance management
	• Resource utilization • Chargeback accounting • Problem diagnosis
Interval of Presentation	On demand
Presentation Method	Tabular data
Data Source	*/dev/kmem*
Kernel Data Collection	Turned on by *"/usr/lib/acct/turnacct on"*
Type of Data	Process
Metrics	CPU (process) Disk space utilization (user)
Summarization	By user
Logging	To binary disk file
Overhead Dependencies	• Number of active processes • Frequency of report generation
Advantages	• Summarizes CPU and disk space utilization by user • Customizable reports
Disadvantages	Consumes significant amount of CPU to collect and record the data

A.6.18 Process Resource Manager (PRM)

Tool Source	Hewlett Packard Company
Documentation	Man pages, manual
Common Uses and Tasks	Load balancing, workload management
	• Definition of CPU, disk and memory entitlements • Dynamically reset by Workload Manager
Interval of Presentation	N/A
Presentation Method	
Data Source	
Kernel Data Collection	
Type of Data	Process
Metrics	• CPU (process) • Disk I/O (LVM volume group) • Memory
Summarization	• By PRM group • Family of commands (*prm**) for reporting and control
Logging	None
Overhead Dependencies	Very little; integrated with kernel
Advantages	• Integrated with Serviceguard for changing entitlements upon failover • Permits any user-defined model for choosing entitlements • Entitlements are enforced by the kernel • Groups can be defined by username and/or process name
Disadvantages	• Limitations on multi-processor systems (see Tools Chapter) • Requires a PRM-specific configuration file

A.6.19 prof

Tool Source	System V Unix
Documentation	Man page
Common Uses and Tasks	Performance Management
	Application Optimization
Interval of Presentation	Process completion
Presentation Method	Tabular data
Data Source	• Kernel sampling • Call to counting procedure inserted into code
Kernel Data Collection	Turned on when process starts
Type of Data	Procedure
Metrics	• CPU (by procedure) • Call counts
Summarization	At process termination
Logging	To binary disk file
Overhead Dependencies	None
Advantages	Shows where a process is spending its time
Disadvantages	• Requires special compilation (-p) • No call graph information • Process must terminate normally • Accuracy affected by multitasking • Does not work with shared libraries

A.6.20 *ps* (process status)

Tool Source	System V Unix
Documentation	Man page and kernel source
Common Uses and Tasks	Crisis management
	• Problem diagnosis • Benchmarking • Casual monitoring
Interval of Presentation	On demand
Presentation Method	Tabular data
Data Source	*/dev/kmem*
Kernel Data Collection	Always turned on
Type of Data	Process
Metrics	• Current state • Current priority • Nice value • Start time • Cumulative execution time • PID, PPID
Summarization	None
Logging	Redirect standard output to a file
Overhead Dependencies	Number of running processes
Advantages	• Familiarity • Filters for limiting output
Disadvantages	• Minimal information • No averaging or summarization

A.6.21 *sar* (System Activity Reporter)

Tool Source	System V Unix
Documentation	Man page and kernel source
Common Uses and Tasks	Performance and crisis management
	• Baselines • Problem diagnosis • Benchmarking • Resource utilization
Interval of Presentation	One or more seconds
Presentation Method	Tabular data
Data Source	*pstat*
Kernel Data Collection	Always turned on
Type of Data	Global
Metrics	• CPU • Memory • Disk (physical and logical) • Kernel Resources
Summarization	Averages the samples at the end
Logging	• Binary data to disk (optional) • ASCII data to disk (optional)
Overhead Dependencies	Presentation interval
Advantages	• Lots of data • Familiarity with the tool • Kernel resource overflow statistics • Ipc usage rate statistics
Disadvantages	• No VM paging information • Rudimentary summarization • No graphics or data reformatting • Many lines per interval

A.6.22 scopeux

Tool Source	Hewlett-Packard Company (part of MeasureWare)
Documentation	Man page
Common Uses and Tasks	Performance and crisis management
	• Baselines • Problem diagnosis • Benchmarking • Resource utilization
Interval of Presentation	One and five minutes
Presentation Method	Counters
Data Source	*midaemon* (Measurement Interface)
Kernel Data Collection	Turned on by *midaemon*
Type of Data	• Global • Application • Process
Metrics	• CPU • Memory • Disk • Kernel Resources • Network
Summarization	One and five minutes
Logging	Binary data to disk
Overhead Dependencies	• Number and extent of application definitions • Number of running processes
Advantages	Method for collecting and consolidating data
Disadvantages	Needs another tool to interpret the data

A.6.23 size

Tool Source	System V Unix
Documentation	Man page
Common Uses and Tasks	Performance and crisis management
	Problem diagnosis
Interval of Presentation	On demand
Presentation Method	One line of data
Data Source	*a.out* file
Kernel Data Collection	None
Type of Data	Process
Metrics	Static size of process (text, data, BSS)
Summarization	None
Logging	None
Overhead Dependencies	None
Advantages	Quick look at static process size for resource utilization planning
Disadvantages	Does not include dynamically allocated memory, shared memory, or shared libraries

A.6.24 *swapinfo* (Swap Space Information)

Tool Source	Hewlett-Packard Company
Documentation	Man page
Common Uses and Tasks	Performance and crisis management
	• Problem diagnosis • Resource utilization
Interval of Presentation	On demand
Presentation Method	Tabular data
Data Source	*/dev/kmem*
Kernel Data Collection	Always turned on
Type of Data	Global
Metrics	Swap device space reservation and utilization
Summarization	By swap device Use "*swapinfo -t*" for better formatting and total information
Logging	None
Overhead Dependencies	• Number of swap devices and file systems • Number of processes on swap devices
Advantages	Quick look at swap space utilization
Disadvantages	Limited information

A.6.25 *time, timex*

Tool Source	System V Unix
Documentation	Man page
Common Uses and Tasks	Crisis management
	• Problem diagnosis • Benchmarking • Application optimization
Interval of Presentation	Process completion
Presentation Method	Tabular data
Data Source	*/dev/kmem*
Kernel Data Collection	Always turned on
Type of Data	Process
Metrics	CPU (user, system, and elapsed times). *Timex* optionally includes *sar* and process-accounting information
Summarization	None
Logging	Redirect standard error to a file
Overhead Dependencies	None
Advantages	Minimal overhead
Disadvantages	• Minimal information • *Timex* requires *sadc* to be running in some versions

A.6.26 top

Tool Source	BSD 4.X Unix
Documentation	Man page
Common Uses and Tasks	Performance and crisis management
	• Problem diagnosis • Performance characterization • Benchmarking
Interval of Presentation	One or more seconds
Presentation Method	Screen tabular data
Data Source	*pstat*
Kernel Data Collection	Always turned on
Type of Data	• Global • Process
Metrics	• CPU (Global and Process) • Memory (Global and Process)
Summarization	None
Logging	None
Overhead Dependencies	Presentation interval
Advantages	• Quick look at global CPU and process data • Load average per CPU on SMP system
Disadvantages	• Limited statistics • Uses *curses(3)* for terminal output

A.6.27 uptime

Tool Source	BSD 4.X Unix
Documentation	Man page
Common Uses and Tasks	Performance and crisis management
	• Problem diagnosis • Performance characterization
Interval of Presentation	On demand
Presentation Method	Tabular data
Data Source	*/dev/kmem*
Kernel Data Collection	Always turned on
Type of Data	Global
Metrics	• One-, five- and fifteen-minute load averages • Number of users
Summarization	None
Logging	None
Overhead Dependencies	None
Advantages	Quick look at CPU load averages
Disadvantages	Limited information

A.6.28 vmstat

Tool Source	BSD 4.X Unix
Documentation	Man page, kernel source and *include* files
Common Uses and Tasks	Crisis management
	Problem diagnosis
Interval of Presentation	One or more seconds
Presentation Method	Columnar data to screen
Data Source	*pstat*
Kernel Data Collection	Always turned on
Type of Data	Global
Metrics	• CPU • Memory
Summarization	First line: average since boot or reset; otherwise, none
Logging	Redirect standard output to a file
Overhead Dependencies	Presentation interval
Advantages	• Fast start-up • Minimal overhead • One line per interval
Disadvantages	• Poorly documented • Cryptic headings

A.6.29 Workload Manager (WLM)

Tool Source	Hewlett-Packard Company
Documentation	Man pages, manual
Common Uses and Tasks	Resource management
	• Adjusting PRM configuration based on CPU, memory, and disk metrics to achieve SLOs (service level objectives) • Integrated with Serviceguard for adjusting entitlements upon failover
Interval of Presentation	N/A
Presentation Method	
Data Source	
Kernel Data Collection	
Type of Data	Process
Metrics	• CPU (process) • Disk I/O (LVM volume group) • Memory
Summarization	By PRM group
Logging	
Overhead Dependencies	Very little; integrated with the kernel
Advantages	• Can dynamically adjust PRM settings upon certain conditions (which are monitored) • Can monitor and control multiple systems (but does not coordinate across systems)
Disadvantages	• Requires familiarization with another GUI • Currently, works only on a single-system basis

A.6.30 *xload* (X/Windows-Based CPU Load)

Tool Source	Massachusetts Institute of Technology
Documentation	Man page
Common Uses and Tasks	Performance management
	Casual monitoring
Interval of Presentation	On demand and continuous
Presentation Method	X/Window graph
Data Source	*/dev/kmem*
Kernel Data Collection	Always turned on
Type of Data	Global
Metrics	CPU Load Average
Summarization	One minute
Logging	None
Overhead Dependencies	None
Advantages	Graphic representation
Disadvantages	Minimal information

HP-UX Version Naming
Reference

This appendix contains a list of the various versions of HP-UX which are discussed in this book. The newer versions may be referred to by multiple names. Figure B-1 shows the names used for each version. The version name supplied by the *uname(1)* command is also seen when running the *strings(1)* command on */stand/vmunix*.

Figure B-1 HP-UX Version Naming

Version supplied by the *uname(1)* command	Version referred to in marketing and some technical documentation	Supported architectures and OS integer size
10.20	10.20	PA-RISC (32-bit)
11.0	11.0	PA-RISC (32- and 64-bit)
11.11	11i 11i Version 1 11i v1 NOTE: there has been a series of upgrades to 11i	PA-RISC (32- and 64-bit)
11.20	11i Version 1.5 11i v1.5	IPF (64-bit)
11.22	11i Version 1.6 11i v1.6	IPF (64-bit)
11.23	11i Version 2 11i v2	IPF (64-bit) –Summer 2003 PA-RISC (64-bit) –Summer 2004

Dynamically Tuneable Parameters

T his appendix contains an alphabetized listing of those tuneable parameters that are automatically tuned by the kernal or dynamically tuneable by the system administrator while the kernel is running.

Use the following commands to change the value of a dynamically tuneable parameter:

• *kmtune* with HP-UX 11i v 1, 1.5, and 1.6

• *kctune* with HP-UX 11i v 2.0 and later

When tuning a parameter dynamically, it is important to recall that the change is effective only in the running kernel. If the system were to reboot, the change would be lost. Therefore, it is important to reconfigure the on-disk kernel file (*/stand/vmunix*) if you want the tuneable parameter changes to be permanent and applicable whenever the system reboots. Use the *-u* option to update the tuneable parameters in the kernel file.

HP intends to continue to enhance HP-UX by making more and more parameters dynamically tuneable. An ultimate goal is to make parameters automatically tuned by the kernel itself as loads on the system change.

NOTE:

    Whenever changing tuneable parameters, make sure to review the current HP-UX system administration documentation and release notes. These documents will provide up-to-date information on each tuneable parameter and whether the parameter is dynamically tuneable by the system administrator and possibly automatically tuned by the kernel itself.

As of HP-UX 11i version 1 (11.11), the parameters shown in Figure C-1 are dynamically tuneable by the system administrator in the running kernel. With HP-UX 11i version 1.6 (11.22), the parameters shown in Figure C-2 are dynamically tuneable by the system administrator in the running kernel. Currently, in HP-UX 11i version 2 (11.23), the parameters shown in Figure C-3 are dynamically tuneable by the system administrator in the running kernel:

Figure C-1   Parameters Dynamically Tuneable in HP-UX 11.11

Parameter	Purpose
core_addshmem_read	Readable Shmem in Core Dump
core_addshmem_write	Writeable Shmem in Core Dump
maxfiles_lim	Upper Limit for Maxfiles
maxtsiz	Max Text Segment Size
maxtsiz_64bit	Max Text Segment Size
maxuprc	Max Processes Per User
msgmax	Max Message Queue Size
msgmnb	Max Bytes Per Message
scsi_max_qdepth	Max Outstanding I/Os Per Device
semmsl	Max Semaphores Per Set
shmmax	Max Shared Memory Seg Size
shmseg	Max Num Shd Mem Segs Per Proc

Figure C-2   Parameters Dynamically Tuneable in HP-UX 11.22

Parameter	Purpose
core_addshmem_read	Readable Shmem in Core Dump
core_addshmem_write	Writeable Shmem in Core Dump
executable_stack	Security Feature – See Documentation
ksi_alloc_max	Max Num Queued Signals

Figure C-2 Parameters Dynamically Tuneable in HP-UX 11.22

Parameter	Purpose
max_acct_file_size	Process Accounting
max_thread_proc	Max Threads Per Process
maxdsiz	Max Data Segment Size
maxdsiz_64bit	Max Data Segment Size
maxfiles_lim	Upper Limit for Maxfiles
maxssiz	Max Stack Segment Size
maxssiz_64bit	Max Stack Segment Size
maxtsiz	Max Text Segment Size
maxtsiz_64bit	Max Text Segment Size
maxuprc	Max Processes Per User
msgmax	Max Message Queue Size
msgmnb	Max Bytes Per Message
nkthread	Max Num of Kernel Threads
nproc	Max Num of Processes
physical_io_buffers	Max buffers For physical I/O Operations
scsi_max_qdepth	Max Outstanding I/Os Per Device
secure_sid_scripts	Security Feature – see Documentation
semmsl	Max Semaphores Per Set
shmmax	Max Shared Memory Segment Size
shmmni	Max Num Shared Memory Segments
shmseg	Max Num Shared Memory Segments Per Process

Figure C-3   Parameters Dynamically Tuneable in HP-UX 11.23

Parameter	Purpose
aio_listio_max	Max POSIX Async Requests for Listio
aio_max_ops	Max Num Concurrent POSIX Async I/O Ops
aio_monitor_run_sec	Frequency for POSIX Monitor
aio_prio_delta_max	Max Slowdown Factor for POSIX Async I/O
aio_proc_thread_pct	Percentage of Total Procs Allowed in POSIX Async Pool
aio_proc_threads	Max Num Threads in POSIX Async I/O Pool
aio_req_per_thread	Desirable Ratio of POSIX Async Requests to Servicing Threads
alwaysdump	Type(s) of Kernel Pages to Dump
core_addshmem_read	Readable Shmem in Core Dump
core_addshmem_write	Writeable Shmem in Core Dump
dbc_max_pct	Max Percentage of Main Memory Allowed for Dynamic Buffer Cache
dbc_min_pct	Min Percentage of Main Memory Allowed for Dynamic Buffer Cache
dontdump	Type(s) of Kernel Pages Not Dumped
dump_compress_on	Compress Kernel Dump on Disk
enable_idds	Enable Intrusion Detection (Security Feature)
executable_stack	Security Feature – See System Documentation
fs_symlinks	Enable Fast Symbolic Links for Short Names
fss_maxhorses	Process Resource Manager – max number of slots on carousel
fss_mp_fix_ok	Process Resource Manager
ksi_alloc_max	Max Num Queued Signals
max_acct_file_size	Process Accounting
max_thread_proc	Max Num Threads Per Process
maxdsiz	Max Data Segment Size
maxdsiz_64bit	Max Data Segment Size for 64-bit Process
maxfiles_lim	Upper Limit for Maxfiles
maxssiz	Max Stack Segment Size
maxssiz_64bit	Max Stack Segment Size for 64-bit Process

Figure C-3 Parameters Dynamically Tuneable in HP-UX 11.23

Parameter	Purpose
maxtsiz	Max Text Segment Size
maxtsiz_64bit	Max Text Segment Size for 64-bit Process
maxuprc	Max Number of Processes Per User
msgmax	Max Message Queue Size
msgmnb	Max Bytes Per Message
ncdnode	Max CDFS Open Files
nkthread	Max Num of Kernel Threads (system-wide)
nproc	Max Num of Processes (system-wide)
scroll_lines	Max Num Scrollable Lines on Unix Workstation Monitor
scsi_max_qdepth	Max Outstanding I/Os Per SCSI/FC Device
secure_sid_scripts	Security Feature – See System Documentation
semmsl	Max Semaphores Per Set
shmmax	Max Shared Memory Segment Size for Any Process
shmmni	Max Num Shared Memory Segments (identifiers)
shmseg	Max Num Shared Memory Segments Per Process
st_ats_enabled	Enable Reserving Tape Device on Open
st_fail_overruns	Tapes Must Use Minimum Physical Record Size
st_large_recs	Max Logical Record Size for Tapes
vxfs_ifree_timelag	Min Time for Keeping Inode Free List

The parameters shown in Figure C-4 are automatically tuned by the kernel as the running load on the system dictates in HP-UX 11i Version 2. It should not typically be necessary for the administrator to tune these parameters.

Figure C-4   Parameters Automatically Tuned By the Kernel in HP-UX 11.23

Parameter	Purpose
ncallout	Number of Kernel Callouts
nfile	Max Number of In-Core Inodes
nflocks	Max Number of File Locks
physical_io_buffers	Max buffers For physical I/O Operations

Index

Q

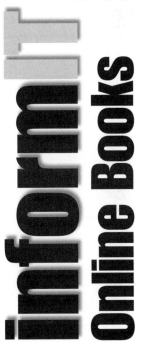

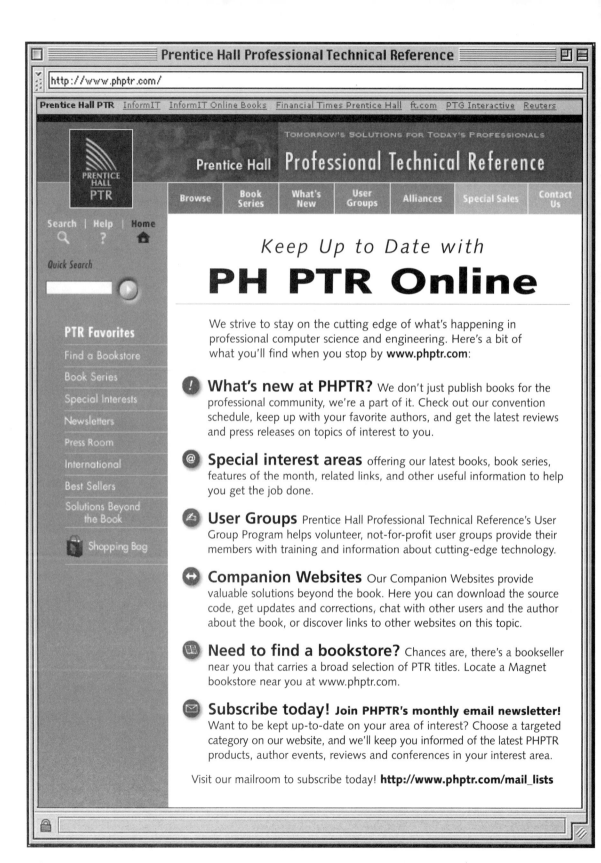